Advanced Maya® Texturing and Lighting

Second Edition

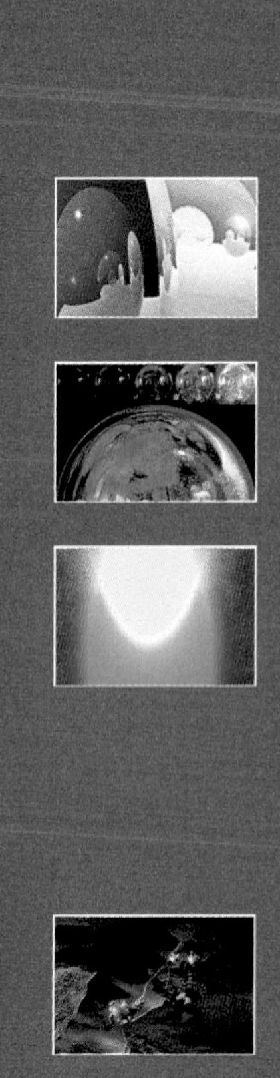

Advanced Maya® Texturing and Lighting

Second Edition

Lee Lanier

WILEY PUBLISHING, INC.

Acquisitions Editor: Mariann Barsolo
Development Editor: Susan Herman
Technical Editors: Keith Reicher, Eric Keller
Production Editor: Laurel Ibey
Copy Editor: Liz Welch
Production Manager: Tim Tate
Vice President and Executive Group Publisher: Richard Swadley
Vice President and Executive Publisher: Joseph B. Wikert
Vice President and Publisher: Neil Edde
Project Manager: Laura Moss-Hollister
Assistant Producer: Kit Malone
Book Designer: Franz Baumhackl, Lori Barra
Compositor: Kate Kaminski, Happenstance Type-O-Rama
Proofreader: Ian Golder, Word One
Indexer: Nancy Guenther
Cover Designer: Ryan Sneed
Cover Image: Lee Lanier

Published simultaneously in Canada

ISBN: 978-0-470-29273-0

Library of Congress Cataloging-in-Publication Data

Lanier, Lee, 1966-
Advanced Maya texturing and lighting / Lee Lanier. — 2nd ed.
p. cm.
ISBN 978-0-470-29273-0 (pbk. : CD-ROM)
1. Computer animation. 2. Maya (Computer file) I. Title.
TR897.7L367 2008
006.6'96—dc22

2008019683

10 9 8 7 6 5 4 3 2 1

Dear Reader,

Thank you for choosing *Advanced Maya Texturing and Lighting, Second Edition.* This book is part of a family of premium quality Sybex books, all written by outstanding authors who combine practical experience with a gift for teaching.

Sybex was founded in 1976. More than thirty years later, we're still committed to producing consistently exceptional books. With each of our graphics titles we're working hard to set a new standard for the industry. From the writers and artists we work with to the paper we print on, our goal is to bring you the best graphics books available.

I hope you see all that reflected in these pages. I'd be very interested to hear your comments and get your feedback on how we're doing. Feel free to let me know what you think about this or any other Sybex book by sending me an email at `nedde@wiley.com`, or if you think you've found an error in this book, please visit `http://wiley.custhelp.com`. Customer feedback is critical to our efforts at Sybex.

Best regards,

Neil Edde
Vice President and Publisher
Sybex, an Imprint of Wiley

To all the dreamers and artists out there.

Acknowledgments

My thanks to the excellent editorial, production, and compositing staff at Sybex and Wiley & Sons, including Acquisitions Editor Mariann Barsolo, Development Editor Susan Herman, Production Editor Laurel Ibey, Technical Editors Keith Reicher and Eric Keller, Copy Editor Liz Welch, and Proofreader Ian Golder.

Special thanks to the faculty, staff, and students at the Art Institute of Las Vegas and Westwood College Online for inspiring me to perfect my craft. Special thanks also to my family and friends who supported my wild ambitions. And the biggest thanks to my beautiful wife, Anita, who encouraged me all the way, despite all those late, late 3D nights.

Several of the photos in this book were provided by the photographers of Stock XCHNG (`www.sxc.hu`). This is a wonderful site that provides royalty-free, restriction-free material simply out of love of the medium. Additional models were purchased from Turbo Squid (`www.turbosquid.com`), another excellent service.

About the Author

Lee Lanier is an award-winning 3D animator and director. His films have played in more than 200 film festivals, museums, and galleries worldwide. Before directing the shorts "Millennium Bug," "Mirror," "Day Off the Dead," "Weapons of Mass Destruction," and "13 Ways to Die at Home," Lee served as a senior animator in the Lighting and Modeling Departments of Pacific Data Images on *Shrek* and *Antz*. He got his start in 3D at Buena Vista Visual Effects at Walt Disney Studios, where he created digital special effects for such films as *Mortal Kombat*. Lee currently lives in Boulder City, Nevada, where he serves as manager of BeezleBug Bit, LLC (`www.BeezleBugBit.com`) and director of the Dam Short Film Festival (`www.DamShortFilm.org`).

Contents

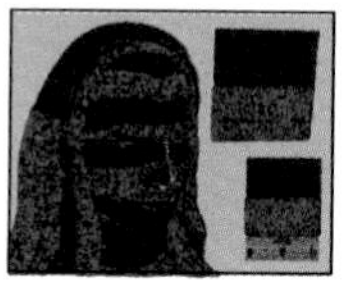

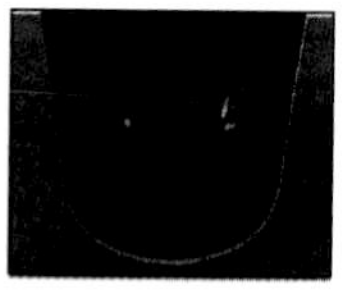

Introduction

Texturing and lighting is a blast. There's nothing quite like turning a gray-shaded model into something that looks real—or that could be real.

I should stress that I am self-taught. In 1994, I sat down at a spare seat of Alias PowerAnimator 5.1 and started hacking away. After several years and various trials by fire, 3D became a livelihood, a love, and an obsession. Along the way, I was fortunate enough to work with many talented artists at Buena Vista Visual Effects and Pacific Data Images. In 2000, I switched from PowerAnimator to Maya and have since logged tens of thousands of hours with the subject of this book.

Due to the unusual combination of an informal and professional background, I do not profess to know everything there is to know about Maya. In fact, you may find a better, quicker, more efficient way to achieve some of the texturing and lighting techniques described in this book. That's the beauty of Maya. There are probably a dozen ways to tackle every problem or challenge. If anything, I hope this book provides you with the theory, the background, and the basic approach you need to come up with *your own* creative solutions.

Second Edition

The first edition of *Advanced Maya Texturing and Lighting* was written with Maya 7.0 and published in 2006. This edition represents a major revision, with every chapter updated for the most recent Maya release and the latest trends and techniques in the animation industry. In addition, material covering fundamental theory that underpins computer animation and the natural world it tries to re-create has been expanded.

Who Should Read This Book

Advanced Maya Texturing and Lighting, Second Edition, is designed for anyone with a working knowledge of Maya. Specifically, this book was written with the following people in mind:

- Students who are reaching the upper levels of their 3D curriculum
- Hobbyists or amateurs who are self-starters and would like to rapidly refine their Maya skills
- Professionals working in other areas of Maya, such as animation or rigging, who would like to expand their knowledge of texturing and lighting

Although most of the information in this book is Maya specific, you can apply the texturing and lighting theories and approaches to other 3D programs. This book

"There's nothing   

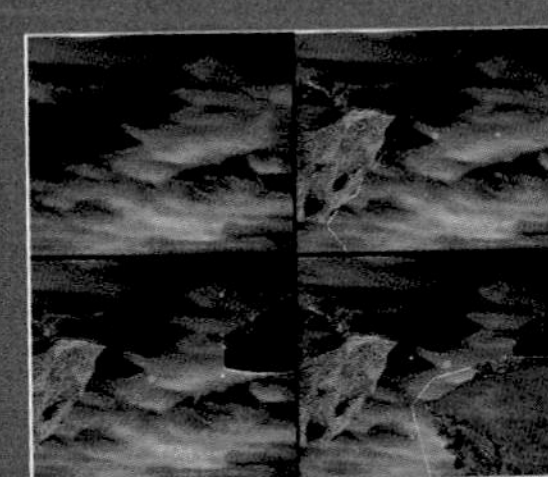 quite like turning a gray-shaded 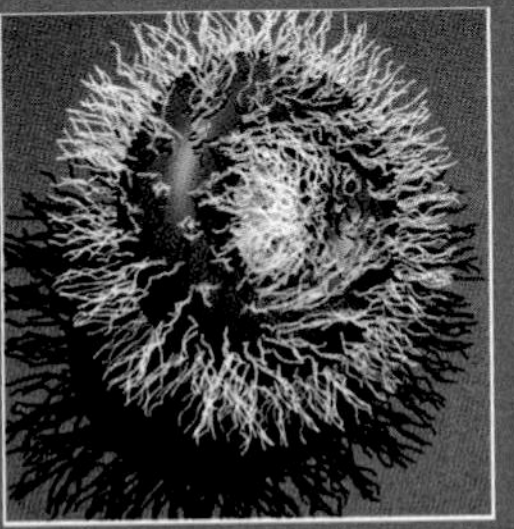 model into something that looks real—or that could be real."

also assumes that you have a basic knowledge of such image manipulation programs as Adobe Photoshop and compositing programs as After Effects.

How to Use This Book

Advanced Maya Texturing and Lighting, Second Edition, is divided into 14 chapters. Thirteen of these chapters are in the book. One of the chapters is provided as a bonus PDF file on the companion CD.

Chapter 1 discusses lighting history, technique, and application, as well as basic color and composition theory. Naturalistic, stylistic, 1-point, 2-point, and 3-point lighting are covered in detail. If you are new to lighting, this is the best place to start.

Chapters 2 and 3 detail Maya lights and shadows and how to properly apply them. Specialized effects, such as Environment Fog, Light Fog, the Toon renderer, Maya Fur, Maya Hair, and nCloth, are also covered.

Chapters 4 through 8 delve deeply into Maya materials and utilities. Most Maya books barely scratch the surface in this area. If you've ever wondered what each Maya node actually *does*, check out these chapters. Custom networks are also discussed at length. Numerous examples are provided with clearly labeled illustrations, and you'll find that the examples are easy to follow (as much as such a complex subject allows).

Chapter 9 takes a detour and discusses UV texture space. UV preparation is a critical component of texturing, but it is often ignored by texturing and lighting books.

Chapters 10 through 12 concentrate on rendering and expend a good deal of text on mental ray, Global Illumination, Final Gather, and other advanced render tools.

Chapter 13 includes advanced tools and techniques, including HDRI lighting, normal mapping, and the Render Layer Editor. A guide to the creation of this book's cover illustration is also provided.

If you're fairly new to Maya or 3D in general, I suggest starting with Chapter 1, then working your way through the book. If you're experienced with Maya, I recommend hitting the chapters that contain information that's poorly documented by other sources. In this case, Chapters 6, 7, and 8 should prove the most interesting. If you'd like to take your Maya knowledge even further, an `Additional_Techniques.pdf` file is included on the companion CD. The file includes extra sections that cover shading networks, NURBS preparation, and advanced rendering techniques.

Each chapter of *Advanced Maya Texturing and Lighting, Second Edition,* contains either a tutorial or examples of industry work. The tutorials are in-depth methods of practicing advanced techniques. Each tutorial is accompanied by ample illustrations and completed Maya scene files. The industry examples, on the other hand, present renders from completed animations and explain the process of their creation. These sections often include "quick and dirty" techniques that were born in the face of production deadlines.

The Companion CD

The CD included in the back of the book is an important part of learning with *Advanced Maya Texturing and Lighting, Second Edition*. A bonus chapter, sample scenes, shading networks, QuickTime movies, and texture bitmaps are included to help you perfect your knowledge. The included materials match many of the illustrations in this book; check the illustration captions for filenames.

As for Maya file locations, the following directory structure is used on the CD:

Project_Files\Chapter_1\scenes	*scene files and shading networks*
Project_Files\Chapter_1\images	*background and HDR images*
Project_Files\Chapter_1\textures	*texture bitmaps*
Project_Files\Chapter_1\movies	*sample QuickTime movies*

Maya Versions

The scene files included on the CD are saved in the Maya 8.5 `.ma` format. The files have been tested with versions 8.5 and 2008. All the techniques discussed in the book have been tested with versions 8.5 and 2008; any significant differences between the two versions have been noted in the text.

Shading Network Figures

A number of figures in this book illustrate custom shading networks. The connections are labeled with the output and input channels. As such, the output channel name is indicated by its placement on top of the connection line (closer to the top of the node icon). The input channel name is placed below the connection line (see Figure I.1). Details concerning attributes, channels, custom connections, nodes, and shading networks are provided.

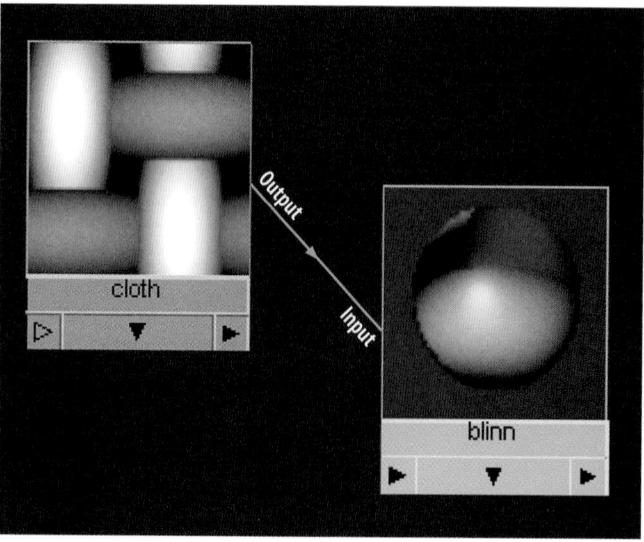

Figure I.1 An example shading network

A number of files saved on the companion CD contain shading networks. When opening a file, you may be surprised to find it void of geometry. Nevertheless, you can access the contained shading network through the Hypershade Materials, Textures, or Utilities tab. If the network is exotic and difficult to access, instructions are included in the text.

Abbreviations

Since Maya requires a three-button mouse for proper operation, the abbreviations LMB, MMB, and RMB are used and respectively stand for Left-Mouse-Button, Middle-Mouse-Button, and Right-Mouse-Button.

Websites

Feel free to contact me at `www.BeezleBugBit.com`. If you're a fan of short films, or have made a short film and would like to find an audience, visit `www.DamShortFilm.org`.

1 Understanding Lighting, Color, and Composition

Lighting is a cornerstone of any 3D project. Although you can easily create and position lights within a scene, an understanding of lighting theory will help you make aesthetically solid choices. The history of art and cinema is full of inspiring examples to choose from. Although 3-point lighting is a mainstay of 3D, 1-point, 2-point, and naturalistic lighting provide alternative lighting methods that better match the real world and the art traditions of the past. On the other hand, stylistic lighting can free an artist from traditional bounds and thereby place no limits on expression.

Chapter Contents

Common lighting terms
An overview of 1-, 2-, and 3-point lighting
An exploration of naturalistic and stylistic lighting
A quick review of color theory, monitor calibration, and composition techniques
Lighting examples

Understanding the Art of Lighting

Like every aspect of 3D, lighting must be created from scratch. Unfortunately, the techniques for emulating the real world are not always obvious or intuitive. Luckily, a wealth of lighting theory exists in the form of historical artwork, photography, and motion pictures.

For the sake of clarity, I've broken the discussion of lighting theory into the following categories: 1-point, 2-point, 3-point, naturalistic, and stylistic. The first three categories refer to the number of lights employed. The last two refer to a particular style. Before delving into 1-point lighting, however, I'll define a few common lighting terms:

Key The most intense light in a scene. The key light's source is generally identifiable (the sun, a lamp, and so on). The key light usually produces the strongest shadow in the scene.

Fill A secondary light that is less intense than the key. This light "fills" in the dark areas of a subject and the shadows produced by the key. Fill lights often represent light from a key that has bounced off a surface, such as a wall.

Rim An intense light source placed behind a subject that strikes the subject along the edge. Rim lights are often employed as hair lights. These lights are commonly known as backlights or kickers.

Using 1-Point Lighting

The 1-point lighting scheme is dramatic, sometimes stark, and often foreboding. The lighting involves a single, easily identifiable key light source, with no significant supplemental sources. You can find 1-point lighting in the following situations:

- A man lights a cigarette in an otherwise dark alley.
- A woman drives a car down a dark country road, lit only by the car's instrument panel.
- Sunbeams burst through the window of an otherwise unlit interior.
- A theater audience is illuminated by the light of the movie screen (see Figure 1.1).

The motion picture genre that most closely emulates 1-point lighting is film noir. Film noir is a style historically associated with crime dramas of the 1940s and 1950s. The style is typified by black-and-white film stock, sparsely lit characters, and deep black shadows. Aesthetically, the lighting stemmed from stories with cynical, paranoid, or nihilistic outlooks. Technically, the stark lighting was the result of placing only a few lights on the set, in some cases because of budgetary restrictions. Although multiple lights were generally needed for any given shot for proper exposure, the result often *appears* as if a single light source exists (see Figure 1.2).

PHOTO © 2008 JUPITERIMAGES CORPORATION

Figure 1.1 A theater audience is lit by a movie screen in a 1-point lighting setup.

PHOTO © 2008 JUPITERIMAGES CORPORATION

Figure 1.2 Stark lighting in a film noir–style film.

Classic film noir films include *The Maltese Falcon* (1941), *Double Indemnity* (1944), and *Touch of Evil* (1958). More recent examples include *Blade Runner* (1982) and *Sin City* (2005). The lighting style employed by film noir is often referred to as low-key lighting, where there is a strong key light and little, if any, fill.

Film noir is closely related to German expressionism, which was an art movement popular in Germany from 1905 to 1925. German expressionism was dominated by the dark, sinister aspects of the human psyche. The movement is known for its bold, simplified woodcuts (see Figure 1.3) and its atmospheric horror cinema (for example, *The Cabinet of Dr. Caligari*, 1919).

Figure 1.3 Emil Nolde (1867–1956). *Prophet*. 1912. Woodcut print.

The roots of expressionism can be traced to the chiaroscuro painting style of the 15th and 16th centuries in Italy and Flanders. Chiaroscuro is defined by a bold contrast between lights and darks (the word is Italian for light-dark). This is often characterized by figures in bright pools of light jutting through dark spaces. Chiaroscuro reached its pinnacle with the baroque art movement (17th and 18th centuries in Europe) and is exemplified by master painters Caravaggio (1573–1610) and Rembrandt (1606–69). For example, in Figure 1.4, Jesus and his disciples are lit by the light of a single high window from the left. A fill light reaches the front of the table and the sides of their faces; however, the result is fairly subtle.

When painters push for stronger contrast, unlit areas of the scene are rarely painted with pure black. In Figure 1.5, an unidentified key light arrives from the left. No other source of light is apparent. Yet, a background wall is visible due to a faint fill. In addition, the head of a central character is seen in the shadow. Hence, the paintings illustrated in Figures 1.4 and 1.5 bridge the gap between 1- and 2-point lighting.

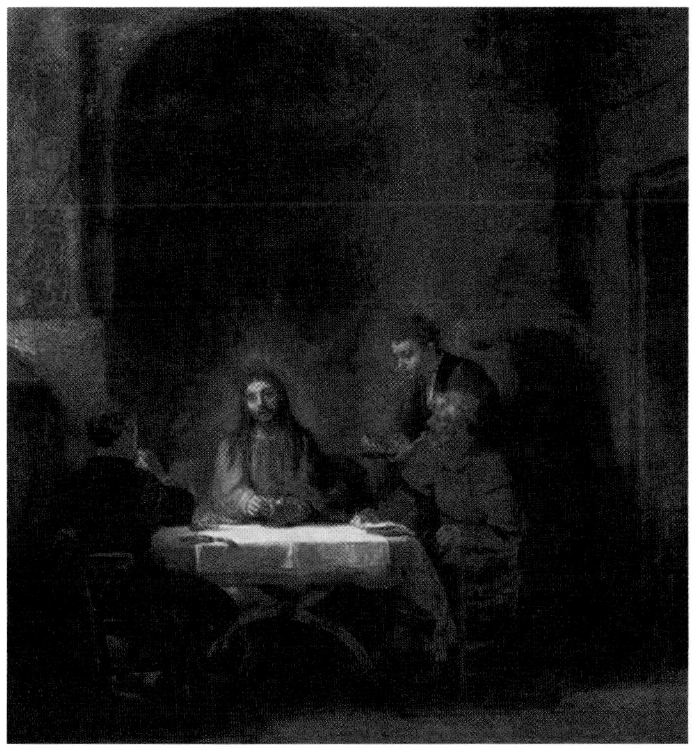

PHOTO © 2008 JUPITERIMAGES CORPORATION

Figure 1.4 Rembrandt. *The Supper at Emmaus*. 1648. Oil on wood. Louvre, Paris.

PHOTO © 2008 JUPITERIMAGES CORPORATION

Figure 1.5 Rembrandt. *The Return of the Prodigal Son*. 1662. Oil on canvas. The Hermitage, St. Petersburg. Note that the wall and central character in the background are barely visible.

In comparison, true 1-point lighting is sometimes found in portraiture. For example, in Figure 1.6 there is a single light source in front of and higher than the man. A secondary light source is not identifiable. The painter, Anthony Van Dyck (1599–1641), was an influential baroque portraitist.

Figure 1.6 Van Dyck. *Portrait of Cornelis van der Geest*. c. 1621. Oil on oak. National Gallery, London.

You'll see 1-point lighting in contemporary photography and videography. In particular, this technique is used in work created for the fashion industry, commercial advertising, and music videos. A strong, diffuse key light, sometimes in the form of a "soft box" light diffuser or a large ring of fluorescent lights, is placed around, beside, or above the camera. This setup creates evenly lit faces with little sense of additional lighting (see Figure 1.7).

Figure 1.7 A fashion photograph displays 1-point lighting.

Modern painters have also made use of 1-point lighting. For example, in Figure 1.8 a boxing match is lit by a single strong source from frame left. As with the work illustrated in Figures 1.4 and 1.5, there is an extremely soft fill present; the fill lights the back of the rightmost boxer. The painter, George Bellows (1882–1925), was a member of the Modern School movement; he sought to portray the gritty reality of urban life.

Figure 1.8 Bellows. *Club Night*. 1907. Oil on canvas. National Gallery of Art, Washington, D.C.

It's easy to set up 1-point lighting in 3D. The most difficult aspect of the scheme is the creation of aesthetic patterns of light and dark. For example, in Figure 1.9 a film noir–style photo is re-created in Maya. A series of trial-and-error renders were necessary to position a directional light in a satisfactory manner. The intensity of the key should be high enough to illuminate the parts not in shadow but not so high as to "blow out" or overexpose some areas.

Figure 1.9 (Left) Film noir photo. (Right) 1-point lighting re-creation in Maya. The scene is included on the CD as `1_point.ma`.

Using 2-Point Lighting

The 2-point lighting scheme matches many of the lighting scenarios we encounter in our everyday lives. The scheme often involves a strong key and an extremely diffuse fill. The following are examples of 2-point lighting:

- Sunlight streams through a window. The light bounce from the interior walls serves as a fill.
- Office workers sit in a windowless room lit with overhead fluorescent lights. The light bounce from the walls, desks, and floor serves as a fill.
- A couple walks down a sidewalk on a sunny day. The light bounces off the concrete, providing fill to the bottom of their hands, the underside of their chins, and their eye sockets (see Figure 1.10).

You'll often see 2-point lighting in painted portraits. For example, in Figure 1.11 a man is lit by a strong key light arriving from the left. A second light source delivers fill from the right; thus, no part of the person or his outfit is left unlit. This painting was created by Frans Hals (1582–1666), a baroque painter whose loose, powerful brushstrokes inspired the impressionism movement. This style of lighting is called short lighting in studio photography; the side of the head facing away from the camera receives the key. The opposite style of lighting is called broad lighting, in which the side of the head facing the camera receives the key.

Photo © 2008 Jupiterimages Corporation

Figure 1.10 A couple receives sunlight from above and as a bounced fill from the sidewalk. The lighting is a 2-point setup.

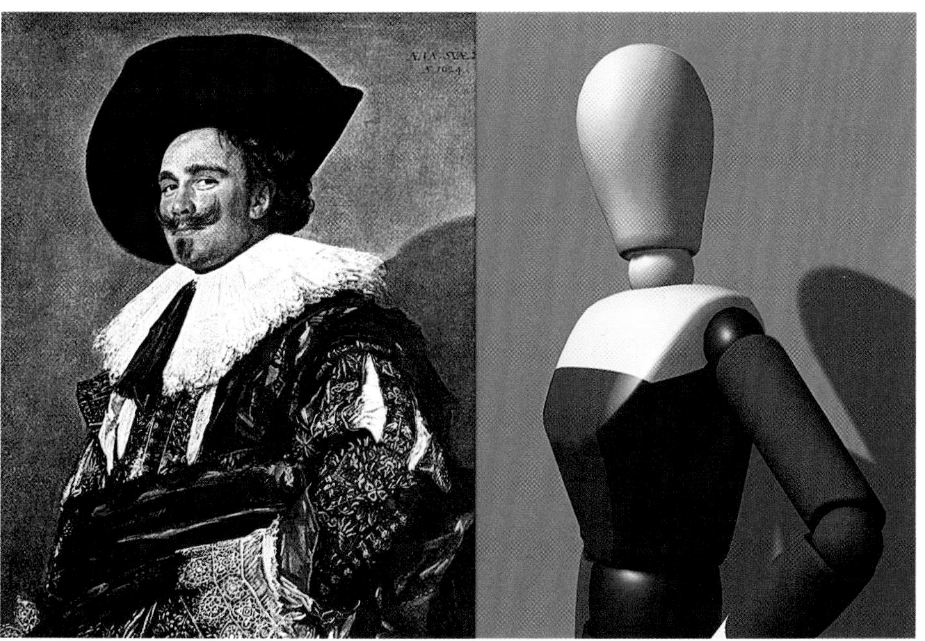

Left Photo © 2008 Jupiterimages Corporation

Figure 1.11 (Left) Hals. *The Laughing Cavalier*. 1624. Oil on canvas. The Wallace Collection, London. (Right) 2-point lighting re-creation in Maya. The scene is included on the CD as `2_point.ma`.

The intensity of the key light as compared to the fill (key-to-fill ratio) should vary with the subject and location. The optimum intensity of any light used in a scene depends on its position and the qualities of the materials involved. Nevertheless, as a rough rule of thumb for an initial lighting pass, you can set the intensity of a fill light to at least half that of the key. For the 3D reproduction illustrated in Figure 1.11, a directional light serves as the key. The directional light's Intensity value is set to 1.75. An ambient light, which serves as the fill, is placed screen right with its Intensity value set to 0.6 (see Figure 1.12).

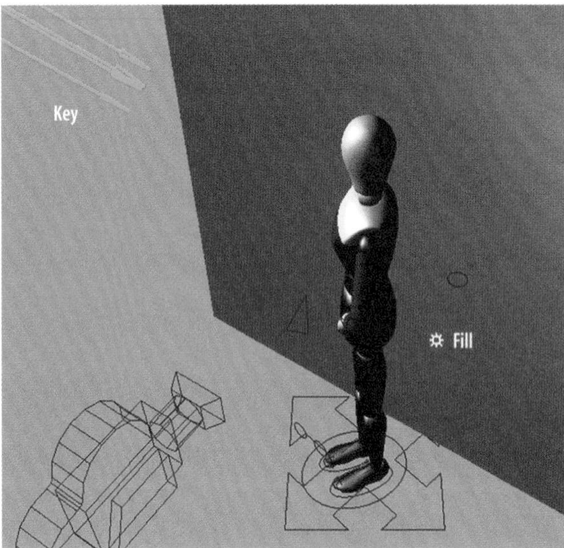

Figure 1.12
Two-point lighting set up for the Hals painting re-creation

The 2-point lighting scheme is not limited to portraits. Many outdoor scenes exhibit two distinct sources of light. For example, in Figure 1.13 a watercolor street scene portrays a strong key light in the form of the sun. An even fill along the backs of the house and other structures represents the bounced sunlight, which serves as the second light source.

Figure 1.13 Harry Leith-Ross (1886–1973). Untitled. c.1945. Watercolor on paper. Whereabouts unknown.

Using 3-Point Lighting

Perhaps the most commonly discussed and applied lighting technique is 3-point lighting. Descriptions can be found in numerous 3D, film, and video instructional materials. Although 3-point lighting is a reliable way to light many scenes, it has inherent drawbacks.

In the standard 3-point lighting scheme, a strong key is placed to one side of a subject (approximately 15 to 45 degrees off the camera axis). A fill light is placed on the opposite side and is at least half the intensity of the key (see Figure 1.14). A rim light is placed behind the subject so that it grazes the subject's edge.

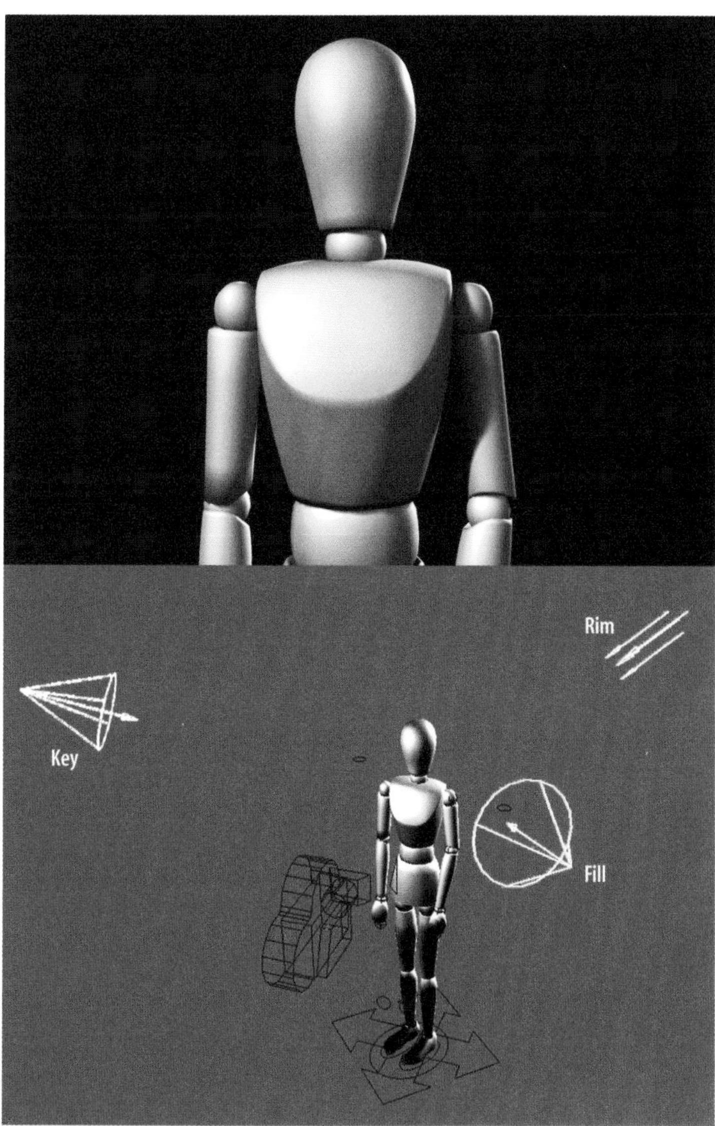

Figure 1.14 Standard 3-point lighting applied to a mannequin. This scene is included on the CD as `3_point_man.ma`.

Note: Four-point lighting simply adds a fourth light to illuminate the background or set behind the subject.

The 3-point lighting scheme is popular in the realm of 3D because it lends depth to a potentially flat subject. For example, in Figure 1.15 a sphere is given additional roundness with three lights. A spot light, which serves as the key, is placed screen left. An ambient light, which serves as a fill, is placed screen right. A directional light, which functions as a rim light, is placed behind the sphere. The balance between the key and fill creates a slightly dark "core" down the center of sphere. The bright edge created by the rim helps separate the sphere from the dark background.

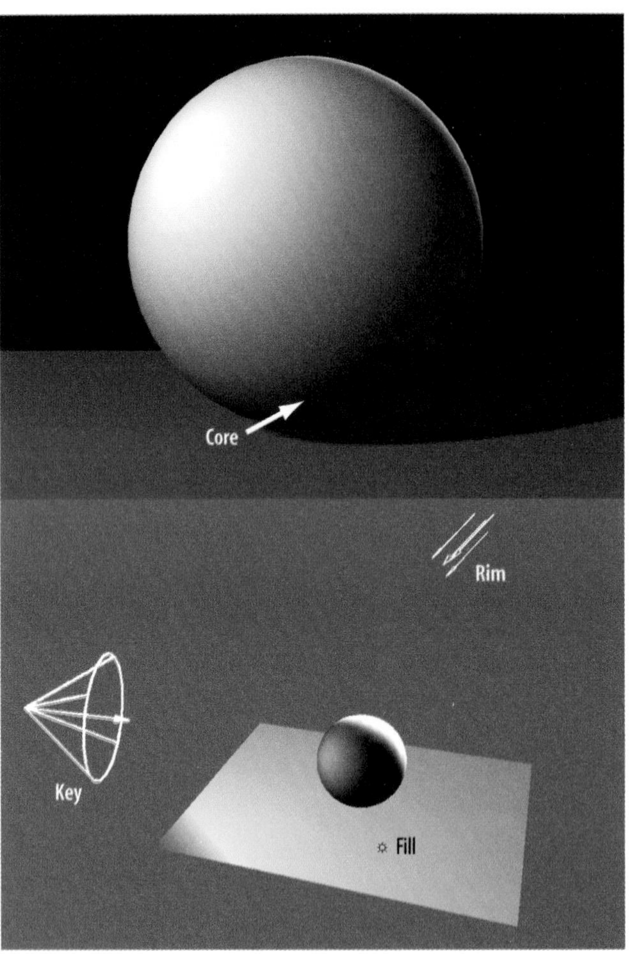

Figure 1.15 Standard 3-point lighting applied to a primitive sphere. This scene is included on the CD as `3_point_sphere.ma`.

Three-point lighting was developed in the "Golden Age of Hollywood," which refers to the period between the advent of "talkies" and the years immediately following World War II. Studio cinematographers developed the technique as an efficient way to light scenes when time was somewhat limited and production schedules had to be met. When lighting actors, cinematographers often sought out the "Rembrandt patch," which is a triangular patch of light on the cheek opposite the light source (see Figure 1.16). The patch was named after the painter, who often featured such a pattern in his portraits.

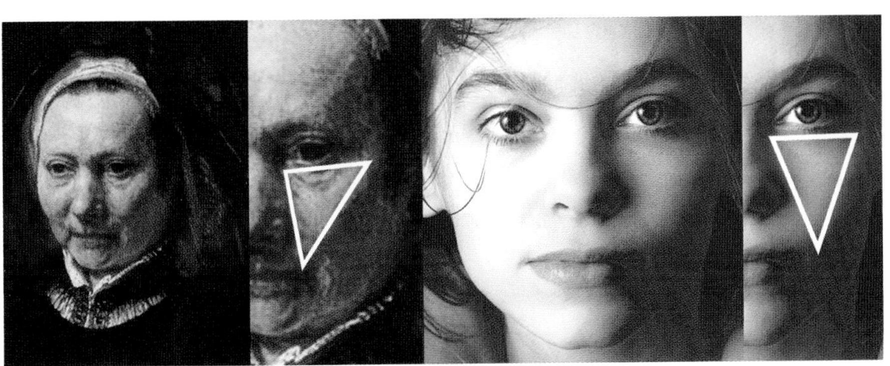

Figure 1.16 (Left) Rembrandt. *Portrait of an Old Woman*. c. 1650. Oil on canvas. Pushkin Museum of Fine Arts, Moscow. (Right) Modern photo with similar "Rembrandt patch" on subject's left cheek.

Rim lights, in particular, were developed to separate the actor from a dark or cluttered background. Rim lights (and other fundamental aspects of lighting design) can trace their roots to early theatrical stage lighting. Early examples of their use in motion pictures include, but are not limited to, *Old and New* (1929), directed by Sergei Eisenstein, and the 1920s comedies of Charles Chaplin (*A Woman of Paris*, *Gold Rush*, and so on). Eventually, rim lights were used to impart a fantastic glow to the hair of heroines such as Ingrid Bergman in *Casablanca* (1942), Rita Hayworth in *Gilda* (1946), and Grace Kelly in *Rear Window* (1954). The use of rim lights does not necessitate the use of a definitive fill light. Glamour lighting, a name loosely given to the lighting style of publicity photography of American motion picture studios from the 1920s to the 1940s, often used only a key and a rim (see Figure 1.17). A variation of this technique, known as butterfly lighting or Paramount lighting, places a high key directly in front of the subject (thereby creating a shadow in the shape of a butterfly under the nose).

Figure 1.17 Three variations of glamour lighting, as seen in photographs of Jane Wyman (left), Ida Lupino (center), and Mary Pickford (right).

Proper 3-point lighting is fairly difficult to find in the world of painting. Clearly defined rims are not generally painted in. In many cases, a portion of a subject that is dark is allowed to blend into a dark background (see Figures 1.4, 1.5, and 1.6). In other situations, the chosen background is bright enough to delineate the outline of the subject. In Figure 1.18, the man's dark hair and the shadow on his left shoulder are offset by a pool of light on the back wall. This strategically placed pool serves the same function as a rim light, but isn't part of the modern 3-point lighting method.

On the other hand, rim lighting can often be found in nature. For example, in Figure 1.19 a cloud covers the sun and picks up a bright rim. Intense sunlight strikes a cactus from behind, thereby illuminating its spines. A woman's hair is lit from light streaming through a window. These natural occurrences, however, do not fit the standard 3-point lighting system. None of the subjects are affected by more than two distinct sources of light.

Many contemporary cinematographers and videographers consider 3-point lighting either antiquated or unsatisfactory for many lighting situations. The necessity of specific positions for key, fill, and rim lights guarantees that 3-point lighting does not match many real-world situations. The alternative to 3-point lighting is thus naturalistic lighting.

Photo © 2008 Jupiterimages Corporation

Figure 1.18 Giovanni Battista Moroni (1520–78). *The Tailor.* c. 1565. Oil on canvas. National Gallery, London.

Photos © 2008 Jupiterimages Corporation

Figure 1.19 Naturally occurring examples of rim lighting

Using Naturalistic Lighting

Naturalistic lighting is an adaptable scheme that matches the natural lighting scenario of the subject location. Any light that is visible is logically driven by a recognizable source. Naturalistic lighting is sometimes called "transparent" in that no artificial lighting methods can be detected. Another way to define naturalistic lighting is to list what it *lacks*:

- Unmotivated shadows
- Impossibly distinct rim light
- Perfectly placed lights that never permit a character to fall into shadow or be unglamorously lit

In the field of motion pictures, there are numerous examples of non-naturalistic lighting. Many films feature stylized or exaggerated lighting. This is particularly evident with musicals, which are fantastic by their very nature. Such films as *The Band Wagon* (1953) and *Silk Stockings* (1957) employ high-key lighting, in which the fill light is intense and there is a low key-to-fill ratio. The characters in these films are therefore evenly lit and carry a minimum number of deep, dark shadows. High-key lighting is also evident in many television sitcoms, in which it is necessary to keep a character well lit at all positions on the set. Similar lighting is employed for advertising and catalog art (see Figure 1.20).

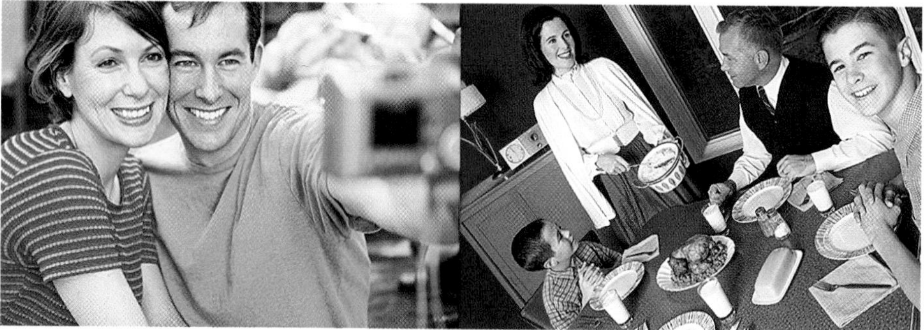

Figure 1.20 High-key lighting demonstrated by ad photography

In other situations, non-naturalistic lighting is a result of technical limitations or time and budget restrictions. A common problem with older motion pictures is the unintended creation of unmotivated, multiple shadows. For example, light representing the sun casts multiple shadows of a character on the ground. More commonly, a lamp casts multiple, distinct shadows of its own fixture (see Figure 1.21). This is caused by a need to illuminate a set with multiple lights to attain correct exposure even though the desired light source—in terms of the story—is singular.

Figure 1.21 A lamp unrealistically casts three sharp shadows of itself (as seen in a frame blowup from a 1950s motion picture).

In contrast, naturalistic lighting is often found in post-1950s historical dramas, particularly those set in times before the advent of the lightbulb. Prime examples include *Barry Lyndon* (1975), directed by Stanley Kubrick (1928–99), and *1492* (1992), directed by Ridley Scott (1937–). In these works, lighting is motivated by combinations of sunlight, moonlight, candlelight, and firelight. Keys, fills, and their resulting shadows are often extremely soft. The naturalistic lighting approach is not limited to historical drama, however. Kubrick also employed naturalistic lighting in such films as *A Clockwork Orange* (1971) and *The Shining* (1980).

In the world of art, naturalistic lighting can be found in any of the painting genres that placed a premium on accurate lighting. For example, Jan van Eyck (1385–1440) was an early adopter of physically accurate painting. In Figure 1.22, the light from several windows bounces through a room, creating soft shadows along the way. Van Eyck helped to establish the style of the Early Renaissance, which placed an importance on the study of the natural world.

In addition to chiaroscuro works, the baroque movement produced many naturalistic paintings. The movement placed an emphasis on emotionally and physically accurate portrayals of subjects. Two Dutch painters, Jan Vermeer (1632–75) and Pieter de Hooch (1629–84), were particularly successful at rendering soft, naturally lit interiors and exteriors. For example, in Figure 1.23 a sunset sky provides a diffuse light within a building's shadow for a threesome at a table, yet brightly lights buildings in the distance.

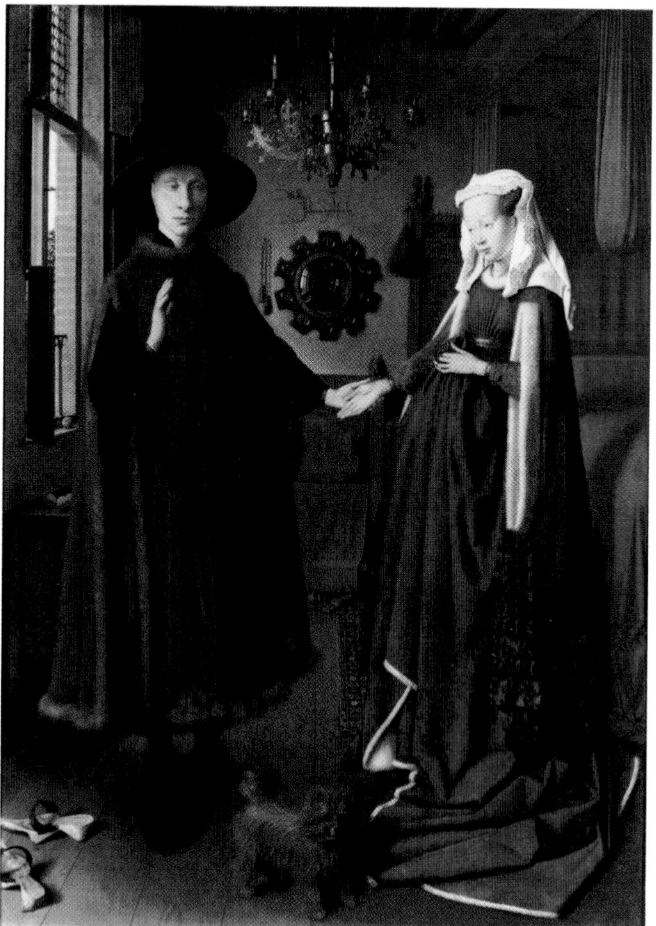

Figure 1.22 Van Eyck. *Giovanni Arnolfini and His Wife Giovanna Cenami*. 1434. Tempura on wood. National Gallery, London.

Realism, as an art movement, appeared in the mid-19th century and placed a premium on an accurately portrayed world with no hint of idealism or romanticism. Realist artists include George Caleb Bingham (1811–79) and Jules Breton (1827–1906), both of whom are noted for their accurately rendered outdoor scenes. Impressionism, centered in France in the 1860s and considered a branch of realism, sought to faithfully portray light and color as perceived by the human eye. This attention to light is illustrated by Figure 1.24. A woman stands at a bar in front of a large mirror. The painting was created at a real location and was not staged in the artist's studio (this preference was known as "plein-air," or "open-air"). Although the scene is quite cluttered with detail, little attempt has been made to separate the woman from her surroundings. That is, there is no artificial rim light or artifacts of a specific lighting scheme. This is equally true of the bottles at the lower left; their forms begin to merge into a single mass. (Although the lighting is accurately portrayed, the mirror's reflection lacks the artist and skews the entire background for compositional convenience.) Famous impressionistic painters include Edgar Degas (1834–1917), Claude Monet (1840–1926), Pierre-Auguste Renoir (1841–1919), and Édouard Manet (1832–83).

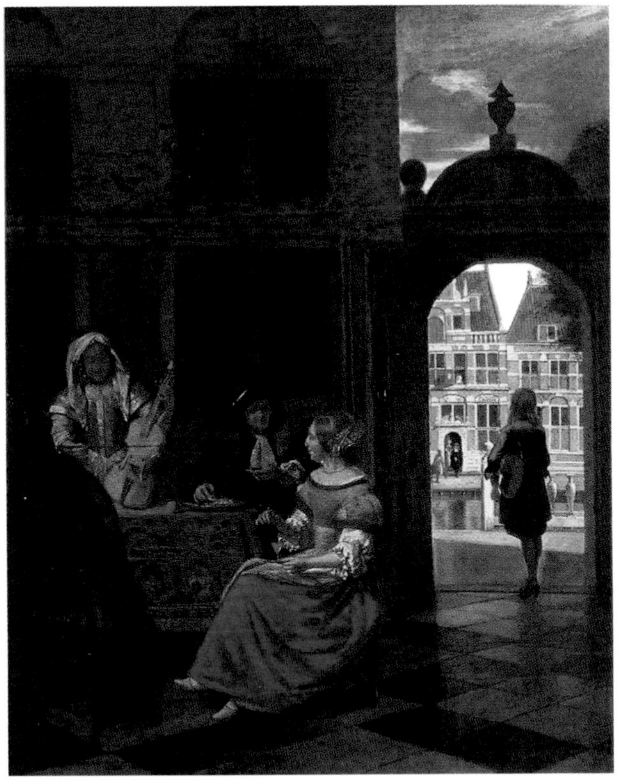

PHOTO © 2008 JUPITERIMAGES CORPORATION

Figure 1.23 De Hooch. *A Musical Party in a Courtyard*. c. 1677. Oil on canvas. National Gallery, London.

PHOTO © 2008 JUPITERIMAGES CORPORATION

Figure 1.24 Manet. *A Bar at the Foiles-Bergére*. 1882. Oil on canvas. Courtauld Institute Galleries, London.

Naturalistic lighting, by its very nature, does not dictate a fixed number of lights or specific light locations or intensities. However, you can use the following guidelines to assist you during setup:

- Determine what the strongest light is and where it should be coming from. Is the light source visible within the frame or is it arriving from offscreen? Set one or more key lights in appropriate locations. Match the type of light to the type of source. (See Chapter 2 for more information on Maya light types.) Render tests to determine the appropriate intensities of the key or keys *before* adding fill lights.
- Determine what secondary light sources are needed. Are these sources physical (that is, a lamp, a candle, and so on), or are they actually the bounced light of the strongest light source? Set fill lights in the appropriate locations. If you are copying an existing location, replicate the key-to-fill ratio. If the scene you are creating does not exist in the real world, apply a key-to-fill ratio that is similar to an *equivalent* location in the real world.
- When applying shadows, replicate the type of shadow that is naturally produced by a specific light source. For example, midday sunlight creates hard-edged parallel shadows (see Figure 1.25). An artificial source close to the subject, such as a lightbulb, produces a shadow that widens and softens over distance. (See Chapter 3 for information on shadow creation in Maya.)

Figure 1.25 (Left) The sun creates parallel shadows of stone columns. (Right) An artificial light source creates a shadow that widens and softens over distance.

- Color is equally important when reproducing a particular location. Different light sources create different wavelengths of light, which in turn produce specific hues that are perceived by the human eye or recorded on a medium such as film or video. (See Chapter 2 for information concerning Maya light color. For information on color temperature, see "A Note on Color Temperature" at the end of this chapter.)

For practice, you can always re-create existing images. For example, in Figure 1.26 the lighting of a Vermeer painting is replicated in 3D.

Figure 1.26 (Left) Vermeer. *A Lady Standing at a Virginal.* 1673. Oil on canvas. National Gallery, London. (Right) Naturalistic lighting re-creation in Maya. The scene is included on the CD as `naturalistic.ma`.

Using Stylized Lighting

Stylized lighting pays no heed to the real world but fabricates fantastic sources of light or simply ignores the lighting information altogether.

The oldest form of stylized lighting can be called 0-point lighting. In this case, lighting plays no part in the artistic representation. You can see this in prehistoric art, as well as in the art of ancient or primitive cultures (see Figure 1.27). To this day, 0-point lighting survives as line-art cartoons.

Figure 1.27 Petroglyphics and hieroglyphics carry no lighting information.

You can find stylized lighting in numerous pieces of modern art. Many times, this style is evident even when distinct modeling is given to the subject. (That is, the subject is painted to have three-dimensional form.) For example, in Figure 1.28, a man is completely disconnected from his environment. Although it can be assumed to be night, there is no way to tell for sure. No shadows of lighting clues exist to establish a real-world lighting scheme.

Figure 1.28 Vincent Willem van Gogh (18590). *Portrait of Dr. Gachet.* 1890. Oil on canvas. Whereabouts unknown.

Stylized lighting is well suited for 3D animation, since the medium places no limitation on the type of lighting employed. For 3D examples of this style, see the section "Step-by-Step: 3D Lighting Examples" at the end of this chapter.

Understanding Color and Composition

Successful lighting is not dependent on appropriate light placement alone. One crucial component is color. Unfortunately, it is beyond the scope of this book to cover the bulk of color theory. However, a discussion of the RYB and RGB color models, color wheels, color space, color temperature, and light color is worth a look.

At the same time, composition is a critical component of any animation that is rendered. Composition—the aesthetic arrangement of objects within a frame—can be reduced to the golden mean and the rule of thirds.

Color Theory Overview

In the traditional color theory model, red, yellow, and blue are considered primary colors. As such, they follow these rules:

- No combination of any two primary colors can produce a third primary color.
- Combinations of all three primaries can produce a wider range of colors than any other combination of colors.

You can form secondary colors by mixing together primary colors, which produces orange, green, and violet (purple). You can form tertiary colors by mixing primary colors and secondary colors; the resulting colors are generally given hyphenated names, such as blue-green. The primary, secondary, and tertiary colors are often represented by a 12-step color wheel (see Figure 1.29).

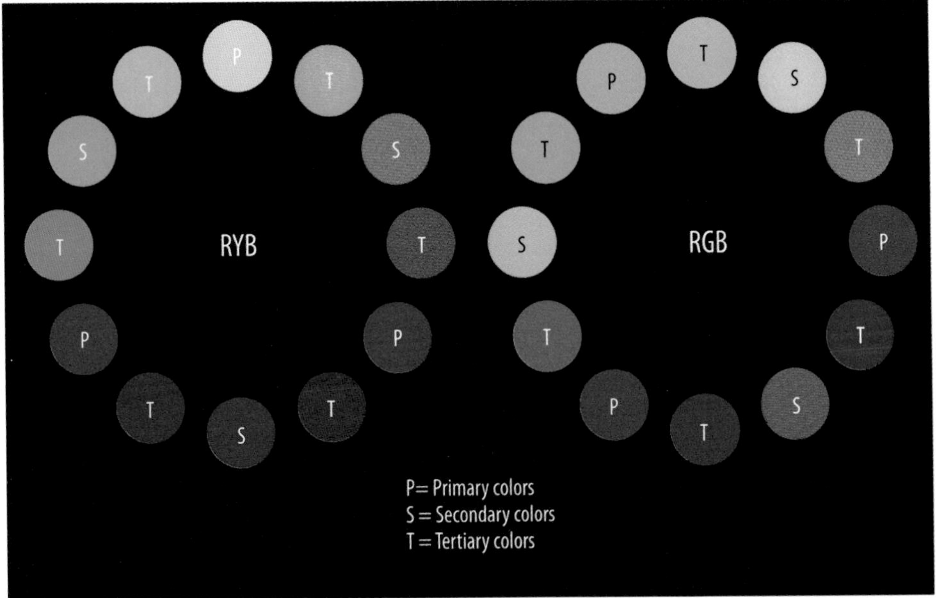

Figure 1.29 (Left) Red-yellow-blue (RYB) color wheel re-created in Maya. The scene is included on the CD as RYB_wheel.ma. (Right) Red-green-blue (RGB) color wheel re-created in Maya. The scene is included on the CD as RGB_wheel.ma.

The red-yellow-blue (RYB) color theory model evolved in the 18th century and was based on color materialism, which assumes that primary colors are based on specific, indivisible material pigments found in minerals or other natural substances. The popularization of specific RYB colors was aided by printmakers such as Jakob Christoffel Le Blon (1667–1741), who developed the color separation printing process. The color wheel itself was invented by Sir Isaac Newton (1642–1727) in 1704, although his variation contained seven hues visible when white light was split by a prism.

The development of computer graphics, however, has added a new set of primary colors: red, green, and blue, or RGB. This produces its own unique color wheel (see Figure 1.29). Through an additive process, computer monitors mix red, green, and blue light to produce additional colors. Added in equal proportions, RGB primaries produce white. In contrast, the RYB color theory model is subtractive in that the absence of red, yellow, and blue produces white (assuming that the blank paper or canvas is indeed white). In this case, if colored paint or ink pigments are present, they absorb certain wavelengths of light, thus preventing those wavelengths from being reflected back at the viewer. When combined in equal proportions, the RYB primaries produce black (having absorbed *all* visible wavelengths of light). Modern printing techniques follow the subtractive model by utilizing cyan, magenta, and yellow primary inks, with the addition of black ink (CMYK, where K is black). Cyan, magenta, and yellow happen to be secondary colors on the RGB color wheel. Maya's Color Chooser window represents the RGB color wheel as a hexagon shape; primary and secondary colors are located at the corners of the hexagon. (For more information on the Color Chooser, see Chapter 6.)

Despite the disparity between color theory models, methods of using a RYB color wheel are equally applicable to RGB color wheels. As such, the goal of color selection is color harmony, which is the pleasing selection and arrangement of colors within a piece of art. The most common methods of choosing harmonic colors produce the following color combinations with the RGB color wheel:

Complementary colors A pair of colors at opposite ends of the color wheel. For example, in Figure 1.30, the blue-cyan body and red-orange head of a bizarre character compose a complementary color set.

Figure 1.30 A blue-cyan body and a red-orange head form complementary colors. This still is taken from *7 Deadly Sins for the 21st Century* (2005).

Split complement One color plus the two colors that flank that color's complementary color (for example, green, blue-violet, and red-violet).

Analogous colors Colors that are side-by-side. For example, in Figure 1.31 the cloaks of two women are red-orange and yellow-orange. In RGB, red-orange is a mixture of primary red and tertiary orange; yellow-orange is the mixture of secondary yellow and tertiary orange. (If compared to the RYB color wheel, the colors correspond to secondary orange and tertiary yellow-orange, which are also analogous.)

Figure 1.31 Antonio da Correggio (1489–1534). *The Mystic Marriage of Saint Catherine.* c. 1520. Oil on canvas. National Gallery, London. The women's cloaks form analogous colors.

Diad Two colors that have a single color position between them (for example, secondary violet and primary red on the RGB color wheel).

Triad Three colors that are equally spaced on the wheel.

Note: A common mistake made by many 2D and 3D animators is the overuse of pure primary and secondary colors in their designs. Colors located between the secondary and tertiary elements will provide a more diverse palette. For instance, instead of choosing 1, 0, 1 in Maya RGB color space, try selecting 0.5, 0.4, 0.8 for a more muted variation of violet.

Checking Color Calibration

Maya operates in RGB color space. Color space represents all the colors that a device can produce. The color space available to various output devices varies greatly. For example, the color space that a television can display is significantly different from the color space available to a computer monitor or a printer.

Never assume that a computer monitor is displaying your renders correctly. If you are creating an animation for video, it's best to check the resulting edit on a professional broadcast monitor. If you are creating a render for print, bring the render into Photoshop or a similar program, convert the RGB color space to CMYK color space, and choose the correct color profile (see the next paragraph). If you are creating the animation for motion picture film, calibrate your monitor based on the suggestions of the service transferring the frames. Larger animation houses often maintain their own transfer equipment. In many cases, a lookup table (LUT) is developed to properly map the gamma of the computer monitors used by animators. Portable calibration hardware is also used to check the calibration result. (The color displayed by a monitor "drifts" over time.) Although this process may be too costly for an independent animator, calibration shortcuts can be taken.

Many digital-imaging programs are bundled with calibration software. Adobe Gamma is perhaps the most common. Launching the program will step you through an interactive calibration process. Although useful, Adobe Gamma is designed for print projects, so it might not provide accurate settings for some animation. In addition, Photoshop, along with other digital-imaging programs, offers multiple color profiles based on the color standards of the International Color Consortium (ICC). Color profiles represent the color reproduction capabilities of a device. Hence, you can work within the color limitations of a specific printer while in Photoshop. Unfortunately, the standard profiles are not designed for film or video.

A quick-and-dirty method of checking the color calibration of a monitor involves the use of a chip chart. For example, in Figure 1.32 a chart runs from black to white in 11 distinct steps and in a continuous gradient. When displayed on a monitor, a portion of the chart may appear "crushed." (Certain steps may no longer be visible, and the gradient may no longer be smooth.) If this is the case with your monitor, you might unintentionally base a scene's lighting on an inaccurate view of the scene's actual color space. The end result might be an animation that appears too dark and muddy on video or too bright and washed out on film. Adjusting the brightness, contrast, gamma, and color temperature of the monitor can alleviate this problem. Although you can usually adjust the brightness and contrast through a monitor's external control panel, the gamma and color temperature are usually controlled through a piece of calibration software (for example, Adobe Gamma). (For more information on gamma, see Chapter 6.)

Figure 1.32 A calibration chip chart. This file is included on the CD as `chip_chart.tif`.

A Note on Color Temperature

Color temperature is based on the wavelength of light emitted by a material when it is heated. Technically speaking, if a light source is said to be 5500 kelvin, it emits the same wavelength of light, and the same color of light, as a black body radiator heated to 5500 kelvin. A black body radiator is a theoretical material that absorbs 100 percent of the radiation that strikes it when the body is at absolute zero (–273 C°). Although there are no true black bodies in the real world, graphite and various metals come close. In the original experiments by William Kelvin (1824–1907), a block of heated carbon was used. The kelvin, on the other hand, is a measurement of temperature that adds 273 to the temperature read in Celsius. The kelvin measurement only refers to the thermal temperature of the theoretical black body radiator and is not the actual temperature of a light source. In other words, a fluorescent lightbulb does not have to reach a real-world 4000 degrees kelvin to produce the same color of light as the black body radiator at 4000 kelvin; instead, the color of the bulb is roughly correlated to the color of the heated black body.

When a material is heated to a temperature above 700 K (700 kelvin), it emits visible light. At temperatures close to 700 K, the light wavelength is long and the perceived light is red. At temperatures above 6000 K, the wavelength becomes shorter and the perceived color shifts to blue. The chart in Figure 1.33 indicates the color temperature of various light sources and their perceived colors. The colors represented are only a rough approximation. In addition, the color temperatures listed for each light source are an average; depending on the circumstance or the method of manufacture, color temperatures can easily vary by hundreds of kelvin.

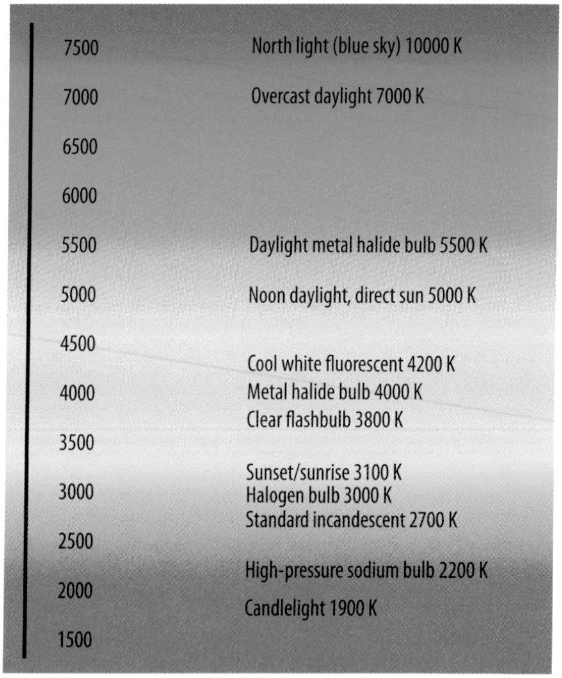

7500 North light (blue sky) 10000 K
7000 Overcast daylight 7000 K
6500
6000
5500 Daylight metal halide bulb 5500 K
5000 Noon daylight, direct sun 5000 K
4500
Cool white fluorescent 4200 K
4000 Metal halide bulb 4000 K
Clear flashbulb 3800 K
3500
Sunset/sunrise 3100 K
3000 Halogen bulb 3000 K
Standard incandescent 2700 K
2500
High-pressure sodium bulb 2200 K
2000
Candlelight 1900 K
1500

Figure 1.33 Color temperatures of common light sources. This image is included on the CD as `color_chart.tif`.

Setting a White Point

In the case of monitor calibration, color temperature is used to set the white point of the hardware. A white point is a coordinate in color space that defines what is "white." If a monitor is given a white point with a high kelvin value, the display has a blue cast. If a monitor is given a white point with a low kelvin value, the display has a yellow cast. The flexibility of the white point is necessary to match potential output formats. For example, graphic artists who use offset printing might set their monitors to 5500 K. For 3D animation intended for video, 6500 K generally works because broadcast-quality video monitors have a hardware white point set to 6500 K. In contrast, older consumer televisions may have a white point set as high at 9300 K. Many plasma and LCD televisions now offer the option to switch to 5400 K to better match motion picture film.

When lighting in Maya, you do not need to know the kelvin temperature of a light source. What is important, however, is that the color of the light logically fits the type of source. For example, daytime sunlight varies from white to blue. Firelight varies from red to orange. Incandescent lightbulbs are yellowish. If a light color is out of place, a scene may appear incorrect to the viewer. This should not be confused with the way colors are recorded on film, where colors are often exaggerated. For example, daylight film (balanced for 5500 K) will make the yellow of an incandescent bulb more orange. Tungsten film (balanced for 3200 K) will make sunlight extremely blue. Professional photographers and cinematographers reduce this problem by employing color corrective filters and gels. However, the end result is rarely the same as the way it was originally perceived by the human eye. Obviously, if you are matching 3D to a live-action plate, colors should be replicated regardless of what they might be. However, if the 3D is only meant to *look* real, colors—as they're perceived by the human eye—should be matched.

For more information on color manipulation, see Chapter 6. For information on color bit depth, see Chapter 10.

Applying the Golden Mean

The golden mean was extolled by Pythagoras (580–500 BC) and his fellow Greeks. The mean is a number, 1.618 . . . , that is irrational and cannot be converted to a fraction. The golden mean defines a golden rectangle, which has an aspect ratio of roughly 1.618:1. Mathematically, a golden rectangle is a rectangle that can be partitioned into a square and a smaller rectangle that has the same aspect ratio of the original rectangle (see Figure 1.34). The golden mean is represented as the Greek letter phi and is commonly referred to as the golden ratio, golden section, or golden proportion. Although the Greeks are often given credit for discovering the golden mean, some historians suggest that it was employed by earlier civilizations (for example, Babylonia and Egypt).

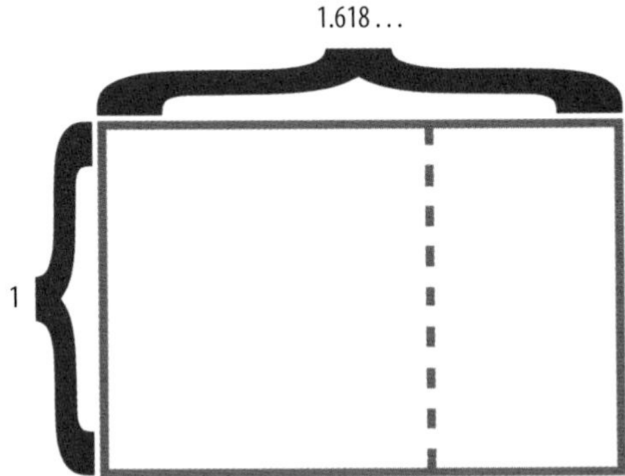

Figure 1.34 The golden rectangle

Greek architects determined that the golden rectangle was aesthetically superior to other ratios and employed the shape in many building designs. This determination has persisted for the past two millennia in the architecture of Western civilization. As for fine art, the golden mean was rediscovered by artists of the Renaissance, including Leonardo da Vinci (1452–1519) and Raphael (1483–1520). Variations of the golden mean can also be found in Medieval Islamic architecture and tile work. Many 19th- and 20th-century artists, including Georges Seurat (1859–91), Piet Mondrian (1872–1944), and Salvador Dali (1904–89), applied the compositional technique (see Figure 1.35). The golden rectangle survives to this day as the approximate aspect ratio of credit and debit cards (1.6:1). The 1.66:1 motion picture aspect ratio, used extensively outside North America, also comes close to the golden rectangle. (For more information on aspect ratios, see Chapter 10.)

Figure 1.35 The golden mean and golden rectangle used in a composition by Seurat. (*Circus Sideshow.* 1888. Oil on canvas. Metropolitan Museum of Art, New York.) The painting is repeated twice.

The golden mean has many natural occurrences. For example, the Fibonacci series, a series of numbers in which the division of any two adjacent numbers is roughly the golden mean, can be used to accurately predict the growth of flower petals, seeds, seashells, pine cones, and various plant leaves.

Numerous psychological studies have been undertaken since the late 1800s to determine if humans have a natural bias toward the golden rectangle. Conclusions have been varied; on average, they've recognized the rectangle's slight advantage. Nevertheless, since the golden mean and its geometric corollaries have consciously or unconsciously been used in such a large body of popular art, you can benefit from its judicious use.

In addition to the golden rectangle, the golden mean can be expressed as a golden triangle, a pentagram, or a decagon. For example, in Figure 1.36 the golden triangle and pentagram are used in the composition of paintings by Raphael and Leonardo da Vinci.

Figure 1.36 (Left) Raphael. *Madonna del Cardellino*. 1506. Oil on wood. Uffizi, Florence. (Right) da Vinci. *Virgin and Child with St. Anne*. 1508. Oil on wood. Louvre, Paris.

Rule of Thirds

The rule of thirds is a compositional technique developed for modern photography and videography. Simply put, you can take any frame and divide it into three horizontal and vertical sections to determine the alignment of subjects (see Figure 1.37). For example, you can align a tree, a person, or other vertical element with a vertical line. You can align the horizon or a building with a horizontal line. The four points at which the lines cross are considered prime compositional spots and should feature important details in a shot (for example, a person's face, the moon, and so on).

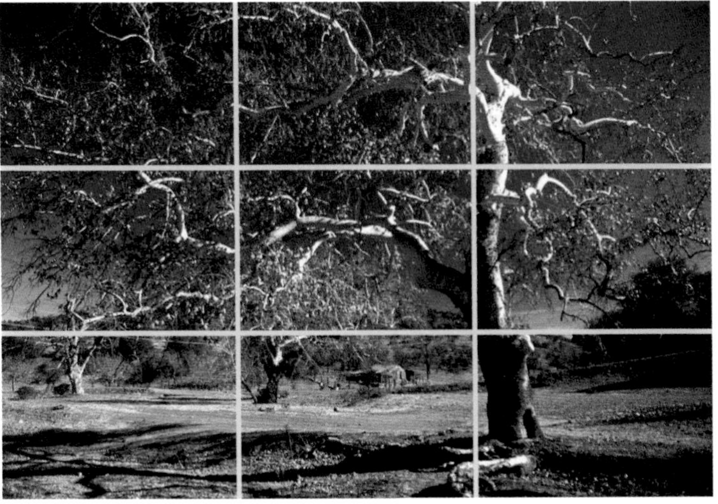

Figure 1.37 A photo divided in accordance to the rule of thirds

The rule of thirds is not an accurate representation of the golden mean (see Figure 1.38). However, the rule may have evolved as a simplified variation of the golden rectangle subdivided according to the golden mean. (Unfortunately, the exact origin of the rule of thirds technique remains murky.) The rule of thirds is useful for modern media, such as videography, that often require quick compositional decision making. The golden mean, on the other hand, is appropriate for painting and 3D since more time can be spent contemplating composition. In any case, attention to compositional detail will improve any animation you choose to tackle.

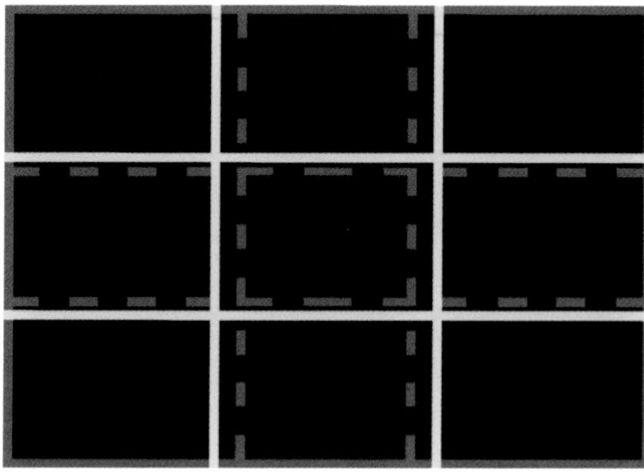

Figure 1.38 A golden rectangle (red) divided in accordance to the rule of thirds (yellow)

Note: Screen direction, a system of motion picture rules developed over the last 100 years, dictates how and where characters, vehicles, and props should be positioned and/or be allowed to move through a series of shots. A strong knowledge of this system will allow you to make proper choices when setting up an animation with multiple shots. You can find information on screen direction from sources that discuss storyboarding, film direction, or editing.

Step-by-Step: 3D Lighting Examples

In this section, I'll discuss the lighting approach of various independent animations. The lighting style varies from naturalistic to stylized.

Millennium Bug featured a series of otherworldly characters inserted into photographs of San Francisco. Simple naturalistic lighting was employed to match the cloudy, overcast weather conditions of the photos. In one shot (see Figure 1.39), a 3D head was added to a preexisting crane. A single spotlight, positioned high and to the right, served as a key. A very low intensity fill light was placed low and to the left. The shadow of the head on the building was added in the composite. Film grain and an artificial camera move were also added in postproduction. *Millennium Bug* was created with Alias PowerAnimator on Silicon Graphics machines.

Figure 1.39 *Millennium Bug*, 1998

Mirror employed an extreme example of chiaroscuro lighting. Many shots possessed only a single key with a limited cone size and no fill. In Figure 1.40, a woman is lit with a single spotlight from screen left. The shadow directly behind the woman was fabricated in the composite and is hence less dense than other shadows in the shot. *Mirror* was created with the original beta release of Maya.

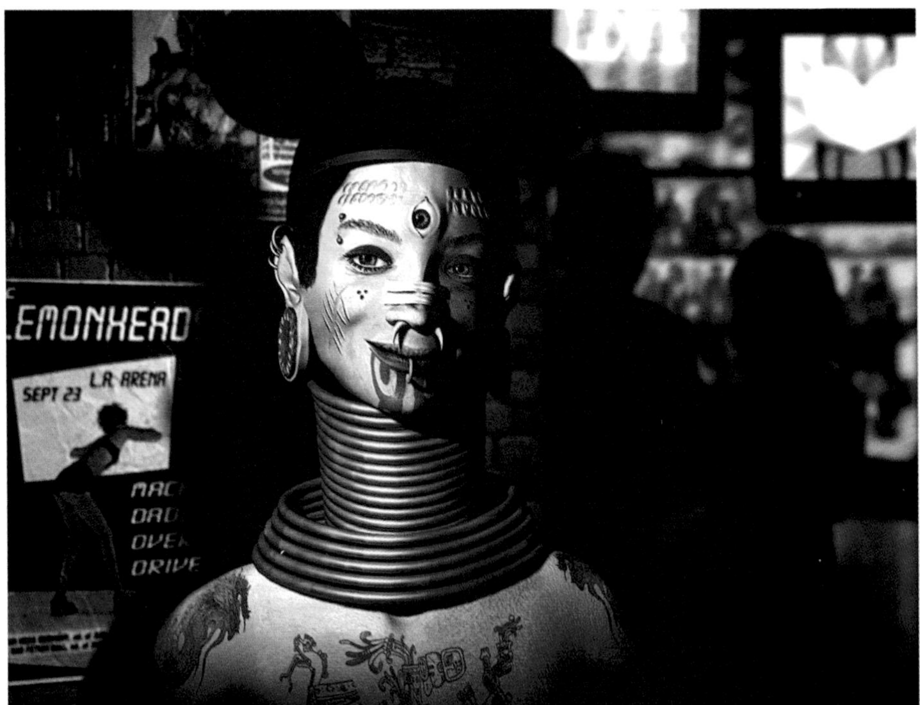

Figure 1.40 *Mirror*, 2000. A QuickTime movie excerpt is included on the CD as `mirror.mov`.

In *Day Off the Dead*, a combination of naturalistic and 2-point lighting was used. For exteriors, one to four lights were placed to emulate a bright, sunlit day (see the top of Figure 1.41). For the interiors, rarely more than two lights were used; in each case, there was always a strong key. Many of the shadows were created during the composite, which allowed the shadow shapes to go off in unrealistic and inappropriate directions (see the bottom of Figure 1.41). This lent a dreamlike feel to the piece. Depth of fields were added for many shots in postproduction.

Figure 1.41 *Day Off the Dead*, 2003. A QuickTime movie excerpt is included on the CD as `dotd.mov`.

Weapons of Mass Destruction employed high-key lighting with supersaturated colors. The film was constructed as a series of short vignettes, many of which served as bizarre commercials from the future. In one shot (see Figure 1.42), a worm was lit with a strong key from the front. The ambience and incandescence of the character's material prevented the need for any additional lights. The background, which started as a 3D piece, was eventually converted to a digital matte painting.

Little Dead Girl made use of stylistic lighting. In many cases, the light hitting the characters had little to do with the environment. In the two shots featured in Figure 1.43, the Little Dead Girl, the Lab Frog, and the Eyeball Child were given their own sets of key lights, fill lights, and rim lights. The goal of the lighting was simply to model the characters in an interesting fashion. In the end, the animation took on the feel of stop-motion cinematography.

Figure 1.42 *Weapons of Mass Destruction*, 2004. A QuickTime movie excerpt is included on the CD as womd.mov.

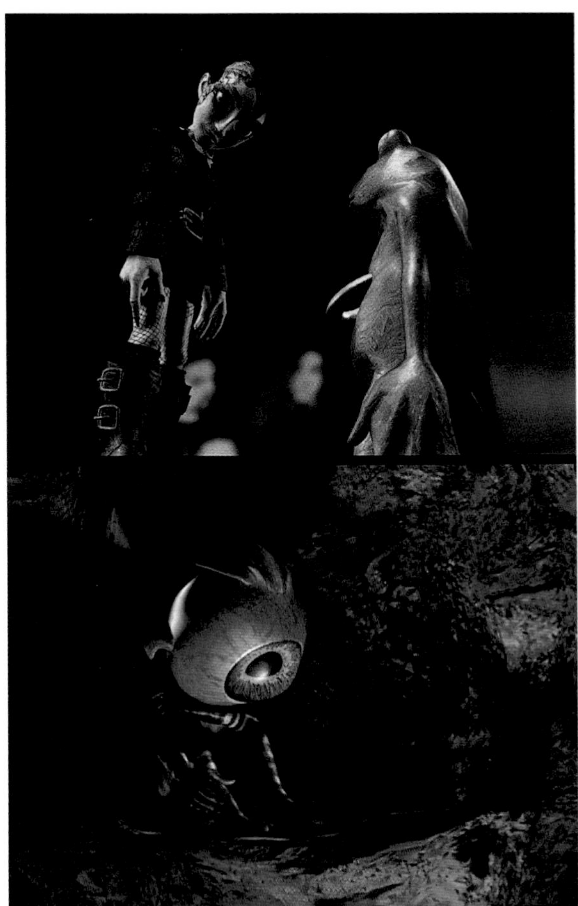

Figure 1.43 *Little Dead Girl*, 2005

Applying the Correct Maya Light Type

Maya offers six types of lights that emulate a wide range of real-world lighting situations. Familiarity with the way light interacts with various environments will benefit your 3D lighting. Light Fog and Light Glow effects are also available through Maya lights, giving you even more flexibility when re-creating specific lighting situations. The Relationship Editor can link lights to objects, allowing you to create multiple lighting setups in a single scene.

2

Chapter Contents

Qualities of each of the six Maya light types
Real-world equivalents for each light type
Linking and unlinking lights
Creating Light Fog and Light Glow
A review of Environment Fog and Volume Fog

Maya Light Types

The six Maya light types have unique sets of qualities and are thus appropriate for different situations. Although spot and ambient lights receive the most use, directional, point, area, and volume lights are equally valuable. Despite their differences, the six types share many common attributes, which are discussed in the next section.

If no lights are present in a scene, Maya creates a default lighting scheme. Once a light is created, the default lighting scheme is overridden. You can turn off the default scheme at any time by unchecking the Enable Default Light attribute in the Render Options section of the Render Settings window.

When you choose Shading > Smooth Shade All from a workspace view menu, Maya uses default lighting even if new lights are created. To see the actual lighting in the Smooth Shade All mode, choose Lighting > Use All Lights from the workspace view menu.

Common Light Attributes

The following attributes are common to all Maya lights:

Color Sets the color of the light. If you map a texture to this attribute, the result is similar to a slide projector and the texture appears on the surfaces that the light strikes.

You can emulate the shadow of an object that does not exist by mapping a black-and-white texture to the Color attribute. For example, in Figure 2.1 a bitmap featuring black leaves on a white background is mapped to a spot light, which creates a simulated, treelike shadow. In this case, the Color Gain of the File texture that carries the bitmap is tinted blue to replicate moonlight. (When mapping the Color of a point or ambient light, the texture becomes pinched due to the omnidirectional nature of those two lights.)

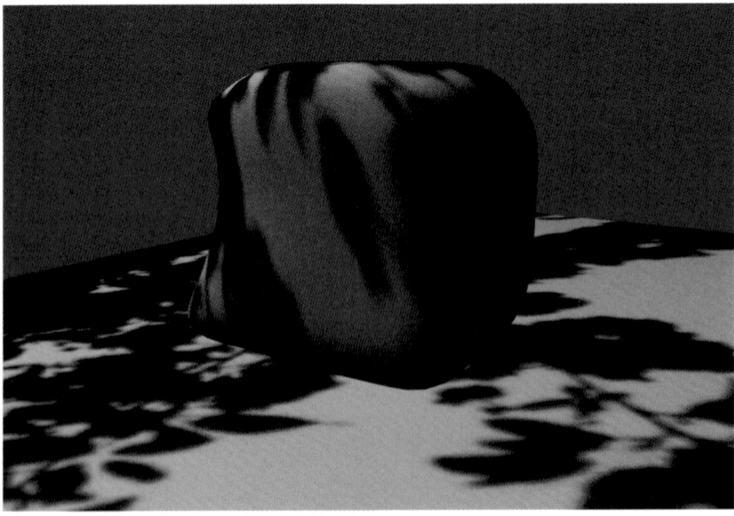

Figure 2.1 The shadow of a tree is created by mapping the Color of a spot light. The scene and image are included on the CD as `spot_leaves.ma` and `leaves.tif`.

In addition, you can animate the Color attribute by left-clicking the color swatch, choosing a new color from the Color Chooser window, right-clicking the color swatch or the word *Color* in the Attribute Editor tab, and choosing Set Key from the shortcut menu. To edit the resulting animation curves, select the light and open the Graph Editor (choose Window > Animation Editors > Graph Editor).

Intensity Controls the brightness of the light. You can apply a texture to this attribute to vary the intensity across the throw of the light. The texture serves as a multiplier. If Intensity is set to 2 and the texture is 50 percent gray, the intensity of the light will only be 1 when it strikes a surface.

Illuminates By Default Serves as an on/off switch for the light.

Emit Diffuse and Emit Specular Determines whether the light will affect the diffuse and specular calculations of a material during a render. Each attribute can be checked off independently. If only Emit Specular is checked, the specular highlights will render by themselves; however, the alpha channel will include the entire surface.

Maya lights offer manipulator handles to make the positioning of the light icons easier. You can activate a manipulator by selecting the light and choosing Display > Rendering > Camera/Light Manipulator > *manipulator name*. (To hide the manipulator, choose it again it from the menu.) The following manipulator handles are available for all six lights:

Cycling Index Displays an upside-down Q-shaped icon that, when clicked, cycles through all the other available manipulators (see Figure 2.2). This is perhaps the most efficient way to use the light manipulators.

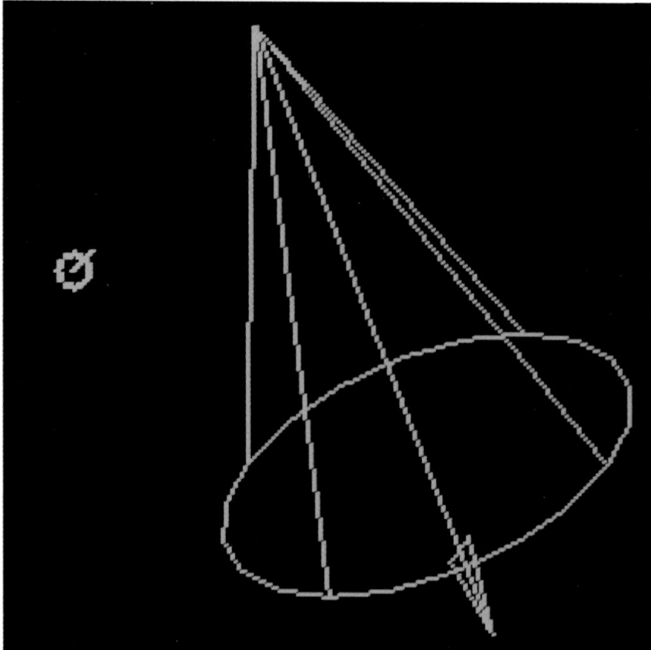

Figure 2.2 A spot light's Cycling Index manipulator

Center Of Interest Displays a Center Of Interest manipulator and an Origin manipulator (see Figure 2.3). When the Center Of Interest is translated, the light rotates automatically to follow. You can also translate the Origin manipulator and thus move the body of the light.

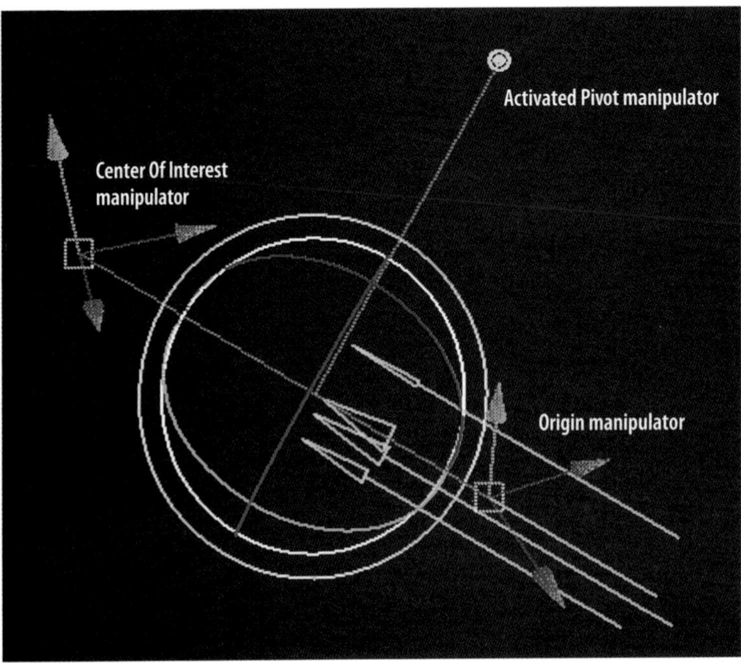

Figure 2.3 A directional light's Center Of Interest and Pivot manipulators. The Pivot manipulator handle is activated so that the Rotate tool operates around the new pivot point.

Pivot Displays a handle that sets the light's pivot point. You can drag the handle's small circle across the light's Center Of Interest line, which is automatically displayed with the Pivot manipulator (see Figure 2.3). You can set the pivot in front of or behind the light. To rotate the light with the new pivot point, click the small circle so that its center becomes solid yellow. To return the rotation to the light's origin, click the small circle a second time. If the Pivot manipulator is hidden while it is active (that is, solid yellow at the center), the Rotate tool will continue to operate around the new pivot point.

By default, the light of ambient, directional, point, and spot lights never decays. That is, its intensity appears the same whether an object struck by the light is one world unit from the light or a million world units from the light. However, with point and spot lights you can force the light to lose intensity by changing the Decay Rate attribute to Linear, Quadratic, or Cubic. The Decay Rate options are ordered from the mildest to the harshest (see Figure 2.4). With Quadratic, the intensity decreases proportionally with the square of the distance (Intensity = 1/distance*distance), which matches the real world. When using decay, you will need to raise the Intensity value of the light. For example, in Figure 2.4 each light is given an Intensity value of 150. Even so, the light with the Cubic Decay Rate manages to illuminate no more than 12 world units from its origin.

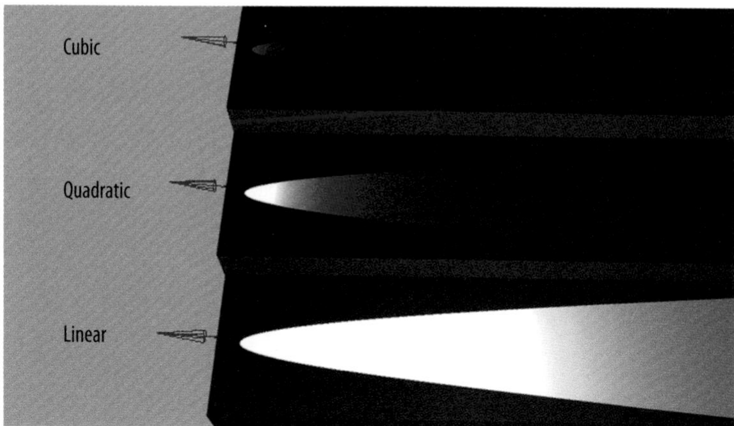

Figure 2.4 Linear, Quadratic, and Cubic decay rates for a spot light. This scene is included on the CD as `spot_decay.ma`.

Note: Area lights naturally decay over distance. Nevertheless, area lights carry a Decay Rate attribute to speed the decay process. In contrast, directional and ambient lights have no natural decay. However, you can create decay through a custom shading network. See Chapter 7 for an example using the Light Info utility. Volume lights, on the other hand, are constrained by their sphere, box, cylinder, or cone light shape.

Using Spot Lights

Maya spot lights are named after the spotlights used on stage and in motion pictures. As opposed to their real-world counterparts, however, the light rays from a Maya spot light are born at an infinitely small point in space. The light rays quickly diverge and follow the shape of the spot light cone. Although the cone has a finite length, the light rays continue on indefinitely. The scale of the light icon does not affect the light's intensity.

Spot lights are ideal for emulating light that possesses one or more of the following traits:

- Naturally divergent rays
- Close proximity to the subject
- Identifiable transition between 0 and 100 percent intensity

Hence, flashlights, car headlights, recessed lighting, table lamps with shades, overhead lighting that "pools," and sunlight diffusely bounced through a window are all good candidates for spot lights (see Figure 2.5).

Figure 2.5 Real-world lighting situations that match the qualities of Maya spot lights

Spot lights are unable to accurately emulate daytime sunlight, since the spot light rays can never be parallel. Additionally, if the Cone Angle of a spot light is set to a large value, such as 120, the resulting shadows are distorted. (For more information on shadows, see Chapter 3.)

In addition to standard light manipulators, Maya spot lights include Cone Angle, Penumbra, Look Through Barn Doors, and Decay Regions manipulators. You can activate these by selecting the light and choosing Display > Rendering > Camera/Light Manipulator > *manipulator name*.

Cone Angle Creates a circular handle at the edge of the light cone that allows you to interactively increase or decrease the Cone Angle attribute. If you click-drag the small cyan cube, the cone size will change.

Penumbra Creates a circular handle at the center of the light cone that allows you to interactively increase or decrease the Penumbra attribute. The Penumbra represents the transition from full light intensity to no light intensity. The larger the Penumbra value, the softer the edge of the spot light. If the Penumbra is smaller than the Cone Angle, the Cone Angle establishes the outermost limit of the spot light's illumination (see Figure 2.6). If the Penumbra value is larger than the Cone Angle, the Penumbra establishes the outermost limit of the spot light's illumination.

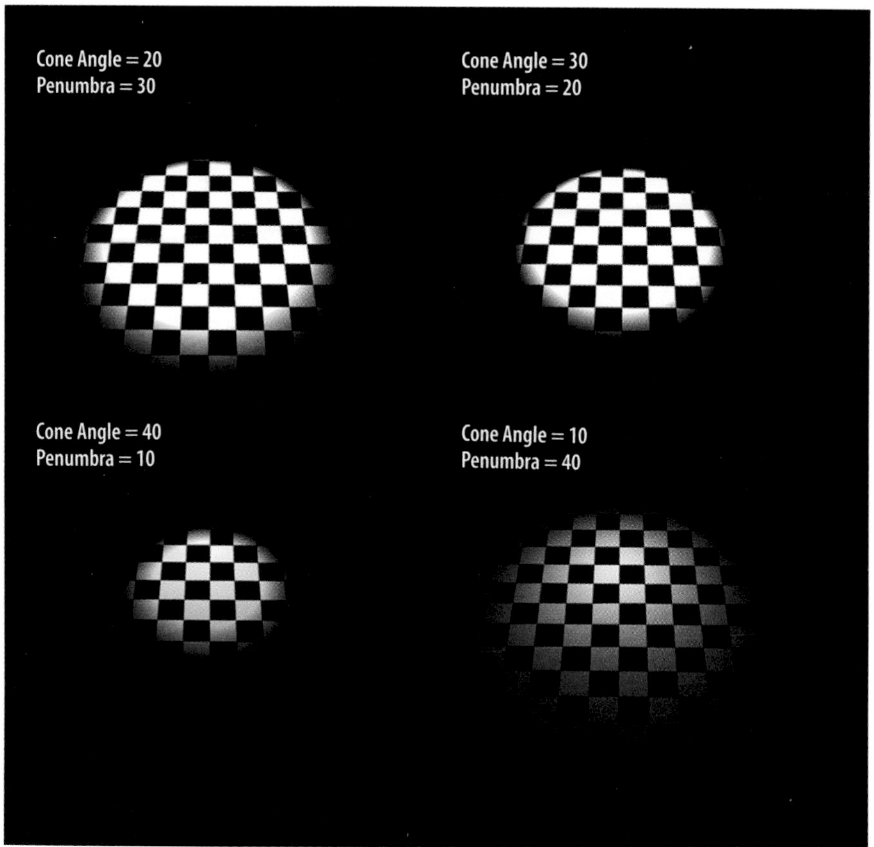

Figure 2.6 Four Cone Angle and Penumbra settings for the same spot light

Look Through Barn Doors Toggles on virtual barn doors for the spot light. In the real world, barn doors are rectangular metal flaps that control the light throw of a spotlight (see Figure 2.7).

Photo © 2008 Jupiterimages Corporation

Figure 2.7 Barn doors on a spotlight

In Maya, barn doors allow a normally circular light to be square. To see the Look Through Barn Doors manipulator, you must check the Barn Doors attribute in the Light Effects section of the spot light's Attribute Editor tab, choose Panels > Look Through Selected in a workspace view, and choose Display > Rendering > Camera/Light Manipulator > Look Through Barn Doors. The barn doors are represented by two horizontal and two vertical cyan lines. If you reduce the values of the Left Barn Door, Right Barn Door, Top Barn Door, or Bottom Barn Door attributes in the Light Effects section, the barn door lines move closer to the center of the light. The smaller the remaining "hole," the smaller the rectangular light shape when the light strikes a surface. If a barn door line extends past the circular edge of the light, the circular edge serves as the cutoff point for that section of the light (see Figure 2.8). You can interactively click and drag the barn door lines in the workspace view when Panels > Look Through Selected is activated for the light.

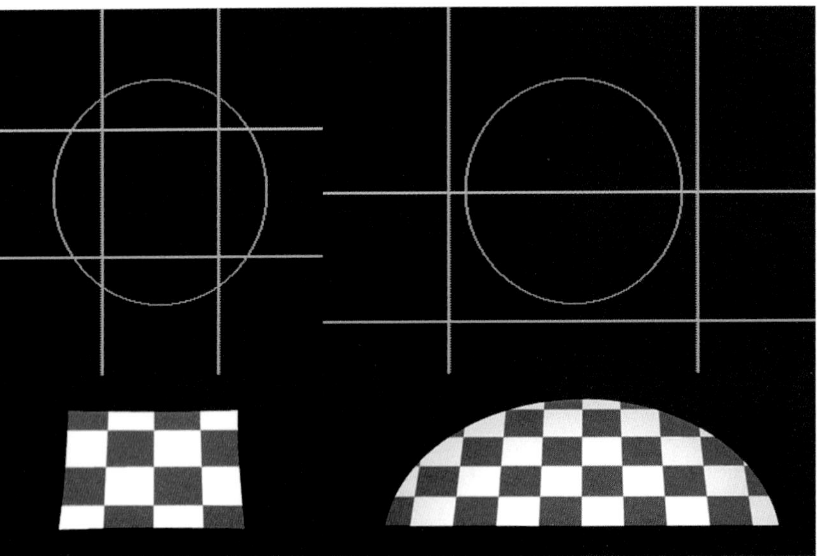

Figure 2.8 (Top) Look Through Barn Door manipulators for two spot lights. (Bottom) The corresponding light shapes made by the spot lights.

Decay Regions Displays circular handles that represent decay regions. You can force the light to possess specific decay regions by checking the Use Decay Regions attribute in the Decay Regions section of the spot light's Attribute Editor tab. Three regions, labeled 1, 2, and 3, are provided. Each region has a Start Distance and an End Distance attribute. Both attributes represent a specified number of world units from the light's origin. The section between the Start Distance and End Distance represents the area where the light is active. The gaps between these sections represent the areas that receive no light. Hence, you can force the light to "skip" across surfaces (see Figure 2.9). You do not have to use all three regions. If the End Distance and Start Distance values of two neighboring regions are identical, the decay between the regions is nonexistent. You can click-drag the Decay Regions manipulator circles to interactively resize the regions. The Use Decay Regions and Decay Rate attributes are compatible. However, shadows are unaffected by the use of the Use Decay Regions attribute.

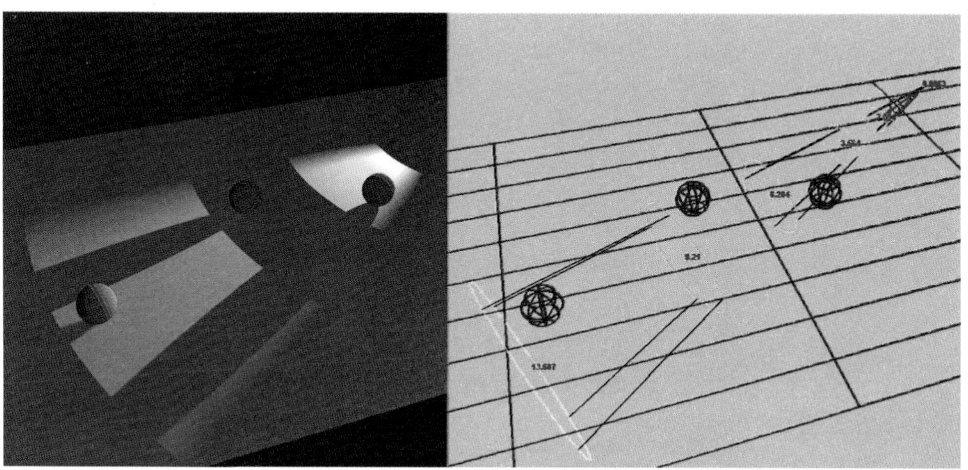

Figure 2.9 Light "skips" across a plane when the Use Decay Regions attribute for a spot light is checked.

For a more subtle decay, you can create custom curves with a spot light's Intensity attribute. To do this, click the Intensity Curve Create button in the Light Effects section of the light's Attribute Editor tab. A curve node is automatically created (see Figure 2.10). By default, the curve is given an excessive number of keyframes. Nevertheless, you can delete or add keys as necessary in the Graph Editor (choose Window > Animation Editors > Graph Editor). The Intensity of the light is represented by the down to up Y direction of the graph. The distance the light travels in world units from its origin is represented by the left-to-right X direction of the graph. The distance is determined with the aid of a Light Info utility. (For more information, see Chapter 7.) By default, the curve starts at 1 and ends at 100 in the X direction, but you can scale the curve or move keyframes if necessary.

You can create similar curves for the light's Color. To do this, click the Color Curves Create button in the Light Effects section of the light's Attribute Editor tab. In this situation, separate curve nodes are created for the Red, Green, and Blue channels. Once again, the default curves will have an excessive number of keyframes; these can also be edited in the Graph Editor.

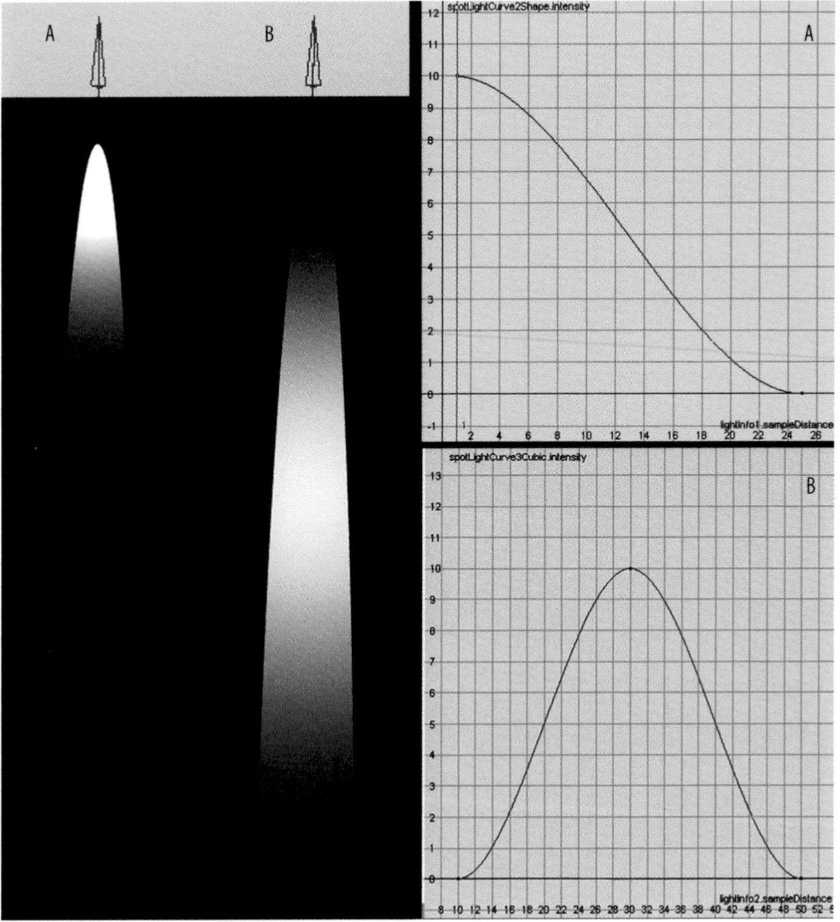

Figure 2.10 Two spot lights are given custom Intensity curves. This scene is included on the CD as `spot_curves.ma`.

Using Directional Lights

Directional lights provide light direction without light position. That is, they are infinite and constant in one direction. The position and the scale of the directional light icon do not affect the light's intensity.

Directional lights are ideal for emulating light that possesses one or more of the following traits:

- Naturally parallel rays
- A source that is a great distance from the subject
- No identifiable edge or falloff

Hence, direct sunlight and moonlight are the best candidates for directional lights (see Figure 2.11).

Directional lights are ideal for set pieces that are large in world space. In the same situation, a spot light would have to be placed extremely far from the subject or have its Cone Angle increased to a very large value, which in turn would cause the light's shadows to become even less parallel (see Chapter 3 for a comparison of shadows).

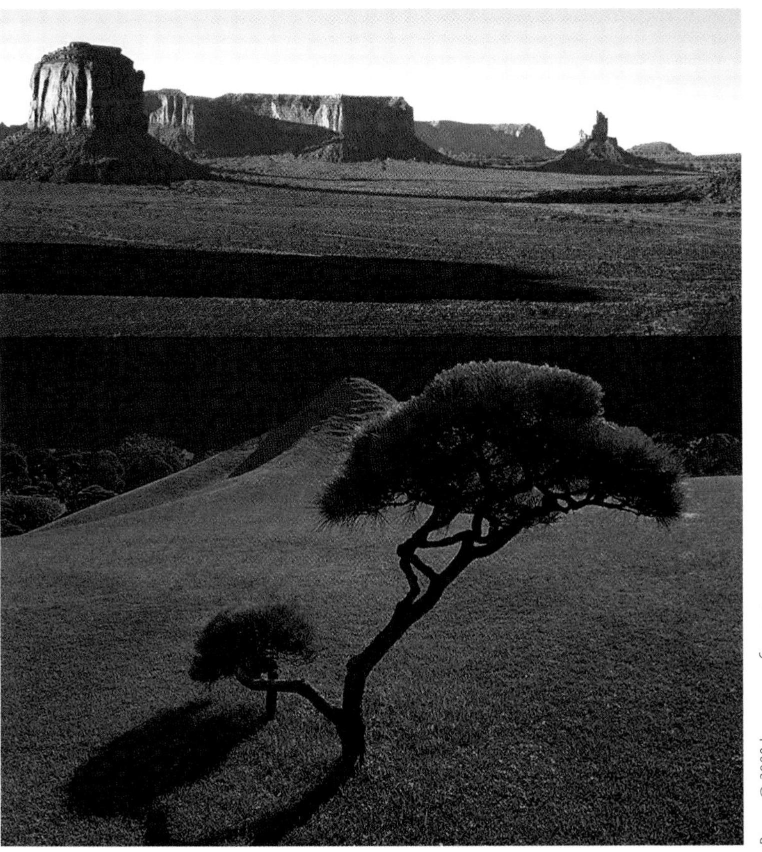

Figure 2.11 Real-world lighting situations that match the qualities of Maya directional lights

Using Ambient Lights

Ambient lights create a soft light emanating in all directions. The ambient light icon cannot be scaled. Ambient lights do not contribute to specular or bump map calculations. If a scene is lit solely with ambient lights and a material has a bump map, the bump map will not be visible.

Ambient lights are ideal for emulating light that possesses one or more of the following traits:

- Extremely diffuse or random rays
- Little, if any, variation in intensity
- Visible in areas that are shadowed by other lights

Hence, ambient lights are well suited for fill light. In particular, light that bounces off walls and light that bounces off the ground are appropriate for ambient lights (see Figure 2.12).

Figure 2.12 Real-world lighting situations that match the qualities of Maya ambient lights. The camel, building, and couple are visible in the shadow of the key light (the sun) thanks to the presence of fill light (reflected sun light).

By default, ambient lights are not truly omnidirectional. The Ambient Shade attribute controls the balance between omnidirectional and directional light rays for the light. The default Ambient Shade value of 0.45 mixes omnidirectional and directional rays (see Figure 2.13). If Ambient Shade is 0, the light is read with equal intensity at all points in the scene. If Ambient Shade is 1, the light emanates from the current position of the light icon; in this case, the light is identical to a point light. If Ambient Shade is 0, it does not matter where the light icon is placed.

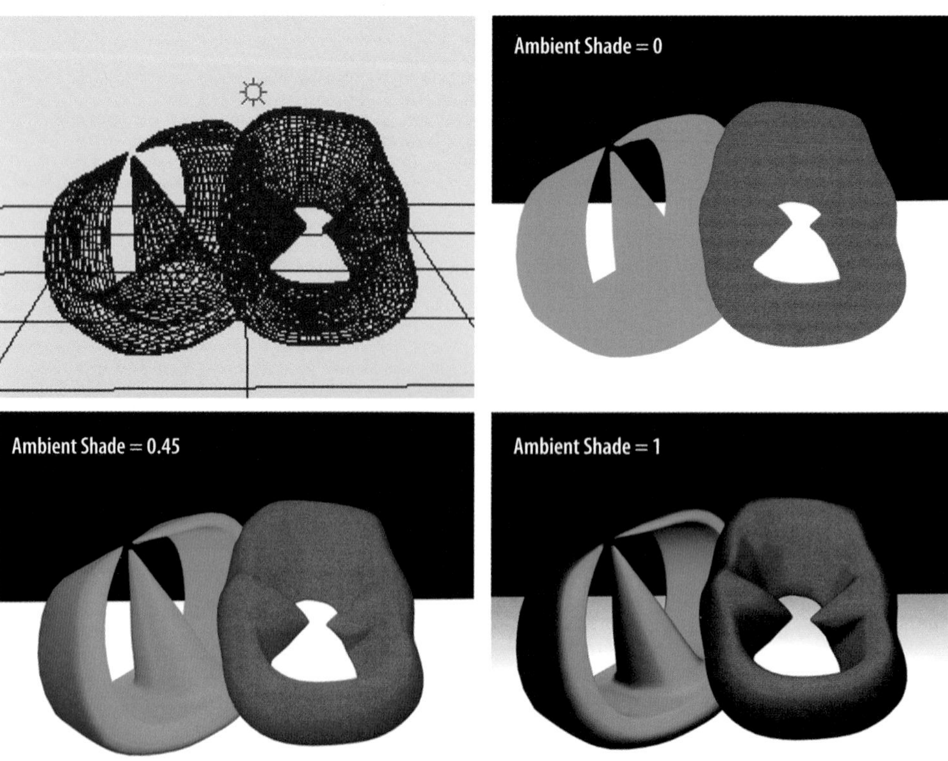

Figure 2.13 Various Ambient Shade values for an ambient light. This scene in included on the CD as `ambient_shade.ma`.

Using Point Lights

Point lights represent a light source at a fixed position. Light emanates in all directions from the light icon. As with a spot light, the light is generated from an infinitely small point at the center of the icon. The icon cannot be scaled.

Point lights are ideal for emulating light that possesses one or more of the following traits:

- Omnidirectional
- Physically represented by a spherical shape

Hence, incandescent lightbulbs are the perfect candidate for point lights. Point lights can also emulate LEDs and compact fluorescent lighting (see Figure 2.14).

Figure 2.14 Real-world lighting situations that match the qualities of Maya point lights

Using Area Lights

Area lights are physically based lights that emanate from a confined, flat area. Area lights can be scaled in two directions (X and Y). Area lights have a center pointer that indicates the direction in which the light is flowing.

Area lights are ideal for emulating light that possesses one or more of the following traits:

- Emanates from a flat or narrow source
- Bounces off or transmits through a large, flat surface
- Possesses decay that is affected by distance and angle

Hence, area lights match light filtering through a window or bouncing off a large wall. Area lights can also re-create fluorescent lighting fixtures, strips of neon light, back-lit signs, and large, dense banks of incandescent bulbs (see Figure 2.15).

Figure 2.15 Real-world lighting situations that match the qualities of Maya area lights

Area lights do not produce parallel light rays. Instead, area lights create a series of rays that emanate from the light icon at sampled positions along the height and width. In essence, area lights function as an array of stacked point lights (see Figure 2.16).

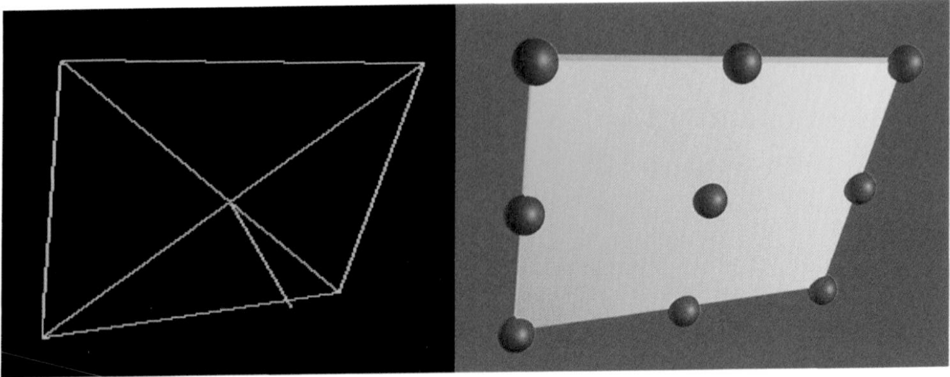

Figure 2.16 (Left) Area light icon (Right) A simplified representation of an area light array. Red spheres represent sampled positions that generate light rays.

The intensity of an area light is affected by its Intensity attribute *and* its relative angle. That is, if the angle between the surface normal and the light direction vector of a single ray is large, the light intensity contribution of the ray is low. If the angle between the surface normal and the light direction vector of a single ray is small, the light intensity contribution of that ray is high. Since area lights produce a series of rays that are sampled across the height and width of the light icon, a unique light direction vector exists for each ray of the series.

Because the light rays of an area light diverge from their origins, the edge of the area light's throw is soft. The degree of softness depends on the distance between the light and the surface. For example, the higher the light is raised above a surface, the more diffuse the edge (the divergent rays have the opportunity to overlap to a greater degree). Although area lights are either square or rectangular, the edge is always rounded at the corners. For a perfectly square pattern, you can use a spot light with barn doors.

Area lights, due to their nature, decay automatically. Nevertheless, a Decay **Rate** attribute is provided to accelerate the decay process. Although you can map a texture to an area light's Color attribute, the resulting light pattern will not be predictable; specific patterns of a bitmap will not be visible.

Using Volume Lights

Volume lights possess a shape icon that dictates the extent of their light throw. You can scale and translate the shape icon to achieve different light falloffs. By default, the light's Light Shape attribute is set to Sphere. You can switch the attribute to Box, Cylinder, or Cone. You can find the Light Shape attribute in the Volume Light Attributes section of the light's Attribute Editor tab.

By default, a volume light shoots light rays from the center of its shape icon in an outward direction; in this way, the volume light is similar to a point light. However, the light will never escape from or exceed the boundary of the shape icon. You can force the light rays to shoot inward from the boundary of the shape by changing the Volume Light Dir attribute to Inward. On the other hand, if Volume Light Dir is set to Down Axis, the light rays will be generated in parallel and will all follow the light shape's down axis. By default, the down axis points toward negative Y. The axis is indicated by the shape icon's green arrow when Down Axis is chosen (see Figure 2.17). You can rotate the shape icon if need be.

By default, the volume shape is closed. However, if Light Shape is set to Sphere, Cylinder, or Cone, you can reduce the Arc attribute and thus use only a section of the light. For example, if Light Shape is set to Sphere, Volume Light Dir is set to Outward, and Arc is set to 90, a pie-shaped wedge of light is created on an intersecting plane.

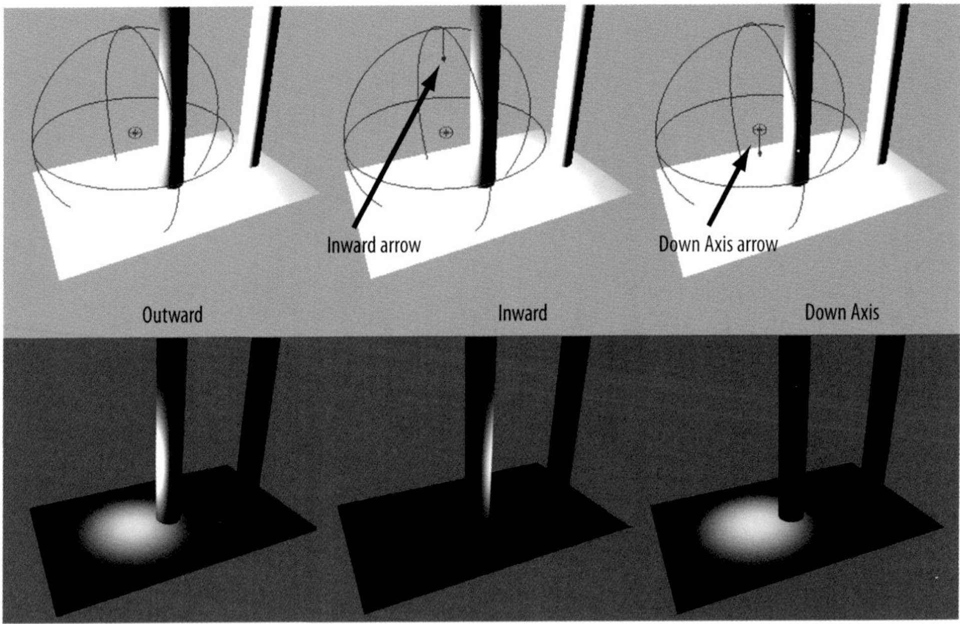

Figure 2.17 Volume light with Volume Light Dir set to Outward, Inward, and Down Axis. The light intersects a plane and one of two cylinders. This scene is included on the CD as `volume_axis.ma`.

You can add additional ambient light to the volume shape by checking the Emit Ambient attribute in the Color Range section. In this situation, ambient light is added to all points within the volume shape.

The quality of the light produced by a volume light is controlled by two gradients: Penumbra and Color Range. The Penumbra gradient, which is available to Cylinder and Cone shapes, controls the light falloff. The left side of the gradient represents the intensity of the light at the volume shape's outer edge. The right side of the gradient represents the intensity of the light at the shape's center. You can insert additional handles into the Penumbra gradient by clicking the gradient field. If a handle is pulled down to 0, the light will have zero intensity at that point. Additionally, you can widen the end of the Cone shape by raising the value of the Cone End Radius attribute. In its default state, the Cone shape's down axis extends from the point of the cone.

The Color Range gradient controls the color of the light. As with the Penumbra gradient, the left side corresponds to the volume shape's outer edge. You can insert additional handles into the Color Range gradient by clicking the gradient field. The color of each handle is set by the Selected Color swatch. If a handle is set to black, it effectively reduces the light's intensity to zero at that point. For example, in Figure 2.18 Light Shape of a volume light is set to Box. Volume Light Dir is set to Outward, and Emit Ambient is checked. Three additional color handles are inserted into the Color Range gradient. The result is a stylized light emanating from the center of the cube.

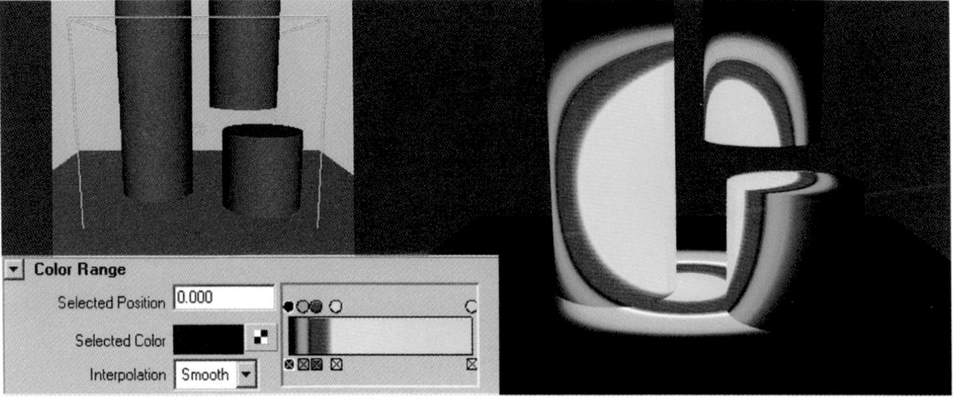

Figure 2.18 A custom Color Range gradient tints the light of a cube shape volume light. This scene is included on the CD as `volume_color.ma`.

The main advantage of a volume light is the ease with which the light falloff can be adjusted through the shape icon and the Color Range and Penumbra gradients. Thanks to the flexibility of the light's attributes, a volume light can function in a similar manner to an ambient, a point, or a directional light.

Linking and Unlinking Lights

In Maya, there are several ways to link and unlink lights and surfaces. By default, a light is linked to all surfaces within a scene when it is created. If a light is unlinked from a surface, it no longer illuminates that surface. The option is useful for lighting complex scenes where a light may be adversely affecting some surfaces while lighting others properly. In addition, it allows different elements within a scene to have the dedicated set of lights. For instance, one character may be given one set of lights with specific settings, while a second character is given a separate set of lights with a completely different set of settings.

The quickest way to unlink a light is to select the light and surface, switch to the Rendering menu set, and choose Lighting/Shading > Break Light Links. (Unlinking affects the Render View and Batch Render, but is not reflected in the Smooth Shade All workspace view.) To relink the light and surface, choose Lighting/Shading > Make Light Links.

When linking and unlinking multiple lights and surfaces, it is often more efficient to use the Relationship Editor. For example, to unlink a light from multiple surfaces, follow these steps:

1. Select a light. Choose Window > Relationship Editors > Light Linking > Light-Centric. The Relationship Editor window opens (see Figure 2.19).

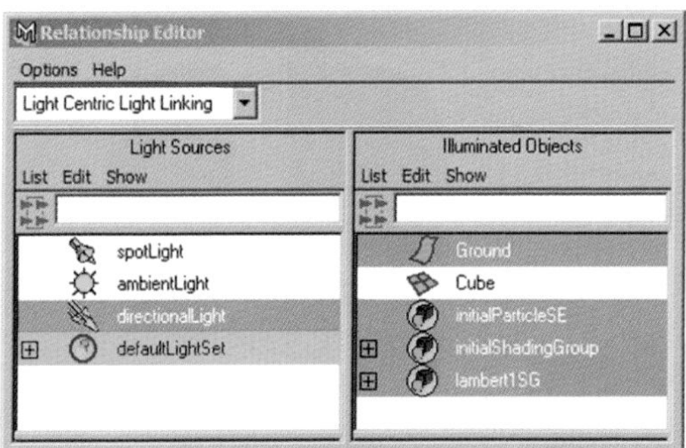

Figure 2.19 The Light-Centric view in the Relationship Editor

2. The left column of the window lists all the lights in the scene. The right column lists all the geometry and shading group nodes in the scene. To see only the light you selected, choose List > Manual Load from the left-column menu. This option will load into the column only the lights that are currently selected. The Manual Load option is also available in the right-column List menu.
3. Click the light name in the left column. A gray bar will highlight it. At the same time, each surface in the right column will receive a gray bar, indicating that the light is linked to it. To break a link, click a name in the right column, which will remove the gray bar, as with the Cube object in Figure 2.19. You can restore a link by re-clicking a name in the right column. If a long list exists in the right column, you do not have to click each name individually. Instead, click the topmost name and drag the mouse downward; all the names under the mouse arrow are automatically highlighted or unhighlighted.

You can also choose Window > Relationship Editors > Light Linking > Object-Centric, which will open the Relationship Editor with the surfaces on the left and the lights on the right. In this situation, you can break the links by clicking the light names. You can switch from Light-Centric to Object-Centric at any time by choosing the option from the window's upper-left drop-down menu.

If you click a highlighted shading group name, all the surfaces assigned to the shading group are unlinked. If you click a surface name, only the surface is unlinked; the other surfaces assigned to the shading group are unaffected.

To simplify the view within the columns of the Relationship Editor window, choose Show > Objects > *object type* from the column menu. If an object type has a check mark beside it, the object type is displayed in the column.

In addition, it's possible to link and unlink shadows from surfaces. For more information, see Chapter 3.

Using Light Fog and Light Glow

Maya spot lights, point lights, and volume lights support Light Fog and Light Glow. In addition, Maya area lights support Light Glow. Light Fog creates a virtual fog in a specific volume. Light Glow creates a post-process light effect.

Creating Light Fog

To create Light Fog, click the Light Fog checkered attribute button in the Light Effects section of the light's Attribute Editor tab. A Light Fog material, named lightFog, is automatically created and is accessible in the Materials tab of the Hypershade window. The lightFog material node is connected to a new light fog shading group node but will have no visible connection to the light itself.

If the light is a spot light, a cone-shaped fog icon will instantly extend itself from the original light cone. The new cone, drawn in blue in the workspace view, represents the area in which the fog will appear (see Figure 2.20). Scaling the entire spot light will increase or decrease the fog area. The fog will not extend past the end of the fog icon but will abruptly end. A utility node named coneShape generates the fog icon.

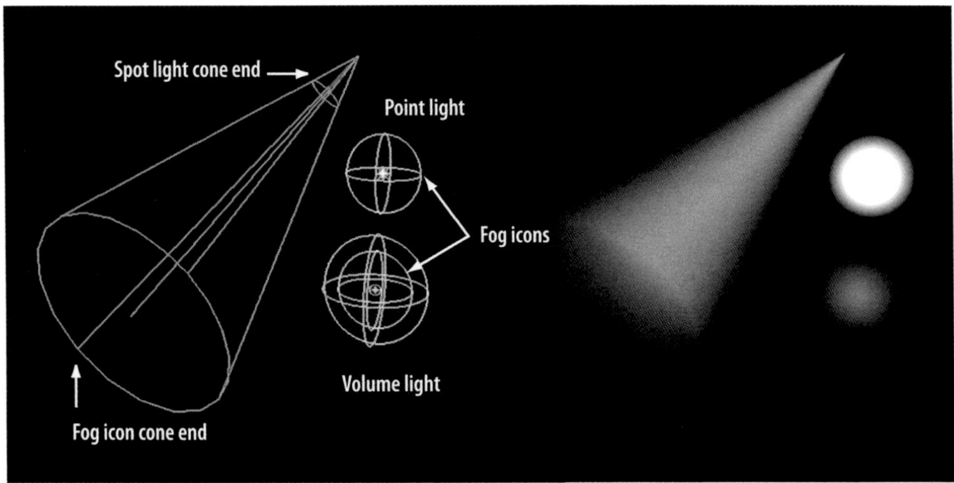

Figure 2.20 Fog icons and default fog renders for a spot light, point light, and volume light. This scene is included on the CD as `light_fog.ma`.

If the light is a point light or a volume light, a sphere-shaped fog icon is added. Initially, the fog icon for a volume light is the same size as the volume light itself, but the fog icon can be scaled. (It's a separate utility node parented to the light shape node.) However, if the fog icon for a volume light is scaled larger than the volume light, the fog will no longer be illuminated and the fog will no longer appear in the alpha channel. You can also scale the fog icon of a point light, in which case the size of the icon is not restricted.

The Light Fog material has the following attributes:

Color Is multiplied by the light's Color attribute to determine the color of the fog. For instance, if the Light Fog material Color is set to yellow and the light's Color attribute is set to cyan, the fog will appear green and the illuminated objects will be struck by cyan light. If the light's Color attribute is left as white, the fog will pick up the color of the Light Fog material Color.

Density Sets the density of the fog. The higher the value, the more opaque the fog. The density is consistent throughout the entire fog volume. You can set the Density value higher than 1.

Color Based Transparency If checked, bases the fog's transparency on its color. Bright areas of the fog are the most opaque and dark areas are the most transparent. If unchecked, the fog becomes 100 percent opaque and the colors of the surfaces trapped within the fog are ignored (see Figure 2.21).

Figure 2.21 Spot light fog with different Density, Color Based Transparency, and Fast Drop Off settings.

Fast Drop Off When checked, causes the occlusion of objects within the fog to vary with their distance from the camera (see Figure 2.21). This closely copies the physical nature of real fog. If unchecked, the amount of occlusion is consistent and the object's distance from the camera is ignored. If checked, the Density attribute is ignored.

Matte Opacity Mode Determines how the fog will render in the alpha channel. (*Matte*, *mask*, and *alpha* are interchangeable words when discussing rendering.)

Opacity Gain, which is the default option, renders alpha based on the fog transparency. Opacity Gain is appropriate for most renders. Pixel values used for the Opacity Gain calculation are multiplied by the Matte Opacity attribute.

The second option, Solid Matte, ignores transparency information and bases the alpha solely on the Matte Opacity value. If Matte Opacity is set to 1, the fog will be 100 percent opaque in the alpha channel.

The third option, Black Hole, works like Solid Matte, but in reverse. By default, the fog is rendered as 100 percent transparent in the alpha, "punching" a hole into all objects that intersect its throw.

In addition to the options available through the Light Fog material, spot lights possess Fog Spread and Fog Intensity attributes in their Light Effects section. Fog Spread controls the width of the fog within the fog icon; low values cause the fog to form at the icon's center, away from the icon edges. Fog Intensity controls the fog's brightness; higher values cause the fog to become more opaque. The Fog Intensity attribute is provided for point lights and volume lights. In place of Fog Spread, point lights have Fog Radius. Fog Radius interactively scales the fog icon of the point light. In addition, point lights have the Fog Type attribute. When Fog Type is switched from

Normal to Linear or Exponential, there are minor variations in the fog quality at the edge of the fog icon.

When a texture is mapped to the Color of a light with Light Fog, the color of the texture is streaked through the fog, making the effect similar to a movie projector in a smoky room (see Figure 2.22).

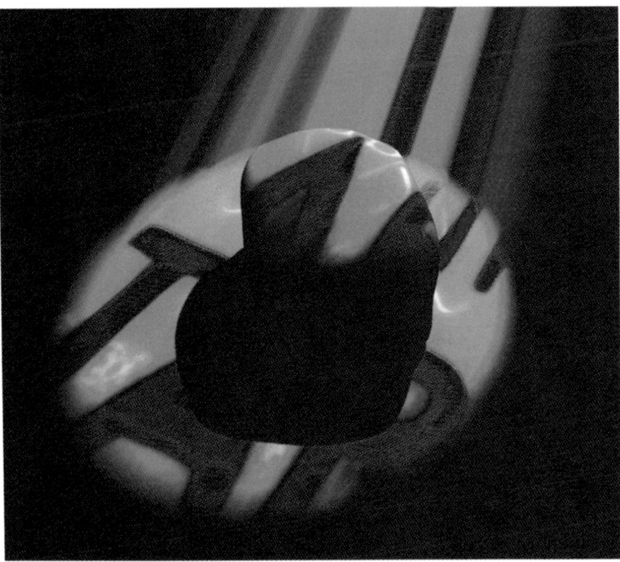

Figure 2.22 Light Fog with a bitmap mapped to the Color attribute of a spot light. This scene and image is included on the CD as `fog_bitmap.ma` and `countdown.tif`.

By default, Light Fog ignores all surfaces in a scene and passes through objects. However, if shadows are turned on for the light, the fog stops appropriately. For details on rendering fog with shadows, see Chapter 3.

Note: The brightness of Light Fog is ultimately dependent on the light's Intensity value. If the light's Intensity is set to 0 or is reduced to 0 through a bitmap, the fog ceases to exist.

A Note on Environment and Volume Fog

Environment Fog produces a fog effect similar to Light Fog. Environment Fog, however, occurs at all points within the camera view between a camera's near to far clipping planes. You can create Environment Fog by clicking the Environment Fog attribute button in the Render Options section of the Maya Software tab in the Render Settings window.

Environment Fog consists of four nodes: envFogLight, environmentFog, environmentFogShape, and envFogMaterial. The envFogLight node is an ambient light placed to illuminate the fog. The environmentFogShape node is a render utility that connects the fog to a shading group node; in the workspace view, it is represented by a disc that surrounds the ambient light. The environmentFog node carries the fog's transform information. (For more information on nodes, see Chapter 6.) The env-FogMaterial node controls the look of the fog and carries the following sections and attributes:

Simple Fog This section represents the default Environment Fog type. Simple Fog has a limited number of attributes and is efficient to render. Color sets the fog color. Color Based Transparency works the same way as the Light Fog attribute. Saturation Distance determines the distance from the camera at which the fog becomes 100 percent opaque. The Use Layer attribute, when checked, acts as a multiplier for the fog's density. If a 3D texture is mapped to the Layer attribute, the fog density varies throughout its mass (see Figure 2.23). (For more information on 3D textures, see Chapter 5.)

Figure 2.23 Simple Fog with Color set to green, Saturation Distance set to 1, Use Height checked, Min Height set to 0, Max Height set to 1, Blend Range set to 0.5, and Cloud texture mapped to the Layer attribute. This scene is included on the CD as `ground_fog.ma`.

The Use Height attribute, when checked, limits the fog to a certain height off the "ground" (the XZ plane). Min Height and Max Height determine the fog's range in Y. Blend Range determines the speed with which the fog transitions at the borders of Min Height and Max Height. A value of 1 causes the fog to end abruptly. Lower values create a more gradual transition between fog and no fog.

Physical Fog Toggles off and on physically based Environment Fog. If Physical Fog is checked, Simple Fog attributes cannot be accessed. Physical Fog has seven Fog Type fogs. Uniform Fog creates fog with density equal in all directions. Atmospheric, Sky, Water, Water/Fog, Water/Atmos, and Water/Sky fogs are designed to emulate real-world situations (see Figure 2.24). The attributes for these fogs are listed in the Air, Water, and Sun sections of the Env Fog material's Attribute Editor tab. These attributes control color, opacity, density, and light scatter, as well as the color, intensity, and position of an artificial sun.

Figure 2.24 (Left) Physical Fog with Water/Atmos Fog Type. Camera is below the virtual water level. (Right) Same fog, but with the camera placed just above virtual water level. This scene is included on the CD as `physical_fog.ma`.

Note: You can apply Environment Fog as a post-process by checking the Apply Fog In Post attribute in the Render Options section of the Maya Software tab in the Render Settings window. In this section, you also have the option to artificially increase the softness of the fog by increasing the Post Fog Blur attribute. When checking Apply Fog In Post, you may need to increase the Saturation Distance value, as the fog will become extra dense through the post-process composite.

Volume Fog, on the other hand, is designed to fill a volume primitive shape. You can create a volume primitive by choosing Create > Volume Primitives > *shape*. The resulting primitive, whether it is a sphere, cube, or cone, is automatically assigned to a Volume Fog material that is named after the shape (for example, cubeFog). The Volume Fog material carries standard material and fog attributes such as Color, Transparency, Incandescence, and Density. In addition, the material provides a Color Ramp gradient. If the Color Ramp Input attribute is set to Ignore, the color of the fog is taken from the Color attribute. However, if Color Ramp Input is set to Transparency, Concentric, or Y Gradient, the color of the fog is taken from the gradient (see Figure 2.25). The left side of the gradient represents the color of the fog at its center (Concentric) or bottom (Y Gradient). If Color Ramp Input is set to Transparency, the most transparent areas of the fog receive colors from the left side of the gradient and the more opaque regions of the fog receive colors from the right side of the gradient. The Transparency attribute affects this calculation.

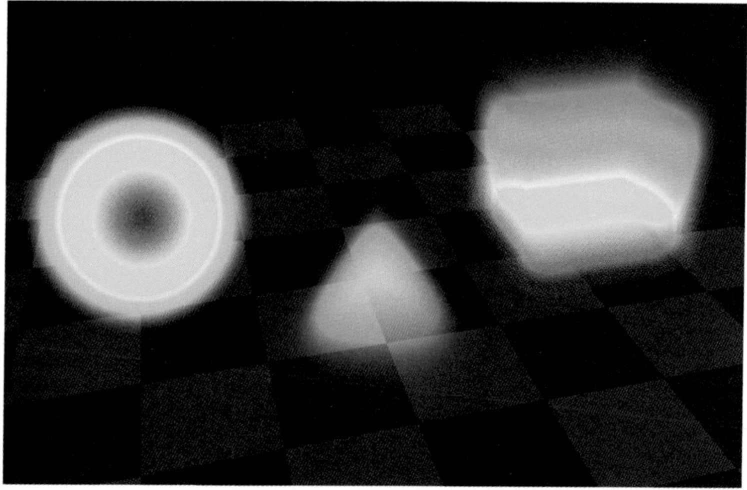

Figure 2.25 Left to Right: Sphere volume with Concentric fog, Cone volume with Transparency fog, and Cube volume with Y Gradient fog. This scene is included on the CD as `volume_fog.ma`.

Light Glow

Light Glow is a post-process that creates various lighting effects. To create a Light Glow, click the checkered Map button beside the Light Glow attribute in the Light Effects section of a spot, point, volume, or area light's Attribute Editor tab. An Optical FX utility is automatically connected to the light. The controls for the Light Glow are broken into five sections in the Optical FX utility's Attribute Editor tab: Optical FX, Glow, Halo, Lens Flare, and Noise.

The Optical FX Attributes section controls the global qualities of the Optical FX utility (see Figure 2.26). By default, the node creates a four-pointed star with a glow at the center of the light. Star Points sets the number of "arms" visible on the star. You can remove the star point effect by setting Star Points to 0. Rotation controls the orientation of the star points. The glow is controlled by the Glow Type attribute. In addition, you can add a halo glow with the Halo Type attribute.

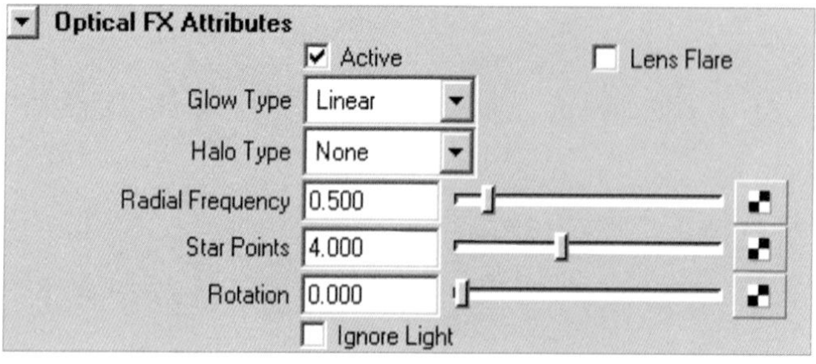

Figure 2.26 The Optical FX Attributes section of the optical FX utility's Attribute Editor tab

You can choose one of six Glow Type glows: None, Linear, Exponential, Ball, Lens Flare, and Rim Halo. None turns the glow off. Linear creates a ball-style glow that decays in a linear fashion. Exponential decays in an exponential manner and therefore appears smaller. Ball creates a large glow that truncates the star points. Lens Flare creates a multicolored ball-style glow. Rim Halo renders only a multicolored version of the star points; the colors shift from lavender at the base to red at the tips, traveling clockwise through the RGB color wheel.

You can choose one of six Halo Type halos: None, Linear, Exponential, Ball, Lens Flare, and Rim Halo. The halos roughly correspond to the glows with the same name. The halos, however, are more diffuse and extend farther from the light's center. The exceptions to this are the Lens Flare and Rim Halo options, which do not render in multiple colors. Halo Type does not have to match Glow Type (see Figure 2.27). If Glow Type is set to None, Halo Type will not produce star points.

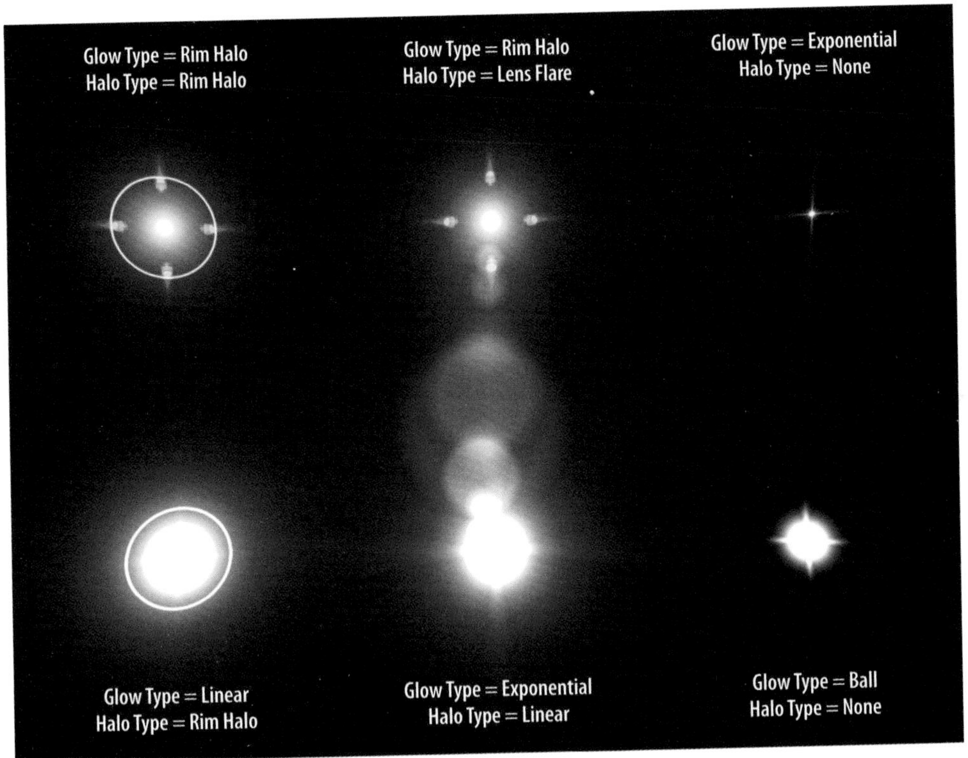

Figure 2.27 Six point lights with six combinations of Glow Type and Halo Type attributes. This scene is included on the CD as `glow_halo.ma`.

Glow and halo descriptions in the previous two paragraphs are based on default settings. Both glow and halo effects have their own sections in the Optical FX utility's Attribute Editor tab. The attributes in these sections are fairly self-explanatory and determine the intensity, spread, internal noise, and additional star arms of the glow and halo. The color of the glow or halo is derived from the multiplication of the light

Color value and the Glow Color and Halo Color attributes of the Optical FX utility. For example, if the light's Color is yellow and the Glow Color is cyan, the center of the glow is yellow and the body of the glow is green.

You can create a lens flare with the Optical FX utility by checking the Lens Flare attribute in the Optical FX Attributes section. The quality of the flare is controlled by the attributes in the Lens Flare Attributes section. Once again, the attributes are fairly self-explanatory and determine the flare's color, intensity, spread, and included components.

There are several Optical FX utility attributes that add noise to the glow effect. To take advantage of this noise, follow these steps:

1. Raise the value of Glow Noise, in the Glow Attributes section, above 0.
2. Adjust the value of the Noise Threshold attribute, in the Noise section, to fine-tune the strength of the noise.
3. Adjust Noise Uscale and Noise Vscale, in the Noise section, to adjust the size of the noise. To offset the noise pattern left, right, down, or up, adjust Noise Uoffset and Noise Voffset.
4. To randomize the strength of the star arms, as well as fragment the individual arms, increase the Glow Radial Noise, in the Glow Attributes section, above 0. In addition, increase the value of Radial Frequency, in the Optical FX Attributes section. To maximize the fragmentation, choose a lower value for Glow Star Level, in the Glow Attributes section.

When the Optical FX utility is created for a point or volume light, a sphereShape render utility node is also placed in the scene. This node connects the opticalFX node to a shading group node and is necessary for the glow or halo to render. A spot light receives a directedDiscShape node. Although you can scale these specialized utility nodes, the scale does not affect the size of the glow or halo. That said, the glow and halo of a spot light is not visible unless the spot light is pointing toward the camera.

You can graft Optical FX utilities onto geometry. The Ignore Light attribute in the Optical FX Attributes section supports this function. For a description of this process, see Chapter 8.

Chapter Tutorial: Lighting an Interior

In this tutorial, you will light the interior of a room, mixing daylight with incandescent light and candlelight (see Figure 2.28). You will use point lights, volume lights, and a spot light. In addition, you will apply Light Fog and Light Glow effects.

1. Open `room.ma` from the Chapter 2 scene folder on the CD. Spend a few minutes familiarizing yourself with the model's various parts. All the surfaces have been assigned to Blinn materials with simple procedural and bitmap textures.

Figure 2.28 The lit room.

2. Select the persp camera, either in the workspace view or in the Hypershade window. Open its Attribute Editor tab. Set the Background Color attribute (found in the Environment section) to a sky blue. Render a test frame. The blue should appear through the circular window. You'll also notice that the lightbulbs in the lanterns have a glow; this is provided by the Glow Intensity attribute of their assigned material.

3. Create three point lights. Name the lights **LanternLightA**, **LanternLightB**, and **LanternLightC**. Place one light in the center of each hanging lantern (see Figure 2.29). For each light, set the Intensity to 1.75, the Color to a pale orange, and the Decay Rate to Linear. If Decay Rate is set to No Decay, a large portion of the room is brightly and inappropriately lit. In addition, check Use Depth Map Shadows (in the Depth Map Shadow Attributes section). Change Resolution to 256 and Filter Size to 24 to soften the resulting shadow's edge. Render a test frame.

4. Create two new point lights. Name one light **CandleL** and the other **CandleR**. Place CandleL above the candle geometry held by the screen left wall sconce (see Figure 2.30). Place CandleR above the candle geometry held by the screen right wall sconce. For each light, set the Color to orange, the Intensity to 1.25, and Decay Rate to Linear. This will make the light falloff more believable. In addition, check Use Depth Map Shadows (in the Depth Map Shadow Attributes section). Change Resolution to 256 and Filter Size to 12 to soften the resulting shadow's edge. Render a test frame.

Figure 2.29 Point light placed at center of hanging lantern

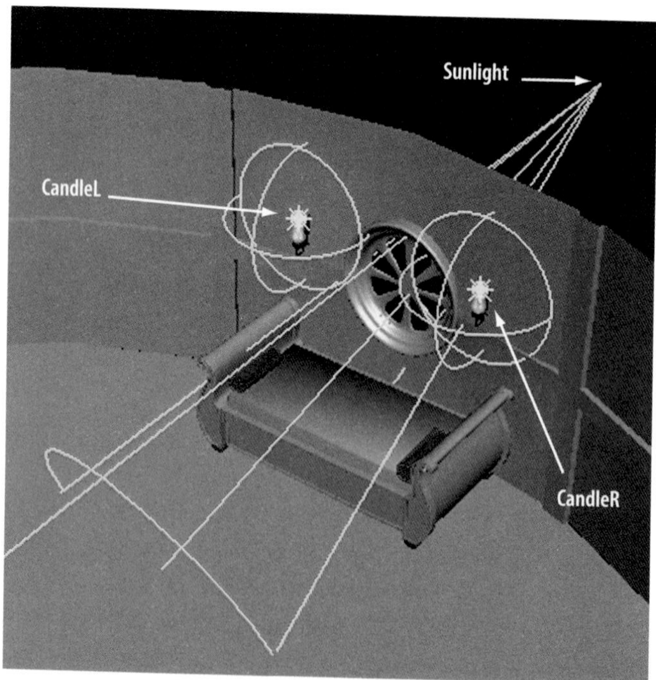

Figure 2.30 Point lights placed over wall sconces and spot light pointed through window

5. Create a spot light. Scale the spot light so that it easy to work with. The scale of the light does not affect its intensity. Rename the spot light **Sunlight**. Place Sunlight outside the circular window at an angle. Use Figure 2.30 as a reference for light placement. Change Sunlight's Intensity to 4.5 and Cone Angle to 25. Render a test frame. Initially, Sunlight will ignore the wall. Open Sunlight's Attribute Editor tab. Check Use Depth Map Shadows (in the Depth Map Shadow Attributes section). Change Resolution to 256 and Filter Size to 12 to soften the resulting shadow's edge. Render another test frame. The light should form a pattern of the window on the ground. Try different positions and rotations for Sunlight until the light pattern is satisfactory.
6. Create a new volume light and name it **CandleAmbient**. Change its Color to a saturated orange. Change the Intensity attribute to 0.6. Check Use Depth Map Shadows. Set Resolution to 256 and Filter Size to 6. Transform CandleAmbient so it is centered under the arches and in front of the daybed area. Scale the light so that it encloses most of the room. Use Figure 2.31 as a reference. This light provides a soft fill for the area lit by the candles. Render a test frame.

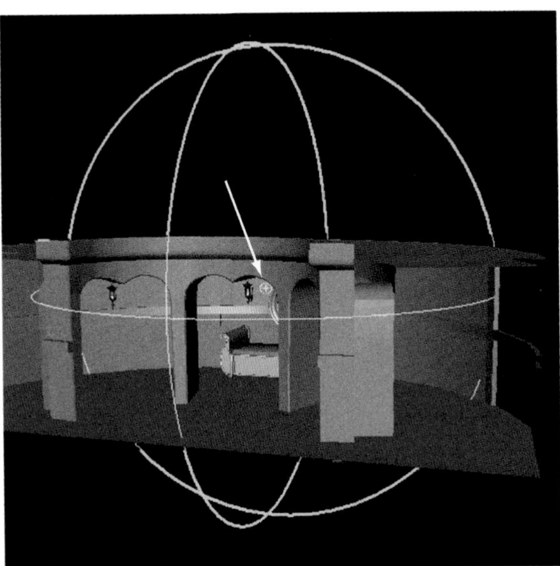

Figure 2.31 Volume light placed at the center of the room

7. Create a new volume light and name it **SunlightAmbient**. Change its Color to a pale blue and its Intensity to 0.6. Move the light so that it is near the model's edge and is relatively close to the camera. Scale the light so that it encloses the

right side of the room. Use Figure 2.32 as a reference. This light provides a faint fill that represents sunlight bounced from the floor and helps to prevent unlit areas from becoming too dark.

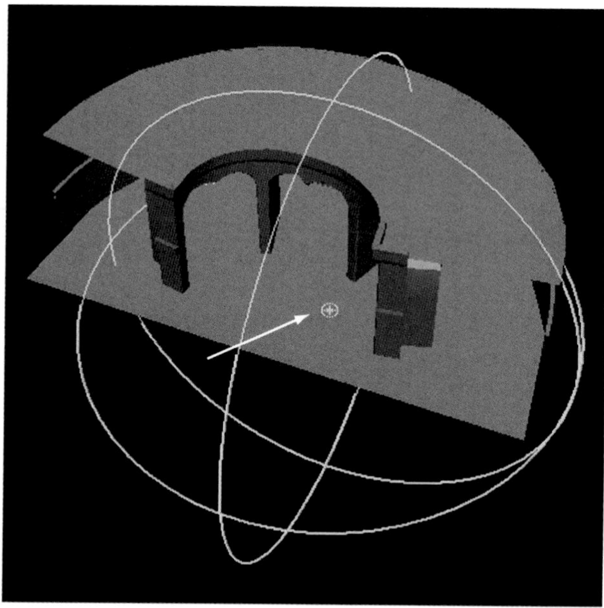

Figure 2.32 Volume light placed near the camera at the edge of the model

8. Select Sunlight and open its Attribute Editor tab. Click the Light Fog checkered attribute button in the Light Effects section. The fog icon will extend itself from the spot light cone. Scale the spot light until the fog icon is large enough to pass through the wall and floor. Render a test frame. Initially, the fog may appear grainy. The graininess will go away when the render quality is raised. Open the Hypershade window and switch to the Materials tab. Select the lightFog1 material and open its Attribute Editor tab. Set Color to a pale sky blue and Density to 1.3.

9. Select CandleL and open its Attribute Editor tab. Click the Light Glow checkered attribute button in the Light Effects section. An Optical FX utility is automatically created. Open the Hypershade window and switch to the Lights tab. Select the opticalFX1 node and open its Attribute Editor tab. Set Glow Color to saturated orange. Set Glow Intensity to 3 and Glow Spread to 0.5. This will create a small, hot glow that will emulate the candle flame. Repeat this process for CandleR. Render a test frame. At this stage, the glass of the two sconces is too dark. In the Hypershade, select the LampGlass material and open its Attribute Editor tab. Change the Incandescence attribute to a dark orange. This will create the illusion that the glass is lit by the candles.

10. The lighting is complete! Open the Render Settings window, switch to the Maya Software tab, and change the Edge Anti-Aliasing attribute to Highest Quality and render a final frame. The render should look similar to Figure 2.28. If you get stuck, take a look at a finished version of this scene saved as `room_finished.ma` in the Chapter 2 scene folder on the CD.

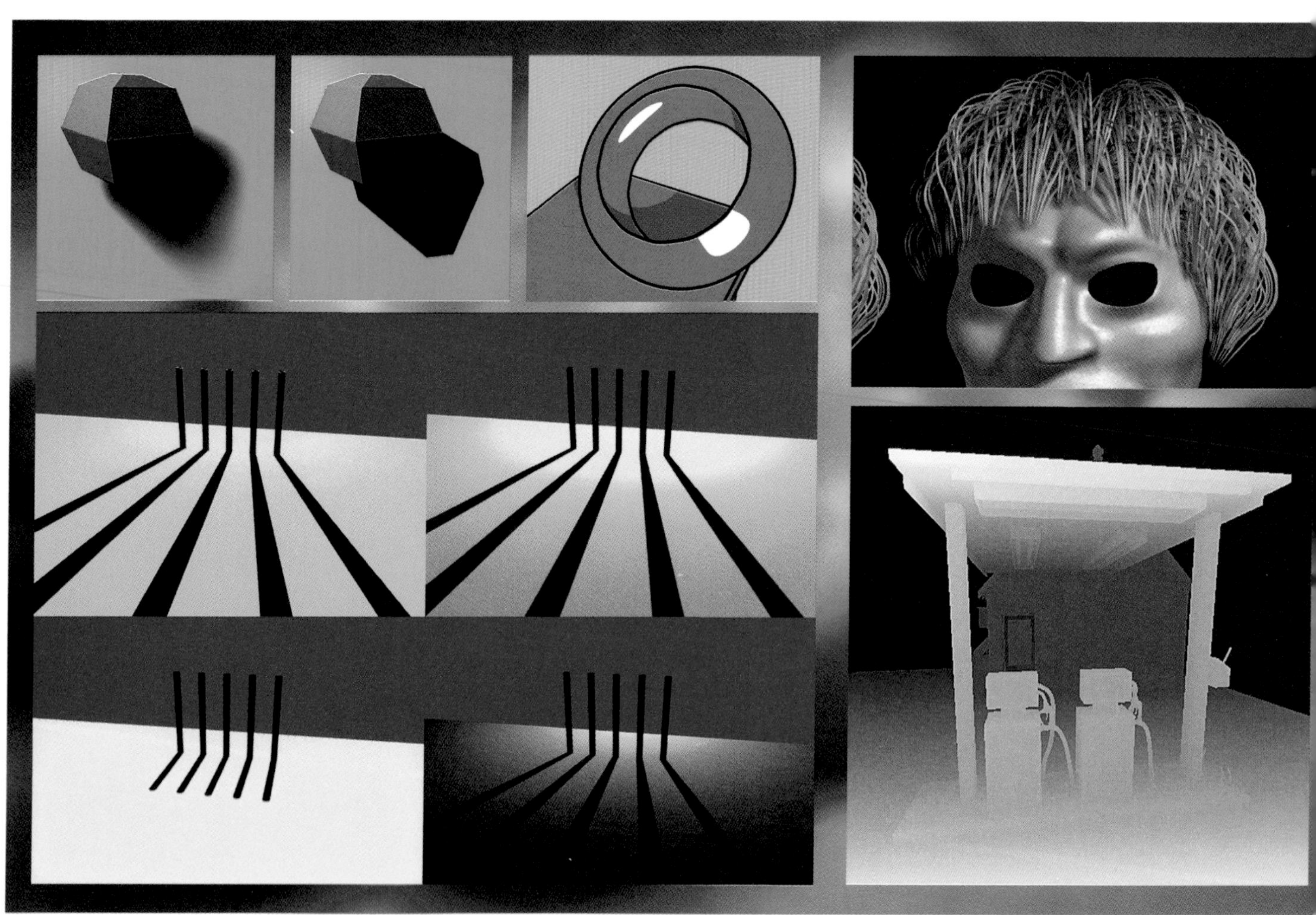

Creating High-Quality Shadows

Shadows are an inescapable part of the physical world. Unless an animation is intended for a stylized look, high-quality shadows are a necessity for a professional render. Depth map and raytrace shadows can be fine-tuned to match many lighting scenarios. In addition, you can shadow advanced effects in Maya, including Light Fog, Maya Fur, Paint Effects, Maya Hair, nCloth, and the Toon system. To make the shadow-rendering process more efficient, you can link shadows.

3

Chapter Contents

Depth map methodology
Fine-tuning and troubleshooting depth maps
Adjusting raytrace shadows
Linking and unlinking shadows
Applying shadows to Light Fog
Creating shadows with Paint Effects
Creating shadows with Maya Fur and Hair System
Using shadows with nCloth and the Toon system

Rendering Depth Maps

Depth maps are easy to apply and efficient to render. Unfortunately, their default quality is generally poor. You can improve the quality by adjusting various attributes and applying specific lighting strategies.

Understanding Depth Maps

When the Use Depth Map Shadows attribute is checked for a spot, directional, point, area, or volume light, Maya creates a temporary depth map (see Figure 3.1).

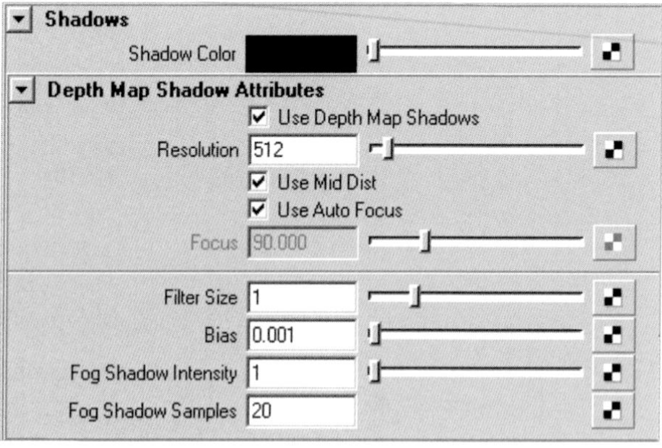

Figure 3.1 The Depth Map Shadow Attributes section of a spot light's Attribute Editor tab

The depth map represents the distance between surfaces in the scene and the shadow-casting light from the light's point-of-view. This information is stored as a monochromatic Z-depth buffer (see Figure 3.2). Objects far from the light receive dark pixels, and objects closer to the light receive light pixels.

Figure 3.2 A depth map

When a surface point is rendered, its distance to the shadowing light is compared to the distance encoded in the corresponding depth map pixel. If the distance is greater than that encoded in the depth map pixel, it's assumed that another surface occludes the surface point's view of the light and the surface point is therefore shadowed. For example, in Figure 3.2 a distant building is partially occluded by a pair of gas pumps. The gas pumps are assigned brighter pixels because they are fairly close to the light. The part of the building that's not occluded has fairly dark pixels. Since the distance value of the dark pixels is equal to the actual distance that the surface points are from the light, no shadows occur in that area (with the exception of self-shadowing, which is discussed later in this section).

By default, depth maps are temporarily written to disk during a render but are not saved. You can force Maya to save the depth map as a Maya IFF bitmap, however, by switching the Disk Based Dmaps attribute (found in the shadow-casting light's Attribute Editor tab) from Off to one of the two following options:

Reuse Existing Dmap(s) With this option, the first time a frame is rendered, the depth map is written to the project folder with a name established by the Shadow Map File Name field (see Figure 3.3). (This attribute is called dmapName in version 8.5.) You can automatically add suffixes to the map name by checking the Add Scene Name and Add Light Name attributes. Each subsequent time the same frame is rendered, the written depth map is retrieved. This option is appropriate if the light position does not change between renders. You can change light attributes, such as Intensity, and material attributes (with the exception of displacement maps) between renders with no penalty. In addition, cameras can be repositioned.

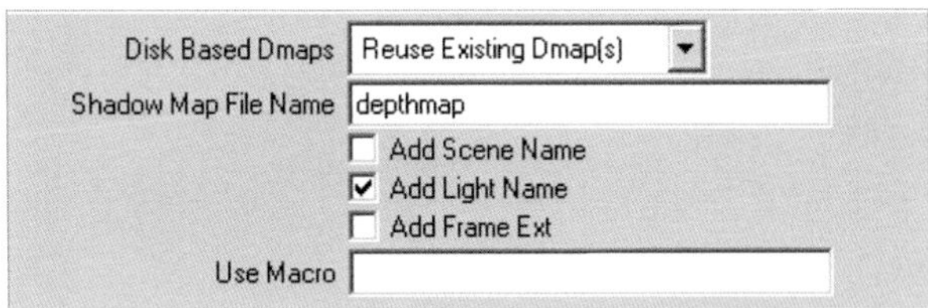

Figure 3.3 The Disk Based Dmaps section of a spot light's Attribute Editor tab

If you batch-render an animation, the Reuse Existing Dmaps(s) option will render only the depth map for the first frame and apply it to all the frames. This is appropriate if objects are static (however, you can animate the camera). If objects are in motion, and their motion does not change between batch renders, check the Add Frame Ext attribute. Add Frame Ext adds a frame number to the depth map filename. The first time the animation is rendered, a depth map is rendered for each frame. For each subsequent render, the series of depth maps is retrieved and reused.

Overwrite Existing Dmap(s) This option assumes that a depth map has been written out at least one time. The new depth map is written over the old one with the name set by the Shadow Map File Name attribute. This option allows you to destroy old depth maps without seeking out the actual files.

By default, Maya writes out at least two IFF files per depth map per frame. The following naming convention is used:

```
ShadowMapFileName_lightName_sceneName.SM.iffframeNumber
ShadowMapFileName_lightName_sceneName.MIDMAP.SM.iffframeNumber
```

When a depth map is calculated, Maya shoots a shadow ray from the light view plane through each pixel of the depth map. The first surface point that the ray encounters is recorded in the SM map. The `MIDMAP.SM` map is created by the Use Mid Dist attribute.

Note: The depth map scene name suffix used by the batch render process differs from the scene name suffix used by the Render View window. The batch render uses the temporary scene file name, such as `shadowtest__1740`, whereas the Render View uses the letters `int`. Maya writes temporary scene files to disk with every batch render, even when no depth map shadows are present. This difference in suffix names can confuse the Reuse Existing Dmap(s) and Overwrite Existing Dmap(s) options.

Adjusting Use Mid Dist and Bias

By default, Use Mid Dist is checked for each light type that supports depth map shadows. This attribute significantly reduces self-shadowing artifacts, which often appear as bands across flat surfaces or a degradation of the shadow as it wraps around a curved surface (see Figure 3.4).

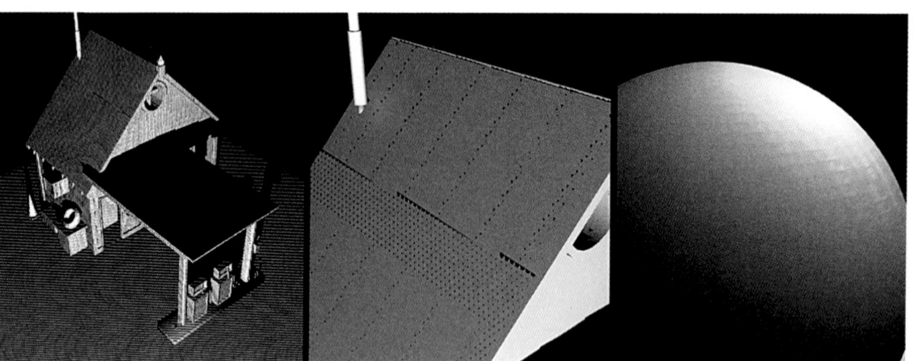

Gas station model created by Matt Orlich.

Figure 3.4 Extreme to subtle depth map artifacts

The artifacts are generally caused by one of two reasons:

- Surface points are misinterpreted as existing "below" or "behind" adjacent surface points. This can occur when surface points are sampled within the boundary of a depth map pixel and are discovered to be farther from the light than the distance value encoded in that pixel (see Figure 3.5). Since the distance value stored in a depth map pixel is based on a single sample—one taken at the point which the shadow ray intersects the surface—this problem occurs frequently.

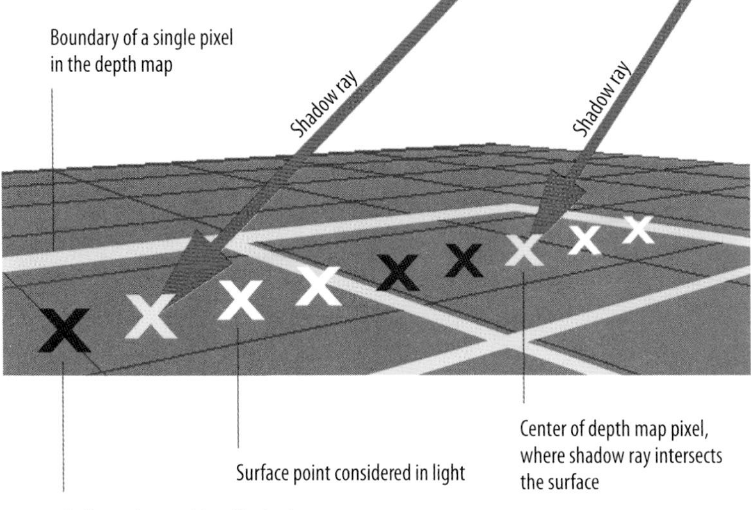

Figure 3.5 A simplified representation of the depth map artifacts

- The pixels of a depth map, which may cover relatively large surface areas, are unable to accurately sample areas of high curvature. In such a case, surface points are incorrectly considered "behind" or "below" adjacent surface points.

In either of these situations, the artifacts are not visible in the depth map bitmap itself. The artifacts occur only during the render of the final image. As a solution, you can increase the depth map Resolution value. Unfortunately, this will reduce the size of the artifacts but will not necessarily eradicate them.

The Use Mid Dist attribute, on the other hand, artificially pushes the surface points closer to the light by comparing the distance from the light to the surface point and the distance from the light to a point halfway between the first surface encountered by the shadow ray and the second surface encountered (see Figure 3.6). The second surface encounters are recorded in the `MIDMAP.SM` depth map.

If a second surface is not encountered, the light's far clipping plane value is used. Again, the basic depth map algorithm works in the following manner:

- If the distance between a surface point and the light is *less* than or *equal* to the distance encoded in the depth map pixel that contains the surface point in its boundary, the surface point is in light.
- If the distance between a surface point and the light is *greater* than the distance encoded in the depth map pixel that contains the surface point in its boundary, the surface point is shadowed.

In this situation, Use Mid Dist forces the depth map to encode distances that are greater than the actual distance to the first surface encountered. Hence, surface points sampled during the render have a greater likelihood of possessing a smaller distance value when compared to the distance encoded in the corresponding depth map pixel.

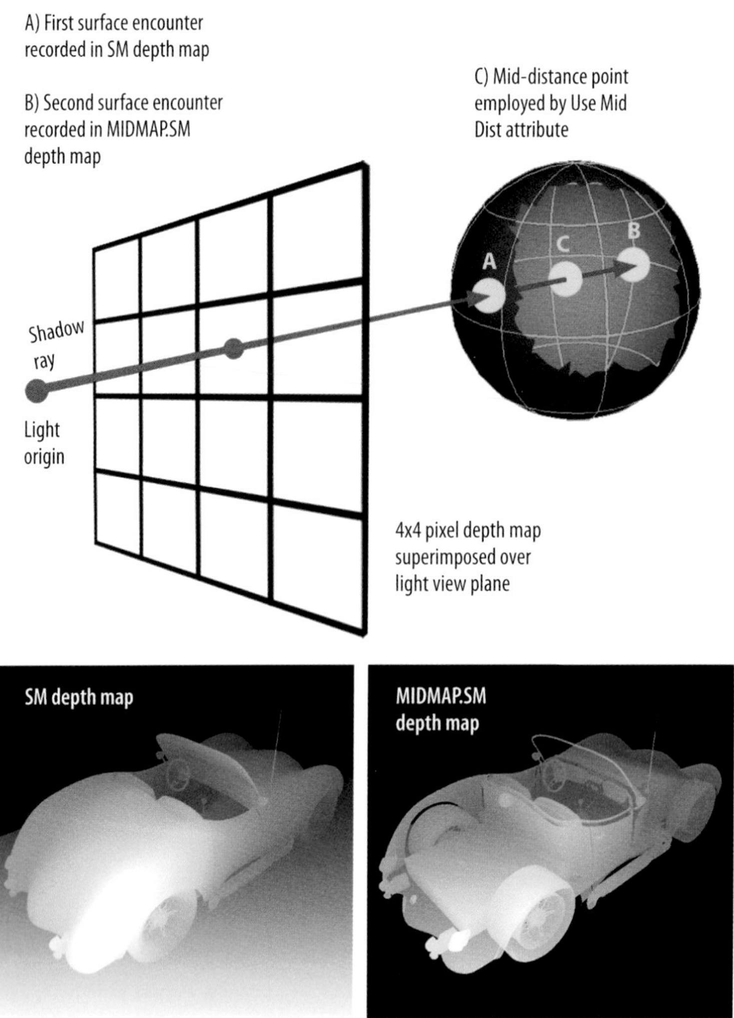

Figure 3.6 A simplified representation of the Use Mid Dist process

Although Use Mid Dist is responsible for a huge improvement in the quality of the render, it cannot eliminate 100 percent of the artifacts. The Bias attribute, which operates on similar principles, is designed to work in conjunction with Use Mid Dist.

Bias holds true to its name and "biases" the surface points toward the light casting the shadow. Whereas Use Mid Dist forces the depth map to take its distance value from a point midway between the first encountered surface and the second, Bias simply multiplies the actual surface point position by a factor that transforms it closer to the light. For spot and point lights, the number entered into the Bias field is multiplied by the distance value derived from the depth map, the result of which is used to determine how far to offset the surface point in world space. Hence, large Bias numbers tend to make the shadow disappear or develop large holes. For directional lights, the Bias attribute is not multiplied by the depth map values but is used as is.

Trial and error is often the best solution when choosing a Bias value. When changing the value, incrementally step from 0.001 to 1. For example, in Figure 3.7 depth map artifacts appear along the edge of a convoluted surface. Although a 0.25 Bias value reduces the problem, a value of 0.5 removes the artifacts completely. Higher values erode the self-shadowing on the surface.

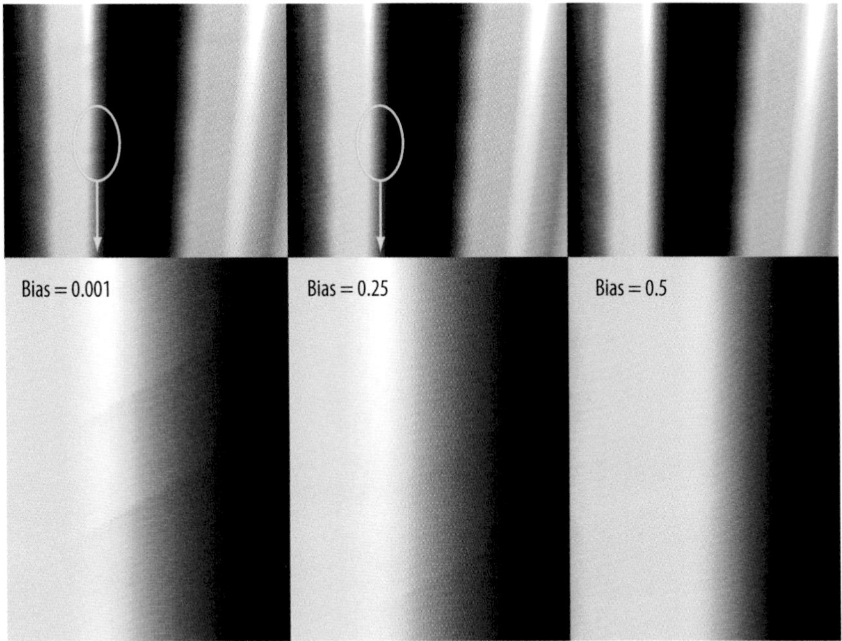

Figure 3.7 Depth map artifacts are eliminated by adjusting the Bias attribute. This scene is included on the CD as `bias_values.ma`.

With most scenarios, checking Use Mid Dist and leaving Bias at its default value is satisfactory for a scene. However, if you find it necessary to change the Bias value, proceed with caution. A Bias value that removes an artifact at one point on a surface can introduce an artifact at another point. For example, an incorrect Bias value will often "disconnect" a surface from a ground or floor. In Figure 3.8, a thin NURBS leg loses its connection with a plane.

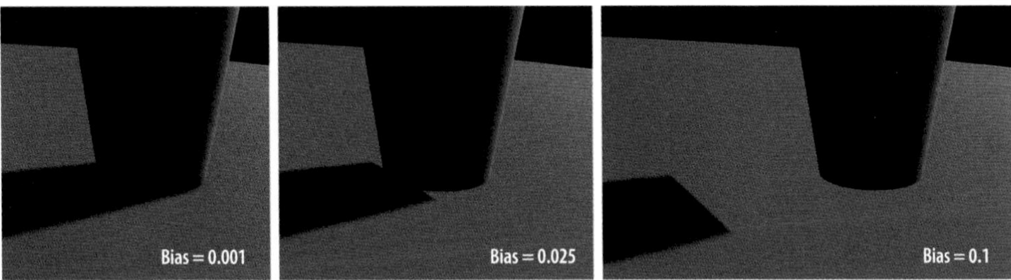

Figure 3.8 Three Bias values affect the connection of a depth map shadow to a NURBS leg. This scene is included on the CD as `bias_leg.ma`.

Note: The Depth Map Shadow Attributes section includes a Use Macro field, which is designed to call externally scripted macros to control the creation of depth maps. You can write the macros in such scripting languages as Perl or Python.

Creating Multiple Depth Maps

If necessary, you can generate more than two depth maps per spot light. If a scene is large in world space or necessitates a large Resolution size, you can uncheck the Use Only Single Dmap attribute. When this attribute is unchecked, six additional attributes become available with the following naming convention: Use *Axis*+/– Map (see Figure 3.9).

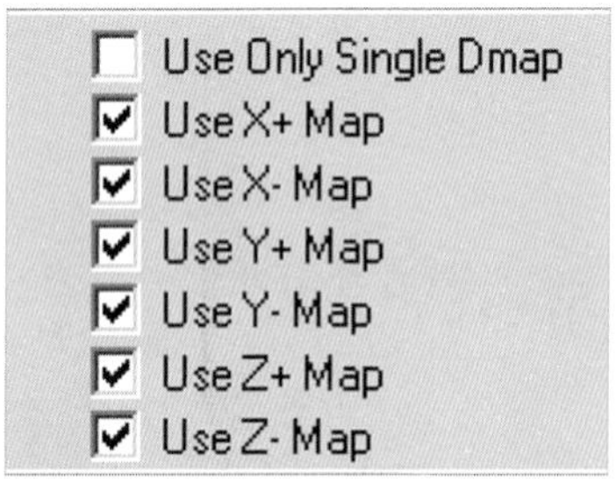

- [ ] Use Only Single Dmap
- [x] Use X+ Map
- [x] Use X- Map
- [x] Use Y+ Map
- [x] Use Y- Map
- [x] Use Z+ Map
- [x] Use Z- Map

Figure 3.9
The Use Only Single shadow-casting spot light's section of the Attribute Editor tab

If one of these new attributes is checked, a depth map is rendered from the point of view of the light in one axis direction. For example, Use X+ Map writes a depth map aligned to the positive X axis. In this case, if Use Mid Dist is checked and Disk Based Dmaps is not set to Off, two depth maps are written out to the disk with the following names:

`ShadowMapFileName.XP.iff`

`ShadowMapFileName.MIDMAP.XP.iff`

`P` stands for positive axis direction. `P` is replaced by `N` if the axis direction is negative. The ability to choose direction is particularly useful for a spot light that must cover a large model. For example, in Figure 3.10 a spot light with a 120-degree Cone Angle value is placed close to the model of a building. Use X+ Map, Use X– Map, and Use Z– Map are checked. The resulting render creates two depth maps—one standard and one for Use Mid Dist—in each axis direction. If Use Only Single Dmap had been checked, the left and right sides of the model would have been excluded from the depth map. If the spot light were moved farther from the model to avoid this problem, a significantly larger Resolution would be required to maintain the map's detail.

By default, point lights create six standard depth maps and six corresponding depth maps for Use Mid Dist. These maps surround the point light in a virtual cube. You can turn off particular directions to save render time. For example, if no critical geometry exists below the point light, you can uncheck Use Y– Map. If a particular direction is completely empty, the corresponding depth map is ignored automatically.

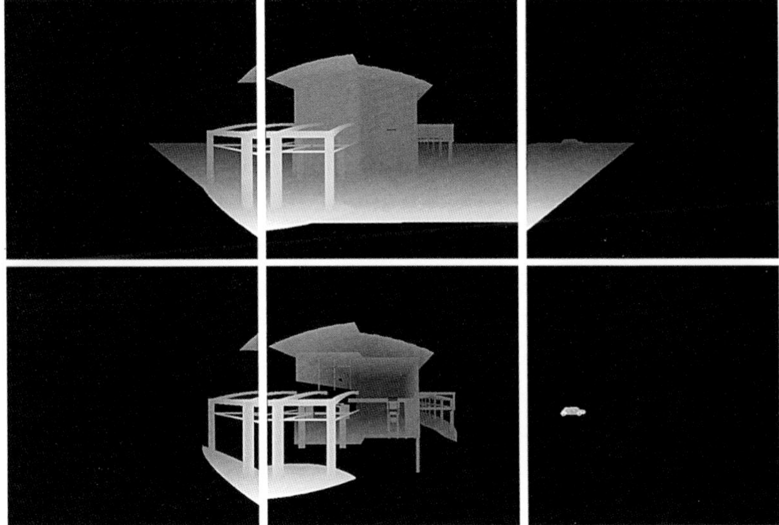

Figure 3.10 Six depth maps are generated for one spot light.

You can view a depth map IFF file by choosing File > View Image and browsing for the filename. The FCheck window opens. Press the Z key while the mouse arrow is over the window or click the Z Buffer button. Since the depth information is stored in the Z channel of the IFF file, the depth map cannot be seen in Photoshop or other standard digital-imaging program. However, if you choose File > Save Image in FCheck while the depth map is visible, you can export the monochromatic image to any of the image formats supported by Maya. In this case, the information is written as RGB. Unfortunately, the converted file cannot be read by a Maya renderer because a depth map with an IFF extension and a Z channel is expected during the shadow-casting process.

Refining Depth Maps

Maya depth maps possess other attributes that are critical to the quality of their render. These include Resolution, Filter Size, Shadow Color, and Use Auto Focus. In addition, a specialized mental ray depth map and area light offers an alternative approach to creating shadows.

Setting the Resolution, Filter Size, and Shadow Color

Resolution sets the pixel size of the depth map. Filter Size controls the amount of edge blur applied to the shadow. As a general rule of thumb, you can follow this guideline:

- A crisp edge requires high Resolution and low Filter Size.
- A soft edge requires low Resolution and high Filter Size.

Aside from softening the shadow's edge, the Filter Size attribute is designed to disguise depth map limitations. Since depth maps are restricted by a fixed number of pixels, the pixels are often visible in the render. For example, in Figure 3.11 three different Filter Size values are applied to a depth map with its Resolution set to the default value of 512.

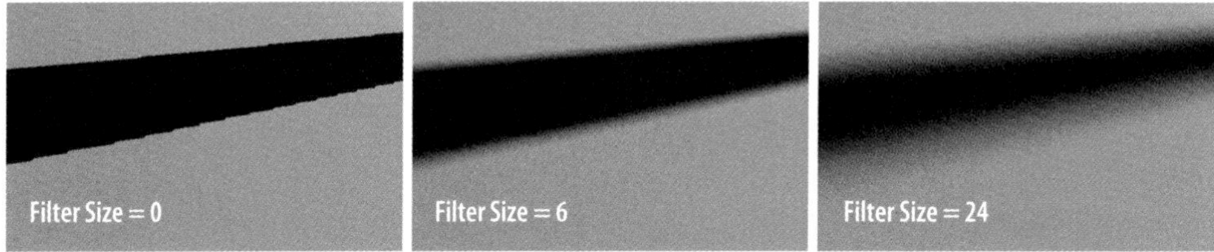

Figure 3.11 A depth map with a 512 Resolution and three different Filter Size values

The blur created by Filter Size is applied to the shadow map equally at all edge points. Hence, it cannot replicate a diffuse shadow that changes edge quality over distance. You can overcome this limitation, however, by creating a custom shading network. For a demonstration of this, see Chapter 7.

Shadow Color tints the color of the shadow, thus emulating bounced light. Choosing a lighter color also creates a shadow that is less intense and gives the appearance that a greater amount of fill light is present.

Setting a Light's Focus

The Use Auto Focus attribute automatically fits objects in the light's view to the resolution of the depth map. That is, if the objects are surrounded by empty space, the light view is "zoomed" in to maximize the number of pixels dedicated to the objects. Use Auto Focus is available on spot, directional, and point lights. Area and volume lights do not possess the attribute.

Note: If the cone of a spot light cuts objects out of the spot light's view, the Use Auto Focus attribute will not widen the view for the depth map. To avoid this problem, you will have to increase the light's Cone Angle, move the light backward, or manually set the light's Focus attribute.

In some situations, a scene will benefit if Use Auto Focus is unchecked and the light's Focus value is set manually. For example, if a depth map shadow is not critical for objects on the fringe of a scene, you can choose a Focus value that allows the light to concentrate on the scene's most important elements.

To choose an appropriate Focus value for a spot light, use the following steps:

1. Select the spot light and open its Attribute Editor tab. Uncheck Use Auto Focus. The Focus attribute becomes available.
2. With the light selected, choose Display > Rendering > Camera/Light Manipulator > Cone Angle. In a workspace view, choose Panels > Look Through Selected. The view through the light appears.
3. Click-drag the Cone Angle manipulator until the cone circle surrounds the objects in the scene that require a depth map shadow. Do not allow the cone circle to "split" a shadow-casting object in half; the resulting shadow will come

to an abrupt stop in the render. Note the Cone Angle value and enter the number in the Focus attribute field. Move the manipulator back to its original position so that the original Cone Angle value is once again achieved.

4. Switch Disk Based Dmaps to Reuse Existing Dmap(s), enter a name into the Shadow Map File Name field, and render out a test frame. (This assumes that no depth maps have been written out.) Double-check the resulting depth map with FCheck. In the workspace view used to look through the light, choose an orthographic view through the Panels menu; this removes the temporary camera attached to the light by the Look Through Selected command.

Although directional lights possess the Focus attribute, choosing an appropriate value requires a different strategy. By default, directional lights possess direction but have no true position; despite the location of the light icon, they are considered to be an infinite distance from the subject. Hence, a directional light automatically includes all the objects in a scene for a depth map shadow. As a result, two new attributes become available when Use Auto Focus is unchecked: Width Focus and Use Light Position. Use the following steps to set these attributes:

1. Select the directional light and open its Attribute Editor tab. Uncheck Use Auto Focus and check Use Light Position.
2. In a workspace view, choose Panels > Look Through Selected. The view through the light appears. With Alt+RMB, dolly the light in or out so that the shadow-casting objects fill the view.
3. Using the workspace view menu, choose View > Camera Attribute Editor. In the camera's Attribute Editor tab, note the value in the Orthographic Width field in the Orthographic Views section. The Orthographic Width attribute represents the width of the visible scene as measured from the left side to the right side of the current view. Enter the value into the Width Focus field of the directional light.
4. Switch Disk Based Dmaps to Reuse Existing Dmap(s), enter a name into the Shadow Map File Name field, and render out a test frame. (This assumes that no depth maps have been written out.) Double-check the resulting depth map with FCheck. If the foreground appears clipped, the light icon is below, intersecting, or otherwise too close to the clipped surface. Simply dolly the light back in the workspace view and render another test. If shadow-casting objects are cut off at the left or right side of the depth map, gradually increase the Width Focus value and render additional tests.

The process of setting the focus for a point light is also unique. The point light Focus attribute does not correspond to either the Cone Angle or Orthographic Width attribute. You can determine an appropriate Focus value, however, by employing the following formula:

```
Focus = depth map world space width * 12
```

You can determine the world space width of a desired depth map by measuring across a scene with the Distance tool (choose Create > Measure Tools > Distance Tool). For example, in Figure 3.12 a desired depth map includes three center cones but not the outer two cones. The Distance tool is used to determine the maximum distance between the outer cones. The number, approximately 6.1, is multiplied by 12. The result is rounded off to 73 and entered into the Focus field. This formula represents a rough approximation. Multiple tests may be necessary to determine the best value.

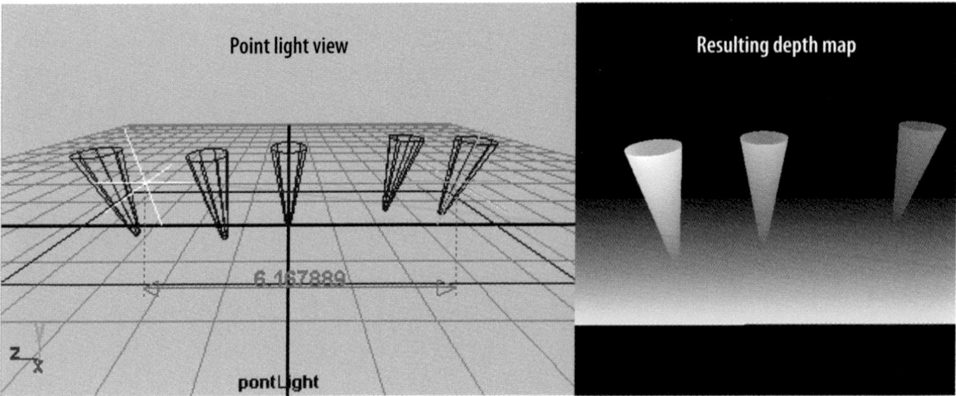

Figure 3.12 The Focus value of a point light is determined with the assistance of the Distance tool. This scene is included on the CD as `point_focus.ma`.

Using mental ray Shadow Maps and Area Lights

The mental ray renderer supports standard Maya depth maps. In addition, mental ray can produce its own shadow map variation. You can also adapt a standard spot or area light by activating the mental ray area light options. (To render the mental ray light and shadow variations, switch the Render Using attribute, in the Render Settings window, to mental ray.)

When checked, the Use mental ray Shadow Map Overrides attribute (found in the Shadows subsection of the mental ray section of a spot, directional, area, or point light's Attribute Editor tab) overrides the standard Maya depth map shadow. (With Maya 8.5, you must uncheck the Derive From Maya attribute.) The Shadow Map Format attribute, found just above Use mental ray Shadow Map Overrides, controls the type of mental ray shadow map. The Regular Shadow Map option produces mental ray depth maps, which are more advanced than the Maya equivalent due to additional attributes. The Detail Shadow Map option supports object transparency and is discussed in Chapter 11. If you click the Take Settings From Maya button, the applicable values from the Depth Map Shadow Attributes section are transferred to the mental ray Shadow Map Overrides subsection. The following attributes control the look of the resulting mental ray shadow:

Resolution Sets the pixel size of the depth map.

Samples Sets the number of subpixel samples taken per pixel. Low values create grainy results.

Softness Controls the spread of the light. Values above 0 create a softer, more diffuse shadow edge. Higher values necessitate higher Samples values to create acceptable results (see Figure 3.13). High values tend to smear the shadow at surface corners.

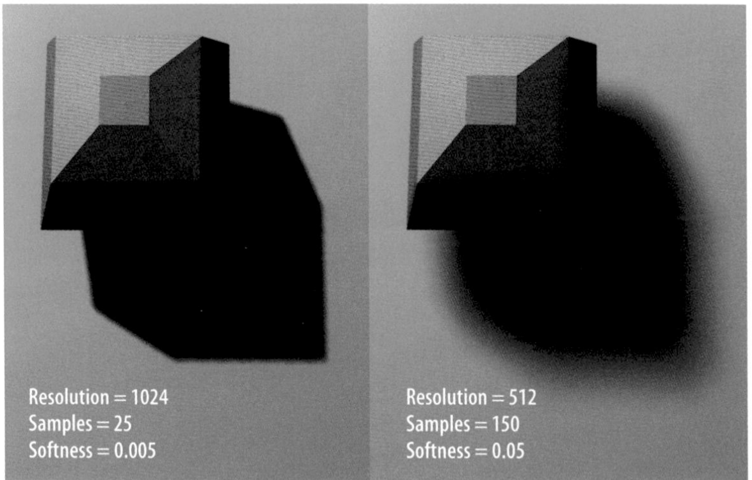

Figure 3.13 mental ray depth map shadows with two attribute settings

Bias Functions in the same manner as the default Maya depth map Bias attribute by offsetting surface points to avoid self-shadowing artifacts. This attribute, if above 0, overrides the Shadow Map Bias attribute in the Shadow Map subsection of the Render Options section of the mental ray tab in the Render Settings window. Maya documentation recommends a Bias value that is less than the world distance between the light and the shadowed object. (Additional shadow attributes, including those found in the mental ray tab of the Render Settings window, are discussed in detail in Chapter 11.)

Shadow Map File Name When a name is entered into this field, mental ray shadow maps are written to disk in the `renderData\mentalray\shadowMap` folder within the project directory. The maps are overwritten with each new render. The depth map files are written in a native mental ray format and cannot be viewed with FCheck. Point lights automatically produce six depth map files, while other lights produce one each.

You can convert a spot light into a mental ray area light by checking the Area Light attribute (found in the Area Light subsection of the mental ray section of a spot light's Attribute Editor tab). You can convert a standard Maya area light into a mental ray area light by checking Use Light Shape (found in the same subsection). In both cases, mental ray adapts the chosen light by grafting a specialized mental ray area light onto the light icon (see Figure 3.14).

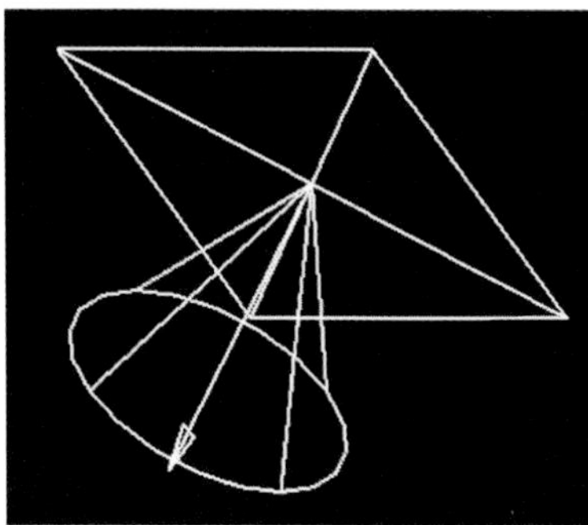

Figure 3.14
When the Area Light attribute is checked, a mental ray light is grafted onto the spot light icon.

The added area light acts as a light spread, thus creating a diffuse, soft-edged shadow. The result is most noticeable when combined with a default raytrace shadow, which produces a hard edge in its default state (see Figure 3.15).

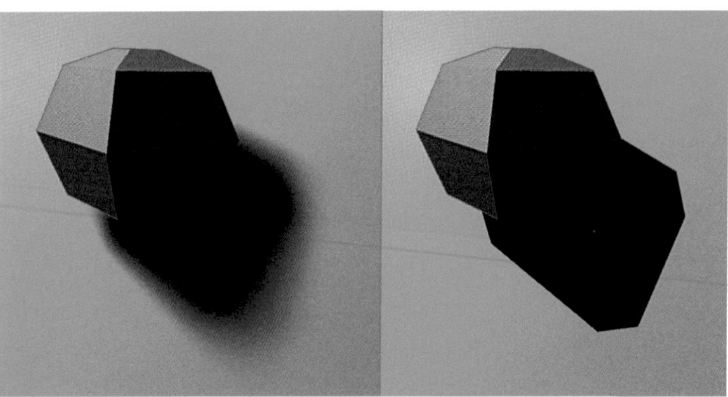

Figure 3.15 (Left) Raytrace shadow with a mental ray area light grafted onto a spot light. (Right) Default raytrace shadow with same spot light. This scene is included on the CD as `area_spot.ma`.

You can adjust the resulting shadow with the following attributes:

Type Determines the shape of the area light. Options include Rectangle, Disc, Sphere, Cylinder, and User. If Type is set to Cylinder, the area light sends shadow rays above, below, and behind the parent light. If Type is set to Sphere, the area light sends shadow rays in all directions. The User option allows you to apply a custom mental ray light shader to the area light.

High Samples Sets the number of shadow rays emitted from the area light, as measured in the X and Y direction of the light's icon. Default values leave the shadow very grainy. High values create an excellent result but slow the render.

High Sample Limit Represents the maximum number of times a shadow ray is permitted to reflect or refract before it must employ the Low Samples attribute. By switching to Low Samples, fewer shadow light rays are involved when calculating reflections and refractions.

Low Samples The number of shadow rays employed when the High Sample Limit is reached.

Visible If the parent light is a Maya area light, the Visible attribute determines whether the mental ray area light icon is visible in the render. If Visible is checked, Shape Intensity becomes available and controls the strength of the visibility. If Shape Intensity is set above 0, the icon renders as a solid white rectangle but does not affect the light striking surfaces in the scene. Maya documentation recommends using the mental ray area light in conjunction with the Maya area light as it requires lower sampling levels to produce higher-quality shadows.

Solving Light Gap Errors

Light gaps, which look like thin, bright lines, often appear along the intersection of two surfaces. For example, in Figure 3.16 two primitive planes sit at a right angle and intersect slightly. A spot light, placed behind the surfaces, casts a default depth map shadow. A light gap appears along the intersection seam. Such gaps are due to a mismatch of the depth map to the render of the geometry. Depth maps do not receive anti-aliasing, which leads to stair-stepping. (See Chapter 10 for information on render quality issues.) In this situation, the depth map will not accurately line up with the anti-aliased render, and the bright surface appears in the resulting "gap." The light's Filter Size attribute, which blurs the shadow edge, widens the gap if raised above 0.

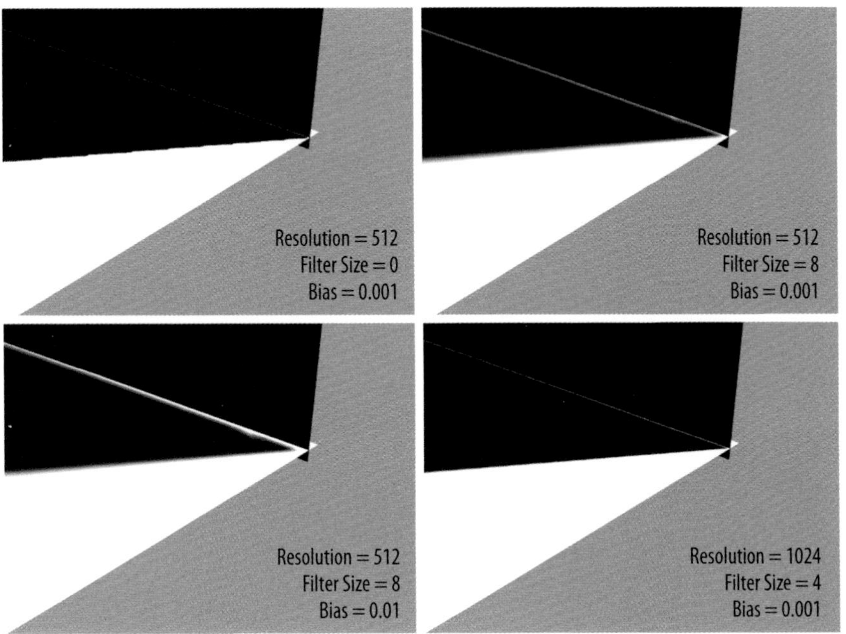

Figure 3.16 A light gap is visible at the intersection of two planes. This scene is included on the CD as `light_gap.ma`.

In this situation, higher Bias values make the error worse. You can increase the light's Resolution, which will reduce the strength of the light gap. However, the increased Resolution will not make the error disappear completely (see Figure 3.16). Switching to raytrace shadows will solve the problem but requires a more time-intensive render. Another solution involves the following steps:

1. Open the shadow-casting light's Attribute Editor tab. In the Depth Map Shadow Attributes section, set the shadow attributes to create a satisfactory shadow.
2. Switch Disk Based Dmaps to Reuse Existing Dmap(s). Enter a name into the Shadow Map File Name field. (This assumes that no depth maps have been written out.) Render a test frame. The render will write the depth maps to the project folder.
3. Select the vertical surface in a workspace view. Translate the surface away from the light. In the example illustrated in Figure 3.16, the plane needs to be translated only 0.2 units in the Z direction. When the plane is moved away from the light, the gap is covered by the geometry and is no longer visible in the render. The depth map is not updated since the Reuse Existing Dmaps(s) option retrieves the map after it has been written out the first time.

In another common depth map scenario, a shadow stops short of a hard corner on a surface. For example, in Figure 3.17 a tire-shaped polygon casts a depth map shadow onto a stand. The shadow stops short of the stand edge, producing a thin white line. In addition, a similar white line is visible along the inner edge of the tire that is in shadow. When the Filter Size is raised, the artifacts become worse. Once again, this problem arises from the mismatch of the aliased depth map with the anti-aliased final render. In this case, an increased Resolution value will reduce the intensity of the white lines.

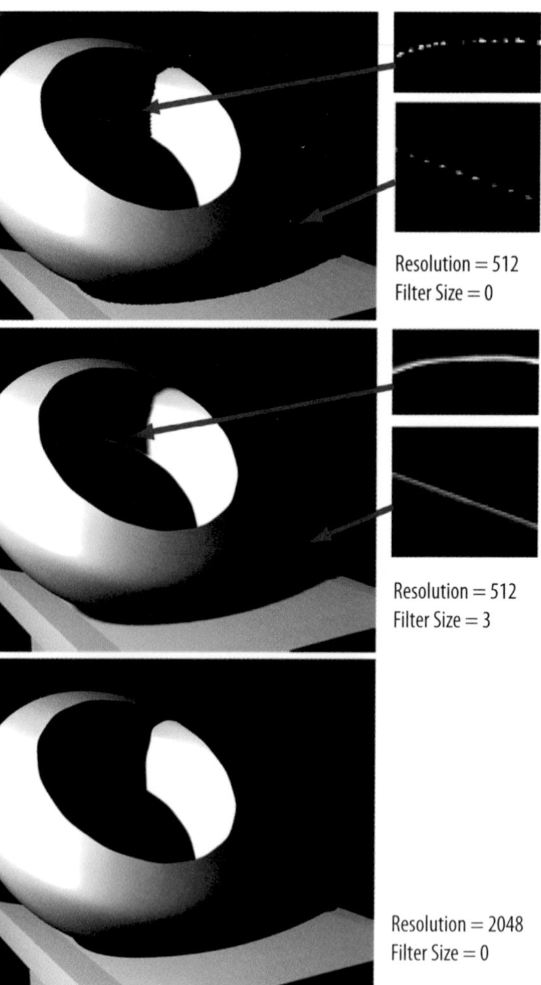

Figure 3.17 Edge artifacts of two objects are reduced by increasing the depth map Resolution. This scene is included on the CD as `depth_edge.ma`.

Unfortunately, an increased Resolution cannot remove the artifacts along the surface edges completely. Raytrace shadows, on the other hand, do not produce this type of artifact.

Comparing Shadows

Each light in Maya imparts distinctive qualities to the shadow it casts. Familiarity with the quirks and strengths of each light will help you make the proper decisions when lighting a scene. As a side-by-side comparison, each light type has been placed in an identical location on a test set (see Figure 3.18). A row of vertical cylinders illustrates the omnidirectional or multidirectional qualities of many of the lights.

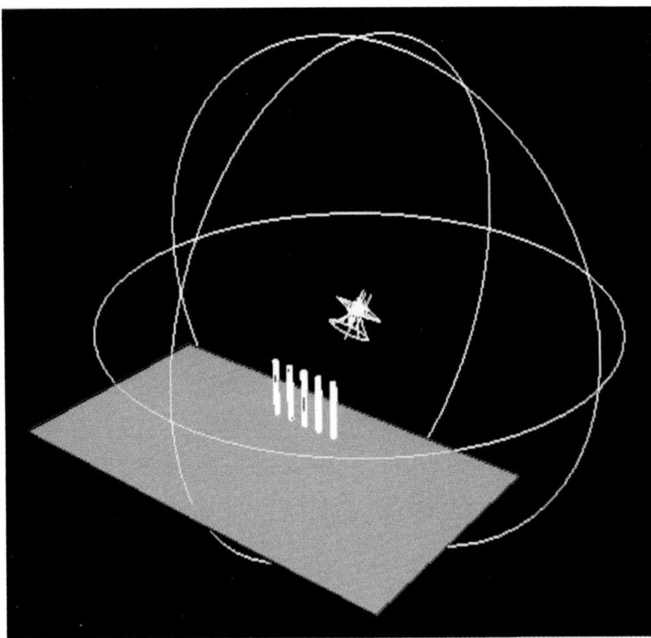

Figure 3.18 The light test set

All the lights, except for the ambient, cast depth map shadows with a Resolution set to 2048 and a Filter Size set to 2 (see Figure 3.19). The ambient light, which cannot cast depth map shadows, casts raytrace shadows with default setting. The area light casts both depth map and raytrace shadows since it possesses a unique, physical-based lighting method. The spot light is rendered with two cone sizes. All the lights, except for the volume, are left at their default scale. The volume light is scaled to surround the test set. The lights are turned on, one at a time, with the Illuminates By Default check box.

When the shadows of each light are compared, many qualities are identical; a few, however, stand out. In particular, the short shadows of the directional display the parallel quality of the light type. Even though the directional has the same Intensity value as all the other lights, it imparts the most illumination to the surface. In terms of realism, the area light with raytrace shadows is by far the best. Even though the raytrace attributes are left at their default settings, the area shadows become more diffuse with distance, mimicking light properties in the real world. In comparison, the area light with a depth map shadow creates a look similar to the volume light. Both the area and the volume have the most aggressive light decay.

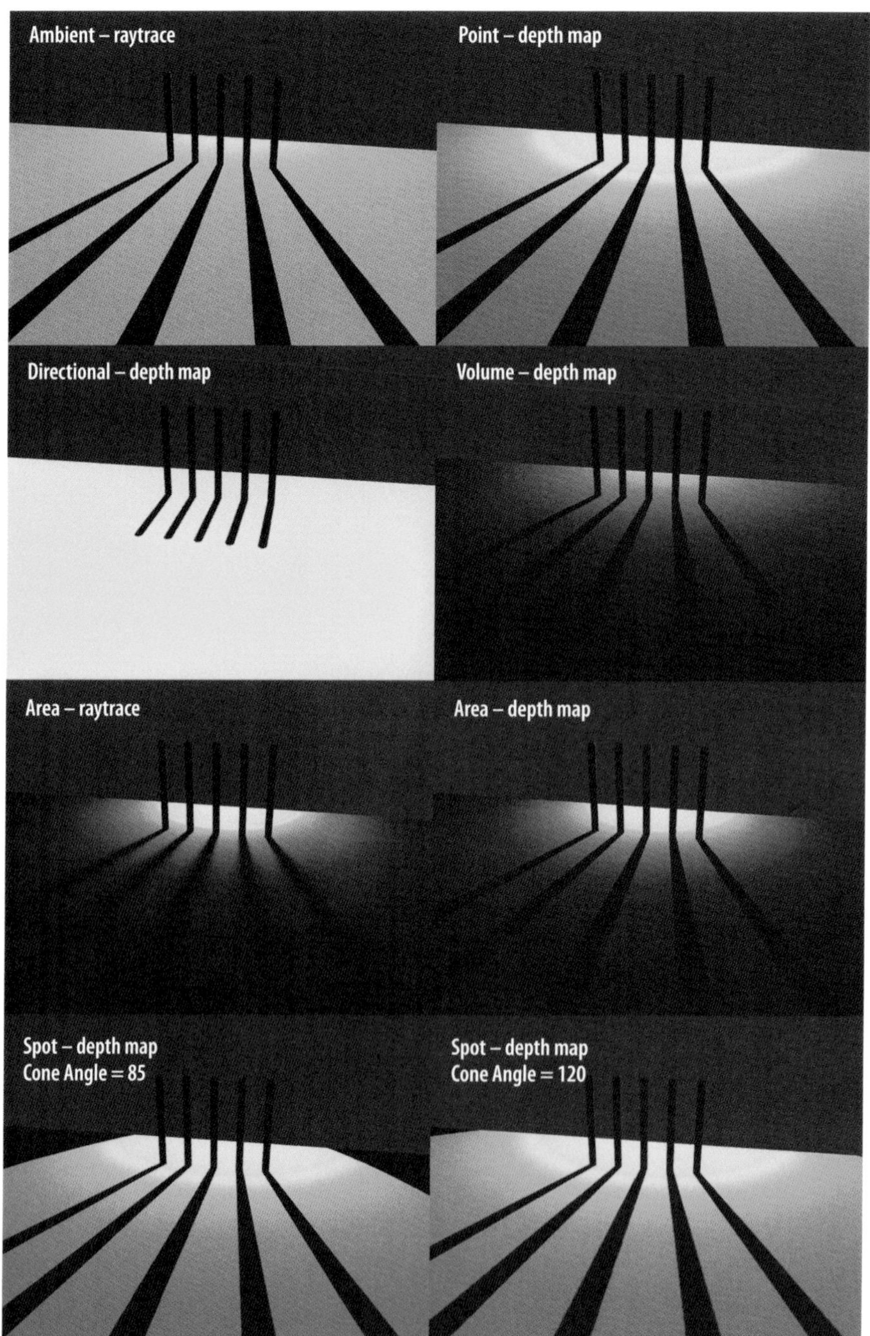

Figure 3.19 The shadow qualities of Maya's six light types. This scene is included on the CD as `light_set.ma`.

Aside from the directional light, all the other lights have almost identical shadow patterns. In all these cases, if the light were moved farther from the cylinders, the shadows would become more parallel and less spread out. The spot light shows slight variations in the pattern when its Cone Angle is increased from 85 to 120. The directional and ambient lights provide the most even lighting, with the intensity of the surface changing little over its length and width. All the other lights create hot spots near the cylinders.

Raytracing Shadows

Raytrace shadows are more physically accurate than depth map shadows but are generally more processor intensive. Raytrace shadows represent the one type of shadow that is available to all light types, including ambient. For a raytrace shadow to be calculated, the Raytracing attribute must be checked in the Maya Software tab of the Render Settings window. When using the mental ray renderer, the Ray Tracing attribute must be checked. (For information on the raytracing process, see Chapter 11.)

Each light carries a set of raytrace shadow attributes:

Shadow Radius/Light Radius/Light Angle Control the softness of the shadow edge by virtually scaling the size of the light (see Figure 3.20). Large light sources, such as a theater marquee or a window with sheer curtains, produce naturally diffuse, soft-edged shadows. Shadow Radius is provided for ambient lights. Light Radius is provided for spot, point, and volume lights. Light Angle is provided for directional lights. With each of these attributes, the larger the value, the softer the resulting shadow. Shadow Radius and Light Radius have a range from 0 to 1. Light Angle has a range from 0 to 360. Area lights do not possess any of these attributes; the softness of their shadows is determined by the position and rotation of the light icon.

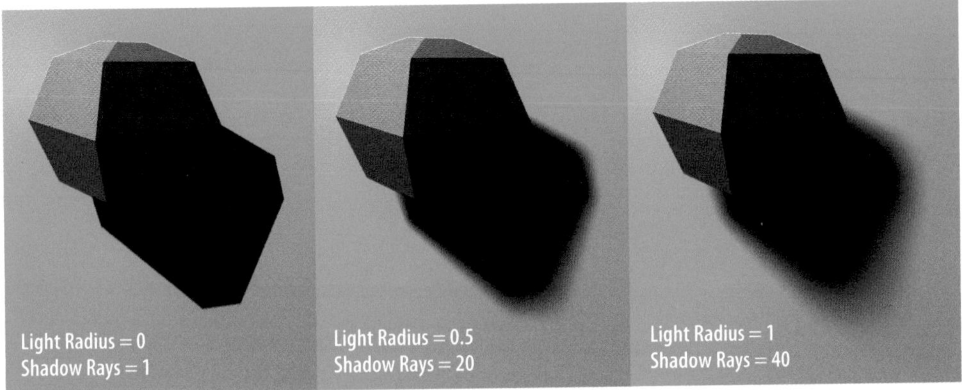

Figure 3.20 A raytrace shadow created by a spot light with three different Light Radius and Shadow Rays attribute values

Shadow Rays Sets the number of rays employed to calculate the shadow edge. The higher the value, the more refined the result.

Ray Depth Limit Sets the number of times a camera eye ray can reflect and/or refract and still cause reflected or refracted objects to cast raytrace shadows within the reflections or refractions. That is, higher values allow raytrace shadows to appear within a greater number of recursive reflections and refractions. If Ray Depth Limit is set to 1, no shadows appear in reflections or refractions.

You can find additional depth map and raytrace shadow attributes in the mental ray tab of the Render Settings window. These will be discussed in great detail in Chapter 11.

Linking and Unlinking Shadows

With Maya, you can make or break shadow links between lights and surfaces. If a shadow link is broken, the surface no longer casts a shadow for that light. For complex scenes, the ability to pick and choose which surfaces cast shadows can save render time and improve render quality.

By default, all surfaces cast shadows for shadow-producing lights that strike them. To break a shadow link for a surface while using the Maya Software or mental ray renderer, follow these steps:

1. If you are using Maya Software, open the Render Settings window, switch to the Maya Software tab, and expand the Render Options section. Change Shadow Linking to Shadows Obey Shadow Linking.
2. If you are using mental ray, open the Render Settings window, switch to the mental ray tab, and expand the Shadows section. Switch Shadow Linking to On.
3. Select the light and the surface whose shadow link you want to break. Switch to the Rendering menu set, and choose Lighting/Shading > Break Shadow Links. The surface will no longer cast a shadow for the selected light. To restore the shadow, select the surface and light and choose Lighting/Shading > Make Shadow Links.

Breaking a shadow link does not prevent a surface from receiving a shadow from another object. If Shadow Linking is set to Shadows Obey Light Linking (Maya Software) or Obeys Light Linking (mental ray), the surface will *not* cast a shadow *only* if it is unlinked from the light in the Relationship Editor or through the Break Light Links tool (see Chapter 2).

Note: To prevent a surface from casting a shadow for any and all lights, regardless of shadow linking, uncheck Casts Shadows in the Render Stats section of the surface's Attribute Editor tab. To prevent a surface from receiving shadows from all other surfaces, uncheck Receive Shadows.

Creating Effects Shadows

Maya's Light Fog, Paint Effects, Fur, Hair, nCloth, and Toon systems create an amazing range of render effects. Although it is beyond the scope of this book to go into great detail for these effects, shadow creation for each is covered. Simple Paint Effects, Fur, Hair, nCloth, and Toon tutorials are included so that prior knowledge is not a prerequisite. (Light Fog is introduced in Chapter 2.)

Shadowing with Light Fog

Light Fog supports depth map shadows with the Maya Software renderer. More important, Light Fog will fail to interact properly with objects in a scene unless Use Depth Map Shadows is checked. Unfortunately, raytrace shadows and the mental ray renderer will not work with Light Fog. However, several mental ray shaders produce their own volume fog. (For more information, see Chapter 12.)

Two additional fog attributes, Fog Shadow Intensity and Fog Shadow Samples, are included in the Depth Map Shadow Attributes section of spot, point, and volume lights. Fog Shadow Intensity dictates the darkness of shadows appearing in the body of the fog (see Figure 3.21).

Figure 3.21 Light Fog shadow with three different Fog Shadow Intensity settings. This scene is included on the CD as `fog_shadow.ma`.

The higher the Fog Shadow Intensity value, the less fog remains in the shadowed area. A value of 10 generally removes all the fog in the shadowed area and leaves a clean alpha channel (assuming there are no objects behind the fog).

Fog Shadow Samples, on the other hand, reduces potential fog graininess by applying additional sampling. Although there is no built-in maximum for the attribute, the default value of 20 is generally sufficient for a smooth render.

Shadowing with Paint Effects

Paint Effects is a powerful tool that allows you to interactively paint specialized strokes that create complex geometry as a post-process. Numerous Paint Effects brushes are included with Maya and are grouped in such categories as grasses, trees, fire, and fibers. To create a simple Paint Effects scene, you can follow these basic steps:

1. Create a primitive, such as a sphere. Select the primitive, switch to the Rendering menu set, and choose Paint Effects > Make Paintable.
2. Choose Paint Effects > Get Brush. The Visor window opens. Select a brush folder, such as trees. Select a brush style by clicking a Paint Effects icon. Close the Visor.
3. Click-drag the mouse arrow over the primitive. The Paint Effects stroke is laid over the surface, and the Paint Effects tube or sprite will grow from it.
4. Render a test with the Maya Software renderer. The Paint Effects brush is laid over the geometry at the end of the render. (Unfortunately, mental ray does not support Paint Effects.)

A Paint Effects stroke is a specialized set of nodes. The *stroke* shape and transform nodes generate the geometry visible in the workspace view. The hidden *curve* node controls the shape of the stroke path. If you select the curve node in the Hypergraph Hierarchy or Outliner window, you can scale, translate, and rotate it like any other curve. You can also manipulate or animate the vertices of the curve to change the shape. The stroke geometry automatically follows the curve. Curve-editing tools, however, cannot be applied to the curve node. If a Paint Effects brush is applied to a surface through Make Paintable, the stroke geometry automatically deforms and moves with the surface. You can apply Paint Effects brushes to any surface that has valid UVs. Last, the brush node, which carries all the brush attributes, is connected to the stroke shape node. You can view the brush node in the Hypergraph Connections window; in addition, the brush node appears beside the stroke shape node in the Attribute Editor. The brush node is named after the brush type (for example, *rope1*).

The majority of Paint Effects brushes grow special tube geometry as part of the post-process. This is most noticeable with brushes that create plant life. A long list of attributes controls the tube growth; these can be found in the Tubes section of the brush node's Attribute Editor tab. Tubes can generate excellent shadows. In contrast, a few Paint Effects brushes create sprites. With these brushes, a bitmap is applied to a flattened tube with alpha information. No matter what direction the camera points, the sprite bitmap always faces the camera. Although sprites can cast shadows, the results are rough.

Paint Effects strokes cannot cast raytrace shadows. However, two attributes are provided to create depth map and fake shadows. They can be found in the Shadow Effects section of the brush node's Attribute Editor tab (see Figure 3.22).

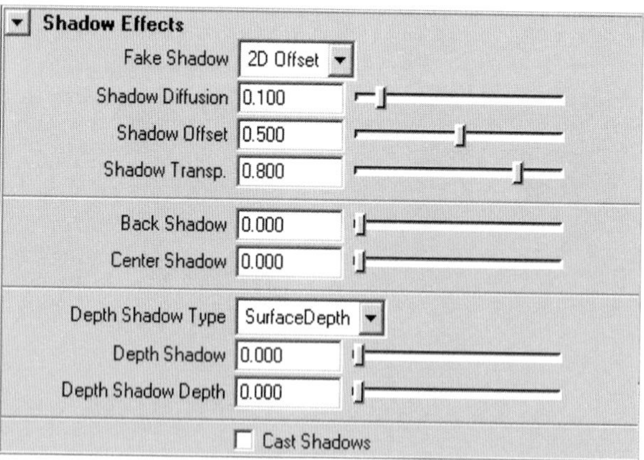

Figure 3.22 The Shadow Effects section of a Paint Effects brush node's Attribute Editor tab

Cast Shadows If checked, the Paint Effects stroke is included in the depth map calculation. If the depth map's Resolution is sufficiently large, the result is quite accurate.

Fake Shadow Provides two methods by which to create shadows without using depth maps: 2D Offset and 3D Cast.

2D Offset creates a drop-shadow effect by replicating the shape of the stroke as viewed by the camera and offsetting it in screen space (see Figure 3.23). This is the least convincing shadow but may be suitable for dense strokes that lie close to a surface, such as eyebrow hair or short grass. 2D Offset will potentially reduce the render time of scenes with a large number of complex strokes. When Fake Shadow is switched to 2D Offset, the Shadow Diffusion, Shadow Offset, and Shadow Transp. attributes become available. Shadow Diffusion controls the softness of the shadow and affects the blending of individual tube shadows. Higher values produce slightly soft results but make the shadows more cohesive. Shadow Offset sets the distance that the shadow is offset. If Shadow Offset is 0.5, the fake shadow is approximately 50 percent visible. If Shadow Offset is above 1, the fake shadow is no longer rooted to the stroke. Positive Shadow Offset values move the fake shadow to the screen right of the stroke. Negative values move the fake shadow to the screen left of the stroke. Shadow Transp. determines the opacity of the shadow. Although you can use 2D Offset in conjunction with Cast Shadows, the results are generally better if Cast Shadows is unchecked. 2D Offset is the one style of shadow that works with sprite Paint Effects.

Figure 3.23 Paint Effects flowers with cast and fake shadows

The 3D Cast option creates a shadow by defining an unseen, flat plane below the stroke and casting a shadow onto it. This option provides good results when the stroke itself is flat or is applied to a fairly smooth surface (see Figure 3.23). 3D Cast shadows are refined by the Shadow Diffusion and Shadow Transp. attributes. Although you can use 3D Cast in conjunction with Cast Shadows, the results are better if Cast Shadows is unchecked. Although 3D Cast shadows are relatively accurate, they have a tendency to separate from the root of the stroke.

In addition to shadow effects, Paint Effects strokes include several attributes to create self-shadowing:

Back Shadow Darkens Paint Effects tubes that are farthest from the light. The higher the value, the darker the result.

Center Shadow Darkens the tubes that are formed closest to the stroke path. The higher the value, the darker the result.

Depth Shadow Darkens the stroke tube along its length based on the distance from a tube point to the corresponding surface or stroke path. If Depth Shadow Type is set to SurfaceDepth, the distance is measured from the tube point to the surface on which the Paint Effects stroke is drawn. If Depth Shadow Type is set to PathDist, the distance is measured from the tube point to the nearest point on the stroke path. Depth Shadow Depth defines the maximum distance that the Depth Shadow shading effect is permitted to act within.

Note: Paint Effects brushes can be adapted or written from scratch. Each Paint Effects brush exists as a MEL text file in the brushes folder of the Maya program directory.

Shadowing with Maya Fur

The Maya Fur system grows numerous hairs over a surface. You can use depth map shadows with fur if special attributes are added to a spot light. If the special attributes are added to other light types, self-shadowing is available. In addition, you can create raytrace fur shadows with the mental ray renderer.

To create a simple fur setup and cast depth map shadows, follow these steps:

1. Create a NURBS, polygon, or subdivision surface. Switch to the Rendering menu set and choose Fur > Attach Fur Description > New. (If you are running Maya Unlimited but do not see the Fur menu, check the `Fur.mll` plug-in in the Plug-In Manager window.) The default fur appears on the surface. You can attach fur to any surface that has valid UVs. Create a primitive plane and place it under the surface so that shadows can be cast.
2. Create a spot light for the surfaces and check Use Depth Map Shadows in the light's Attribute Editor tab.
3. With the light selected, choose Fur > Fur Shadowing Attributes > Add To Selected Light. Attributes are added to the Fur Shading/Shadowing section of

the light's Attribute Editor tab (see Figure 3.24). Switch the Fur Shading Type attribute to Shadow Maps. Leave the Threshold attribute set to 0. Threshold is designed to eliminate the shadows of extra-fine hairs; a hair is only included in a pixel of a depth map if it covers a percentage of the pixel greater than the Threshold value.

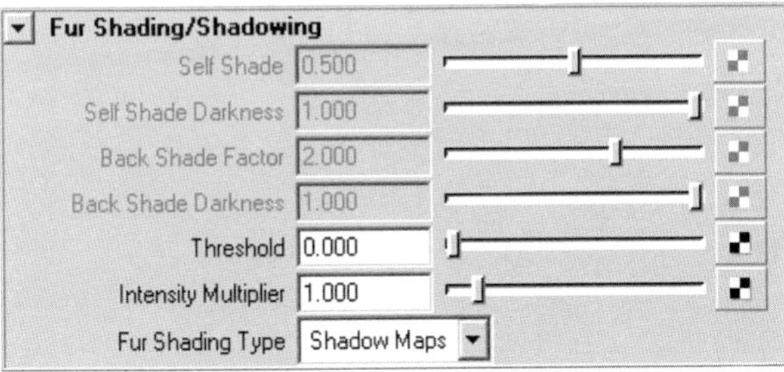

Figure 3.24 The Fur Shading/Shadowing section of a spot light's Attribute Editor tab

4. Render a test frame with the Maya Software renderer. The fur will create an appropriate shadow (see Figure 3.25). Open the Render Settings window and switch the Render Using attribute to mental ray. Render out a second test frame. The shadow continues to appear. If the shadow appears grainy with mental ray, check the Use mental ray Shadow Map Overrides attribute in the Shadows subsection of the light's Attribute Editor tab and adjust the attributes within the Shadow Map Overrides subsection. (See the section "Using mental ray Shadow Maps and Area Lights" earlier in this chapter.)

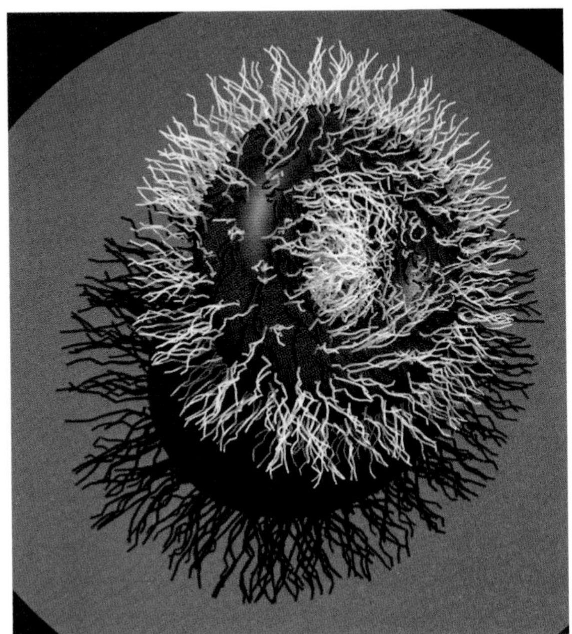

Figure 3.25 Fur with depth map shadows. This scene is included on the CD as `fur.ma`.

Maya Fur supports raytrace shadows only if the renderer is switched to mental ray. To see raytrace shadows, check Use Ray Trace Shadows in the light's Attribute Editor tab and switch the Quality Presets attribute to Draft or Production in the mental ray tab of the Render Settings window. (The default settings of the mental ray ProductionRapidFur preset are designed for depth map shadows and will not produce raytrace shadows.)

Note: Maya may incorrectly place fur shadows if Auto Focus is checked in the light's Attribute Editor tab. For best results, uncheck Auto Focus and enter a value into the Focus field. Maya documentation recommends that you derive the Focus value from this formula: **`Cone Angle`** + **`(Penumbra Angle`** × 2).

If Maya Software is the renderer of choice, Add To Selected Light must be applied to each spot light that is creating a shadow. You can remove the Fur Shading/Shadowing attributes of a light by selecting the light and choosing Fur > Fur Shadowing Attributes > Remove From Selected Light. If mental ray is the renderer of choice, Add To Selected Light is not needed. If the Fur Shading/Shadowing attributes already exist, mental ray ignores them. Whereas the Maya Software renderer creates the fur as a post-process, mental ray integrates the fur directly into the scene. In general, mental ray raytrace shadows are more accurate than Maya Software depth map shadows, which have a tendency to separate individual hair shadows from the hair bases. You can use any light type when raytracing fur shadows with mental ray. In addition, mental ray possesses the following render capabilities:

- Fur appears in reflections and refractions.
- Fur casts colored shadows.
- Fur motion blurs.

If Fur Shading Type is switched to Auto Shading, self-shadowing attributes become available (see Figure 3.24 earlier in this chapter). Auto Shading is available to every light type except volume (which does not support fur shadowing). As with a spot light, the Fur Shading/Shadowing section must be added to the light by choosing Fur > Fur Shadowing Attributes > Add To Selected Light. The following attributes accompany Auto Shading:

Self Shade Defines the percentage of the fur hair length that is darkened. The percentage is anchored at the root. Thus, if Self Shade is 0.5, a fur hair is darkened from the root to its mid-length point. If Self Shade is 1, the entire hair is darkened. A value of 0 effectively turns the Self Shade attribute off. Self Shade Darkness controls the amount of black mixed with the fur hair's original color. A value of 0.5 will equally mix black with the fur hair color. A value of 1 will make the fur hair pure black.

Back Shade Factor Artificially darkens the fur hair that lies on the surface side opposite the light source. A Back Shade Factor value of 0 creates a harsh transition from the lit side of the fur to the dark side. Values between 0 and 1 create a more natural falloff from the lit side to the dark side. Values above 1 make the falloff more rapid. A value of 0 effectively turns the Back Shade Factor attribute off. Back Shade Darkness controls the amount of black mixed with the fur hair's original color. A value of 0.5 will equally mix black with the fur hair color.

Intensity Multiplier Serves as a multiplier for the light intensity read by the fur. Fur strongly reflects light and is thereby often rendered inappropriately bright. Reducing this attribute below 1 will darken the fur without affecting other objects in the scene. Intensity Multiplier functions even if Fur Shading Type is set to No Shading.

Shadowing with Maya Hair

The Maya Hair system generates a series of dynamic curves that can simulate hair, ropes, chains, and other thin but long elements. The quickest way to generate hair in Maya is to switch to the Dynamics menu set, choose Hair > Get Hair Example, select a hair icon in the Visor window, right-click, and choose Import Maya File *name of hair file* from the shortcut menu. A complete scene with a polygon model and hair system is brought in. Otherwise, you can create a hair system from scratch following these steps:

1. Create a NURBS or polygon primitive. Choose Hair > Create Hair with default settings. A hair system is attached. You can attach hair to any NURBS or polygon surface that has valid UVs. If you would like to add hair to a specific location on the surface, choose Hair > Paint Hair Follicles > ❑ instead. The Paint Hair Follicles tool allows you to determine where hair grows by interactively painting across the surface.
2. Relax the hair by playing back the Timeline. Once the hair has fallen and has come close to rest, stop the playback. You can set the hair's current position as a new start position by selecting the hair curves and choosing Hair > Set Start Position > From Current. The hair will not collide with the surface unless you select the hair curves and the surface and choose Hair > Make Collide.
3. Create a light and check Use Depth Map Shadows. Render a test frame. A shadow appears across the surface. Open the Render Settings window and switch the Render Using attribute to mental ray. Render out a second test frame. The shadow continues to appear (see Figure 3.26). If the resulting mental ray shadow appears grainy, check the Use mental ray Shadow Map Overrides attribute in the Shadows subsection of the light's Attribute Editor tab and adjust the attributes within the Shadow Map Overrides subsection. (See "Using mental ray Shadow Maps and Area Lights" earlier in this chapter.)

When a hair system is created, many new nodes are included. The hairSystemFollicles node is a group node to which all the follicle shape nodes belong as children. Follicles are small, red circles along the hair-generating surface that create individual clumps of dynamic curves. The hair that is rendered is actually a Paint Effects tube. Hence, pfxHair, pfxHairShape, and hairSystemShape are included. pfxHair serves as a transform node for the hair system. pfxHairShape carries global Paint Effects attributes such as Display Quality. hairSystemShape carries a specialized set of Paint Effects attributes designed for rendering hair.

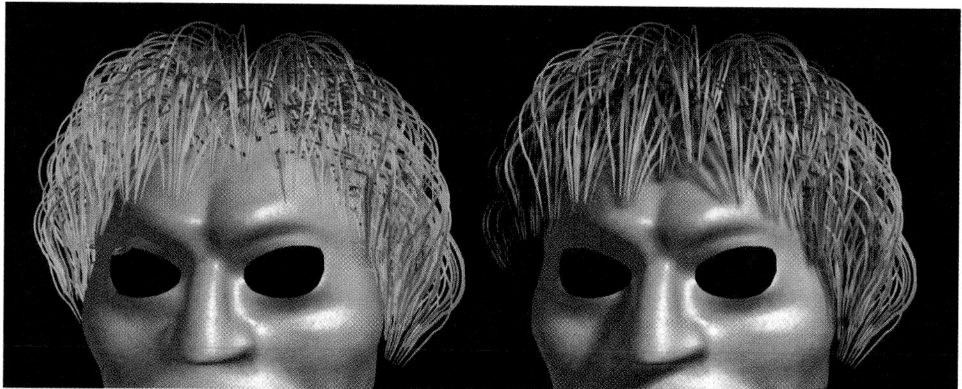

Figure 3.26 (Left) Maya Hair without shadows. (Right) Maya Hair with depth map shadows rendered with mental ray. This scene is included on the CD as `hair.ma`.

Note: A specialized material, Hair Tube Shader, is designed for a hair system that is converted from Paint Effects to polygons (you can choose Modify > Convert > Paint Effects To Polygons). The material is automatically assigned to the resulting polygons and includes specialized color gradients and specular controls designed specifically for human and animal hair. The material is unique in that it ignores surface normals and instead bases its shading on the camera view and Tube Direction attribute. Since the Hair Tube Shader material is a variation of the Anisotropic material, you can assign it to any surface. (For more information on Maya materials, see Chapter 4.)

You can render hair with raytrace shadows if the mental ray renderer is selected. Whereas the Maya Software renderer creates hair as a post-process, mental ray integrates the hair directly into the scene. As such, mental ray possesses the following render capabilities:

- Hair appears in reflections and refractions.
- Hair motion blurs.

You can turn on or off the hair's reflection visibility, refraction visibility, and the ability to receive shadows by checking the Visible In Reflections, Visible In Refractions, and Receive Shadows attributes in the Render Stats section of the hairSystemShape node's Attribute Editor tab.

Shadowing with nCloth

With nCloth, Maya provides a robust dynamic simulation system with which you can realistically emulate cloth objects. nCloth adapts preexisting polygon surfaces. To create a simple scene with nCloth, follow these steps:

1. Create a polygon plane and position it above a polygon sphere.
2. Switch to the nCloth menu set (you must be running Maya Unlimited). Select the plane and choose nCloth > Create nCloth. The plane is tessellated and converted into an nCloth dynamic mesh. This is indicated by a small circle icon at the plane's center.

3. Return to frame 1 and play back the Timeline. At this point, the nCloth plane falls but fails to interact with the sphere. To prevent this, select the sphere and choose nCloth > Create Passive > ❑, select Nucleus1 from the Solver drop-down list, and click Apply. Nucleus1 is the default Nucleus dynamic simulation solver that is assigned to the nCloth mesh when the Create nCloth tool is applied with default options. (You can employ multiple Nucleus solvers in the same scene.) Return to frame 1 and play back the Timeline. The nCloth mesh now interacts with the sphere.

When the Create nCloth tool is applied, an nCloth shape node is created. The original polygon shape node is connected to the nCloth shape node and is used as an input mesh. Because the original polygon surface is not destroyed, it provides UV and other material information to the nCloth mesh. Therefore, you can render nCloth with standard materials and depth map or raytraced shadows (see Figure 3.27).

Figure 3.27 An nCloth plane with mental ray depth map shadows. This scene is included on the CD as `ncloth.ma`.

Shadowing with the Toon System

The Maya Toon system emulates the "ink and paint" method of traditional 2D cel animation. Solid "ink" outlines are applied to areas of solid-color "paint." The outlines are specialized tube geometry that is applied to the assigned surfaces. The areas of color are created by Surface Shader and Ramp Shader materials, which are assigned by the Toon system.

The quickest way to apply the Toon system is to switch to the Rendering menu set, choose Toon > Get Toon Example, select a Toon icon in the Visor window, right-click, and choose Import Maya File *name of Toon file* from the shortcut menu. A complete scene with a Toon system is brought in. Otherwise, you can apply the Toon system with the following steps:

1. Create several NURBS or polygon primitives. Allow them to partially intersect. Choose Toon > Assign Outline > Add New Toon Outline. Toon outline tubes are created and applied to all the outer edges and corners of the primitives.
2. At this point, the primitives remain assigned to the default Lambert material. To create the paint-like quality, select the primitives again and choose Toon > Assign Fill Shader > Solid Color. A Surface Shader material is automatically assigned to the primitives. You can change the Out Color attribute of the material to change the "paint" color.

Surface Shader materials ignore all lighting and shadowing information in a scene. Therefore, the Solid Color fill shader does not create shadows. However, if you choose Toon > Assign Fill Shader > Shaded Brightness Two Tone or Shaded Brightness Three Tone, shadows are generated. In this situation, a Ramp Shader is assigned to the surfaces. The Color Input of the Ramp Shader is set to Brightness, which forces Maya to apply the colors of the Ramp Shader's Color gradient based on the brightness of the surface. Shadowed surface areas, which receive little or no light, pick up the left-hand side of the gradient (see Figure 3.28). This works with both depth map and raytrace shadows. Although the mental ray renderer supports the Ramp Shader material, it does not render the Toon outlines. (For more information on the Ramp Shader material, see Chapter 7.)

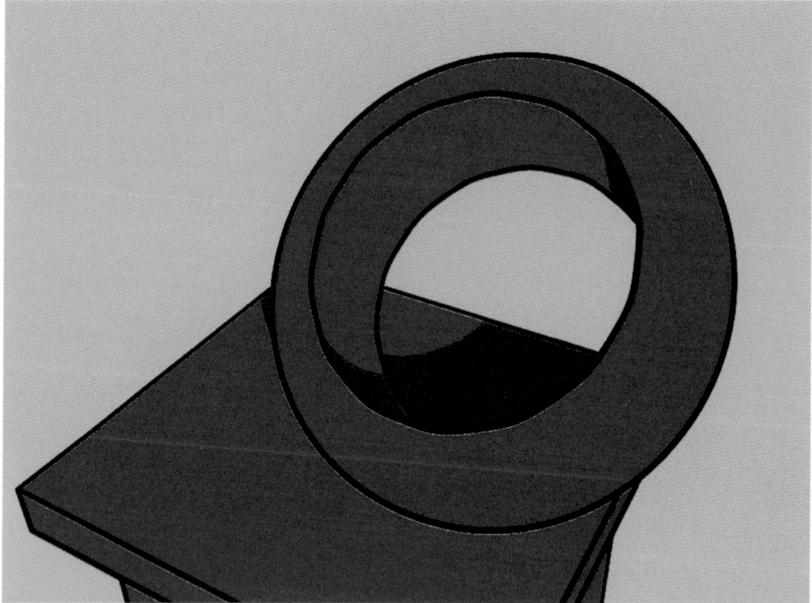

Figure 3.28 A pair of primitives are assigned a Toon outline and the Shaded Brightness Two Tone fill shader. The render is raytraced. This scene is included on the CD as `toon_shadow.ma`.

Other Fill Shaders are accessible through Toon > Assign Fill Shader > *name of shader*. Light Angle Two Tone applies a Ramp Shader, but sets the Color Input attribute to Light Angle. The Light Angle option chooses colors from the gradient based on the angle between the surface normals and the illuminating lights. Oddly enough, Light Angle Two Tone generates shadows. Rim Light, on the other hand, uses a Ramp Shader material, but adds a white color handle to the Incandescence gradient and therefore creates a thin white line around the surface's edge. Circle Highlight is similar, but inserts a white handle into Specular Color gradient, thereby creating an artificial specular highlight on the brightest potion of the surface. Both Rim Light and Circle Highlight options generate shadows.

When the Add New Toon Outline tool is applied, a pfxToon transform and pfxToon shape node are created. The pfxToon shape node generates the tube geometry for the "ink" outline and hosts a long list of attributes that affect the outline position, color, and behavior.

Chapter Tutorial: Lighting a Flickering Fire Pit with Shadows

In this tutorial, you will create a fire with soft, flickering shadows (see Figure 3.29). You will use Paint Effects fire with a volume, ambient, and directional light.

FIRE PIT MODEL COURTESY OF KRISTEN SCALLION

Figure 3.29 Fire created with a Paint Effects brush and lit with a directional, ambient, and volume light. A QuickTime movie is included on the CD as `fire_pit.mov`.

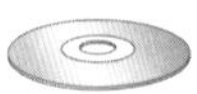

1. Open the `fire.ma` file from the Chapter 3 scene folder on the CD. Create a directional light. Open its Attribute Editor tab. Change the Color to a pale blue. This will serve as the scene's moonlight.
2. Move the directional light above the set and to screen right. Rotate it toward the fire pit. Render out a test frame. Adjust the light's Intensity and Color until satisfactory. Although this light will not be the key light, the sand and rocks should be appropriately visible for nighttime.
3. In the directional light's Attribute Editor tab, check Use Depth Map Shadows. Set Resolution to 512 and Filter Size to 6. This combination of medium Resolution and moderate Filter Size will create a slightly soft shadow. Render a test frame. Experiment with different light positions and shadow settings.
4. Create an ambient light and open its Attribute Editor tab. Set the Intensity attribute to 0.2, or approximately 1/10th the Intensity value of the directional. Tint the ambient light's Color to pale blue. Move the ambient light to screen left, just above the set. This light serves as a low fill that will prevent the backside of the rocks from becoming too black.
5. Create a volume light and open its Attribute Editor tab. Change Light Shape to Cylinder. Change the Color to a deep orange. In the Penumbra section, click the

left handle of the gradient. Once the handle is selected, change the Interpolation attribute to Smooth. This will change the linear gradient to one that has a slow start and a slow end; ultimately, this will make the falloff of the volume light more subtle.

6. Move the volume light to the center of the fire pit. Scale the light so that it is approximately twice the length, width, and height of the fire pit. In this case, the volume light will look oval from the top and short and squat from the side. Render a test frame to see how far the light from the volume light is traveling.

7. In the volume light's Attribute Editor tab, check Use Depth Map Shadows. Set Resolution to 128 and Filter Size to 6. This creates a soft shadow emanating from the center of the pit. Render out a test frame. The rocks should produce shadows similar to the shadows in Figure 3.29.

8. Select the cone-shaped ash geometry, which lies in the center of the fire pit. Choose Paint Effects > Make Paintable. Choose Paint Effects > Get Brush. The Visor window opens. In the Paint Effects tab, click the brush category folder named fire. Several fire brush icons become visible. Click the largeFlames icon. Close the Visor window. In the top view, click-drag the pencil mouse icon over the ash geometry. When the mouse button is released, a Paint Effects stroke is created. Keep the stroke fairly short.

9. Render out a test frame. Fire will appear where the stroke is drawn. Initially, the fire is too small to be seen over the top of the sticks and rocks. Select the stroke curve and open its Attribute Editor tab (which is labeled largeFlames1). Change the Global Scale attribute to 60. Render out a test frame. The flame should be clearly visible. If the flames appear too bright or saturated, adjust the stroke's Color1 and Color2 attributes (found in the Shading section of the stroke's Attribute Editor tab). In addition, you can darken the Glow Color (found in the Glow section of the stroke's Attribute Editor tab). Initially, the flames will move too slowly. To speed up the fire, change the Flow Speed attribute to 0.8. You can find Flow Speed in the Flow Animation section of the stroke's Attribute Editor tab.

10. Following the process detailed in steps 8 and 9, paint additional Paint Effects strokes on the ash geometry. Multiple strokes are necessary to make the fire convincing. Experiment with different fire styles with different scales. The version illustrated in Figure 3.29 uses three strokes and employs the following brushes: largeFlames and flameMed.

11. Paint Effects fire is preanimated and will automatically change scale and shape in a convincing manner. To match this animation, you can keyframe the Intensity, TranslateX, and TranslateZ of the volume light. To do this, move the Timeline slider to frame 1. Select the volume light. Set a key by pressing Crtl+S or choosing Animate > Set Key from the Animation menu set. A red key frame line will appear at frame 1 of the Timeline. Move the Timeline slider to frame 5. Translate the volume light slightly in the X or Z direction (no more than 1 world unit). Set another key. Repeat the process through the duration of the Timeline.

You'll want to add keyframes every 3 to 12 frames in a random pattern (see Figure 3.30). In the end, the volume light should move back and forth in an unpredictable manner. This will cause the volume shadows to move over time in a fashion similar to actual flickering fire light.

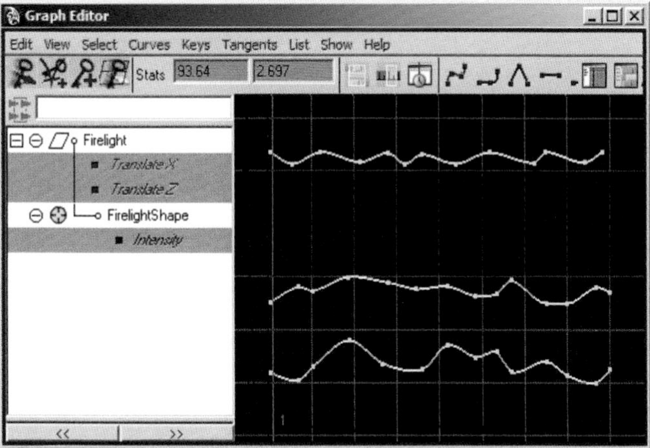

Figure 3.30 The Graph Editor view of the volume light's Intensity curve (top) and TranslateX and TranslateZ curves (bottom)

12. To animate the volume light changing its Intensity over time, move the Timeline slider to a desired frame and right-click the Intensity field. In the shortcut menu, choose Set Key. For the duration of the Timeline, set Intensity keys every 3 to 12 frames. Randomly vary the Intensity from 2 to 3 (see Figure 3.30).

13. The fire pit is complete! Render out a low-resolution AVI as a test. The fire and corresponding light should flicker. If you get stuck, a finished version has been saved as `fire_finished.ma` in the Chapter 3 scene folder on the CD.

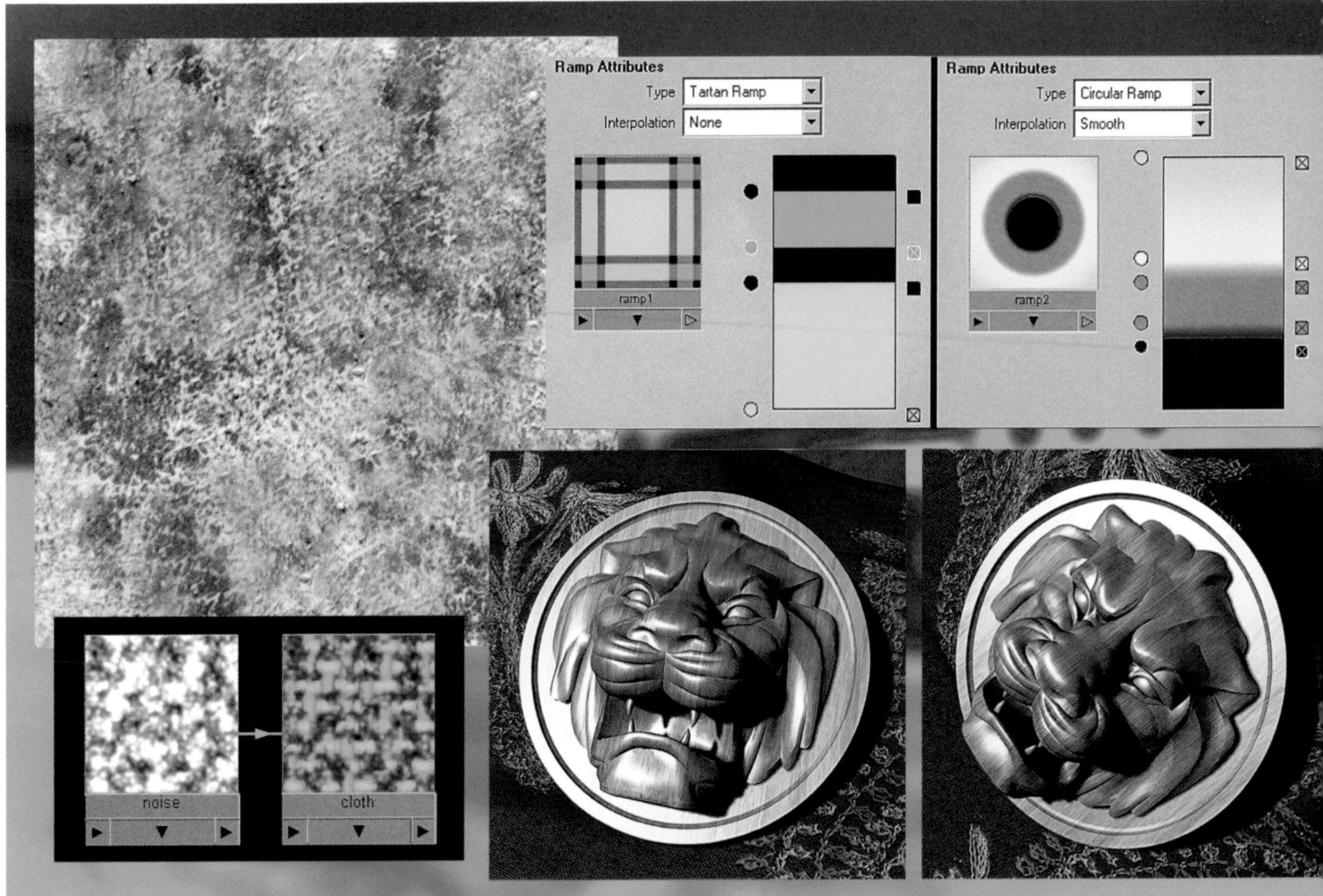

Ramp Attributes
Type Tartan Ramp
Interpolation None
ramp1
Ramp Attributes
Type Circular Ramp
Interpolation Smooth
ramp2
noise
cloth

Applying the Correct Material and 2D Texture

Simply put, a material determines the look of a surface. Although it's easy enough to assign a material and a texture to a surface and produce a render, many powerful attributes and options are available to you. At the same time, a rich historical legacy has determined why materials and textures work the way they do. You can map a wide range of 2D textures to materials, creating an almost infinite array of results. Simple combinations of textures and materials can lead to believable reproductions of real-world objects.

4

Chapter Contents

Theoretical underpinnings of shading models
Review of Maya materials
Review of 2D textures
Descriptions of extra texture attributes
Material and texture layering tricks
Using common mapping techniques to reproduce real materials

Reviewing Shading Models and Materials

A shader is a program used to determine the final surface quality of a 3D object. A shader uses a shading model, which is a mathematical algorithm that simulates the interaction of light with a surface. In common terms, surfaces are described as rough, smooth, shiny, or dull.

In the Maya Hypershade and Multilister windows, a shading model is referred to as a material and is represented by a cylindrical or spherical icon. Ultimately, you can use the words *shader* and *material* interchangeably.

A shading group, on the other hand, is connected to the material as soon as it's assigned. The shading group's sole function is to associate sets of surfaces with a material so that the renderer knows which surface is assigned to which material. The shading group does not provide any definition of surface quality. If the connection between a shading group node and material is deleted, the assigned surface appears solid green in the workspace view and is skipped by the renderer (see Figure 4.1). When a material is MMB-dragged into the Hypershade work area, it is automatically connected to a new shading group. If you select a material through the Create Render Node window, however, you have the option to uncheck the With Shading Group attribute; in this case, no new shading group is created.

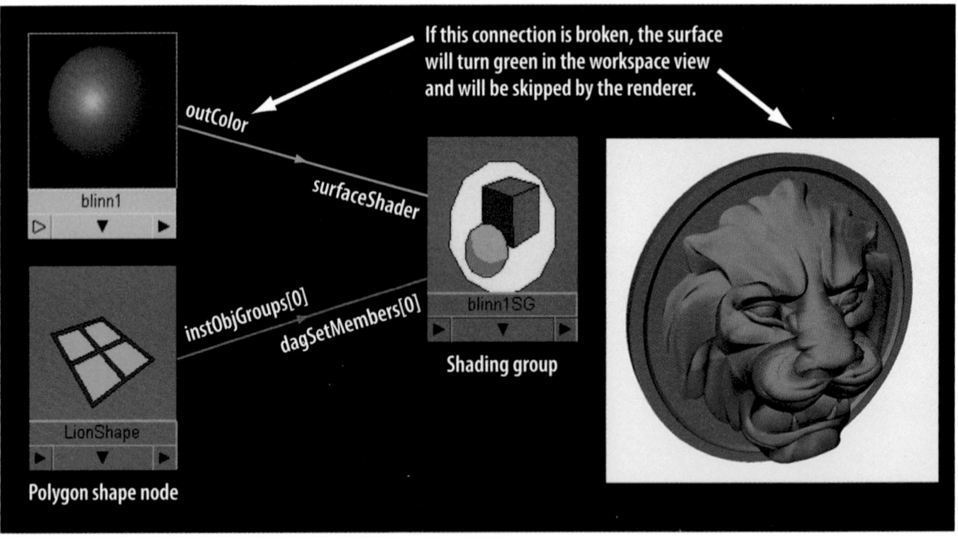

Figure 4.1 A shading group network

Shading with Lambert

The Lambert material carries common attributes: Color, Transparency, Ambient Color, Incandescence, Bump Mapping, Diffuse, Translucence, Translucence Depth, and Translucence Focus. In Maya, the Lambert node is considered a "parent" node. That is, Phong, Phong E, Blinn, and Anisotropic materials inherit their common attributes from the Lambert material. In each case, the attributes function in an identical manner. (For a more detailed discussion of nodes and the Transparency attribute, see Chapter 6. For information on the Bump Mapping attribute, see Chapter 9.) Maya's Lambert material uses a diffuse-reflection model in which the intensity of any given surface point is based on the angle between the surface normal and light vector. In order for Maya's Lambert material to smoothly render across polygon faces, it borrows from other shading models, such as interpolated or Gouraud shading. With Gouraud, the intensity of any given point on a polygon face is linearly interpolated from the intensities of the polygon's vertex normals and two edge points intersected by a scan line.

Note: The Smooth Shade All option (Shading > Smooth Shade All through a workspace view menu) is able to interpolate across polygon faces to produce a smooth result. In contrast, the Flat Shade All option (Shading > Flat Shade All through a workspace view menu) applies a single illumination calculation per polygon face, which leads to faceting.
NURBS surfaces, while based on Bezier splines, are converted to polygon faces at the point of render by the renderer. Hence, all the shading model techniques in this chapter apply equally to NURBS surfaces. If Flat Shade All is checked through a workspace view menu, a NURBS primitive sphere appears nearly identical to its polygon counterpart.

Calculations involving diffuse reflections utilize Lambert's Cosine Law. The law states that the observed radiant intensity of a surface is directly proportional to the cosine of the angle between the viewer's line of sight and the surface normal. As a result, the radiant intensity of the surface, which is perceived as surface brightness, does not change with the viewing angle. Hence, a Lambertian surface is perfectly matte and does not generate highlights or specular hot spots. Physically, a real-world Lambertian surface has myriad surface imperfections that scatter reflected light in a random pattern. Paper and cardboard are examples of Lambertian surfaces. The law was developed by Johann Heinrich Lambert (1728–77), who also served as the inspiration for the Lambert material's name.

The term *diffuse* refers to that which is widely spread and not concentrated. Hence, the Diffuse attribute of the Lambert material represents the degree to which light rays are reflected in all directions. A high Diffuse value produces a bright surface. A low Diffuse value causes light rays to be absorbed and thereby makes the surface dark.

The Ambient Color attribute represents diffuse reflections arriving from all other surfaces in a scene. To simplify the rendering process, the diffuse reflections are assumed to be arriving from all points in the scene with equal intensities. In practical terms, Ambient Color is the color of a surface when it receives no light. A high Ambient Color value will cause the object to wash out and appear flat.

The Incandescence attribute, on the other hand, creates the illusion that the assigned surface is emitting light. The color of the Incandescence attribute is added to the Color attribute, thus making the material appear brighter.

Note: You can use the Ambient Color and Incandescence attributes as irradiant light sources when rendering with Final Gather. For more information, see Chapter 12.

The Translucence attribute simulates the diffuse penetration of light into a solid surface. In the real world, you can see this effect when holding a flashlight to the back of your hand. Translucence naturally occurs with hair, fur, wax, paper, leaves, and human flesh. Advanced renderers, such as mental ray, are able to simulate translucence through subsurface scattering (see Chapter 12 for an example). Maya's Translucence attribute, however, is a simplified system. The higher the attribute value, the more the scene's light penetrates the surface (see Figure 4.2).

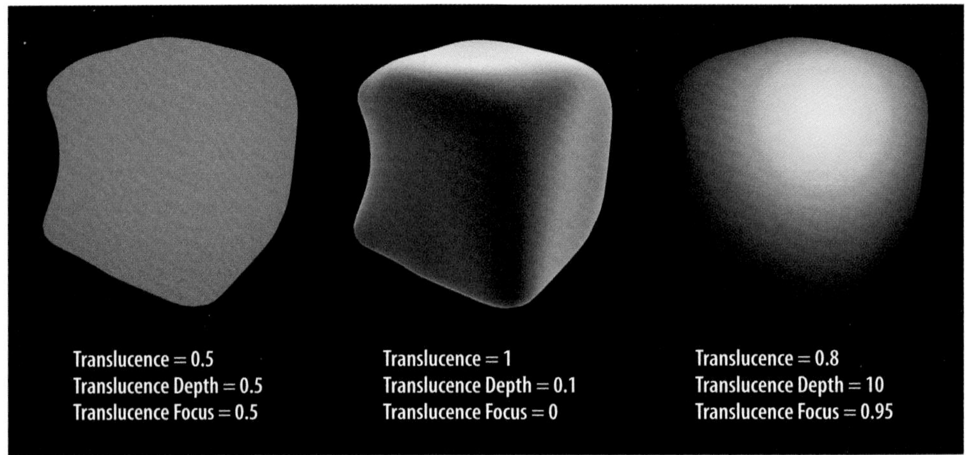

Figure 4.2 Different combinations of Translucence, Translucence Depth, and Translucence Focus attributes on a primitive lit from behind. This scene is included on the CD as `translucence.ma`.

A Translucence value of 1 allows 100 percent of the light to pass through the surface. A value of 0 turns the translucent effect off. Translucence Depth sets the virtual distance into the object to which the light is able to penetrate. The attribute is measured in world units and may be raised above 5. Translucence Focus controls the scattering of light through the surface. A value of 0 makes the scatter of light random and diffuse. High values focus the light into a point.

Shading with Phong

The Phong shading model uses diffuse and ambient components but also generates a specular highlight based on an arbitrary shininess. In general, specularity is the consistent reflection of light in one direction that creates a "hot spot" on a surface. With the Phong model, the position and intensity of a specular highlight is determined by reading the angle between the reflection vector and the view vector (see Figure 4.3). A vector, in this situation, is a line segment that runs between two points in 3D Cartesian space that represents direction. (For a deeper discussion of vectors and vector math, see Chapter 8.)

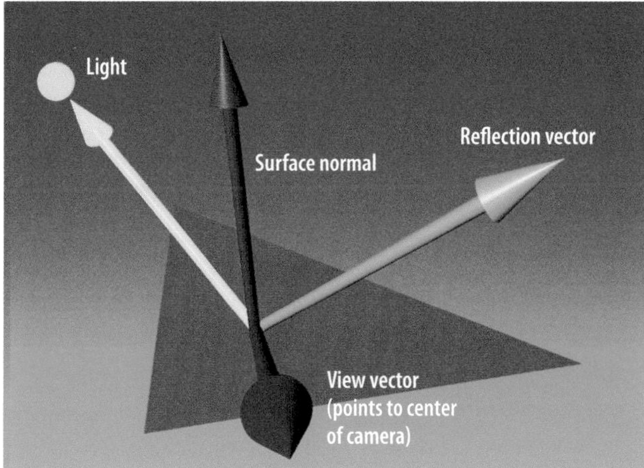

Figure 4.3 A simplified representation of a specular shading model

If the angle between the light vector and the surface normal is 60 degrees, the angle between the reflection vector and the surface normal is also 60 degrees. In this way, the reflection vector is a mirrored version of the light vector. If the angle between the reflection vector and view vector is large, the intensity of the specular highlight is either low or zero. If the angle between the reflection vector and view vector is small, the intensity of the specular highlight is high. The speed with which the specular highlight transitions from high intensity to no intensity is controlled by the Cosine Power attribute. The higher the Cosine Power value, the more rapid the falloff, and the smaller and "tighter" the highlight.

Both Gouraud and Phong shading models produce specular highlights. However, Phong produces a higher degree of accuracy, particularly with low-resolution geometry. As with the Gouraud technique, Phong reads vertex normals. Phong goes one step further, however, by interpolating new surface normals across the scan line. The angle between a surface normal at the point to be rendered (*c*) and the light vector determines the intensity of that point (see Figure 4.4).

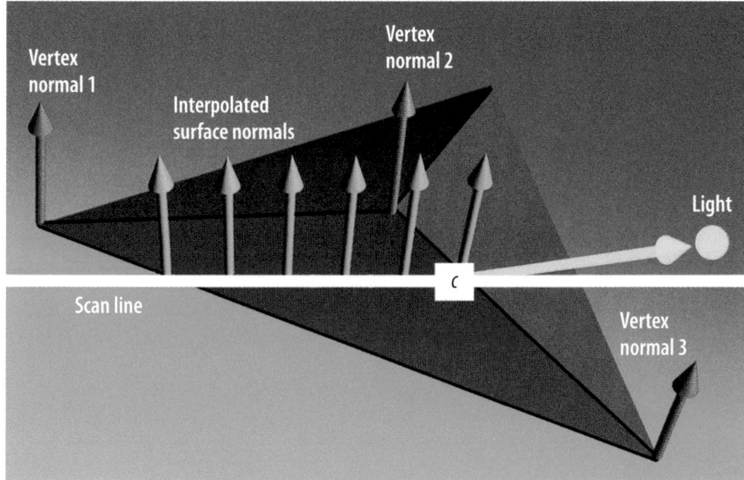

Figure 4.4 A simplified representation of the Phong shading model

Ultimately, 3D specular highlights are an artificial construct. Real-world specular highlights are reflections of intense light sources (see Figure 4.5).

Figure 4.5 (Top left) A classic specular highlight appears on an eye. (Top right) A closer look at the eye reveals that the specular highlight is the reflection of the photographer's light umbrella. (Bottom left) A glass float with a large specular highlight. (Bottom middle) With the exposure adjusted, the float's specular highlight is revealed to be the reflection of a window. (Bottom right) The window that creates the reflection.

Shading with Blinn

The Blinn shading model borrows the specular shading component from the Phong model but treats the specular calculations in a more mathematically efficient way. Instead of determining the angle between the reflection vector and view vector, Blinn determines the angle between the view vector and a vector halfway between the light vector and view vector. This frees the specular calculation from specific surface curvature. In practical terms, you can make the Maya Phong and Blinn materials produce nearly identical highlights (see Figure 4.6). Maya's Blinn material uses the Eccentricity attribute to control specular size and the Specular Roll Off attribute to control specular intensity.

When it comes to the position of the specular highlight, both Phong and Blinn re-create Fresnel reflections, whereby the amount of light reflected from a surface depends on the angle of view (which is the opposite of diffuse reflections). That is, when the view changes, the highlight appears at a different point on the surface (see Figure 4.7).

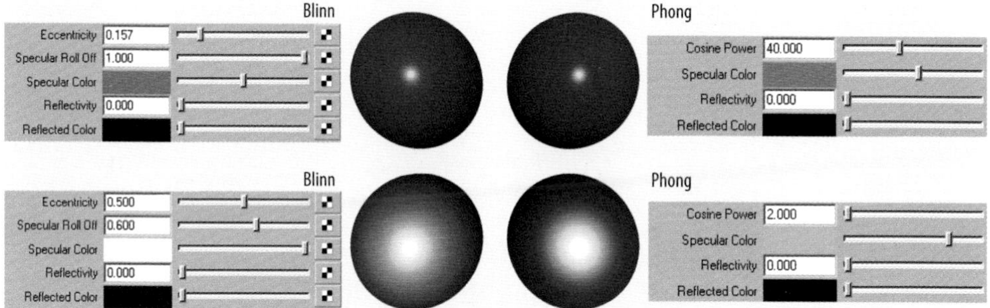

Figure 4.6 Small and large specular highlights on Blinn and Phong materials. This scene is included on the CD as `blinn_phong.ma`.

Model created by PixWATT Studio

Figure 4.7 Specular highlights appear at different points on the medallion as the view changes.

Note: Although Maya's Blinn and Phong materials are able to change the location of the specular highlight as the view changes, they are unable to accurately change the inherent intensity of the specular highlight. The Studio Clear Coat utility plug-in, however, solves this limitation. For a demonstration, see Chapter 7.

Shading with Phong E

Maya's Phong E material is a variation of the Phong shading model. Phong E's specular quality is similar to both Phong and Blinn. The Roughness attribute controls the transition of the highlight core to the highlight edge. A low Roughness value will cause the highlight to fade off quickly, whereas a high Roughness value causes the highlight to have a diffuse taper in the style of a Blinn material. The Highlight Size attribute controls the total size of the highlight. The Whiteness attribute allows an additional color to be blended into the highlight between the colors established by the Color and Specular Color attributes. The Specular Color attribute is the color of the highlight at its greatest intensity.

Blinn, Phong, and Phong E highlights will become distorted as they approach the edge of a surface with a high degree of curvature. In addition, Blinn, Phong, and Phong E produce elongated highlights on cylindrical objects (see Figure 4.8).

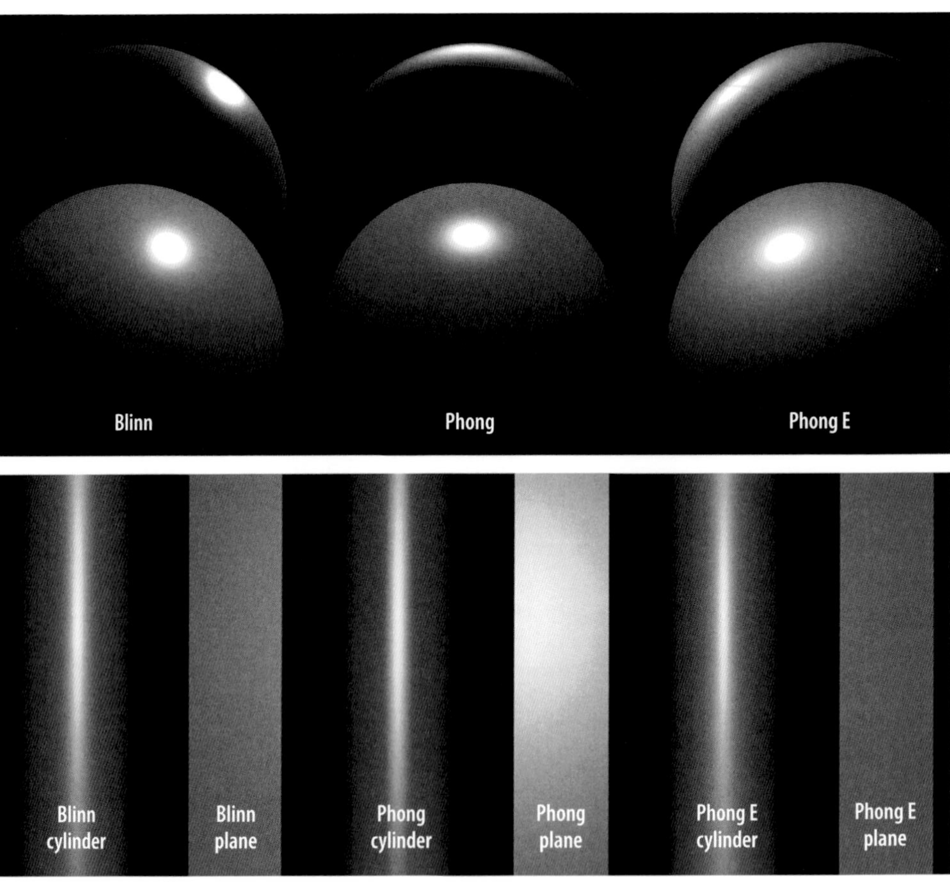

Figure 4.8 Blinn, Phong, and Phong E materials assigned to primitive spheres, cylinders, and planes. This scene is included on the CD as `blinn_phong_cylinders.ma`.

When comparing the material's highlights to photographs of real-world equivalents, it's apparent that the Blinn, Phong, and Phong E models are fairly realistic (see Figure 4.9). Phong and Phong E materials do have a slight advantage on the edge of a spherical surface, where specular reflections naturally grow in width.

Note: Fresnel reflections are named after Augustin-Jean Fresnel (1788–1827), who drafted theories on light propagation. The Gouraud shading model was presented by Henri Gouraud in 1971. The Phong shading model was created by Bui Tuong Phong in 1975. The Blinn shading model was developed in 1977 by James Blinn, who was also a pioneer of bump and environment mapping.

Figure 4.9 (Left) Various cylindrical objects lit by a single overhead light. (Right) A billiard ball with specular reflections of windows on its top edge.

Shading with the Anisotropic Material

The anisotropic shading model produces stretched reflections and specular highlights. The model simulates surfaces that have microscopic grooves, channels, scratches, grains, or fibers running parallel to one another. In such a situation, specular highlights tend to be elongated and run perpendicular to the direction of the grooves. The effect occurs on choppy or rippled water, brushed, coiled, or threaded metal, velvet and like cloth, feathers, and human hair (see Figure 4.10).

Figure 4.10 Anisotropic specular highlights on water, metal, and hair

The anisotropic shading model is opposite that of isotropic shading models used by such materials as Blinn or Phong. With isotropic models, the quality of the specular highlight does not change if the assigned surface is moved or rotated. With anisotropic models, a change in the surface's translation or rotation can significantly alter the resulting highlight. As a simple demonstration, two NURBS spheres are assigned to default Blinn and Anisotropic materials and are translated and rotated (see Figure 4.11).

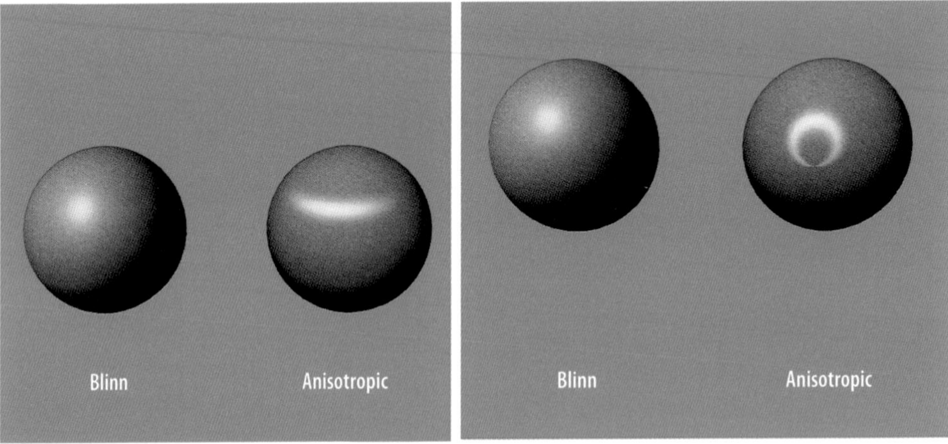

Figure 4.11 The specular highlight of an Anisotropic material changes with translation and rotation of the assigned sphere on the right. This scene is included on the CD as `anisotropic_spin.ma`. A QuickTime movie is included as `anisotropic_spin.mov`.

CDs and DVDs produce strong anisotropic highlights due to their method of manufacture. You can re-create these in Maya with the following steps:

1. Create a new scene. Choose Create > NURBS Primitives > Circle with the default settings. Select the resulting circle and choose Edit > Duplicate.
2. Select the duplicated circle and reduce the scale so that it is the appropriate size for the CD's center hole. Select both circles, switch to the Surfaces menu set, and choose Surfaces > Loft.
3. Select the new surface and assign it to a new Anisotropic material. Open the material's Attribute Editor tab. Set Spread X to 100, Spread Y to 1, Roughness to 0.8, and Fresnel Index to 9.5.
4. Create a point light and place it above the surface. Render a test. At this point, the specular highlight is white. To insert colors into the highlight, click the checkered Map button beside Specular Color. From the Create Render Node window, choose Ramp. Open the new ramp texture in the Attribute Editor tab. Set the Interpolation to Smooth. Render a test. The highlight now emulates the color shift of real CDs (see Figure 4.13). If the colors run in a direction opposite that of a real CD, switch the top and bottom handles of the ramp texture.

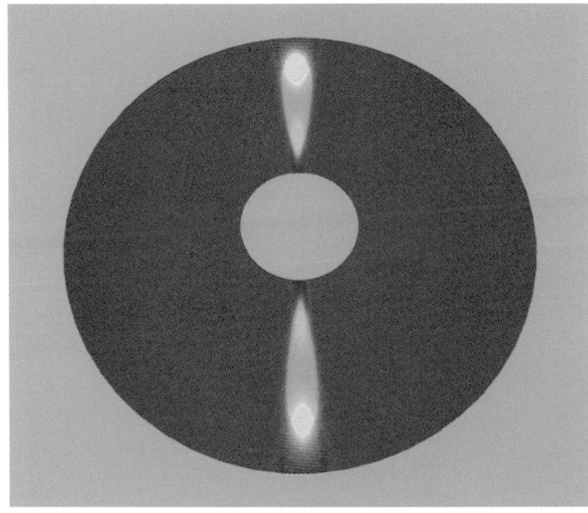

Figure 4.12
The anisotropic highlight of a CD is re-created in Maya. This scene is included on the CD as `anisotropic_cd.ma`.

The Anisotropic attributes work in the following way:

Angle Determines the angle of the specular highlight.

Spread X Sets the width of the grooves in *x* direction. The *x* direction is the U direction rotated counterclockwise by the Angle attribute.

Spread Y Sets the width of the grooves in *y* direction, which is perpendicular to the *x* direction. If Spread X and Spread Y are equal, the specular highlight is fairly circular.

Roughness Controls the roughness of the surface. The higher the value, the larger and the more diffuse the highlights appear.

Fresnel Index Sets the intensity of the specular highlight.

Anisotropic Reflectivity If checked, bases reflectivity on the Roughness attribute. If unchecked, the standard Reflectivity attribute determines reflectivity.

For information on raytracing and an additional example of an Anisotropic material used to create the specular highlights on glass, see Chapter 11.

Shading with a Shading Map

Maya's Shading Map material remaps the output of another material. In other words, the Shading Map discreetly replaces the colors of a material, even after the qualities of that material have been calculated. In a basic example, the Out Color attribute of a Blinn material is mapped to the Color of a Shading Map material (see Figure 4.13). The Out Color of a Ramp texture is mapped to the Shading Map Color of the Shading Map material. In turn, the Shading Map material is assigned to a polygon frog. Where the Blinn material normally shades the model with a dark color, the bottom of the Ramp is sampled. Where the Blinn normally shades the model with a light color, such as a specular highlight point, the top of the Ramp is sampled.

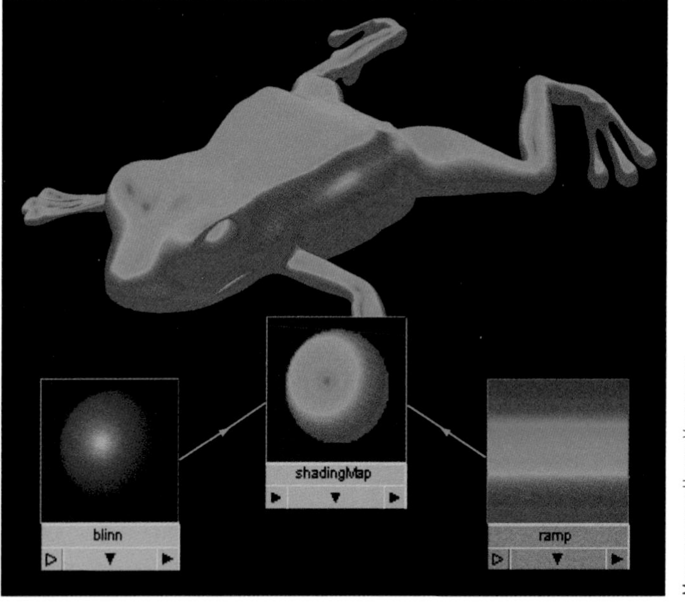

Figure 4.13 A polygon frog is assigned to a Shading Map material. A simplified version of this scene is included on the CD as `shading_map.ma`.

Shading with a Surface Shader

Maya's Surface Shader material is a "pass through" node. That is, the material was designed to make arbitrarily named inputs recognizable to the renderer. The material does not contain shading properties and will not take into account any light or shadow information. A surface assigned directly to a Surface Shader material appears self-illuminated. Any texture mapped to the Out Color attribute of the Surface Shader comes through the render with all its original vibrancy intact (see Figure 4.14). This makes the Surface Shader ideal for background skies and brightly lit signs. The material is also well suited for custom cartoon materials in which shadowing and highlights are provided by a custom network and not by actual lights. For a cartoon material example, see Chapter 7.

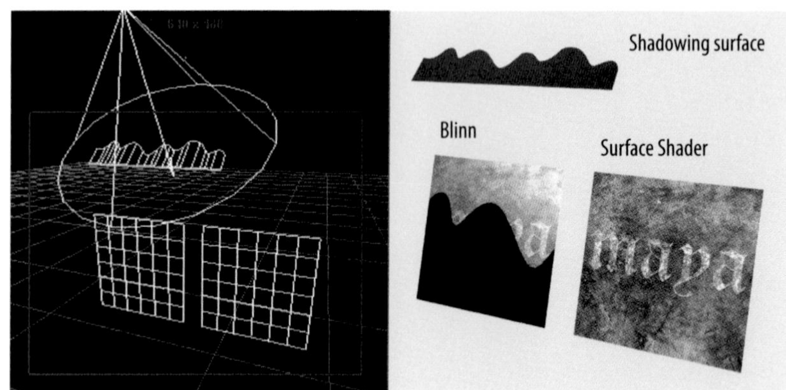

Figure 4.14 A plane assigned to a Blinn material picks up shadows and highlights, whereas a plane is assigned to a Surface Shader material and ignores all lighting information. This scene is included on the CD as `surface_shader.ma`.

Shading with Use Background

Maya's Use Background material allows the assigned surface to pick up color from a camera's Background Color attribute or image plane. For example, in Figure 4.15 a photo of a quiet town is loaded into the default persp camera as an image plane (choose View > Image Plane > Import Image from the camera's workspace view menu). A NURBS plane is aligned to the perspective of the photo's street. The plane is assigned to a Use Background material. The resulting render places the shadow of a polygon craft on top of the street.

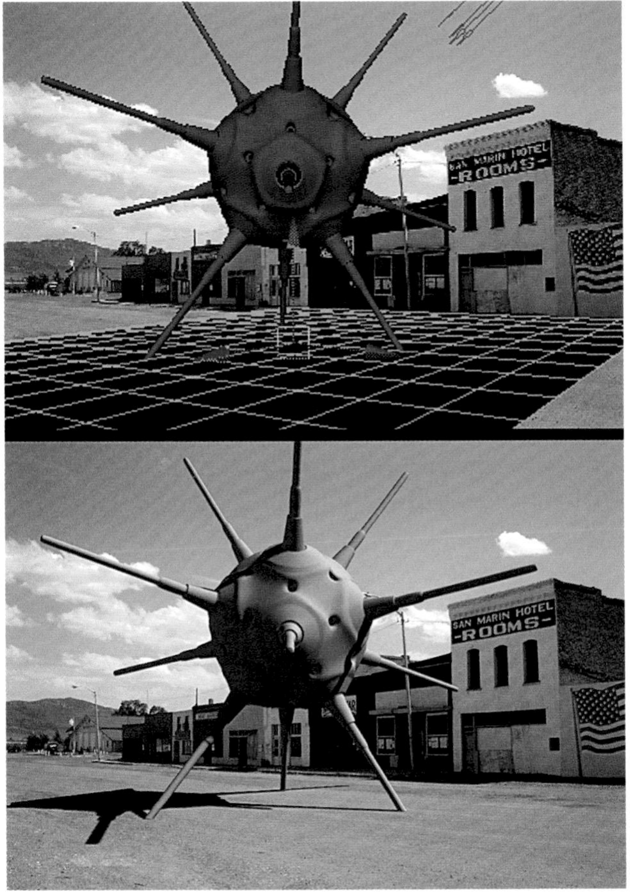

MODEL CREATED BY KONSTANTINOFF

Figure 4.15 The Use Background material is assigned to a primitive plane, thus placing a shadow on a photo of a street. A simplified version of this scene is included on the CD as `use_background.ma`. The image is also included in the `textures` folder as `street.tif`.

If the image plane is removed from the camera and the polygon craft is assigned to a 100 percent transparent Lambert material, the shadow is rendered by itself and appears in the alpha channel (see Figure 4.16). This offers an excellent means to render shadows out on their own pass. If shadows are rendered separately, you can composite them back onto a static background. For an example of this technique, see Chapter 10. For more information on alpha channels, see Chapter 6.

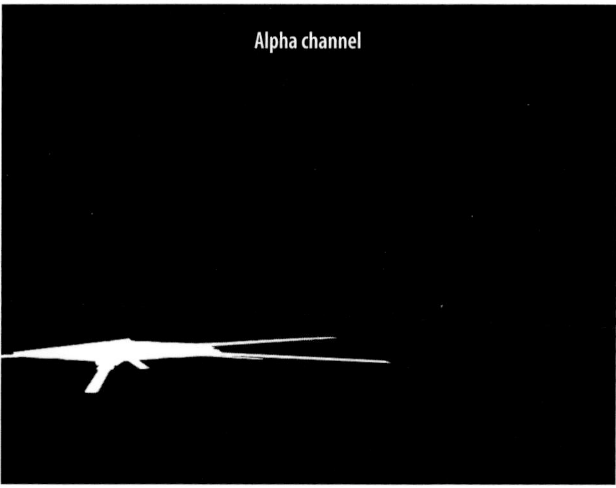

Figure 4.16 The Use Background material isolates a shadow in the alpha channel. A simplified version of this scene is included on the CD as `background_shadow.ma`.

The Use Background material also serves as an "alpha punch" that cuts holes into other objects. For this to work, the camera's Background Color attribute (found in the Environment section of the camera's Attribute Editor tab) should be set to black. For example, in Figure 4.17 three polygon gorillas stand close together, partially occluding each other. In a first render pass (see the top of Figure 4.17), a Use Background material is assigned to the center gorilla while the other surfaces are assigned to several Blinn materials. As a result, the center gorilla cuts a hole into the other two. As a second render pass (see the middle of Figure 4.17), the Use Background material is assigned to the two outer gorillas and the ground plane. The center gorilla is assigned to a Blinn. As a result, the two outer gorillas cut a hole into the center gorilla. When the two render passes are brought into a compositing program, they fit together perfectly (see the bottom of Figure 4.17). This works whether the objects are static or are in motion. When used in this fashion, the Use Background material allows characters and objects in a scene to be rendered separately without any worry of which object is in the front and which is in the back.

Note: You can isolate shadows with Maya's Render Layer Editor. For a detailed description of the editor, see Chapter 13.

Note: Three materials—Hair Tube Shader, Ocean Shader, and Ramp Shader—are not discussed in this chapter. The Hair Tube Shader is designed for the Maya Hair System, which is covered briefly in Chapter 3. The Ocean Shader is designed specifically for fluid dynamic ocean simulations and has no other general purpose. The Ramp Shader is reviewed in Chapter 7.

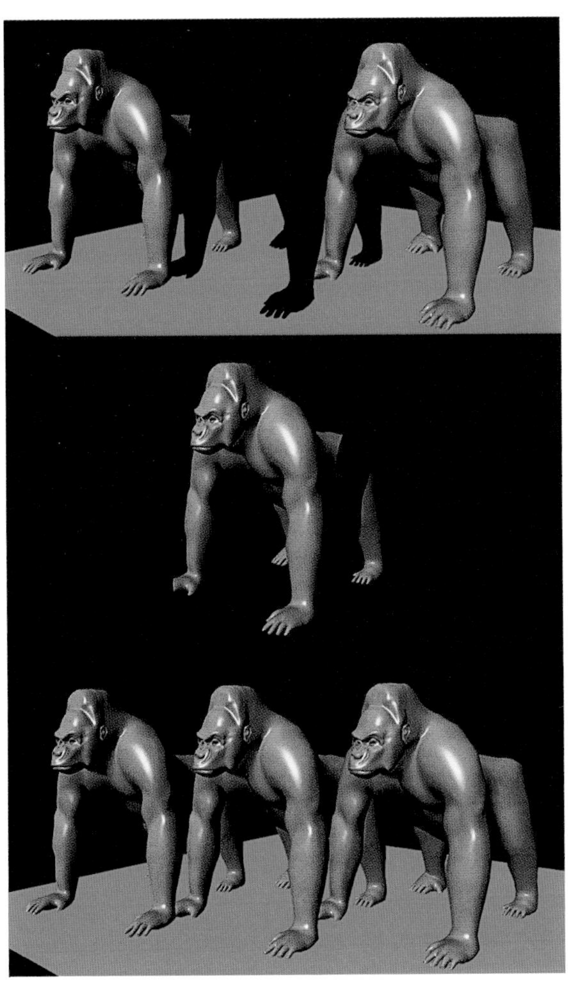

Figure 4.17 The Use Background material cuts holes into the alpha of two renders. When the renders are composited back together, they fit perfectly. A simplified version of this scene is included on the CD as `background_alpha.ma`.

Reviewing 2D Textures

Maya 2D textures can be grouped into the following categories: cloth, water, Perlin noise, ramp, bitmap, and square. Aside from bitmaps, all these textures are generated procedurally. That is, Maya creates these textures with specialized algorithms that create repeating patterns.

Applying Cloth

The Cloth texture is unique in that it generates interlaced fibers. Aside from obvious use in clothing, it can be adjusted to generate various organic patterns such as reptile scales. For example, in Figure 4.18 a Cloth texture is mapped to the Bump Mapping attribute of a Blinn material.

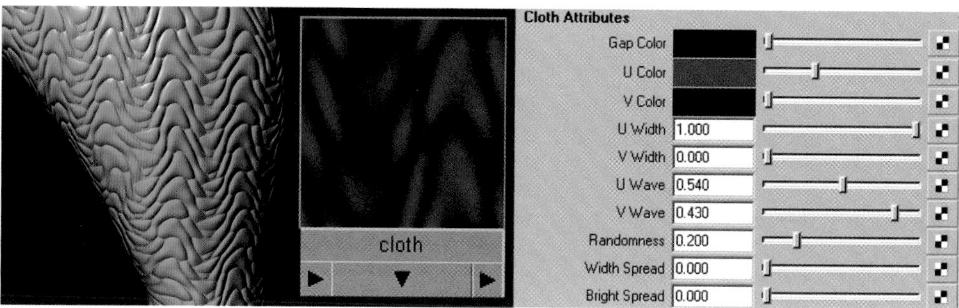

Figure 4.18 The Cloth texture is adjusted to create scales. This material is included on the CD as `cloth_scales.ma`.

The regularity, or irregularity, of the cloth pattern is controlled by ten attributes. Gap Color, U Color, and V Color set the color of the virtual threads. U Width and V Width determine the width of the threads in the U and V direction. U Wave and V Wave insert wave-like distortion into the cloth pattern. Randomness harshly distorts the pattern in the U and V directions. Width Spread randomly changes the thread widths. Bright Spread randomly darkens of lightens the thread colors.

Applying Water

By default, the Water texture produces overlapping wave patterns. Although the default is not particularly suited for realistic liquid, you can adjust the attributes to create other patterns found in nature. For example, in Figure 4.19 a Water texture is applied to a plane as a bump map and is adjusted to emulate wind-blown sand.

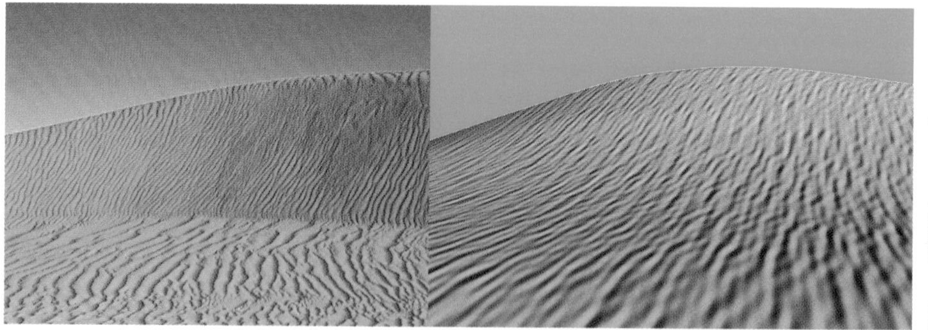

Figure 4.19 (Left) Wind-blown sand forms patterns on a dune. (Right) A 3D facsimile utilizing the Water texture. This scene is included on the CD as `water_sand.ma`.

Critical attributes of the Water texture include:

Number Of Waves Sets the number of waves used to create the pattern.

Wave Time and Wave Velocity Wave Time controls the placement of the waves. Gradually increasing the value will cause the waves to "roll" across the texture as if part of a body of water. Wave Velocity sets the speed by which the waves move if Wave Time is changed. Both attributes are designed for keyframe animation.

Wave Amplitude Controls the height of the waves. Higher values introduce greater degree of contrast into the pattern.

Wave Frequency and Sub Wave Frequency Wave Frequency sets the fundamental frequency of the waves. Higher values create waves that are narrower and more tightly packed. Sub Wave Frequency overlays a higher frequency onto the base waves, which makes the wave pattern more irregular.

Smoothness Smoothness blurs the wave pattern. A higher value makes the pattern softer and less detailed. (The generated pattern is never hard-edged, even when Smoothness is turned down to 0.)

The Concentric Ripple Attributes section sets aside another ten attributes for creating and controlling circular ripples. You can isolate the concentric ripples by setting Number Of Waves to 0.

In addition, you can use the Water texture to distort flags and other cloth-like surfaces. For example, in Figure 4.20 a Water texture is mapped to the Bump Mapping attribute of a Blinn material. The Repeat UV attribute of the Water's 2D Placement utility is kept below 1 in the U and V direction.

Figure 4.20 A Water texture is applied to a plane as a bump map, giving the cloth texture extra dimension. This scene is included on the CD as `water_cloth.ma`.

Note: The Ocean texture is designed for Maya's Ocean System. The Fluid Texture 2D texture uses Maya's fluid dynamic simulation. For more information, refer to the "Fluid Effects" Maya help file.

Applying Perlin Noise

Perlin noise was invented by Ken Perlin in the early 1980s as a means of generating random patterns from random numbers. You can use Perlin-based 2D textures to break up surface regularity. For example, you can map the Maya Noise texture to a material's Specular Color to make a specular highlight appear more irregular (see Figure 4.21).

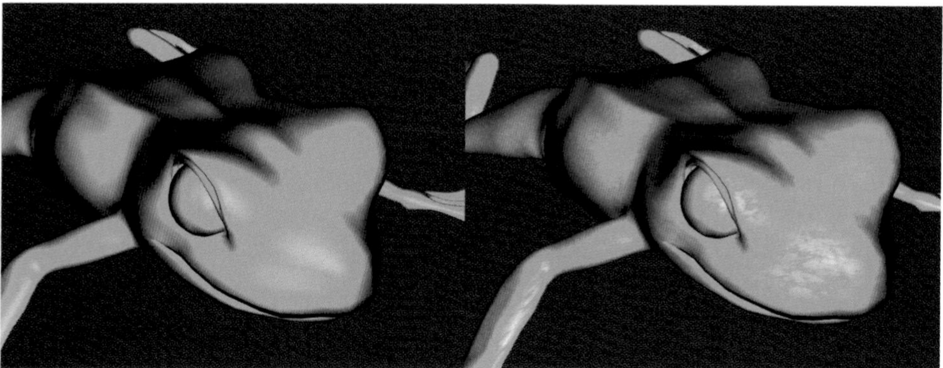

Figure 4.21 (Left) A Blinn assigned to a polygon frog shows little variation in the specular highlight. (Right) A Noise texture mapped to the Specular Color of the same Blinn produces a more complex result. A simplified version of this scene is included on the CD as `specular_noise.ma`.

In addition, you can map a Noise texture to a File texture's Color Gain to dirty up an otherwise clean bitmap. For an example, see "Stacking Materials and Textures" later in this chapter.

Maya's Fractal texture is a more complex variation of classic 2D Perlin noise in which turbulence (the averaging of multiple scales) is added for detail. The majority of attributes are identical to the Noise texture. The attribute list for both the Noise and Fractal texture is quite long but will be detailed in Chapter 5.

Maya's Mountain texture, on the other hand, is a variation of Perlin noise that lacks a smoothing function. It simulates a simplified mountain range where snow occurs at a particular elevation (as viewed from above). Although it's not possible to create a realistic mountain with the Mountain texture, you can use the texture to create granular patterns. For example, in Figure 4.22 two Mountain textures are respectively mapped to the Color and Bump Mapping attributes of a Phong material, creating the illusion of green debris and scum on a floor. A Checker texture is mapped to the Snow Color of the Mountain connected to the Phong's Color attribute, thus providing the red and white tiles.

The Mountain texture's unique attributes follow:

Amplitude, Snow Color, and Rock Color Amplitude sets the amount of Rock Color that appears "through" the Snow Color. A low value favors Snow Color in the coloring scheme. As demonstrated in Figure 4.22, Snow Color can be mapped with another texture. The same is true for Rock Color.

Boundary Controls the raggedness of the Snow Color to Rock Color transition. A low value creates smoother transitions and favors the Snow Color. A high value creates numerous interlocking nooks and crannies.

Snow Altitude, Snow Dropoff, and Snow Slope Snow Altitude determines the "altitude" at which Snow Color appears. Higher values increase the overall amount of snow. Snow Dropoff controls the rapidity at which the snow disappears at lower altitudes. The lower the Snow Dropoff value, the less snow there is. Snow Slope is the angle at which snow sticks to the virtual mountain. The higher the Snow Slope value, the more snow there is.

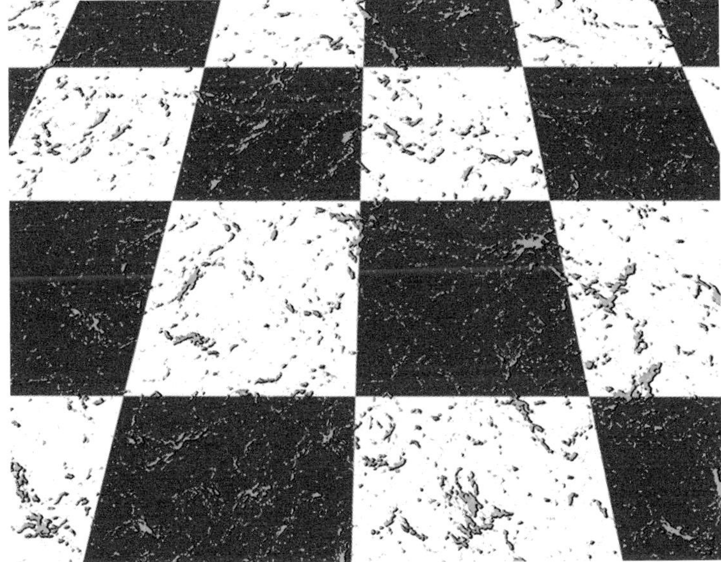

Figure 4.22 A Mountain texture creates green debris and scum on a floor. This scene is included on the CD as `mountain_dirt.ma`.

Applying Ramps, Bitmaps, and Square Textures

The Ramp texture allows selected colors to transition in the U or V direction. The texture carries a total of nine ramp Type attribute options and seven Interpolation attribute options, supporting a wide range of results (see Figure 4.23).

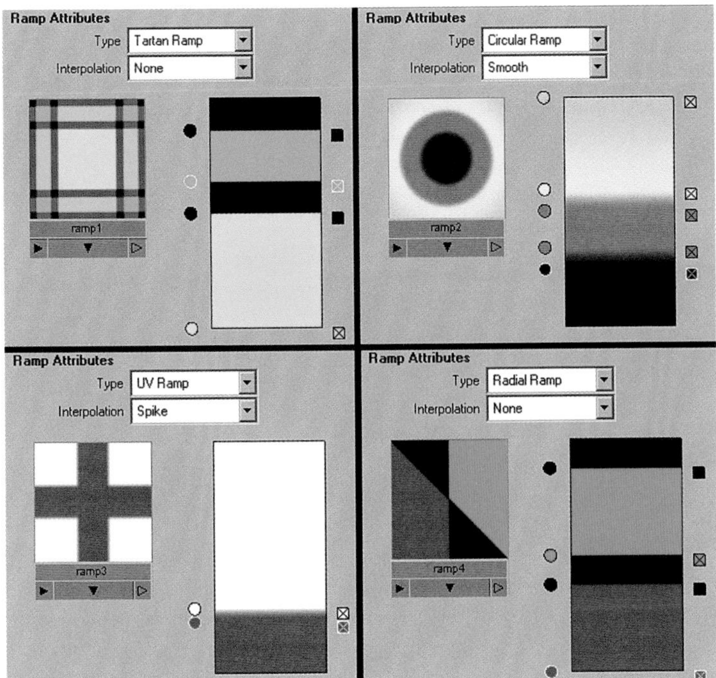

Figure 4.23 Unusual combinations of ramp types and interpolations. These textures are included on the CD as `ramps.ma`.

Note: Ramp textures are often employed in custom shading networks. For a demonstration of a Ramp used to create a custom wireframe render, see Section 4.1 of the `Additional_Techniques.pdf` on the CD. For a demonstration of a Ramp used to create a window reflection in an eye, see Section 4.2 of the same file. Ramp textures are also used to create an iron shading network later in this chapter, a custom cartoon material in Chapter 7, and per-particle colors in Chapter 8.

Importing custom bitmaps, whether as File, PSD File, or Movie textures, is the most powerful way to achieve realism and detail in Maya. File textures are used extensively in the custom shading networks demonstrated in Chapters 5 through 7. Movie textures are simply variations of File textures. Movie textures will read any movie format supported by Maya, including Windows Media Player AVI files on Windows systems and QuickTime on Macintosh systems. In order to use all the frames contained within the movie, you must check the Use Image Sequence attribute. Both File and Movie textures are able to accept numbered image sequences. Once again, Use Image Sequence must be checked for all the frames to be read.

Square textures are generated by repeating color blocks or lines in the U and V directions. Square textures include Bulge, Grid, and Checker. The Bulge texture can be thought of as a blurry Grid texture. Both Bulge and Grid are often useful for bump mapping. If either the U Width or V Width attribute of the Grid texture is set to 0, parallel grooves are generated in one direction. The Checker texture is handy for checking UV distortions on surfaces (see Chapter 9).

Mastering Extra Map Options

Several texture attributes are often overlooked, but are nonetheless quite useful. These include Filter, Filter Offset, Filter Type, Invert, and Color Remap.

Setting the Filter Type

By default, many Maya textures are filtered, whether they are procedural or bitmap. This is necessary to prevent aliasing problems. In general, aliasing artifacts occur when the detail contained within a texture is smaller than corresponding screen pixels. The problems are most noticeable when textures have a high degree of contrast and the camera or surface is in motion. In this situation, a moiré pattern is often formed (see Figure 4.24 for an extreme example). Although many of the anti-aliasing attributes in the Render Settings window reduce such problems (see Chapter 10), texture filtering remains a necessity of the 3D process.

In Maya, the filtering process is controlled by the Filter and Filter Offset attributes, found in the Effects section of the texture's Attribute Editor tab. Filter forces the renderer to employ a lesser or greater degree of filtering. In essence, filtering averages the texture pixels, thus blurring the texture. The lower the Filter value, the lesser the degree of filtering and the sharper the texture. The higher the Filter value, the greater the degree of filtering and the blurrier the texture. You can stylistically add or subtract detail from a texture by adjusting the Filter attribute. For example, in Figure 4.25 the effect of a large Filter value is a blurry Grid texture. Whereas Filter controls the degree of filtering in camera space, Filter Offset controls the amount of blur in texture space. In practical terms, the Filter Offset value is added to the Filter value for an extra degree of blurring.

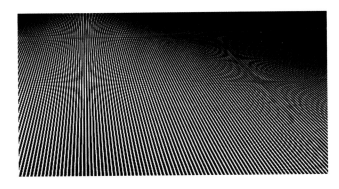

Figure 4.24
Moiré patterns formed by texture details that are smaller than corresponding screen pixels

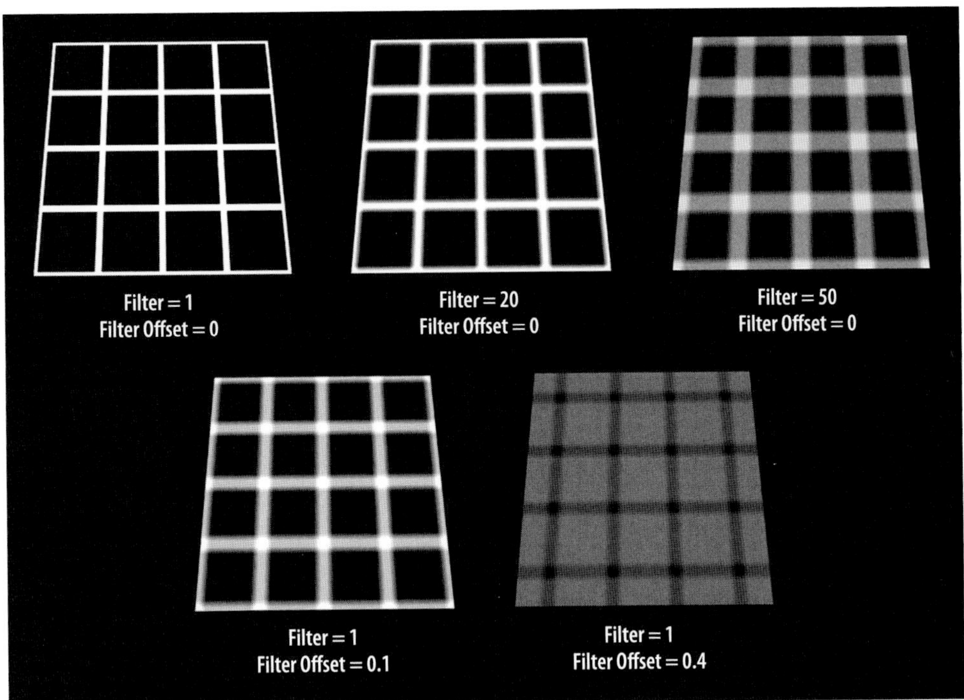

Figure 4.25 A Grid texture with six different Filter and Filter Offset settings. This scene is included on the CD as `grid_filter.ma`.

Note: Cloth, Bulge, Ramp, Water, Fluid Texture 2D, Fluid Texture 3D, Granite, Leather, and Snow textures do not possess filtering attributes.

File, Movie, and PSD File textures offer additional controls for the filtering process. You can set the Filter Type attribute, found at the top of the textures' Attribute Editor tab, to Off, Mipmap, Quadratic, Quartic, Gaussian, and Box.

Off turns off the filtering process and removes the Filter and Filter Offset attributes. Although this will speed up the render, moiré and stair-stepping artifacts will most likely appear.

Mipmap applies the mipmapping process. In this case, Maya stores averaged color values for multiple sizes of each texture. The sizes linearly decrease (for example, 512 × 512, 256 × 256, 128 × 128, and so on). When the renderer tackles an individual screen pixel, it determines the most appropriately sized mipmap. If the pixel falls over a distant surface, it recalls a small size. If the pixel falls over a surface in the immediate foreground, it recalls a large size. The angle between the surface and the camera is part of the equation. An oblique surface (one that is not perpendicular to the line of sight) induces a smaller mipmap, and a non-oblique surface induces a larger one. To increase the accuracy of the mipmap selection, Maya often averages a consecutive pair of mipmaps (for example, 512 × 512 and 256 × 256).

Gaussian shares its name with filters common to digital paint programs, such as Adobe Photoshop. Gaussian filters blur an image by convolving an array representing the original image and a second, smaller array known as a kernel. In simple terms, convolution allows the arrays to be multiplied together by "sliding" the kernel across the image array. The kernel itself contains a bell-shaped distribution of values that causes a predictable effect on different frequencies within the image. Higher frequencies equate to small details. Low frequencies equate to large image features. The end effect of a Gaussian filter is a blur that softens fine details without destroying large image features or negating edges.

Quadratic and Quartic are approximations of the Gaussian filter type that employ different bell-shaped distributions in their kernels. Both filters are optimized for speed. Quadratic offers the best balance of efficiency and quality, and is therefore the default option for Filter Type.

Box is the simplest filtering option available. Box gives equal weight to all sampled image pixels; hence, it does not preserve edges as well as other filter types. As a comparison, a TIFF image of a street is loaded into a File texture (see Figure 4.26). The File texture is mapped to the Out Color attribute of a Surface Shader material, which is assigned to a plane. The plane is rendered with Off, Mipmap, Quadratic, and Box Filter Type options. Off produces the most contrast; unfortunately, the sharp edges are likely to cause stair-stepping artifacts when the camera or plane is animated. Mipmap produces a softer result while allowing the building's "Meat Market" sign to be fairly readable. Quadratic is very close to Mipmap, but offers a slight increase in edge contrast. In this example, Quadratic erodes away the center horizontal line of the sign's first "E." Box creates the blurriest result, which make the sign difficult to read. In addition, Box creates harsh kinks in vertical lines. In particular, the left vertical edge of the sign has a severe stair-step artifact.

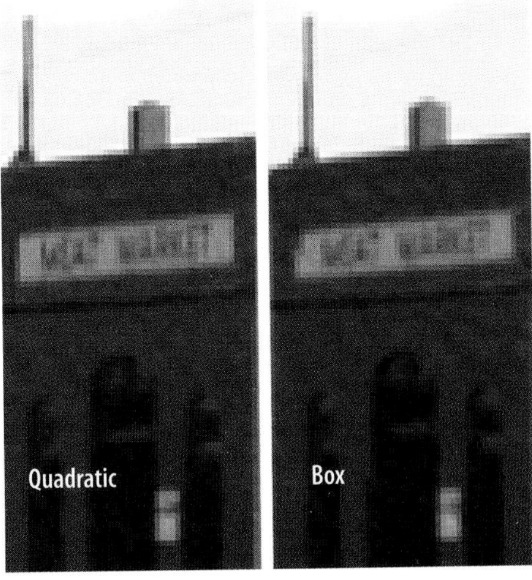

Figure 4.26
Detail of a 1024 × 768 bitmap, loaded into a File texture and rendered with four Filter Type options. This scene is included on the CD as `filter_comparison.ma`.

Two extra attributes are available to File, Movie, and PSD File textures: Pre Filter and Pre Filter Radius. Pre Filter, if checked, applies additional image-space filtering to the loaded map. The filtering occurs before any other operation is applied to the map. The higher the Pre Filter Radius value, the blurrier the image.

Note: If a texture's Filter Type is set to Box, Quadratic, Quartic, or Gaussian and the texture's Filter is set to an excessively high value, the texture will become pixilated and blocky. To intentionally create a heavy blur on a texture, leave Filter at its default value and raise Filter Offset by small increments (such as 0.1). Although Pre Filter will blur the texture, its blur cannot reach the strength supplied by the Filter Offset.

Shifting Color with Invert and Color Remap

The Invert check box, found in the Effects section of a texture's Attribute Editor tab, inverts the colors of the texture. The result is identical to the Reverse utility (see Chapter 8). If a color is pure white (RGB: 1, 1, 1), the inverted result is black (RGB: 0, 0, 0). If a color is yellow (RGB: 1, 1, 0), the inverted result is blue (RGB: 0, 0, 1). You can predict the results by picking an opposite side of the Maya color wheel.

The Color Remap Insert button, also found in the Effects section, attaches an Rgb To Hsv utility and a Ramp texture to the shading network. The new network color-shifts the original texture (see Figure 4.27). The portion of the texture that has low color values is given colors from the bottom of the Ramp. The portion of the texture that has high color values is given colors from the top of the Ramp. If you change the Ramp colors, the colors of the texture automatically change. (See Chapter 6 for a demonstration of the Rgb To Hsv utility in a custom network.)

Figure 4.27
The result of an activated Color Remap Insert button as applied to a File texture. This scene is included on the CD as `color_remap.ma`.

Stacking Materials and Textures

The Layered Shader material offers an easy method by which to combine two or more materials. For example, in Figure 4.28 a Blinn and a Lambert material are mapped to a Layered Shader material. The Blinn's Color is set to red with a hot specular highlight. The Lambert's Color is set to yellow and carries no specularity. The Blinn and Lambert are represented by the purple box icons in the icon field of the Layered Shader Attributes section of the Layered Shader's Attribute Editor tab. The Blinn and Lambert each receive a Transparency attribute. Which set of attributes is visible depends on which box icon is highlighted. You can switch between the box icons at any time by clicking them. If you hold your mouse over an icon, the name of the connected material is revealed. Although only two materials are connected to the Layered Shader in this example, you can connect three, four, five, or more. You can disconnect materials by clicking the small × below the corresponding icon. How the materials are mixed depends on each material's Transparency value. In the case of Figure 4.28, the Blinn, represented by the left icon, has a Transparency value set to 50 percent gray. The Lambert, represented by the right icon, has a Transparency value set to 0 percent black. The resulting Layered Shader contains a 50 percent mix of each material, producing an orange color. The specular highlight becomes more intense since the colors are added.

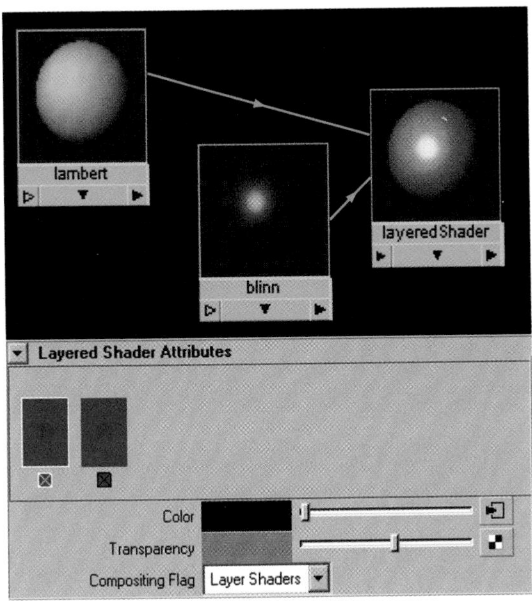

Figure 4.28 Two materials are blended with the Layered Shader material. This material is included on the CD as `layered_shader.ma`.

To choose the correct value for the various Transparency sliders in the Layered Shader material, follow these guidelines:

- The horizontal row of purple box icons is similar to a vertical stack of layers in Adobe Photoshop. The leftmost icon is equivalent to the highest layer in Photoshop, and the rightmost box is equivalent to the lowest layer.
- If the Transparency value of the first material (the one that is represented by the leftmost icon) is set to 0 percent black, the first material obscures all other materials.
- The last material mapped to the Layered Shader (represented by the rightmost icon) does not need its Transparency adjusted above 0 percent black. If the Transparency value is raised above 0 percent black, the resulting material becomes semitransparent.

The Layered Shader material works equally well with textures. As such, the material provides the Compositing Flag attribute to determine how to output the blended items. If you are blending materials, set Compositing Flag to Layer Shaders. If you are blending textures, set Compositing Flag to Layer Texture.

Note: You can map materials and textures to the Layered Shader material by MMB-dragging material and texture icons into the Layered Shader Attributes icon field of the Layered Shader's Attribute Editor tab. A purple box icon appears for each material or texture added.

The Layered Texture texture is almost identical to the Layered Shader material. However, it prefers connections from textures and will not function with materials. Any mapped texture receives a purple box icon. In the place of Transparency sliders, Layered Texture includes Alpha sliders. In addition, each texture connected to the Layered Texture receives a Blend Mode attribute. The Blend Mode attribute determines how each texture will combine with the texture just below it. In terms of icons, the Blend Mode attribute controls how each icon will be combined with the icon to its immediate right. A number of Blend Mode options (Add, Subtract, Multiply, Difference, Lighten, Darken, Saturate, Desaturate, and Illuminate) are identical to the equivalent layer blend modes in Adobe Photoshop and other digital-imaging programs. The None option makes the texture 100 percent opaque, preventing any lower texture (or right-hand icon) from appearing. If an Alpha attribute is mapped with a black and white texture, the In option cuts out the lower texture in the shape of the Alpha map; black areas become holes in the lower texture. With the same alpha map, the Out option inverts the cut. The Over option places the texture with the Alpha map on top of the lower texture as if it were a decal; black areas become holes for the upper map.

Although the Layered Texture texture offers a great deal of control when blending separate textures, you can simply map the Color Gain attribute of a texture (found in the Color Balance section of a texture's Attribute Editor tab). Color Gain works as a scaling factor—the texture's Out Color attribute is multiplied by the Color Gain color or map. For example, in Figure 4.29 a Noise texture is mapped to the Color Gain of Cloth texture, thus dirtying it. Conversely, the Color Offset attribute works as an offset factor. Whereas Color Gain functions as a multiplier, Color Offset simply adds its value to Out Color. Thus, a black Color Offset will have no effect on the texture. A 50 percent gray Color Offset will brighten the texture by adding RGB values of 0.5, 0.5, 0.5 to the texture's Out Color.

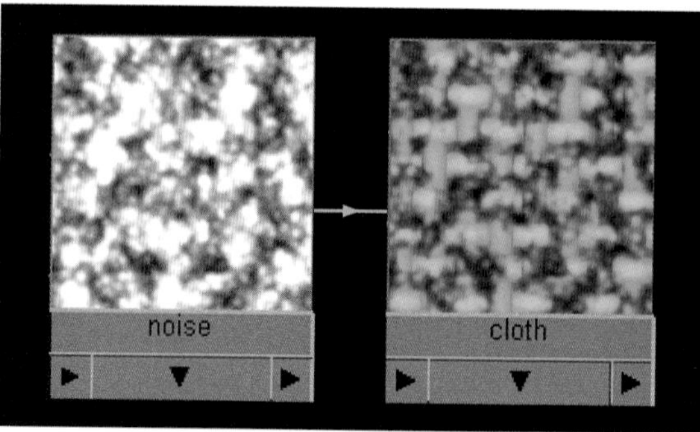

Figure 4.29 A Noise texture is mapped to the Color Gain of a Cloth texture. This material is included on the CD as `color_gain.ma`.

Mastering the Blinn Material

You can adjust a Blinn material to emulate a wide range of surfaces. In this section, steps for achieving wood, metal, and plastic using common map attributes are detailed. To simplify the demonstration, a single bitmap texture, `rusty.tif`, is used in each case (see Figure 4.30). (For details on creating glass, water, and ice, see Chapter 11.)

Figure 4.30 A noisy, dirty, rusty bitmap texture that can be applied in numerous ways. This bitmap is included on the CD as `rusty.tif`.

Before I discuss specific texturing examples, a quick look at placement utilities and naming conventions is necessary. The 2D Placement utility is connected automatically to a shading network when a material's checkered Map button is clicked and any 2D texture is selected from the Create Render Node window. If a 3D texture is selected from the Create Render Node window, a 3D Placement utility is connected automatically. Both utilities control the UV tiling of the texture. At the same time, MMB-dragging a 2D or 3D texture into the Hypershade work area automatically connects the appropriate placement utility.

Materials, textures, and utilities, once connected to a shading network or MMB-dragged into the Hypershade work area, pick up a new naming convention. For example, a 2D Placement utility may be named place2dTexture1. In general, the spelling and capitalization will vary slightly. This applies to attributes as well. For example, the Out Color attribute may appear as outColor or blinn.outColor when connected to a shading network.

For the purpose of this chapter and Chapter 5, I will use the full name of the material, texture, or utility as it appears in Create Maya Nodes menu and Create Render Node window. In addition, I will use the full attribute name as it appears in the corresponding Attribute Editor tab. Starting with Chapter 6, however, custom connections are covered in great detail, and I will use the specific node and connection names.

Re-Creating Wood

For realistic wood, it's best to use an actual photo or scan. However, if a decent photo or scan is not available, you can generate the illusion of wood grain by adjusting the UV tiling of an otherwise inappropriate bitmap. For example, in Figure 4.31 `rusty.tif` is loaded into a File texture, which in turn is mapped to the Color attribute of a Blinn material (named Wood).

Figure 4.31 (Top left) 3D wood. (Top right) Reference photo of wood. (Bottom) Wood shading network. This scene is included on the CD as `wood.ma`.

The Blinn has the following custom settings:

Diffuse	0.95
Eccentricity	0.35
Specular Roll Off	0.22
Specular Color	light orange

The File texture's 2D Placement utility has the following custom settings:

Mirror U	On
Mirror V	On
Repeat UV	0.25, 14
Rotate UV	70
Noise UV	0.001, 0.001

The Noise UV attribute creates subtle distortions in the File texture, making the texture repeat less obvious. The Mirror U and Mirror V attributes flip the texture each time it's repeated, adding even more variety. In addition, the Color Gain of File texture is tinted brown. The Filter Offset of the File is set to 0.02, which softens the texture slightly. The File texture is also applied as a bump map. The Bump 2D utility's Bump Depth value is set to 0.005.

Note: If Noise UV is raised above 0, 0, the only Filter Type available to the renderer is Mipmap.

Re-Creating Metal

Metal is perhaps the most difficult surface to re-create. Chrome, polished silver, stainless steel, and similar metals can be reproduced with raytraced reflections. (See Chapter 11 for raytracing tips.) Many metal finishes, however, do not create coherent reflections. In such a situation, believability comes from the metal's color and the contrast of the metal to its specular highlight. For instance, cast iron is a very "dark" metal. Although iron has a moderately bright secular highlight, the section of the surface that does not receive direct light becomes dark quickly. In this situation, the iron is a poor light reflector. You can create this look by creating a dark surface color with a diffuse specular highlight. For example, in Figure 4.32 a Blinn material is assigned to a torus with the following custom settings:

Diffuse	0.09
Eccentricity	0.47
Specular Roll Off	0.5
Reflectivity	0.25

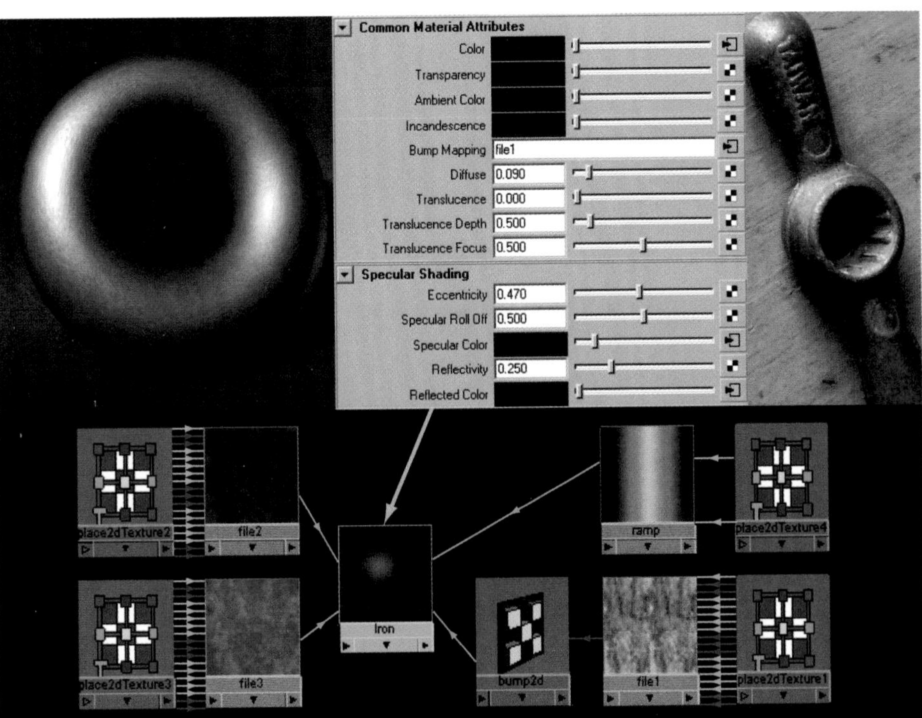

Figure 4.32 (Top left) 3D iron. (Top middle) Blinn material settings. (Top right) Reference photo of iron. (Bottom) Iron shading network. This scene is included on the CD as `iron.ma`.

The rusty.tif file is loaded into three File textures. The first File (file1) is mapped to the Bump Mapping attribute of the Blinn material (named Iron). The Bump 2D utility's Bump Depth value is set to 0.01, creating a subtle roughness to the surface. The Placement 2D utility for file1 has its Repeat UV set to 2, 1. The second File texture (file2) is mapped to the Blinn's Color. The Color Gain of file2 is lowered to darken the bitmap and thereby reduce the contrast visible as a color. When a File texture is mapped to the Blinn's Color, more variation is present in the render than could be provided by a solid color. The third File (file3) is mapped to the Blinn's Reflected Color. The Reflected Color attribute creates the illusion of reflection without the need to raytrace. The Filter Offset of file3 is set to 0.5, blurring the bitmap. The Invert attribute of file3 is checked, thereby tinting the surface color blue and reducing the contrast. With these settings, the Reflected Color attribute creates a subtle, bluish ambient reflection across the surface. The Reflectivity attribute controls the strength of the Reflected Color effect. Last, a Ramp texture is mapped to the Specular Color of the Blinn. The Ramp has the following custom settings:

Type	U Ramp
Interpolation	Smooth
Noise	0.017
Noise Freq	1.25

The Ramp has five handles running from black to light gray. This creates a light band across the center of the torus.

Re-Creating Plastic

Plastic should never be thought of as a solid color. Even the most finely manufactured plastic product will contain numerous surface imperfections and variations in the specularity. The quickest way to emulate dark plastic is to apply a bitmap as a bump and a specular color. For example, in Figure 4.33 rusty.tif is loaded into a File texture (named file1). The Color Offset of file1 is set to a light blue, which reduces the bitmap's contrast; file1 is mapped to the Specular Color attribute of a Blinn material (named Plastic), which is assigned to a sphere.

The 2D Placement utility for file1 has the following custom settings:

Repeat UV	40, 40
Noise UV	0.1, 0.2
Stagger	On

The combination of a high Repeat UV value with a relatively high Noise UV value creates very small, near-random detail. Stagger, when checked, offsets each repeat by the half-length of the texture, creating an even more uneven pattern. rusty.tif is also loaded into a second File texture (file2), which is mapped to the Bump Mapping attribute of the Blinn. The Bump 2D utility's Bump Depth is set to 0.01. The 2D Placement utility of file2 also has a high Repeat UV value of 20, 20, a

Noise UV value of 0, 0.005, and a Rotate UV value of 90. Last, the Color of the Blinn itself is set a dark gray. The Blinn has the following custom settings:

Diffuse	0.52
Eccentricity	0.34
Specular Roll Off	0.24

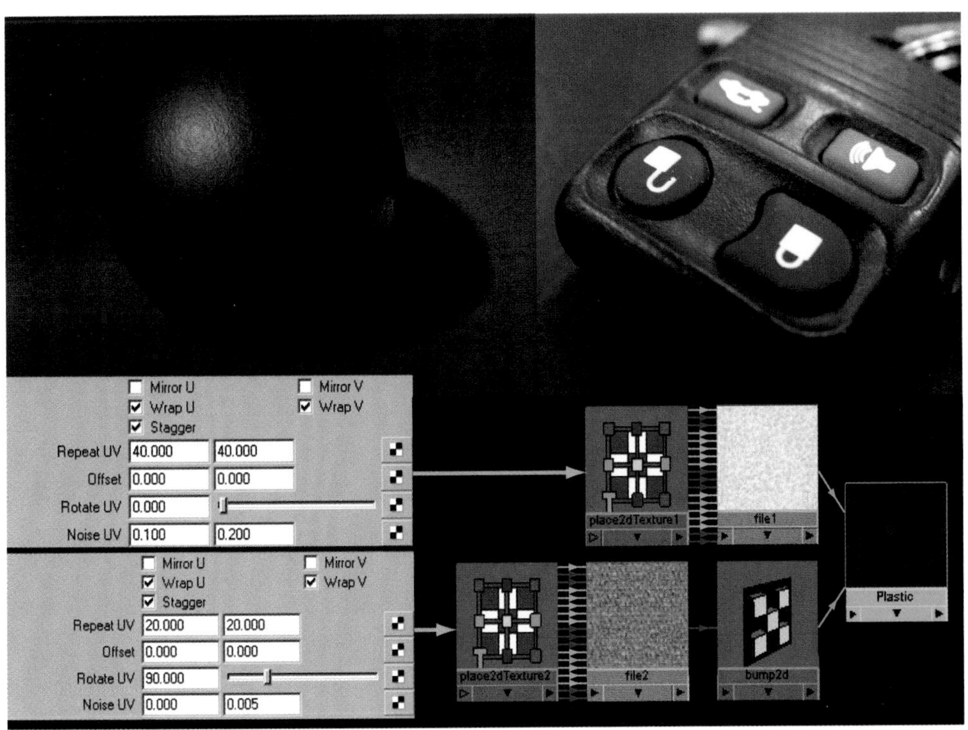

Figure 4.33 (Top left) 3D plastic. (Top right) Reference photo of plastic. (Bottom) Plastic shading network. This scene is included on the CD as `plastic.ma`.

Note: Highly repeated texture maps, such as those described in the previous example, can lead to buzzing and other anti-aliasing problems. The trick is to keep the Repeat UV value as low as possible while maintaining the correct look. A proper Repeat UV value depends on the camera placement, how the surface is lit, if the surface and/or camera is animated, and if motion blur is present. For an additional discussion on anti-aliasing issues, see Chapter 10.

Chapter Tutorial: Re-Creating Copper with Basic Texturing Techniques

In this tutorial, you will re-create the look of copper with basic texturing techniques. You will use a generic noisy bitmap (`rusty.tif`) as a color and bump map for a Blinn material.

Copper is a "bright" metal and is highly reflective. If copper has not been polished, however, it creates a highly diffuse reflection. This is due to numerous, microscopic imperfections. Unpolished copper is therefore slightly "glowy" and has an unfocused specular highlight (see Figure 4.34).

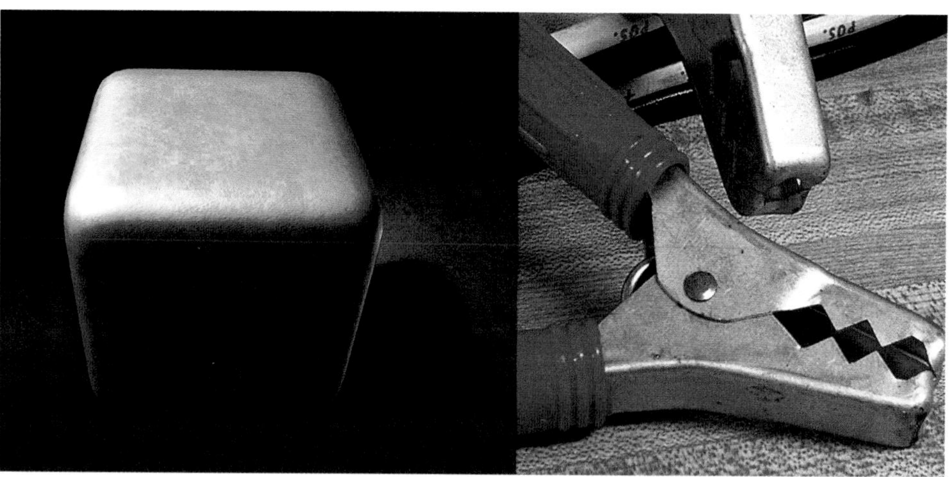

Figure 4.34 (Left) Finished 3D copper. (Right) Reference photo of copper.

1. Open `copper.ma` from the Chapter 4 scene folder on the CD.
2. Open the Hypershade window. MMB-drag a Blinn material into the work area and rename name it **Copper**. Assign Copper to the polygon cube.
3. Open Copper's Attribute Editor tab. Set the Color attribute to a semidark, reddish brown. Use Figure 4.35 as reference. Set the Ambient Color attribute to a lighter reddish brown. A high Ambient Color value replicates the bright quality of the metal. Set Diffuse to 0.7, Eccentricity to 0.49, Specular Roll Off to 0.85, and Reflectivity to 0.15. This combination of settings creates an intense specular highlight that spreads over the edge of the cube without overexposing the top face. Render a test frame. Adjust the Color and Ambient Color attributes to emulate the distinctive copper look.
4. Click the Bump Mapping attribute's checkered Map button. Click the File button in the Create Render Node window. The Bump 2D utility appears in the Attribute Editor. Set the Bump Depth attribute to –0.003.
5. In the work area, select the newly created File texture and rename it **File1**. Click the file browse button beside the Image Name attribute and retrieve `rusty.tif` from the Chapter 4 texture folder on the CD. In the work area, select the 2D Placement utility (now named place2dTexture1) connected to File1 and open its Attribute Editor tab. Set Repeat UV to 3, 3 and check Stagger. Custom UV settings ensure that the scale of the texture detail is appropriate for the model. Render a test frame.
6. Select Copper and open its Attribute Editor tab. Click the Reflected Color attribute's checkered Map button. Click the File texture button in the Create Render Node window. The new File texture appears in the work area with a 2D Place-

ment utility. Rename the new File texture **File2**. Click the file browse button beside the Image Name attribute and retrieve `rusty.tif` from the Chapter 4 texture folder on the CD. Set File2's Filter Offset to 0.005. The Filter Offset value will blur the texture and resulting simulated reflection. The strength of the reflection is controlled by Copper's Reflectivity. The simulated reflection is most noticeable in the dark front face of the cube. Render a test frame.

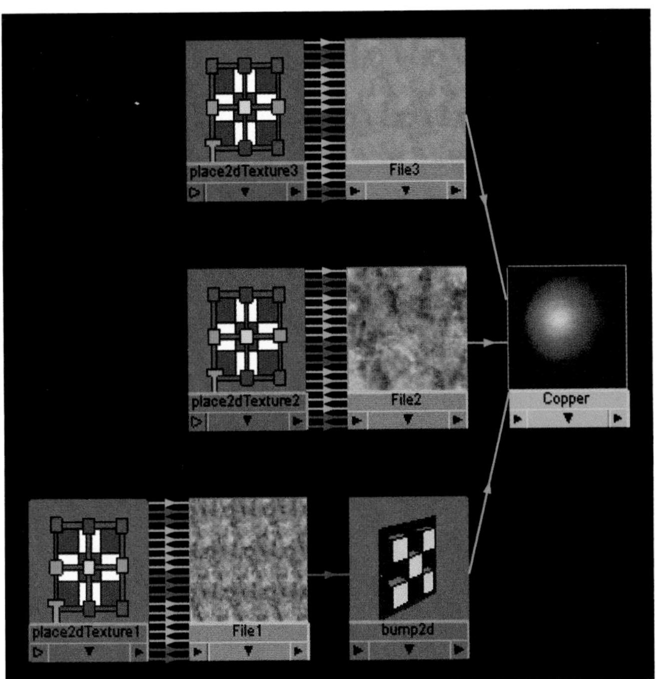

Figure 4.35 The copper shading network

7. Open Copper's Attribute Editor tab. Click the Specular Color attribute's checkered Map button. Click the File button in the Create Render Node window. The new File texture appears in the work area with a 2D Placement utility. Rename the new File texture **File3**. Set File3's Filter Offset to 0.005. Change the Color Gain attribute to an RGB value of 66, 62, 72. You can enter color values by clicking the Color Gain color swatch and opening the Color Chooser window (set the color space drop-down to RGB and the color range drop-down to "0 to 255"). This tints the Color Gain with a washed-out lavender, which balances the red of Copper's Color and Ambient Color and creates a copperlike look. Change the Color Offset attribute to a 50 percent gray.
8. Render a test frame. If the material's color does not look correct, change Copper's Color attribute to an RGB value of 82, 44, 35 and the Ambient Color attribute to an RGB value of 116, 48, 38.
9. In the work area, select the newest 2D Placement utility (now named place2dTexture3) connected to File3 and open its Attribute Editor tab. Set Repeat UV to 2, 2 and check Stagger. The copper material is complete! If you get stuck, a finished version is saved as `copper_finished.ma` in the Chapter 4 scene folder.

5

Applying 3D Textures and Projections

The 3D Placement utilities generated by 3D and environment textures possess unique application traits. Projection utilities, on the other hand, are designed to work with 2D textures. Three-dimensional textures procedurally create a wide range of solid patterns; that is, they have height, width, and depth. In addition, you can convert 3D textures into 2D bitmaps with the Convert To File Texture tool.

Chapter Contents

Review and application of 3D textures
Attributes of 2D and 3D noise textures
Review of environment textures
Application of 2D texture Projection utilities
Strategies for placing placement boxes and projection icons

Exploring 3D Textures

Maya 3D textures are procedural. That is, they are generated mathematically through predefined algorithms. Procedural textures are resolution independent and do not have defined edges or borders. Many of the algorithms employed by Maya make use of fractal math, which defines nonregular geometric shapes that have the same degree of nonregularity at all scales. Thus, Maya 3D textures are suitable for many shading scenarios found in the natural world. For example, the addition of 3D textures to a shading network can distress and dirty a clean floor and wall (see Figure 5.1).

Figure 5.1 (Left) Set with standard textures. (Right) Same set with the addition of 3D textures to the shading networks. This scene is included on the CD as `dirty_set.ma`.

When you MMB-drag a 3D texture into the Hypershade work area or choose it through the Create Render Node window, a 3D Placement utility is automatically connected to the texture and named place3dTexture (see Figure 5.2). The scale, translation, and rotation of the 3D Placement utility's placement box affects the way in which the texture is applied to the assigned object. If the assigned object is scaled, translated, or rotated, it will pick up different portions of the texture. By default, new placement boxes are positioned at 0, 0, 0 in world space and are 2 × 2 × 2 units large. If the 3D Placement utility is deleted or its connection is broken, Maya assumes that the 3D texture sample is at its default size and position.

The 3D Placement utility determines the color of each surface point by locating the point's position within the placement box. Each position derives a potentially unique color. This process is analogous to a surface dipped into a square bucket of swirled paint or a surface chiseled from a solid cube of veined stone. Should the surface sit outside the placement box, the surface continues to receive a unique piece of the 3D texture. Since 3D textures are generated procedurally, there isn't a definitive texture border at the edge of the placement box. A significant advantage of 3D textures, and the use of the 3D Placement utility, is the disregard of a surface's UV texture space. In other words, the condition of a surface's UVs does not impact the ability of a 3D texture to map smoothly across the surface.

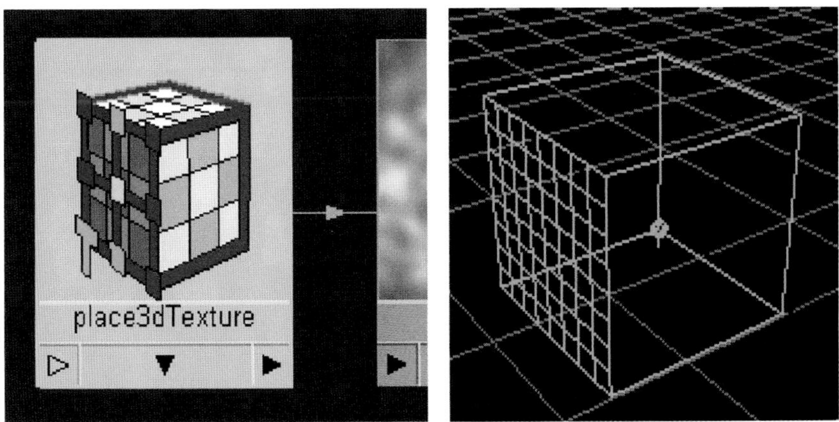

Figure 5.2 (Left) 3D Placement utility. (Right) Corresponding placement box.

You can group Maya 3D textures, found in the 3D Textures section of the Create Maya Nodes menu in the Hypershade window, into four categories: random, natural, granular, and abstract.

Applying Random Textures

Random 3D textures follow their 2D counterparts by attempting to produce a random, infinitely repeating pattern.

Using the Brownian Texture

The Brownian texture is based on Brownian Motion, which is a mathematical model that describes the random motion of particles in a fluid dynamic system. A key element of the model is the "random walk," in which each successive step of a particle is in a completely random direction. Brownian Motion was discovered by the biologist Robert Brown (1773–1858).

In general, the Brownian texture is smoother than other fractal-based textures. As such, the texture can replicate a sandy beach or similar surface. One disadvantage of the Brownian texture, however, is its tendency to produce rendering artifacts when viewed up close. For example, in Figure 5.3, a faint grid is visible on the middle plane.

The distinctive attributes of the Brownian texture follow:

Lacunarity Represents the gap between various noise frequencies. A higher value creates more detail. A lower value makes the texture smoother. *Lacunarity*, as a term, refers to the size and distribution of holes appearing in a fractal.

Increment Signifies the ratio of fractal noise used by the texture. A higher value reduces the contrast between light and dark areas.

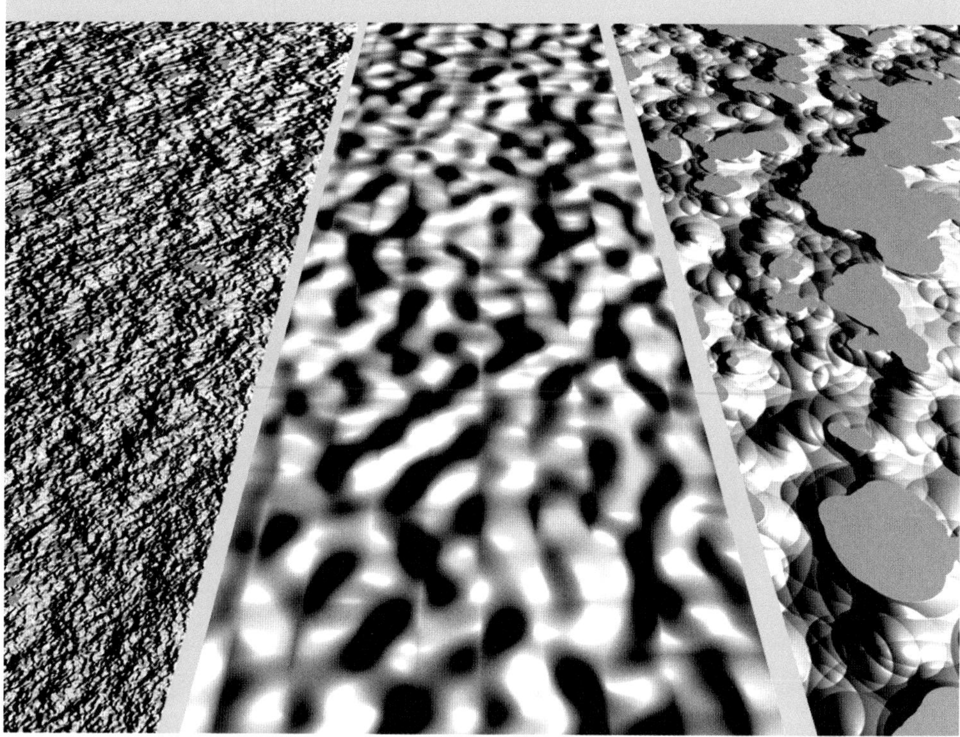

Figure 5.3 2D Fractal texture applied as a bump map to left plane. Brownian texture applied as a bump map to middle plane. Noise texture applied as a bump map to right plane. This scene is included on the CD as `brownian_noise.ma`.

Octaves Sets the number of calculation iterations. A higher value creates more detail in the map.

Weight3d Determines the internal fundamental frequency of the fractal pattern. A low value in the X, Y, or Z field causes the texture to smear in that particular direction.

Using Volume Noise

The Volume Noise texture is a 3D variation of the Noise texture. The following attributes are shared by both Volume Noise and Noise:

Threshold and Amplitude The Threshold value is added to the colors produced by the fractal pattern, which raises all the color values present in the pattern. If any color value exceeds 1, it's clamped to 1. The colors produced by the fractal are also multiplied by the Amplitude value. If the Amplitude value is 1, the texture does not change. If the Amplitude value is 0.5, all the color values are halved.

Note: Noise and Fractal textures, at their default settings, often contain too much contrast to be useful in many situations. A quick way to reduce this contrast is to pull the Amplitude and Threshold sliders toward each other to the slider center.

Noise Type There are five types of noise (see Figure 5.4). Billow is the default and contains sharper, disc-like blobs. Billow provides additional attributes, including Density, Spottyness, Size Rand, Randomness, and Falloff. Each of these attributes controls what its name implies. Perlin Noise uses Ken Perlin's classic 2D model, which produces a fairly soft pattern. Wave produces patterns similar to the Wave texture and will undulate if Time is animated. (The Wave noise type is listed as Volume Wave with the Volume Noise texture.) Num Waves sets the number of waves used by the Wave noise type. Wispy uses classic Perlin Noise but adds smeared distortions with a second noise layer. SpaceTime is a 3D version of classic Perlin Noise. Changing the Time attribute will select different 2D "slices" of SpaceTime noise.

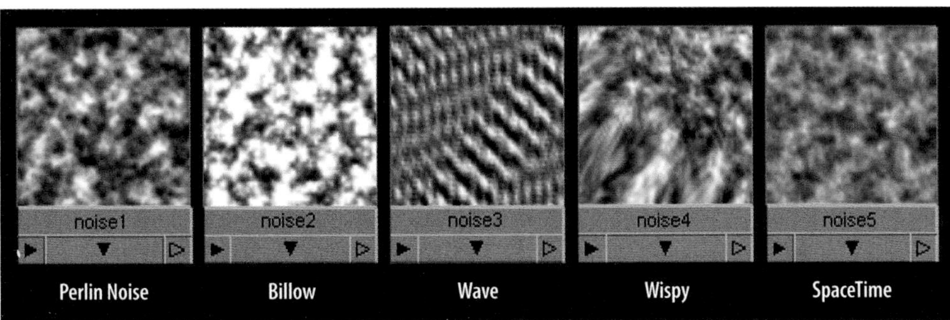

Figure 5.4 The five types of noise available to Noise and Volume Noise textures

Ratio, Depth Max, and Frequency Ratio Ratio controls the ratio of low- to high-frequency noise. If the value is 0, only low-frequency noise is visible. The low-frequency noise creates the large black and white noise "blobs." If the Ratio value is high, multiple layers of noise with higher and higher frequencies are added to the low frequency. The number of layers added depends on the Depth Max attribute. Depth Max controls the number of iterations the texture undertakes in its calculations and therefore determines the number of potential frequency layers. The higher the Depth Max value, the more complex the resulting noise. Frequency Ratio, on the other hand, establishes the scale of the frequencies involved in the Ratio calculation. Higher values create noise with finer detail.

Inflection If Inflection is checked, it inserts a mathematical "kink" into the noise function. In effect, this creates dark borders around various blobs of noise and injects white into the dark gaps. Inflection has no affect on the Billow noise type.

Time For the Noise texture, Time establishes which "slice" of the noise pattern is viewed. The Noise texture can be visualized as a 3D noise pattern from which 2D slices are retrieved. Each layer that is added with the Depth Max attribute is a slice from a noise pattern at a different frequency. The Time attribute creates a slightly different result for each Noise Type. For example, with Perlin Noise, higher Time values force Maya to choose a slice that is lower in the V direction and to the left in the U direction. With SpaceTime, higher values force Maya to choose a slice that is "deeper"; that is, raising the Time value moves the slice view "through" the three-dimensional noise.

You can see movement through the three-dimensional noise by keyframing the Time attribute. For example, in Figure 5.5 a cube is assigned to a Surface Shader material. A Volume Noise texture is mapped to the Out Color of the Surface Shader. The Noise Type attribute is set to SpaceTime. The Time attribute is animated, changing from 0 to 3 over 90 frames. Frequency Ratio is set to 1, Frequency is set to 4, and Scale is set to 5, 5, 5, making the pattern larger and easier to see.

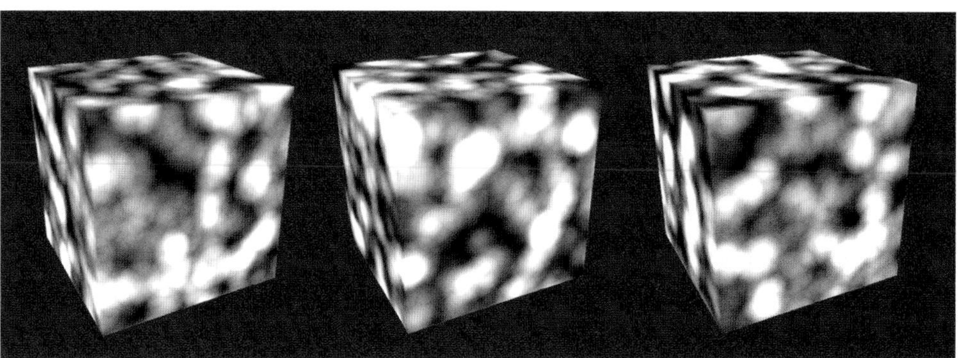

Figure 5.5 Three frames from a Volume Noise texture with a keyframed Time attribute. This scene is included on the CD as `noise_slice.ma`. A QuickTime movie is included as `noise_slice.mov`.

For the Volume Noise texture, Time establishes which section of the noise pattern, defined as a cube, is used. As with the Noise texture, the style of noise established by the Noise Type attribute affects the way in which Time moves across or through the 3D noise pattern.

Frequency Frequency defines the fundamental frequency of the noise. A high value "zooms out" from the texture. A low value "zooms in" to the texture. A value of 0 creates a dark gray. High values add detail to the noise.

Implode and Implode Center Implode warps the noise around a point defined by Implode Center. With the Noise texture, a high Implode value streaks the noise away from the viewer. A low value bulges the noise outward in a spherical fashion. With the Volume Noise texture, a high Implode value stretches the pattern or creates a wave-like warp depending on the Implode Center values. (If Implode Center is set to 0, 0, 0, Implode has no effect on Volume Noise.)

In addition, the Volume Noise texture has two unique attributes:

Scale Determines the scale of the noise in the X, Y, and Z directions. You can choose different values for each axis. For instance, a Scale of 1, 10, 1 stretches the noise detail in the Y direction.

Origin Offsets the noise in the X, Y, and Z directions. In other words, the cube that cuts out a section of the 3D noise pattern is moved through the noise to a new location.

Whether a Volume Noise or Noise texture should be selected depends on the nature of the object assigned to the texture's shading network. Since Volume Noise depends on a 3D Placement utility, it is not suited for an object that deforms or is in motion. On the other hand, the Noise texture, which is mapped directly to the surface, is restricted by the quality of the surface UVs. For example, in Figure 5.6 a polygon frog has a Noise and Volume Noise mapped to the Color attribute of an assigned Blinn material. In both cases, the Color Gain and Color Offset attributes of the noise texture are tinted green. Since the frog is split into multiple UV shells (groups of UV points), shell borders are noticeable on the Noise texture version. The Volume Noise version, by comparison, ignores the inherent UV information in favor of the 3D Placement process. Hence, the Volume Noise version renders cleanly with no shell borders. To improve the quality of the Noise version, more time must be spent refining the UVs. To make the Volume Noise version acceptable for animation and deformation, you must use the Convert To File Texture tool or the Transfer Maps window. (Convert To File Texture is described at the end of this chapter; the Transfer Maps window is discussed in Chapter 13.) The same dilemmas occur when choosing between Fractal and Solid Fractal textures.

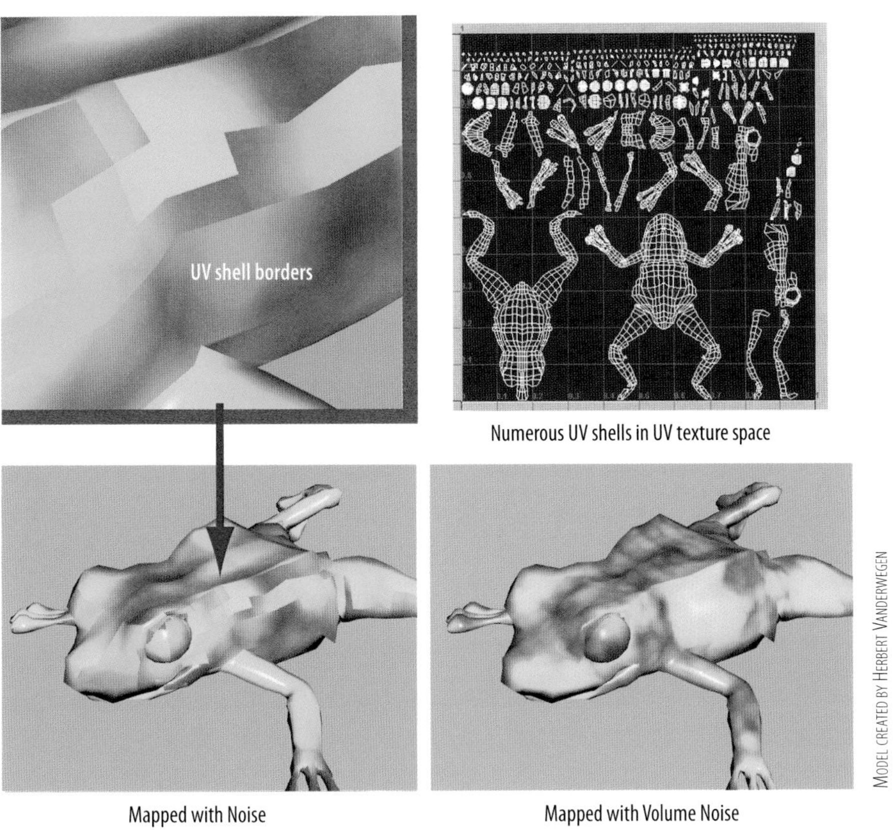

Figure 5.6 A polygon frog with Noise and Volume Noise textures mapped to the color of the assigned Blinn

On a more technical level, Perlin Noise, and thus Noise and Volume Noise texture variations, are graphic representations of multiple noise functions, each at a different scale (frequency), added together. You can emulate the addition of noise functions in the Hypershade window by connecting two Noise textures to a Plus Minus Average utility. For example, in Figure 5.7 the Out Color attributes of two

Noise textures are connected to input3D[0] and input3D[1] of a Plus Minus Average utility. The Operation of the utility is set to Average. To see the result, the utility's output3D is connected to a Layered Texture. The Layered Texture icon reveals a new, more complex noise pattern, which is a combination of Noise1 and Noise2. Noise1's Frequency is set to 3 and Noise2's Frequency is set to 10, guaranteeing that the scale of each noise pattern is different.

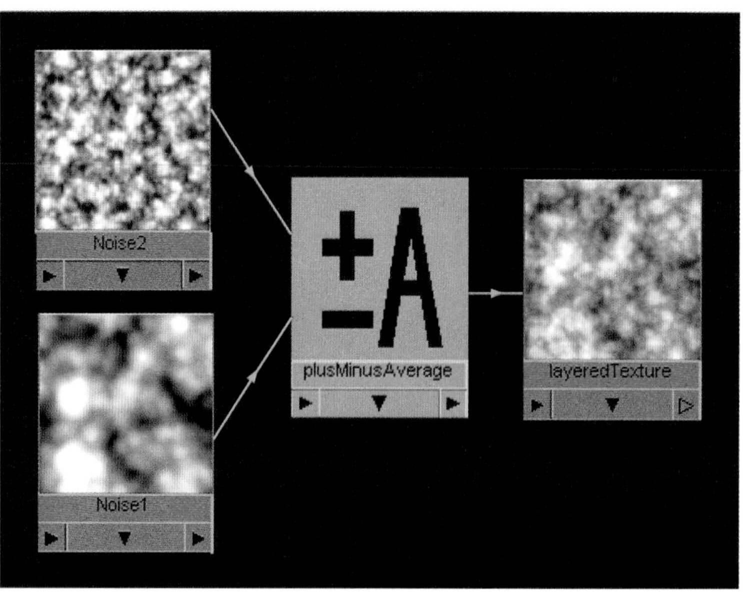

Figure 5.7 Two Noise textures are averaged to produce a more complex noise pattern. This shading network is included on the CD as `noise_average.ma`.

Using Solid Fractal

The Solid Fractal texture is a 3D variation of the Fractal texture. Both Solid Fractal and Fractal share attributes with Volume Noise and Noise. These attributes include Amplitude, Threshold, Ratio, Frequency Ratio, and Inflection. For descriptions of each attribute, see the previous section in this chapter. At the same time, Solid Fractal and Fractal share the following unique attributes:

Bias Controls the amount of contrast in the texture. A high value creates more contrast. A value of –1 creates a solid 50 percent gray.

Animated If checked, makes the Time and Time Ratio attributes available. Time retrieves different "slices" of the noise. With the default settings, slight variations in the Time value make changes to the noise pattern drastic and seemingly random (equivalent to television static). However, you can control the degree of change with the Time Ratio attribute. The lower the Time Ratio value, the more gradual the change to the noise pattern. To see a truly incremental change in the noise pattern, Time must be raised or lowered by less than 0.01 per frame and Time Ratio must be kept near 1. As with the SpaceTime noise type available for the Noise texture, the movement is through the noise pattern (as opposed to left to right or down to up).

In addition, the Fractal texture carries the Level Min and Level Max attributes. These two attributes control the number of iterations the texture undertakes in its calculations. A high Level Max value will produce finer detail in the resulting noise. Solid Fractal, on the other hand, carries the Ripples and Depth attributes. The Ripples fields, which represent Ripples X, Ripples Y, and Ripples Z attributes, control the fundamental noise frequency of the Solid Fractal. In basic terms, Ripples creates waviness in the texture in the X, Y, and Z directions. A high value in any one of the three fields causes the noise to stretch. High values in all three fields inserts a greater number of dark "holes" into the noise. The Depth fields, which represent Depth Min and Depth Max attributes, set the minimum and maximum number of iterations used in the Solid Fractal calculation. The higher the values, the finer the detail. The lower the values, the blurrier the texture.

Using the Cloud Texture

The Cloud texture uses Perlin and fractal noise techniques to create soft, wispy noise suitable for smoke or clouds. To create a cloud in a sky, follow these steps:

1. Create a NURBS sphere. Scale the sphere in one direction so that it becomes elongated.
2. Open the Hypershade window. MMB-drag a Lambert material into the work area. Assign the Lambert to the sphere.
3. Open the Lambert's Attribute Editor tab. Change the Color attribute to a suitable cloud color. Click the Transparency checkered Map button and choose the Cloud texture from the Create Render Node window.
4. With the Cloud texture open in the Attribute Editor, change Color1 and Color2 to 100 percent white. In the Effects section, select Invert. This ensures that the edges, and not the sphere's center, are transparent. Render a test frame. The sphere looks like a puff of smoke.
5. In the perspective workspace view, choose View > Camera Attribute Editor. The camera's Attribute Editor tab opens. In the Environment section, change Background Color to a more suitable sky color. Render a test frame.
6. Open the Cloud texture's Attribute Editor tab. To prevent the edges of the sphere from appearing too opaque or too black, incrementally raise the Edge Thresh attribute value. This erodes the cloud's edges so that a spherical outline can no longer be seen. Render a series of tests to check this. If the cloud appears too granular or noisy, lower the Ratio attribute slightly. This makes the noise pattern blurrier.
7. Open the Lambert's Attribute Editor tab. Slowly raise the Ambient Color until the majority of dark spots on the cloud disappear. Render a series of tests to check this.
8. Open the Cloud texture's Attribute Editor tab. Incrementally raise the Color Offset attribute in the Color Balance section. This thins the cloud and makes it appear more wispy (see Figure 5.8). Render a series of tests to check this. For

additional realism, move the vertices of the sphere to make the resulting cloud's shape more random.

Figure 5.8 A Cloud texture creates a wispy cloud. This scene is included on the CD as `cloud.ma`.

In addition, you can use the Cloud texture to quickly create a moon or other planetary body. For example, in Figure 5.9 a Cloud texture is mapped to the Incandescence of a Lambert material, which is assigned to a sphere.

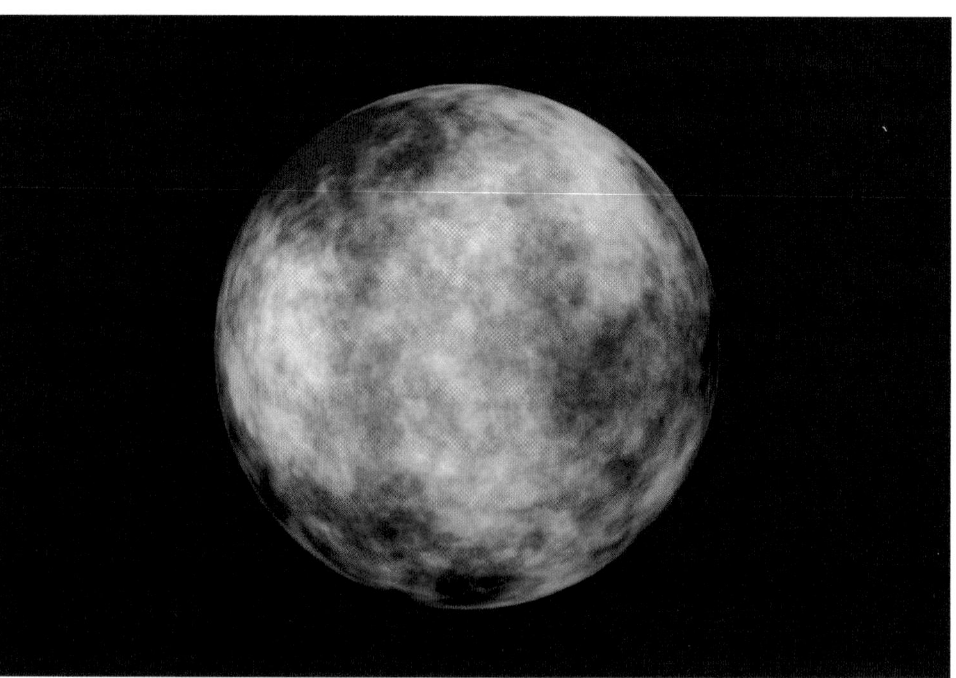

Figure 5.9 A Cloud texture is mapped to the Incandescence attribute of a Lambert material, creating a moonlike texture. This scene is included on the CD as `cloud_moon.ma`.

As for the Cloud texture attributes, Color1 and Color2 are mixed to create the noise. Edge Thresh and Center Thresh control the density of the noise. Low Edge Thresh values create a denser noise pattern along the edges of the 3D Placement box by biasing Color2. High Center Thresh values create a less dense noise pattern at the center of the placement box by biasing Color1. If both Edge Thresh and Center Thresh are low, Color2 is favored in the pattern. Contrast fine-tunes the color mixture. If the Contrast value is 0, the colors are averaged across the entire texture. If the value is 1, the colors maintain a harder separation. Amplitude scales the resulting noise; that is, the noise color values are multiplied by the Amplitude value. The Depth and Ripples fields, which represent the Depth Min, Depth Max, Ripples X, Ripples Y, and Ripples Z attributes, function in the same manner as those belonging to the Solid Fractal texture (see the previous section). Soft Edges, when checked, creates a more gradual transition between Color1 and Color2. This attribute also reduces the amount of contrast and allows more detail to survive. Transp Range controls the rapidity with which the colors transition between each other and become opaque. A low value creates a harsher transition. A high value creates a subtler, tapered transition. Ratio controls the ratio of low- to high-frequency noise. This attribute is identical to the Ratio attribute used by the Noise, Volume Noise, Fractal, and Solid Fractal textures.

Applying Natural Textures

Natural textures attempt to create specific patterns visible in the natural world. These include the Marble, Wood, Leather, and Snow textures.

Using Marble

The Marble texture creates a stonelike pattern that includes virtual mineral veins. The Marble texture isn't designed to match a specific marble type, nor is the texture capable of replicating a realistic marble by itself. However, if the Marble texture is combined with other 2D and 3D textures, it becomes more convincing. For example, in Figure 5.10 a Marble texture is mapped to the Color of a Blinn material, which in turn is assigned to a cube. When the marble is used by itself, it betrays its procedural origin. When Leather, Noise, Fractal, and Cloud textures are mapped to the Color Gain, Color Offset, Vein Color, and Filler Color attributes of the Marble texture as well as the Bump Mapping attribute of the Blinn, the results become more complex. This technique of combining procedural textures makes any single procedural texture more believable.

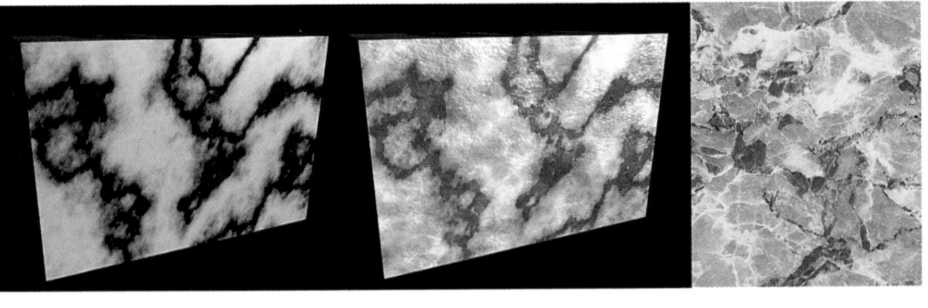

Figure 5.10 (Left) Marble texture. (Center) Marble texture with other procedural textures mapped to various attributes. (Right) Reference photo of real marble. This scene is included on the CD as `marble.ma`.

As for attributes, Filler Color sets the color of the stone's bulk. Vein Color sets the color of the thin veins. Vein Width sets the width of the veins. If the value is high, the veins become large spots. Diffusion controls the color mixture of the stone. Low values produce a high level of contrast between the Filler Color and Vein Color. High values allow the Vein Color to spread and mix into the Filler Color. Contrast increases or decreases the amount of contrast set by Diffusion. A Contrast value of 1 is equal to a Diffusion value of 0. Amplitude controls the complexity of the veins. Higher values create thinner veins with more kinks. You can raise the Amplitude value above the default maximum of 1.5. Ratio controls the ratio of low- to high-frequency noise. This attribute is similar to the Ratio attribute used by the Noise, Volume Noise, Fractal, and Solid Fractal textures. If the Marble texture's Ratio is raised above 0.9, however, detail is removed. The Depth and Ripples fields, which represent the Depth Min, Depth Max, Ripples X, Ripples Y, and Ripples Z attributes, function in the same manner as those belonging to the Cloud and Solid Fractal textures (see the previous section).

Using Wood

The Wood texture replicates the rings found in a cross-section of a tree trunk or a branch. The Wood texture is not well suited for realistic wood. However, the texture can create convincing painted or stained wood when applied as a low-intensity bump map. For example, in Figure 5.11 a Wood texture is mapped to the Bump Mapping attribute of a Blinn material, which in turn is assigned to a flattened polygon cube.

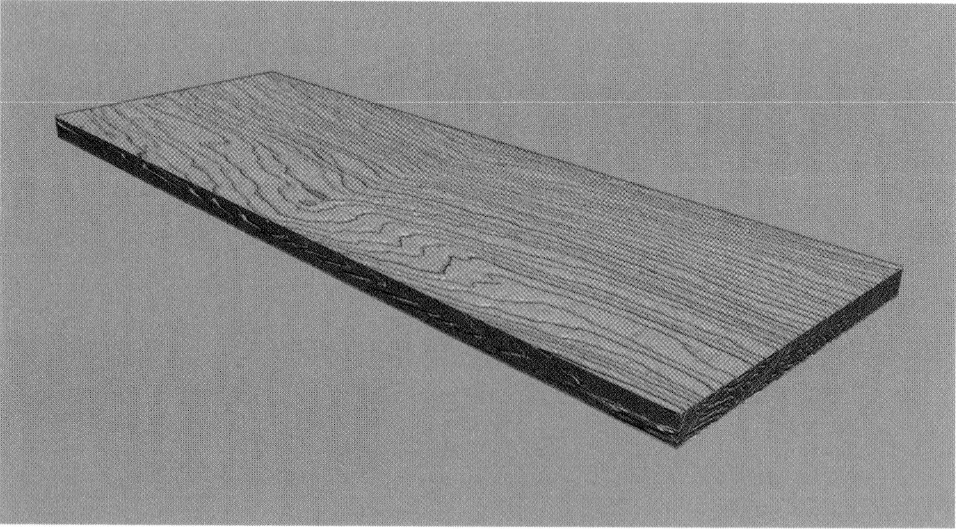

Figure 5.11 A Wood texture applied to a cube as a bump map. This scene is included on the CD as wood.ma.

On a more technical level, Vein Color establishes the color of the rings. Filler Color establishes the color of the wood between rings. Vein Spread determines how far the Vein Color will bleed into the Filler Color. A Vein Spread value of 0 will remove the Vein Color from the texture (with the exception of extremely thin ring lines). Layer Size "zooms" in and out of the pattern. Higher values create fewer rings. Randomness varies the width of each ring. When raised, Age adds more rings. Grain Color and Grain Contrast control the color and intensity of "grains" within the wood. These appear as tiny dots throughout the wood. Grain Spacing controls the distance between individual grain dots. Center sets where the circular heart of the wood is in the U and V directions.

The patterns created by the wood rings are controlled by a set of attributes in the Noise Attributes section of the Wood texture's Attribute Editor tab. Amplitude X sets the strength of noise function in the X direction. Amplitude Y does the same for the Y direction. When the 3D Placement box is at its default position, X direction corresponds with the world X axis and Y direction corresponds with the Y axis. The Ratio, Depth Min, Depth Max, Ripples X, Ripples Y, and Ripples Z attributes are identical to those of the Solid Fractal, Cloud, and Marble textures.

Using Leather

Although the Leather texture is not designed to create realistic animal hide, it can create interesting organic and cellular patterns (see Figure 5.12). Cell Color sets the color of the circular cells. Crease Color sets the color found between the cells. Cell Size determines the size of individual cells. Density determines how closely the cells are packed together. High values create less empty space between the cells and thus less color provided by Crease Color. Spottyness randomly kills off cells. High values create larger areas colored by the Crease Color. Randomness varies the pattern of cells. Low values make the distance between cells and the cell size more consistent. Threshold controls the intensity of the cell growth. High values increase the intensity of the Cell Color.

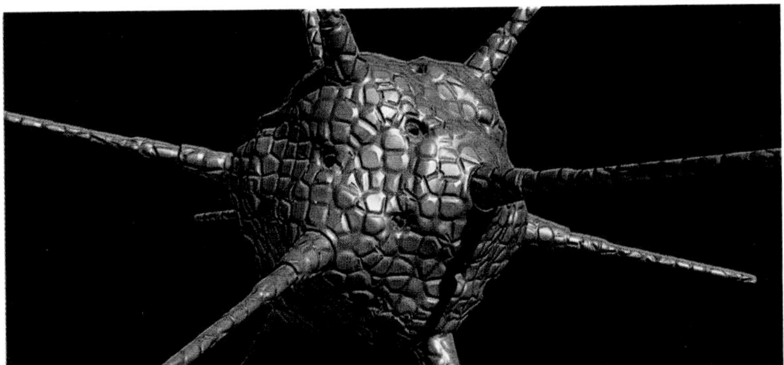

Figure 5.12 A Leather texture, with default settings, applied as a color and bump map to an assigned Blinn material

Using Snow

The Snow texture places a virtual snow on the areas of a surface that point toward the positive Y axis and do not possess too great a slope. The Snow texture works in conjunction with bump and displacement maps. For example, in Figure 5.13 a Fractal texture is used as a displacement map on a primitive plane. The Snow texture is mapped to the Color attribute of the Blinn connected to the displacement. As a result, all the parts of the surface that point upward are colored white. (For more information on bump and displacement mapping, see Chapter 9.)

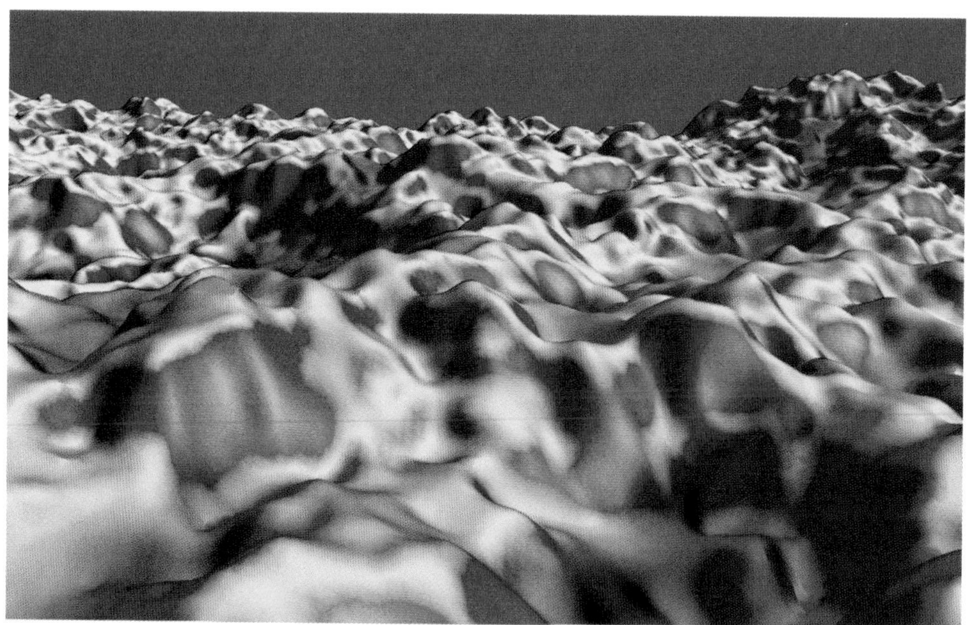

Figure 5.13 A Snow texture colors the peaks of a displaced plane. This scene is included on the CD as `snow_displace.ma`.

You can adjust the Snow texture to emulate fallen dust, dirt, or other debris. For example, in Figure 5.14 a Snow texture is mapped to the Color attribute of a Blinn, which is assigned to a plate and bowl. A Mountain texture is mapped to the Snow Color attribute of the Snow texture, producing white bits of debris instead of solid snow. The Threshold attribute of the Snow texture is set to 0.75, causing the debris to appear only on surface faces whose normals lie roughly between 0 and 22 degrees off the Y axis.

MODEL COURTESY OF KEVIN ELMER

Figure 5.14 A Snow texture creates a debris-like effect over a pair of dishes. This scene is included on the CD as `dish_debris.ma`.

As for the Snow texture attributes, Snow Color sets the color of the virtual snow. Surface Color sets the color of the surface where the snow does not stick. (In the case of Figure 5.14, Surface Color is set to blue.) You can map this attribute with another texture for more realism. Whether or not snow sticks to a surface face is determined by the Threshold attribute. A value of 0.5 allows the snow to stick to any surface point whose surface normal lies roughly between 0 and 45 degrees off the positive Y axis. A value of 0 allows the snow to stick to any surface point whose surface normal lies roughly between 0 and 90 degrees off the positive Y axis. For example, a value of 0 would cause the snow to appear on the top half of a sphere. Depth Decay controls the transition from snow to lack of snow. High values make the transition fairly hard, and low values make the transition tapered and soft. A Depth Decay value of 0 removes the snow completely. Thickness determines the thickness of the virtual snow. High values make the snow more opaque.

The positive Y axis used by the Snow texture is defined by the Snow texture's 3D Placement box, and not the world axis. If the box is left at its default position, the positive Y axis runs "up" in world space. However, if the box is rotated, the positive Y axis used by the Snow texture changes. When viewing the 3D Placement box, remember that the Y axis runs in the same direction as the small "tail" on the corner diamond icon (see Figure 5.2 earlier in this chapter and Figure 5.29 in the section "Placing Placement Boxes and Projection Icons").

Applying Granular Textures

Granular textures employ noise as grains or dots. These include Rock and Granite textures.

Using Rock

The Rock texture is similar to the Mountain texture in that it creates a hard-edged pattern (see Figure 5.15).

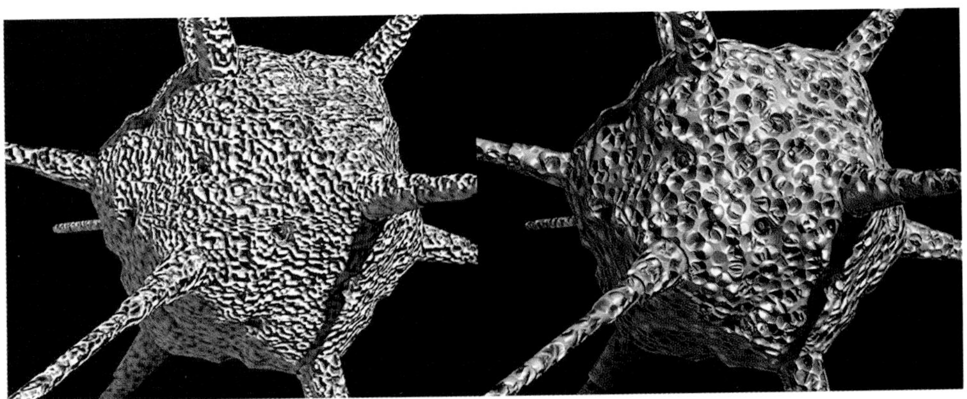

Figure 5.15 (Left) Default Rock texture applied as color and bump. (Right) Default Granite texture applied as color and bump.

Mix Ratio sets the ratio of Color 1 to Color 2. If the Mix Ratio value is below 0.5, Color 2 becomes the grain color. If the Mix Ratio value is above 0.5, Color 1 becomes the grain color. Grain Size controls the size of the individual grains. Diffusion controls the hardness of the grain edges. Higher values blur the grains. If you increase the Grain Size and Diffusion values, you can create a stylized tile (see Figure 5.16).

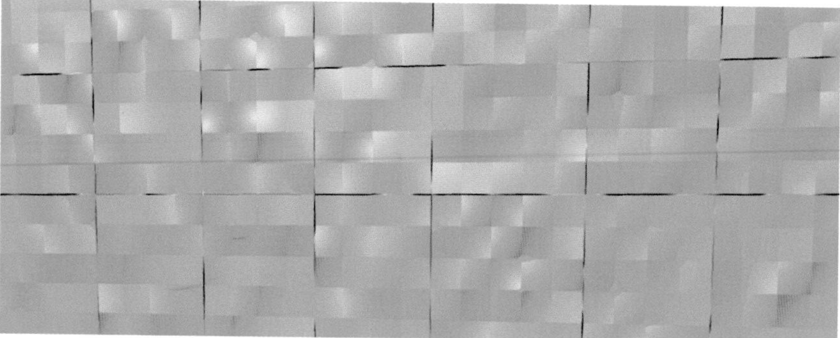

Figure 5.16 Rock texture with raised Grain Size and Diffusion values applied as a bump map. This scene is included on the CD as `rock_tiles.ma`.

Using Granite

The Granite texture is similar to the Leather texture in that it creates a series of colored, semicircular cells. At the same time, you can adjust the Granite texture to produce abstract patterns (see Figure 5.17).

Figure 5.17 The Granite texture is adjusted to produce an abstract pattern. This scene is included on the CD as `granite_pattern.ma`.

On a technical level, the texture combines three sets of cells, the color of which is determined by Color 1, Color 2, and Color 3. Cell Size determines the size of individual cells. Filler Color determines the color of the space between cells. Density controls the intensity of the cell color. High Density values reduce the amount of empty space between cells and therefore decrease the amount of Filler Color visible. Mix

Ratio controls the visible ratio of the three cell colors. A value of 0 prevents the use of Color 2 and Color 3 cells. Values between 0.001 and 0.5 create a relatively equal mix of all three cell colors. Values closer to 1 favor Color 1 and Color 3. Spottyness reduces the cell density. Randomness controls the regularity of the cells. A value of 0 will align the cells in a grid. Higher values make the cells more chaotic. Threshold determines the amount of contrast between cells. Lower values reduce the contrast. Creases, when checked, inserts honeycomb-style division lines between the cells, making their shapes more irregular.

Applying Abstract Textures

Abstract textures are not intended to replicate any real-world object. Nevertheless, they offer an interesting alternative to other textures. Stucco and Crater textures fall into this category.

Using Stucco

The Stucco texture mixes two colors, Channel 1 and Channel 2. The Shaker attribute determines the ratio of the two colors. A high value biases Channel 1. A low value biases Channel 2.

Two Stucco attributes, Normal Depth and Normal Melt, will not function unless the Out Normal attribute of the texture is connected to the Normal Camera attribute of a material. Since this requires a custom connection, the following steps are recommended:

1. Create a new scene. Create a primitive object. Open the Hypershade window. MMB-drag a Blinn material into the work area. Assign the Blinn to the primitive.
2. MMB-drag a Stucco texture into the work area and drop it on top of the Blinn. The Connect Input Of menu opens. Choose Color from the menu. A connection line appears between the Stucco and Blinn icons. Note that the Stucco icon is named stucco1 and the Blinn icon is named blinn1.
3. MMB-drag the stucco1 icon on top of the blinn1 icon a second time. The Connect Input Of menu opens. Choose Other from the menu. The Connection Editor window opens.
4. In the left column, click Out Normal so that it becomes italicized and highlighted. Out Normal is at the very end of the list. In the right column, click Normal Camera so that it becomes italicized and highlighted. Close the Connection Editor. This connection has the effect of turning the Stucco texture into a bump map without the need for a Bump 2d or Bump 3d utility. In fact, the Bump Mapping attribute of blinn1 lists stucco1 as its connection. Close the Hypershade and render a test frame.

The Normal Depth attribute controls the depth of the bump. The Normal Melt attribute controls the smoothness of the bump. Low Normal Melt values create a rough bump with small detail, and high values create a smooth bump with large features. For information on standard bump mapping, see Chapter 9.

Using Crater

The Crater texture functions in a manner similar to the Stucco texture but adds extra attributes. The Crater texture mixes three colors defined by Channel 1, Channel 2, and Channel 3. The Shaker attribute controls the mixture. Shaker values below 0.1 favor Channel 1. Values from 0.1 to 0.5 favor Channel 1 and Channel 2. Values above 0.5 mix all three colors. When the value is raised above 2, the detail is reduced in scale and Channel 3 is favored. Melt controls the smoothness of the resulting pattern. Low values introduce a greater number of kinks into the threads of color. Balance controls the ratio of the three colors. As the Balance value gets higher, a greater portion of the Channel 2 color is added to the mixture. Frequency controls the scale of detail created by the color mix. High values create a finer, more convoluted pattern. Frequency is similar to the Frequency Ratio attribute of the Noise, Volume Noise, Fractal, and Solid Fractal textures.

The Out Normal attribute of the Crater texture must be connected to the Normal Camera attribute of a material for the Norm Depth, Norm Melt, Norm Balance, and Norm Frequency attributes to work. Norm Depth controls the strength of the resulting bump and is identical to the Normal Depth attribute of the Stucco texture. Norm Melt controls the smoothness of the bump and is identical to the Normal Melt attribute of the Stucco texture. Norm Balance controls the ratio between high and low points on the resulting bump. High values reduce the number of deep pits created by the bump mapping process. Norm Frequency controls the noise frequency used to generate the bump. High values create finer bump detail and introduce a greater variation between high and low points.

Although the default Crater and Stucco textures are quite vivid and match few surfaces in the real world, you can easily adjust their attributes to create a more complex result (see Figure 5.18).

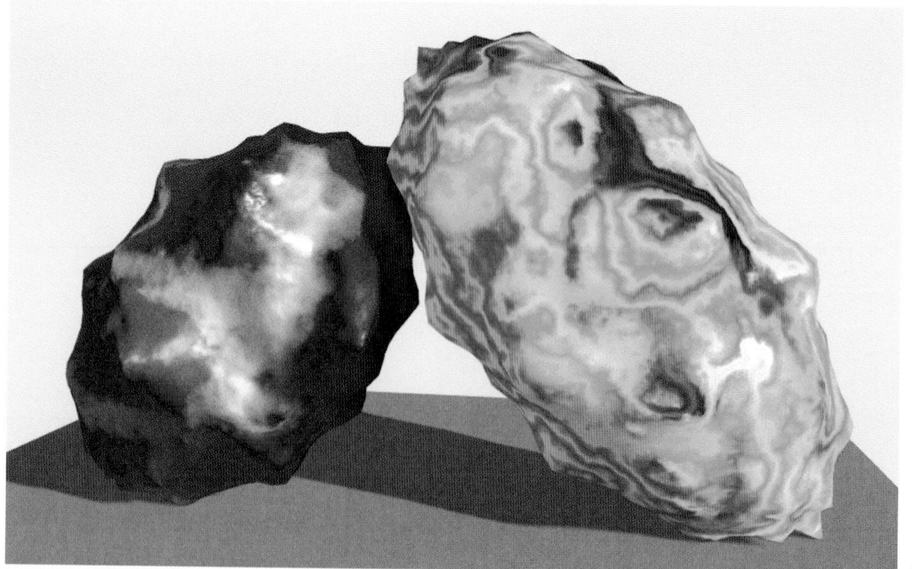

MODEL COURTESY OF KEVIN ELMER

Figure 5.18 Stucco texture (left) and Crater texture (right) applied with custom attribute settings. This scene is included on the CD as `crater_stucco_custom.ma`. A version with default texture settings is included as `crater_stucco.ma`.

Applying Environment Textures

Environment textures, found in the Env Textures section of the Create Maya Nodes menu in the Hypershade window, are designed to surround an object or enclose an entire scene. Environment textures require a unique rendering process. In the process, a reflection vector is derived from the camera eye vector and the surface normal of a rendered surface point (see Figure 5.19). (The angle of reflection is equal to the angle of incidence created by the camera eye vector.) Where the reflection vector strikes a placement sphere (or cube), the pixels of the texture mapped to the sphere are noted. The noted pixels are consequently used in the color calculation of the surface point. Environment textures were developed as an inexpensive way to simulate reflections.

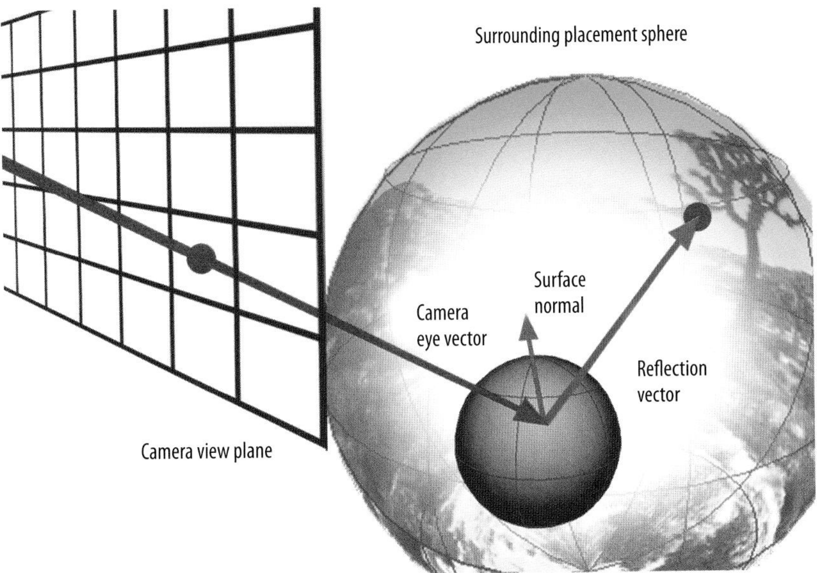

Figure 5.19 A simplified representation of the environment texture process

With Maya, you can successfully simulate reflections by mapping an environment texture to the Reflected Color attribute of a material. For example, in Figure 5.20 the materials assigned to a polygon car's glass, chrome, and paint have an Env Sphere texture mapped to their Reflected Color. A bitmap photo of a desert landscape is mapped to the Env Sphere's Image. As a result, a simulated reflection appears in appropriate places. Environment textures are not limited to the Reflected Color attribute, however. Any attribute is fair game. For example, an environment texture mapped to a material's Color applies the color of the Image bitmap through the camera eye vector and reflection vector process.

When you MMB-drag an environment texture into the Hypershade work area or choose it through the Create Render Node window, a 3D Placement utility is automatically connected to the texture node. This utility creates the placement sphere or cube that appears in the workspace view. Each of the five environment texture types creates a unique placement sphere or cube with specialized attributes. Although the 3D Placement utility node created for an environment texture looks similar to the 3D Placement utility node created for a 3D texture, the utilities are not identical. The 3D

Placement used for a 3D texture defines the volume in which a surface point is plotted in the X, Y, and Z directions to determine a color. The 3D Placement used for an environment texture employs camera eye and reflection vectors.

Model created by Pumpkinhead 3D

Figure 5.20 A car's reflections are provided by an Env Sphere texture. A simplified version of the scene is included on the CD as `car_env_sphere.ma`.

The Env Sphere texture simulates an environment by applying a map to the inner surface of an infinite sphere. You can map any texture to the Env Sphere's Image attribute. The placement icon created for the Env Sphere texture is drawn as a full circle and a half circle enclosed by two planes (see Figure 5.21). The translation and scale of the placement icon does not affect the application of the Env Sphere texture. However, the rotation of the icon will change the texture placement. The Env Sphere texture carries two unique attributes: Shear UV and Flip. Shear UV twists the mapped texture in the U and V directions (producing a barber pole effect). Flip swaps the U direction with the V direction, thus turning the mapped texture 90 degrees. Since the Env Sphere texture is based on a spherical placement, the mapped texture is pinched at the top and bottom pole.

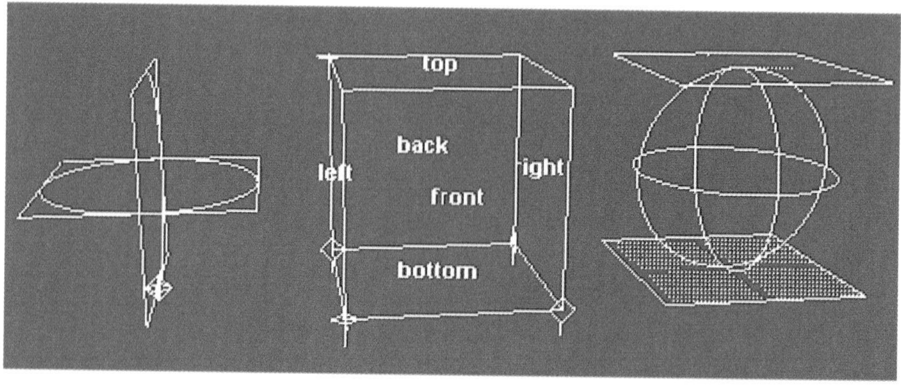

Figure 5.21 (Left) Env Sphere placement icon. (Middle) Env Cube placement icon. (Right) Env Chrome placement icon.

The Env Cube texture maps six textures to the six sides of a cube placement icon (see Figure 5.21). The scale and translation of the icon affects the application of the texture unless the Env Cube's Infinite Size attribute is checked. In either situation, the rotation of the icon changes the texture placement. The six attributes to which you can map six textures are intuitively named Right, Left, Top, Bottom, Front, and Back. The Env Cube texture is ideal for simulating an interior room.

The Env Chrome texture creates stylized chrome with a procedural ground plane and sky. The placement icon is differentiated by a top and bottom plane (see Figure 5.21). Env Chrome has an extremely long list of attributes. Nevertheless, to make the texture more realistic, I suggest the following guidelines:

- Turn off the light boxes in the virtual sky by reducing Light Width and Light Depth to 0.
- Turn off the dark grid on the virtual floor by reducing the Grid Width and Grid Depth to 0.
- Map more realistic textures to Sky Color, Zenith Color, Horizon Color, and Floor Color. Use the same texture for Sky Color and Zenith Color as the two attributes determine the color of the virtual sky. Use the same texture for Horizon Color and Floor Color as the two attributes determine the color of the virtual ground plane.

Once you turn off the virtual light boxes and grid, you can use the Env Chrome texture to create a simulated reflection with a distinct ground plane and sky (see Figure 5.22).

Figure 5.22 An Env Chrome texture is mapped to the color of a Blinn material, creating a simulated reflection on the surface of the sphere. This scene is included on the CD as `chrome_custom.ma`.

The Env Sky texture creates a procedural ground and sky, complete with a virtual sun. The placement icon is a half sphere attached to a plane. The attribute list for the Env Sky texture is as long as the Env Chrome texture. Fortunately, the attributes are intuitively named and fairly straightforward.

The Env Ball texture is designed for High Dynamic Range Image (HDRI) rendering techniques. In this case, special "light probe" images are prepared by photographing a highly reflective chrome ball in order to capture specific reflection information. For a demonstration using the Env Ball texture, see Chapter 13.

2D Texture Projection Options

You can apply any 2D texture in three ways: Normal, As Projection, and As Stencil. The Normal method maps the texture directly to the surface with tiling controlled by the 2D Placement utility, which is connected automatically. The As Stencil method creates a shading network with a Stencil utility (see Chapter 8). The As Projection method creates a Projection utility in addition to a 3D Placement utility and a 2D Placement utility. You can check one of these three methods in the 2D Textures section of the Create Maya Nodes menu or in the Create Render Node window.

By default, when As Projection is checked and a texture selected, the Out Color attribute of the texture is connected to the Image attribute of the Projection utility. The Projection utility defines the style and coverage of the projection. The 3D Placement utility, in this scenario, stores the transform information of the Projection utility and provides the interactive projection icon. During a render, a projection ray is shot out from each pixel of the projected texture in a direction defined by the 3D Placement utility. If a projection ray strikes a surface, the pixel of the ray is noted and thereafter used in the color calculation of the struck surface point. To relate the 3D Placement utility to the Projection utility, the World Inverse Matrix attribute of the 3D Placement utility is connected to the Placement Matrix attribute of the Projection utility. (For more information on Maya matrices, see Chapter 7.)

By default, the Projection utility creates a Planar projection. The utility provides a total of nine projection styles. You can switch between these styles by changing the Proj Type attribute in the Projection utility's Attribute Editor tab. The projection styles follow:

Off Disables the projection. The texture connected to the Projection utility is ignored.

Planar Places the texture on a projection plane. Its main disadvantage is its inability to match complex shapes. For example, in Figure 5.23 a Planar projection appears correct on a plane but streaks through a cube, sphere, and torus.

Spherical Places the texture inside a projection sphere. By default, the sphere is incomplete and covers only 180 degrees along the U direction and 90 degrees along the V direction. This creates a projection shape similar to a piece of paper pressed against one side of a ball. Whatever section of the assigned surface is not covered by the projection receives a repeated portion of the texture. You can create complete coverage of the projection sphere by raising the Projection's U Angle attribute to 360 and V Angle attribute to 180. Regardless of the U Angle and V Angle values, "pinched poles" will appear. That is, the upper edge of the texture is pinched into a single point, as is the lower. For example, in Figure 5.24 a Checker texture is mapped to a Surface Shader material as a Spherical projection. The top and bottom portion of the Checker is collapsed at the poles. A similar problem occurs with a NURBS sphere; even though all NURBS surfaces have four edges, two of the edges are collapsed into single points at the sphere's top and bottom pole.

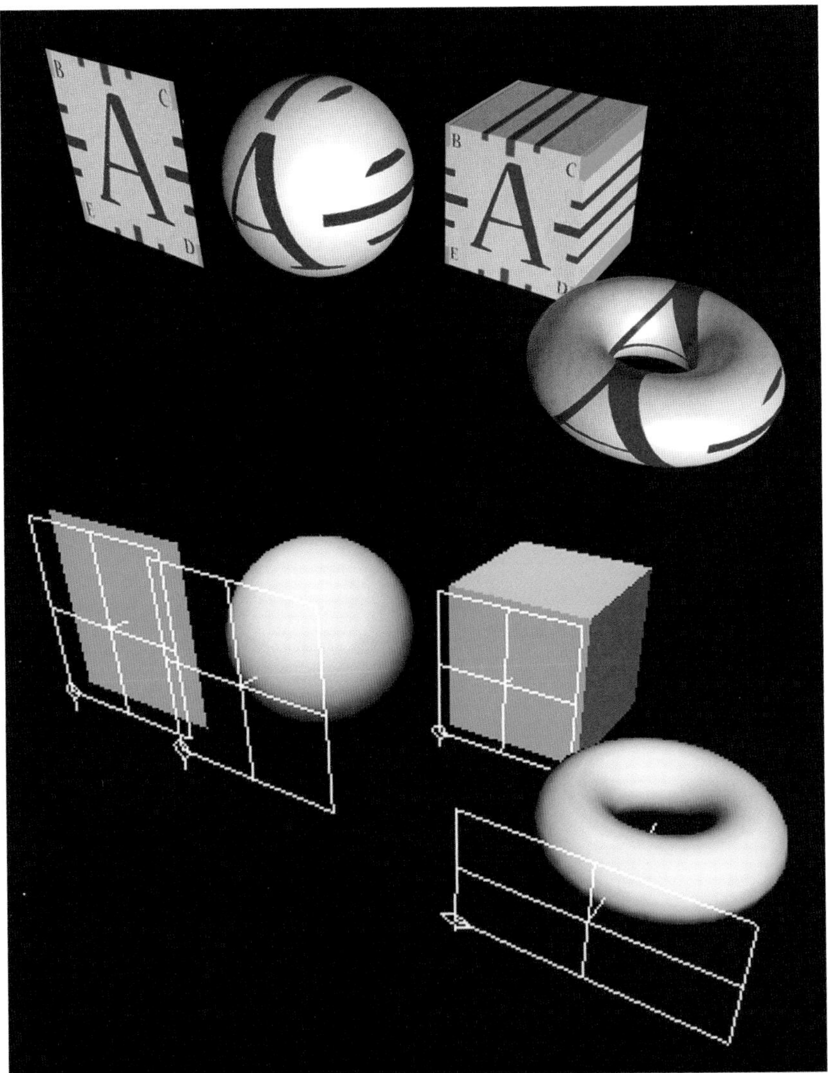

Figure 5.23 Planar projections mapped to various primitive surfaces. This scene is included on the CD as `proj_plane.ma`.

Note: Although always visible, a Projection utility's V Angle attribute is functional only for a Spherical projection type. U Angle is functional only for Spherical and Cylindrical projections.

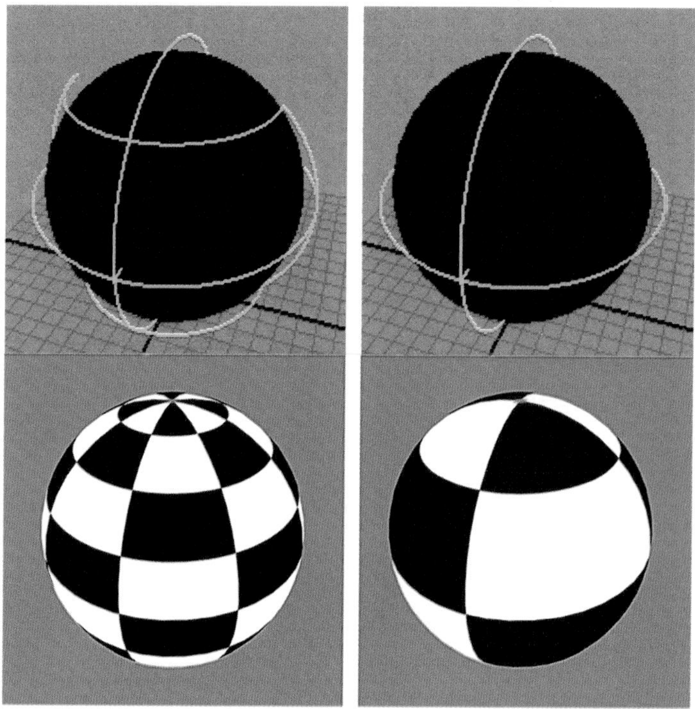

Figure 5.24 (Left) A Spherical projection with default settings is applied to a sphere. (Right) The Spherical projection's U Angle is set to 360 and its V Angle is set to 180. This scene is included on the CD as `proj_spherical.ma`.

Ball Places the texture inside a projection sphere. The projection pinches the texture at only one pole. A real-world equivalent is a blanket draped over a ball with the blanket's four corners twisted together at one spot. The pole is indicated by the diamond-shaped UV origin symbol on the projection icon (see Figure 5.25).

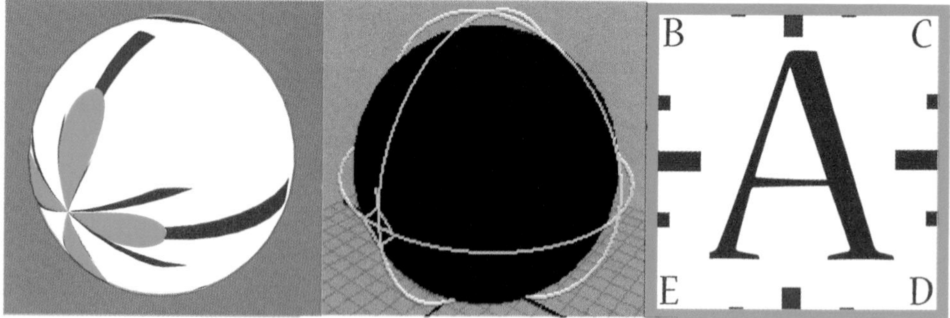

Figure 5.25 (Left) A Ball projection is applied to a sphere. (Middle) The Ball projection icon. (Right) The test bitmap. This scene is included on the CD as `proj_ball.ma`.

Cylindrical Places the texture inside a cylinder. The left and right edges of the texture will meet if the projection's U Angle is set to 360 degrees. The Cylindrical type creates two pinched poles at the top and bottom of the projection (see Figure 5.26).

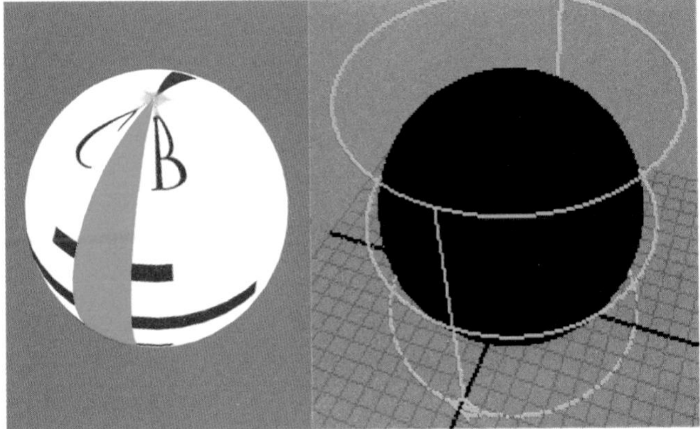

Figure 5.26 A Cylindrical projection applied to a sphere. This scene is included on the CD as `proj_cylinder.ma`.

Cubic Places a texture onto the six faces of a cube (see Figure 5.27).

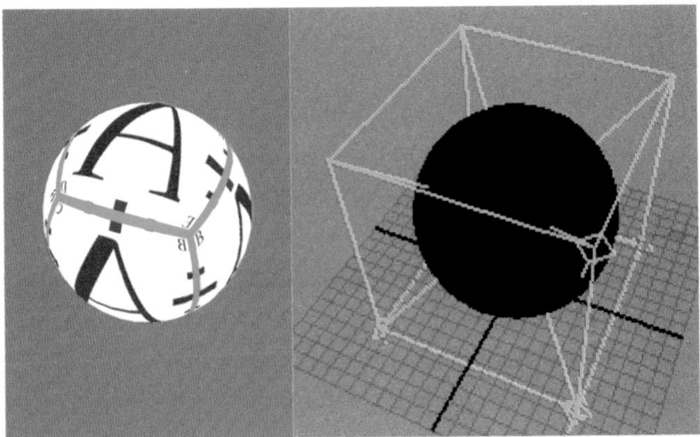

Figure 5.27 A Cubic projection applied to a sphere. This scene is included on the CD as `proj_cubic.ma`.

Concentric Randomly selects vertical slices from the texture and projects them in a concentric pattern.

TriPlanar Projects the texture along three planes based on the surface normal of the object that is affected.

Perspective Projects the texture from the view of a camera (see Figure 5.28). For this to work, a camera must be selected from a drop-down list provided by the Link To Camera attribute (found in the Camera Projection Attributes section of the Projection utility's Attribute Editor tab). The projection icon will take the form of a camera frustum but will not be aligned to the chosen camera in 3D space. The frustum can be "snapped" to the camera, however, by connecting the Translate, Scale, and Rotate attributes of the camera's transform node to the same attributes of the 3D Placement node connected to the Projection utility node. (For more information on custom connections, see Chapter 6.)

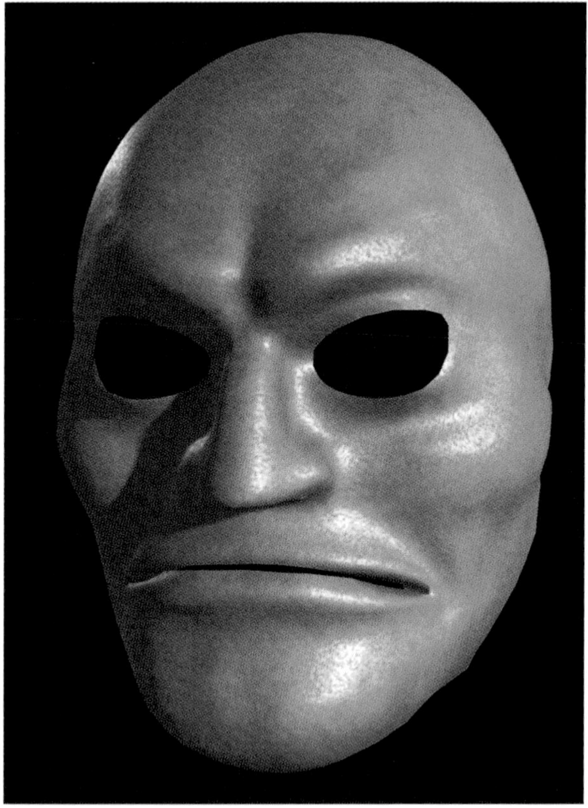

Figure 5.32 A skin material created with 2D and 3D procedural textures.

3. To properly judge the results, create several lights. Follow either the 2- or 3-point lighting techniques discussed in Chapter 1. Render a series of tests until the lighting is satisfactory.
4. Open the Blinn's Attribute Editor tab. Click the Specular Color checkered Map button and choose a Fractal texture from the Create Render Node window. Double-click the place2dTexture1 icon in the work area, which opens its Attribute Editor tab. Set Repeat UV to 15, 15 and check Stagger. This reduces and randomizes the scale of the fractal pattern so that it can emulate pores.
5. Open the Blinn's Attribute Editor tab. Adjust the Eccentricity and Specular Roll Off attributes. Correct values depending on the lighting of the scene. The goal is to create a strong specular highlight without losing the detail provided by the Fractal texture. Be careful not to raise the Eccentricity value too high; this will spread out the highlight and make the skin look dull.
6. In the work area, double-click the Fractal icon (named fractal1), which opens its Attribute Editor tab. Reduce the Amplitude and raise the Threshold slightly. This reduces the amount of contrast in the fractal pattern and makes its effect subtler. Tint the Color Gain attribute a pale blue. This inserts a color other than red into the material and helps make the skin color more varied.

Creating Custom Connections and Applying Color Utilities

Creating custom shading networks is a powerful way to texture and render with Maya. You can connect hundreds of material, texture, geometry, light, and camera attributes through the Hypershade window for unique results. In addition, you can apply specialized color utilities that can customize the hue, saturation, value, gamma, and contrast of any input and output.

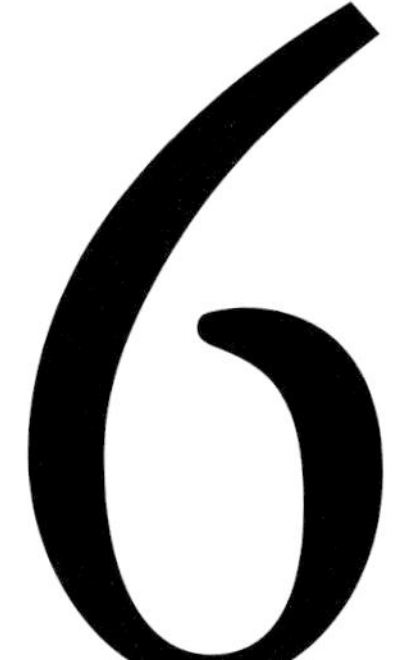

Chapter Contents

A quick review of the Hypershade window
Multiple approaches for creating connections
Tips for keeping the Hypershade organized
Practical applications of each color utility

Mastering the Hypershade Window

The Hypershade window is the heir to the Multilister domain. Although the Multilister window is a legacy tool from PowerAnimator, the Hypershade was created specifically for Maya. Everything that can be done in the Multilister can be done in the Hypershade, but not vice versa. You can access the Hypershade by choosing Window > Rendering Editors > Hypershade. You can access the Multilister by choosing Window > Rendering Editors >Multilister.

Reviewing the Basics

The Hypershade window allows the connection of various Maya nodes. Technically speaking, a node is a construct that holds specific information plus any actions associated with that information. A node might be a curve, surface, material, texture, light, camera, joint, IK handle, and so on. Any box that appears in the Hypergraph or Hypershade window is a node. (For a differentiation between transform and shape nodes, see Chapter 7.) A node's information is organized into specific attributes. If an attribute can be animated, it is called a channel (and appears in the Channel Box). For example, the Scale X of a sphere is a channel.

You can connect attributes in an almost endless fashion. A series of connected nodes is a node network. If the network is designed for rendering, it's called a shading network. Any node connected to any other node is considered upstream or downstream. An upstream node is a node that outputs information. A downstream node is a node that receives or inputs information. The node icons themselves will show if an upstream or downstream connection exists. If the bottom-left arrow is solid, the node is downstream of another node. If the bottom-right arrow is solid, the node is upstream of another node. If either arrow is hollow, a connection does not exist in the direction in which the hollow arrow points (see Figure 6.1).

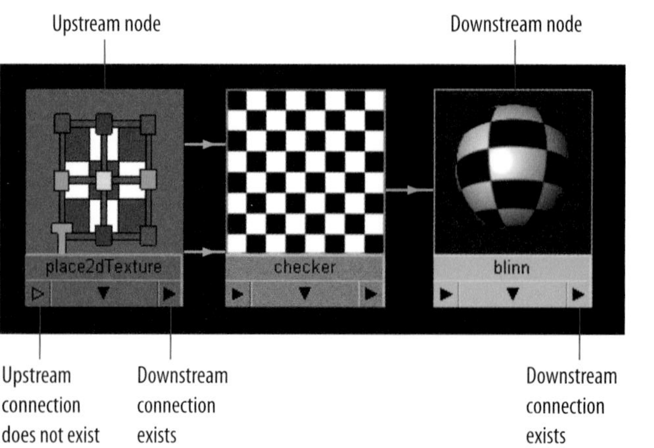

Figure 6.1
Upstream and downstream node connections

You can create new nodes at any time by clicking a node icon in the Create Maya Nodes menu of the Hypershade window. You can also MMB-drag nodes from the Create Maya Nodes menu into the work area. To copy individual nodes, choose

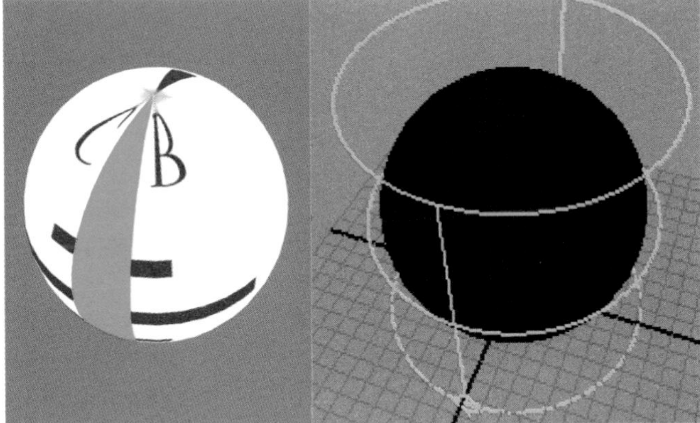

Figure 5.26 A Cylindrical projection applied to a sphere. This scene is included on the CD as `proj_cylinder.ma`.

Cubic Places a texture onto the six faces of a cube (see Figure 5.27).

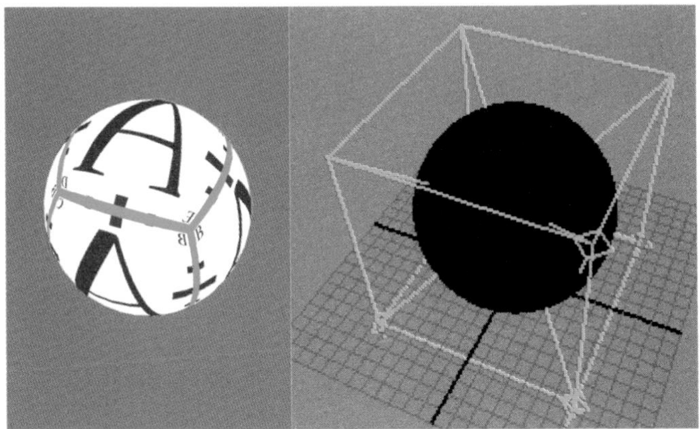

Figure 5.27 A Cubic projection applied to a sphere. This scene is included on the CD as `proj_cubic.ma`.

Concentric Randomly selects vertical slices from the texture and projects them in a concentric pattern.

TriPlanar Projects the texture along three planes based on the surface normal of the object that is affected.

Perspective Projects the texture from the view of a camera (see Figure 5.28). For this to work, a camera must be selected from a drop-down list provided by the Link To Camera attribute (found in the Camera Projection Attributes section of the Projection utility's Attribute Editor tab). The projection icon will take the form of a camera frustum but will not be aligned to the chosen camera in 3D space. The frustum can be "snapped" to the camera, however, by connecting the Translate, Scale, and Rotate attributes of the camera's transform node to the same attributes of the 3D Placement node connected to the Projection utility node. (For more information on custom connections, see Chapter 6.)

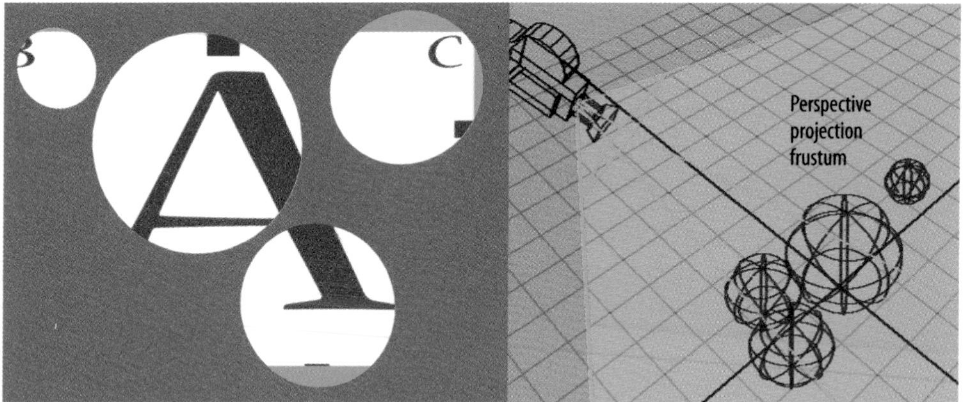

Figure 5.28 A Perspective projection applied to a series of spheres. This scene is included on the CD as `proj_persp.ma`.

Placing Placement Boxes and Projection Icons

The translation, scale, and rotation of a 3D Placement utility's placement box or projection icon affect the application of the texture mapped to it. For 3D textures, I suggest the following tips for placing the placement box:

- If a surface is already assigned to the material to which the 3D Placement utility belongs, click the Fit To Group BBox button in the 3D Texture Placement Attributes section of the 3D Placement utility's Attribute Editor tab. This snaps the placement box to the bounding box of the surface.
- If you need to translate, scale, or rotate the placement box, select the place3dTexture icon in the Hypershade window. You can also click the Interactive Placement button found in the 3D Placement utility's Attribute Editor tab. The Interactive Placement button selects the placement box and displays an interactive translate, rotate, and scale handle.
- Unfortunately, the 3D texture icons, as they appear in the Hypershade window, are not accurate representations of the way in which the texture will render. This remains true if the placement box is scaled to fit the assigned surface. Trial and error renders provide the best fine-tuning method in this situation.

For 2D textures mapped with the As Projection option, the following tips are suggested for placing the 3D Placement utility's projection icon:

- The Fit To Group BBox button found in the 3D Placement utility's Attribute Editor tab is identical to the Fit To BBox button found in the Projection utility's Attribute Editor tab. You can use either button to snap the projection icon to the assigned object or assigned group's bounding box.
- If you need to translate, scale, or rotate the projection icon, select the place3dTexture icon in the Hypershade window. You can also click the Interactive Placement button found in the Projection or 3D Placement utility's Attribute Editor tab. The Interactive Placement button selects the projection icon and displays an interactive translate, rotate, and scale handle.

The projection icon created for projected 2D textures indicates the employed UV orientation. For example, a Planar projection icon features a diamond-shaped symbol at one corner (see Figure 5.29). This represents the 0, 0 origin in UV texture space. (For more information on UV texture space, see Chapter 9.) Using the origin symbol as a reference, you can orient the icon and predict the resulting render. For example, if a Planar projection icon is viewed from a front workspace view and the origin symbol is at the bottom-left corner, V runs down to up and U runs left to right, matching a texture's icon in the Hypershade window.

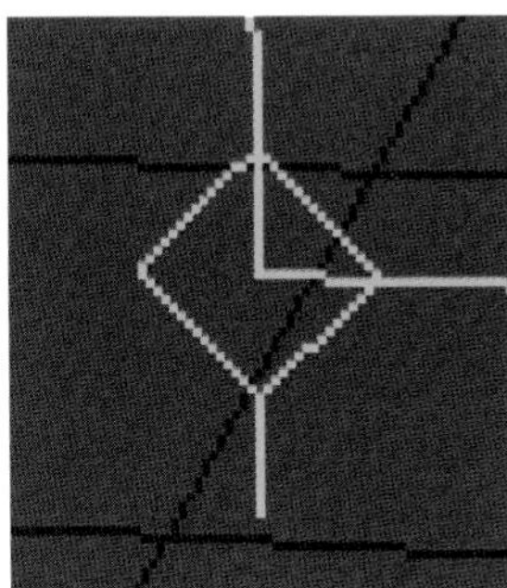

Figure 5.29
The UV origin symbol of a projection icon

Spherical, Cylindrical, Ball, TriPlanar, and Cubic projection icons also carry an origin symbol. For Ball projections, the diamond shape represents the point where all four corners of the texture converge. TriPlanar projections carry three origin symbols, one at the corner of each plane. Each plane is identical to a Planar projection. Cubic projections carry six symbols, although three of them overlap at one corner. Concentric projections carry no symbols since standard UV interpretation does not apply.

For each and every example in this section, animation of the assigned surface can adversely affect the projection. If either the surface or the projection icon is moved, the surface picks up a different portion of the texture. If the surface is larger than the projection icon or is not aligned to the icon, it receives a repeated portion of the texture. To avoid this problem, you can parent the 3D Placement utility to the surface. However, this will not prevent errors when a surface deforms. Fortunately, the Convert To File Texture tool is available.

Applying the Convert To File Texture Tool

The Convert To File Texture tool allows you to convert projected 2D textures, as well as 2D and 3D procedural textures, into permanent bitmaps. To apply the tool, follow these steps:

1. Select a material that has a projected or procedural texture assigned to one or more of its attributes. Shift+select the surface to which the material is assigned.
2. Choose Edit > Convert To File Texture (Maya Software) > ❑ from the Hypershade window menu. The Convert To File Texture Options window opens (see Figure 5.30).
3. The X Resolution and Y Resolution attributes determine the size of each bitmap written out. Choose appropriate sizes and specify a File Format value. Then click the Convert And Close button.

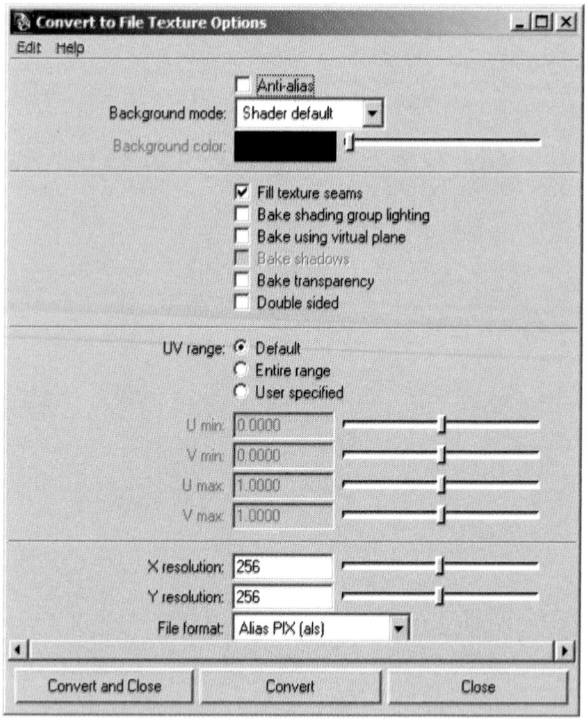

Figure 5.30
The Convert To File Texture Options window

For each projected 2D texture, procedural 2D texture, and procedural 3D texture mapped to the material, a bitmap is written to the following location with the following name:

project_directory/texture_name-surface_name.format

At the same time, the original material is duplicated with the original shading network structure. In place of the projected and procedural textures, however, File textures are provided with the new bitmaps preloaded. The new material is automatically assigned to the surface. When compared side by side, the converted bitmap surface is virtually identical to the original (see Figure 5.31). Once the converted bitmaps are applied to the surface through the duplicated material, you can delete the original material. Thereafter, you can animate or deform the surface; the textures will not slide.

Note: Oddly enough, the Convert To File Texture tool also converts all nonprocedural bitmaps. This offers the advantage of locking in any custom UV settings. In addition, any bitmap mapped to a single channel attribute, such as Transparency or Diffuse, is converted to grayscale. The original bitmaps are not harmed.

Note: The Convert To File Texture tool will not work if the surface is assigned to the default Lambert material or if the surface is connected to more than one shading group. In general, the default Lambert material should not be used in the texturing process. You can delete connections to unneeded shading groups in the Hypershade window.

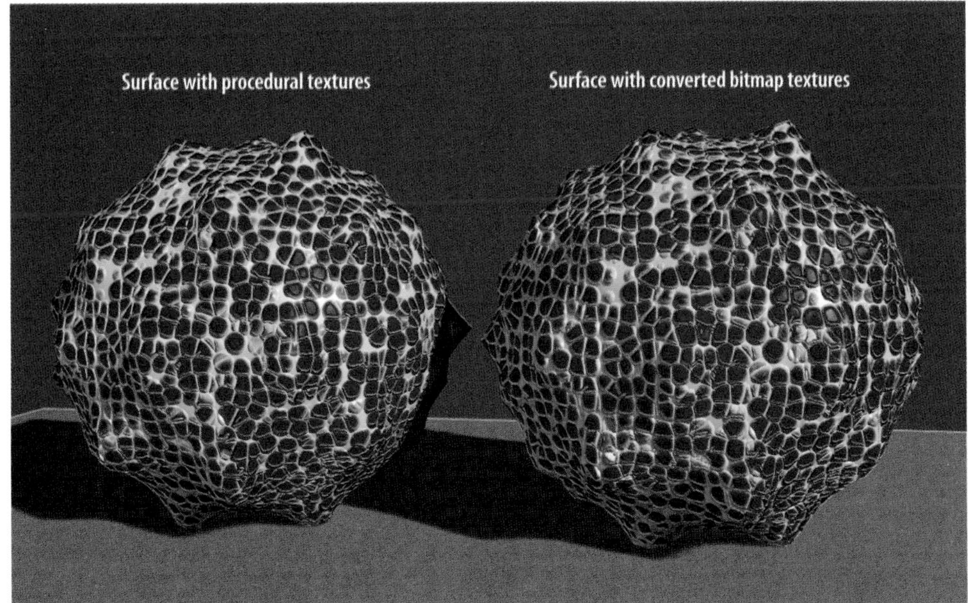

Figure 5.31 Procedurally mapped surface compared to surface with converted bitmaps. This scene is included on the CD as convert.ma.

The Convert To File Texture tool carries additional attributes for fine-tuning. Anti-Alias, if checked, anti-aliases the bitmap. Background Mode controls the background color used in the conversion. Fill Texture Seams, when checked, extends the color of any UV shell past the edge of the shell boundary; this prevents black lines from forming at the boundaries when the surface is rendered. Bake Shading Group Lighting, Bake Shadows, and Bake Transparency, when checked, add their namesake elements to the converted bitmap. Double Sided must be checked for Bake Shadows to function correctly. UV Range allows the custom selection of a non-0-to-1 range. (It is also possible to bake lighting information through the Transfer Maps window, which is discussed in Chapter 13.)

Chapter Tutorial: Creating Skin with Procedural Textures

In this tutorial, you will texture a character's head using nothing more than 2D and 3D procedural textures (see Figure 5.32). Although custom bitmaps generally create the highest level of realism, the proper use of procedural textures can save a significant amount of time on any production.

1. Open `head.ma` from the Chapter 5 scene folder on the CD. This file contains a stylized polygon head.
2. Open the Hypershade window. MMB-drag a new Blinn material into the work area. Assign the Blinn to the head. Open the Blinn's Attribute Editor tab. Change the Color attribute to a flesh color of your choice. Change the Ambient Color to a dark red. This will give the surface a subtle, skinlike glow in the shadows. The Ambient Color slider should not be more than ⅛ of the slider length from the left side. If the Ambient Color is too strong, the surface will look washed out and flat.

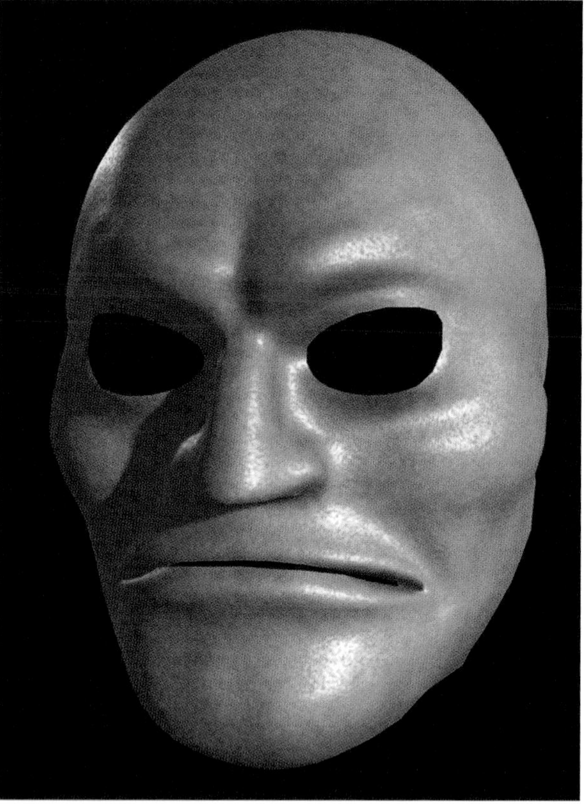

MODEL CREATED BY TRAVIS FIELDS

Figure 5.32 A skin material created with 2D and 3D procedural textures.

3. To properly judge the results, create several lights. Follow either the 2- or 3-point lighting techniques discussed in Chapter 1. Render a series of tests until the lighting is satisfactory.
4. Open the Blinn's Attribute Editor tab. Click the Specular Color checkered Map button and choose a Fractal texture from the Create Render Node window. Double-click the place2dTexture1 icon in the work area, which opens its Attribute Editor tab. Set Repeat UV to 15, 15 and check Stagger. This reduces and randomizes the scale of the fractal pattern so that it can emulate pores.
5. Open the Blinn's Attribute Editor tab. Adjust the Eccentricity and Specular Roll Off attributes. Correct values depending on the lighting of the scene. The goal is to create a strong specular highlight without losing the detail provided by the Fractal texture. Be careful not to raise the Eccentricity value too high; this will spread out the highlight and make the skin look dull.
6. In the work area, double-click the Fractal icon (named fractal1), which opens its Attribute Editor tab. Reduce the Amplitude and raise the Threshold slightly. This reduces the amount of contrast in the fractal pattern and makes its effect subtler. Tint the Color Gain attribute a pale blue. This inserts a color other than red into the material and helps make the skin color more varied.

7. Open the Blinn's Attribute Editor tab. Click the Bump Mapping checkered Map button. Choose a Granite texture from the Create Render Node window. In the work area, double-click the bump3d1 icon, which opens its Attribute Editor tab. Change Bump Depth to 0.005. In a workspace view, select the 3D Placement utility's placement box and scale it down to 0.5, 0.5, 0.5 in X, Y, Z. Render a test. The Granite texture provides a subtle bumpiness/fuzziness to the parts of the skin that do not have specular highlights.
8. Return to the Blinn's Attribute Editor tab. Click the Incandescence checkered Map button and choose a Solid Fractal texture from the Create Render Node window. In the work area, double-click the Solid Fractal icon (named solid-Fractal1), which opens its Attribute Editor tab. Change the Ratio value to 1 and the Frequency Ratio value to 4. Change Color Gain to a dark purple. Render a test frame. The Solid Fractal texture introduces variation within the basic skin color. If the result is too bright or the color is not quite right, adjust the Color Gain and render additional tests.

The skin material is complete! If you decide to apply this material to a character that moves or deforms, you can use the Convert To File Texture tool to change the 3D procedural textures into bitmaps. If you get stuck with this tutorial, a finished version is included as `head_finished.ma` in the Chapter 5 scene folder on the CD.

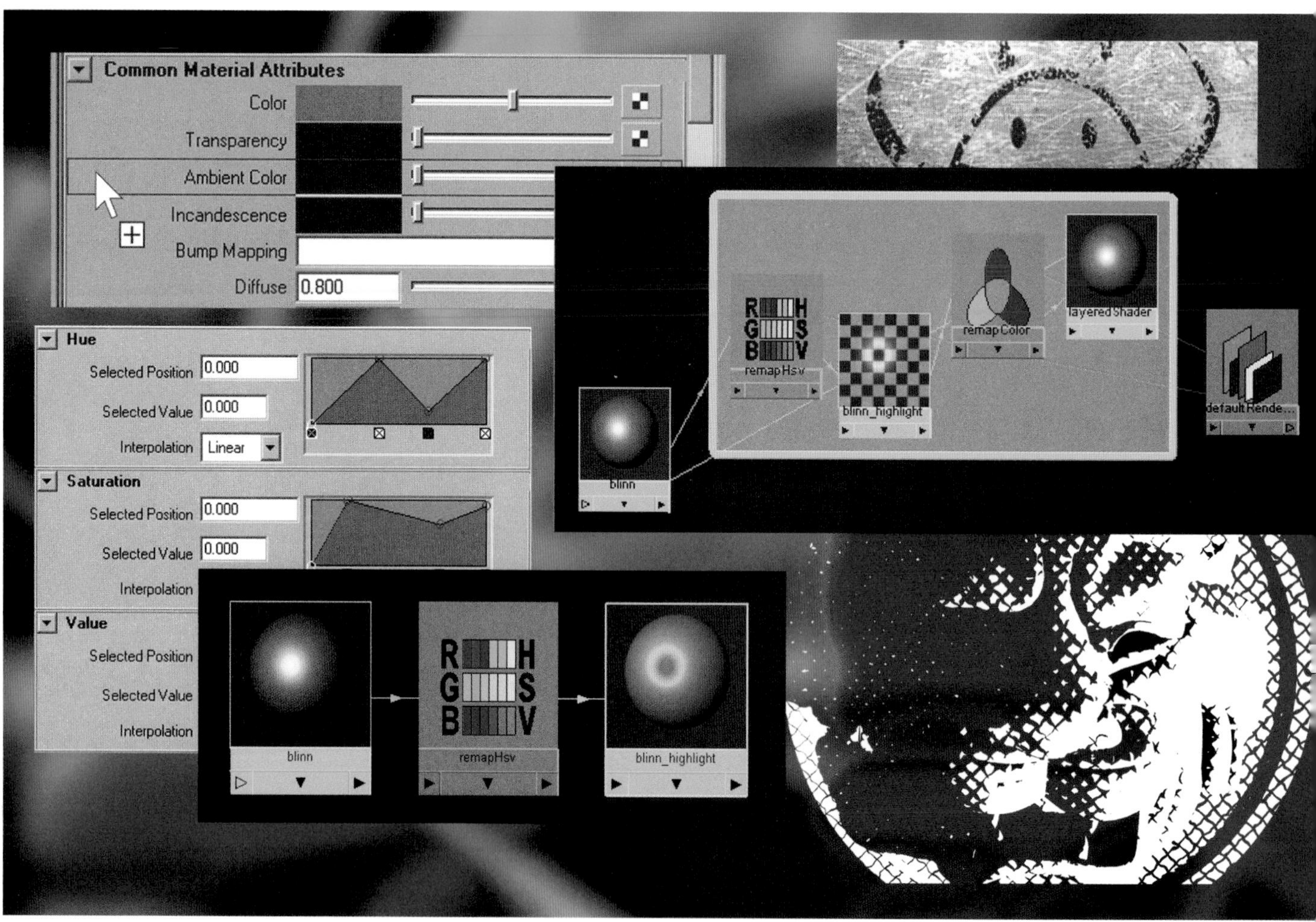
Common Material Attributes
Color
Transparency
Ambient Color
Incandescence
Bump Mapping
Diffuse 0.800
Hue
Selected Position 0.000
Selected Value 0.000
Interpolation Linear
Saturation
Selected Position 0.000
Selected Value 0.000
Interpolation
Value
Selected Position
Selected Value
Interpolation
blinn
remapHsv
blinn_highlight
remapColor
layeredShader
defaultRende...
blinn
remapHsv
blinn_highlight

Edit > Duplicate > Without Network from the Hypershade menu. To copy entire shading networks, choose Edit > Duplicate > Shading Network.

You can export shading networks. Choosing File > Export Selected Network saves the selected network, by itself, in a file with the `.mb` or `.ma` extension. You can then bring networks back into the Maya scene by choosing File > Import from the Hypershade menu.

To assign materials, MMB-drag them on top of geometry in a workspace view. Alternatively, you can follow these steps:

1. Select the surface.
2. With the mouse over the material icon, right-click and choose Assign Material To Selection from the marking menu.

Creating Custom Connections

You can create custom connections through the Connection Editor (choose Window > General Editors > Connection Editor) or the Hypershade window's work area. Descriptions of various approaches follow.

Using the Connection Editor

The Connection Editor is divided into two sections. By default, the left side contains outputs (upstream) and the right side contains inputs (downstream). A single node can be displayed on each side. To load a selected material, texture, surface, or any other Maya node, click the Reload Left or Reload Right button.

To make a connection, simply select an attribute on the left and an attribute on the right. Once a connection is made, the names of the attributes become italicized. A number of attributes are grouped into sets of three, as represented by the plus sign (see Figure 6.2). This grouping is a type of vector. (See Chapter 8 for a discussion on vectors.) It occurs most commonly with the Color attribute, which is composed of Red, Green, and Blue channels, but it also applies to color-driven attributes such as Transparency and Incandescence. You can reveal the individual channels of any given vector attribute by clicking the plus sign.

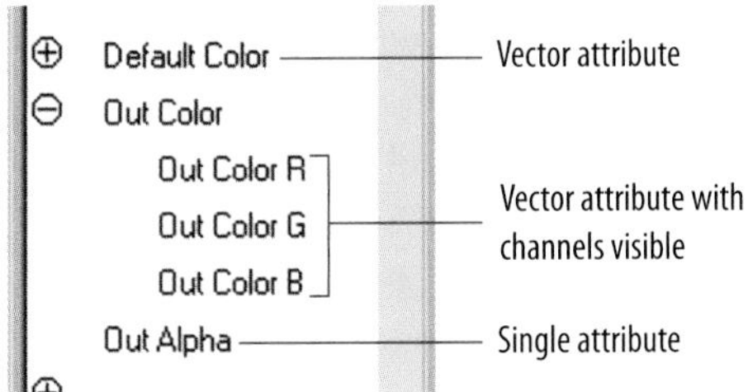

Figure 6.2 Vector attributes and a single attribute in the Connection Editor

Other attributes, such as Translate or Normal Camera, represent a spatial vector with X, Y, and Z coordinates. Any vector attribute can be connected to any other vector attribute. However, a vector attribute cannot be connected to a single attribute.

Nevertheless, a single attribute can be connected to any single channel of the vector (see Figure 6.3). If any attribute is dimmed out, it is nonkeyable and thereby off limits for a custom connection.

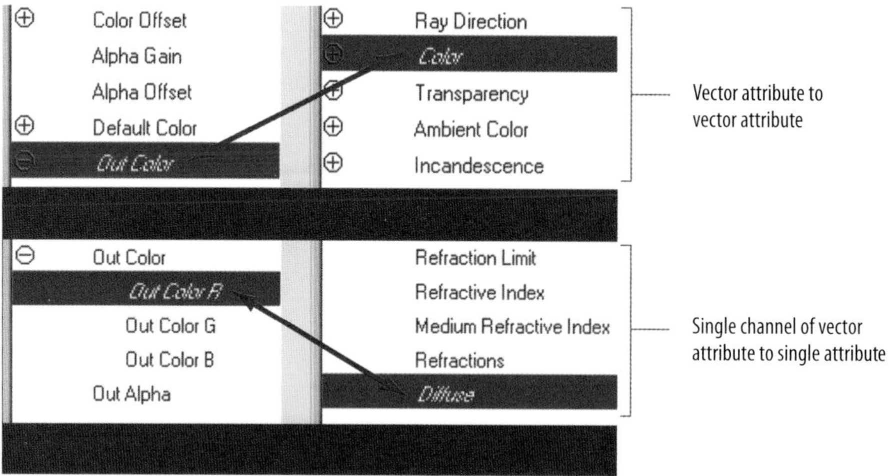

Figure 6.3 (Top) A vector attribute connected to second vector attribute. (Bottom) The single channel of a vector attribute connected to a single attribute.

Color, the most common attribute, is predictably named Color on the input (downstream) side of a node. However, it is named Out Color on the output (upstream) side. Similarly, there is Out Glow Color, Out Alpha, and Out Transparency. See the end of this section for a discussion of Out Alpha and Out Transparency.

Employing Drag and Drop

Dragging and dropping one node on top of another using the MMB automatically opens the Connect Input Of menu (see Figure 6.4). The default attribute (usually Color) of the output (upstream) node is automatically used for the connection. The Connect Input Of menu makes no distinction between vector and single attributes. If a Connect Input Of menu selection is made that confuses the program, the Connection Editor automatically opens. The attributes listed by the Connect Input Of menu is incomplete (although they are the most common and often the most useful). To see the full list, choose Other to open the Connection Editor. Dragging and dropping one node on top of another using the MMB while pressing Shift opens the Connection Editor immediately.

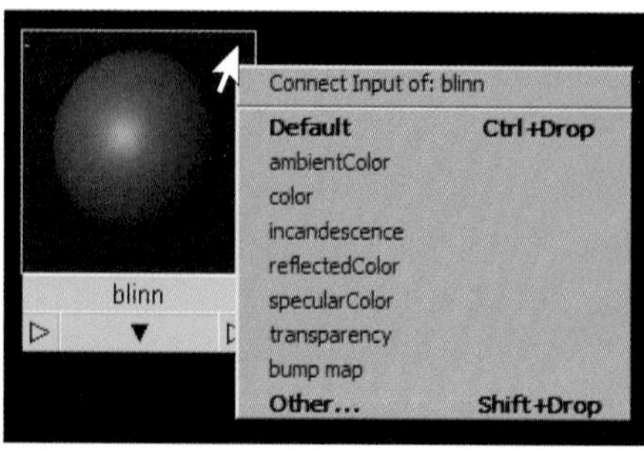

Figure 6.4 The Connect Input Of menu for a Blinn material

Dragging and dropping one node on top of another using the MMB while pressing Ctrl instantly makes a connection. In this situation, the default attribute for both nodes is used. For instance, the default input attribute of a Blinn material is Color. The default input attribute of a bump2d node is Bump Value. If the two nodes involved in the connection are not a standard pair, Maya will not be able to make a decision. For example, dragging one texture on top of another texture with the MMB and Ctrl forces Maya to open the Connection Editor.

You can also MMB-drag nodes from the Hypershade window to the Attribute Editor. An outlined box appears around any valid attribute when the mouse arrow hovers over it (see Figure 6.5). Releasing the mouse button over an attribute automatically creates a connection. In this case, it's best to double-click the downstream node first to open the node's Attribute Editor tab, and then MMB-drag the upstream node without having actually selected it. Of course, clicking the standard checkered Map button on an Attribute Editor tab opens the Create Render Node window and creates a connection once a material, texture, or utility is selected.

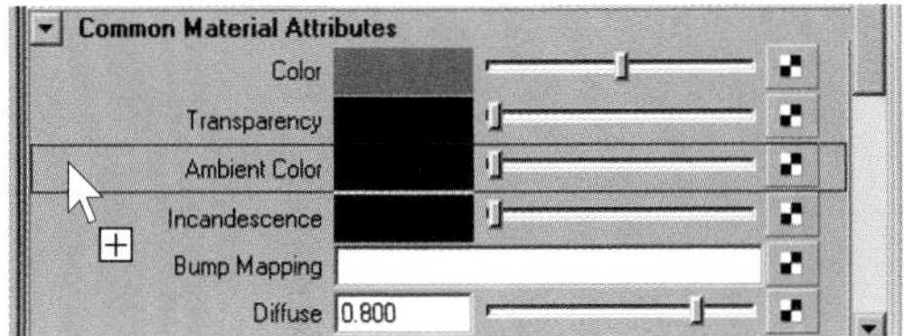

Figure 6.5
A node MMB-dragged to the Attribute Editor. The outlined box around the attribute signifies a potentially valid connection.

Duplicating a Line

Left mouse button (LMB)-clicking and -dragging an existing connection line creates a brand-new ghost line. If the ghost line is dropped onto another node, the Connect Input Of menu opens. If you click the original line behind the arrowhead, the ghost line starts at the input (downstream) node. If you click the original line ahead of the arrowhead, the ghost line starts at the output (upstream) node. The attribute for the node from which the ghost line extends will be the same as the original connection line (see Figure 6.6).

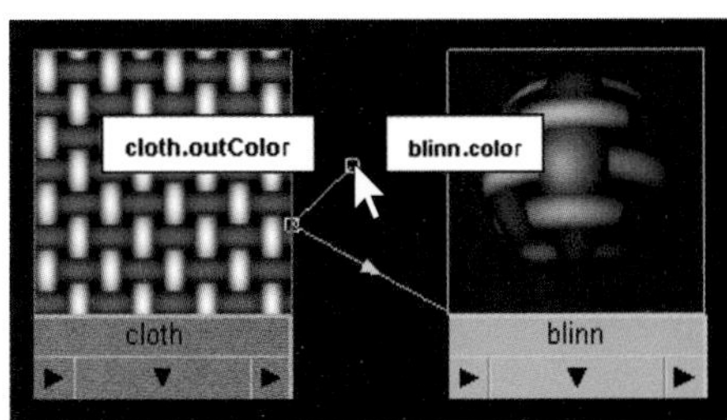

Figure 6.6
LMB-clicking an existing connection line creates a ghost line.

You can display the white label boxes in Figure 6.6 at any time by clicking an existing connection line. Regardless of the way nodes are arranged in the work area, the output (upstream) attribute is displayed in the white label box to the left of the mouse arrow, while the input (downstream) attribute is displayed in the white label box to the right of the mouse arrow. For example, when examining the connection in

Figure 6.6, cloth.outColor appears in the left label box, while blinn.color appears in the right label box. Along these lines, output channels often carry an *out* prefix and therefore appear on the left, or output, label box.

Right-Clicking a Node Corner

Right-clicking the bottom-right corner of a node opens the Connect Output Of menu (see Figure 6.7). Vector attributes are represented by an arrow on the right side; you can choose either the vector attribute or any single channel. Once an attribute is chosen, a connection line attaches itself to the mouse arrow. When you click another node, the Connect Input Of menu opens. Once you choose an input attribute, the connection is made. This technique works best if the camera is zoomed in fairly close to the node.

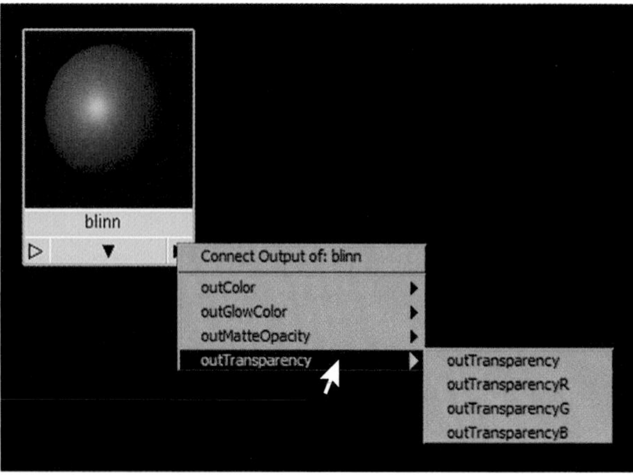

Figure 6.7 Right-clicking the bottom-right corner of a node opens the Connect Output Of menu.

A Note on Alpha and Transparency

Alpha information is stored by DDS, Maya IFF, Maya16 IFF, OpenEXR, PNG, RLA, SGI, SGI16, Targa, TIFF, TIFF16, and PSD files as RGB+A and can be used by compositing programs such as Adobe After Effects and The Foundry's Nuke. Alpha represents the opacity of any given pixel in a bitmap.

You can use alpha as transparency information in Maya in two ways. The quickest method is to load the bitmap into a File texture and connect the File's Out Transparency attribute to the Transparency attribute of a material node. The second method involves the use of the PSD File texture. For example, in Figure 6.8 the transparency surrounding a frog is supplied by the alpha channel of a PSD file. In this case, `alpha.psd` is loaded into a PSD file texture node named psdFileTexAlpha. The outTransparency of psdFileTexAlpha is connected to the transparency of a lambert material node named LambertAlpha. The drop-down menu of psdFileTexAlpha's Alpha To

Use attribute is set to Alpha 1. Last, the outColor of the psdFileTexAlpha is connected to the color of LambertAlpha.

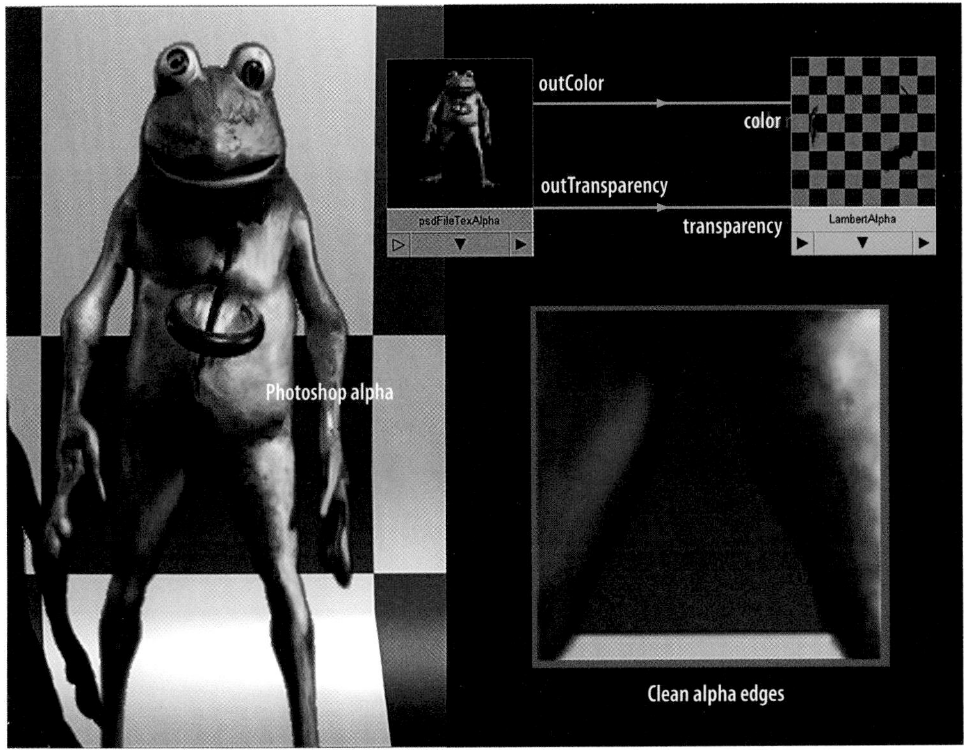

Figure 6.8 The alpha channel of a PSD file is used for transparency. This example is included on the CD as `transparency.ma`.

The PSD File texture can also read Photoshop layer transparency. For example, in Figure 6.9 the transparency surrounding the frog is supplied by the layer information of a second PSD file. In this case, `layer.psd` is loaded into a PSD file texture node named psdFileTexLayer. The outColor of psdFileTexLayer is connected to the color of a lambert material node named LambertLayer. The outTransparency of psdFileTexLayer is connected to the transparency of LambertLayer. This time, the Alpha To Use attribute of psdFileTexLayer is set to Transparency. The layer transparency technique tends to create a fine white line along the image edge, as can be seen along the frog's inner legs. This is due to Photoshop's flattening of the image as it saves (the transparency becomes premultiplied white).

Out Alpha, on the other hand, is used most commonly as a grayscale, single-channel version of a texture. A bump2D node, for example, will connect outAlpha to its own bumpValue attribute by default. (See Chapter 9 for a discussion on bump mapping.) As an additional example, the outAlpha of a stucco texture node is connected to the colorR, colorG, and colorB of a blinn material node. The result is a grayscale version of the stucco pattern (see Figure 6.10). Out Alpha and similar single-channel attributes are sometimes referred to as *scalar*, whereby they possess only magnitude.

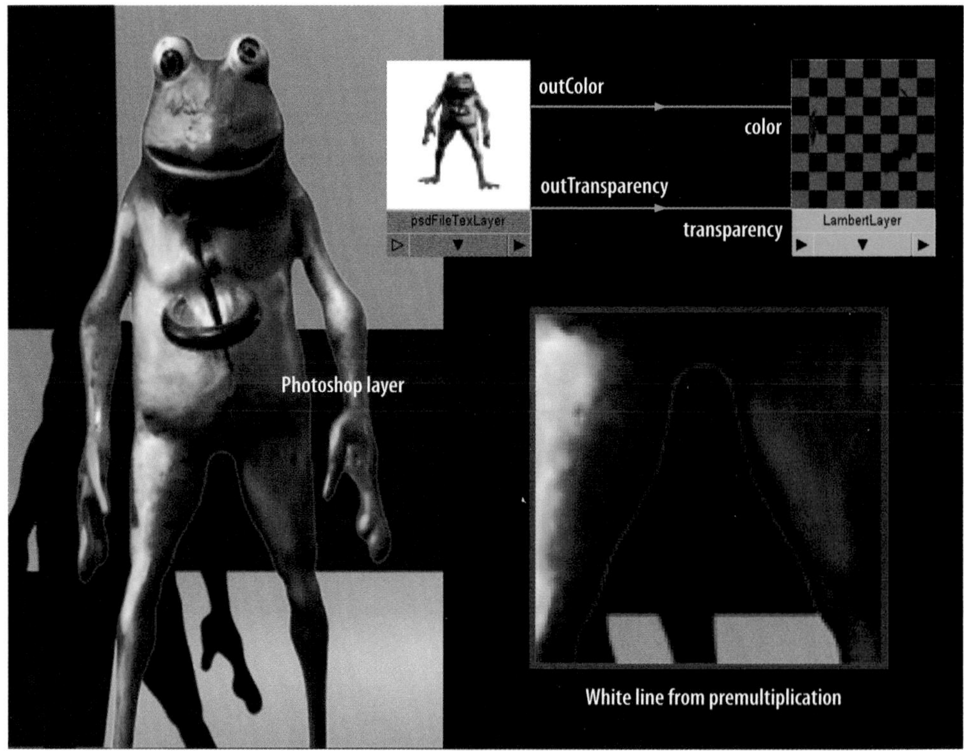

Figure 6.9 The layer information of a PSD file is used for transparency. This example is included on the CD as `transparency.ma`.

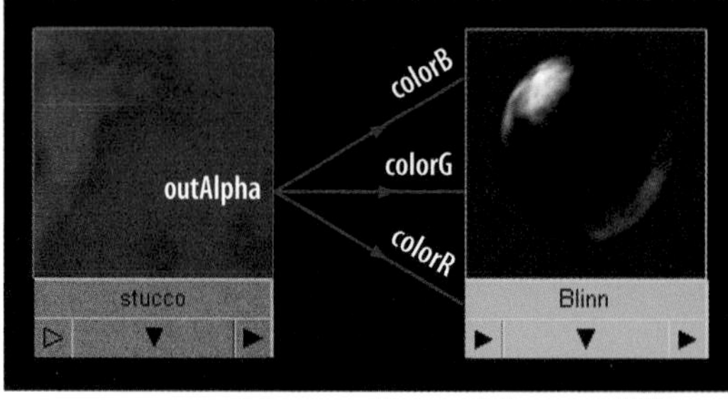

Figure 6.10 Connecting outAlpha of a Stucco texture to colorR, colorG, and colorB of a Blinn material creates a grayscale version of original texture. This material is included on the CD as `alpha_grayscale.ma`.

Cleaning Up

Shading networks can become complex in the Hypershade window. Hence, they are often difficult to work with unless you take steps to organize all the various nodes. A few tips for keeping the Hypershade easy to navigate follow.

Filling Bins, Containers, and Tabs

Bins are containers for nodes; the contents of only one bin can be seen in the tab area at any given time. By default, there is one Master Bin. To create new bins, click the Create Empty Bin button (see Figure 6.11). To assign a node to a bin, MMB-drag-and-drop the node from the tab area onto the bin icon. You can also select the node, RMB-click over the bin icon, and choose Add Selected from the shortcut menu. You can remove a node from a bin by choosing Remove Selected from the same shortcut menu. If necessary, a node can be assigned to multiple bins. (The entire shading network that is connected to a node will be added to any bins that the node has been assigned to.) By default, all nodes belong to the Master Bin.

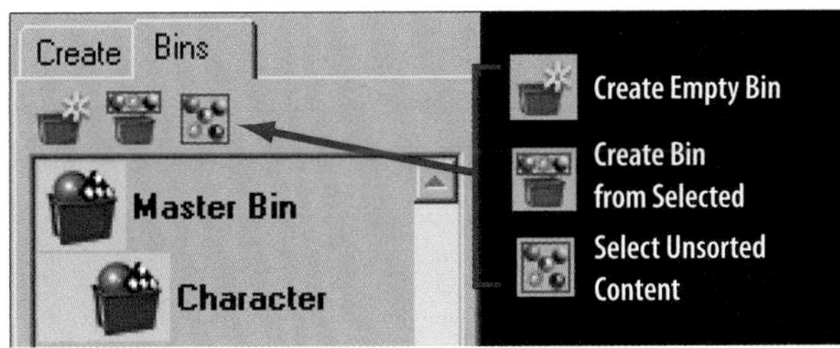

Figure 6.11 The Hypershade window bin icons

Containers, on the other hand, are specialized node groupings. A container is represented by a thick, rounded edge (see Figure 6.12).

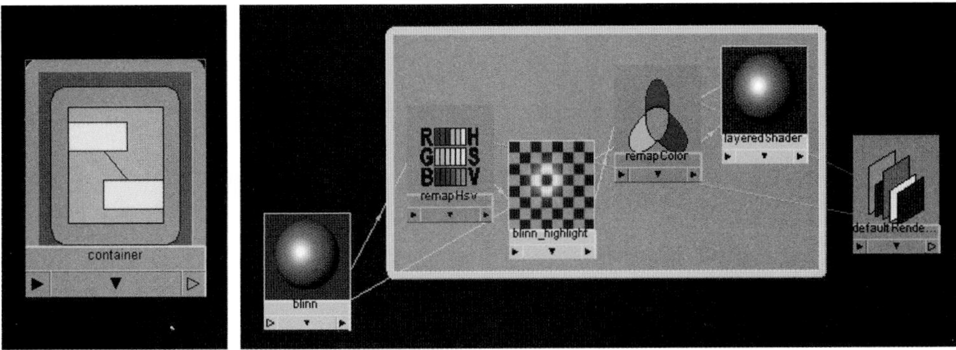

Figure 6.12 (Left) A collapsed container. (Right) An expanded container with connections to nodes not included in the container.

In terms of texturing, you can use containers as a method of organization. For example, you can select all the nodes that make up a shading network and convert them to a container with the following steps:

1. Select the shading network nodes in the Hypershade work area.
2. RMB-click one of the nodes and choose Create Container From Selected from the shortcut menu. The nodes are collapsed into a single container.
3. To view the original nodes, double-click the container. To hide the original nodes, double-click again.

If only a portion of a network is converted to a container, connections run from the nodes within the container to nodes outside the container. If you move the nodes that belong to a container while the container is expanded, the container automatically resizes itself. The container does not possess any of its own attributes, although you can add attributes through the Attribute Editor menu. (See Chapter 9 for information on adding attributes.) You can rename a container by opening it in the Attribute Editor tab and changing the name in the Container field. To remove selected nodes from a container, RMB-click a selected node and choose Remove From Container from the shortcut menu. You can view container nodes in the Hypergraph Hierarchy and Hypergraph Connections windows.

As for tabs, you can create, rename, or reorder custom tabs through the Hypershade window Tabs menu.

Focusing the Work Area

The Show Previous Graph and Show Next Graph buttons toggle through work area views. At the same time, the connection buttons offer a quick way to frame other components of a shading network (see Figure 6.13). This is particularly useful when a portion of a network has been "lost" and is no longer in view. The connection buttons also serve as a quick way to view normally hidden downstream nodes. In addition, you can find the Input Connections and Output Connections buttons can at the top of every Attribute Editor tab.

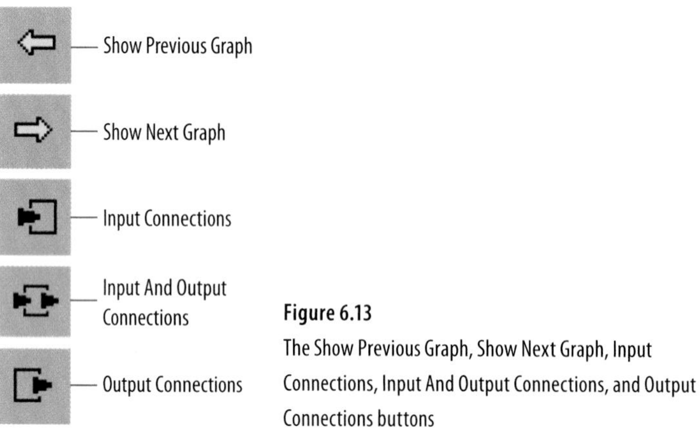

Figure 6.13
The Show Previous Graph, Show Next Graph, Input Connections, Input And Output Connections, and Output Connections buttons

Unless a scene contains complex custom connections, you can view the majority of its node network within the Hypershade window's work area. You can even find rarely viewed nodes that represent render partitions, light linking, Timeline time, expressions, construction history, UV mappings, and Paint Effects brushes. To achieve such a view, select any node in the Hypershade work area and click the Input And Output Connections button. Select all the nodes that appear and click the button again. Repeat this process two or three times. A complex node network soon appears (see Figure 6.14). Blue lines run downstream to the renderPartition and lightLinker nodes, as well as to various utilities. Purple lines run from geometry shape nodes to shading group nodes. Cyan lines run from place2dTexture nodes to textures. Green lines run downstream to shading groups and between textures.

Occasionally, the Hypershade window will not display all the components of a custom shading network. This is particularly true when the network contains a mixture of materials, lights, and cameras. In addition, the Hypershade fails to automatically display transform nodes. Should this situation arise, the Hypergraph Connections window offers a reliable alternative. To view the entire node network of a scene within the Hypergraph, follow these steps:

1. Choose Window > Hypergraph: Connections. From the Hypergraph Connections window menu, choose Show > Auxiliary Nodes.

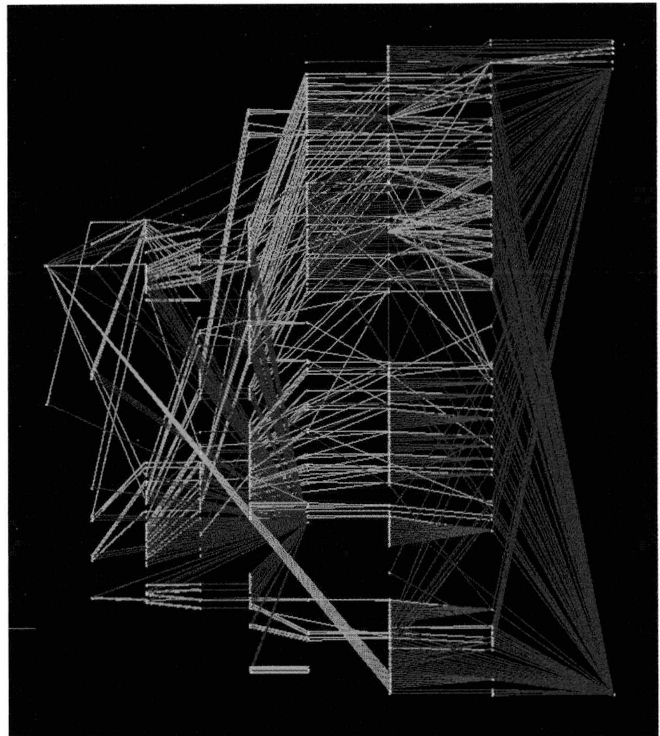

Figure 6.14 The node network of this book's cover illustration as displayed in the Hypershade work area

2. In the Auxiliary Nodes window, click-drag the mouse arrow over the nodes listed in the Node Types That Are Hidden In Editors field. With the nodes highlighted, click the Remove From List button. This guarantees that no node types are hidden in the Hypergraph Connections window. Close the Auxiliary Nodes window.
3. Choose Show > Auxiliary Nodes from the Hypergraph menu so that the menu item is checked. Select all the nodes that are visible. Choose Graph > Input And Output Connections from the Hypergraph menu. Select all the nodes that are visible. Choose Input And Output Connections again. Repeat the process until there is no change in the view.

Returning to the Hypershade window, right-clicking while the mouse arrow hovers over a node in the work area opens a marking menu with a Graph Network option. Choosing Graph Network reveals and frames all the upstream connections of a selected node (see section B of Figure 6.15). By default, Graph Network clears all other networks from the work area. To avoid this, right-click over an empty portion of the work area and choose (and therefore uncheck) Clear Before Graphing. A disadvantage of Graph Network is its inability to reveal nodes downstream from the selection. Right-clicking over an empty portion of the work area and choosing Graph > Rearrange Graph arranges nodes in a pattern identical to choosing Graph Network from the marking menu (although it can arrange only the nodes that are already visible).

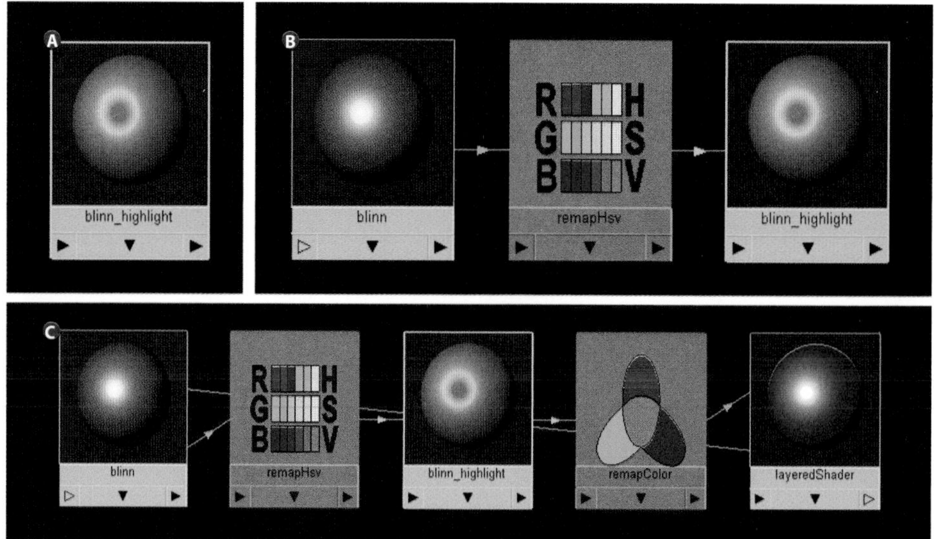

Figure 6.15 (A) A lone blinn node in the work area. (B) The work area after the application of Graph Network. (C) The work area after the alternate application of the Input And Output Connections button.

The most thorough way to organize the work area is to use the Input And Output Connections button. The resulting network is very orderly (see section C of Figure 6.15). In general, the resulting order will only break down once large swaths of the scene are viewed. The Input And Output Connections button will clear unselected shading networks from the work area. Nevertheless, the button will arrange all connected nodes if multiple shading networks are selected simultaneously.

Deleting Unused Nodes

Choosing Edit > Delete Unused Nodes from the Hypershade menu is an excellent way to thin out the Hypershade. Complex or lengthy projects often produce redundant nodes. Delete Unused Nodes deletes any node that is not assigned to a surface or is part of an assigned shading network.

Shifting Colors

Twelve utility nodes in Maya are designed to shift colors. These utilities can convert color space, remap color ranges, adjust brightness and contrast, and even read the luminance of a surface within a scene.

Converting RGB to HSV

The Rgb To Hsv utility converts a Red/Green/Blue vector into a Hue/Saturation/Value vector. The Hsv To Rgb utility does the opposite. In Maya, Red, Green, and Blue channels have a numeric range of 0 to 1. In HSV color space, Hue corresponds to a pure color and has a range of 0 to 360. Saturation, which represents the amount of white mixed into a color, has a range of 0 to 1. Value, which represents the amount of black mixed into a color, also has a range of 0 to 1. With the Hsv To Rgb utility, inHsvR carries the hue, inHsvG carries the saturation, and inHsvB carries the value. In contrast, the Rgb To Hsv utility offers inRgbR, inRgbG, and inRgbB, which represent the standard red, green, and blue color components.

The Rgb To Hsv and Hsv To Rgb utilities allow calculations to stay in HSV color space. In addition, the Hsv To Rgb utility can serve as a color "dial." For example, in Figure 6.16 a bitmap is tinted different colors as the Timeline progresses.

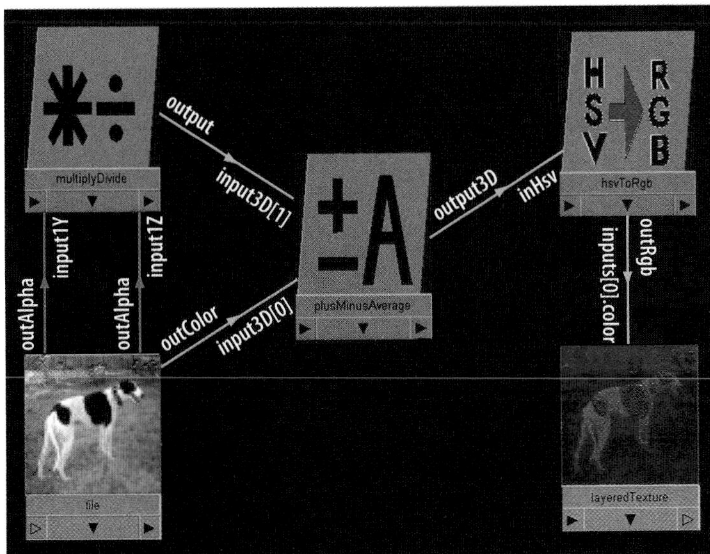

Figure 6.16 An Hsv To Rgb utility is used to create a color dial. This scene is included on the CD as `hsvtorgb.ma`.

To view the shading network, follow these steps:

1. Open the `hsvtorgb.ma` file from the CD. Open the Hypershade window.
2. Switch to the Utilities tab. MMB-drag the hsvToRgb node into the work area.
3. With the hsvToRgb node selected, click the Input And Output Connections button. The network becomes visible.

A bitmap named `greyhound.tif` is loaded into a File texture. The outColor of the file node is connected to the input3D[0] of a plusMinusAverage node. The output3D of the plusMinusAverage node is connected to the inHsv of an hsvToRgb node. As a test, outRgb of the hsvToRgb node is connected to the inputs[0].color of a layeredTexture node. The output of a multiplyDivide node is connected to input3D[1] of the plusMinusAverage node. The plusMinusAverage node's Operation is set to Average. (For information on the Multiply Divide and Plus Minus Average utilities, see Chapter 8.) Last, the outAlpha of the file node is connected to input1Y and input1Z of the multiplyDivide node.

The multiplyDivide node serves as the color dial controller. The multiplyDivide node's Input1X attribute determines the outgoing hue since it is connected to inRgbR. Input1X is animated with keyframes so that the value changes from 0 to 359. This creates a complete clockwise revolution of the HSV color wheel (which is a counterclockwise spin on Maya's RGB color wheel). The plusMinusAverage node averages the hue value provided by the multiplyDivide node and the outColorR channel value of the texture. In this way, the final texture is not washed out or completely overtaken by the new hue value. The outAlpha of the file node determines the saturation of the final texture as it is connected to the input1Y of the multiplyDivide node, which in turn is connected to inRgbG of the hsvToRgb node. The outAlpha also determines the value (the amount of mixed-in black) of the final texture as it is connected to the input1Z of the multiplyDivide node, which in turn is connected to inRgbB of the hsvToRgb node.

Table 6.1 shows what happens to different color pixels of the original texture if the Input1X of the multiplyDivide node is set to 100.

Table 6.1 Colors Resulting from Different Texture Pixel Values

Texture Pixel RGB	multiplyDivide Output	plusMinusAverage Output	hsvToRgb Output
0, 0, 0	100, 0, 0	50, 0, 0	0, 0, 0 (black)
0.5, 0.5, 0.5	100, 0.5, 0.5	50.25, 0.5, 0.5	0.5, 0.459, 0.25 (brown)
1, 0.6, 1	100, 0.6, 1	50.5, 0.6, 1	1, 0.905, 0.4 (light orange)

Converting RGB to Luminance

The Luminance utility converts RGB values into luminous values. In Maya, a luminous value signifies the apparent brightness of a color as seen by the human eye. The Luminance utility's Out Value attribute outputs a scalar (a single channel) version of the input. For example, in Figure 6.17 the outColor of a file texture node is connected to the value of a luminance node. The outValue of the luminance node is connected to the colorR, colorG, and colorB of a blinn material node. The result is a grayscale version of the original bitmap. The Out Value attribute varies from the common Out Alpha attribute in that it biases the green channel. Colors are not perceived equally by the human brain; hence, the Luminance utility uses the following formula:

```
outColor = (0.3 × Red) + (0.59 × Green) + (0.11 × Blue)
```

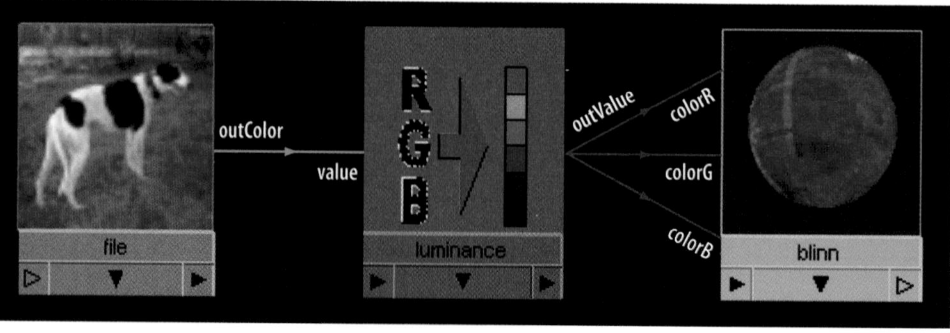

Figure 6.17 The Luminance utility converts RGB values into luminous values that are represented as a grayscale. This material is included on the CD as `luminance.ma`.

Blending Colors

The Blend Colors utility blends two colors or textures together using a third color or texture as a control. The Blend Colors formula is as follows:

```
outColor = (Color1 × Blender) + (Color2 × (1 - Blender))
```

If the Blender attribute is 1, Color1 is the resulting output. If Blender is 0, Color2 is the resulting output. If Blender is 0.5, a percentage of Color1 and Color2 are added. For example, in Figure 6.18 the Blend Colors utility is used to create a logo stenciled onto a wall. `logo_mask.tif` is loaded as a File texture. The outAlpha of the file node is connected to the blender of a blendColors node. `wall.tif` is brought in as a second File texture. The outColor of the second file node is connected to color1 of the blendColors node. `logo_color.tif` is brought in as a third File texture. The outColor of the third file node is connected to color2 of the blendColors node. The output of the blendColors node is finally connected to the color of a blinn material node. The raggedness of the logo is generated by `logo_mask.tif`. (For a discussion on the Stencil utility, which can provide results similar to this example, see Chapter 8.)

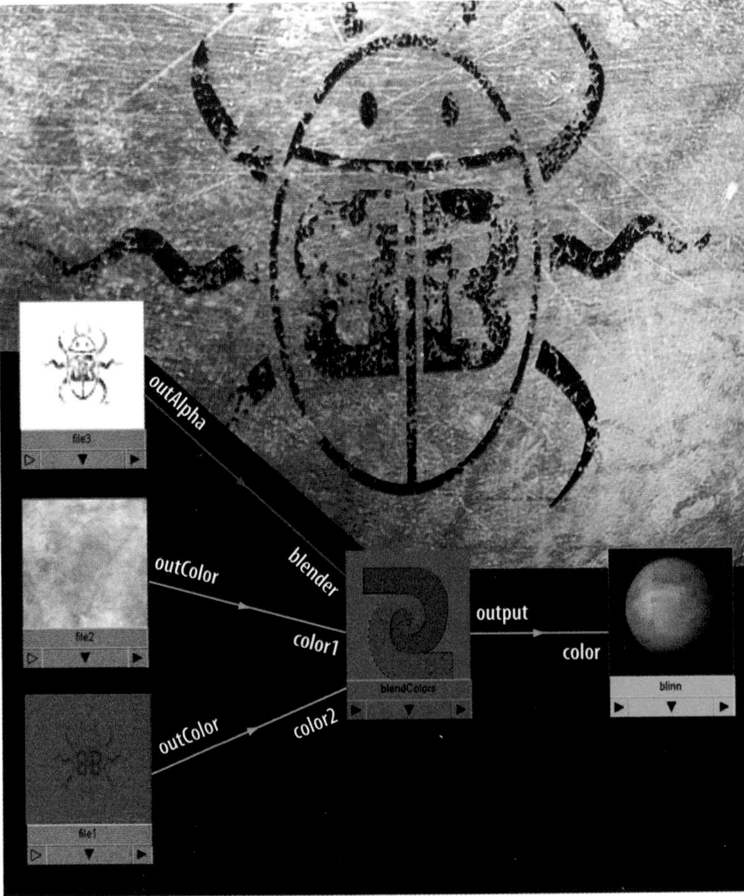

Figure 6.18 A logo is added to a wall with the Blend Colors utility. This scene is included on the CD as `blend_colors.ma`.

Remapping Color

The Remap Color utility allows the adjustment of a color attribute through the use of interactive gradients. A gradient functions like a horizontal ramp. Technically speaking, a gradient is a graphic representation of the transition between two colors. The far-left side of a gradient represents the output color value that will be given to the lowest values of the input color. The far-right side of the gradient represents the output color value that will be given to the highest values of the input color. With the default upward slope, 0 is given 0, 0.5 is given 0.5, and 1 is given 1, and thus there is no change.

The simplest way to see the Remap Color utility functioning is to reverse the gradient slope. In Figure 6.19, the outColor of a grid texture node is connected to the color of a remapColor node. The outColor of the remapColor node is connected to the color of a lambert material node. When the slope direction is reversed on each gradient, the whites become black (RGB: 1, 1, 1 to 0, 0, 0) and the blacks become white (0, 0, 0 to 1, 1, 1).

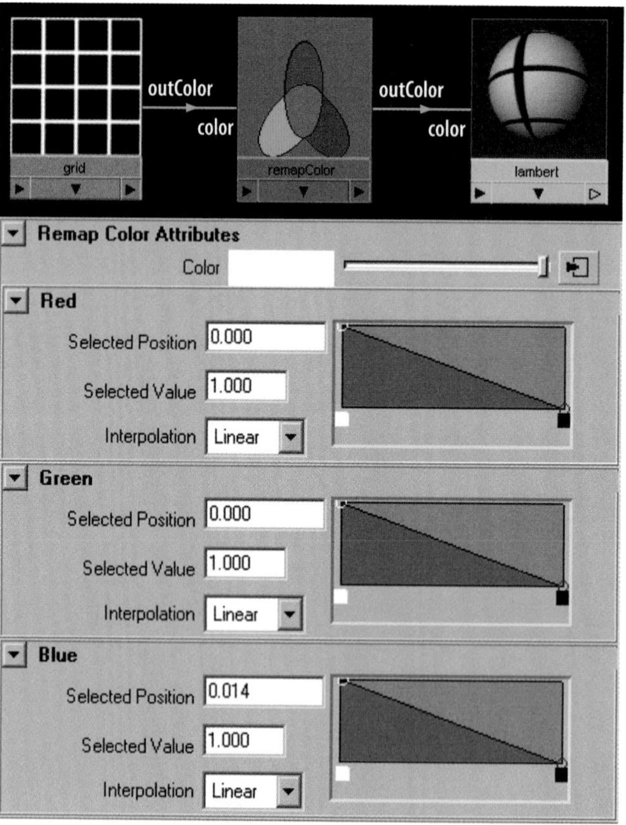

Figure 6.19 A Grid texture is inverted with a Remap Color utility. This material is included on the CD as `remap_invert.ma`.

In a second example, a Noise texture is used (see the top of Figure 6.20). The far left handle of the Red gradient is moved to the top. This forces the texture to carry the maximum amount of red at all points. Thus, black becomes pure red (0, 0, 0 to 1,

0, 0). White is unchanged since it already contained the maximum amount of red (1, 1, 1 to 1, 1, 1). Gray turns into a pale red (0.5, 0.5, 0.5 to 1, 0.5, 0.5).

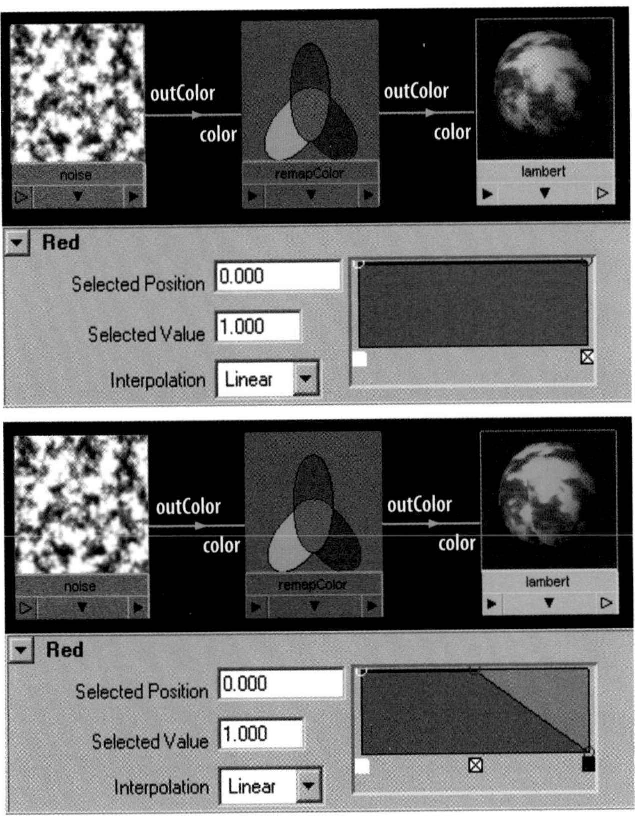

Figure 6.20 (Top) Black is shifted to red with a Remap Color utility. This material is included on the CD as `remap_red_1.ma`. (Bottom) White is shifted to cyan with a Remap Color utility. This material is included on the CD as `remap_red_2.ma`.

In a third example (see the bottom of Figure 6.20), a Noise texture is used again. This time, the Red gradient is reversed and then given a plateau by inserting an additional handle. Any part of the Noise texture that has a red value of 0.5 or less receives the maximum amount of red. Any part of the Noise texture that has a red value greater than 0.5 receives less red, allowing the green and blue to triumph and thus produce a cyan color.

You can insert additional handles into any of the three gradients by clicking in the dark gray area. You can move any handle up/down and left/right by LMB-dragging. Any handle can be deleted by clicking its × box. You can change the transition from handle to handle by switching the gradient's Interpolation attribute from Linear to Smooth, Spline, or None.

The Remap Color utility is not limited to color attributes. For example, in Figure 6.21 the translate of a sphere transform node is connected to the color of a remapColor node. The outColor of remapColor is connected back to the transform node's rotate. The gradients on the remapColor node are set to numerous jagged peaks and valleys. As a result, the sphere automatically undergoes an erratic rotation when moved in any direction. The Remap Color utility's Input Min and Input Max are set to –10 and 10, respectively. This prevents the rotation from continuing when the sphere's translation exceeds 10 units in the X, Y, or Z direction. The Output Min and Output Max are set to –360 and 360, respectively. This forces the remapped translate values to stay between –360 and 360, which permits the sphere to rotate in any direction for a single revolution.

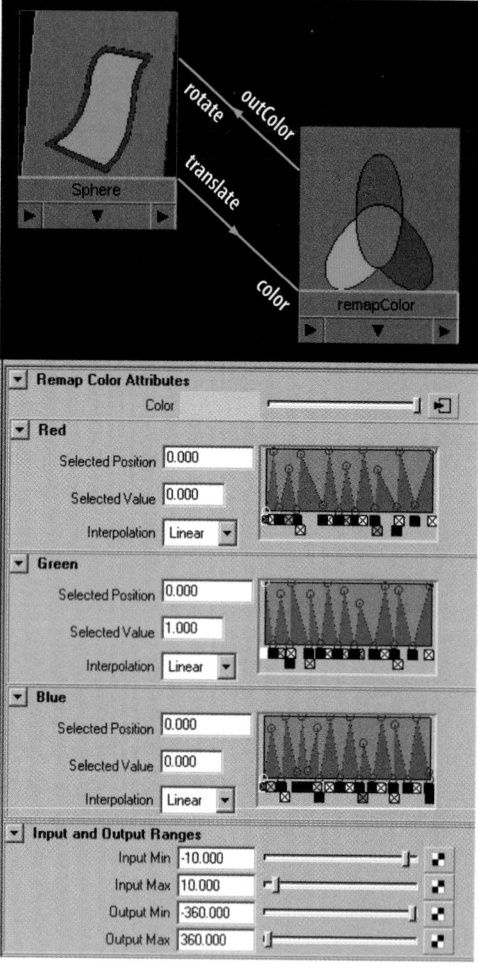

Figure 6.21
The rotation of a sphere is automatically driven, and made erratic, with a Remap Color utility. This scene is included on the CD as `remap_rotate.ma`. A QuickTime movie is included as `remap_rotate.mov`.

To view the custom shading network, follow these steps:

1. Open `remap_rotate.ma` file from the CD. Open the Hypershade window.
2. Switch to the Utilities tab. MMB-drag the remapColor node into the work area.
3. With the remapColor node selected, click the Input And Output Connections button. The network becomes visible.

Note: You can MMB-drag any node that is visible in the Hypergraph into the Hypershade work area. This includes geometry. Any node that appears in any tab of the Hypershade can be MMB-dragged into the work area as well. This includes cameras, lights, and shading groups.

Remapping HSV

The Remap Hsv utility works in the same fashion as the Remap Color utility. Instead of offering Red, Green, and Blue gradients, however, it carries Hue, Saturation, and Value gradients. By separating Hue from Value, it's possible to isolate very narrow sections of a texture or material. For example, in Figure 6.22 the specular highlight of a Blinn material is given an artificial chromatic aberration. Optically, chromatic aberration is the inability of a lens to focus various color wavelengths on the same focal plane. This artifact often appears in both traditional and digital color photography and is referred to as "purple fringing."

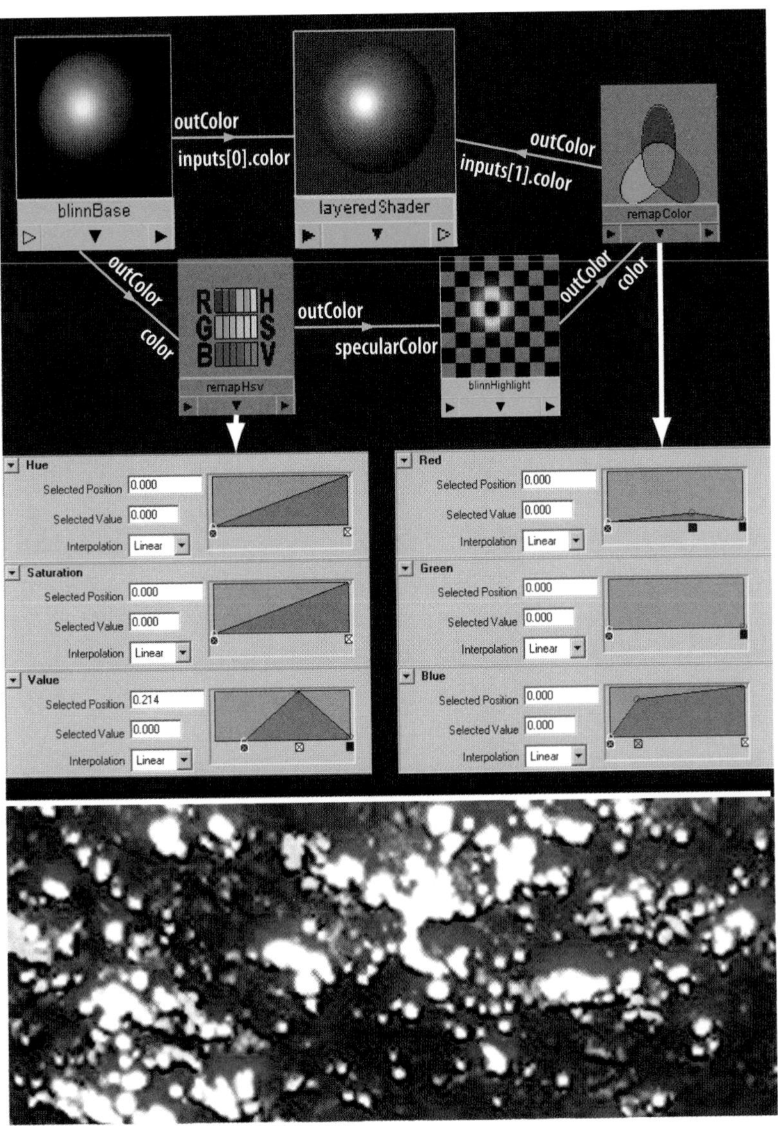

Figure 6.22 (Top) The specular highlight of a Blinn is given an artificial chromatic aberration with a Remap Hsv utility. This material is included on the CD as `remap_hsv.ma`. (Bottom) Chromatic aberration is visible as a "purple fringing" in a photograph of tree foliage.

To achieve the purple fringe on the highlight, the outColor of a blinn material node, named blinnBase, is connected to the color of a remapHsv node. The outColor of remapHsv is connected to the specularColor of a second blinn material node named blinnHighlight. The outColor of blinnHighlight is connected to the color of a remapColor node. The outColor of remapColor is connected to the inputs[1].color of a layeredShader material node. The outColor of blinnBase is connected to the inputs[0].color of the layeredShader node. By adjusting the remapHsv Value gradient, a narrow sliver of the blinnBase specular highlight is retrieved. This is visible on the icon of blinnHighlight (which has its Transparency attribute set to 100% white). The remapColor node tints the pulled highlight a purplish color. The layeredShader node is able to combine the isolated purplish highlight and the original blinn.

Remapping Value

Although the Remap Value utility controls color through two gradients, its basic functionality is different from Remap Color and Remap Hsv utilities. Remap Value provides a single-channel Value gradient that can be used by itself. (See Chapter 7 for an example of the Remap Value utility used in such a way for car paint.)

The Remap Value utility also provides a Color gradient. The Color gradient is controlled by the Input Value attribute. That is, if a texture mapped to the Input Value attribute provides the color black, the left side of the Color gradient is sampled. If a texture mapped to the Input Value attribute provides the color white, the right side of the Color gradient is sampled. Hence, the Remap Value utility supports an additional method of blending two sources together.

For example, in Figure 6.23 `maya.tif` is brought in as a File texture. The outColor of the file texture node is connected to color[0].color_Color of a remapValue node. This connection attaches the file node to a handle within the Color gradient. The outColor of a crater texture node is connected to color[1].color_Color of the remapValue node. This connection attaches the crater node to a second Color gradient handle. The handles are arranged so that the file node handle is at the far right of the gradient and the crater node handle is at the far left. The outAlpha of a fractal texture node is connected to inputValue of the remapValue node. Thus, the fractal node becomes a controller for the Color gradient. Black spots within the fractal cause the remapValue node to select color from the crater node. White spots within the fractal cause the remapValue node to add the file and crater together to determine a color. The outColor of the remapValue node is finally connected to the color of a lambert material node, which in turn is assigned to a plane. In the end, the lambert color is a mixture of the crater and file based on the pattern provided by the fractal.

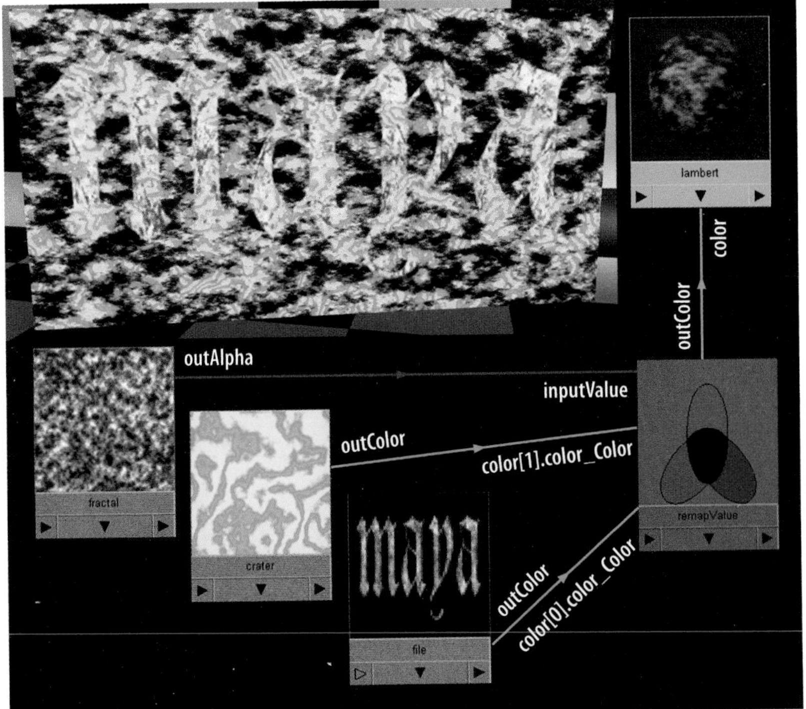

Figure 6.23 Two textures are blended together with a Remap Value utility. This scene is included on the CD as `remap_value.ma`.

Smearing Colors

The Smear utility allows one texture to be distorted by another. If Smear is combined with a Ramp texture, it creates a stylized vision effect that might be appropriate for an alien, a monster, or a robot. For example, in Figure 6.24 a sequence of video images is loaded into a File texture. The Use Image Sequence attribute is checked so that the images are automatically loaded as the Timeline moves forward. The outColor of the file node is connected to the inRgb of a smear node. The outU of the smear node is connected to the offsetU of the place2dTexture node of a ramp texture node. The outV of the smear node is also connected to the offsetV of the place2dTexture node of the ramp node. The outColor of the ramp node is finally connected to the outColor of a surfaceShader material node, which is assigned to a primitive plane. The ramp has three handles: one red and two orange. The higher the values are in the video image bitmaps, the farther the smear node "pulls" the ramp down in the V direction. For instance, if a bitmap provides a pixel with RGB values 0.5, 0.5, 0.5, the ramp is pulled downward so that the top rests at the center of the ramp field. If a bitmap provides a pixel with RGB values 0.9, 0.9, 0.9, the ramp is pulled downward so that the top rests one tenth above the bottom of the ramp field. When the ramp is called upon by the surfaceShader material, every pixel of the ramp is offset in the V direction by a unique amount. Hence, the ramp appears as a colored version of the video bitmap.

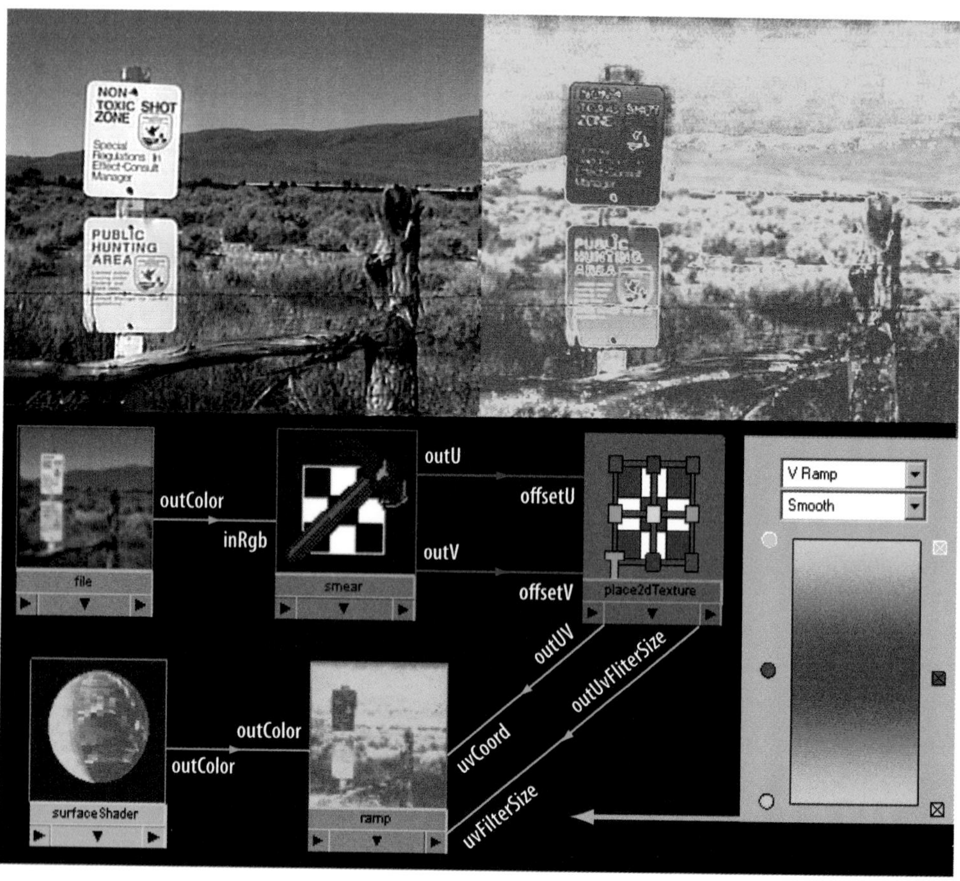

Figure 6.24 An image sequence and a Ramp texture are combined with the Smear utility. This scene is included on the CD as `smear.ma`. A QuickTime movie is included as `smear.mov`.

Internally, the Smear utility converts the input RGB to HSV. New UV coordinates are generated by plotting values on an HSV color wheel. For another example of the Smear utility, see the tutorial at the end of this chapter.

Correcting Gamma

Gamma correction is the adjustment of an image to compensate for the physical limitations of a computer monitor. With a monitor, the intensity (brightness) of a screen pixel does not linearly increase with the application of additional voltage. Because of this, uncorrected images may appear inappropriately dark or washed-out. Gamma correction solves this by applying a complementary intensity curve to the image to negate the monitor's intensity curve. Different operating systems apply gamma correction in different ways, whether through hardware or software controls. Microsoft-based systems generally operate with a gamma value set to 2.2, whereas Macintosh systems operate with a gamma value set to of 1.8. Some programs, like Adobe Photoshop, allow you to apply different gamma values to the system on the fly.

Gamma correction is applied to the image with the following standard formula:

```
new pixel value = image pixel value  ^ (1.0 /  gamma value)
```

Thus, if an image pixel has a value of 0.5, 0.5, 0.5 and the gamma value is set to 2.2, the new pixel value, which is sent to the screen, is roughly 0.73, 0.73, 0.73.

Maya's Gamma Correct utility also applies the standard gamma formula:

```
outValue = value ^ (1.0 / Gamma)
```

In this case, the Gamma Correct utility adjusts the values of the value input and outputs the result through outValue. No other node is affected. As a rule of thumb, the higher the Gamma attribute values are, the more washed out the mid-range values become. High- and low-range values (white whites and black blacks) are affected to a lesser degree.

An interesting side effect of the Gamma Correct utility is the increase or decrease of saturation. For example, in Figure 6.25 `face.tif` is loaded into a File texture. The outColor of the file node is connected to the value of a gammaCorrect node. As a test, the outValue of the gammaCorrect node is connected to the inputs[0].color of a layeredTexture node. The Gamma attribute of the gammaCorrect node is set to 0.5, 0.5, 0.5. As a result, the washed-out bitmap gains a good deal of saturation. Raising the Gamma above 1 would have the opposite effect—less saturation.

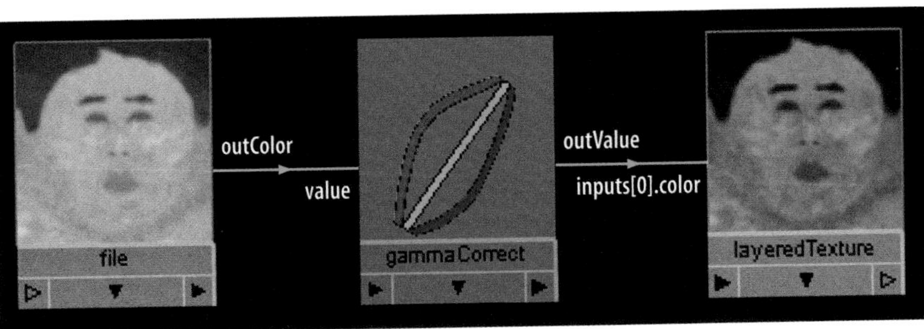

Figure 6.25 A washed-out face bitmap is given extra saturation with a Gamma Correct utility. This shading network is included on the CD as `gamma_correct.ma`.

To view the custom shading network, follow these steps:

1. Open the `gamma_correct.ma` file from the CD. Open the Hypershade window.
2. Switch to the Utilities tab. MMB-drag the gammaCorrect node into the work area.
3. With the gammaCorrect node selected, click the Input And Output Connections button. The network becomes visible.

Note: Many Maya utilities feature vector attributes that are represented by three number fields (for example, Gamma). These fields are read left to right when representing color (red, green, blue) or position (X, Y, Z). When one of these fields is used in a custom shading network, the connection is made to a single channel of the attribute (for example, gammaX).

Adjusting Contrast

The Contrast utility does exactly what its name implies. The higher the Contrast attribute value of the Contrast utility, the whiter the whites and the blacker the blacks become. The lower the Contrast attribute value, the more the colors converge toward each other. The Bias attribute determines the RGB values that the colors converge to. For example, in Figure 6.26 `face_2.tif` is loaded into a File texture. The outColor of the file node is connected to the value of a contrast node. As a test, the outValue of the contrast node is connected to the inputs[0].color of a layeredTexture node. The Contrast attribute of the contrast node is set to 4, 4, 4. The Bias attribute is set to 0.4, 0.4, 0.4. The resulting image has extremely white whites and black blacks and few colors in the mid-ranges.

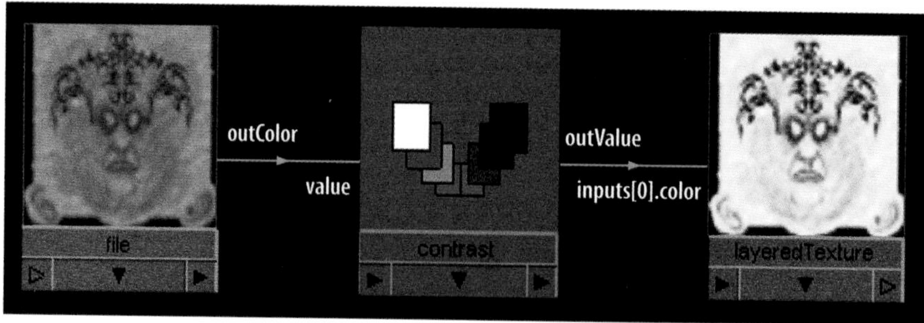

Figure 6.26 A washed-out face bitmap is given a great deal of contrast with the Contrast utility. This shading network is included on the CD as `contrast.ma`.

A Contrast value of 1 and a Bias value of 0.5 leaves the texture unchanged. Lowering the Contrast value reduces the contrast. Raising the Bias value darkens the texture overall.

A Note on Sliders and Super-White

In Maya, many sliders that include number fields can readjust themselves. For instance, a Diffuse attribute slider normally runs from 0 to 1. However, if you enter 2 into the field, the slider automatically readjusts itself to run between 0 and 4. For the Diffuse attribute, higher values result in a predictably brighter surface. Other sliders, when pushed past their default range, will not display a perceptible change. Any Maya color channel can exceed the standard bounds of 0 to 1. Although it's not possible to do this directly through the Attribute Editor, you can enter extra-high values into the fields of the Color Chooser window. To do so, follow these steps:

1. In the Attribute Editor tab, click the color swatch of an attribute. The Color Choose window opens.
2. Choose either RGB or HSV from the color space drop-down menu. If you choose RGB, enter a value into the Red, Green, or Blue field. There is no practical limit to the size of the number you enter. If you choose HSV, enter a value into the Hue, Saturation, or Value field. Although Hue and Saturation accept large numbers, the Value field is generally the most useful for custom values.
3. Click the Accept button to close the window.

In addition, you can create extra-high values, either intentionally or unintentionally, through custom connections. As a demonstration, the Line Color and Filler Color attributes of a grid texture node are set to 0.5, 0.5, 0.5 in RGB, creating a solid gray (see Figure 6.27). The outColor of the grid node is connected to the input1 of a multiplyDivide node (see Chapter 8 for a description). The output of the first multiplyDivide node is connected to the input1 of a second multiplyDivide node. The output of the second multiplyDivide node is connected to a blinn material node. The Input2 attribute of the first multiplyDivide node is set to 4, 4, 4. The end result, as seen in the second multiplyDivide node, is an RGB color with values of 2, 2, 2. These inappropriately high values are often referred to as *super-white*. From a practical standpoint, Maya simply clamps any color over 1.0 to 1.0 when rendering standard images. Even though the RGB is 2, 2, 2, it's rendered as if it's 1, 1, 1 (as seen on the blinn icon). Nevertheless, the super-white values can cause problems with custom connections if they are not taken into account. Fortunately, the Clamp utility can solve this problem (see the next section).

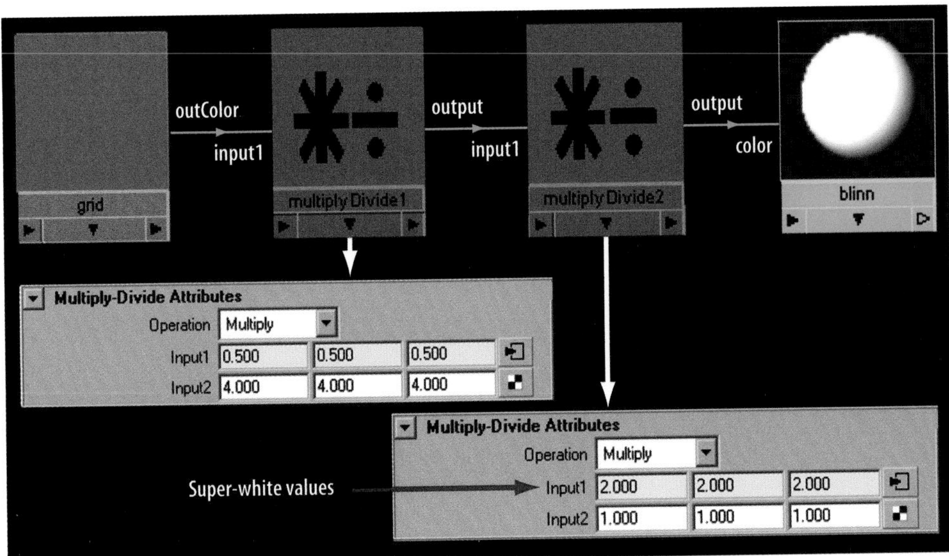

Figure 6.27 A shading network designed to test super-white values. This network is included on the CD as `superwhite.ma`.

To view the custom shading network, follow these steps:

1. Open the `superwhite.ma` file from the CD. Open the Hypershade window.
2. Switch to the Utilities tab. MMB-drag the multiplyDivide1 node into the work area.
3. With the multiplyDivide1node selected, click the Input And Output Connections button. The network becomes visible.

Note: Maya supports high-dynamic range (HDR) image formats, which are able to store super-white values. See Chapter 13 for details.

Note: The term *super-white* was coined to describe the disparity between the standard definition of video white (100 IRE units in YUV color space) and the RGB color space used by Maya and other digital-imaging programs. Basically, Maya creates whites that are 9 percent above the color range that a television can actually display. For more details on color space and monitor calibration, see Chapter 1. For a discussion of 8-bit versus 16-bit rendering, see Chapter 10.

Clamping Values

The Clamp utility is designed to keep a value within a particular range. If a value is too low or too high, it "clamps" it. As an example, Table 6.2 shows what happens to inputR values if MinR is set to 0.3 and MaxR is set to 1.0.

Table 6.2 Clamped Output Values Resulting from Different Input Values

inputR	0	0.2	0.8	1.1	4.5	9.0
outputR	0.3	0.3	0.8	1.0	1.0	1.0

In this example, if the inputR value is less than 0.3, the outputR value is 0.3. If inputR is greater than 1.0, outputR is 1.0. If inputR is between 0.3 and 1.0, outputR is the same value. The Clamp utility has three inputs and three output channels (inputR, inputG, inputB, outputR, outputG, and outputB); you can connect single attributes to any of these. Otherwise, you can connect vector attributes directly to Input or Output. In a similar fashion, Min and Max, which set the clamp range, are vector attributes that carry three channels each (minR, minG, minB, maxR, maxG, and maxB). You can enter negative or positive values into the Min and Max fields.

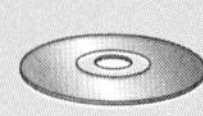

Note: For an example of the Clamp utility used to drive a character bicep, see Section 6.1 of the `Additional_Techniques.pdf` file on the CD. For an example of the Clamp utility used to create disco ball glitter, see Chapter 7.

Reading Surface Luminance

During a render, the Surface Luminance utility automatically reads the luminance of every single rendered point on the surface assigned to a material that is part of the same shading network. That is, the utility can determine the total amount of light a point on a polygon face receives and outputs a value from 0 to 1 that represents this.

As an example, in Figure 6.28, a custom crosshatch material is applied to a medallion model. The crosshatch pattern is generated by a Ramp texture and a Surface Luminance utility.

The outValue of a surfaceLuminance node is connected to the colorEntryList[0].position of a ramp texture node. The colorEntryList[*n*].position attribute controls the vertical position of a color handle in a ramp texture. In this case, the surfaceLuminance node drives the black color handle up and down the ramp based on how much light a surface point receives. If a surface point receives the maximum amount of light, the outValue of the surfaceLuminance node is 1, which forces the black handle up to the top of the ramp (leaving the entire ramp field white). If a surface point receives a little light, the outValue is a lower value, which allows the black handle to stay low, thus creating a mix of black and white within the ramp color field.

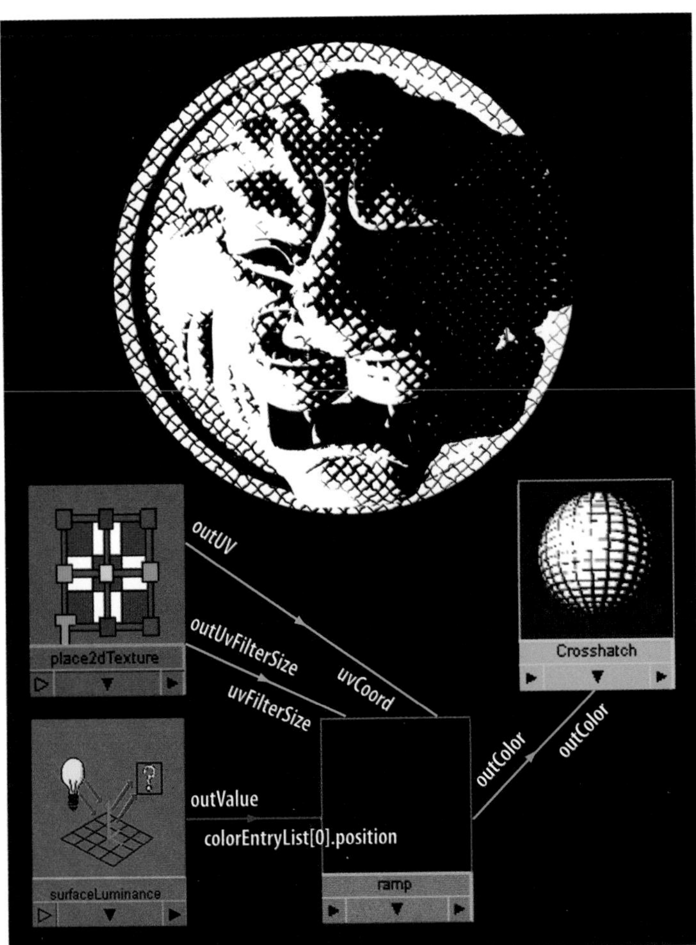

Figure 6.28 A crosshatch material is created with a standard Ramp texture and a Surface Luminance utility. This material is included on the CD as `crosshatch.ma`. A QuickTime movie is included as `crosshatch.mov`.

The ramp's Type attribute is set to UV Ramp; this allows the pattern to repeat on the surface vertically and horizontally. The ramp's Interpolation attribute is set to None, giving the rendered lines a hard edge. The ramp's Noise attribute is set to 0.1 and Noise Freq is set to 0.05 in order to give the lines some squiggle. The ramp node has a standard place2dTexture node with a Repeat UV set to 25, 25. Higher repeat values will produce finer lines. The place2dTexture node also has its Rotate Frame set to 45 in order to angle the pattern. Last, the outColor of the ramp node is connected to the outColor of a surfaceShader material node, which is assigned to the medallion.

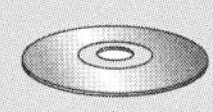

Note: For an additional application of the Surface Luminance utility, see Section 6.2 of the `Additional_Techniques.pdf` file on the CD. In Section 6.2, a stylized metal is created with super-white values.

Chapter Tutorial: Creating a Custom Paint Material

In this tutorial, you will create a custom material that transforms a photo into a stylized painting (see Figure 6.29). You will use the Smear, Remap Hsv, and Contrast utilities.

Figure 6.29 (Left) A digital photo. (Right) The same photo after the application of a custom paint material.

1. Create a new Maya scene. Open the Hypershade window.
2. MMB-drag a new Layered Texture utility (located in the Other Textures section of the Create Maya Nodes menu) into the work area.
3. MMB-drag two Remap Hsv utilities (located in the Color Utilities section of the Create Maya Nodes menu). Place them to the left on the layeredTexture node. Use Figure 6.30 as a reference. Rename the top remapHsv node **remapHsvA.** Rename the bottom remapHsv node **remapHsvB.**
4. Connect the outColor of remapHsvA to inputs[1].color of the layeredTexture node. (For a review of how to create custom connections, refer to the beginning of this chapter.)
5. Connect the outColor of the remapHsvB to inputs[0].color of the layeredTexture node.

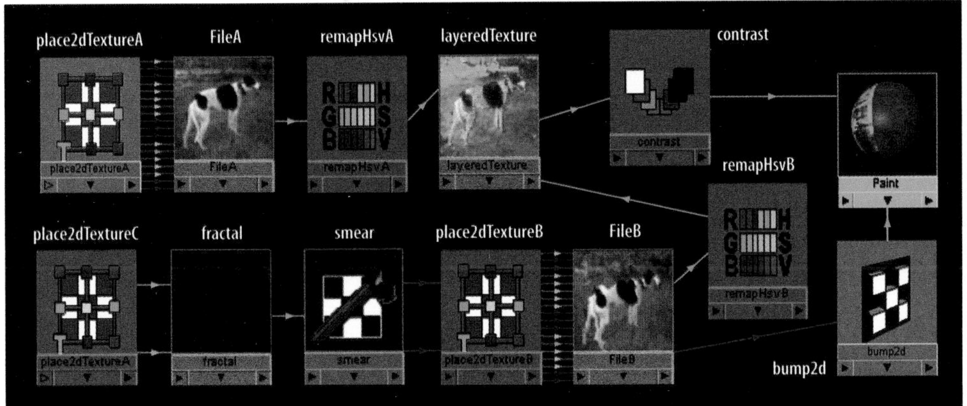

Figure 6.30 The shading network of the custom paint material

6. Select remapHsvA and open its Attribute Editor tab. Click the Color checkered Map button and select a File texture from the Create Render Node window. A place2dTexture node is automatically created along with a file texture node. Rename this place2dTexture node **place2dTextureA**. Rename the file node **FileA**.
7. Select remapHsvB and open its Attribute Editor tab. Click the Color checkered Map button and select a File texture from the Create Render Node window. A second place2dTexture is automatically created along with a second file texture node. Rename the new place2dTexture node **place2dTextureB**. Rename the new file node **FileB**.
8. Select FileA and open its Attribute Editor tab. Click the File Browse button beside Image Name and choose `greyhound.tif` from the Chapter 6 textures folder on the CD.
9. Select FileB and open its Attribute Editor tab. Click the File Browse button beside Image Name and choose `greyhound.tif` from the Chapter 6 textures folder on the CD.
10. MMB-drag a Smear utility (located in the Color Utilities section of the Create Maya Nodes menu) into the work area. Place it to the left of place2dTextureB.
11. Connect the outU of the smear node to the offsetU of place2dTextureB. Connect the outV of the smear node to the offsetV of place2dTextureB.
12. Select the smear node and open its Attribute Editor tab. Click the In Rgb checkered Map button and choose a Fractal texture from the Create Render Node window. A new place2dTexture node is automatically created. Name this latest place2dTexture node **place2dTextureC**.
13. Select the fractal node and open its Attribute Editor tab. Change the Amplitude attribute to 0.7 and the Threshold attribute to 0.2. This will wash out the

fractal pattern and reduce the contrast. If the fractal node is left with default values, the distortion created by the smear node will be extremely intense and the greyhound bitmap will no longer be recognizable. Move the Color Gain attribute slider (located in the Color Balance section) until it's barely above black. This will also reduce the intensity of the distortion. Try different positions on the Color Gain slider. Small changes will produce greatly different results.

14. Select place2dTextureC and open its Attribute Editor tab. Change the Repeat UV attribute to 0.6, 0.6. When the Repeat UV value is reduced, the blobs with the Fractal become larger; this, in turn, creates larger waves in the smear node's distortion. Try different Repeat UV values to see different variations of the effect.

15. Select remapHsvA and open its Attribute Editor tab. Change the Hue, Saturation, and Value gradients to roughly match the left side of Figure 6.31. To move points on a gradient, select the little circles and LMB-drag. To insert new points, click inside the dark gray area of each gradient. To delete a point, click the × box below it. These adjustments are shifting the hue, saturation, and value of the undistorted greyhound bitmap.

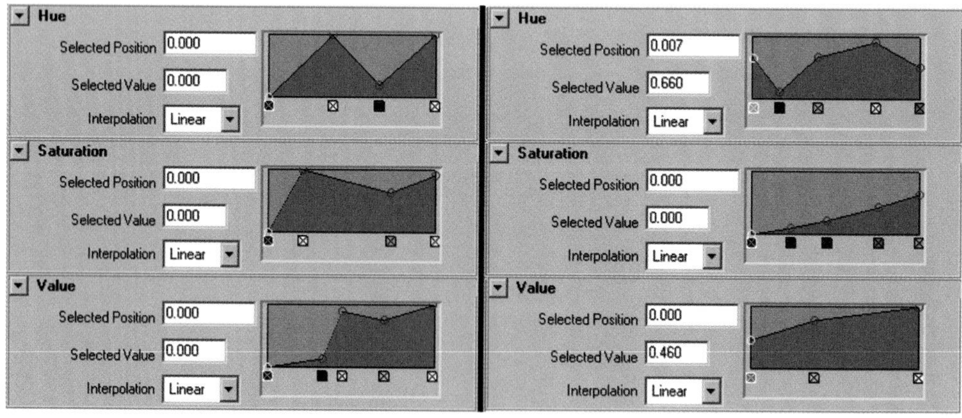

Figure 6.31 (Left) The gradients of the remapHsvA node. (Right) The gradients of the remapHsvB node.

16. Select remapHsvB and open its Attribute Editor tab. Change the Hue, Saturation, and Value gradients to roughly match the right side of Figure 6.31. These adjustments are shifting the hue, saturation, and value of the distorted greyhound bitmap.

17. Select the layeredTexture node and open its Attribute Editor tab. Click the leftmost purple box. This displays the options for remapHsvB. Change the Alpha attribute to 0.5. This allows a 50-50 mix between the remapHsvA and remapHsvB nodes. (The Blend Mode attribute should be set to Over.)

18. MMB-drag a Contrast utility (located in the Color Utilities section of the Create Maya Nodes menu) into the work area. Place it to the right of the layeredTexture node. Connect the outColor of the layeredTexture node to the value of the contrast node.
19. MMB-drag a new Blinn material into the work area. Place it to the right of the contrast node. Connect the outValue of the contrast node to the color of the blinn node. Select the contrast node and open its Attribute Editor tab. Change the Contrast attribute to 1.5, 1.5, 1.5 and the Bias attribute to 0.7, 0.7, 0.5. This adjusts the contrast of the layeredTexture node. Try different numbers to see different results.
20. Select place2dTextureB and open its Attribute Editor tab. Change the Translate Frame attribute to 0, 0.1. This raises the FileB up a tiny amount in the V direction, which counteracts the downward pull of the smear node.
21. MMB-drag a Bump 2D utility (located in the General Utilities section of the Create Maya Nodes menu) into the work area. Connect outAlpha of FileB to the bumpValue of the bump2d node. Connect outNormal of the bump2d to normalCamera of the blinn node. Since outNormal is not a default attribute of a Blinn material, you will have to use the Connection Editor. Select the bump2d node and open its Attribute Editor tab. Change the Bump Depth value to 0.3. This bump mapping will give the smear distortion a sense of thickness.
22. The custom paint material is complete! Assign the blinn material node to a primitive NURBS plane; add a directional, point, or spot light and render out a test. It should look similar to Figure 6.29. If you get stuck, a finished version of the material is saved as `paint.ma` in the Chapter 6 scene folder on the CD.

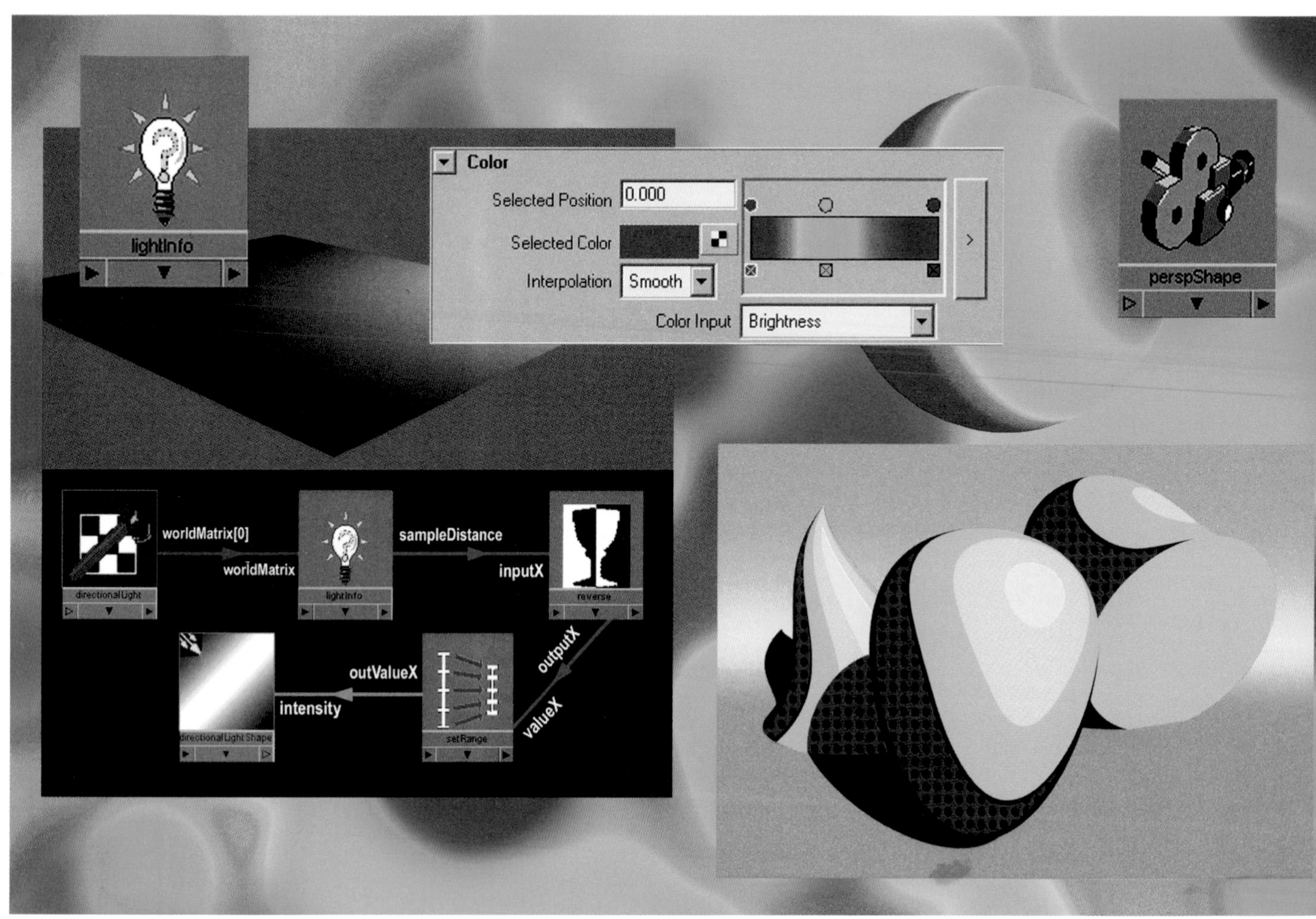

lightInfo
Color
Selected Position
0.000
Selected Color
Interpolation
Smooth
Color Input
Brightness
perspShape
worldMatrix[0]
worldMatrix
directionalLight
lightInfo
sampleDistance
inputX
reverse
outputX
valueX
outValueX
intensity
directionalLightShape
setRange

Automating a Scene with Sampler Nodes

Sampler utilities can automate a render. They can evaluate every surface point for every frame and return unique values that other nodes can use. At the same time, you can connect cameras, lights, and geometry for unique shading networks. Along similar lines, the Studio Clear Coat plug-in utility creates surface qualities unavailable to standard materials.

7

Chapter Contents

Review of the Ramp Shader material and coordinate spaces
Practical applications of sampler utilities
Review of software-rendered particles
Connecting materials to nonmaterial nodes
Creating shading networks with multiple materials
The unique functionality of the Studio Clear Coat plug-in utility

Employing Samplers

The Sampler Info, Light Info, Particle Sampler, and Distance Between utilities can all be described as samplers. They sample surface points, object transforms, or particle transforms automatically throughout the duration of an animation. You can find the Sampler Info, Light Info, and Distance Between utilities in the General Utilities section of the Create Maya Nodes menu in the Hypershade window. You can find the Particle Sampler utility in the Particle Utilities section. Before I discuss the Sampler Info or Light Info utilities, however, a look at the Ramp Shader material and a review of coordinate space is warranted.

A Review of the Ramp Shader Material

The Ramp Shader material has a Color Input attribute that has Light Angle, Facing Angle, Brightness, and Normalized Brightness options (see Figure 7.1).

Figure 7.1 (Left) The Selected Color gradient and Color Input attribute of a Ramp Shader material. (Right) The resulting material assigned to a primitive sphere lit from screen right. To see a larger version of the gradient, click the large button to the gradient's right. This scene is included on the CD as `ramp_shader.ma`.

The Color Input attribute allows the Ramp Shader to sample different points along the Selected Color gradient based on feedback from the environment. With Light Angle, the material compares the angle of the surface normal to the direction of the light. If the angle between the two is small, a high value is returned and the right side of the gradient is sampled. If the angle between the two is large, a small value is returned and the left side of the gradient is sampled. On a technical level, the surface normal vector and the light direction vector are put through a dot product calculation, producing the cosine of the angle between the two vectors. For a deeper discussion on vectors and vector math, see Chapter 8.

This technique is also used for the Facing Angle option, whereby the angle of the surface normal is compared to the camera direction. The Brightness option, on the other hand, calculates the luminous intensity of a surface point. If the surface receives the maximum amount of light, the right side of the gradient is sampled. If the surface receives a moderate amount of light, the middle of the gradient is sampled. The gradient runs 0 to 1 from left to right. The Light Angle, Facing Angle, and Brightness calculations are normalized to fit to that scale.

The disadvantage of the Ramp Shader is its inflexibility. Although colors can be changed on the Selected Color gradient, the Facing Angle, Light Angle, and Brightness calculations cannot be fine-tuned. Sampler Info, Light Info, and Surface Luminance utilities solve this problem by functioning as separate nodes. The Sampler Info utility replaces the Facing Angle option. The Light Info utility replaces the Light Angle option. The Surface Luminance utility, as detailed in the previous chapter, replaces the Brightness option. Although the Normalized Brightness option normalizes all the light intensities in the scene, its basic function is identical to Brightness and can be replicated with the Surface Luminance utility in a custom shading network. Most important, the Sampler Info, Light Info, and Surface Luminance utilities provide a wide array of supplementary attributes.

Coordinate Space Refresher

In general, four coordinate spaces are used in 3D software—object, world, camera, and screen. The term *coordinate space* simply signifies a system that uses coordinates to establish a position. For a surface to be rendered, it must pass through the following spaces in the following order:

Object space A polygon surface is defined by the position of its vertices relative to its center. By default, the center is at 0, 0, 0 in object space (sometimes called model space). A NURBS spline has its origin point at 0, 0, 0 in object space. The axes of a surface in object space are rotated with the surface.

World space World space represents the virtual "world" in which the animator manipulates objects. A surface is moved, rotated, and scaled in this space. To do this, the vertex positions defined in object space must be converted to positions in world space through a world matrix. A matrix is a table of values, generally laid out in rows and columns.

Camera space World space must be transformed into camera space (sometimes called view space) in order to appear as if it is viewed from a particular position. In Maya's camera space, the camera is at 0, 0, 0 with an "up" vector of 0, 1, 0 (positive Y) while looking down the negative Z axis.

Screen space Three-dimensional camera space must be "flattened" so that it can be seen in 2D screen space on a monitor.

In addition, Maya uses local space, parametric space, and raster space. Local space (sometimes called parent space) is similar to object space, but uses the axes and origin of a parent node. This is feasible due to Maya's DAG node system. (See the section "A Transform and Shape Node Refresher" later in this chapter.)

To determine the color of a particular pixel when rendering a surface assigned to a material that uses a texture map, the renderer compares the parametric spaces of both the texture and the surface. Texture and surface parametric spaces are commonly referred to as UV texture space. For more information on UVs and UV texture space, see Chapter 9.

Note: A parametric surface is one that has undergone parameterization. In general terms, parameterization is the mapping of a surface to a second surface or domain. For example, when representing the spherical earth on a rectangular map, specific features of the earth are drawn at specific positions on the map. Depending on the style of parameterization, distortions that affect either feature angles or feature areas occur. (For instance, on common Mercator-style maps, Greenland is unnaturally large.) For more information on surface parameterization, see Chapter 9.

Raster space is a coordinate system used to calculate individual pixel locations on a screen. In addition, the mental ray renderer uses internal space, which relates surface points and vectors to mental ray shaders. Object, world, and camera spaces within Maya are based on a "right-handed" Cartesian space.

Using the Sampler Info Utility

The Sampler Info utility carries the Facing Ratio attribute, which is identical to the Facing Angle option of the Ramp Shader material. The Sampler Info utility also offers such attributes as Ray Direction and Normal Camera. Two examples of its use follow.

Applying Car Paint

Many surfaces, including clear-coat car paints, produce Fresnel reflections (see Chapter 4). In this situation, the intensity of a reflection or specular highlight varies with the angle of view. For instance, at the top of Figure 7.2, the sky reflection is more intense along the roof and hood of the car than it is along the doors and fenders. To create this effect, you can use the Facing Ratio attribute of a Sampler Info utility. At the bottom of Figure 7.2, a polygon car is lit with default lighting. The persp camera's Background Color attribute is set to a light blue. Raytracing is checked in the Render Settings window so that the background color is picked up as a reflection. The car body is assigned to a Blinn material named CarPaint. CarPaint's Color is set to black. CarPaint's Diffuse and Eccentricity are set to 0. Reflectivity is set to 0.3. Specular Roll Off is increased to an artificially high value of 5. These settings leave the paint a deep black with highlights derived solely from reflections.

As for the custom shading network, the facingRatio of the samplerInfo node is connected to the inputValue of a remapValue node. The outValue of the remapValue node is connected to the specularColorR, specularColorG, and specularColorB of the CarPaint node. If a surface point faces away from the camera (such as one on the top of the hood), it receives a low facingRatio value. This low value is increased, however, by the reversed Value gradient slope of the remapValue node. Conversely, if the facingRatio is high (from the door or fender), the gradient lowers it. Thus, the top of the hood receives the most reflection and the doors and fenders receive the least. Additional handles are inserted into the Value gradient in order to increase the rapidity of the reflection falloff. The handles are all set to Spline in order that the gradient take on a smooth shape. In this case, the Color gradient of the remapValue node is not used at all. The shading network works equally well with the Maya Software or mental ray renderer. The Studio Clear Coat plug-in also addresses the Fresnel nature of car paint and is discussed at the end of this chapter.

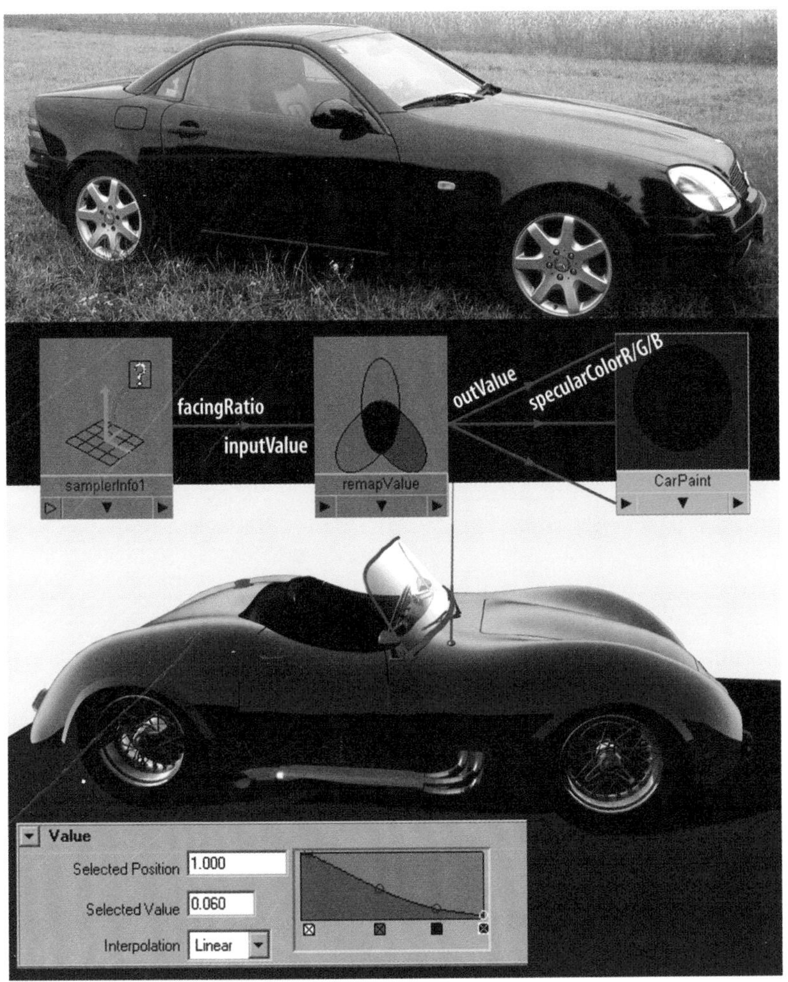

Figure 7.2 (Top) A car shows signs of Fresnel reflections. (Bottom) A reflection changes intensity over a surface with the aid of a Sampler Info utility. A simplified version of this scene is included on the CD as `paint.ma`.

Creating Disco Ball Glitter

In Figure 7.3, a disco ball is given a glittery reflection. A Sampler Info utility controls the location of the glitter. The disco ball is composed of two polygon primitive spheres. The inner sphere is animated to spin. The outer sphere is static. Both spheres are faceted. (Choose Normals > Set To Face from the Polygons menu set to create the faceted effect.) The inner sphere is assigned to a Blinn material named InnerBlinn with the Color set to black and an Env Chrome texture mapped to the Reflected Color attribute. (See Chapter 5 for a discussion of environment textures.) The outer sphere is assigned to a second Blinn named OuterBlinn with a custom shading network. This network starts with the outColor of a mountain texture node connected to the colorIfTrue of a condition node. (See Chapter 8 for a description of the Condition utility.)

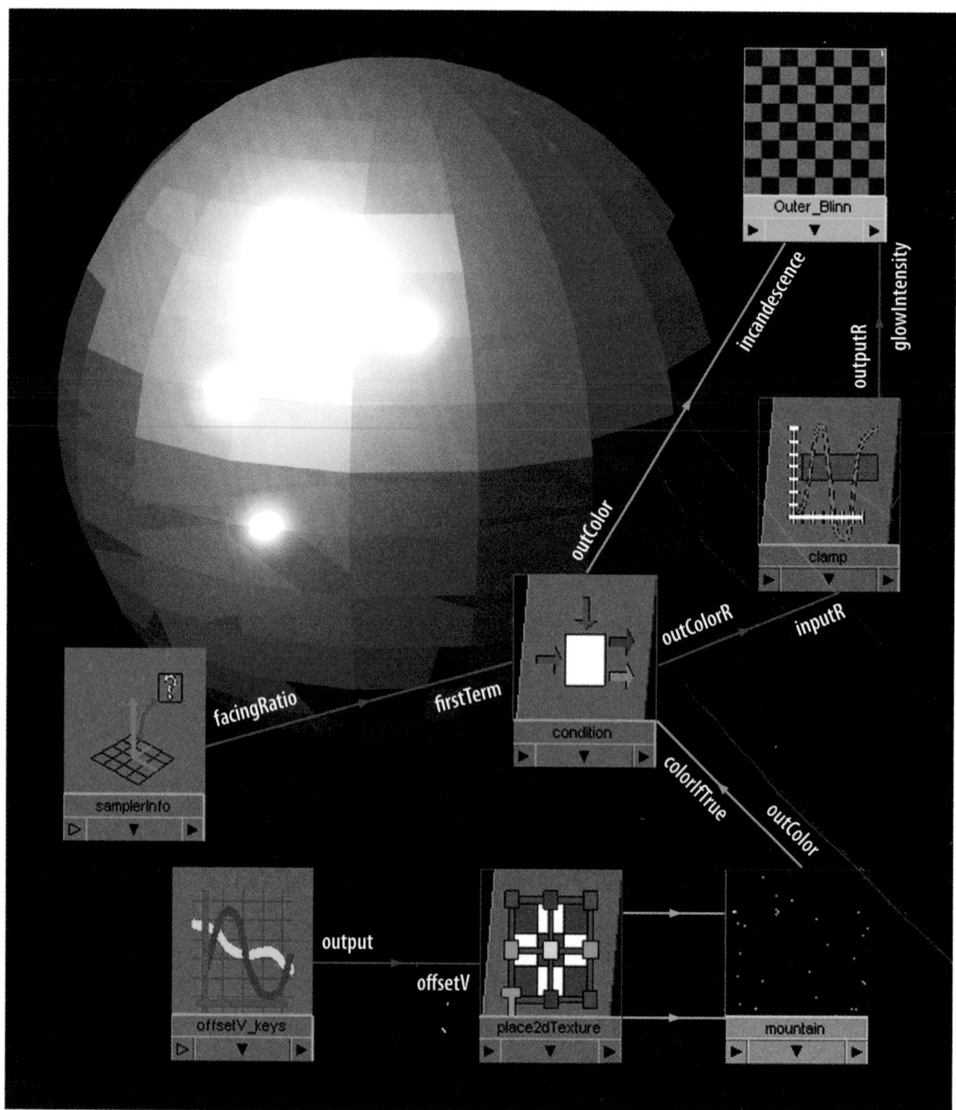

Figure 7.3 The glitter of a disco ball is created with the help of a Sampler Info utility. This scene is included on the CD as `discoball.ma`. A QuickTime movie is included as `discoball.mov`.

The Mountain texture has the following custom settings:

Snow Color: Black

Rock Color: White

Amplitude: 0.6

Snow Roughness: 0

Rock Roughness: 0

Snow Altitude: 1

Depth Max: 2.3

The net effect of these settings is a texture with a few white specks on a black background. The Offset V of the mountain's place2dTexture node is animated to run from 0 to 15. This rapidly changes the pattern of specks as the Timeline moves forward. The facingRatio of a samplerInfo node is connected to the firstTerm of the condition node. The outColorR of the condition node is connected to the inputR of a clamp node. The outputR of the clamp node is connected to the glowIntensity of OuterBlinn. Last, the outColor of the condition node is also connected to the incandescence of OuterBlinn.

The condition node, with the help of the samplerInfo node, tests whether or not surface normals of the outer sphere point toward the camera. If they do, they receive incandescent white specks from the mountain texture node. If they don't, they are unaffected by the condition node (the condition node's Color If False attribute is left at 0, 0, 0). Since the outputR of the clamp node is also connected to the glowIntensity of OuterBlinn, a post-process glow is placed wherever the incandescent white specks appear. The Hide Source attribute of the OuterBlinn is checked on; therefore, the glow and not the surface of OuterBlinn is rendered. The final result is a disco ball that produces small, intense bits of "reflected" light on the part that faces the camera.

Note: For an example of the Sampler Info utility used to create simulated iridescence, see section 7.1 of the `Additional_Techniques.pdf` file on the CD.

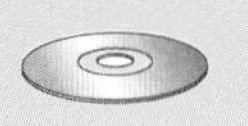

Using the Light Info Utility

The Light Info utility retrieves directional and positional information from a light connected to it. The utility can function like the Light Angle option of the Ramp Shader material, but is more flexible. Before showing a few examples, however, a review of transform nodes, shape nodes, DAG objects, and instanced attributes is worth a closer look.

A Transform and Shape Node Refresher

In Maya, cameras, lights, and surfaces are represented by two nodes: a transform node and a shape node. For example, *spotlight* is a transform node that carries all the light's transform information (Translate, Rotate, Scale), and *spotLightShape* is a shape node that possesses all the nontransform light attributes (Intensity, Cone Angle, and so on). As for geometry, *nurbsSphere* is the transform node, and *nurbsSphereShape* is the shape node.

Transform and shape nodes are also known as DAG objects. DAG (Directed Acyclic Graph) is a hierarchical system in which objects are defined relative to the transformations of their parent objects. *Acyclic* is a graph theory term that declares that the graph is not a closed loop. At the same time, Maya uses a dependency graph system, which simply supports a collection of nodes connected together. Technically, DAG objects are dependency graph nodes. However, not all dependency graph nodes are DAG objects since dependency graph nodes can be cyclic and do not need the parent/child relationship.

By default, there is no visible connection between a transform node and its corresponding shape node. However, every shape node must have one transform node as a parent. A transform node cannot have more than one shape node as a child, although it can have multiple transform nodes as children. A shape node is considered a "leaf level" node and cannot have any node as a child.

The worldMatrix[0] attribute, utilized by many of the example shading networks in this book, includes the [0] to indicate the index position within an array that stores the attribute. World Matrix is an "instanced attribute," whereby it can be used at different positions within a DAG hierarchy. The [*n*] appears automatically after a World Matrix attribute is connected in the Hypershade window. For more detailed information on the World Matrix attribute, see Chapter 8.

Creating Falloff for Directional and Ambient Lights

Directional and ambient lights do not decay naturally, nor do they possess a Decay Rate attribute. However, you can employ a Light Info, Reverse, and Set Range utility to overcome this. For example, in Figure 7.4 a directional light has an extremely short throw despite its proximity to a nearby primitive plane.

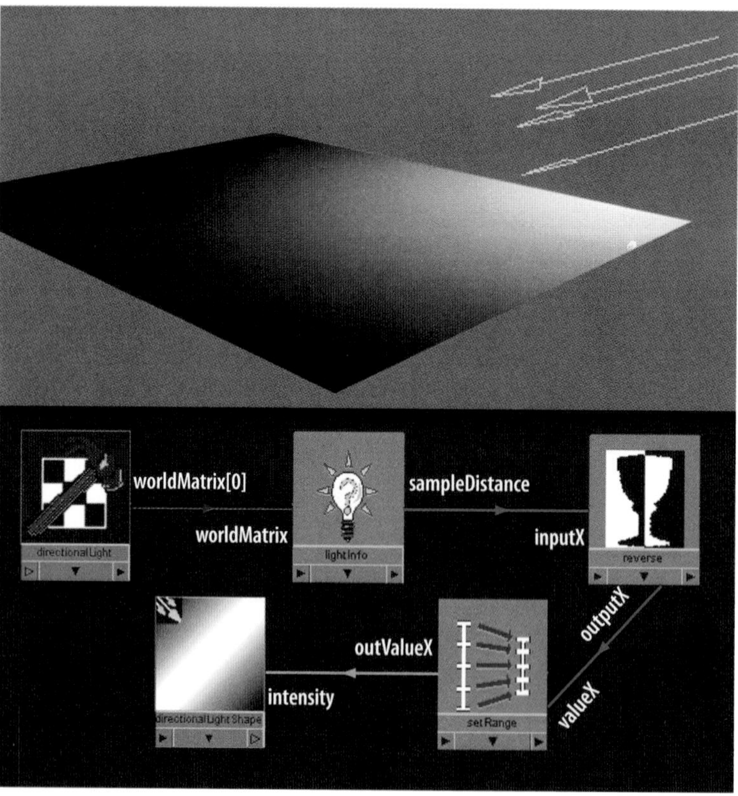

Figure 7.4 A directional light is given decay with a Light Info utility. This scene is included on the CD as `directional_decay.ma`.

For this to work, the worldMatrix[0] of the light's transform node is connected to the worldMatrix of a lightInfo node. The sampleDistance of the lightInfo node is connected to the inputX of a reverse node. The Sample Distance attribute returns a value that represents the distance from the connected light to the surface point being rendered. The outputX of the reverse node is connected to the valueX of a setRange node, which has its Max X attribute set to 10 and its Old Min X attribute set to –5. Last, the outValueX of the setRange node is connected to the intensity of the light's shape node. Thus, if a surface point is a great distance from the light's origin, the Intensity attribute receives a low value. If the surface point is close, it receives a high value. The following math occurs:

```
intensity = (((1 - sampleDistance)  + 5) / 5) * 10
```

If the Sample Distance value is greater than 6 units, the outValueX value is negative and is thus interpreted as 0 by the light. This network functions equally well for ambient lights. For more information of the Set Range utility, see Chapter 8.

Note: You can give a Maya light a negative Intensity value, such as –1. This causes the light to negate other lights in the scene. Wherever the negative light strikes an object, it reduces the net effect of other lights in proportion to its Intensity. That said, this does not happen if the light is connected to a shading network similar to the one described in this section. Instead, the negative Intensity value is essentially clamped to 0.

Making Objects Glow in the Dark

In Figure 7.5, a NURBS squid begins to glow once a light has passed it by. This trait, known as phosphorescence, is normally caused by the emission of light following the removal of a radiation source. In this reproduction, a standard spot light serves as the "radiation." The spot light's Intensity attribute is set to 15 and its Decay Rate is switched to Linear, forcing the light to have a fairly short throw.

The squid is assigned to a shading network that starts with a Light Info utility. The worldMatrix[0] of the spotLightShape node is connected to the worldMatrix of a lightInfo node. The sampleDistance of the lightInfo node is connected to the input1X of a multiplyDivide node. The outputX of the multiplyDivide node is connected to the glowIntensity of a blinn material node. The Input2X of the multiplyDivide node is set to 1000, and the Operation attribute is set to Divide. Dividing by a large number allows the glow of the blinn node to increase as the light moves farther away but will never allow the glow value to become excessively large.

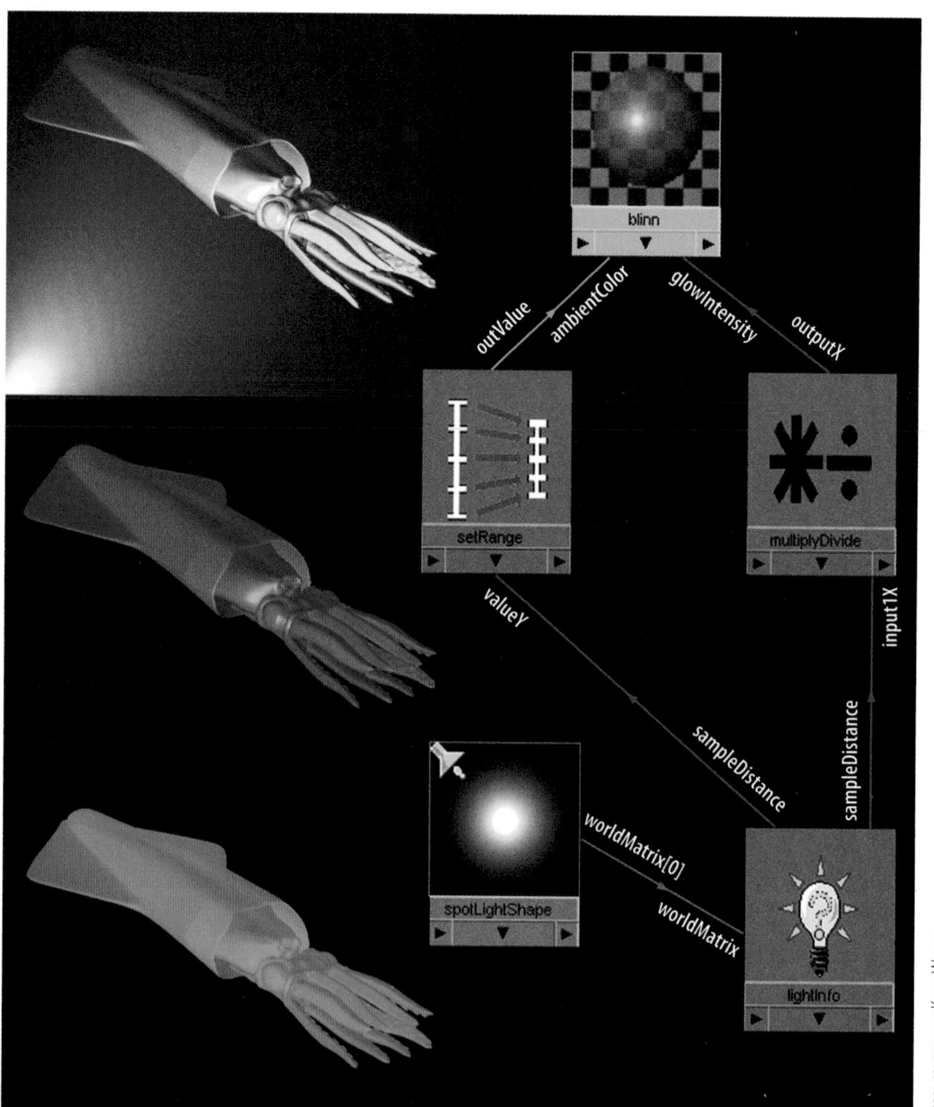

Figure 7.5 A Light Info utility allows a squid to glow when a spot light is withdrawn from its presence. A simplified version of this scene is included on the CD as `glow.ma`. A QuickTime movie is included as `glow.mov`.

The sampleDistance of the lightInfo node is also connected to the valueY of a setRange node (see Chapter 8 for a description of the Set Range utility). The outValue of the setRange node is connected to the ambientColor of the blinn node. This increases the amount of greenish ambience as the light gets farther away. The setRange Old Max attribute is set to 100, 100, 100 and the Max attribute is set to 0, 2, 0. Hence, if the light is 0 units from the squid, the Ambient Color is 0, 0, 0. If the light is only 50 units from the squid, the Ambient Color is 0, 1, 0. If the light is 100 units from the squid, the Ambient Color is 0, 2, 0.

Deriving Color from a Spatial Vector

In a second example of the Light Info utility, a camera is connected in order to retrieve world space directional information. This information is then used to control the color of an "in camera" display. In Figure 7.6, the worldMatrix[0] of the default camera's perspShape node is connected to the worldMatrix of a lightInfo node. The camera's worldMatrix[0] is also connected to the matrix of a vectorProduct node. The lightDirection of the lightInfo node is connected to the input1 of the vectorProduct node as well.

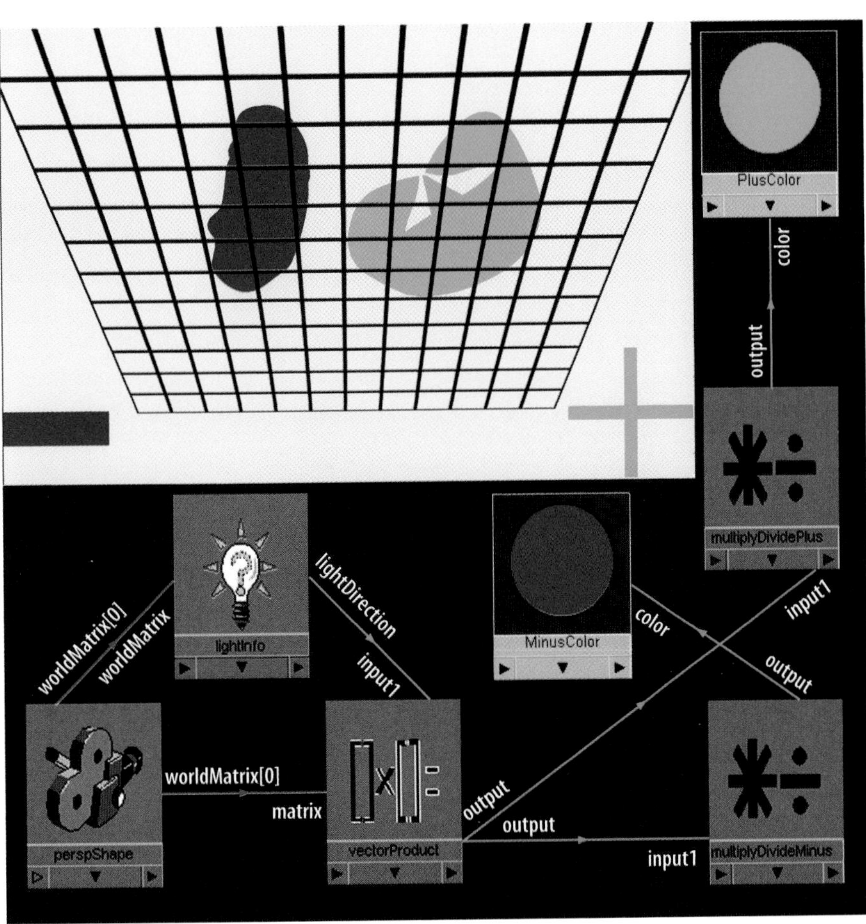

Figure 7.6 An "in camera" display that indicates which direction a camera is pointing is created with a Light Info utility. This scene is included on the CD as `camera_display.ma`. A QuickTime movie is included as `camera_display.mov`.

The Vector Product utility is designed to perform mathematical operations on two vectors. In addition, it can multiply a vector by a matrix. This function allows the Vector Product utility to convert a vector in one coordinate space to a second coordinate space. In this case, the vectorProduct node's Operation attribute is set to Vector

Matrix Product, which undertakes this task. Since the worldMatrix[0] of the camera is used as the input matrix, the output of the vectorProduct node is the camera direction vector in world space. The output vector runs between –1, –1, –1 and 1, 1, 1 in X, Y, and Z. (For a deeper discussion on vectors and vector math, see Chapter 7.)

Note: If lightDirection is connected directly to either multiplyDivide node, the network will not function. Instead, the minus sign will remain blue regardless of camera rotation. This indicates that the lightInfo node outputs a 0, 0, 1 vector, which infers that the camera lens is pointing down the negative Z axis with no rotation in X or Y (which is the same as the default state of a new camera).

The output of the vectorProduct node is connected to the input1 attributes of two multiplyDivide nodes. The multiplyDividePlus node has its Input2 set to –1, –1, –1, guaranteeing that it produces a negative value. The multiplyDivideMinus node has its Input2 left at 1, 1, 1. Last, the output of each multiplyDivide node is connected to the outColor of two different surface shader material nodes. The PlusColor material is assigned to a plus sign created as a text primitive. The MinusColor material is assigned to a minus sign. Both signs are placed near the bottom of the camera and parented to the camera itself. As the camera is rotated, the colors of the symbols change in correspondence to the direction the camera points. (If the colors are not visible with Hardware Texturing checked on, you will have to render out a test frame.)

As with the axis display found in Maya's workspace views, red corresponds to X, green corresponds to Y, and blue corresponds to Z. Hence, if the camera points in the positive X direction, the plus sign becomes red. If the camera points in the negative X direction, the minus sign becomes red. Table 7.1 reveals what happens mathematically when the camera is given other rotations.

Table 7.1 Colors resulting from different camera rotations.

Camera rotation	vectorProduct output	MinusColor RGB (output × 1, 1, 1)	PlusColor RGB (output × –1, –1, –1)
0, 0, 0	0, 0, 1	0, 0, 1 (bright blue)	0, 0, 0 (black)
45, –45, 0	–0.5, –0.7, 0.5	0, 0, 0.5 (blue)	0.5, 0.7, 0 (yellow-green)
–90, 0, 0	0, 1, 0	0, 1, 0 (bright green)	0, 0, 0 (black)

Any RGB value less than 0 is clamped to 0 by the renderer (negative color values are rendered black). You can use this coloring technique on any object (as can be seen by the two primitive shapes in the camera's view). In addition, you can connect any object that possesses a World Matrix attribute—such as a camera, light, or NURBS surface—to the Light Info and Vector Product utilities so that its direction can be derived in this fashion.

Using the Particle Sampler Utility

The Particle Sampler utility has the unique ability to graft a UV texture space onto a particle mass. Before I suggest specific applications, however, let's take a quick look at particle texturing.

Particle Refresher

In Maya, particles are either hardware or software rendered. This section focuses on software-rendered particles since they can accept standard materials. The three software-rendered particle types are Blobby Surface, Cloud, and Tube. Their software-rendering capability is symbolized by the "s/w" beside the particle name listed by the Particle Render Type drop-down menu, which is found in the Render Attributes section of the particle shape node Attribute Editor tab (see Figure 7.7). Although Cloud particles are excellent for smoke, Blobby Surface particles can replicate a wide range of liquid and semiliquid materials.

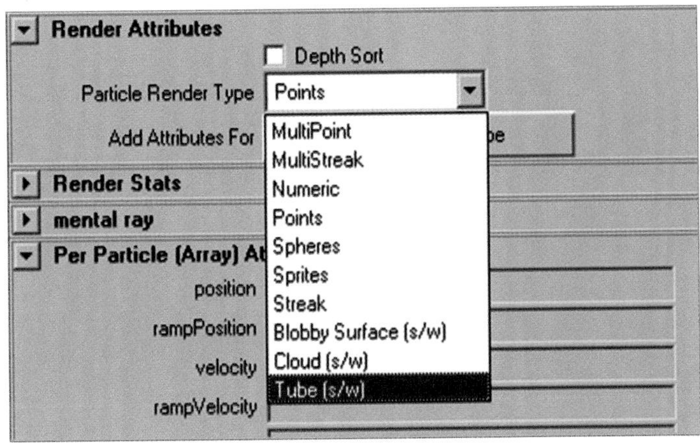

Figure 7.7 The Particle Render Type drop-down menu

By default, Blobby Surface particles derive their color from the lambert1 material via the initialParticleSE (Initial Particle Shading Engine) shading group node. You can assign Blobby Surface particles to Lambert, Blinn, Phong, Phong E, Anisotropic, Layered Shader, and Ramp Shader materials.

Cloud and Tube particles derive shading information from the default particleCloud1 material (see the next section). Cloud and Tube particles cannot be assigned to any other standard material. However, you can assign the particles to a new Particle Cloud or Volume Fog material (found in the Volumetric section of the Create Maya Nodes menu).

Texturing Particles

To apply a texture to a Cloud or Tube particle, you can map the Color or Life Color attribute of a Particle Cloud material. If you map the Color, the texture is applied to each particle but will be oriented toward the camera. For example, in Figure 7.8 a Checker texture with a Repeat UV of 1, 1 is used.

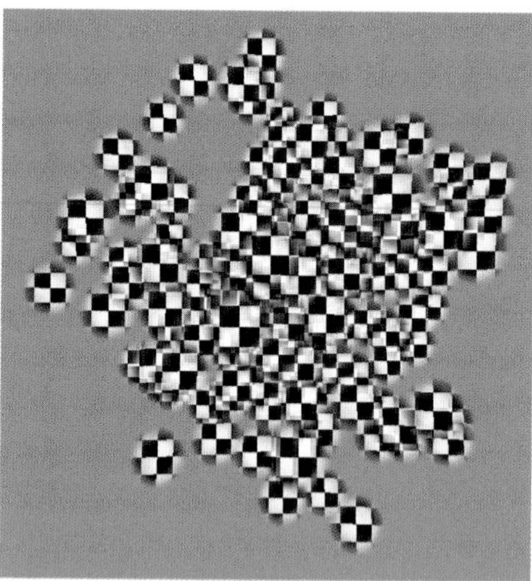

Figure 7.8 A Checker texture material is mapped to the Color attribute of a Particle Cloud material. This scene is included on the CD as `cloud_checker.ma`.

On the other hand, if you map a texture to the Life Color attribute, colors are sampled along the V axis of the texture. To create an example, follow these steps:

1. Switch to the Dynamics menu set. Choose Particles > Create Emitter. Play back the Timeline until the particles are visible.
2. Select the particles. Press Ctrl+A to open the Attribute Editor. Switch to the particleShape1 tab. Scroll down to the Render Attributes section and change Particle Render Type to Cloud (s/w). Click the Current Render Type button and reduce the Radius value so that individual particles are easier to see.
3. Go to the Lifespan Attributes section and change Lifespan Mode to Constant (see Figure 7.9). Change Lifespan to 5 so that the particles live 5 seconds. If Lifespan Mode is set to the default Live Forever option, Life Color cannot use the ramp color information.

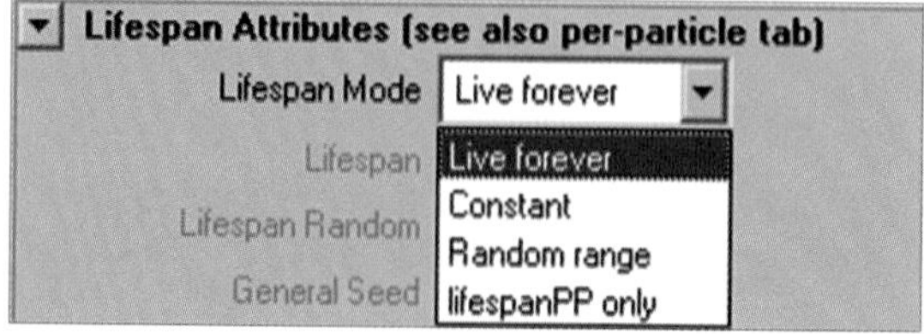

Figure 7.9 The drop-down menu of a particle shape node's Lifespan Mode attribute

4. Open the Hypershade window. Choose the particleCloud1 material and bring up its Attribute Editor tab. Click the checkered Map button beside Life Color and choose a Ramp texture from the Create Render Node window.
5. A ramp node is connected to the particleCloud1 material. However, it is represented by a spherical icon. In addition, a Particle Sampler utility is connected to the ramp. Render a test. Young particles render red (see Figure 7.10). Old particles render blue. An example scene is included as `cloud_ramp.ma` in the Chapter 7 folder on the CD.

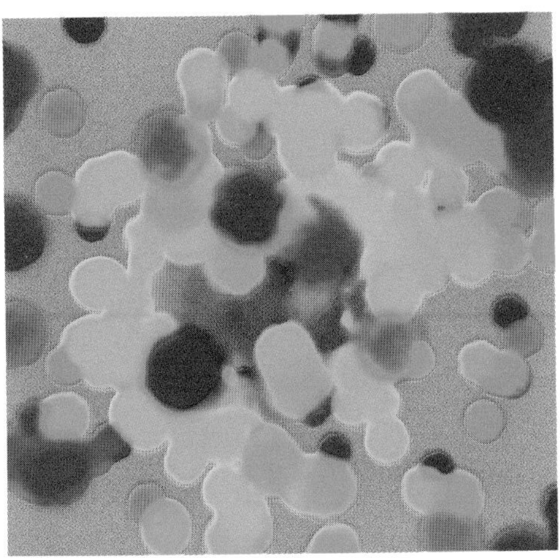

Figure 7.10 A ramp texture is mapped to the Life Color attribute of a Particle Cloud material.

In contrast, a Blobby Surface particle node that is assigned to a material that uses a texture will pick up that texture. Oddly enough, each particle receives the entire texture twice—once for the top and once for the bottom (see Figure 7.11). In addition, the Blobby Surface particles will show bump and transparency maps. The texture will appear even when the Threshold attribute is raised and the particles begin to stick together.

You can prevent each Blobby Surface particle from carrying the complete texture by manually assigning the node to a shading network that uses a Particle Sampler utility. For example, in Figure 7.12 a NURBS plane is used as an Emit From Object particle emitter. The Emitter Type attribute of the emitter is set to Directional. Rate (Particles/Sec) is set to 25. Direction X, Direction Y, and Direction Z are set to 0, 1, 0, respectively. Speed is set to 1. The particleShape's Particle Render Type attribute is set to Blobby Surface with a Radius value of 0.1 and a Threshold value of 0.5. The particleShape's Lifespan Mode attribute is set to Constant with a Lifespan value of 1.

Figure 7.11 One Blobby Surface particle node is assigned to a Phong material with a Checker texture. A second is assigned to a Phong with an iris bitmap. This scene is included on the CD as `particle_eye.ma`.

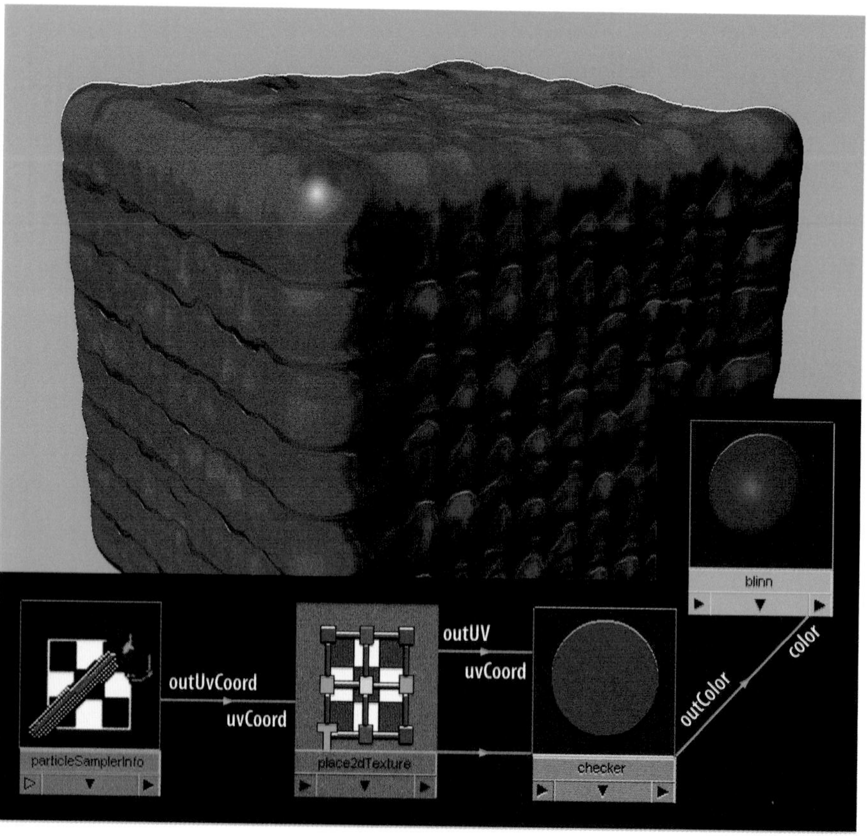

Figure 7.12 A Blobby Surface particle mass picks up the red and blue of a Checker texture with the help of a Particle Sampler utility. This scene is included on the CD as `particle_checker.ma`.

As for the shading network, a red and blue Checker texture is mapped to the Color of a Phong material. The Phong is assigned to the Blobby Surface particle node. The outUvCoord of a particleSamplerInfo node is connected to the uvCoord of the checker's place2dTexture node. (The UV Coord attribute is hidden until you choose Right Display > Show Hidden in the Connection Editor.) This connection fits the UV texture space of the checker node to the particle mass. As with the Life Color attribute of the Particle Cloud material, the texture is sampled at a single point along the V direction during the particle's life. Hence, details in the U direction (left to right on the screen) are lost. The relatively high particle count and a Threshold value of 0.5 turns the blue of the checker texture into thin horizontal lines.

You can correct the U direction smearing with a slight change to the connections. In Figure 7.13, a similar shading network is laid out. This time, instead of a Checker texture, a bitmap of the word *Maya* is loaded into a File texture. The outVCoord of a particleSamplerInfo node is connected directly to the vCoord of the file texture node. The outUCoord attribute, however, is not connected at all. Instead, the worldPositionZ of the particleSamplerInfo node is connected to the input1X of a multplyDivide node. The outputX of multiplyDivide is connected to the uCoord of the file node. Since the particles are born along the Z axis of the world, the worldPositionZ attribute serves as a crude Repeat U tiling control. The Input2X attribute of the multiplyDivide node is set to 0.08, which creates the following math:

```
uCoord = worldPositionZ x 0.08
```

Figure 7.13 Blobby Surface particles display the word *Maya* with the help of a Particle Sampler utility. This scene is included on the CD as `particle_word.ma`. A QuickTime movie is included as `particle_word.mov`.

If a particle is born at the far right of the emitter, it has a Z position of 12. Hence, the uCoord becomes roughly 1, which is the right edge of the *Maya* bitmap. If the Z position is 6, the uCoord becomes roughly 0.5, or the center of the bitmap. This technique works with particles that have a chaotic or random motion (although the texture will be more difficult to recognize and will ultimately repeat). In addition, this technique works when the Blobby Surface particle Threshold value is raised and the particles begin to stick together.

The Particle Sampler utility can also command various per-particle attributes. For a discussion of this feature and the Array Mapper utility, see Chapter 8.

Using the Distance Between Utility

The Distance Between utility does exactly what its name implies. It returns a value that represents the distance between any two objects. You can automatically apply this utility by choosing Create > Measure Tools > Distance Tool and clicking in two different locations in any workspace view. Two locators are placed in the scene, and the distance is measured between them by a Distance Between utility. The distance value is displayed on a line drawn between the two locators. Although this method is convenient, it is possible to manually connect a Distance Between utility to a custom shading network.

For example, in Figure 7.14 the color of two primitive polygon shapes changes from blue to red as they approach each other. In this shading network, the center attribute of ShapeA's transform node is connected to point2 of a distanceBetween node. The center of ShapeB's transform node is connected to point1 of the distanceBetween node (the Translate attribute will not work in this case). The distance attribute of the distanceBetween node is connected to the input1X of a multiplyDivide node. The Input2X attribute of the multiplyDivide node is set to 0.05, guaranteeing that the result will be well below 1 even when the shapes travel a significant distance apart. The outputX of the multiplyDivide node is connected to the inputX of a reverse node. This ensures that the shapes will become redder as they approach each other and not vice versa. Last, the output of the reverse node is connected to the color of a blinn material node. The InputY and InputZ attributes of the reverse node are set to 0.5 since they have no inputs. This creates the green-blue color when the ouputX of the multiplyDivide node, which controls the inputX of the reverse node, provides a low value.

Tying into Nonmaterial Nodes

Custom connections are not limited to materials, textures, and geometry transform nodes. Any node that can be MMB-dragged from the Hypergraph to the Hypershade is fair game. A few examples that employ geometry, cameras, construction history, and default shading nodes follow.

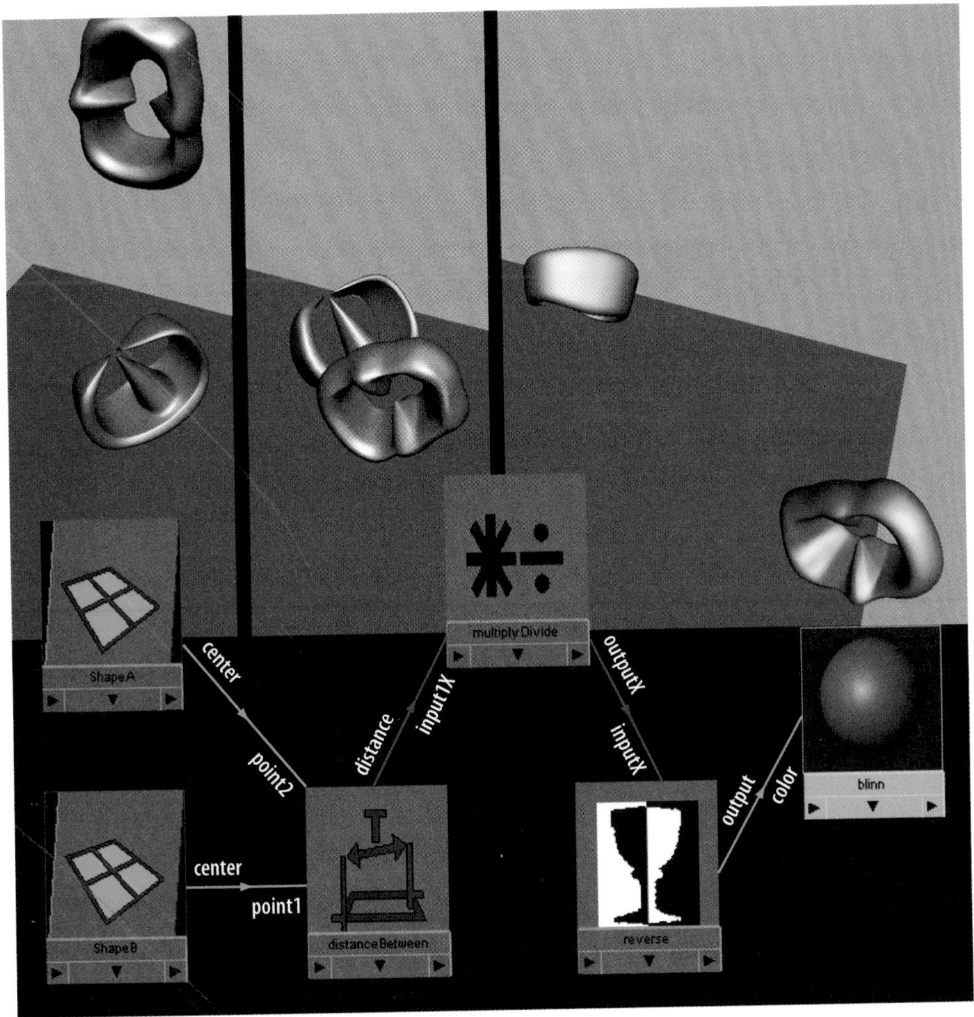

Figure 7.14 The colors of two abstract shapes are controlled by a Distance Between utility. This scene is included on the CD as `distance.ma`. A QuickTime movie is included as `distance.mov`.

Creating Simulated Propeller Spin

A spinning plane propeller is basically a blurred disc. Although the prop is visible with the correct point-of-view or proper frame rate, its shape is generally indistinct. You can emulate a spinning propeller in Maya by having a propeller disc drive its own transparency. For example, in Figure 7.15 a NURBS disc is animated rotating from 0 to 10,000 degrees in Z over a period of 90 frames.

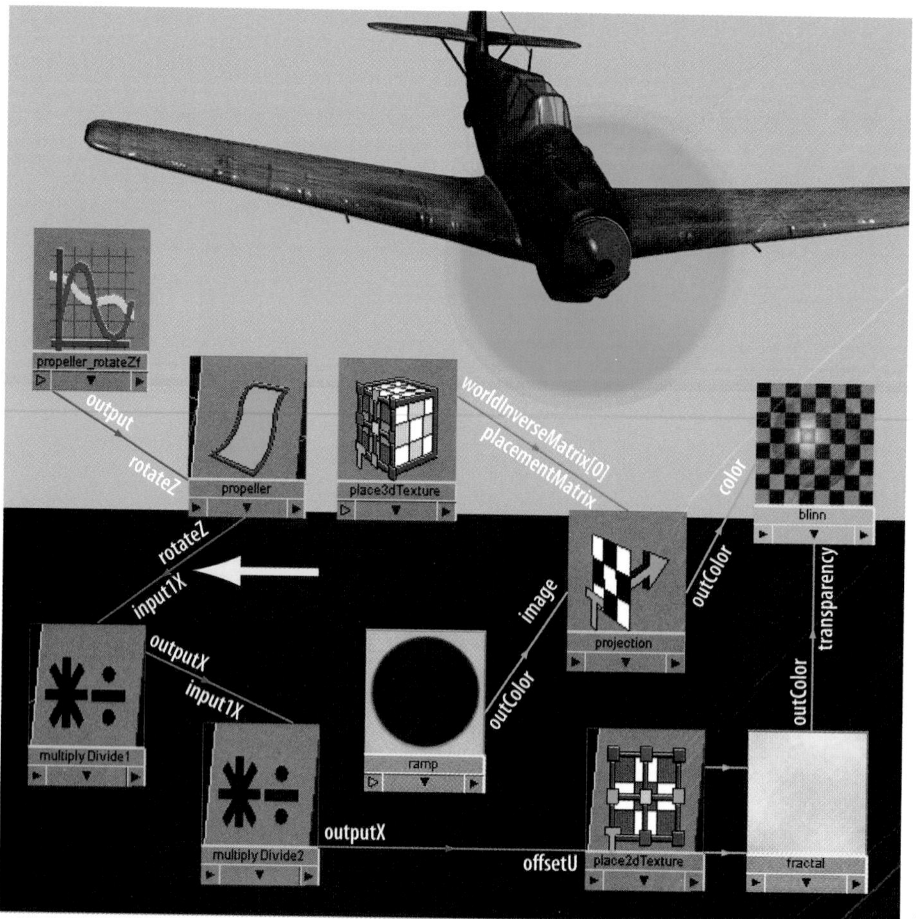

Model courtesy of Jason Martin

Figure 7.15 A NURBS disc serves as a spinning propeller. The opacity flicker is driven by its own geometry. The yellow arrow indicates the point at which Maya inserts a unitConversion node. A simplified version of this scene is included on the CD as `propeller.ma`. A QuickTime movie is included as `propeller.mov`.

The rotateZ of the disc's transform node is connected to the input1X of a multiplyDivide node named multiplyDivide1. The outputX of multiplyDivide1 is connected to the input1X of a second multiplyDivide node named multiplyDivide2. The Input2X of multiplyDivide1 is set to 0.01. The Input2X of multiplyDivide2 is set to 0.005. This sequence converts a potentially large rotation value into an extremely small one. The outputX of multiplyDivide2 is connected to the offsetU of the place2dTexture node belonging to a fractal texture node. Thus, the rotation of the disc automatically pushes the fractal texture node in the U direction. The Repeat UV of the place2dTexture node is set to 0.001, 0.001, which reveals only a small section of the fractal. The custom settings for the fractal texture node are as follows:

Ratio: 0.5

Frequency Ratio: 10

Bias: –0.3

Filter: 5

These adjustments create a softer version of the fractal pattern. The outColor of the fractal node is connected to the transparency of a blinn material node named PropellerColor. As the disc rotates, the fractal moves left, revealing darker and lighter sections. Hence, the propeller disc flickers during the animation. The color of the disc is derived from a circular ramp texture with brown and yellow handles. The ramp is projected onto the disc for a more exact lineup of colors. While this technique might not work for close-ups, it can be used successfully for wider shots and flybys. It also serves as an extremely efficient method of rendering since no motion blur is involved.

Reproducing the Hitchcock Zoom-Dolly

Alfred Hitchcock introduced a famous zoom-dolly camera move in the film *Vertigo* (1958). Steven Spielberg later popularized the same motion in *Jaws* (1978). If a camera zooms out while simultaneously dollying forward, the background distorts over time. This is due to the optical nature of the camera lens. Telephoto lenses (for example, 300 mm) flatten a scene, but wide lenses (for example, 24 mm) give a scene more depth. It's possible to change the focal length of a zoom lens with a twist of the hand (for example, 200 mm to 50 mm).

You can automate the Hitchcock zoom-dolly with custom connections. For example, in Figure 7.16 the transform node of a single-node camera, named HitchCam, is parented to a group node named HitchCamGroup. To view the custom shading network, open `hitchcock.ma` and follow these steps:

1. Open the Hypershade window and switch to the Utilities tab.
2. MMB-drag the multiplyDivide node into the work area.
3. With the multiplyDivide node selected, click the Input And Output Connections button.

HitchCamGroup is animated along the Z axis. HitchCamGroup's translateZ attribute is connected to the input1X of the multiplyDivide node. The outputX of the multiplyDivide node is connected to the focalLength of the camera's shape node, named HitchCamShape. The multiplyDivide node's Operation is set to Multiply, and its Input2X is set to 10. When HitchCamGroup is at its start position of 0, 1, 10, the focalLength of HitchCamShape is 100. When HitchCamGroup is at its end position of 0, 1, 1, the focalLength of HitchCamShape is 10. Scrubbing the Timeline will quickly show the high degree of distortion that happens to the background and foreground objects. An animation curve node—seen at the top of the network—appears because an attribute is keyframed. Even though HitchCamGroup is the parent of HitchCam, there is no visible connection in the Hypershade window.

Note: Strangely enough, it is possible to connect a node to itself. MMB-dragging a node on top of itself is the quickest way to do this. Choosing Other from the Connect Input Of menu opens the Connection Editor and reveals that the node is listed in both the Output and the Input column. That said, an attribute cannot be connected to itself (for example, focalLength to focalLength). Nevertheless, two different attributes can be connected (for example, focalLength to shutterAngle).

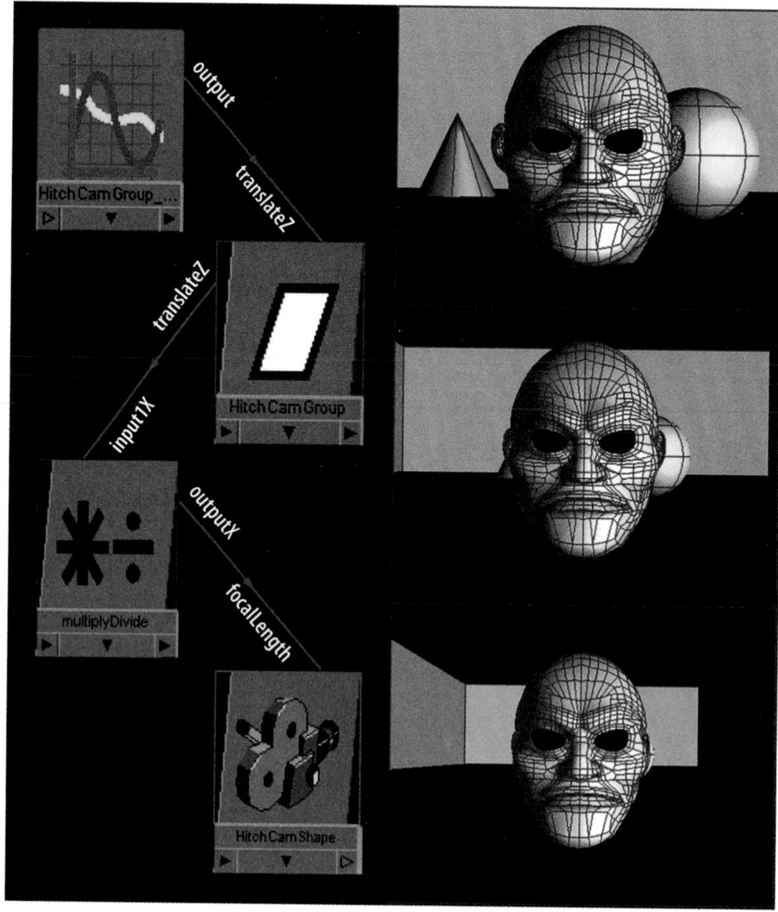

Figure 7.16 A Hitchcock zoom-dolly is created by connecting a camera's translation to its focal length. This scene is included on the CD as `hitchcock.ma`. A QuickTime movie is included as `hitchcock.mov`.

Tapping into Construction History Nodes

You can put construction history nodes to work in the Hypershade window. In Figure 7.17, an asteroid model automatically receives more surface detail as it approaches the camera along the X axis.

To view the entire custom network, open `history.ma` and follow these steps:

1. Open the Hypershade window and switch to the Utilities tab.
2. MMB-drag the clamp node into the work area.
3. With the clamp node selected, click the Input And Output Connections button. A portion of the network becomes visible.
4. Select all the visible nodes and click the Input And Output Connections button a second time.

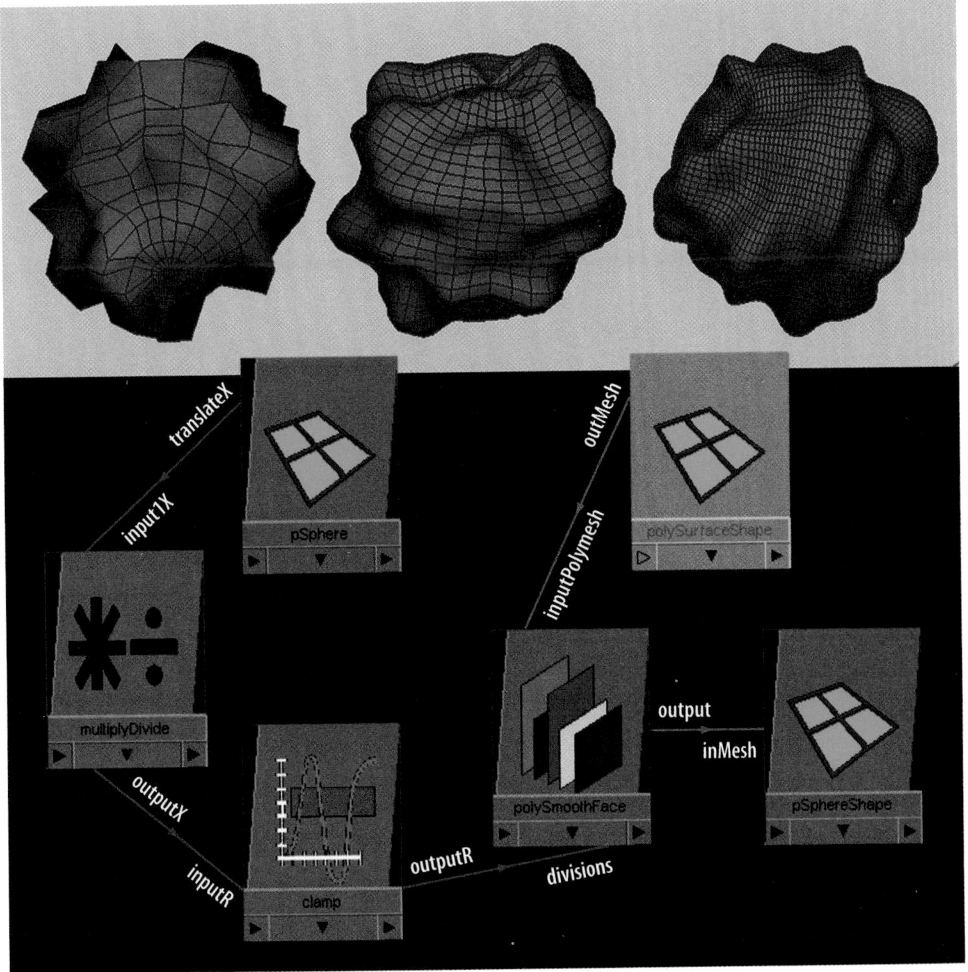

Figure 7.17 A polygon asteroid receives more detail as it approaches the camera. Iterations of a Smooth tool are driven by custom connections. This scene is included on the CD as `history.ma`. A QuickTime movie is included as `history.mov`.

For the network to function, the animated translateX attribute of the pSphere polygon transform node is connected to the input1X of a multiplyDivide node. The multiplyDivide node's Operation is set to Divide and its Input2X attribute is set to 15. This division increases the amount of distance the asteroid must travel before the detail is increased. The outputX of the multiplyDivide node is connected to the inputR of a clamp node. The outputR of the clamp node is connected to the divisions attribute of a polySmoothFace node. The polySmoothFace node is a product of choosing Mesh > Smooth. Whenever the Smooth tool is applied, it creates two new nodes: polySmoothFace and polySurfaceShape. The Divisions attribute of polySmoothFace controls the number of iterations the Smooth tool undertakes. The clamp node's MaxR attribute is set to 3 so that the iterations stay between 0 and 3. The surface's pre-Smooth state is retained by polySurfaceShape. Both polySmoothFace and polySurfaceShape nodes, like all construction history nodes, will exist until history has been deleted on the polygon surface (Edit > Delete By Type > History).

Redirecting the Initial Shading Group Node

By default, Maya assigns all new geometry to the Initial Shading Group and the Lambert material connected to it (named lambert1). You can replace the Lambert with a Blinn or any other material by deleting the connection between the outColor of the default lambert material node and the surfaceShader attribute of the initialShadingGroup node. You can locate the initialShadingGroup node by clicking the Input And Output Connections button while lambert1 is selected. You can then connect the outColor of a new material to surfaceShader of the initialShadingGroup. From that point forward, all new surfaces are automatically assigned to the new material (see Figure 7.18). The outColor of the default lambert material node is also connected to the surfaceShader of the initialParticleSE node. A different material can be connected to this as well. The initialParticleSE node determines the default material qualities of software-rendered Blobby Surface, Cloud, and Tube particles.

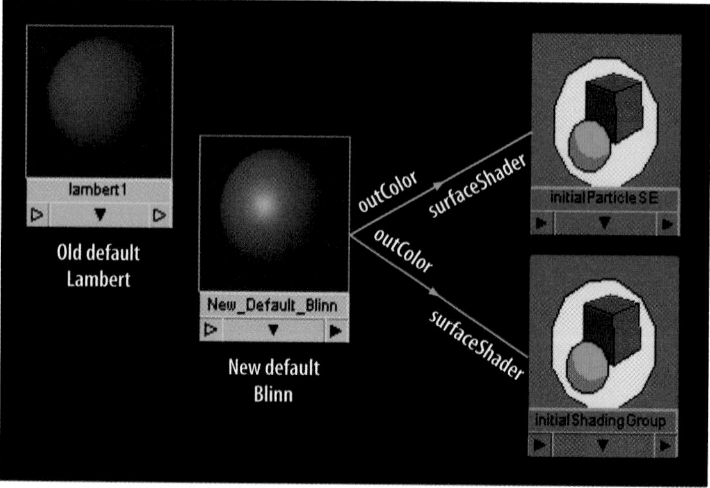

Figure 7.18 The default Lambert material is replaced with a Blinn. This scene is included on the CD as `initial_shading.ma`.

Note: Whenever a new material is assigned to a surface, it automatically receives its own shading group node with a name along the lines of blinn1SG. These material-specific shading group nodes can be deleted and replaced if necessary. For additional information on shading groups, see Chapter 4.

Connecting Multiple Materials in One Network

A custom shading network is not limited to a single material. In some situations, connecting one material to a second material can force the renderer to apply an additional layer of evaluation to the assigned surface. As a simple demonstration of this, the outColor of a phong material node is connected to the color of a lambert material node (see Figure 7.19). Although the lambert node does not have the ability to produce a specular highlight, it picks up the *look* of a specular highlight from the phong.

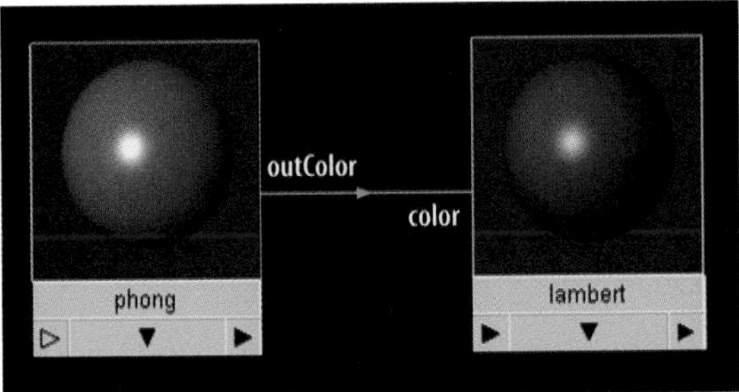

Figure 7.19 A Lambert material inherits the qualities of a Phong.

To achieve this, the renderer evaluates the assigned surface as if a Phong material was assigned to it. The renderer takes the color information from this evaluation and applies it to the color of the Lambert material. This evaluation occurs at each pixel and the color is assigned at each pixel. If a pixel is white with the Phong shading model, then the Lambert color is white. Hence, a false specular highlight is produced. Any attribute of the phong material node that is mapped will carry through. For example, if a texture is mapped to the Bump Mapping attribute of the phong node, the bump will appear automatically on the lambert node.

Note: For a demonstration of a complex, custom skin shader that uses the majority of techniques in this chapter (including multiple materials), see section 7.2 of the `Additional_Techniques.pdf` file on the CD.

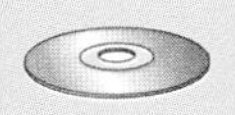

Using the Studio Clear Coat Utility

Studio Clear Coat is a plug-in utility that's in its own category. Its sole function is to create reflections with uneven intensity. As opposed to the car paint shading network detailed in Figure 7.2, this utility functions as a single node.

For example, in Figure 7.20 the outValue of a studioClearCoat node is connected to the reflectivity of a blinn material node (named Car_Paint). The same lighting and environment that was used in Figure 7.2 is applied here. The studioClearCoat node has an Index value of 1.7, a Scale value of 1.55, and a Bias value of –0.1. The resulting render is almost identical to Figure 7.2. The main difference is the rapidity with which the Studio Clear Coat utility transitions between the hood reflection and fender reflection. Although this is not necessarily better or worse, the Studio Clear Coat utility is extremely easy to apply. Unfortunately, it will not work with the mental ray renderer. The custom paint network used in Figure 7.2, on the other hand, offers more flexibility with the addition of the Value gradient and will work with Maya software or mental ray renderers.

Figure 7.20 The reflective falloff of car paint is controlled by a Studio Clear Coat utility. A simplified version of the scene is included on the CD as `clearcoat.ma`.

The Studio Clear Coat utility's attributes follow:

Index Represents the refractive index of the surface. A refractive index is a constant that relates the speed of light through a vacuum to the speed of light though a material (such as car paint). The constant follows:

```
speed of light through a vacuum
÷
speed of light through a material
```

Water has a refractive index of 1.33, which equates to `1/0.75`. The speed of light through water is only 0.75 times as fast as the speed of light through a vacuum. The refractive index of air is extremely close to 1 and is considered 1 when working in 3D.

As light passes between two materials that possess different refractive indices, the angle of refraction does not match the angle of incidence (the angle between the incoming light ray and the material boundary normal, which is perpendicular to the boundary surface). If the light passes from a material with a low refractive index to a high refractive index, the angle of refraction is rotated toward the material boundary normal. Hence, objects appear bent (for example, when a pole is dipped into water). The clear-coat paint systems on modern cars produce a refractive index somewhere between 1.4 and 1.8. The amount of perceived distortion is minimized by the extreme thinness of the transparent clear-coat layer (an average of 50 to 100 microns).

Scale Serves as a multiplier for the final result. Higher values will make the reflection more intense.

Bias Offsets the intensity of the reflection. Lower values decrease the intensity of the reflection and increase the contrast within the reflection. Higher values increase the intensity and lower the contrast. The default value is –0.1.

Note: If the Studio Clear Coat utility is not visible in the General Utilities section of the Hypershade window, choose Window > Settings/Preferences > Plug-In Manager and click the Loaded check box for the `clearcoat.mll` plug-in.

Note: Refractive indices are derived from Snell's Law, which describes the relationship between angles of incidence and angles of refraction. The law is named after Willebrord Snell (1580–1626), who developed a mathematical model based on earlier investigations by Claudius Ptolemy (ca. 100–170) and others. For more information on Snell's Law, see Chapter 12.

Chapter Tutorial: Building a Custom Cartoon Shading Network

In this tutorial, you will create a custom cartoon shading network that combines solid colors with a simulated halftone print (see Figure 7.21). Sampler Info, Surface Luminance, Condition, and Multiply Divide utilities will be used.

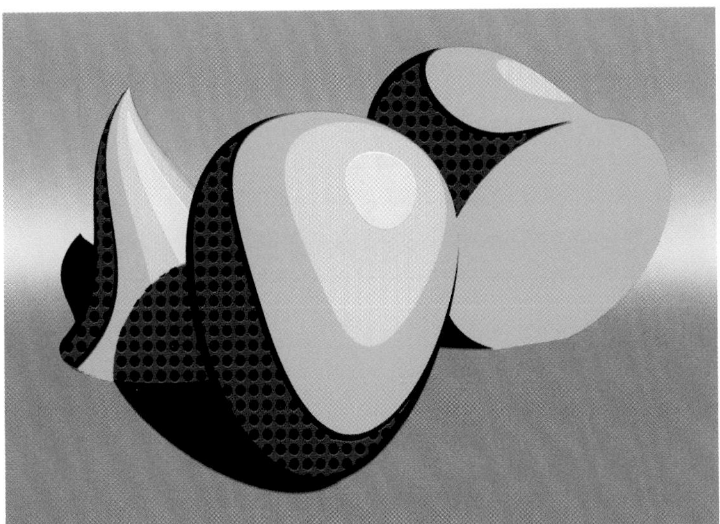

Figure 7.21 A custom cartoon shading network applied to primitives. A QuickTime movie is included on the CD as `cartoon.mov`.

1. Create a new Maya scene. Open the Hypershade window.
2. MMB-drag a Surface Shader material into the work area and rename it **Cartoon**. MMB-drag a Condition utility (found in the General Utilities section of the Create Maya Nodes menu) into the work area. Place it to the left of the Cartoon node. Use Figure 7.22 as a reference.

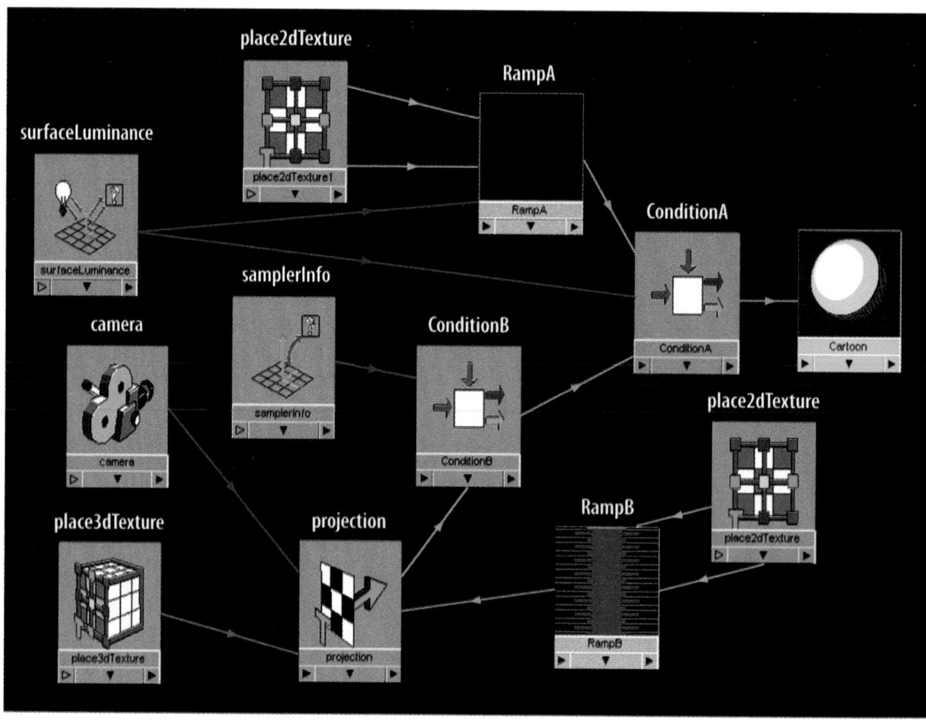

Figure 7.22 The shading network of the custom Cartoon material

3. Connect the outColor of the condition node to the outColor of the Cartoon node. You will have to open the Connection Editor to do this.
4. Select the condition node and rename it **ConditionA**. Open its Attribute Editor tab. Click the Color If False Map button and choose a Ramp texture from the Create Render Node window. A place2dTexture node will automatically appear with the new ramp node. Rename the ramp node **RampA**.
5. Select RampA and open its Attribute Editor tab. Create four color handles that go from black to green to white (see Figure 7.23). Change RampA's Interpolation attribute to None.
6. MMB-drag a Surface Luminance utility (found in the Color Utilities section of the Create Maya Nodes menu) into the work area. Place it to the left of the other nodes. Connect the outValue of the surfaceLuminance node to the firstTerm of ConditionA.
7. Connect the outValue of the surfaceLuminance node to the vCoord of RampA. You will have to use the Connection Editor. This connection forces the render to select different pixels in the V direction of the ramp based on the amount of light any given point on the assigned surface receives. If a surface point is dark, it gets its color from the bottom of the ramp. If a surface point receives a moderate amount of light, it gets its color from the center of the ramp.
8. MMB-drag a second Condition utility into the work area. Place it to the left of ConditionA. Rename the new condition node **ConditonB**. Connect the outColor of ConditionB to colorIfTrue of ConditionA.

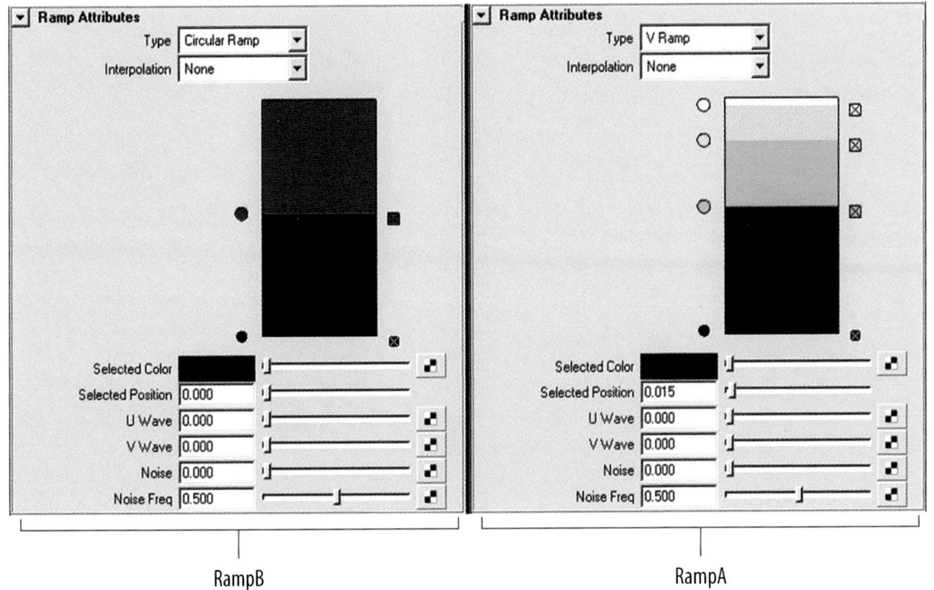

Figure 7.23 (Left) RampB (Right) RampA

9. MMB-drag a Sampler Info utility (found in the General Utilities section of the Create Maya Nodes menu) into the work area. Place it to the left of ConditionB. Connect the facingRatio of the samplerInfo node to the firstTerm of ConditionB.

10. Select ConditionB and open its Attribute Editor tab. Set the Color If False attribute to 0, 0, 0. Click the Color If True Map button, select As Projection in the 2D Textures section of the Create Render Node window, and click the Ramp texture button. Selecting As Projection creates the Ramp texture with a projection node and a place3dTexture node (see Figure 7.22). Rename the new ramp node **RampB.**

11. Create a new one-node camera by choosing Create > Cameras > Camera from the main Maya menu. Create several primitives and place them in the view of the camera. Assign all the primitives to the Cartoon material. Feel free to change the camera's Background Color attribute to white or add a white ground plane.

12. Select the projection node and open its Attribute Editor tab. Change the Proj Type attribute to Perspective. MMB-drag the new camera node, named camera, from the Cameras tab area to the work area and drop it on top of the projection node. Choose Other from the Connect Input Of drop-down menu. The Connection Editor window opens. Connect the Message of the camera node to the linkedCamera of the projection node. The Message attribute is normally hidden. When you choose Left Display > Show Hidden in the Connection Editor, the Message attribute becomes visible at the top of the list. When the camera node is connected to the projection node, the projection node will know to project from the view of the new camera and not the default persp camera.

13. Look at the camera icon in a workspace view. There should be a projection frustum (a pyramid shaped icon representing a camera's view) extending from the camera icon toward the primitive objects (Figure 7.24). If not, select the place3dTexture node that is connected to the projection node. This will select the frustum icon and allow you to translate it to a suitable location. If you would like to animate the camera moving, parent the place3dTexture node to the camera. Ultimately, this projection will allow the halftone dots to appear continuously across multiple surfaces without distortion.

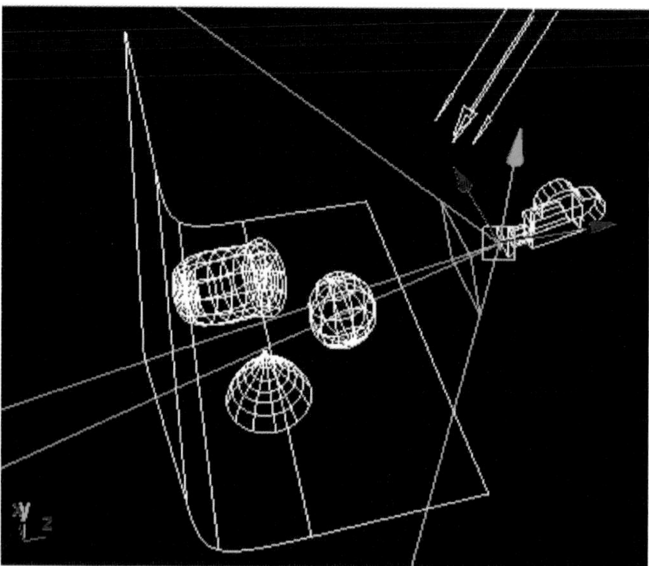

Figure 7.24 Selected camera frustum

14. Select RampB and open its Attribute Editor tab. Place two color handles in the color field. A black handle should be at the bottom. A dark purple handle should be at the center (Figure 7.23). Set Type to Circular Ramp and Interpolation to None. RampB will produce a halftone print pattern. Select the place2dTexture node of RampB. Open its Attribute Editor tab and change the Repeat UV value to 65, 40. Choose larger numbers to create smaller halftone circles.

15. Select ConditionB and open its Attribute Editor tab. Set the Second Term attribute to 0.3 and the Operation to Greater Than. ConditionB works as an if statement. If the facingRatio of the samplerInfo node is greater than 0.3, ConditionB will output the halftone pattern of RampB as the color. If the facingRatio is 0.3 or less, pure black will be output as the color; ultimately, this creates a black "ink line" around the edge of the objects.

16. Select ConditionA and open its Attribute Editor tab. Set the Second Term attribute to 0.5 and the Operation to Less Than. ConditionA serves as a second if statement. If the outValue of the surfaceLuminance node is less than 0.5, the

color output by ConditionB is selected (black or halftone dots). If the outValue of the surfaceLuminance node is equal to or greater than 0.5, the color output by RampA (various shades of green) is selected. The surfaceLuminance node also controls the vCoord of RampA, so that the selection of different shades of green is based on the amount of light the surface receives.

17. The custom cartoon material is complete! Render out a test. It should look similar to Figure 7.21. If you get stuck, a finished version of the material is saved as `cartoon.ma` in the Chapter 7 scene folder on the CD.

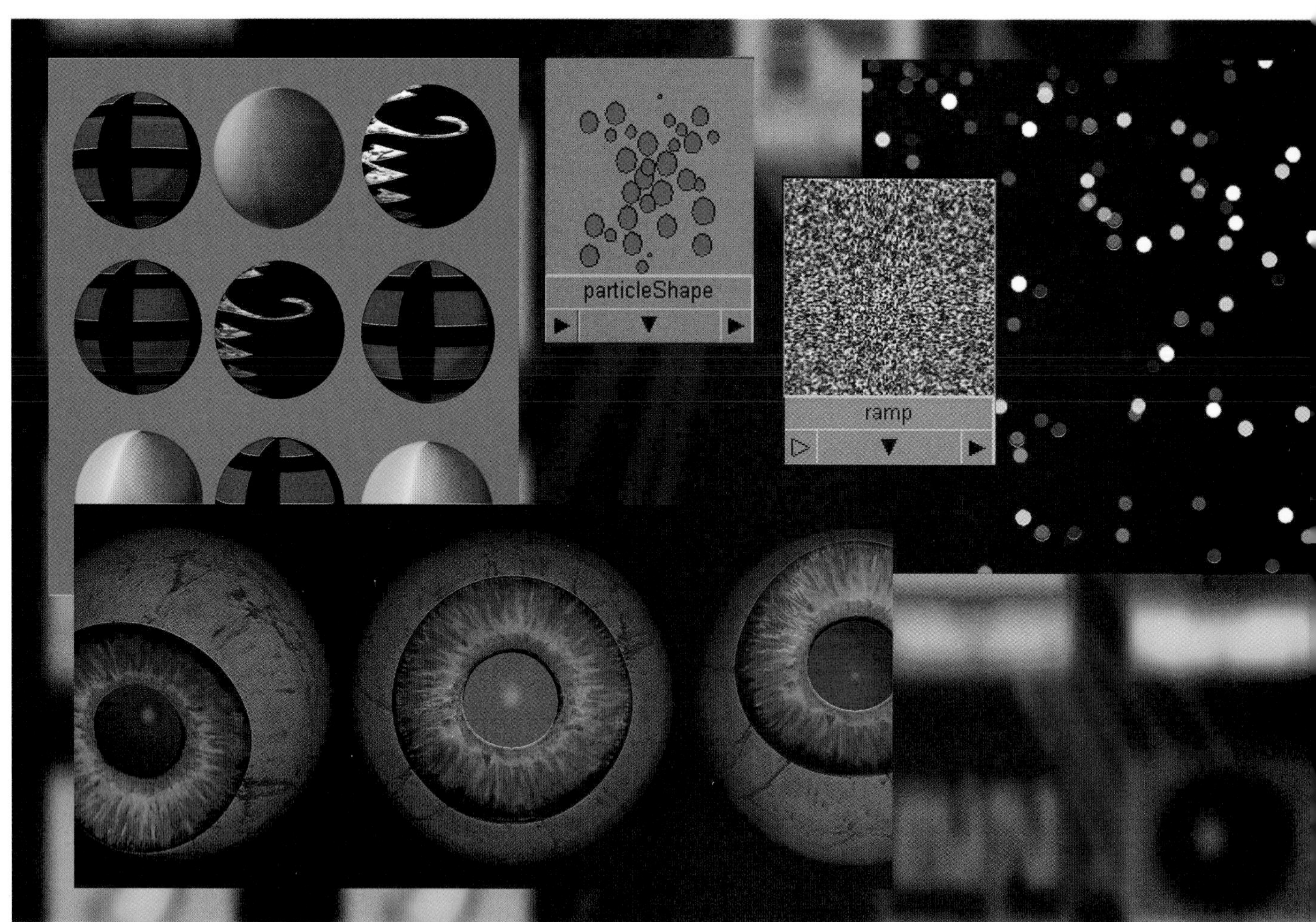

particleShape
ramp

8 Harnessing the Power of Math Utilities

Math utilities refine outputs and emulate complex mathematics. Switch utilities let you create numerous texture variations with a single material. With Array Mapper and Particle Sampler utilities, you can control a particle's material and movement on a per-particle basis. You can also create unique effects with Stencil and Optical FX utilities.

Chapter Contents

Practical applications of each math utility
A general approach to using per-particles attributes
The functionality of the Array Mapper and Particle Sampler utilities
Uses for Stencil and Optical FX utilities
The purpose of Unit Conversion and other scene nodes

Math Utilities

The values provided by various attributes in Maya are often unusable in a custom shading network. The numbers are too large, too small, or negative when they need to be positive. Hence, Maya provides a host of math utilities designed to massage values into a usable form. The utilities vary from simple (Reverse, Multiply Divide, and Plus Minus Average) to advanced (Array Mapper, Vector Product, and others). Switch utilities, on the other hand, provide the means to texture large groups of objects with a limited number of materials.

Reversing Input

The Reverse utility simply reverses an input. The following math occurs:

```
Output = 1 - Input
```

Thus, an input of 1 produces 0 and an input of 0 produces 1. At the same time, the Reverse utility will make larger numbers negative or positive. For instance, an input of 100 produces –99 and an input of –100 produces 101. Only an input of 0.5 will lead to an unchanged output.

For example, in Figure 8.1 the Specular Roll Off of a material is automatically reduced as it becomes more transparent. The transparency attribute of a blinn material node is connected to the input of a reverse node. The outputX of the reverse node is connected back to the specularRollOff of the blinn. If a vector attribute (RGB) is connected to the reverse node, it is not necessary to utilize all three channels on the output. Without this network, a specular highlight of the blinn will remain visible even if its transparency is turned up to 100 percent. Although you can keyframe the Specular Roll Off attribute, this network is easy to set up.

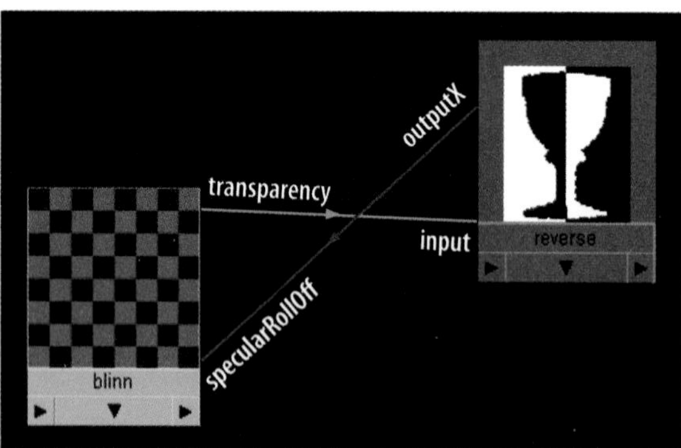

Figure 8.1 The Specular Roll Off of a Blinn material is driven by its Transparency attribute with the aid of a Reverse utility. This scene is included on the CD as `reverse.ma`.

Multiplying and Dividing

The Multiply Divide utility applies multiplication, division, or power operations to zero, one, or two inputs. If no inputs exist, you can enter numbers into the Input1 and Input2 attribute fields. If the Multiply Divide utility has one input, you can enter numbers into the unconnected Input1 or Input2 attribute fields. Regardless of the number of inputs, the Multiply Divide utility follows this logic:

```
Input1 / Input2
Input1 * Input2
Input1 ^ Input2
```

If the utility's Operation attribute is set to Multiply, the order makes no difference. If the utility's Operation is set to Divide or Power, however, the order is critical, as in this example:

```
10 / 2 = 5 while 2 / 10 = 0.2
10 ^ 2 = 100 while 2 ^ 10 = 1024
```

A chain of Multiply Divide nodes can emulate fairly complex math. Although Maya expressions can easily handle math work, the Multiply Divide utility offers an alternative method that allows the user to stay within the Hypershade window. For example, in Figure 8.2 the generic formula `y = 1 / (x^(x / 2))` is re-created.

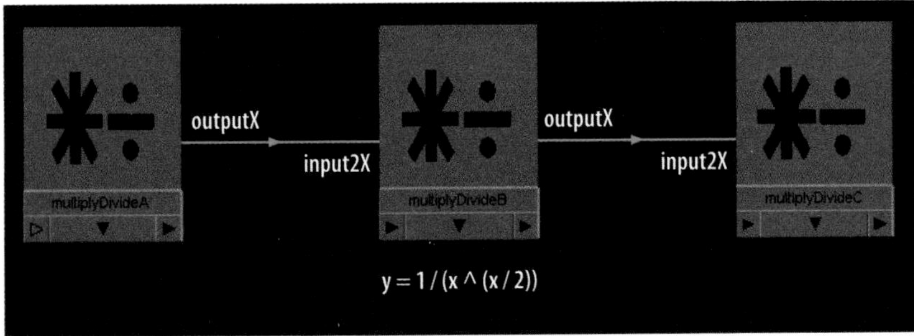

Figure 8.2 A generic formula is re-created with Multiply Divide utilities. This network is included on the CD as `multiply_generic.ma`.

To view the custom network, follow these steps:

1. Open the `multiply_generic.ma` file from the CD. Open the Hypershade window and switch to the Utilities tab.
2. MMB-drag multiplyDivideA into the work area.
3. With multiplyDivideA selected, click the Input And Output Connections button. The network becomes visible.

In this case, `(x / 2)` is provided by multiplyDivideA. `x` is entered manually into the Input1X field. Input2X is set to 2. The Operation attribute is set to Divide.

`x ^` is provided by multiplyDivideB. `x` is entered manually into the Input1X field. The Operation attribute is set to Power. outputX of multiplyDivideA is connected to input2X of multiplyDivideB.

`1 /` is provided by multiplyDivideC. Input1X is set to 1. Operation is set to Divide. outputX of multiplyDivideB is connected to input2X of multiplyDivideC. Ultimately, outputX of multiplyDivideC equals the answer, or in this case, `y`. If `x` is 1, then `y` equals 1. If `x` is 4, then `y` equals 0.0625. If `x` is 15, then `y` = 1.51118e-009. In Maya, e-009 is equivalent to $\times 10^{-9}$. If the outputX of multiplyDivideC is connected to the input1X of a fourth multiplyDivide node, the input1X field will display 0.000. Since the Input1 and Input2 fields of the Multiply Divide utility are limited to three floating points, they will not display numbers with an excessive number of digits. However, the correct value of multiplyDivideC's outputX can always be retrieved by entering `getAttr multiplyDivideC.outputX` in the Script Editor.

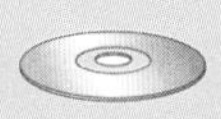

Note: For an additional application of the Multiply Divide utility, see section 8.1 of the `Additional_Techniques.pdf` file on the CD. In section 8.1, the rotation of a tire is automatically and accurately driven by its translation.

Adding, Subtracting, and Averaging Values

The Plus Minus Average utility supports addition, subtraction, and average operations. It operates on single, double, and vector input attributes. If single attributes are connected, they are not visible in the Plus Minus Average utility's Attribute Editor tab. However, double and vector attributes are indicated by input fields (see Figure 8.3).

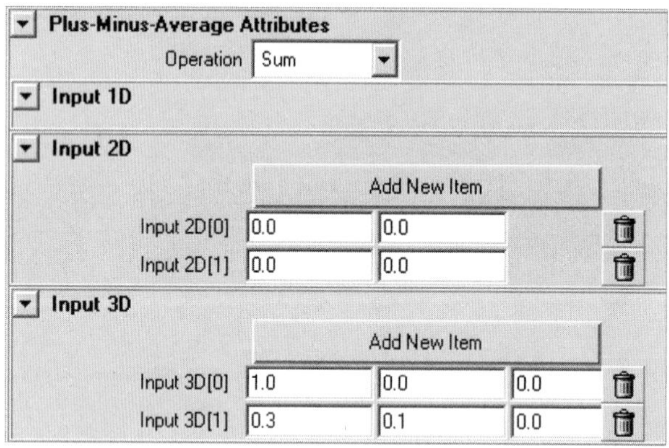

Figure 8.3 A Plus Minus Average utility with single, double, and vector inputs

The Plus Minus Average utility provides Add New Item buttons in the Input 2D and Input 3D sections of its Attribute Editor tab. When you click one of these buttons, a new set of input fields is added to the appropriate section. The input fields are not connected to a node, which allows you to enter values by hand. However, you can choose to make a custom connection to the new input.

You can connect single attributes to input1D[*n*] of a plusMinusAverage node. You can connect double attributes, such as uvCoord, to input2D[*n*]. You can connect vector attributes, such as outColor, to input3D[*n*]. *n* represents the order with which attributes have been connected, with the [0] position being the first. There is no limit to the number of attributes that may be connected. For example, in Figure 8.4 the translateX attributes of four primitive polygon shape transform nodes are connected to input1D[*n*] of a plusMinusAverage node with the node's Operation set to Subtract.

To illustrate the result, the output1D of the plusMinusAverage node is connected to the translateX of a locator. To see this custom network, follow these steps:

1. Open the `plus_simple.ma` file from the CD. Open the Hypershade window and switch to the Utilities tab.
2. MMB-drag plusMinusAverage1 into the work area.
3. With plusMinusAverage1 selected, click the Input And Output Connections button. The network becomes visible.

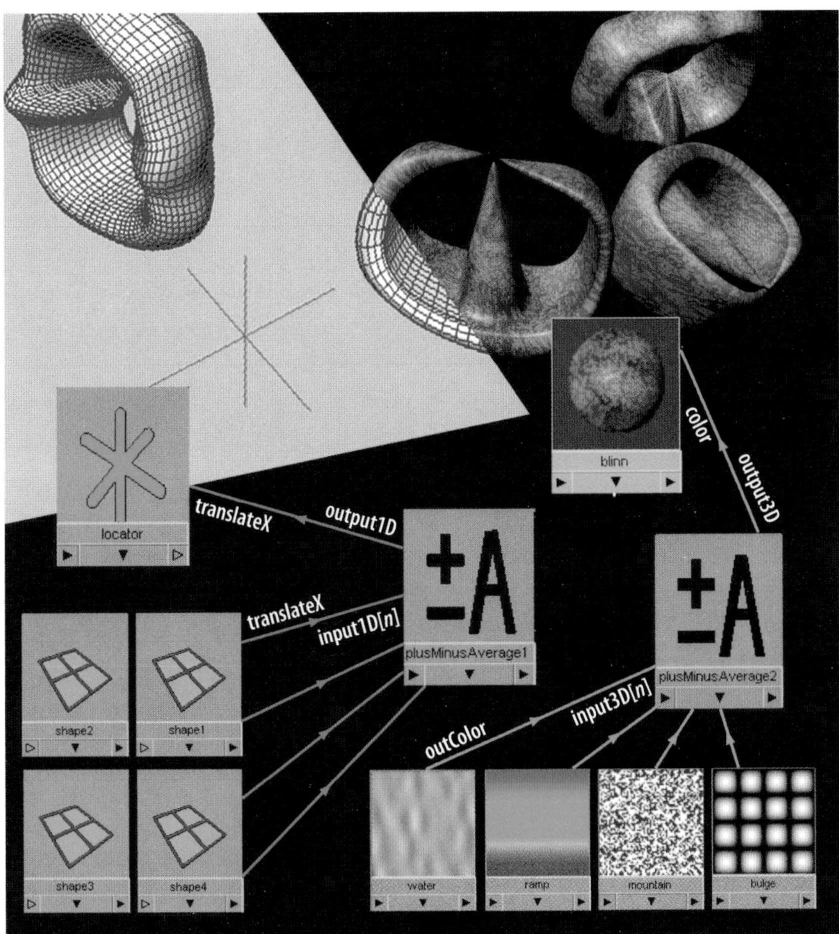

Figure 8.4 Two Plus Minus Average utilities subtract translation and average texture color for four polygon shapes. This scene is included on the CD as `plus_simple.ma`.

The locator position represents the result of the following math:

```
shape1.tx - shape2.tx - shape3.tx - shape4.tx
```

If the Operation attribute of the plusMinusAverage node is switched to Sum, the same logic applies. However, if the Operation attribute is switched to Average, the following math occurs:

```
(shape1.tx + shape2.tx + shape3.tx + shape4.tx) / 4
```

You can apply the Average operation to color attributes as well. In the same example, the outColor attributes of four textures are connected to the input3D[*n*] of a second plusMinusAverage node. The utility's output3D is connected to the color of a blinn material node, which is assigned to all four shapes. The following happens to the red channel of an individual pixel:

```
(water.colorR + ramp.colorR + mountain.colorR + bulge.colorR ) / 4
```

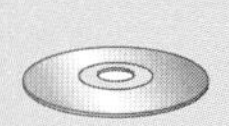

Note: For an additional application of the Plus Minus Average utility, see section 8.2 of the `Additional_Techniques.pdf` file on the CD. In section 8.2, the length of a triangle's edge is solved with the application of the Pythagorean Theorem.

Using Expressions

Maya expressions offer the most efficient and powerful way to incorporate math calculations into a custom shading network. Although a deeper discussion on expressions is beyond the scope of this book, here are a few items to keep in mind:

Create New Expression Right-clicking an attribute field in the Attribute Editor and choosing Create New Expression from the shortcut menu opens the Expression Editor window. The attribute that was chosen will be highlighted in Expression Editor's Attributes list. Once a valid expression is created and the Create button is clicked, an expression node and appropriate connections are created. The attribute field, as seen in the Attribute Editor, turns purple to indicate the connection to an expression. The expression node is not immediately visible in the Hypershade work area. However, if you select the node to which the expression was applied in the work area and click the Input And Output Connections button, the expression node is revealed.

Time A master Time node (time1) is automatically connected to each expression node and is undeletable. This node manages the flow of time for the Maya Timeline. You can connect the node's outTime to any single attribute of any node; however, a connection line will not necessarily appear in the Hypershade window.

Nodes and Channels You can reference any channel of any node in an expression. The naming convention will always follow the formula *node.channel*.

Functions For a list of Maya math, vector, array, and other functions available to expressions, choose the Insert Functions menu of the Expression Editor window.

Duplication You can duplicate expression nodes by choosing Edit > Duplicate > Without Network from the Hypershade window menu. The new expression appears in the Expression Editor if you choose Select Filter > By Expression Name from the Expression Editor menu. The math functions of the duplicate are identical to the original. However, the channel names are missing. You can display the new expression node by entering the node name, such as *expression3*, into the search field of the Hypergraph Connections window.

Changing the Range of a Value

The Set Range utility maps one range of values to a second range of values. The underlying math for the utility follows:

```
outValue = Min + (((value-oldMin)/(oldMax-oldMin)) * (Max-Min))
```

As an example illustrated by Table 8.1, five different ValueX inputs are processed by a Set Range utility, resulting in new Out ValueX outputs. For this example, Old MinX of the utility is set to –100, Old MaxX is set to 100, Min X is set to 0, and MaxX is set to 1.

Table 8.1 The Result Of Various ValueX Inputs Applied To A Set Range Utility

ValueX	–100	–75	0	21	500
Out ValueX	0	0.125	0.5	0.605	1

The mid-value of the Old MinX and Old MaxX range (0) becomes the mid-value of the new MinX and MaxX range (0.5). Any value greater than the Old MaxX is clamped to the Old MaxX value before it is remapped. Hence, 500 becomes 100, which is then remapped to 1. Min, Max, Old Min, Old Max, and Value are vector attributes. The individual channels (for example MinX, MinY, MinZ) can carry different values.

In a working example, the Set Range utility is used to create diffuse shadows on a directional light. Diffuse shadows are a product of diffuse lighting. A diffuse light source is one that either produces divergent light rays or is physically large enough that it produces multiple overlapping shadows. One feature of a diffuse shadow is an increased edge softness over distance. A second feature is a shadow color that becomes lighter over distance (see the photo at the top of Figure 8.5).

Since depth map shadows are calculated using a single point-of-view of a light, Maya is unable to produce a diffuse effect. A light's Filter Size attribute blurs the edge of a depth map shadow, but the blur is equally intense whether or not it's close to the object casting the shadow. Raytraced shadows, on the other hand, can be adjusted to have a larger spread and thus a softer edge over distance; however, high-quality raytrace shadows can be time intensive. (See Chapter 3 for more information on shadow quality settings.) Nonetheless, you can emulate diffuse shadows with the shading network illustrated in Figure 8.5. To view this custom shading network, follow these steps:

1. Open the `setrange_shadow.ma` file from the CD. Open the Hypershade window and switch to the Lights tab.
2. MMB-drag the KeyShape node into the work area.
3. With KeyShape selected, click the Input And Output Connections button. The network becomes visible.

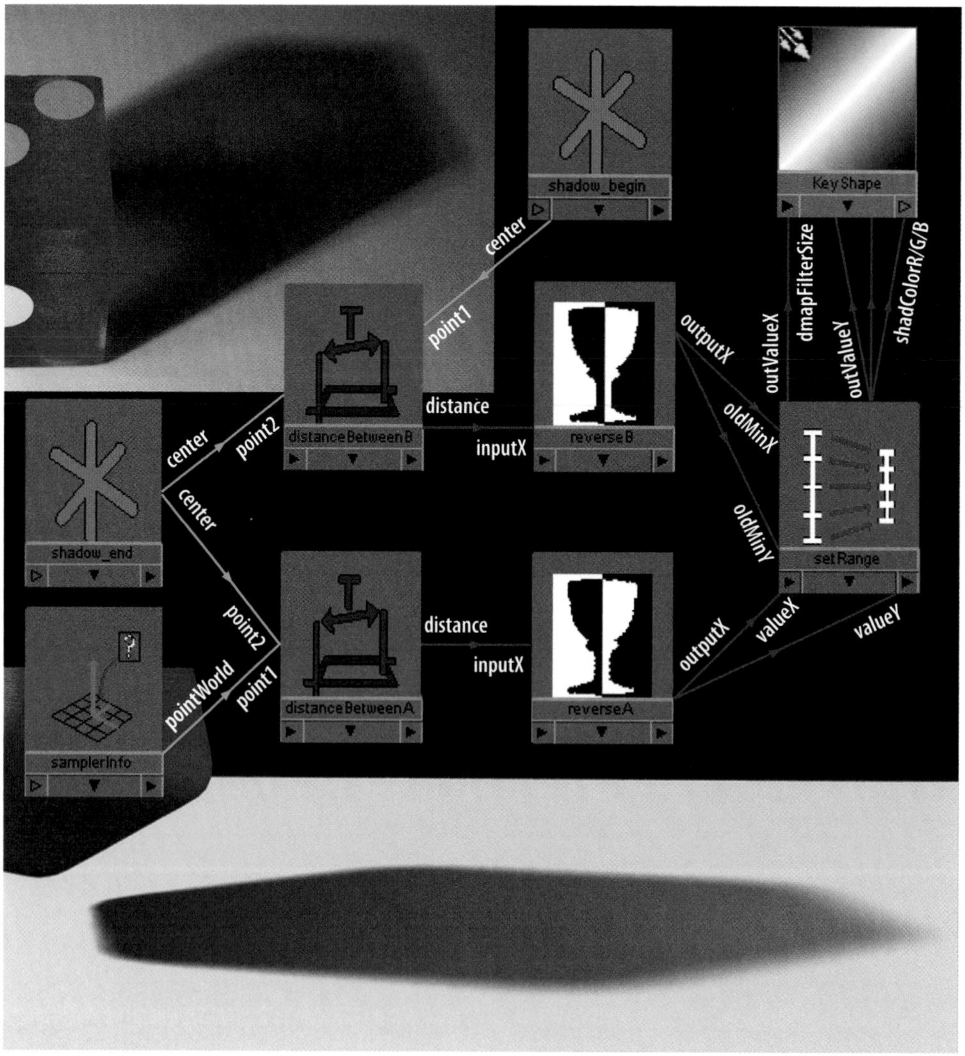

Figure 8.5 The diffuse quality of a depth map shadow is controlled by a Set Range utility. This scene is included on the CD as `setrange_shadow.ma`.

For the 3D render at the bottom of Figure 8.5, a directional light named Key is placed behind a polygon cube. The light's Use Depth Map Shadows attribute is checked. Two locators are placed in the scene. The first locator, named shadow_begin, is placed at a point on the ground where the shadow begins (close to the cube). A second locator, named shadow_end, is placed on the ground where the shadow ends.

Note: To accurately position a locator at the point where a shadow ends, select the shadow-casting light and choose Panels > Look Through Selected from a workspace view menu. The locator will be occluded by an object if it is within a shadow.

The center attribute of the shadow_begin transform node is connected to the point1 of a distanceBetween node (distanceBetweenB). The center of shadow_end is connected to point2 of distanceBetweenB. The Center attribute provides the location of an object's bounding box in world space. Ultimately, distanceBetweenB determines the length of the shadow. The center of shadow_end is also connected to the point2 of a second distanceBetween node (distanceBetweenA). The pointWorld attribute of a samplerInfo node is connected to the point1 of the distanceBetweenA. The Point World attribute stores the world position of the point being sampled during the render. Hence, distanceBetweenA determines the distance between the end of the shadow and the point being sampled. The distance of distanceBetweenA is connected to the inputX of a reverse node (reverseA). The outputX of the reverseA is connected to the valueX and valueY of a setRange node.

In the meantime, the distance of the distanceBetweenB node is connected to its own reverse node (reverseB). The outputX of reverseB is connected to oldMinX and oldMinY of the setRange node. The setRange node's MinX is set to 2 and its MaxX is set to 32. This represents the range of values that can be used as a Filter Size for the directional light. Since the Old Min value is fed by distanceBetweenB, and has been made negative by reverseB, the Old Max is set to 0. This negative range (–*n* to 0) matches the negative distance value provided by reverseA. These negative values are necessary to place the diffuse effect at the shadow end and not the shadow beginning. In this case, if a point near the end of the shadow is sampled, the distance between that point and the shadow_end is small and outputX of reverseA will be a small negative number (for example, –1). As a number, –1 is relatively high in the Old Min and Old Max range (close to 0) and is thus remapped to a number close to 32. Again, distanceBetweenB and reverseB represent the length of the shadow and therefore supply the Old Min values. If a point near the beginning of the shadow is sampled, the distance between that point and the shadow_end is large and outputX of reverseA will be a large negative number, such as –15. As a number, –15 is relatively low in the Old Min and Old Max range (not close to 0) and is thus remapped to a number close to 2.

Returning to the network, the outValueX of the setRange node is connected to the dmapFilterSize of the directional light KeyShape node. A dmapFilterSize of 0 produces no additional blur. A dmapFilterSize value of 32 creates the maximum amount of blur on the shadow. The outValueY of the setRange node is also connected to the shadColorR, shadColorG, and shadColorB of the light KeyShape node. The MinY of the setRange node is set to 0 and the MaxY is set to 0.5. This converts the Old Min and Old Max range into a range usable as a color. The end effect is a shadow that becomes lighter as it travels farther away from the cube. Increasing the value of MaxY will create a lighter shadow. This network works best with depth map shadows that have a relatively large Resolution value (for example, 1024). Smaller Resolution values will reveal the transitions between different Filter Size values. Nevertheless, this offers an alternative way to produce a diffuse shadow effect without the necessity of potentially time-consuming raytracing.

Mapping Per-Particle Attributes

The Array Mapper utility is designed to control per-particle attributes on particle nodes. The attributes can affect particle size, dynamic behavior, color, and opacity. (An array is an ordered list of values.)

The simplest way to see the Array Mapper utility work is to create an RGB PP attribute for hardware-rendered particles. Since the process is a little unusual, I recommend you use the following steps:

1. Create a new scene. Switch to the Dynamics menu set and choose Particles > Create Emitter. Play back the Timeline. Select the resulting cloud of particles.
2. Open the Attribute Editor tab for a selected particle shape node (particleShape1) and expand the Lifespan Attributes section. Set the Lifespan Mode value to either Constant or Random Range and choose a Lifespan length (measured in seconds).
3. Click the Color button in the Add Dynamic Attributes section. The Particle Color window opens. Check the Add Per Particle Attribute option and click the Add Attribute button (see Figure 8.6). This adds an RGB PP attribute to the list in the Per Particle (Array) Attributes section of the particle shape node's Attribute Editor tab.

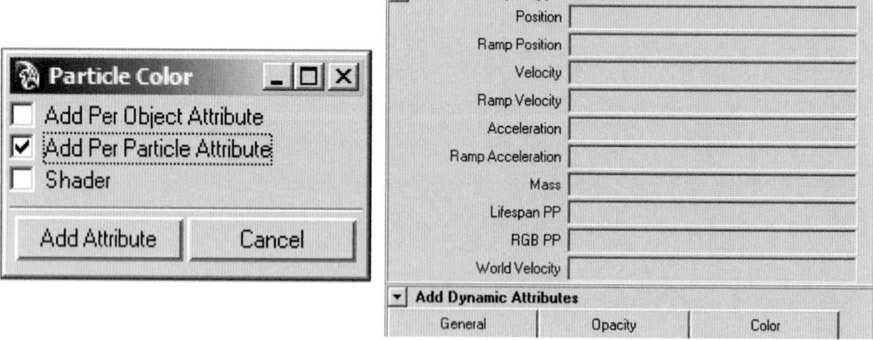

Figure 8.6 (Left) The Particle Color window. (Right) The Per Particle (Array) Attributes and Add Dynamics Attributes sections of a particle shape node's Attribute Editor tab. Note the addition of the RGB PP attribute.

4. Right-click the field next to RGB PP and choose Create Ramp from the shortcut menu. A Particle Array utility and a Ramp texture are automatically connected to the particle shape node. The particles will then pick up the color of the ramp over their lifespan. You can render the default point particles with either the Maya Hardware renderer or the Hardware Render Buffer. (See Chapter 10 for more information on hardware rendering.)

You can manually connect the Array Mapper utility (found in the General Utilities section of the Create Maya Nodes menu). For example, in Figure 8.7 the outColor of a ramp texture node is connected to the computeNodeColor of an arrayMapper node. The message of the ramp is also connected to the computeNode of the arrayMapper. The outColorPP of the arrayMapper node is connected to the rgbPP of the particleShape node. In turn, the ageNormalized of the particleShape node is connected to the vCoordPP of the arrayMapper node. The Min Value and Max Value attributes of the Array Mapper utility serve as a clamp for the outColorPP and outValuePP attributes (outValuePP is the single-attribute version of outColorPP). You can replace the ramp texture with other types of textures, but the results will be unpredictable.

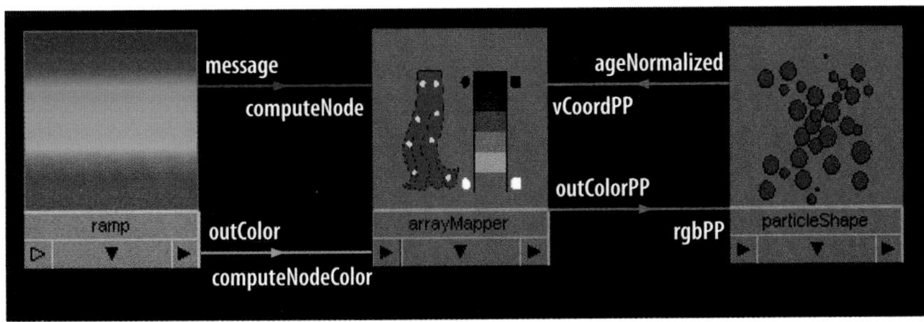

Figure 8.7 The shading network for a per-particle attribute

Although color is used in the previous example, a number of other per-particle attributes are available, including incandescencePP, radiusPP, and opacityPP. You can access these attributes by clicking the General button in the Add Dynamics Attributes section of the particle shape's Attribute Editor tab and choosing the Particle tab of the Add Attribute: particleShape window (see Figure 8.8). In addition to the PP attributes, the Particle tab carries a long list of more esoteric attributes, any of which can be utilized for per-particle operations through an expression.

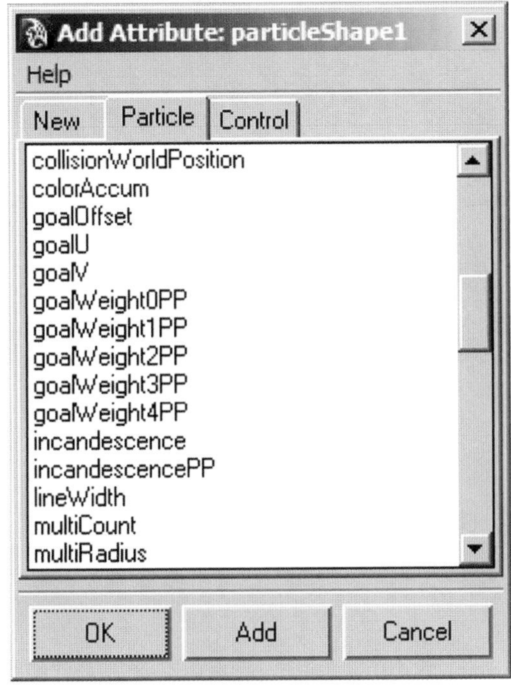

Figure 8.8 The Particle tab of the Add Attribute window. Only a small portion of the available PP attributes are shown.

In a second example, a single Array Mapper utility drives the color, opacity, and acceleration of a point particle node (see Figure 8.9).

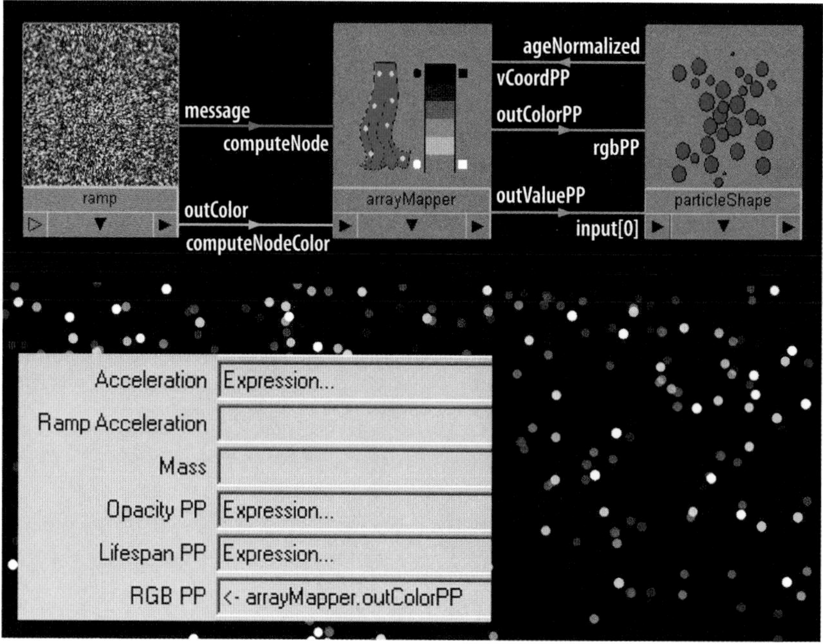

Figure 8.9 A point particle node receives its color, opacity, and acceleration from an Array Mapper utility. This scene is included on the CD as `array_point.ma`. A QuickTime movie is included as `array_point.mov`.

To view the shading network, follow these steps:

1. Open the `array_point.ma` file from the CD. Open the Hypershade window and switch to the Textures tab.
2. MMB-drag the ramp node into the work area.
3. With the ramp node selected, click the Input And Output Connections button. The network becomes visible.

With this network, the Noise attribute of the connected ramp node is set to 1 and its Noise Freq attribute is set to 50, which creates a random pattern throughout the ramp. Although rgbPP receives its color directly from the ramp node, an expression controls the particle node's opacity, acceleration, and lifespan. The expression follows:

```
particleShape.opacityPP=arrayMapper.outValuePP;
particleShape.acceleration=arrayMapper.outValuePP*-500;
particleShape.lifespanPP=rand(1,3);
```

To view the expression, follow these steps:

1. Choose Window > Animation Editors > Expression Editor.
2. Choose Select Filter > By Expression Name from the Expression Editor menu. Click the word *particleShape* in the Objects field.
3. Switch the Particles attribute to Creation. The expression code is revealed in the text field at the bottom of the window.

In the first line of the expression, outValuePP of the arrayMapper node drives opacityPP. In the second line of the expression, outValuePP drives the particle's acceleration attribute. The acceleration attribute controls the rate of velocity change on a per-particle basis (although it's not listed as a "PP"). You can see the effect of the variable acceleration if the particle count is reduced to a low number. Some particles move rapidly, while others fall very slowly. The outValuePP is multiplied by –500, which makes the acceleration more rapid and the particles' direction in the negative X, Y, and Z direction. The ability to use outValuePP as an input for multiple particle attributes eliminates the need for additional arrayMapper and ramp nodes.

In the third line of the expression, the particle lifespan is assigned a random number from 1 to 3 with the `rand()` function. The outValuePP attribute is automatically connected to input[0] of the arrayMapper node; this represents the use of outValuePP in an expression. When an expression is created for a per-particle attribute, the expression is carried by the particle shape node and no separate expression node is generated.

Note: Right-clicking an attribute field in the Per Particle (Array) Attributes section of a particle shape node's Attribute Editor tab provides the Creation Expression option in a shortcut menu. Creation Expression opens the Expression Editor and lists the particle shape and its numerous channels in the editor's Attributes list. Using the Creation Expression option is also a quick way to access preexisting per-particle expressions.

Creation expressions are executed at the start time of an animation. They are not executed as the animation plays. When using particles, a creation expression is applied one time per particle at the frame in which the particle is born. In contrast, a runtime expression executes at each frame during playback. A runtime expression is useful when values need to constantly change over the life of an animation. You can create a runtime expression by right-clicking an attribute field in the Per Particle (Array) Attributes section of a particle shape node's Attribute Editor tab and choosing Runtime Expression Before Dynamics or Runtime Expression After Dynamics.

As for other particle settings, the emitter is set to a cube volume shape with 0, –1, 0 Direction values. A turbulence field with a Magnitude value of 500 is also assigned to the particles. The field adds additional random motion; although the turbulence affects direction, it does not impact the overall acceleration. The end result is a glitter-like fall of particles. The point particles are rendered with the Hardware Render Buffer with Multi-Pass Rendering.

Unfortunately, the Array Mapper utility will not work with software-rendered particles—*unless* it is used in conjunction with a Particle Sampler utility. The Particle Sampler utility serves as a go-between, retrieving attribute information from a particle shape node and passing it on to a material assigned to the software-rendered particles. For example, in Figure 8.10 the example from Figure 8.9 is reused with the addition of a Particle Sampler utility. The Particle Render Type of the particle shape node is switched to Blobby Surface. The particle node is assigned to a blinn material node. The Noise value of the original ramp texture node is reduced and the ramp colors are adjusted. The Rate(Particles/Sec) value of the particle node is reduced for easier viewing. A directional light is added to the scene.

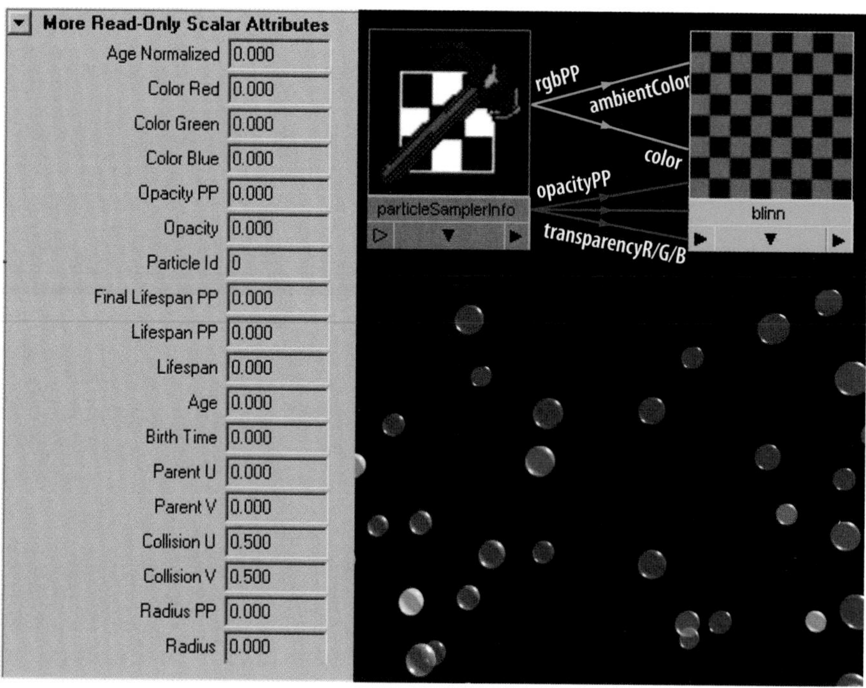

Figure 8.10 A Blobby Surface particle node receives its color, opacity, and acceleration through Array Mapper and Particle Sampler utilities. This scene is included on the CD as `array_blobby.ma`. A QuickTime movie is included as `array_blobby.mov`.

Aside from these adjustments, all the old network connections and the old expression are intact. As an addition, the rgbPP of a particleSamplerInfo node is connected to the color and the ambientColor of the blinn. The opacityPP of the particleSamplerInfo node is also connected to the transparencyR, transparencyG, and transparencyB of the blinn. The end result is a color distribution, opacity, lifespan, and acceleration roughly identical to Figure 8.9 but with a software-rendered particle node. The Particle Sampler utility also carries a long list of read-only attributes (see the left side of Figure 8.10). These attributes remotely read attribute information from the particle shape node that is assigned to the material. (For this to work, the material must share the shading network with the Particle Sampler utility.) The attributes are intuitively named (for example, particleSamplerInfo.rgbPP remotely reads particleShape.rgbPP). You can connect these attributes to any attribute of a material that may prove useful.

Note: You can change various per-particle attributes, such as lifespanPP and opacityPP, through the Particles tab of the Component Editor (Window > General Editors > Component Editor). You can select particle nodes in a workspace view by clicking the Select By Object Type: Dynamics button in the Status Line toolbar. You can select particles individually by clicking Select By Component Type: Points in the Status Line toolbar.

Note: Not all per-particle attributes will work with all particle render types. For instance, radiusPP will only work with Blobby Surface, Cloud, and Sphere particles. For a detailed attribute list, see "List of Particle Attributes" in the Maya help file.

Note: If particles are emitted from a NURBS or polygon object, they can derive their color from that surface. See the "Use a Texture to Color Emission or Scale the Rate" tutorial in the Maya help file.

Working with Vectors and Matrices

Vectors are useful for determining direction within Maya. Matrices, on the other hand, are an intrinsic part of 3D and are necessary for converting various coordinate spaces. Comparing the direction of lights, cameras, and surface components within different coordinate spaces can provide information useful for custom shading networks. Before I discuss such networks, however, a review of vector math, the Vector Product utility, and Maya matrices is warranted.

Understanding Vector Math

In the mathematical realm, a vector is the quantity of an attribute that has direction as well as magnitude. For instance, wind can be represented by a vector since it has direction and speed (where speed is the magnitude).

In Maya, there are several variations of vectors. Vector attributes are simply a related group of three floating-point numbers. Color is stored as a vector attribute (R, G, B). At the same time, Maya vector attributes are used for transforms in 3D space. For instance, the translate of an object is represented as a vector attribute (X, Y, Z).

A second variation of a Maya vector is used to determine direction. That is, a particular point in space (X, Y, Z) has a measurable distance from the origin (0, 0, 0) and a specific angle relative to the origin. In this case, the distance serves as the vector magnitude and the angle is the vector direction. There are a number of specialized attributes that provide this style of vector (which can be loosely described as a "spatial vector"). A more detailed description of commonly used spatial vectors follows:

Normal Camera and Surface Normal The Normal Camera attribute is provided by the Sampler Info utility and material nodes. It represents the surface normal of the point being sampled in camera space. A surface normal is a vector that points directly away from the surface (and at a right angle to the surface). In general, surface normals are normalized so that their length (that is, their magnitude) is 1.

Ray Direction The Ray Direction attribute is provided by the Sampler Info utility and material nodes. It's a vector that runs from the surface point being sampled to the camera in camera space.

Facing Ratio The Facing Ratio attribute is uniquely provided by the Sampler Info utility and is the cosine of the angle between Ray Direction and Normal Camera. (A cosine is the trigonometric function often defined as the ratio of the length of the adjacent side to that of the hypotenuse in a right triangle.) The Facing Ratio is clamped between 0 and 1. A value of 0 indicates that the surface normal is pointing away from the camera. A value of 1 indicates that the surface normal is pointing toward the camera.

Light Direction The Light Direction attribute is provided by the Light Info utility and is a vector that represents the direction in which a light, camera, or other input node is pointing in world space. Lights also have a built-in Light Direction attribute (found in the Light Data section of the light shape node's Connection Editor attribute list). However, the Light Direction attribute of a light is in camera space.

Using the Vector Product Utility

The Vector Product utility accepts any vector attribute, whether it is a color, a transform, or a spatial vector. You can set the utility's Operation attribute to one of four modes:

Dot Product Dot Product multiplies two vectors together and returns a value that represents the angle between them. Its output may be written as

```
output = (a*d) + (b*e) + (c*f)
```


The first input vector is (a, b, c) and is connected to Input 1 of the utility. The second input vector is (d, e, f) and is connected to Input 2 of the utility. The output is a single value. If Normalize Output is checked, the output is the actual cosine and will run between –1 and 1. –1 signifies that the vectors run in opposite directions. 0 signifies that the vectors are perpendicular to each other. 1 signifies that the vectors run in the same direction. When the Operation attribute is set to Dot Product, outputX, outputY, and outputZ attributes are the same value.

Cross Product Cross Product generates a third vector from two input vectors. The new vector will be at a right angle (perpendicular) to the input vectors.

Vector Matrix Product and Point Matrix Product Vector Matrix Product converts the coordinate space of a vector. This becomes useful when input vectors are in different coordinate spaces, such as camera and world. For conversion to work, the utility requires the connection of a transform matrix to its Matrix attribute. You can connect the XForm Matrix attribute of a camera or geometry transform node for this purpose. Xform Matrix is a world space matrix. Maya nodes also carry the World Matrix attribute, which is in world space. (For examples of shading networks using World Matrix, see Chapter 7.) The vector that requires conversion is connected to the Input 1 attribute. The Point Matrix Product operation offers the same space conversion, but operates on points.

An Overview of Maya Matrices

Maya uses a 4 × 4 matrix for transformations (see Figure 8.11). The position of an object is stored in the first three numbers of the last row. The object's scale is stored as a diagonal from the upper left. The object's rotation is indirectly stored within the first three vertical and horizontal positions from the upper-left corner; the rotation values are stored as sine and cosine values. When an object is created, or has the Freeze Transformations tool applied to it, its transform matrix is an *identity matrix*. An identity matrix is one that produces no change when it is multiplied by a second transform matrix. In other words, an object with an identity matrix has no translation, rotation, or increased/decreased scale.

$$\begin{bmatrix} sx & 0 & 0 & 0 \\ 0 & sy & 0 & 0 \\ 0 & 0 & sz & 0 \\ tx & ty & tz & 1 \end{bmatrix}$$

Figure 8.11
Maya's 4×4 transformation matrix

Converting Camera Space to World Space

As an example of camera space to world space conversion, in Figure 8.12 the Xform Matrix of a polygon cube is used to convert a Normal Camera vector of a Sampler Info utility into a world space vector. The results are illustrated by applying the resulting vector to the color of a material.

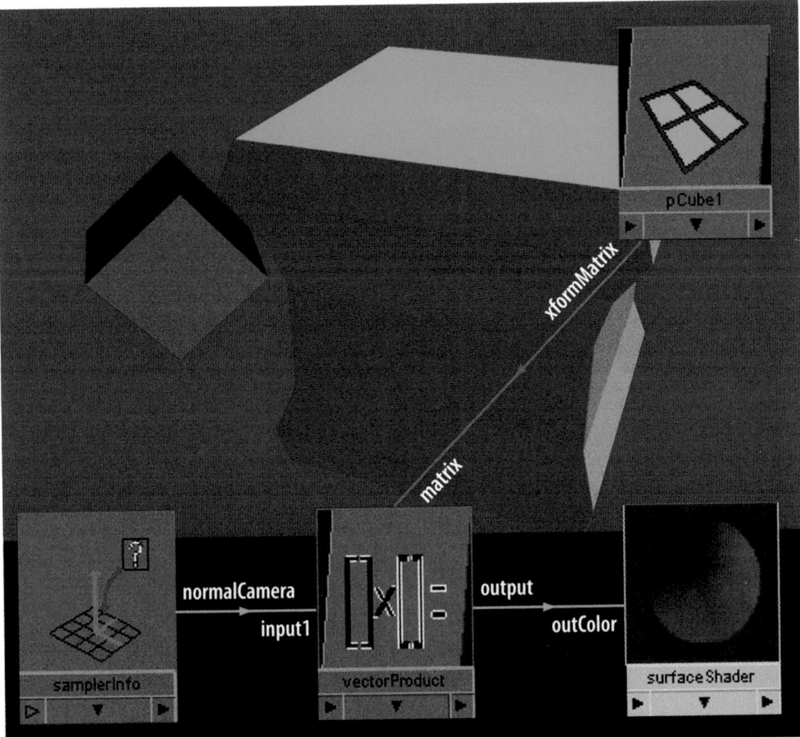

Figure 8.12 The Xform Matrix attribute of a polygon cube drives the color of a material. This scene is included on the CD as `xform_matrix.ma`. A QuickTime movie is included as `xform_matrix.mov`.

The xformMatrix of the pCube1 transform node is connected to the matrix of a vectorProduct node. (pCube1 is the small gray cube in Figure 8.12.) The normalCamera of a samplerInfo node is connected to the input1 of the vectorProduct node. The vectorProduct Operation value is set to Vector Matrix Product. The output of the vectorProduct node is connected directly to outColor of a surfaceShader material node, which is assigned to a second, larger polygon shape.

As a result of the custom connections, the faces of the larger shape that point toward the camera render blue *until* pCube1 is rotated. This is a result of the Normal Camera attribute existing in camera space. A normal that points directly toward the camera always has a vector of 0, 0, 1. At the same time, while pCube1 is at its rest position, its xformMatrix is an identity matrix and has no effect on the normalCamera value. Thus, the values 0, 0, 1 are passed to outColor of the surfaceShader node. When pCube1 is rotated, however, the normalCamera value is multiplied by the new xformMatrix and hence the color of the shape is affected. For instance, if pCube1 is rotated –45, –45, 0, a pale green results on the faces of the larger shape that point toward camera. The resulting math is illustrated in Figure 8.13.

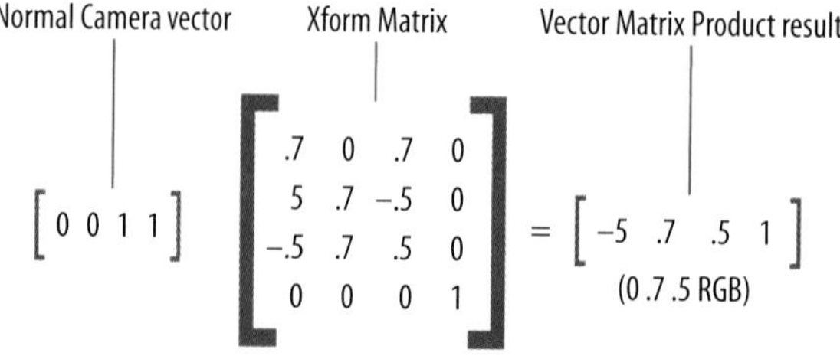

Figure 8.13 A matrix calculation based on pCube1's rotation of –45, –45, 0. The matrix numbers have been rounded off for easier viewing.

When representing the matrix calculation, as with Figure 8.13, the extra number 1 at the right side of the Normal Camera vector (and at the bottom-right corner of the Xform Matrix) is necessary for this type of math operation; however, these numbers do not change as the corresponding objects go through various transformations.

Note: As with many custom networks, the material icon in the Hypershade window, as well as the workspace view, may not provide an accurate representation of the material. To see the correct result for the previous example, use the Render View window.

Note: You can retrieve the current Xform Matrix value of a node by typing **`getAttr`** ***`name_of_node`*****`.xformMatrix;`** in the Script Editor.

Testing a Condition

The Condition utility functions like a programming `If Else` statement. `If Else` statements are supported by Maya expressions and are written like so:

```
if ($test < 10){
     print "This Is True";
} else {
     print "This Is False";
}
```

If the `$test` variable is less than 10, Maya prints "This Is True" on the command line. The `If Else` statement serves as a switch of sorts, choosing one of several possible outcomes depending on the input. The function of the Condition utility, when written in the style of an `If Else` statement, would look like this:

```
if (First Term  Operation  Second Term){
     Color If True;
} else {
     Color If False;
}
```

First Term and Second Term attributes each accept a single input or value, while the Color If True and Color If False attributes accept vector values or inputs. The Operation attribute has six options: Equal, Not Equal, Greater Than, Less Than, Greater Or Equal, and Less Or Equal.

With the Condition utility, you can apply two different textures to a single surface. By default, all surfaces in Maya are double-sided but only carry a single UV texture space. Hence, a plane receives the same texture on the top and bottom. You can avoid this, however, with the shading network illustrated by Figure 8.14.

The flippedNormal of a samplerInfo node is connected to firstTerm of a condition node. The Flipped Normal attribute indicates the side of the surface that is renderable. If the attribute's value is 1, then the "flipped," or secondary, side is sampled. If the value is 0, the nonflipped, or primary, side is sampled. The nonflipped side is the side that is visible when the Double Sided attribute of the surface is unchecked.

Returning to the network, the outColor of a checker texture node is connected to the colorIfTrue of the condition node. The outColor of a file texture node is connected to the colorIfFalse attribute of the same condition node. A bitmap image of a hundred dollar bill is loaded into the file texture node. The condition's Second Term is set to 1 and Operation is set to Equal. Last, the outColor of the condition node is connected to the color of a blinn material node. Thus, the flipped side of a primitive plane receives the Checker texture while the nonflipped side receives the File texture.

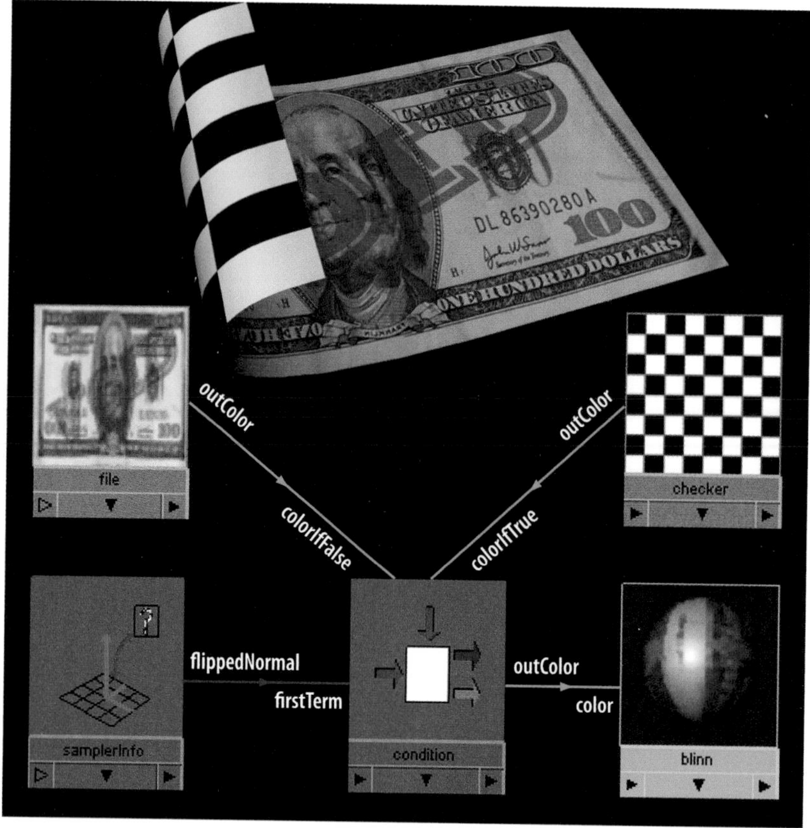

Figure 8.14 A single surface receives two textures with the help of a Condition utility. This scene is included on the CD as `condition_flipped.ma`.

Switching Outputs

Switch utilities provide multiple outputs from a single node. That is, they switch between different values in order to create different results among the geometry assigned to their shading network. Since the application of a Switch utility is unique in Maya, a step-by-step guide for a Triple Switch utility follows:

1. Choose an RGB attribute of a material, such as Color, and click its checkered Map button. Choose a Triple Switch from the Switch Utilities section in the Utilities tab of the Create Render Node window.
2. Assign the material to two or more surfaces.
3. Open the Attribute Editor tab for the tripleShadingSwitch node. Click the Add Surfaces button. All the surfaces assigned to the material appear in the list.
4. Right-click the first surface name in the Switch Attributes list and choose Map from the shortcut menu. The Create Render Node window opens. Choose a texture. The texture node appears in the Hypershade window. The Out Color attribute of the texture node (for example, stucco.outColor) appears in the inTriple column of the Switch Attributes list. Repeat this process for each of the remaining surfaces in the Switch Attributes list.

5. Render a test. Each surface picks up a different texture. An example is included as Figure 8.15.

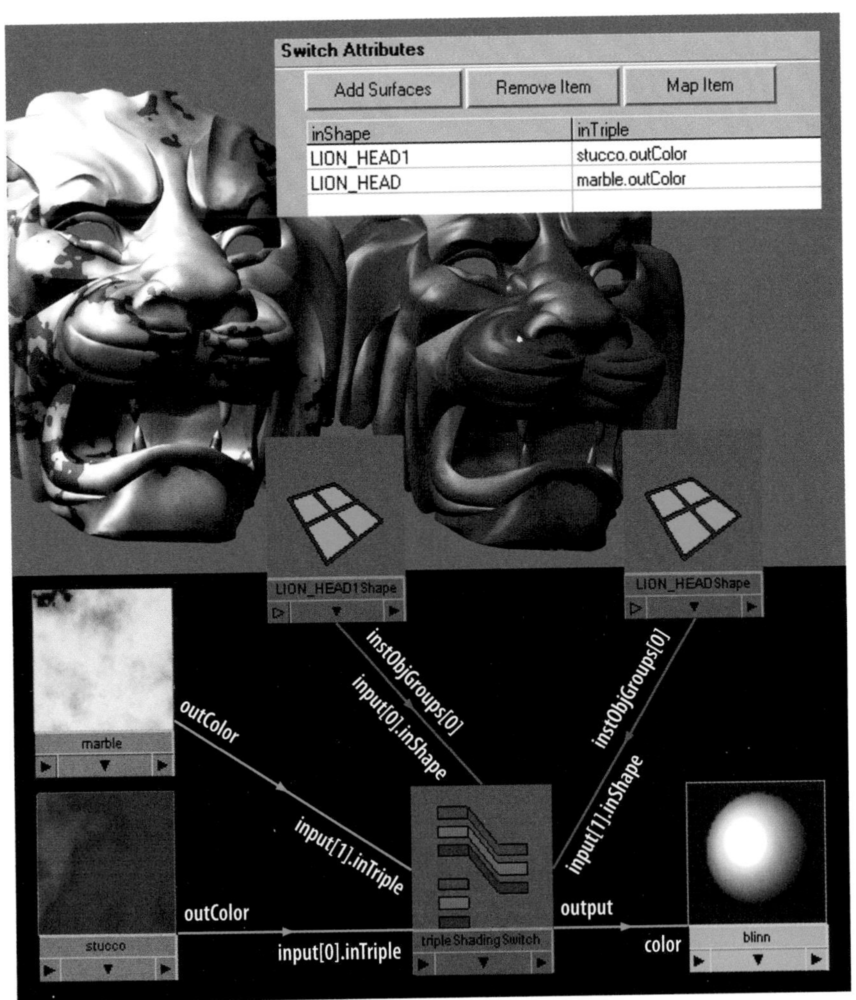

Figure 8.15 Color is controlled by a Triple Switch utility. A simplified version of this scene is included on the CD as `triple_switch.ma`.

Although these steps apply the switch to a material, you can apply them to any node. That said, Triple Switches are designed for vector values and are best suited for any attribute that uses RGB colors or XYZ coordinates.

Single switches, on the other hand, are designed for scalar values and are best suited for such attributes as Diffuse, Eccentricity, Reflectivity, or Bump Value. The Single Switch utility automatically chooses the outAlpha attribute when a texture is chosen. In this case, the outAlpha of each texture connects to the input[*n*].inSingle of the singleShadingSwitch node. The *n* in input[*n*].inSingle corresponds to the slot number of the Switch Attributes list. The first slot is 0, the second is 1, and so on. Although geometry is also connected to the singleShadingSwitch node, the connection lines are initially hidden. Nevertheless, the instObjGroups[*n*] of each geometry shape node must be connected to the input[*n*].inShape of the singleShadingSwitch node. In this situation, the *n* of the instObjGroups[*n*] attribute refers to the hierarchy position of an instanced attribute. (See Chapter 7 for information on attribute instancing.) In most cases, *n* is 0. The instObjGroups[*n*] convention applies equally to Double, Triple, and Quad Switch utilities. In addition, all the switches possess variations of the input[*n*].inSingle input.

Double switches are designed for paired or double attributes. This makes the utility well suited for controlling UVs. For example, in Figure 8.16 a Cloth texture receives standard UV coordinates from a default place2dTexture node. The Repeat UV values, however, are supplied by a Double Switch utility. In this case, the repeatUV attributes of three additional place2dTexture nodes are connected to the input[*n*].inDouble attributes of the doubleShadingSwitch node. place2dTexture1 has a Repeat UV value of 5, 5. place2dTexture2 has a Repeat UV value of 25, 25. place2dTexture3 has a Repeat UV value of 50, 50. This shading network offers the ability to adjust UVs on multiple objects without affecting the base texture or necessitating the duplication of the entire shading network.

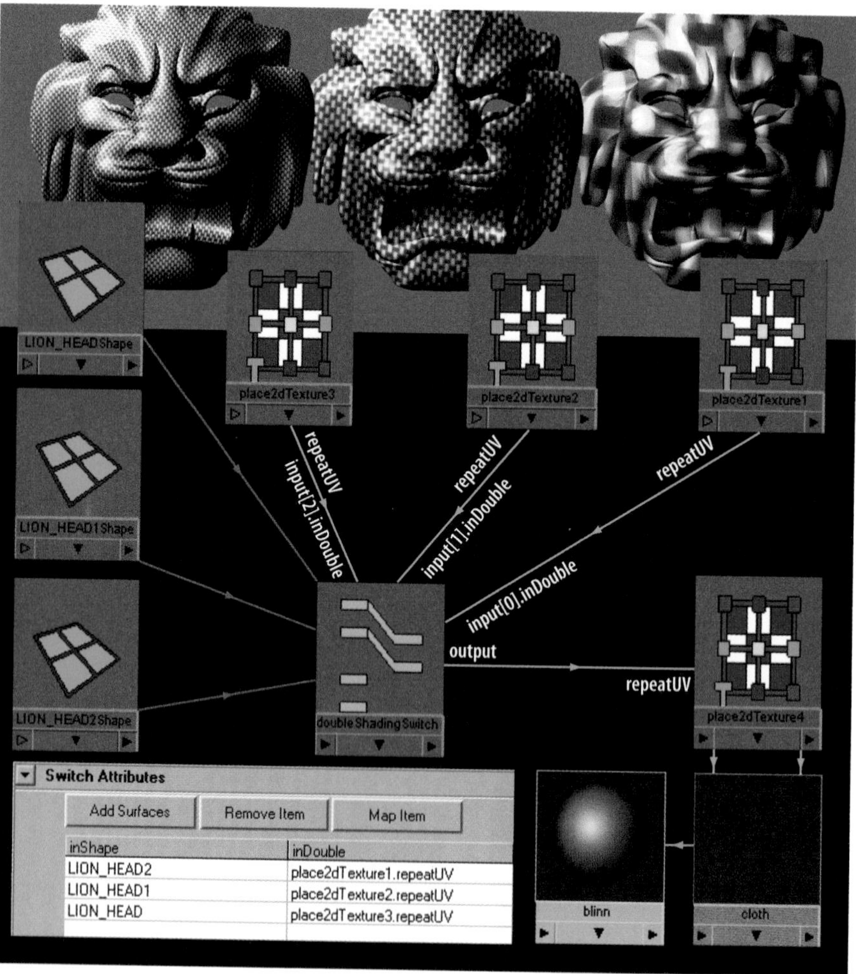

Figure 8.16 Repeat UV is controlled by a Double Switch utility. A simplified version of this scene is included on the CD as `double_switch.ma`.

The Quad Switch utility is suited for handling a vector attribute and a single attribute simultaneously. For example, in Figure 8.17 the outTriple attribute of the quadShadingSwitch node is connected to the color of a blinn material node. The outSingle attribute of the quadShadingSwitch node is connected the diffuse of the same blinn. To split the switch's output in such a way, it is necessary to use the Connection Editor. The color attributes of three additional blinn nodes are connected to the input[*n*].inTriple attributes of the quadShadingSwitch node. The diffuse attributes of the blinn nodes are also connected to the input[*n*].inSingle attributes of the quadShadingSwitch node. Each of the three blinn nodes has the outColor of a different texture connected to their color and diffuse attributes. In this case, the diffuse attributes *do not* need to correspond with the color attributes. For instance, blinn2's color can be connected to input[0].inTriple and blinn2's diffuse can be connected to input[4].inSingle. This ability to mix and match outputs and inputs allows for a great diversity of results. Hence, the Quad Switch provides the flexibility necessary to texture crowds, flocks, and swarms. Although such custom connections will function properly, they do not appear in the Switch Attributes list of the switch's Attribute Editor tab.

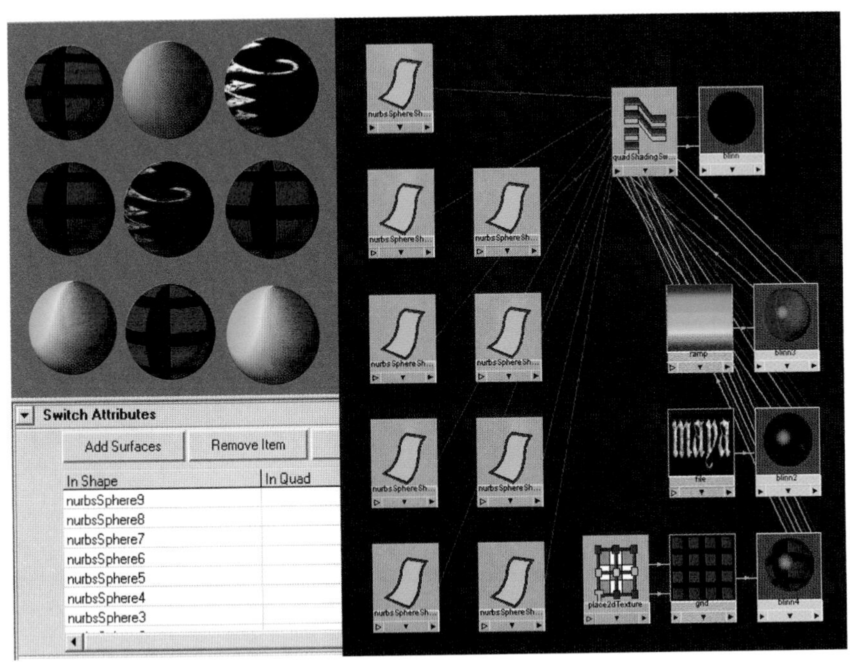

Figure 8.17 Three different Blinn materials are dispersed among nine spheres using a Quad Switch utility. This scene is included on the CD as `quad_switch.ma`.

Using Esoteric Utilities and Scene Nodes

Several utilities and nodes fail to fit into a specific category. Of these, the Stencil utility provides an alternative method of blending maps together. You can repurpose Optical FX and Unit Conversion utilities to fit a custom network. Although scene nodes (those automatically generated by Maya) are not particularly flexible, they provide critical services in a 3D scene.

Stenciling Color

As Stencil is the third texture application radio button listed in the 2D Textures section of the Create Maya Nodes menu (following Normal and As Projection). If a texture is chosen with As Stencil selected, the new texture automatically receives a Stencil utility and two place2dTexture nodes. The Stencil utility stencils the new texture on top of the material color. For example, in Figure 8.18 a red logo is applied to a wall map with this technique. Although the Stencil utility produces results similar to the Blend Colors utility (see Chapter 6), its methodology is fairly different.

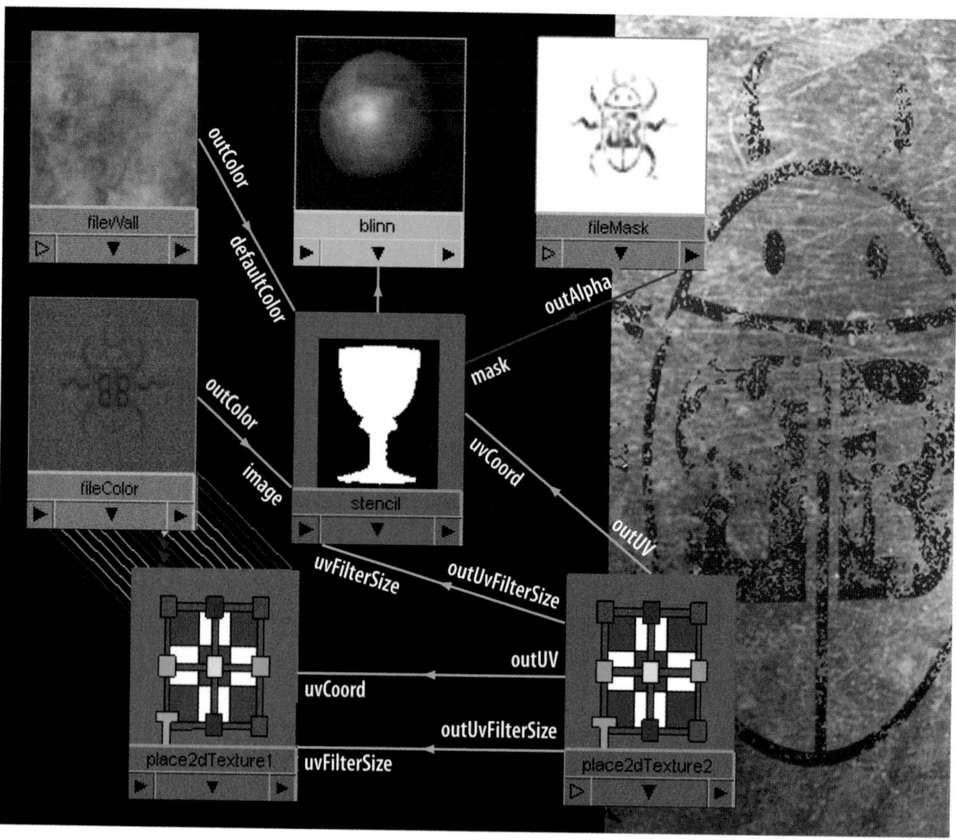

Figure 8.18 A logo is applied to a wall with a Stencil utility. This scene is included as on the CD as `stencil.ma`.

In the example shading network, a red logo bitmap is loaded into a File texture named fileColor. The outColor of fileColor is connected to image of a stencil node. Standard UV connections run from the first place2dTexture node to fileColor. The second place2dTexture node is connected to the stencil node with similar (albeit fewer) standard UV connections. The outUV of the stencil's place2dTexture node is connected to the uvCoord of fileColor's place2dTexture node. The outUvFilterSize of the stencil's place2dTexture node is also connected to the uvFilterSize of fileColor's place2dTexture node.

Normally, this minimal set of connections will cause the fileColor texture to completely overtake the blinn's color. To avoid this, the outAlpha of a second file texture node, named fileMask, is connected to the mask of the stencil node. The Mask attribute controls where the new texture will show over the material color. In this case, a black and white bitmap is loaded into the fileMask node. Where the bitmap is white, the material color shows through; where the bitmap is black, the red logo is rendered.

At this point, the material color that is revealed by the Mask attribute can be only the solid color of the material's Color attribute. To avoid this, the outColor of a third file texture node, named fileWall, is connected to the defaultColor of the stencil node. In this example, a bitmap photo of a wall is loaded into the fileWall node. If fileWall was connected directly to the Color attribute of the blinn, it would not be visible.

Applying Optical FX

The Optical FX utility (found in the Glow section of the Create Maya Nodes menu in the Hypershade window) is automatically created whenever Light Glow is applied to a directional, area, or spot light. The utility controls the look of the glow, halo, or lens flare. (For a discussion on this and other fog effects, see Chapter 2.)

Oddly enough, the Optical FX utility can be "grafted" onto a surface. For example, in Figure 8.19 the worldMatrix[0] attribute of a polygon lightbulb shape node is connected to the lightWorldMat of an opticalFX node. This connection ensures that the optical effect will occur in the center of the lightbulb regardless of the lightbulb's position. The color of the blinn node is connected to lightColor of the opticalFX node. The blinn Color attribute is set to gold, which is picked up by the opticalFX glow. (The lightbulb surface is also assigned to the blinn.) Last, the Ignore Light attribute of the opticalFX node is checked; this informs the program that no light is present. The result is a glow that follows the lightbulb wherever it goes. Unfortunately, since the opticalFX node creates a post-process effect, the size of the glow will not change. You can animate the Glow Spread and Halo Spread attributes of the opticalFX node, however, if necessary.

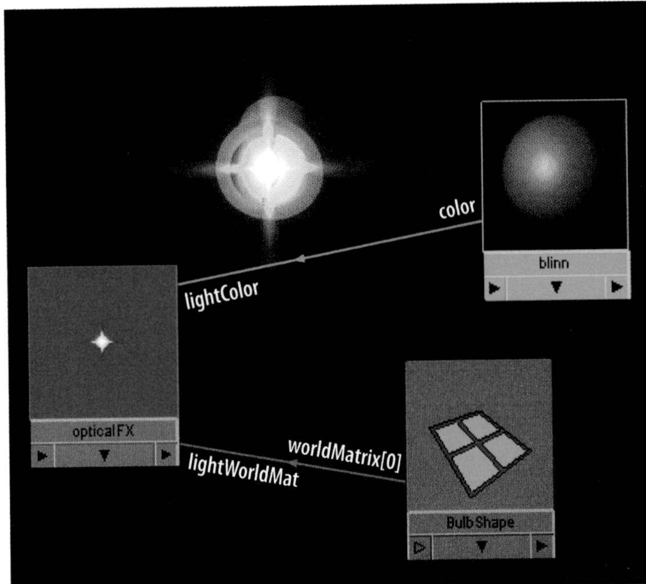

Figure 8.19
An Optical FX utility is attached to a lightbulb model, thereby creating a traveling glow. A simplified version of this scene is included on the CD as `optical_bulb.ma`. A QuickTime movie is included as `optical_bulb.mov`.

Converting Units

The Unit Conversion node, while not accessible in the Create Maya Nodes menu, automatically appears in many custom networks. For example, in Figure 8.20 the translateX of a cone transform node is connected to the rotateX of a sphere transform node. To view the connection, follow these steps:

1. Open `unit_conversion.ma` file from the CD. Select the sphere and cone. Choose Window > Hypergraph: Connections.
2. Choose Show > Show Auxiliary Nodes from the Hypergraph Connections menu (so that the option is checked). A unit conversion node should appear between the sphere and cone transform nodes.
3. If the node fails to appear, choose Show > Auxiliary Nodes from the Hypergraph Connections menu. In the Auxiliary Nodes window, highlight the word *unitConversion* in the Node Types That Are Hidden In Editors field and click the Remove From List button.
4. Alternatively, if you MMB-drag the sphere or cone transform node into the Hypershade work area, clicking the Input And Output Connections button reveals the unit conversion node.

By default, Maya calculates the translation of objects using Linear working units. At the same time, Maya calculates the rotation of objects using Angular working units. Whenever two dissimilar working units, such as Linear and Angular, are used in the same network, Maya must employ a Unit Conversion node to create accurate calculations. In the example illustrated in Figure 8.20, a Unit Conversion node is automatically provided with a Conversion Factor attribute set to 0.017. You can change Conversion Factor to achieve an exaggerated effect. If the Conversion Factor attribute is changed to 1, for example, the sphere will spin at a much greater speed when the cone is transformed.

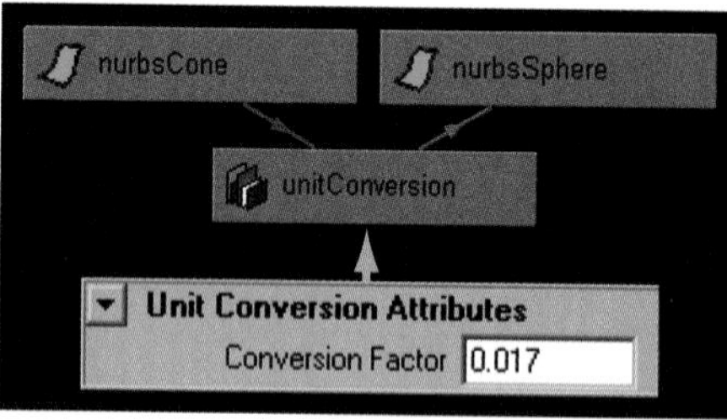

Figure 8.20
A Unit Conversion node converts two dissimilar units of measure. The scene is included on the CD as `unit_conversion.ma`.

Note: You can set a scene's working units by choosing Window > Settings/Preferences > Preferences and switching to the Settings section of the Preferences window. The default Linear working unit is centimeters and the default Angular working unit is degrees.

Note: In general, it's best to work in inches or centimeters. On occasion, calculation errors occur if a scene is set to meter, foot, or yard Linear units. For example, a scene set to foot units can exceed the maximum unit limit of a camera clipping plane and objects will fail to fully draw in the camera view.

Understanding Scene Nodes

Render Partition, Default Light Set, and Light Linker nodes sit the farthest downstream in any shading network (see Figure 8.21). The Render Partition utility defines which shading group nodes are called upon during a render.

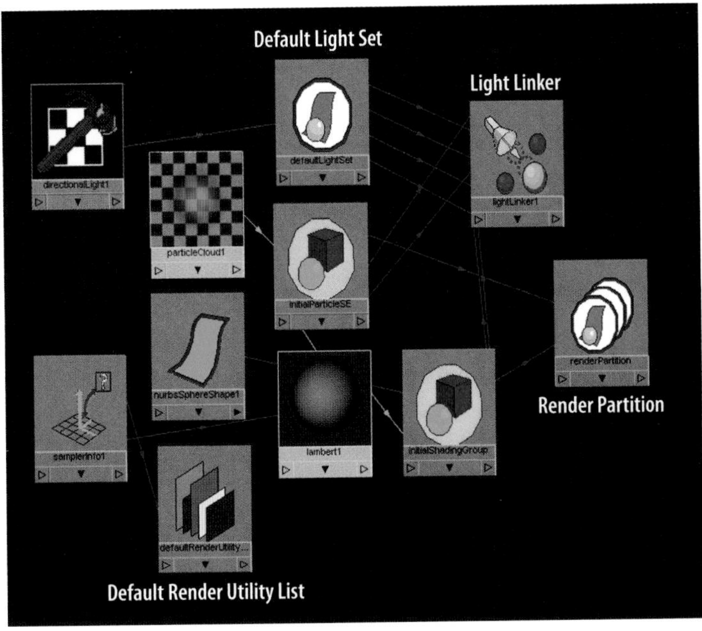

Figure 8.21 Scene nodes in a network

The Default Light Set utility carries a list of lights that illuminate all objects within a scene. The instObjGroups[0] attribute of each light's transform shape node is connected automatically to the dagSetMembers[0] attribute of the defaultLightSet node. If you uncheck the Illuminates By Default attribute in a light's Attribute Editor tab, the connection is removed until the attribute is once again checked.

The message of the defaultLightSet node is connected automatically to link[*n*].light and shadowLink[*n*].shadowLight of the lightLinker utility node. The Light Linker utility defines the relationship between lights and objects. If a light is connected through to defaultLightSet node to the link[*n*].light attribute, the light illuminates all shading groups connected to the lightLinker node. If a light is connected through the defaultLightSet node to the shadowLink[*n*].shadowLight attribute, then the light creates shadows for all shading groups connected to the lightLinker node. All shading group nodes are connected automatically to the lightLinker node. However, if you manually delete the connections, the shading group and the shading group's materials are ignored by the lights in the scene.

The Light Linker utility also stores broken links between lights, shadows, and surfaces. If a light link is broken through the Break Light Links tools, a connection is made between the message attribute of the surface shape node to the ignore[*n*].objectIgnored of the lightLinker node. A connection is also made between the message of the light shape node and ignore[*n*].lightIgnored of the lightLinker node. If the Make Light Links tool is applied, the connections are removed. Similar connections are made between the surface and light shape nodes' message and the lightLinker node when the Break Shadow Links tool is applied.

If a light is linked or unlinked in the Relationship Editor, the connections are identical to those made with the Make Light Links and Break Light Links tools. For more information on the Relationship Editor, Make Light Links, and Break Light Links, see Chapter 2.

The Default Render Utility List node holds a list of all render utilities in Maya. Although it cannot be used for any other purpose, it will show up in custom shading networks connected to each and every utility node.

Chapter Tutorial: Creating Eye Glow with Advanced Math Utilities

In this section, you will re-create the tapetum lucidum of an eyeball. The tapetum lucidum is a highly reflective membrane behind or within the cornea of many mammals and is responsible for the creepy eye glow seen at night. (Although a similar effect occurs when a flash photograph creates "red eye," humans don't possess the membrane.) You will use Light Info, Vector Product, and Multiply Divide utilities, as well as a Ramp texture. The tapetum lucidum of the eyeball geometry will become bright red only when both the camera and the scene's spot light are pointing directly toward it (see Figure 8.22).

1. Open `tapetum.ma` from the Chapter 8 scene folder on the CD. This file contains an eyeball model. A NURBS disc, which sits behind the iris, is named Tapetum and will provide the tapetum lucidum effect. A spot light, named Flashlight, is placed near the eye. It will serve as the scene's single light source and will figure into the calculations.
2. MMB-drag two Light Info utilities into the Hypershade work area. Name the first **lightInfoA** and the second **lightInfoB**. Switch over to the Lights tab of the Hypershade window and MMB-drag the FlashlightShape node into the work area.
3. Open the Hypergraph window. MMB-drag the persp camera transform node, the Flashlight transform node, and the Tapetum geometry transform node into the Hypershade work area. Connect worldMatrix[0] of the camera transform node to the worldMatrix of lightInfoA. Connect the worldMatrix[0] of the Tapetum geometry transform node to worldMatrix of lightInfoB.

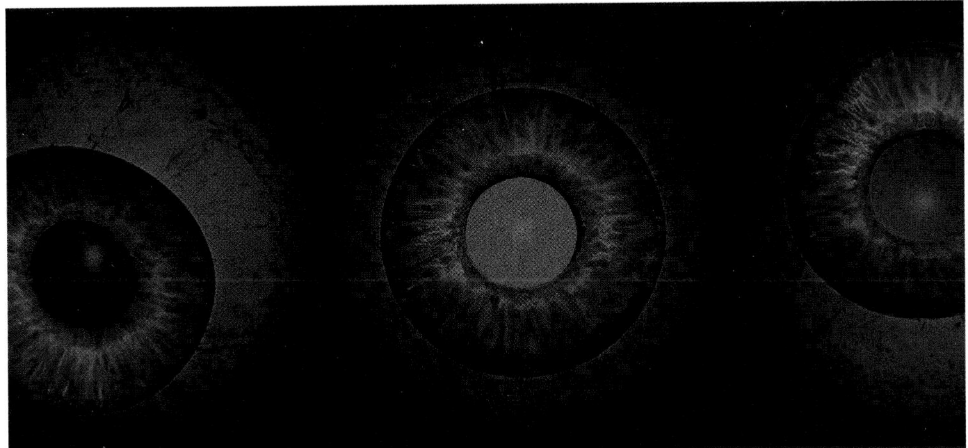

Figure 8.22 The tapetum lucidum of an eye is re-created with the Light Info, Vector Product, and Multiply Divide utilities. A QuickTime movie is included on the CD as `tapetum.mov`.

4. MMB-drag five Vector Product utilities into the work area. Name the first **vectorProductA**, the second **vectorProductB**, the third **vectorProductC**, the fourth **vectorProductD**, and the fifth **vectorProductE**. See Figure 8.23 for the placement of the nodes.

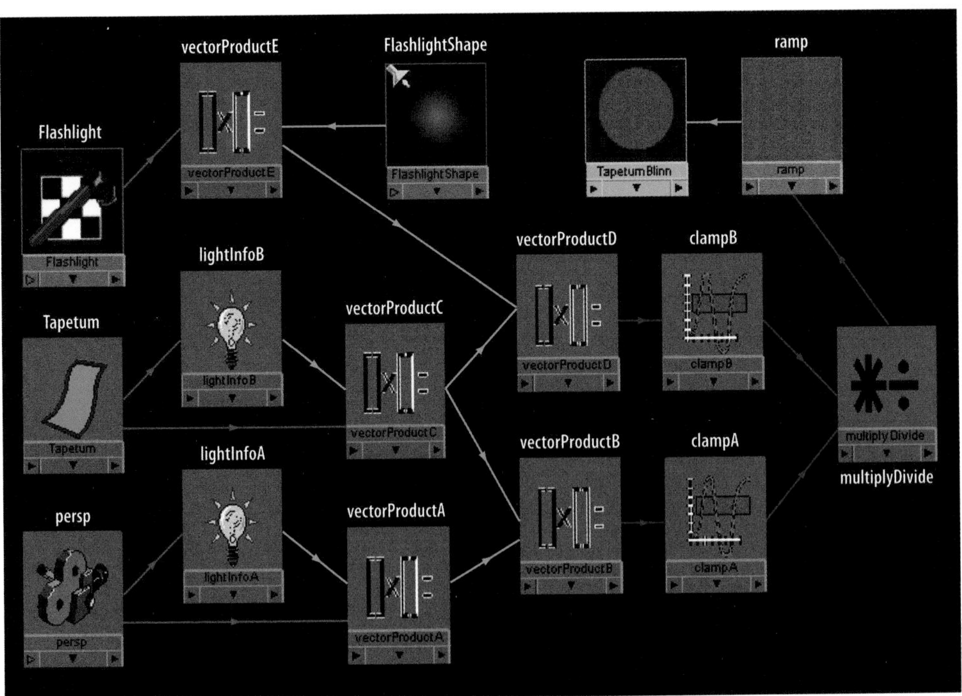

Figure 8.23 The custom shading network for the tapetum effect

5. Connect lightDirection of the FlashlightShape node to input1 of vectorProductE. (The Light Direction attribute is listed within the Light Data section of the light shape node's attribute list when the node is loaded into the Connection Editor.) Connect xformMatrix of the Flashlight transform node to matrix of vector-ProductE. Set vectorProductE's Operation to Vector Matrix Product and check Normalize Output. This will convert the lightDirection vector into a usable world space vector.
6. Connect xformMatrix of the Tapetum transform node to matrix of vectorPro-ductC. Connect lightDirection of lightInfoB to input1 of vectorProductC. Set vectorProductC's Operation to Vector Matrix Product and check Normalize Output. This will convert the direction of the Tapetum geometry into a usable world space vector.
7. Connect xformMatrix of the persp camera transform node to matrix of vectorProductA. Connect lightDirection of lightInfoA to input1 of vector-ProductA. Set vectorProductA's Operation to Vector Matrix Product and check on the Normalize Output button. This will convert the camera direction into a usable world space vector.
8. Connect output of vectorProductC to input2 of vectorProductB. Connect output of vectorProductA to input1 of vectorProductB. Set vectorProductB's Operation to Dot Product and check Normalize Output. This will calculate the angle between the Tapetum geometry direction and the persp camera direction.
9. Connect output of vectorProductC to input2 of vectorProductD. Connect output of vectorProductE to input1 of vectorProductD. Set vectorProductD's Operation to Dot Product and check Normalize Output. This will calculate the angle between the Tapetum geometry direction and the flashlight light direction.
10. MMB-drag two Clamp utilities into the work area. Rename them clampA and clampB. Connect outputX of vectorProductB to inputR of clampA. Connect outputX of vectorProductD to inputR of clampB. For each clamp node, set MinR to 0 and MaxR to 1. This will prevent any negative numbers from reaching the end of the shading network.
11. MMB-drag a Multiply Divide utility into the work area. Connect outputR of clampA to input1X of the multiplyDivide node. Connect outputR of clampB to input2X of the multiplyDivide node.
12. Set the multiplyDivide Operation to Multiply. If the Flashlight points toward the eye, input2X becomes roughly 1. If the eye is "looking" at the camera, input1X also becomes 1. In this the case, the surface normals of the Tapetum are pointing down the negative Z axis, whereby they are actually pointing in the same direction as the camera (you can see this if the Double Sided attribute is unchecked for the surface). If the eye is "looking" away, input1X becomes roughly 0. Similarly, if the light points 90 degrees away from the eye, input2X becomes 0. Hence, when the eye points toward the camera and the light points toward the eye, the multiplyDivide node outputs a large value. If either the

camera or the light points away from the eye, the output value becomes smaller. Only the angles of the light, camera, and geometry are compared. Although object position is part of the Xform Matrix attribute, the position of the object does not affect the output of the Dot Product operation. In other words, the light might produce a normalized cosine of 0.5 whether it's positioned at 0, 0, 0 or 500, 500, 500.

13. MMB-drag a Ramp texture and a Blinn material into the work area. Connect the outputX of the multiplyDivide node to vCoord of the ramp node. Create two handles in the ramp color field, one red and one black. Place the black handle at a Selected Position value of 0.75 and the red handle at a Selected Position value of 1. The ramp should have a thin red strip at the top with the bulk of the color black. Set the ramp's Interpolation attribute to Smooth. Connect outColor of the ramp node to incandescence of the blinn node. Assign the blinn to the Tapetum geometry.

14. Select the iris, cornea, and eyewhite geometry and parent them to the Tapetum. The vector calculations will only be accurate if the Tapetum geometry is at the top of the eye hierarchy.

15. The custom shading network is complete! Render out a few tests. No matter where the camera is, if the eye points toward it and the light points toward the eye, the tapetum lucidum will become bright red. If you get stuck, the finished scene is saved as `tapetum_finished.ma` in the Chapter 8 scene folder.

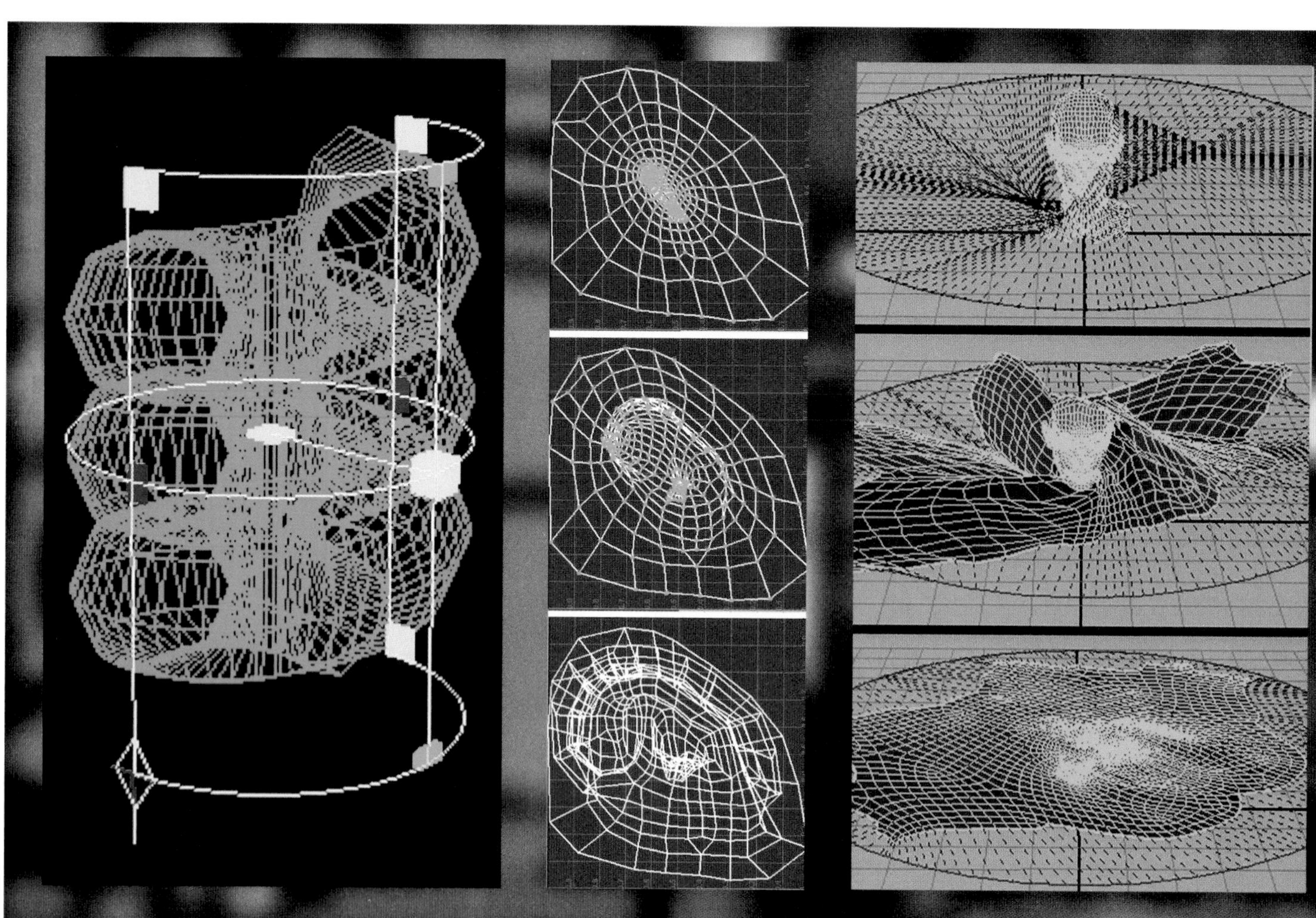

9

Improving Textures through Custom UVs, Maps, and Sliders

Although the Hypershade window provides numerous ways to prepare materials, several important techniques outside the window are worth a look. Preparing proper UVs for any model is a critical step in the texturing process. Using the 3D Paint tool is an efficient way to prepare custom bitmaps. Maya's support of the Photoshop PSD format allows the use of layers. At the same time, the proper use of bump and displacement maps can add realism to a render. Last, custom sliders can automate a material.

Chapter Contents

UV approaches for NURBS and polygon surfaces
Tips and tricks for fixing UV problems
Workflow for the 3D Paint tool
Support of the Photoshop PSD format
Intricacies of bump and displacement maps
Creating custom sliders for materials

Preparing UV Texture Space

The NURBS and polygon surfaces employed in the examples featured by previous chapters carry UV texture spaces that are satisfactory for their corresponding renders. For a render to be successful, the UV texture space of a surface must avoid undue stretching, pinching, or overlapping. Although the modeling steps necessary to create high-quality UVs are numerous and beyond the scope of this book, a few important concepts and techniques are worth reviewing.

To display the UV texture space of a selected surface, choose Window > UV Texture Editor. By default, U runs from left to right; V runs from bottom to top. In the UV Texture Editor, the dark gray area in the upper-right portion of the grid represents the full UV texture space. If a face sits outside this area, it will receive a repeated portion of a texture. UV manipulation of polygon, subdivision, and NURBS surfaces differs greatly. Techniques for dealing with each surface type follow.

Note: UV texture space is a coordinate space that relates pixels of a texture to points on a surface. UV points represent the location of a polygon's vertices within UV texture space; you can transform UV points in the UV Texture Editor. Groups of connected UV points are known as UV shells. *UVs* is a loose term for the current state of UV points in a particular UV texture space.

Prepping NURBS Surfaces

NURBS surfaces automatically receive UV texture information when they are created. 0, 0 in UV texture space occurs at the origin box of the surface. The two vertices appearing closest to the origin box are represented by a tiny U and V, indicating the U and V direction (see Figure 9.1).

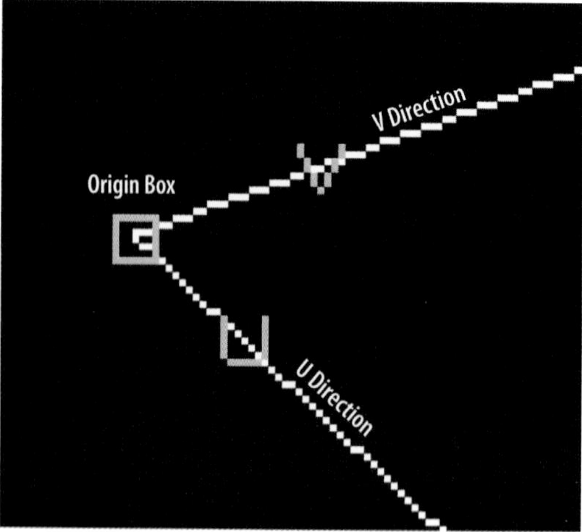

Figure 9.1 The origin box and UV vertices of a NURBS surface

In general, NURBS surfaces are ready to texture as soon as they're created. Nevertheless, an understanding of parameterization, closed and periodic surfaces, stretching, and UV alignment will strengthen your texturing skills.

Adjusting Parameterization

NURBS surfaces are inherently parametric. In general terms, parameterization is the mapping of one domain to a second domain. For example, the Earth, as a spherical planet, is mapped to rectangular travel maps. In terms of NURBS surfaces, parameterization is the method by which values are assigned to curve parameters. Curve parameters are points along the length of a curve or surface that have unique values. As the points get farther away from the origin of the curve or surface, their values increase. The parameter range of a NURBS primitive plane is 0 to 1. The parameter range of other NURBS primitives and custom NURBS surfaces is 0 to the total number of surface spans, which run from edit point to edit point. Ultimately, the parameter points determine the UV value of any given point on the corresponding surface. By default, NURBS surfaces automatically fill the entire UV texture space (see Figure 9.2). Regardless of the surface parameter range, the UV Texture Editor always displays a normalized UV range of 0 to 1.

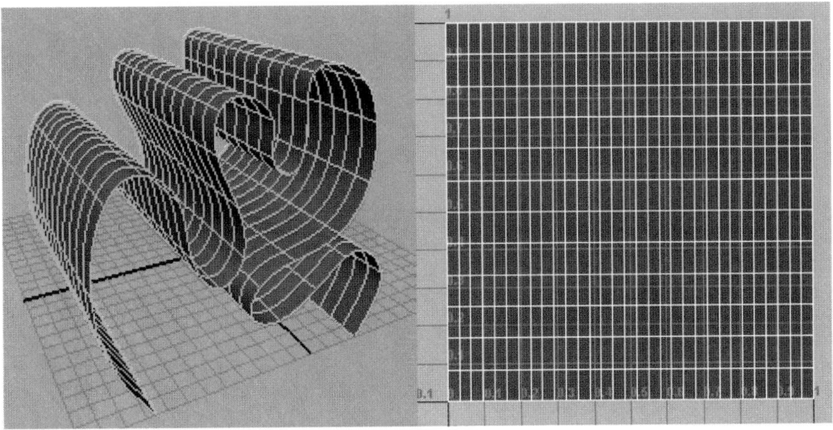

Figure 9.2 (Left) A NURBS loft. (Right) The loft's default UV texture space.

You can apply parameterization in Maya using two methods: uniform and chord length. The uniform method assigns parameter values to each edit point. The assignment does not take into account the length of any given span; instead, the uniform method only considers the total number of spans. Thus, if a curve has four edit points and three spans, the edit points will have the values 0, 1, 2, and 3 (see Figure 9.3). The uniform method is efficient and easy to visualize. However, its interpolation is not as accurate as the chord length method and can lead to unpredictable texture stretching.

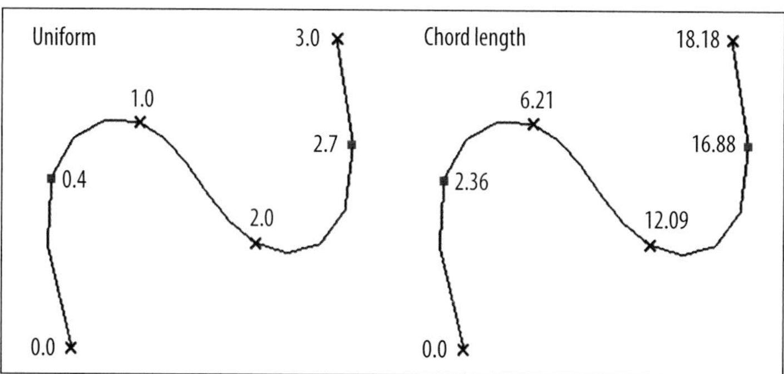

Figure 9.3 Uniform and chord length parameter values on similar curves. These curves are included on the CD as `uniform_chord.ma`.

Technically, chord length is the shortest linear distance between successive edit points. Chord length parameterization assigns parameter values based on these measurements. In other words, the parameter values are distributed unevenly along the curve and are not intrinsically bound to the number of edit points or spans (see Figure 9.3). The parameter values are based on world units and tend to be fairly large. The chord length method is more accurate but is difficult to visualize and predict. Surfaces based on chord length curves can be more complex and potentially flawed. (For example, they can suffer from the addition of extra isoparms, which is known as cross-knot insertion.)

By default, the CV Curve tool creates uniform curves. However, you can create chord length curves by choosing Create > CV Curve Tool > ❑, setting Knot Spacing to Chord Length, and applying the tool. To convert a chord length curve to a uniform curve, switch to the Surfaces menu set, choose Edit Curves > Rebuild Curve > ❑, set Rebuild Type to Uniform, and click Apply.

Note: To normalize the parameter range of a curve, switch to the Surfaces menu set, choose Edit Curves > Rebuild Curve > ❑, set Parameter Range to 0 To 1, and click Apply.

Note: You can observe the parameter values of uniform and chord length curves, as well as NURBS surfaces, by displaying their edit points and clicking the curve or surface isoparm. The Script Editor displays `select -r` *`curve_name`*`.u[`*`parameter_value`*`];` or `select -r` *`surface_name`*`.uv[`*`u_parameter`*`][`*`v_ parameter`*`];`.

Note: For a detailed description of open, closed, and periodic NURBS surfaces and tips and tricks for rebuilding them, see section 9.1 of the `Additional_Techniques.pdf` file on the CD.

Avoiding Texture Stretch

Texture stretching on NURBS surfaces is generally caused by one of the following reasons:

- An uneven distribution of surface isoparms exists due to unevenly spaced curves at the point of surface creation.
- Open/Close Surfaces or Attach Surfaces tools have been applied to the surface.
- Vertices have been moved a significant distance from their neighboring vertices.

You can temporarily fix texture stretching by checking the Fix Texture Warp attribute found in the Texture Map section on the surface's Attribute Editor tab (see Figure 9.4). In this case, the renderer ignores the inherent UV information of the surface and applies a new, nonpermanent chord length parameterization. The Grid Div Per Span U and Grid Div Per Span V attributes set the density of a virtual grid that is placed over the surface to calculate the new UV texture space. Although the default value of 4 works in most situations, you can increase the value for greater accuracy. This fix is supported by the Maya Software and mental ray renderers but will not work with the Hardware Texturing option in a workspace view.

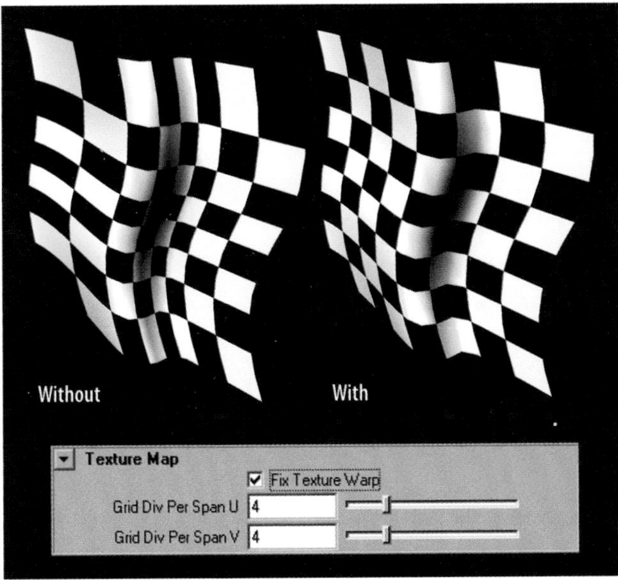

Figure 9.4 The Fix Texture Warp attribute and its effect

A second solution involves a "quick and dirty" method of reconstructing the surface. Using the `stretched_surface.ma` file in the Chapter 9 scene folder of the CD, you can follow these three steps:

1. While pressing the Shift key, insert evenly distributed isoparms across the surface in the direction of the stretching. The greater the number of isoparms, the more accurate the end product will be. Shift-select the two end isoparms. Use Figure 9.5 as a reference for each step.

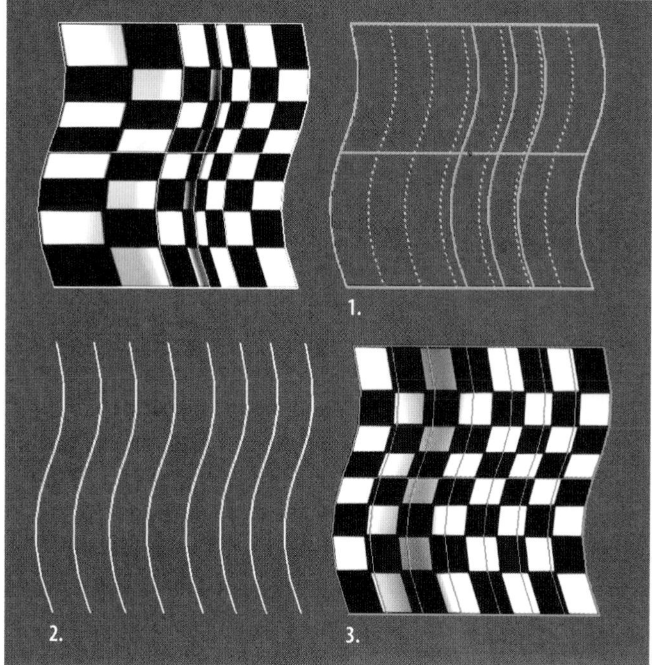

Figure 9.5 Quickly rebuilding a NURBS surface with stretching. This rebuilt surface is included on the CD as `rebuild_stretch.ma`.

2. With the new isoparms and the end isoparms selected, switch to the Surfaces menu set and choose Edit Curves > Duplicate Surface Curves. New curves will appear at all the isoparm locations. Delete the original surface.
3. Select the new curves in logical order (for example, left to right). Choose Surfaces > Loft with the default settings. Delete the curves. The final surface will have an evenly distributed UV texture space (at least in the direction of the loft).

Aligning NURBS Surfaces

To create a complex model with NURBS modeling tools, multiple surfaces are necessary. In this situation, it is important to align the UVs in such a way that they are easily interpreted. One technique employed professionally involves a global alignment of all the surfaces. For example, in Figure 9.6 a character is constructed from numerous NURBS surfaces. A Ramp texture is temporarily assigned to each surface, and Smooth Shade All and Hardware Texturing are checked through a workspace view menu. If the orientation of the ramp on a given surface matches the orientation of the ramp's material icon, the UVs are correctly aligned. That is, U runs left to right and V runs down to up. If a ramp appears sideways or upside down on a surface, you can fix the UVs by switching to the Surfaces menu set and choosing Edit NURBS > Reverse Surface Direction. To choose the correct option on the Reverse Surface Direction tool, it is important to understand the relationship of the NURBS surface normal to the U and V directions.

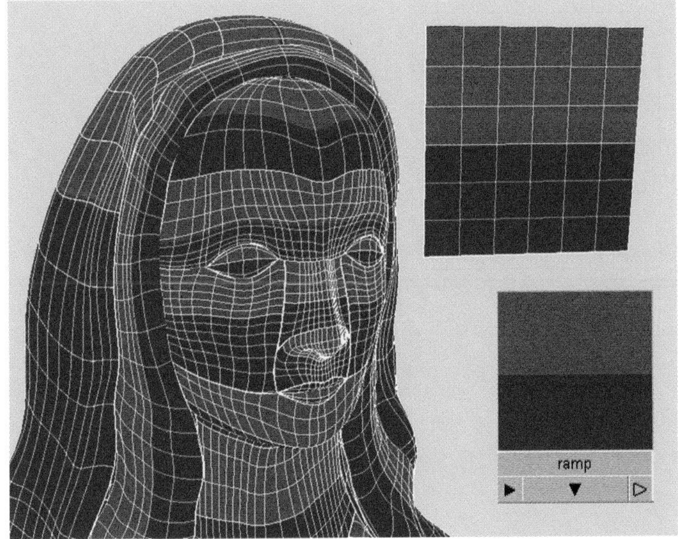

Figure 9.6 A Ramp texture is applied to a NURBS model to check UV alignment.

If U runs left to right and V runs down to up, the normal points toward the camera. If U runs right to left and V runs down to up, the normal points away from the camera. If U is running up and down and V is running left and right, the ramp will appear sideways. One way to remember this is to employ a variation of the right-handed Cartesian coordinate trick. Normally, in right-handed Maya coordinate space, the thumb points toward positive Z, the middle finger points toward positive Y, and the index finger points toward positive X. With a Maya NURBS surface, the thumb points toward positive U, the index finger points toward positive V, and the middle finger represents the direction of the surface normal (see Figure 9.7). All surfaces in Maya are double-sided by default. If the Double Sided attribute is unchecked in the Render Stats section of the surface's Attribute Editor tab, the UV-to-normal relationship is easier to see.

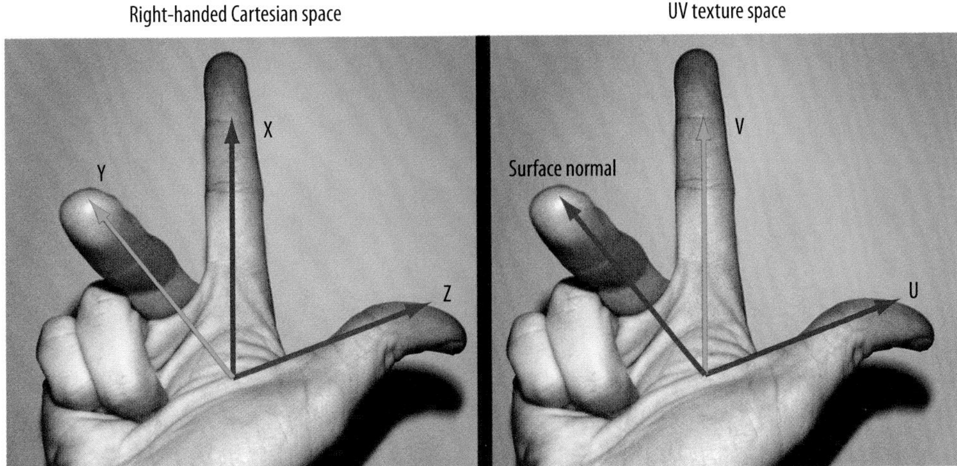

Figure 9.7 The right-handed system for Cartesian space and UV texture space

Note: Some animated productions require that all NURBS surfaces remain single-sided. A quick way to "flip" the normal of any single-sided surface that is pointing away from the camera is to switch to the Surfaces menu set, choose Edit NURBS > Reverse Surface Direction > ❑, set Surface Direction to U, uncheck Keep Original, and click Apply.

Preparing Polygons

Although NURBS surfaces are ready to render with their default UVs, polygon surfaces often need a great deal of adjustment. The use of primitives is the exception since the primitive's inherent UVs are orderly. As soon as various polygon modeling tools are applied to a primitive, however, the resulting UV texture space is cluttered and unusable (see Figure 9.8).

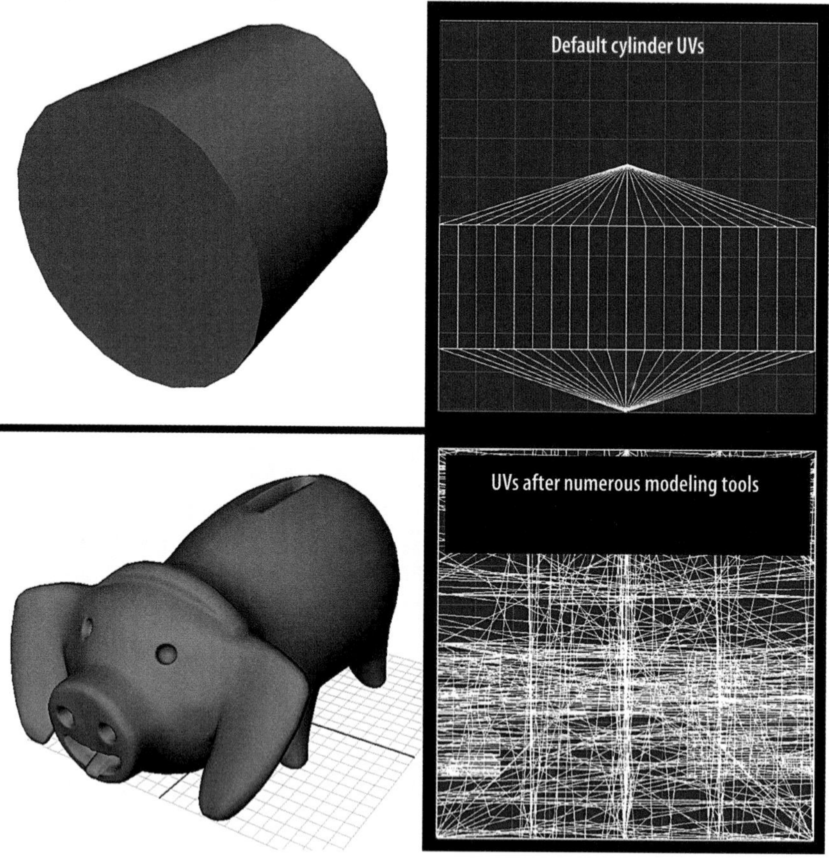

Figure 9.8 A polygon cylinder's default UV texture space and the result of numerous modeling tools

There are two main approaches to preparing UVs within Maya: pelt mapping and mapping tools. Pelt mapping generally requires a specialized MEL script, but can be achieved with standard UV tools through the UV Texture Editor. Mapping tools, on the other hand, are built into the program and represent the most common method of UV preparation.

Pelt Mapping

Pelt mapping unwraps geometry as if it were the pelt or skin of an animal. The goal with this approach is to create a single, large UV shell for the entire surface. This simplifies the texturing process by minimizing the number of resulting edges. In addition, the pelt mapping process creates a UV point distribution that mimics the original mesh. That is, the distance between each point is equivalent to the distance between matching vertices.

Several MEL scripts automate the creation of pelt mapping. For example, `pelt.mel`, available at `http://highend3d.com`, operates in the following manner:

- Creates a duplicate of the target surface.
- Allows you to define seams on the duplicate by cutting edges.
- Creates control clusters for each cut and attaches specialized particles, springs, and radial fields to each vertex.
- Sends the duplicate through a dynamic simulation complete with gravity. A collision plane is provided to "catch" the flattened duplicate.
- Transfers vertex positions from the flattened duplicate to the UV texture space of the original surface. Thus, vertex postions become UV points.

The most difficult aspect of this pelting method is the selection seams. Ultimately, the goal is to create an unfolded, nonoverlapping surface that fits neatly into the UV texture space. As an example of `pelt.mel` in action, a polygon ear is flattened (see Figure 9.9).

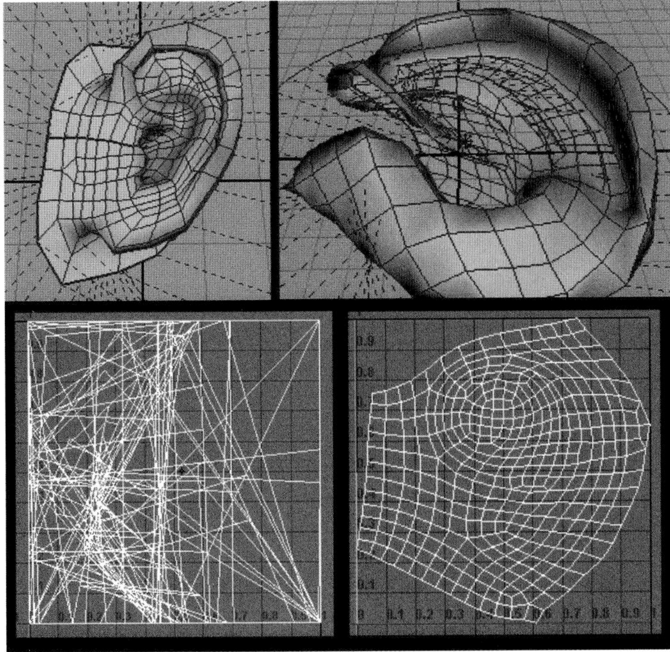

Figure 9.9
(Clockwise, from upper left) A duplicate ear awaits the dynamic simulation provided by `pelt.mel`; the ear dynamically unfolds; the final UV texture space; the UV texture space prior to the operation.

Pelting Tools, available at `http://hydralab.com`, uses a methodology similar to `pelt.mel`. It offers the advantage, however, of interactive tools to define seams and a graphic interface with a greater number of options (see Figure 9.10).

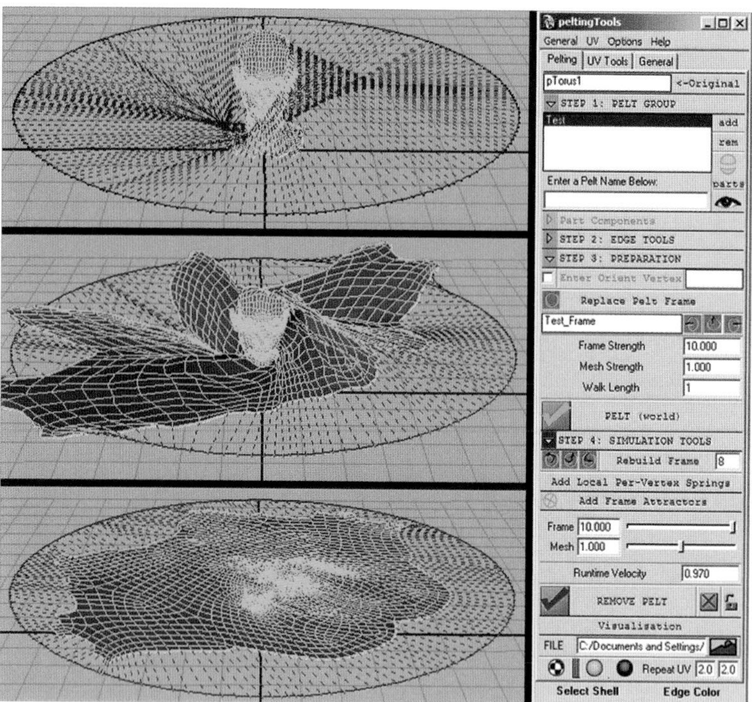

Figure 9.10 (Left) A polygon head goes through a dynamic unfolding. (Right) GUI for Pelting Tools MEL script. A QuickTime movie showing the unfolding is included on the CD as `head_pelt.mov`.

You can also create pelt maps in Maya with the standard set of UV tools. For example, in Figure 9.11 the UV points for the body of a polygon dog are left in one continuous piece. In this case, multiple UV mappings were applied to various parts of the dog. The resulting UV shells were then translated, rotated, scaled, and sewn back together with the Sew UV Edges and Move And Sew UV Edges tools.

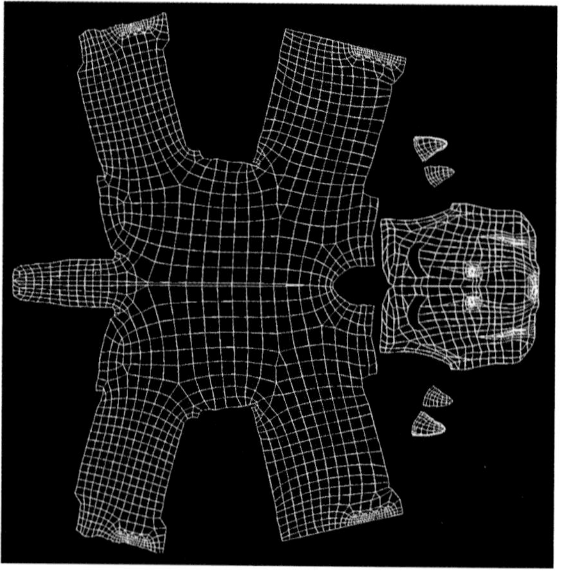

Model courtesy of Kirk Buckendorf

Figure 9.11 The UV texture space of a pelt-mapped polygon dog

Applying UV Mappings

You can find UV mapping tools under the Create UVs menu in the Polygons menu set. The mapping tools include Planar Mapping, Cylindrical Mapping, Spherical Mapping, and Automatic Mapping. To apply a mapping tool, select a polygon surface or set of faces and choose the tool. For example, in Figure 9.12 the Cylindrical Mapping tool is applied to a polygon primitive helix. A projection manipulator instantly appears. You can interactively adjust the sweep, height, translation, and rotation of the manipulator by clicking the various colored handles. The green boxes adjust projection height. The red boxes increase or decrease the horizontal sweep (by default, the cylindrical projection only covers 180 degrees). To access the rotation and translation handles, click the red T and the bottom of the manipulator. As the manipulator is adjusted, the UV points automatically update in the UV Texture Editor (Window > UV Texture Editor).

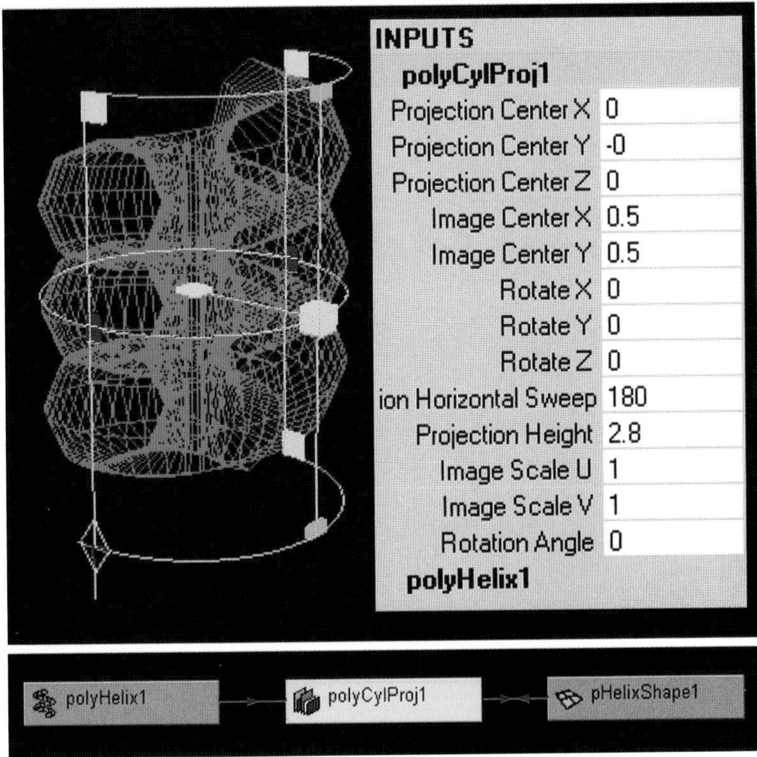

Figure 9.12 (Top left) Cylindrical Mapping projection manipulator applied to a polygon helix. (Top right) The polyCylProj1 node in the Channel Box. (Bottom) The polyCylProj1 node in the Hypergraph Connections window.

Here are a few additional tips for working with mapping tools and their projection manipulators:

Projection Manipulator The manipulator provided by all polygon UV mapping tools is finicky and tends to disappear when a mouse click is slightly off. Fortunately, you can bring back the manipulator by selecting the projection node. You can find the projection node in the Hypergraph Connections window (see Figure 9.12). You can also retrieve the manipulator by selecting the surface and opening the Channel Box.

The projection node will be listed under Inputs (see Figure 9.12). For example, a Cylindrical Mapping projection node will be named polyCylProj1. Clicking the projection node name reveals the projection's attributes and displays the manipulator in the workspace view. If interactive use of the manipulator proves impossible, you can set the projection node's Projection Horizontal Sweep, Projection Height, Rotate, and other projection-specific attributes in the Channel Box. The projection node will remain connected to the surface shape and transform nodes until the surface's history is deleted. At the point of deletion, the UV information is permanently encoded.

Note: Although it is possible to overlap mapping tool projections, it is not recommended. Multiple, active, overlapping projections can lead to flickering textures. If multiple, overlapping projections are deemed necessary, delete the surface's history (Edit > Delete By Type > History) between applications of each mapping. Active mapping tool projections on a skinned, deforming character are equally problematic.

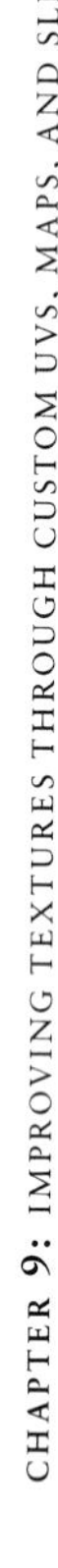

Multiple Projections You can apply UV mapping tools to entire polygon surfaces or to selected faces. On complex models, it often pays to apply separate mappings to various sections; at the same time, it is useful to have all the UV points in a single layout. For instance, if the model is a character, the head is mapped first, then the torso, then one arm, then the next, and so on. This allows different mapping styles and orientations to be applied. For example, the Cylindrical Mapping tool is applied to the head along the Y axis. The Cylindrical Mapping tool is applied a second time to an arm along the X axis. Separate Planar Mapping tools are applied to each hand. To replicate this process efficiently, follow these steps:

1. Select a set of faces. Apply the most appropriate mapping tool. Open the UV Texture Editor. If the projection manipulator is visible in the workspace view, a corresponding translate, scale, and rotate handle is accessible in the UV Texture Editor. Move the selected UV points into an empty area outside the gray area of the full UV texture space (see Figure 9.13). When the UV points are deselected, the entire surface becomes visible once again. The mapping separates the selected faces along the outer edges. (A group of separated UV points is called a UV shell.) If possible, separate the model at a natural border to avoid visible texture seams (for example, between a shirt collar and a neck).
2. Repeat the process for other sets of faces. Once all the faces have been mapped, move, scale, and rotate the individual UV shells back into the gray area.
3. To see how faces have been split in the UV Texture Editor, right-click and choose Edge from the marking menu. Click an outer edge of an UV shell. The corresponding edge that was separated during the mapping process is highlighted.

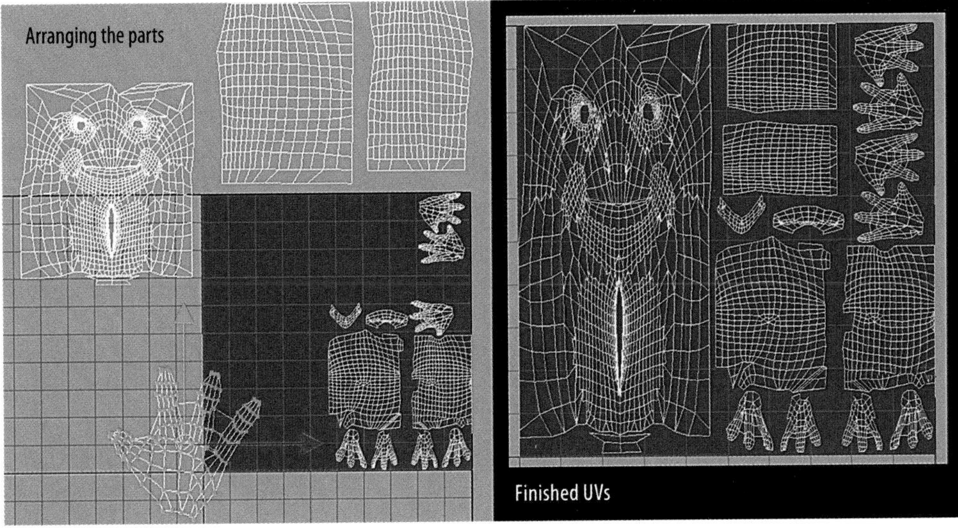

Figure 9.13 Creating and arranging multiple UV shells by applying multiple UV mappings

Although no technical problems will arise from separated faces, the separation can make the texturing process more difficult. To avoid this, you can sew selected faces back together (for example, reattaching a neck and a head). To do this, select one or more edges and choose Polygons > Sew UV Edges in the UV Texture Editor window. The faces that were once separated are rejoined. Sew UV Edges moves the resulting sewn edge to a point halfway between the previously separated faces (see Figure 9.14). This may or may not be useful. An alternative is to choose Polygons > Move And Sew UV Edges, which forces all the faces connected to the selected edge to move up to the second selected edge (see Figure 9.14). Move And Sew UV Edges does not prevent overlapping. If you need to manually split an edge, select the edge and choose Polygons > Cut UV Edges.

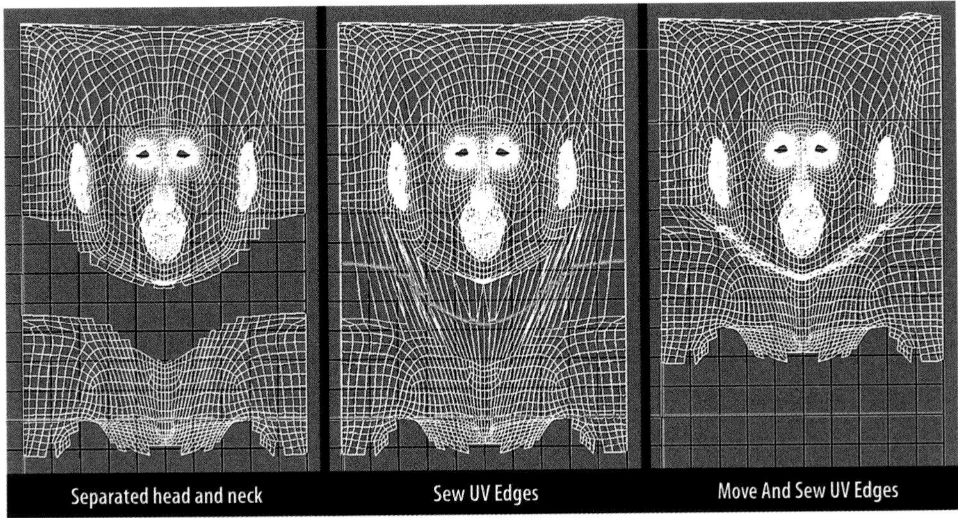

Figure 9.14 Reattaching a neck to a head with Sew UV Edges and Move And Sew UV Edges

Refining UV Points

Ideally, UV points should maximize the UV texture space without overlapping. The amount of space dedicated to each section of a model should be relative to that section's importance. In addition, distances between UV points should be roughly equivalent to the distances between the vertices that they correspond to. That is, if vertices on the model are regularly spaced, the UV points should also be regularly spaced. If the vertices on the model are closer together in the Y direction than they are in the X direction, the UV points should be closer together in the V direction than they are in U direction.

These guidelines are particularly critical for models intended for the video game industry, where textures are hand-painted and the texture resolutions are limited. For example, in Figure 9.15 a low-polygon character and a matching color bitmap are carefully laid out. Ideally, there should be a minimal amount of empty space left between the various UV shells.

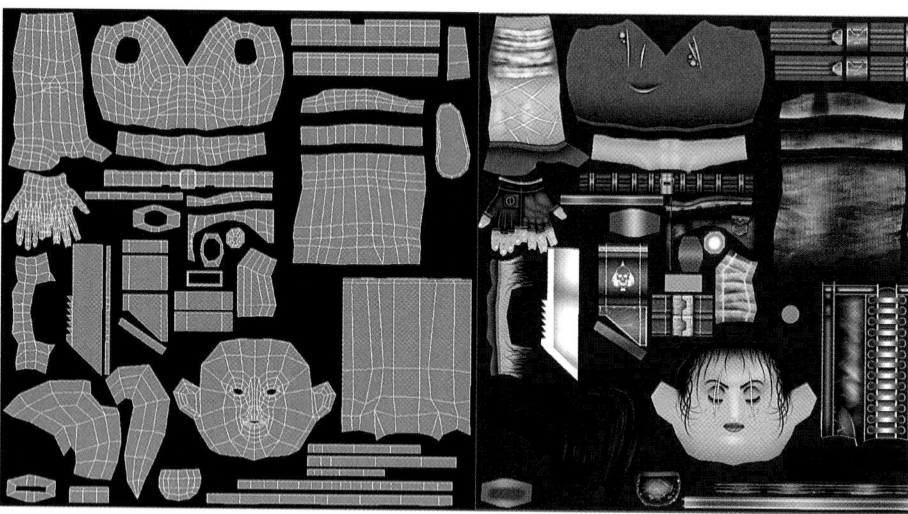

MODEL AND TEXTURE COURTESY OF JASON MARTIN

Figure 9.15 The UV texture space and matching color bitmap of a low-resolution polygon character

A good way to test UVs for potential stretching, pinching, or overlapping problems is to temporarily assign a Checker texture to the surface and choose Shading > Hardware Texturing from a workspace view menu (see Figure 9.16). Once an error has been located or a refinement planned, you can utilize a long list of Maya UV tools. These tools are available through the Polygons menu in the UV Texture Editor window or through the Edit UVs menu found in the Polygons menu set. A few of the more useful UV tools are highlighted in the following sections.

MANIPULATING POINTS

You can select UV points in the UV Texture Editor by right-clicking and choosing UV from the marking menu. Once selected, UV points can be translated, scaled, and rotated with standard Maya transform tools.

Figure 9.16 Testing polygon UVs with a Checker texture

NORMALIZING UVS

Choosing Polygons > Normalize in the UV Texture Editor fits the entire surface (or selected points, edges, or faces) into the full UV texture space. This ensures that a higher percentage of the UV texture space is utilized.

One inherent danger of the Normalize tool is the tool's inability to compensate for "stranded" points. Stranding is an artifact of the Cylindrical Mapping and Spherical Mapping tools (see Figure 9.17). If points are stranded, it's best to manually move them back to the main shell before applying Normalize.

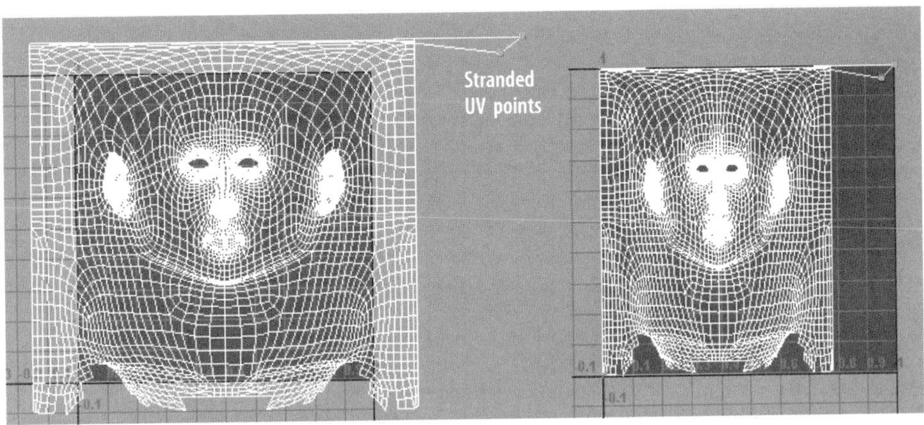

Figure 9.17 (Left) "Stranded" UV points; (Right) Same points after choosing Normalize

RELAXING UVS

Choosing Polygons > Relax in the UV Texture Editor spreads out overlapping and/or high-density clusters of selected UV points. For example, in Figure 9.18 a polygon ear has the Relax tool, with default settings, applied to it multiple times. Parts of the model that were once overlapping are flattened out.

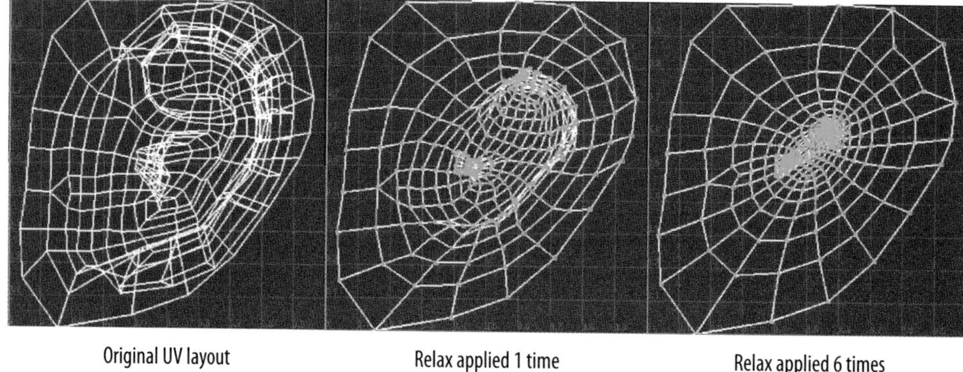

Figure 9.18 A polygon ear before and after applications of the Relax tool

The following options can improve the quality of the relaxation:

Edge Weights If set to World Space, Edge Weights attempts to maintain the original world space angles between faces. If left on Uniform, Edge Weights attempts to make all the edges the same length. Uniform produces a more drastic relaxation than World Space.

Pin UVs and Pin UV Border If Pin UVs is checked, Pin Selected UVs and Pin Unselected UVs options become available. If Pin Selected UVs is then checked, selected UV points will stay in place and unselected UV points will move as they are relaxed. If Pin Unselected UVs is checked instead, the opposite occurs. If Pin UV Border is checked, the outer edges of the UV shell will remain fixed while the rest of the UV points will move. You can check both Pin UVs and Pin UV Border for a more refined result.

Maximum Iterations Sets the number of iterations permitted to the relaxation calculation each time the tool is applied. The lower the value, the more subtle the resulting relaxation. The higher the value, the more extreme the relaxation.

Note: If the vertices at the shared corner of multiple polygon faces have not been merged, the Relax tool will open a hole in the geometry.

LAYING OUT UVS

Choosing Polygons > Layout in the UV Texture Editor automatically arranges UV shells within the UV texture space. For relatively simple models, the resulting arrangement is neat and orderly. The Layout tool will even work across multiple surfaces. (To prevent overlapping, set Layout Multiple Objects to Non-Overlapping.) Since the tool leaves a significant amount of empty space, additional manipulation of the UV points may be required (see Figure 9.19).

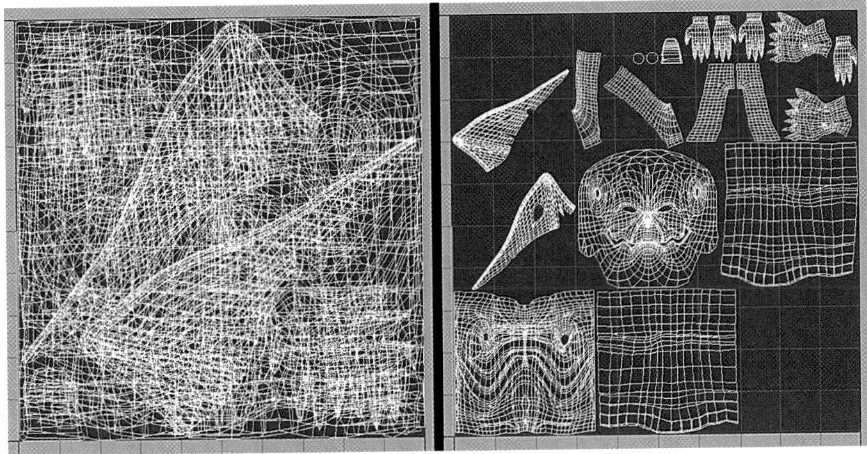

Figure 9.19 Before and after the application of Layout to multiple surfaces

CREATING UV SETS

The creation of UV sets allows a single surface to carry multiple UV layouts. A UV layout is simply a unique arrangement of UV points. Since overlapping is not an issue for UV sets, each UV set and corresponding UV layout can cover the entire UV texture space. Without the use of UV sets, you must carefully arrange individual UV shells belonging to a single surface within the UV texture space (as demonstrated in Figure 9.13 earlier in this chapter). As an additional benefit, each UV set can support a unique UV layout even when polygon faces within the set belong to multiple UV sets. Ultimately, you can assign each UV set to a different texture, thus allowing for a more complex and advanced texturing approach.

To create a UV set during the UV mapping process, open the Options window for the Planar Mapping, Cylindrical Mapping, Spherical Mapping, or Automatic Mapping tool. Check Create New UV Set, enter a name in the UV Set Name field, and click Apply. Once UV sets exist, you can view them, one at a time, in the UV Texture Editor by selecting the surface and choosing UV Sets > *UV_Set_Name* (see Figure 9.20).

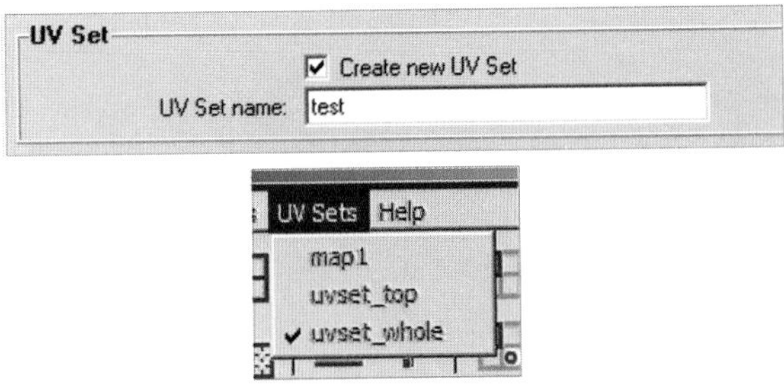

Figure 9.20 (Top) The Create New UV Set attribute within the Planar Mapping Options window. (Bottom) The UV Sets menu in the UV Texture Editor.

In addition, you can create new UV sets in the UV Texture Editor at any time. To do this, select a series of UV points, edges, or faces and choose Polygons > Copy UVs To UV Set > Copy Into New UV Set > ❑, enter a name in the New UV Set Name field, and click Apply. You can also copy UV points into preexisting UV sets by choosing Polygons > Copy UVs To UV Set > *UV_Set_Name.*

You can link UV sets to specific textures by following these steps:

1. Create several UV sets for a surface. Assign the surface to a material that has several textures mapped to it. For example, assign the surface to a Blinn material with a File mapped to its Color and a Noise mapped to its Specular Roll Off.

2. Choose Window > Relationship Editors > UV Linking > UV-Centric. The Relationship Editor window opens. Initially, the UV Sets and Textures columns are empty. Select the surface in a workspace view. The surface, with its UV sets, is listed in the left column. The assigned material, with its texture maps, is listed in the right column.

3. Click the *map1* UV set name in the left column. The map1 UV set is the default UV set that contains all the UV points of the surface. The textures that the map1 set are linked to are highlighted in the right column of with a gray bar. You cannot directly disable the texture links to the map1 UV set.

4. Click a custom UV set name in the left column. The textures listed in the right column remain unhighlighted, which indicates that there is no texture link. Render a test frame. At this point, the render is standard and does not employ the custom UV sets for the selection of textures.

5. Click a texture name in the right column. A link to the UV set is created. Click the map1 UV set name. Note that the texture linked to the custom UV set is now unlinked for the map1 UV set. The texture cannot be linked to the map1 set and the custom set at the same time. Render a test. The texture that is linked to the custom UV set appears *only* on those faces that belong to the custom UV set.

You can link a texture to one UV set at a time. If you wish to have the texture linked to all the UV points, and faces, of a surface, reestablish the link between the texture and the map1 UV set. To reestablish a link, simply click the texture name so that it is highlighted with a gray bar. You can link a UV set to more than one texture. When a link is made between a texture and a custom UV set, a uvChooser utility node is connected automatically to the place2dTexture node that belongs to the texture.

As an example, in Figure 9.21 two UV mappings are applied to a polygon primitive shape. The Planar Mapping tool is applied to the topmost faces and receives a UV set named uvset_top. The Automatic Mapping tool is applied to the entire model and receives a UV set named uvset_whole. The uvset_whole set is linked to a ramp texture node, which in turn is mapped to the Color of a blinn material node. The uvset_top set is linked to a fractal texture node, which in turn is mapped to the Bump Mapping attribute of the same blinn. Since only the top of the model has UV points within the uvset_top set, the bump appears only on the top and nowhere else. The ramp, on the other hand, appears over every polygon since the uvset_whole set contains the entire model in its UV texture space. This technique allows for specific placement of textures on a single surface assigned to a single material.

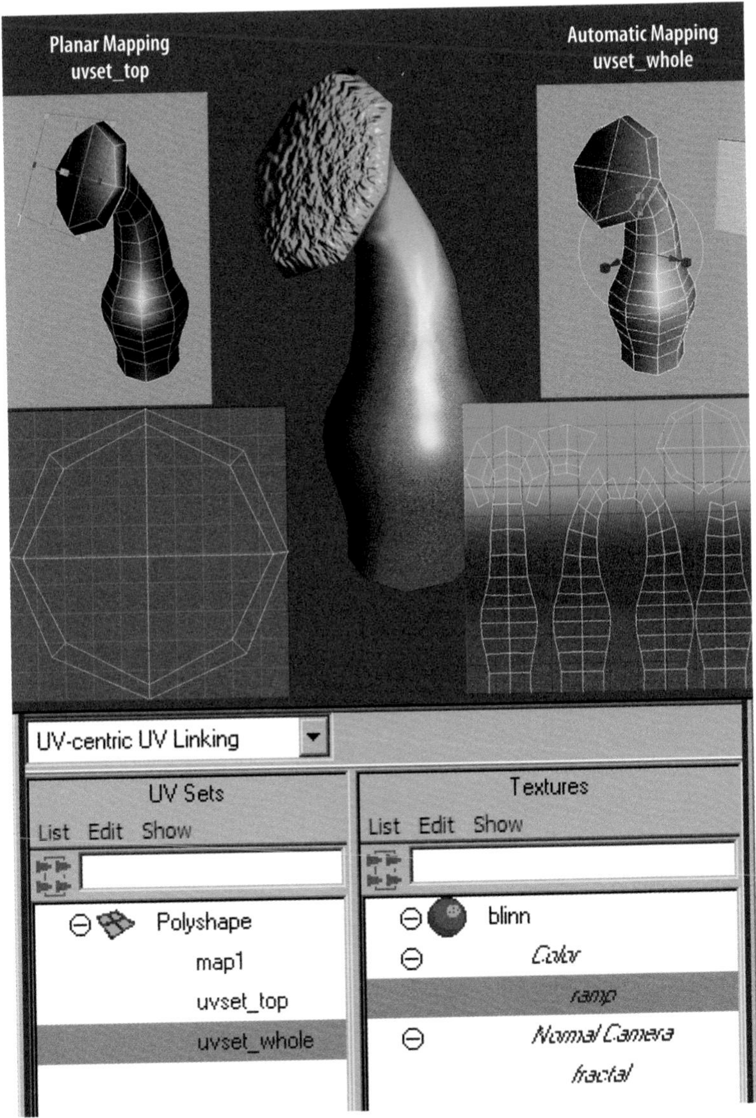

Figure 9.21 Placement of textures on a polygon shape is controlled by two UV sets. This scene is included on the CD as `uv_sets.ma`.

Note: To export a snapshot of the UV layout within the UV texture space, choose Polygons > UV Snapshot or Subdivs > UV Snapshot from the UV Texture Editor menu. The resulting bitmap will contain the full, 0-to-1 UV texture space and may be brought into a paint program.

A Note on Subdivision Surfaces

Subdivision surfaces do not support standard mapping tools. However, if you switch to polygon proxy mode, the mapping and UV tools are applicable. To utilize this method, follow these steps:

1. Right-click the subdivision surface in a workspace view and select Polygon from the marking menu. Polygon proxy mode is activated and is indicated by a polygon cage.
2. Open the surface's Attribute Editor tab. Switch to the PolyToSubdiv tab. Expand the UVs section and switch UV Treatment to Inherit UVs From Poly.
3. Apply polygon modeling tools, mapping tools, or UV tools of your choice. When you are ready to exit the proxy mode, right-click the surface and choose Standard from the marking menu. The subdivision surface will successfully inherit the changes applied in the proxy mode.

A limited number of subdivision UV tools are available through the UV Texture Editor. These include Cut UV Edges, Layout, and Move And Sew UV Edges. The tools are located in the Subdivs menu and function like their polygon counterparts.

Using the 3D Paint Tool

With the 3D Paint tool, you can paint texture maps in a workspace view with a virtual paint brush. In addition, you can rough in bitmaps in preparation for painting the final texture map in Photoshop or other paint program.

The Basic Workflow

Since the steps required by the 3D Paint tool are fairly esoteric, the following guide is provided:

1. Select a NURBS, polygon, or subdivision surface. (Polygon and subdivision surfaces must have nonoverlapping UVs that fit within a normalized UV range of 0 to 1.) Assign a new material to the surface.
2. Select the surface again, switch to the Rendering menu set, and choose Texturing > 3D Paint Tool > ❑. The options window for the 3D Paint tool embeds itself in a new Attribute Editor tab. In the File Textures section, choose a setting from the Attribute To Paint drop-down (see Figure 9.22). Although Color is the default, you can paint Transparency, Incandescence, and many other material attributes. Click the Assign/Edit Textures button. In the Assign/Edit File Textures window, choose Size X, Size Y, and Image Format values for the bitmap that will be written out. Click the Assign/Edit Textures button at the bottom of the window. The window closes and a File texture is mapped automatically to the appropriate attribute of the material assigned to the surface.

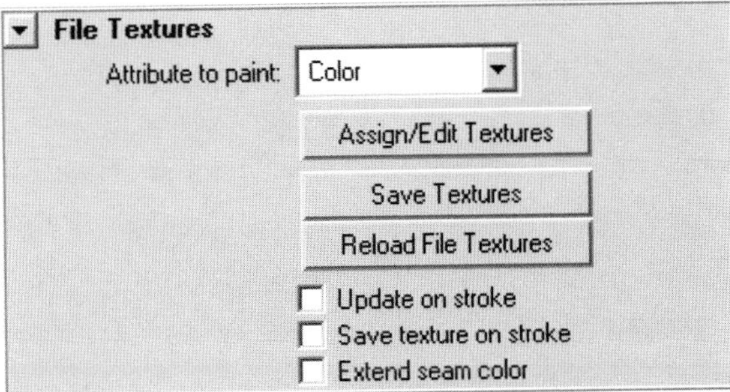

Figure 9.22 The File Textures section of the 3D Paint tool's Attribute Editor tab

3. Adjust the Radius(U) attribute (in the Brush section) to change the size of the brush. The brush is visible as a crosshair within a circle as the mouse pointer crosses the surface. Choose a brush style by clicking one of the Artisan brush icons. Select a Color value and an Opacity value (in the Color section). Click and drag the mouse over the surface. A paint stroke appears as long as Smooth Shade All and Hardware Texturing are checked in the workspace view's Shading menu. The material icon, as shown in the Hypershade window, will not contain the paint strokes at this point.

Note: If a pressure-sensitive stylus and tablet is used, Radius(U) signifies the brush's upper size limit and Radius(L) signifies the brush's lower size limit. If a mouse is used, Radius(L) is ignored.

4. You can change the brush Radius(U), Color, and Opacity values as often as necessary. Two additional Artisan brush options—Erase and Clone—are available in the Paint Operations section (see Figure 9.23). Erase removes old paint strokes and leaves the material's original color. Clone functions in the same manner as a clone brush in a digital paint program. To choose a clone source, click the Set Clone Source button and then click the surface. There are two options for the Clone Brush Mode: Dynamic and Static. Dynamic allows the clone source to move with the brush (the standard Photoshop method). Static fixes the clone source and allows the same sampled area to be painted over and over. In addition, you can set Blend Mode to Lighten, Darken, Multiply, Screen, or Overlay. These modes are similar to those found in Adobe Photoshop.
5. To permanently save the painting, click the Save Textures button (see Figure 9.22). A bitmap is written out in the size and image format specified in step 2. The material icon will update at this point. In addition, the File texture will list a path that points to a default Maya location, as in this example:

    project_directory\3dPaintTextures*scene_name*\sphere_color.iff

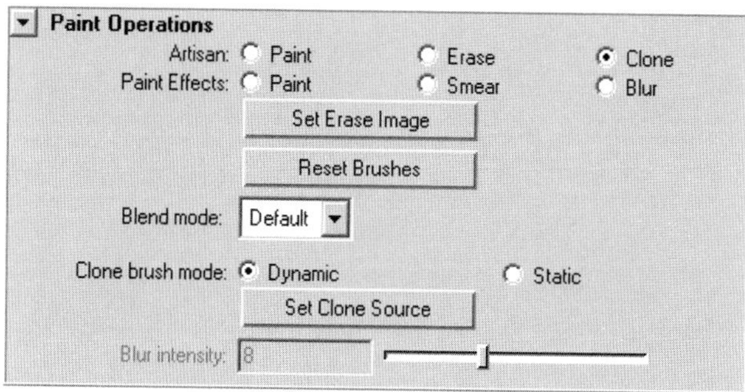

Figure 9.23 The Paint Operations section of the 3D Paint tool's Attribute Editor tab

You can move the resulting bitmap to a different location and reload it into the File texture if necessary. If Save Texture On Stroke is checked, the texture is automatically saved at the end of every stroke. If the Update On Stroke is checked, the material icon constantly updates; in addition, at the end of each stroke, the IPR render window will update. Extend Seam Color extends the paint color at the UV shell borders to prevent seams from appearing on the surface during the render.

6. You can paint multiple textures on a single surface. To create a new texture, choose a different texture type from the Attribute To Paint drop-down menu (see Figure 9.22 earlier in this chapter) and set the options in the Assign/Edit File Textures window. Only one texture is visible on the surface at a time. To return to a previously edited texture, simply choose the appropriate attribute from the Attribute To Paint drop-down menu. If the texture is not visible immediately, click the surface with the brush. Click the Save Textures button to save all the textures at once.

Note: To fill a surface with a single solid color, click the Flood Paint button. The color is set by the Color attribute in the Flood section of the 3D Paint tool's Attribute Editor tab. To erase the latest set of brushwork, click the Flood Erase button.

It's possible to paint across multiple surfaces simultaneously, even when the surfaces are dissimilar (for example, polygons mixed with NURBS surfaces). If multiple surfaces are selected when Assign/Edit Textures is applied, Maya automatically creates a Triple Switch utility (see Chapter 8 for a description). In turn, the Triple Switch utility is connected to a series of File textures that correspond to each surface.

Roughing in a Texture

Although it might be difficult to paint highly intricate bitmaps using only the 3D Paint tool, the tool can provide an invaluable method for roughing in a texture. For example, in Figure 9.24 the bumps and folds of a complex sculpture are marked with the 3D Paint tool. The bitmap is then brought into Photoshop for the fine detail.

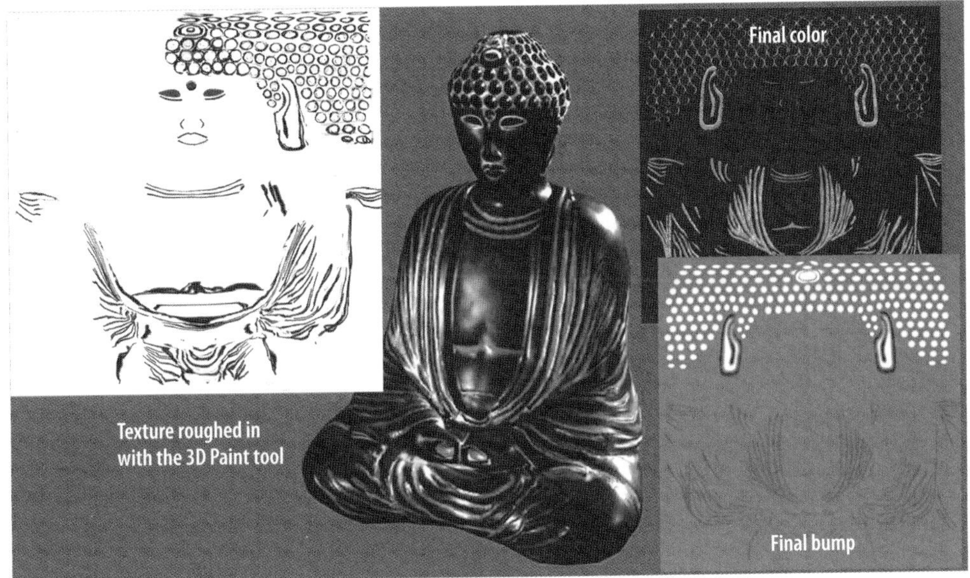

Figure 9.24 The bumps and folds of a sculpture are roughed in with the 3D Paint tool.

PSD Support

Maya supports the Adobe Photoshop PSD file format. Maya's PSD File texture supports the creation of PSD networks in which multiple textures are stored in one file. To achieve this, follow these steps:

1. Create a material and assign it to a NURBS, polygon, or subdivision surface. Apply various textures to the material's Color, Specular Color, Transparency, Diffuse, or other attributes. You can use any 2D or 3D texture, whether they are bitmaps or procedural.
2. Select the surface, switch to the Rendering menu set, and choose Texturing > Create PSD Network to open the Create PSD Network Options window, as shown in Figure 9.25.
3. Enter a filename and path into the Image Name field and specify an image size in the Size X and Size Y fields. If you prefer that Maya provide a snapshot of the UV texture space in the resulting PSD file, check Include UV Snapshot.
4. Choose attributes from the Attributes column and click the right arrow button (between the Attributes and Selected Attributes columns). Clicking the right arrow button lists the selected attributes in the Selected Attributes column (see Figure 9.25). You can choose any combination of attributes (even those with no texture assigned).
5. By default, all procedural textures listed in the Selected Attributes column are converted to a file texture. You can set the options for the conversion by clicking the Convert To File Texture Options button. (See Chapter 5 for more information on the Convert To File Texture tool.)

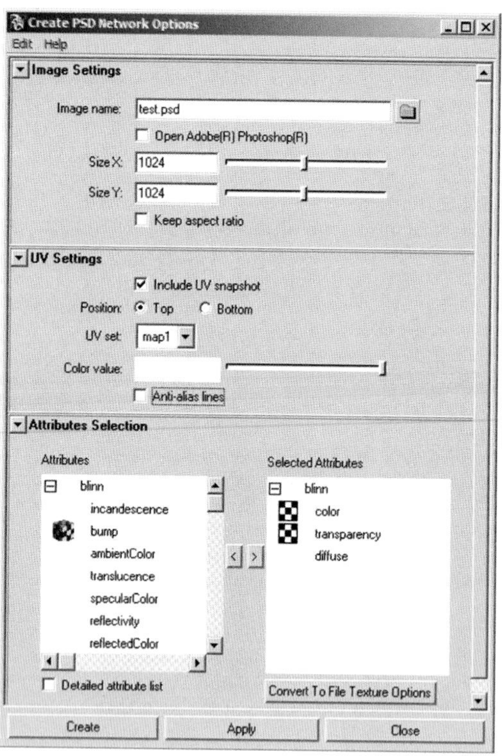

Figure 9.25 The Create PSD Network Options window

6. Click the Create button in the Create PSD Network Options window. Any attribute that is listed in the Selected Attributes column has its old texture node replaced by a psdFileTex node that is named after the material and texture (for example, PSD_blinn_transparency). (An example network is illustrated in Figure 9.26.) If an attribute had no texture mapped to it but was nevertheless listed in the Selected Attributes column, an empty layer is set aside in the resulting PSD file. Each psdFileTex node's Link To Layer Set attribute is set to the appropriate attribute for a connection. For example, if a texture was originally mapped to the Color attribute of a Blinn, the texture node is removed and replaced by a psdFileTex node with its Link To Layer Set attribute set to blinn.color.

You can edit the resulting PSD file in Photoshop. If you make changes and save the file, choose Texturing > Update PSD Networks to ensure that Maya recognizes the changes. You can revise an existing network at any point by selecting the surface and choosing Texturing > Edit PSD Network. At this point, you can add and remove attributes from the Selected Attributes column of the Edit PSD Network Options window. If you remove an attribute, the layer is automatically deleted and the connection to the corresponding psdFileTex node is broken.

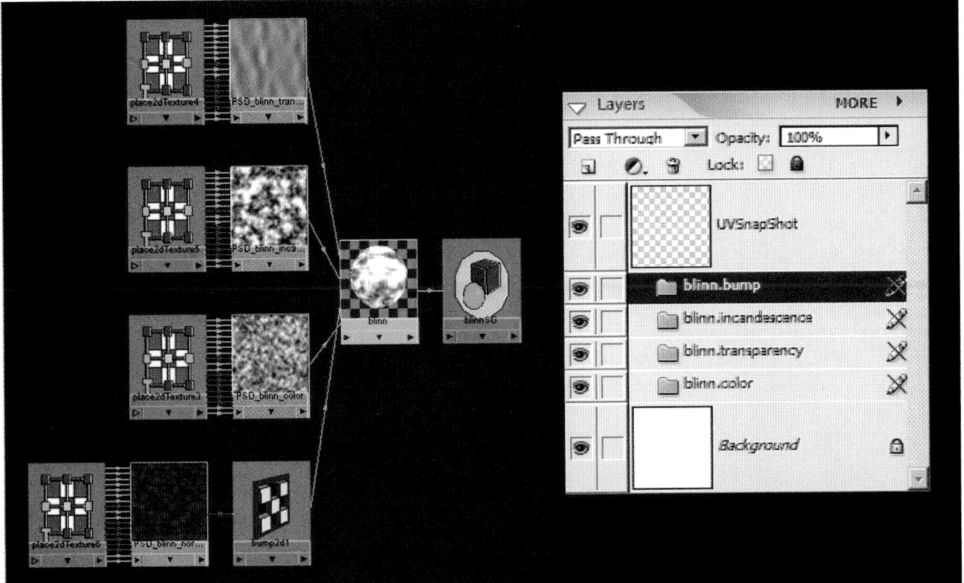

Figure 9.26 (Left) A PSD shading network in the Hypershade window. (Right) The matching PSD file revealed in the Adobe Photoshop Elements Layer window. The scene before the application of Create PSD Network is included on the CD as `psd_network_before.ma`. The scene after the application of Create PSD Network is included as `psd_network_after.ma`. The resulting PSD file is included as `psd_network_Polyshape.psd`.

Bump and Displacement Mapping

Bump and displacement mapping can add an extra level of detail to any material. Each has its own unique strengths, weaknesses, and application. Although the Maya Displacement Shader can be difficult to adjust, the Height Field utility provides a rough preview in a workspace view.

Bump Mapping

Bump maps perturb normals along the interior of a surface at the point of render. They do not, however, affect the outer edges. Nevertheless, the bump effect can easily sell the idea that a surface is rough. When you use a texture as a bump map, middle-gray (0.5, 0.5, 0.5) has no effect. High values cause peaks and low values cause valleys. To set the intensity of a bump map, you can adjust the value of the Bump Depth attribute of the Bump 2D or Bump 3D utility. Bump Depth accepts negative numbers, thus inverting the peaks and valleys.

The simplest way to add a bump map is to click the Bump Mapping checkered Map button in a material's Attribute Editor tab. In this case, a Bump 2D or a Bump 3D utility is automatically connected to the shading network. The Bump 2D utility is designed for standard 2D textures such as File, Checker, or Ramp. The Bump 3D utility is designed for 3D textures such as Brownian, Cloud, or Solid Fractal. If necessary, you can make the bump connections by hand in the Hypershade window. In this case, the outNormal of the bump2d or bump3d node is connected to the normalCamera of the material node. The outAlpha of the texture is connected to the bumpValue of the bump2d or bump3d node. If the outColor of the texture is already connected to another attribute of the material, you can continue to connect the texture's outAlpha to the bumpValue (see Figure 9.27). In this way, only a single place2dTexture node need be adjusted.

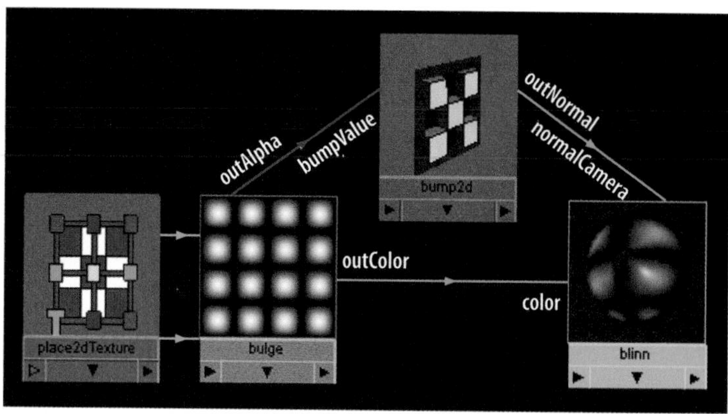

Figure 9.27 A texture is simultaneously connected to a bump2d utility node and a blinn material node.

Bump maps are extremely efficient to render. In fact, bump maps are as convincing as displacement maps in many situations. For example, if a bump map is applied to a surface that sits against a cluttered background, the smooth edges of the surface are difficult to perceive (see Figure 9.28). Motion blur, shadows, and other 3D phenomena also help disguise the bump map's limitations.

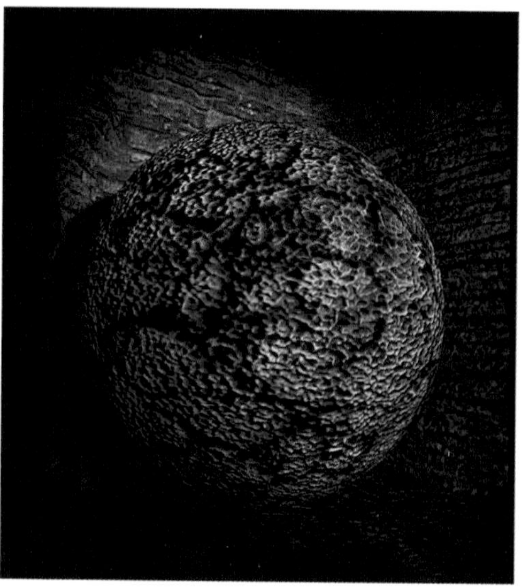

Figure 9.28 A bump mapped surface against two different backgrounds

Note: The mental ray renderer produces superior results when rendering bump maps and normal maps. For information on mental ray rendering, see Chapter 11. For information on normal mapping, which Is related to bump mapping, see Chapter 13.

Displacement Mapping

Displacement maps distort geometry at the point of render. That is, the assigned surface is tessellated and the resulting vertices are translated a distance based on the source texture. Although displacement maps are more processor intensive, they are more realistic than bump maps. Thus, displacement maps provide the following advantages:

- The surface's silhouette is displaced.
- Displaced detail casts and receives shadows.
- A displacement map can create surface features far more detailed than any other common modeling techniques.

Displacement maps cannot be created through standard material connections in Maya. Instead, you must connect a Displacement Shader to a shading group node. Follow these steps:

1. Select a material node in the Hypershade window and open its Attribute Editor tab. Click the Go To Output Connection button at the top of the tab (the button is to the left of the Presets button). The tab for the material's shading group node is loaded into the Attribute Editor. Switch to the Shading Group (SG) tab if it's not already selected.
2. Click the Displacement Mat. checkered Map button in the Shading Group Attributes section. Choose a texture from the Create Render Node window. A displacementShader node is created. The displacement of the displacementShader is connected to the displacementShader of the shading group node (see Figure 9.29). The outAlpha of the texture is connected to the displacement of the displacementShader node. The displacementShader's input and output attribute names are identical.
3. Render a test frame. To increase the intensity of the displacement effect, increase the value of the texture's Alpha Gain attribute (found in the Color Balance section of the texture's Attribute Editor tab). To reduce the intensity, lower the Alpha Gain.

Alpha Gain is a multiplier that's applied to the texture's Out Alpha attribute. The Alpha Gain default value is 1, which has no effect on the Out Alpha value. An Alpha Gain value of 0 removes the displacement completely. An Alpha Gain value of –1 reverses the displacement. Alpha Offset is an offset factor for the texture's Out Alpha. The Alpha Offset value is added to the Out Alpha value, thus increasing the intensity of the displacement. A negative Alpha Offset reduces the displacement intensity.

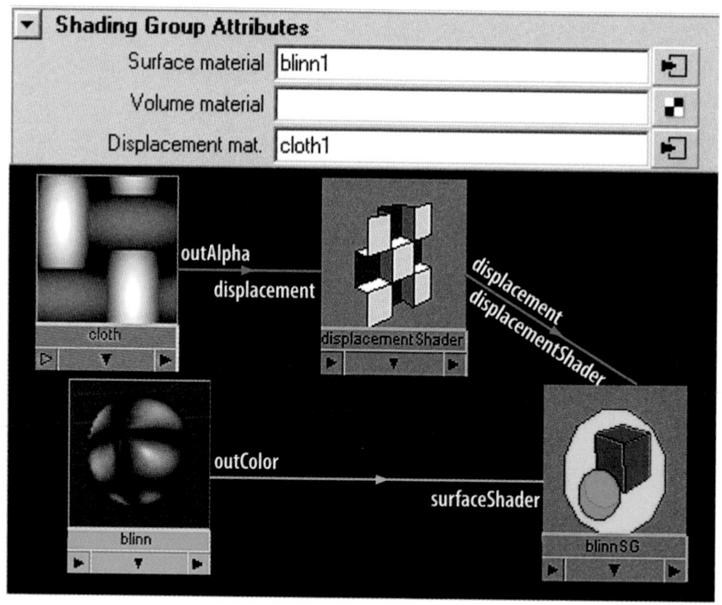

Figure 9.29 A displacement shader node in a shading network

Other aspects of a displacement map can be controlled through the Displacement Map section of the assigned surface's Attribute Editor tab (see Figure 9.30).

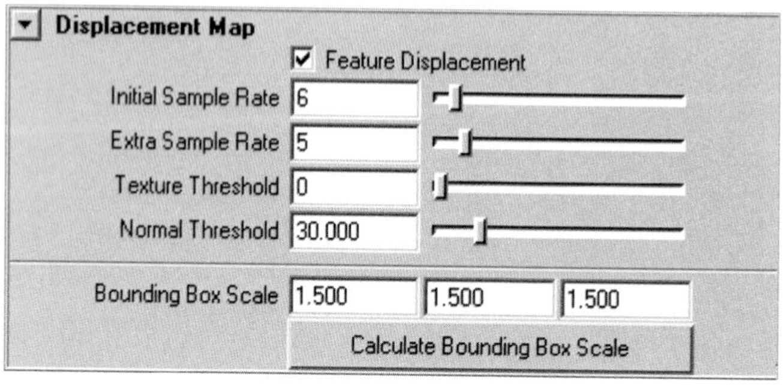

Figure 9.30 The Displacement Map section of a surface's Attribute Editor tab

The following attributes are particularly useful:

Feature Displacement Toggles on or off feature-based displacement. If checked, the Displacement Shader tessellates the assigned surface only in those areas where displaced features occur. If unchecked, the Displacement Shader adds no additional tessellation; in this case, detail contained within the displacement map may be lost if the surface does not have sufficient subdivisions. Maya attempts to make up for the loss of detail inherent with non-feature-based displacement by simultaneously treating the displacement map as a bump map.

Initial Sample Rate and Extra Sample Rate Initial Sample Rate determines the size of a sampling grid laid over each polygon triangle. The grid is used to determine whether the triangle should be tessellated. Tessellation is deemed necessary if the contrast between neighboring texture pixels is sufficient. Extra Sample Rate adds additional sampling. In effect, Extra Sample Rate further subdivides the sampling grid applied by Initial Sample Rate. When setting Initial Sample Rate and Extra Sample Rate, use these guidelines:

- If the surface is highly subdivided, a low Initial Sample Rate is usually satisfactory.
- If the surface is sparsely subdivided and contains large polygon faces, the Initial Sample Rate should be large. Even so, increase the Initial Sample Rate slowly while rendering tests.
- Displacement maps with fine detail and/or a great deal of contrast often necessitate high Initial Sample Rate values.
- If the displacement requires sharp corners or strongly defined transitions between no displacement and high displacement, you should incrementally raise the Extra Sample Rate value. That said, start with an Extra Sample Rate of 0.

Texture Threshold Eliminates unneeded vertices and aims to reduce noise within the displacement. The Texture Threshold value is a percentage of the maximum height variation within the displacement. Any vertex whose difference in height with neighboring vertices is below the Texture Threshold value is removed. The default value of 0 leaves this feature off. When raising the value, do so incrementally. If possible, eliminate any fine noise in the texture map before applying it as a displacement.

Normal Threshold Controls the "softness" of the resulting displacement. This attribute's functionality is identical to that of the Set Normal Angle tool (which you can access by switching to the Polygons menu set and choosing Normals > Set Normal Angle). If the angle between two adjacent triangles is less than the Normal Threshold value, the triangles are rendered smoothly. If not, the triangles are rendered with a sharp edge between them.

Bounding Box Scale Sets the size of the bounding box used to contain a displacement. If a displacement appears cut off at the peaks or carries other render flaws, gradually increase the X, Y, and Z values. The default values of 1.5, 1.5, 1.5 are adequate for most displacements. Large Bounding Box Scale values increase memory usage. The Calculate Bounding Box Scale button estimates an appropriate bounding box size based on the shading network and world scale of the assigned surface.

Note: Environment textures, which require 3D Placement utilities, are not recommended for use as displacement maps. The resulting calculations will be inaccurate.

The Height Field Utility

The Height Field utility previews Displacement Shaders in a workspace view. When a texture node is connected to the utility, it creates a plane at 0, 0, 0 and displaces it with the displacement shading network. The Height Field plane cannot be rendered; however, it can be repositioned. The Height Scale attribute of the Height Field utility

controls the scale of the previewed displacement. If Height Scale is left at 1, the previewed displacement will match the render of the actual Displacement Shader. The Resolution attribute controls the accuracy of the preview. As an example of the shading network, the outAlpha of a fractal texture node is connected to the displacement of a heightField node (see Figure 9.31). The fractal is also used as the displacement input for a displacement shader node. A Blinn is used as a material. Even though the blinn material node is assigned to a primitive plane with only six spans, a great deal of detail is gained. You can find the Height Field utility in the General Utilities section of the Create Maya Nodes menu.

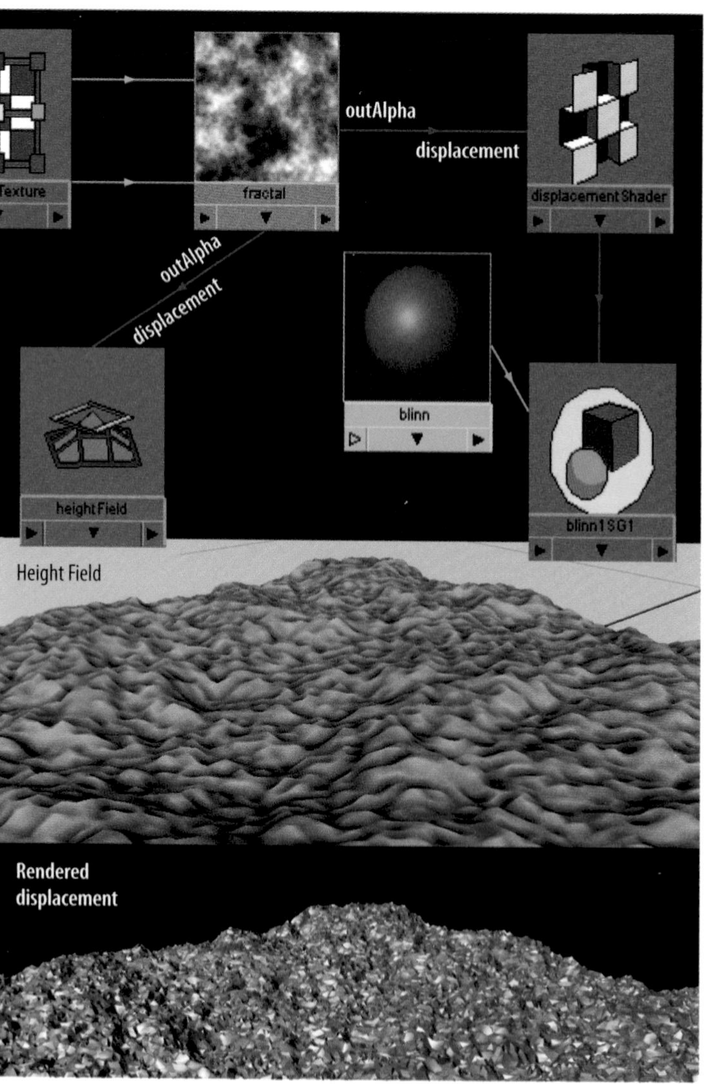

Figure 9.31 (Top) The Height Field utility in a shading network. (Middle) A Height Field utility displacement. (Bottom) The matching software-rendered Displacement Shader. This scene is included on the CD as `displacement.ma`.

Custom Sliders

Every single material, texture, and utility node carries an Extra Attributes section (at the very bottom of the Attribute Editor tab). You can add attributes to this section by choosing Attributes > Add Attributes from the Attribute Editor menu.

In the Add Attribute window, you can set the attribute name with the Long Name field (Maya 2008) or the Attribute Name field (Maya 8.5). Long Name holds the full attribute name as it is used in the Connection Editor and through custom connections (see Figure 9.32). If you check Override Nice Name in Maya 2008, you can set a shorthand name in the Nice Name field. The Nice Name is used in the Channel Box and in the Extra Attributes section of the Attribute Editor tab.

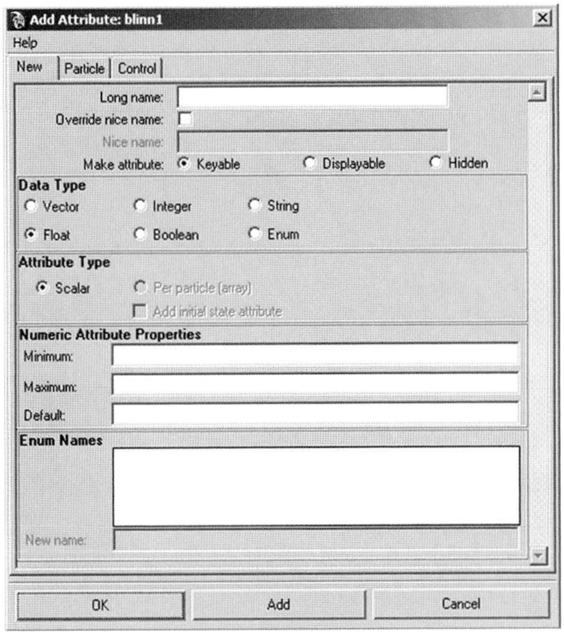

Figure 9.32 The Add Attribute window (Maya 2008)

You can set the attribute type with the Data Type attribute. In most cases, Float (number with decimal places) and Integer (whole number) will suffice, although you can choose Vector (three values), String (text), Boolean (on/off), or Enum (drop-down text list).

If you set Data Type to Float or Integer but do not choose values for the Numeric Attribute Properties attributes, a numeric field is created. If you enter values in the Minimum and Maximum fields, a slider is created with that range. The Default field establishes the start position for the slider. The custom attribute appears in the Extra Attributes section of the Attribute Editor tab as well as at the end of the Channel Box channel list. A custom attribute follows the same naming convention as standard attributes:

```
node_name.attribute_name
```

As such, you can use a custom attribute as part of an expression, MEL script, or custom shading network. In the Connection Editor, the custom attribute appears at the end of the list. You can also keyframe custom attributes.

When a custom attribute with a slider is applied to a shading network, a great deal of flexibility is achieved with a minimum amount of effort. For example, sliders are easily connected to the cartoon material detailed in the Chapter 7 tutorial. In this case, three custom attributes are added to the "Cartoon" blinn material node—Ink_Width, Dot_Width, and Highlight_Color (see Figure 9.33). Ink_Width is connected to secondTerm of the ConditionB node. This controls the thickness of the "ink" outline. Dot_Width is connected to the secondTerm of the ConditionA node. This controls the width of simulated halftone. Ink_Width and Dot_Width are float attributes with a minimum value of 0 and a maximum value of 1. Highlight_Color is connected to colorEntryList[4].color of RampA. This changes the color of the "specular" highlight (the highest color on the ramp). Highlight_Color is a vector attribute that provides RGB fields.

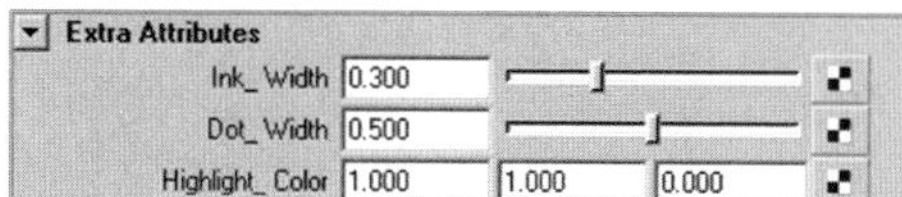

Figure 9.33 Custom float and vector attributes in a custom cartoon shading network. This material is included on the CD as `extra_cartoon.ma`.

Chapter Tutorial: Preparing the UVs of a Polygon Model

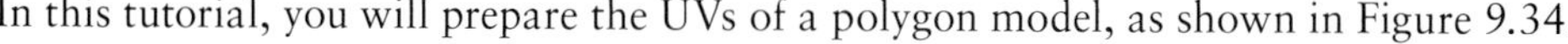

In this tutorial, you will prepare the UVs of a polygon model, as shown in Figure 9.34.

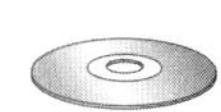

1. Open `piggy_uv.ma` from the Chapter 9 scene folder on the CD. This file contains a polygon model whose UVs are unusable as is.
2. Select the entire surface, switch to the Polygons menu set, and choose Create UVs > Cylindrical Mapping with default options. While the projection manipulator is visible, go to the Channel Box. Change the polyCylProj1 Rotate X value to 270. This orients the projection to the length of the pig. Change Projection Horizontal Sweep to 360. This encloses the surface.
3. Open the UV Texture Editor. Right-click and choose UV from the marking menu. Click an empty space in the Editor to deselect the UV points. Select the UV points that are stranded far from the main body of points and move them in closer. Select all the UV points and scale them down until they fit within the full UV texture space (represented by the dark-gray box in the upper-right corner of the UV Texture Editor's grid).

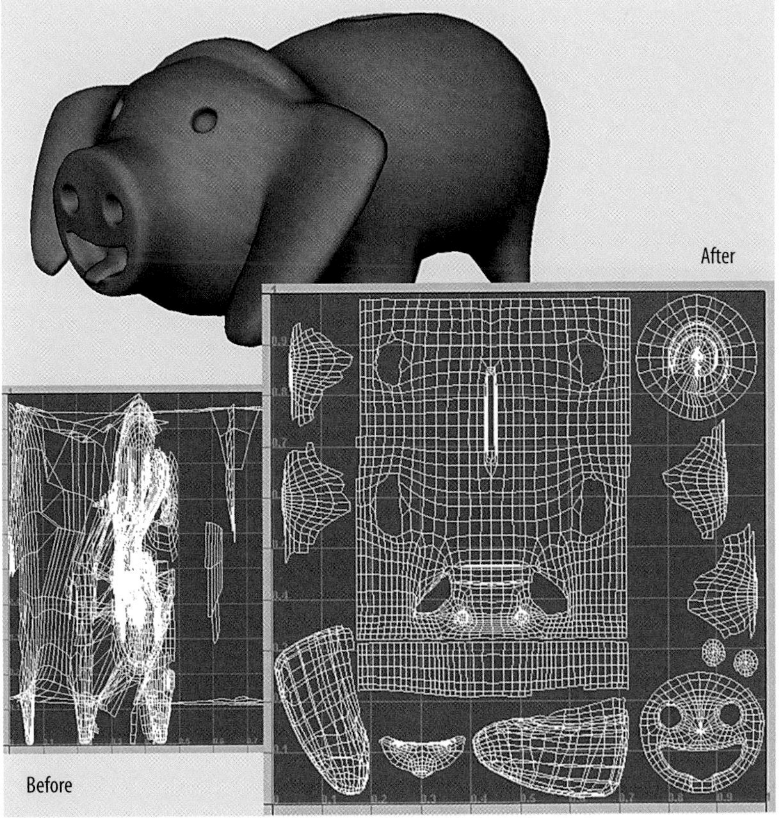

Figure 9.34 A polygon pig and its UVs—before and after

4. At this step, the pig's snout, ears, and legs have significant overlap. To fix this, you can apply additional mappings. Select all the faces that make up the two ears. You can select the faces in a workspace view or inside the UV Texture Editor. If you right-click and choose Face from the marking menu, you can select faces in the Editor. Choose Create UVs > Planar Mapping with the default settings. Interactively rotate the projection manipulator until it is parallel to the front of the ears. While the manipulator remains visible, return to the UV Texture Editor and move the ear UV points off to the side where they won't overlap other points.
5. Select all the faces that make up the snout. This should include the snout front, the snout side, and the parts that make up the interior of the smile and nostrils. Choose Create UVs > Automatic Mapping with the default settings. Although the front of the snout appears intact in the UV texture space, other parts are split into little pieces (see Figure 9.35). For now, this is okay. Select and move the resulting UV points off to the side where they won't overlap other points.

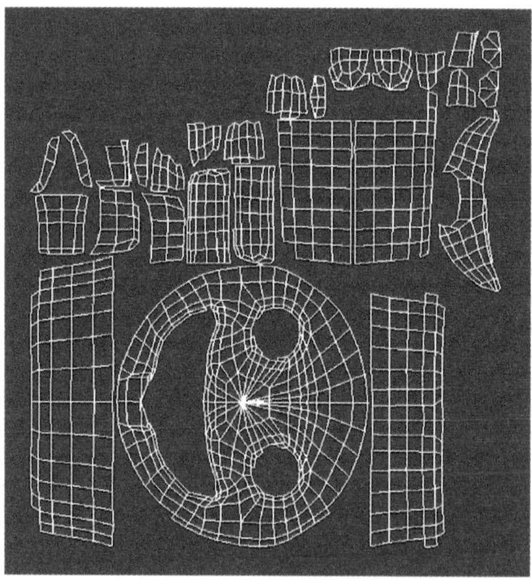

Figure 9.35 The pig's snout after the application of Automatic Mapping

6. Select the faces that make up the front of the snout (the part that looks like a smiley face). Move the faces off to the side where they don't overlap any other parts. Rotate the faces so that they are no longer sideways. Select all the faces that make up the sides of the snout. This might require trial and error. Choose Create UVs > Cylindrical Mapping with the default settings. Move and orient the projection manipulator so that the sides of the snout are fully covered. Move the resulting UV points aside.
7. Select all the faces that make up the inside of the smile and the nostrils. Choose Create UVs > Planar Mapping with the default settings. Move and orient the projection manipulator so that it faces the front of the snout. Select the resulting UV points and move them aside. While the UV points remain selected, choose Edit UVs > Relax six or seven times. This will allow the inner lip to be flattened out.
8. Select all the faces that make up the pig's tail. Choose Create UVs > Planar Mapping with the default settings. Move and orient the projection manipulator so that it faces the back of the pig. Select and move the resulting UV points aside.
9. Select all the faces that make up a single leg. Choose Create UVs > Cylindrical Mapping. With the default settings, move and orient the projection manipulator so that the entire leg is covered. Select and move the resulting UV points aside. Repeat the process for the other legs.
10. Select the surface in a workspace view. With all the UV points visible in the UV Texture Editor, proceed to move, rotate, and scale the UV shells (groups of UV points) back into the full UV texture space. Use Figure 9.34 as a reference. Once you're satisfied with the UV arrangement, select the surface in a workspace view and choose Edit > Delete By Type > History. This will freeze the UVs.

The UV adjustment is complete! This is one of many possible UV preparation approaches and is only a rough pass. You can refine this result in many places. For example, you can reduce the amount of empty space between UV shells. You can fix overlapping UV points on the smile and the bottoms of the legs; re-sew the side of the snout onto the head; and apply additional mappings to separate the front of each ear from its back. Although many fixes require moving points around manually, the technique becomes fairly easy with practice. The final version, as illustrated in Figure 9.34, has been included as `piggy_final.ma` in the Chapter 9 scene folder on the CD.

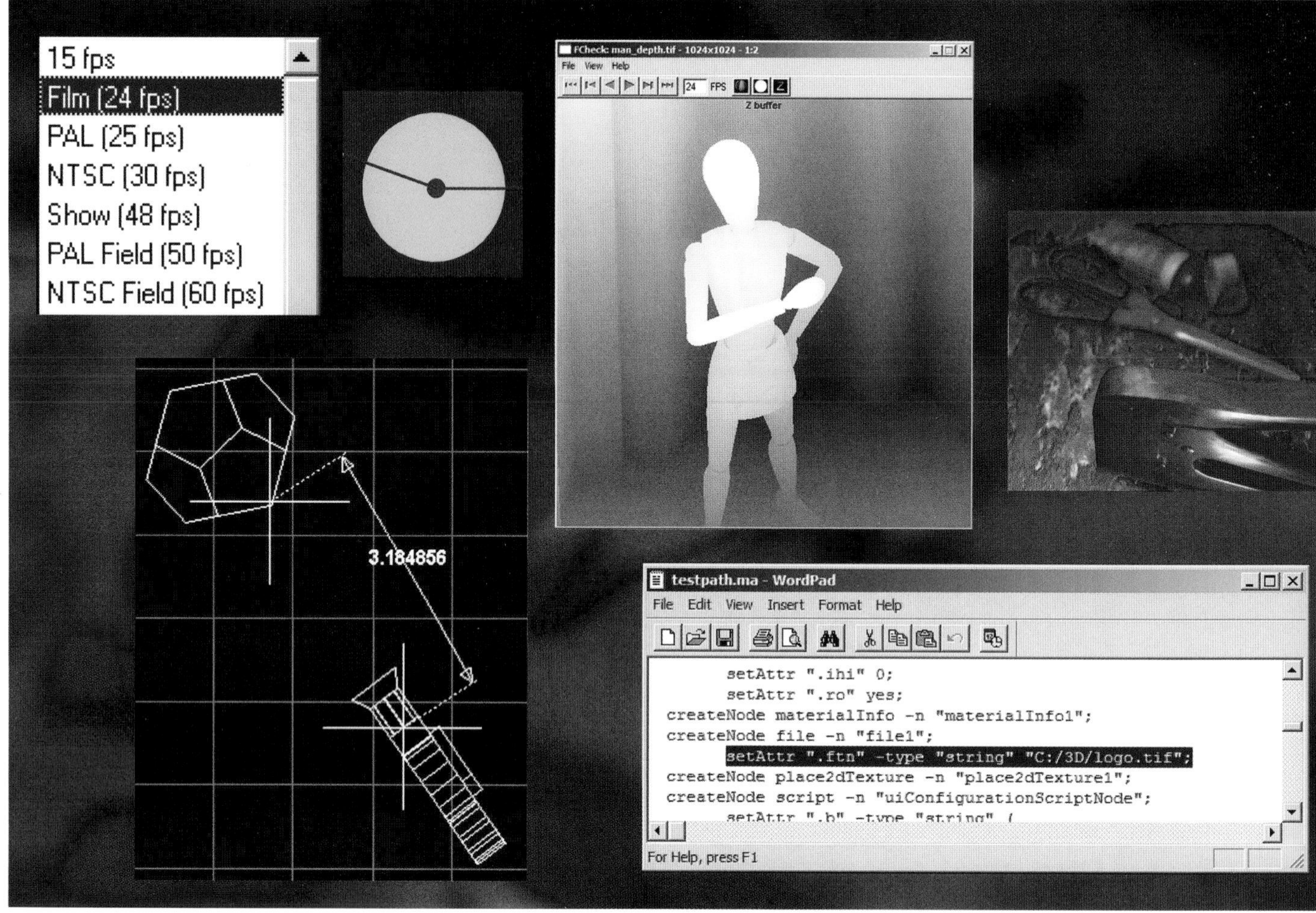

15 fps
Film (24 fps)
PAL (25 fps)
NTSC (30 fps)
Show (48 fps)
PAL Field (50 fps)
NTSC Field (60 fps)
FCheck: man_depth.tif - 1024x1024 - 1:2
File View Help
24 FPS
Z buffer
3.184856
testpath.ma - WordPad
File Edit View Insert Format Help
setAttr ".ihi" 0;
setAttr ".ro" yes;
createNode materialInfo -n "materialInfo1";
createNode file -n "file1";
setAttr ".ftn" -type "string" "C:/3D/logo.tif";
createNode place2dTexture -n "place2dTexture1";
createNode script -n "uiConfigurationScriptNode";
For Help, press F1

Prepping for Successful Renders

Although rendering is the final step of a Maya 3D project, it is often given improper attention. The correct choice of aspect ratios, pixel ratios, frame rates, focal lengths, and film backs at the earliest stage of animation can ensure that the project progresses smoothly. At the same time, careful selection of anti-aliasing, image format, resolution size, depth of field, and motion blur settings will guarantee a successful render. Time-saving techniques, including scene cleanup and command-line rendering, will help you finish projects in a more efficient manner.

10

Chapter Contents

Determining Critical Project Settings

Aspect ratios, frame rates, and film backs are important elements of any animation project and should therefore be selected early in the production process. Although you can change the aspect ratio at any time, such a change can lead to poor compositions. Selecting a different film back midway through a project can also lead to drastic composition changes and interfere with live-action plate matching. Switching frame rates can lead to improperly timed motion and broken lip sync. Camera focal lengths, although less critical than aspect ratios, frame rates, and film backs, should nonetheless be selected early in the animation process.

Deciphering Aspect Ratios

Simply put, an aspect ratio of an image is its displayed width divided by its displayed height. Aspect ratios are commonly represented as x:y (for example, 4:3) or x (for example, 1.33), in which *x* is the width and *y* is the height. A list of popular aspect ratios, their origins, and representative image resolutions follow (see Figure 10.1).

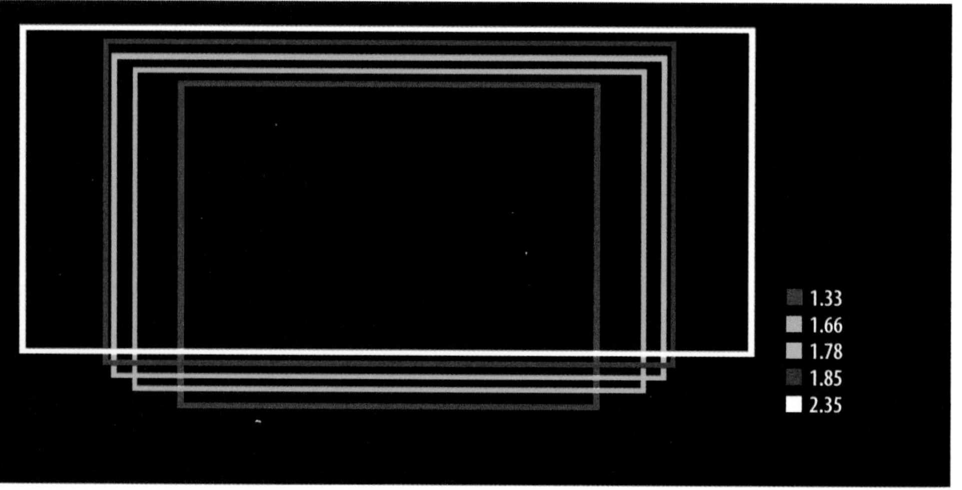

Figure 10.1 Common aspect ratios

16:9 (1.78) Standard widescreen video and the aspect ratio of HDTV. Many digital video cameras offer 16:9 as a recording option. In addition, 16:9 is a popular ratio for animations intended for transfer to 35 mm motion picture film. (In this case, the film is projected with a 1.85 mask.) 16:9 ratio projects require letterboxing when played on 4:3 standard definition televisions. The HDTV video standard uses two resolutions—1280 × 720 and 1920 × 1080. Four variations of these two resolutions exist—720i, 720p, 1080i, and 1080p. The *i* in 720i and 1080i HDTV signifies interlaced frames. The *p* in 720p and 1080p HDTV signifies progressive frames. Progressive frames are whole frames that have not been interlaced.

Note: In the United States, analog television broadcasts will cease as of February 2009. From that point forward, the broadcast standard will be digital television (DTV). Although HDTV has been embraced by many broadcasters, it is simply one format available to DTV. For example, enhanced digital television (EDTV) is a second variation of DTV that runs at 480p or 576p and can be 16:9 or 4:3.

4:3 (1.33) The standard definition television (SDTV) aspect ratio, whose roots can be traced to silent 35 mm motion pictures created by Thomas Edison. NTSC SDTV broadcasts at a resolution of 480 visible lines. (Additional lines contain data such as sync and captioning.) D1, the first professional digital video format, has a NTSC resolution of 720 × 486 with nonsquare pixels. (See the section "Switching between Square and Nonsquare Pixels" later in this chapter.) The square-pixel version of D1 is 720 × 540. DV, a digital variation now in common usage, has a NTSC resolution of 720 × 480 with nonsquare pixels. Digital video editing programs such as Final Cut Pro offer 720 × 480 as an editing format. A common 3D render size, 640 × 480, is a square-pixel variation of the NTSC format.

Note: The NTSC video standard is used throughout North America and parts of South America. PAL, the video standard in Europe and parts of Asia, Africa, and South America, runs at 720 × 576 for SDTV. SECAM, the video standard used in France, Eastern Europe, Russia, and parts of Africa, runs at the same resolution as PAL.

1.66 A masked variation of the 1.37 Academy motion picture format originally developed by Paramount Studios in 1953. A mask is an aperture plate placed behind a projector lens with a cutout "window" that allows only a portion of the film image to reach the screen. 1.66 has since become the standard 35 mm widescreen aspect ratio in many parts of Europe. The 1.37 Academy format was standardized by the American motion picture industry and was used consistently between 1932 and 1953.

1.85 Standard theatrical widescreen in the United States and United Kingdom. Much like 1.66, 1.85 was developed as a method to mask 1.37 in the early 1950s. The SDTV and HDTV broadcast of 1.85 motion pictures requires either letterboxing or cropping through electronic pan-and-scan techniques. The 1.85 aspect ratio was used on *Surf's Up* (2007) and *Shrek the Third* (2007). The render resolution of feature animation varies between studio and project but generally falls between 2K (2,048 vertical lines) and 4K (4,096 vertical lines).

2.35 The aspect ratio of Cinemascope that was developed by 20th Century Fox in the early 1950s. Cinemascope is an anamorphic motion picture format that requires special camera and projector lenses to squeeze and restretch the image for proper viewing. If the anamorphic projector lens is missing, the image will appear excessively tall and skinny. *The Incredibles* (2004) made use of the 2.35 format.

Note: Lens flares, a common artifact of motion picture cameras, are by no means consistent. 2.35 anamorphic flares, for instance, produce thin solid lines across the width of the frame, while 1.66 and 1.85 flares produce the more commonly recognized bright spots.

Switching between Square and Nonsquare Pixels

The NTSC D1 and DV video standards require nonsquare pixels. NTSC D1 and DV nonsquare pixels carry a pixel aspect ratio of 10:11, wherein the height is greater than the width. (10:11 is often expressed as a rounded-off 0.9.) Nonsquare pixels are a legacy requirement of 4:3 SDTV television technology. (The electronic design of a 4:3 SDTV television allows the image to appear normal.) By comparison, computer monitors and HDTV televisions use square pixels. Thus, when a D1 or DV image is displayed on a computer monitor, it appears vertically squished. Editing programs such as Final Cut Pro and Adobe Premiere avoid this problem by offering Show As Square Pixels options.

Note: Each video standard carries its own unique pixel aspect ratio (PAR). For example, PAL D1 and DV have a PAR of 1.066:1 (often expressed as 1.07). 16:9 NTSC D1 and DV have a PAR of 1.2121:1 (often expressed as 1.2). Compositing programs carry the most common pixel aspect ratios as presets.

Note: HDV, a popular high-definition video format, uses the 16:9 aspect ratio. HDV supports 720p and 1080i resolutions. When recording 720p, HDV utilizes a PAR of 1:1. When recording 1080i, HDV uses a resolution of 1440 × 1080 with a PAR of 1.33:1. HDCam, a high-definition variant of Digital Betacam, effectively operates at 1440 × 1080 with a 1.33:1 PAR.

You can set a nonsquare pixel aspect ratio in Maya by changing the Pixel Aspect Ratio attribute in the Render Settings window. For instance, you can set the value to 0.9 for NTSC. However, in order to maximize render quality, it is generally better to render square pixels and "squish" the image in the composite (see Figure 10.2). Thus, when preparing for NTSC DV in Adobe After Effects, a square-pixel 720 × 540 render can be converted to a nonsquare 720 × 480 composite by scaling the image by 90 percent in the X and 88.9 percent in the Y. The size reduction will also serve as an additional form of anti-aliasing. When preparing for NTSC D1, a square-pixel 720 × 540 render can be converted to a 720 × 486 nonsquare composite resolution by scaling by 90 percent in the X and Y.

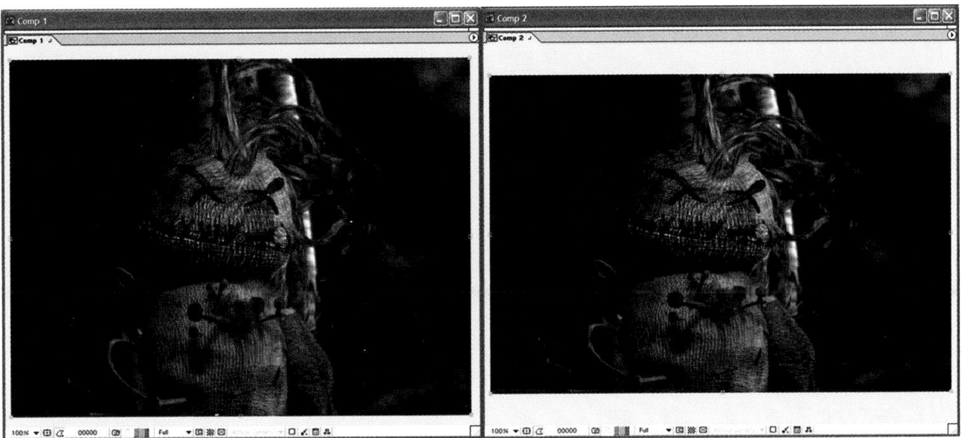

Figure 10.2 (Left) Square-pixel 720 × 540 render in After Effects. (Right) Same render fit into nonsquare 720 × 480 composite.

Selecting a Film Back

In Maya, a camera's virtual optical properties are defined in the Film Back section of the camera's Attribute Editor tab (see Figure 10.3). The most important attribute in this section is Film Gate. With a real-world motion picture camera, a film gate is a plate with a rectangular opening that sits behind the lens and in front of the film stock. The gate controls the exposure of the film by allowing only one frame at a time to be struck by light. Commonly used cameras have distinct lens and film gate setups with specific physical properties. These properties cause light to strike the film in a distinct way. The Film Gate attribute's drop-down menu (see Figure 10.3) provides a selection of common motion picture cameras. When one of these camera presets is selected, the Camera Aperture, Film Aspect Ratio, and Lens Squeeze Ratio attributes automatically update. A description of these attributes follows.

Camera Aperture A "dummy" attribute that drives Horizontal Film Aperture and Vertical Film Aperture, each of which respectively sets the specific width and height of the virtual film gate (measured in world space inches).

Note: *Film back* refers to the plate that holds the film against the film gate. With 3D animation software, the term has come to represent the general qualities of the film gate. In contrast, a real-world camera aperture is the articulated diaphragm that opens or closes to control the amount of light striking the film.

Film Aspect Ratio Sets the width-to-height ratio of Camera Aperture. As you change the value, the Horizontal Film Aperture field automatically updates.

Lens Squeeze Ratio Sets the amount of horizontal squeeze created by a lens. Cinemascope anamorphic lenses require a Lens Squeeze Ratio value of 2. Most lenses do not require a special Lens Squeeze Ratio value and can be left at 1.

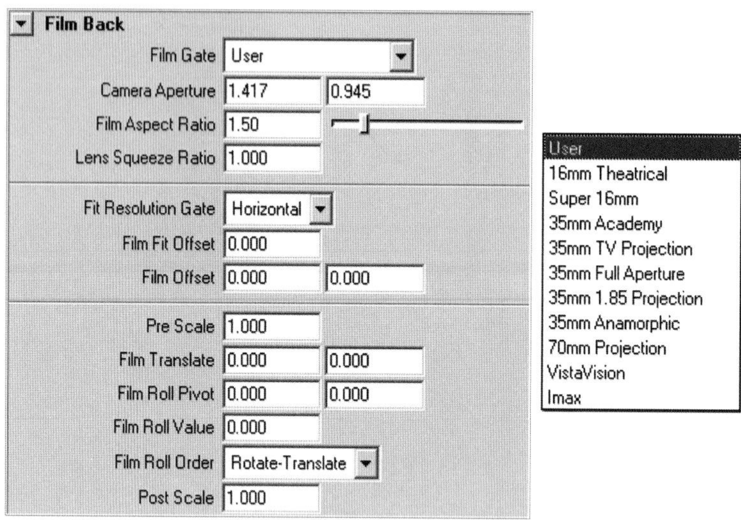

Figure 10.3 (Left) The Film Back section of a camera's Attribute Editor tab; (right) Film Gate presets

If an animation represents an abstract, fanciful, or imaginary scene, you can leave the Film Gate attribute set to the default User. For exaggerated camera effects, you can also enter custom numbers into any of the attributes in the Film Back section. However, if an animation is intended to replicate or fit into preexisting live-action motion picture footage, the Film Gate and associated attributes should be carefully selected.

Note: Video cameras do not have traditional film gates. Their light-gathering CCD or CMOS chips, however, serve the same basic function. When matching a video camera in Maya, you can derive approximate values for Horizontal Camera Aperture and Vertical Camera Aperture. For example, a Canon XL2 camera uses 1/3″ chips with 4:3 aspect ratios. A standard 1/3″ chip has a width of 4.8 mm and a height of 3.6 mm—or 0.19 × 0.14″. (When a chip is labeled 1/3″, it is not an indication of its true width, but a reference to standard designations given to television tubes in the 1950s.) The Canon XL2, like most video cameras, does not utilize the entire chip area, but uses a target area appropriate to the shooting mode. Thus, if the camera is shooting DV at 720 × 480, the actual chip area used is roughly 0.14 × 0.09″. Specifications for such calculations are often available from chip and video camera manufacturers.

As for choosing an appropriate Focal Length value for a video camera, professional-grade lenses generally have the appropriate information marked on the lens housing.

Displaying Gates

As you choose an aspect ratio and a film back for an animation project, it is recommended that you use the camera's various gates. Choosing View > Camera Settings > Resolution Gate through the camera workspace view menu displays the Resolution Gate frame in the perspective view. The Resolution Gate represents the maximum render area (see Figure 10.4). The renderer ignores anything outside the Resolution Gate. For extra security, you can toggle on Safe Action and Safe Title gates by choosing View > Camera Settings > Safe Action and View > Camera Settings > Safe Title. Since the average television set (whether SDTV or HDTV) cuts off a portion of the frame between the Resolution Gate and Safe Action gate, keep critical animation within the Safe Action gate. Keep critical text and titles within the Safe Title gate.

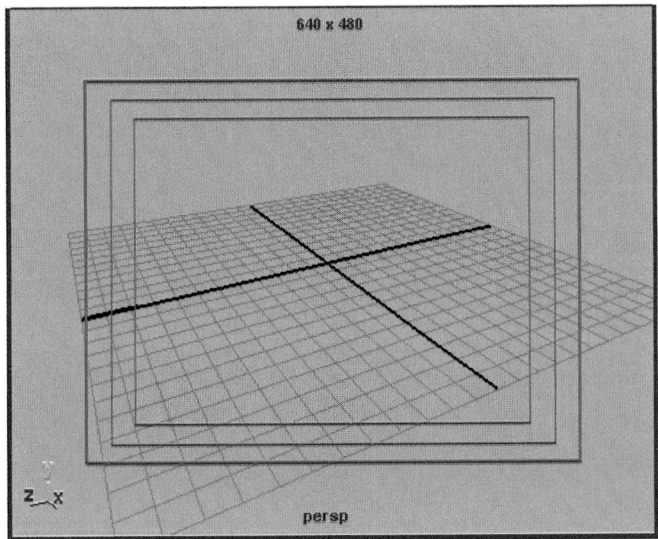

Figure 10.4 The Resolution Gate with Safe Action (middle box) and Safe Title (inner box) toggled on

The Resolution Gate aspect ratio, determined by the Device Aspect Ratio attribute of the Render Settings window, may be different from the Film Aspect Ratio. (See the section "Mastering the Render Settings Window" later in this chapter for more information on Device Aspect Ratio.) Hence, it's recommended that the Fit Resolution Gate attribute, in the Film Back section of the camera's attribute Editor tab, be adjusted. If Fit Resolution Gate is set to Fill, the Film Gate is scaled so that it covers the entire Resolution Gate. Depending on the render resolution, a portion of the Film Gate may be lost outside the Resolution Gate. To see the results of Fit Resolution Gate, you can display the Resolution Gate and Film Gate simultaneously by checking Display Resolution and Display Film Gate in the Display Options section of the camera's Attribute Editor tab. If Fit Resolution Gate is set to Horizontal or Vertical, the Film Gate is scaled in one direction so that it matches the Resolution Gate's dimension in that direction; any gap that appears in the opposite direction will render as normal unless Ignore Film Gate is unchecked in the Render Options section of the Maya Software tab in the Render Settings window. If Fit Resolution Gate is set to Overscan, the Film Gate is fit within the Resolution Gate so that no part is left unrendered; a gap between the gates may appear at the top and bottom. The only way to avoid gaps is to provide the Device Aspect Ratio and Film Aspect Ratio with identical values.

Selecting a Focal Length

Focal length is the distance from the optical center of a lens to its focal point (the point at which the light rays are focused). Once specific shots are determined within an animation project, it's wise to select specific focal lengths. Motion picture and television productions regularly change focal lengths (and even the entire lens) from shot to shot. Different focal lengths can have a significant impact on camera placement, composition, and object distortion. (See Chapter 7 for a demonstration.) Focal length is controlled in the Camera Attributes section of the camera's Attribute Editor tab, which includes Angle Of View, Focal Length, and Camera Scale attributes (see Figure 10.5).

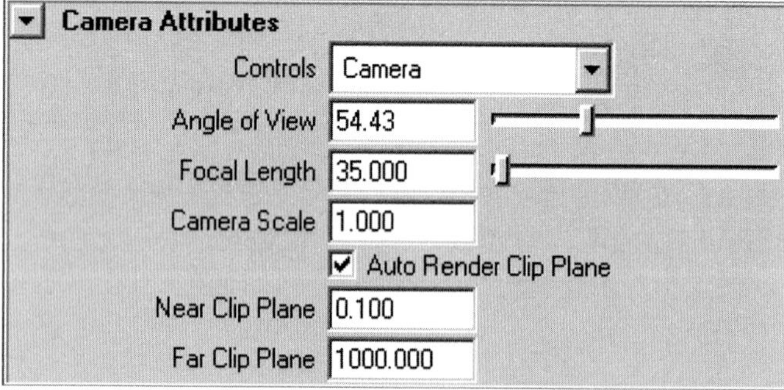

Figure 10.5 The Camera Attributes section of a camera's Attribute Editor tab

Angle Of View A measurement of the angular extent visible through the camera. If this attribute is changed, the Focal Length attribute automatically updates. Since the formula used by Angle Of View is very obscure, it is much more convenient to set the Focal Length attribute.

Focal Length Sets the focal length of a camera lens as measured in millimeters. Common real-world focal lengths include 20 mm, 35 mm, 50 mm, and 135 mm (see Figure 10.6).

Note: Scientific studies have estimated that the human eye has a focal length ranging from 22 mm to 24 mm, although numbers as high as 50 mm are popularly quoted. If you choose a 22 mm lens in Maya, the camera will not necessarily match a human angle of view since there is no "human eye" film gate available.

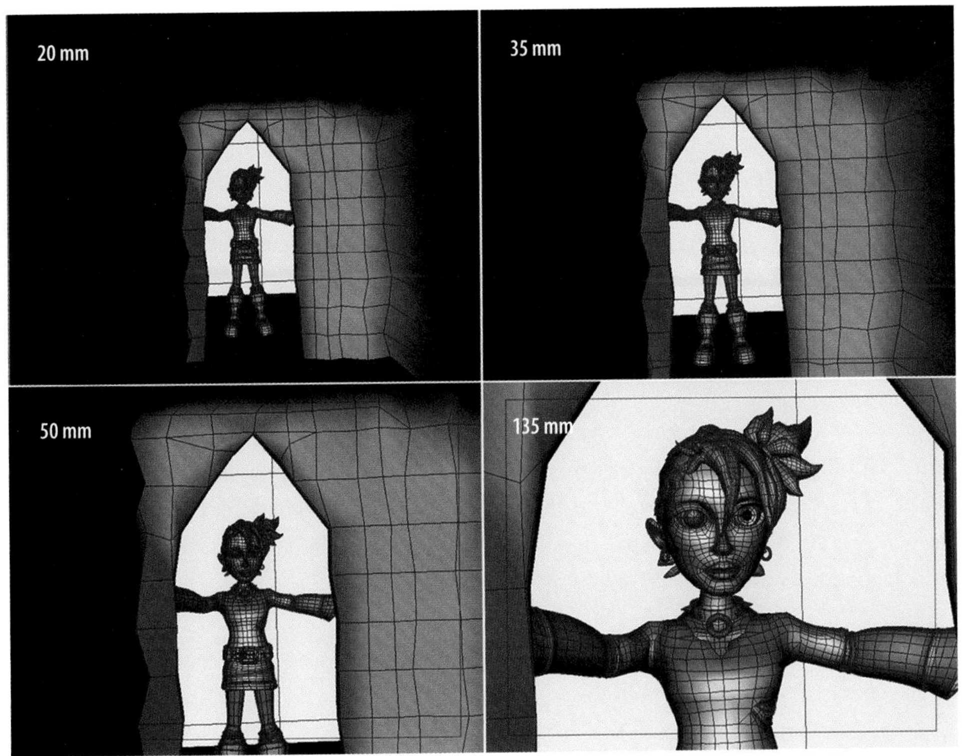

Figure 10.6 Clockwise, from top left: 20 mm, 35 mm, 135 mm, and 50 mm focal lengths in Maya with a 35 mm Academy Film Gate

Camera Scale Scales the Focal Length attribute as if the entire virtual camera mechanism were resized. Objects will appear twice as far away if this attribute is set to 2 and twice as close if this attribute is set to 0.5.

Selecting Frame Rates and Interlacing

A proper frame rate, or frames per second (fps), is critical for smooth animation. To set the rate, choose Window > Setting/Preferences > Preferences, switch to the Settings section, and choose an option from the Time attribute drop-down menu (see Figure 10.7). Maya provides the most common frame rates, including 24, 25, and 30.

24 fps The standard frame rate of motion picture film.

25 fps The standard frame rate of PAL and SECAM video.

30 fps The standard frame rate of NTSC video. 30 fps is a simplification of the more technically accurate 29.97 fps.

Note: To accurately gauge an animation when using the Timeline's playback controls, you must switch the Playback Speed attribute to Real-Time. You can find Playback Speed in the Timeline section of the Preferences window (choose Window > Setting/Preferences > Preferences).

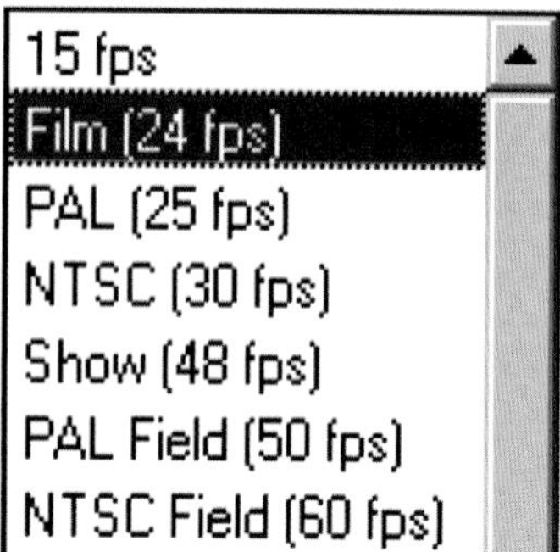

Figure 10.7 A portion of the Time drop-down menu in the Preferences window

Standard television transmission requires the use of interlaced fields. Thus, in reality, PAL runs at 50 interlaced fps and NTSC runs at 60 interlaced fps (or, more accurately, 59.94 interlaced fps). The interlacing process splits any given frame into interlaced upper and lower fields, with one field drawn first and the other field drawn second. Whether the upper field or lower field is drawn first is dependent on the video's field dominance. This varies with video format. You can render interlaced frames in Maya by choosing PAL Field or NTSC Field from the Time drop-down menu in the Settings section of the Preferences window. Compositing programs, such as Adobe After Effects, can also convert noninterlaced frames to interlaced frames at the point of render.

A Note on Frame Rate Conversion

One of the most difficult aspects of rendering is the conversion of one frame rate to another. The conversion of motion picture footage to NTSC video, for instance, requires the 3:2 pulldown process. A 3:2 pulldown converts four film frames into ten interlaced video frames. Two of the frames are repeated three times and two of the frames are repeated twice. 3:2 pulldowns are normally created with telecine machines but can be created with compositing programs such as Adobe After Effects or Autodesk Combustion. Compositing plug-ins, such as RE:Vision Effects Twixtor, offer additional techniques for interpolating and smoothing out frame rate conversions.

To avoid potential fps conversion difficulties, determine the primary presentation format of an animation project early on. If the work is destined for 35 mm transfer and a theatrical release or the film festival circuit, 24 fps would make the most sense. If an animation is created for a television commercial in the United States, 30 fps is necessary. If an animation needs to go to multiple outlets at multiple points around the globe, conversion artifacts should be expected. Even though many postproduction houses can electronically or digitally convert between frame rates, the result is never as smooth as the original. For instance, converting from PAL to NTSC will leave a "judder" in the animation where a slight hesitation appears every few frames.

Note: The average person subconsciously recognizes frame rate conversion. If a motion picture is broadcast on television, it must suffer 3:2 pulldown and have frames repeated. Hence, the motion within the movie does not appear as smooth as similar action shot on video.

Mastering the Render Settings Window

The majority of Render Settings window attributes are intuitive and easy to use. However, several of them are worth a closer look. The attributes are divided into Common and renderer-specific tabs. The Common tab includes Frame Padding, Alpha Channel (Mask), Depth Channel (Z Depth), Resolution, Resolution Units, Device Aspect Ratio, and Pixel Aspect Ratio attributes (see Figure 10.8).

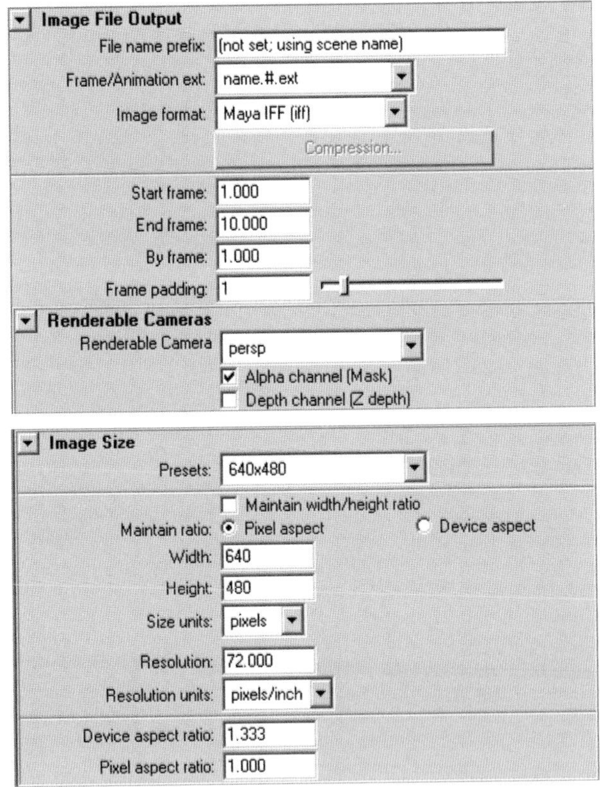

Figure 10.8 The Image File Output and Image Size sections of the Common tab in the Render Settings window

Frame Padding Ensures that each filename carries the same number of numeric placeholders. Many compositing programs, such as Adobe After Effects, expect specific frame numbering conventions. For example, After Effects will incorrectly order the following files:

```
Test.1.jpg
Test.5.jpg
Test.10.jpg
Test.100.jpg
```

However, if the Frame Padding attribute is set to 3, the images will be named in the universally understood manner:

```
Test.001.jpg
Test.005.jpg
Test.010.jpg
Test.100.jpg
```

Alpha Channel (Mask) Toggles on the alpha channel for select image formats (Maya IFF, TIFF, Targa, RLA, and SGI). Alpha represents the opacity of objects in a scene. Alpha is stored as a scalar (grayscale) value in the fourth channel (the *A* in RGBA). In Maya, white indicates opaque objects and black indicates empty space. You can view the alpha channel in the Render View window by clicking the Display Alpha Channel button. Common compositing programs easily read the Maya alpha channel.

Depth Channel (Z Depth) Toggles on the depth channel for select image formats (Maya IFF and RLA). With TIFF, Targa, and SGI images, the attribute causes the depth channel to be written out as a separate file with a *_depth* suffix. Depth channels represent the distance between the camera and objects in the scene. Depth channels (sometimes referred to as Z-depth buffers) are employed by compositing programs to determine object occlusion. For example, a depth channel might be used to properly place 2D fog "into" a rendered 3D scene or to create a depth-of-field effect as part of the compositing process. In another variation, Maya depth map shadows are depth channel maps from the view of the light (see Chapter 3). You can view the depth channel of an image file by choosing File > View Image, browsing for the file, and clicking the Z Buffer button in the FCheck window (see Figure 10.9). Like alpha channels, depth channels are scalar.

Resolution and Resolution Units For video and film, the image size is determined solely by the Width and Height attributes. For projects destined for print, however, the Resolution attribute is added to determine pixels per inch. For example, many print jobs require 300 pixels per inch. You can thus set the Resolution attribute to 300 and the Resolution Units attribute to Pixels/Inch.

Device Aspect Ratio Defines the aspect ratio of rendered images based on the following formula:

Device Aspect Ratio = Image Aspect Ratio × Pixel Aspect Ratio

The image aspect ratio is determined by dividing the Width attribute by the Height attribute. For example, if Width is set to 720, Height is set to 480, and Pixel Aspect Ratio is set to 0.9, the Device Aspect Ratio is set automatically to 1.35. *Device* refers to output device, such a television or computer monitor. (See the section "Deciphering Aspect Ratios" earlier in this chapter.)

Pixel Aspect Ratio Defines the aspect ratio of individual pixels. If set to 1, the pixels are square and do not affect the Device Aspect Ratio calculation. If set to 0.9, the pixels are nonsquare NTSC. (See the section "Switching between Square and Nonsquare Pixels" earlier in this chapter.)

Render-specific attributes reside in the Maya Software, Maya Hardware, and Maya Vector tabs. (See Chapter 11 for a discussion of mental ray attributes.)

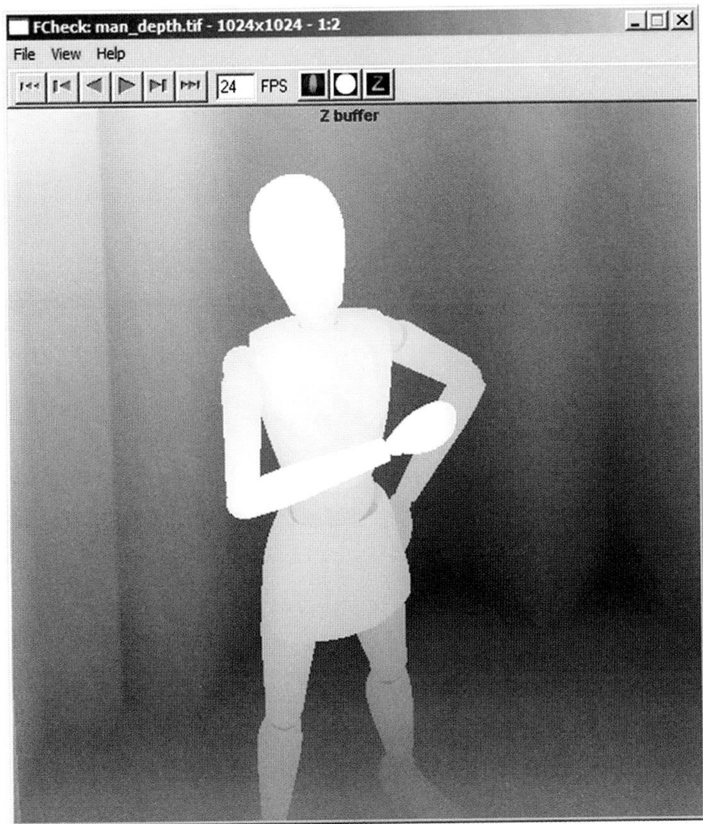

Figure 10.9 A depth channel viewed in FCheck

Prepping Maya Software Renders

The Maya Software renderer is a general-purpose renderer that is suitable for most projects. Critical attributes include Edge Anti-Aliasing, Shading, and Max Shading. Important sections include Multi-Pixel Filtering and Contrast Threshold (see Figure 10.10).

Edge Anti-Aliasing Anti-aliasing is an inescapable necessity of 3D and other computer graphics. Due to the physical limitations of computer monitors and televisions (which possess a limited number of display pixels), normally smooth edges become "jaggy" or "stair-stepped." Maya's anti-aliasing process uses a subpixel sampling technique that computes multiple sample points within a single pixel and assigns the averaged sample values to that pixel. Although Maya offers various anti-aliasing presets, such as Low Quality or High Quality, you can tailor the anti-aliasing by entering values into the Shading and Max Shading attribute fields.

Shading Sets the minimum number of subpixel samples taken within a pixel during the anti-aliasing process. If set to 1, each pixel is sampled one time. If set to 4, each pixel is sampled four times. The number of subpixel samples is not permitted to exceed the Max Shading value.

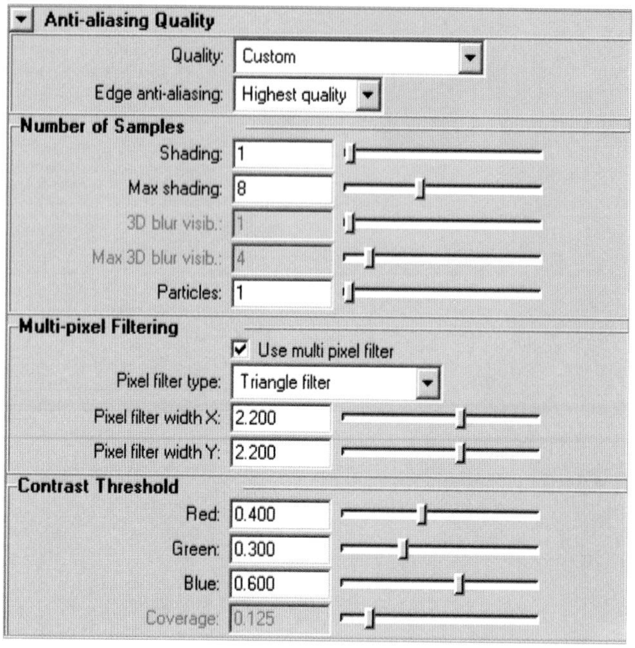

Figure 10.10 A portion of the Maya Software tab in the Render Settings window

Max Shading Sets the maximum number of subpixel samples taken within a pixel during the adaptive shading pass of the anti-aliasing process. This is in effect only when the Edge Anti-Aliasing attribute is set to Highest Quality. Whether or not the Max Shading value is applied is dependent on Contrast Threshold attribute, which controls the adaptive shading pass.

Contrast Threshold This section controls the adaptive shading pass of the anti-aliasing process. The Edge Anti-Aliasing attribute must be set to Highest Quality for the Contrast Threshold section to function. Contrast Threshold tests for pixels whose contrast with neighboring pixels exceeds the Red, Green, or Blue attribute threshold values. For these pixels, additional subpixel sampling is undertaken. In this case, Max Shading sets the maximum number of permitted samples.

Multi-Pixel Filtering Multi-pixel filtering is designed to blend neighboring pixels into a coherent mass. Such filtering helps to prevent common aliasing artifacts. In particular, multi-pixel filtering can improve renders destined for video. The interlaced nature of television is harsh and tends to exaggerate aliasing problems. A slightly soft render, thanks to the multi-pixel filtering process, can look better on video than a nonfiltered render. However, a similar multi-pixel filter applied to a render destined for motion picture film or a web-based movie can prove inferior. In such a case, uncheck Use Multi Pixel Filter. Even if the render is intended for video, it might be wise to reduce the Pixel Filter Width X and Pixel Filter Width Y attributes until the render can be properly tested.

If Use Multi Pixel Filter is checked, you can select five filter styles from the Pixel Filter Type drop-down menu: Box Filter, Triangle Filter, Gaussian Filter, Quadratic B-Spline

Filter, and Plug-in Filter. Of these, Box Filter produces the softest result, while Gaussian Filter produces the sharpest. Triangle Filter, which is the default, produces a moderate degree of softness. Quadratic B-Spline is a legacy filter from the first version of Maya. Plug-in Filter allows you to write a custom filter in Maya's `.mll` plug-in language. The Use Multi Pixel Filter attribute is automatically checked when the Quality attribute (in the Anti-Aliasing Quality section) is set to Production Quality, Contrast Sensitive Production, or 3D Motion Blur Production.

Note: You can adjust and refine the render quality of NURBS surfaces outside the Render Settings window. NURBS tessellation attributes are accessible through the surface's Attribute Editor tab. For a detailed discussion of these attributes, see section 10.1 of the `Additional_Techniques.pdf` file on the CD.

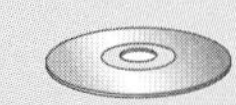

Prepping Maya Hardware Renders

The Maya Hardware renderer provides a quick method of rendering tests and other projects that do not require a high degree of refinement (see Figure 10.11). The Hardware renderer uses the built-in capabilities of the system graphics card.

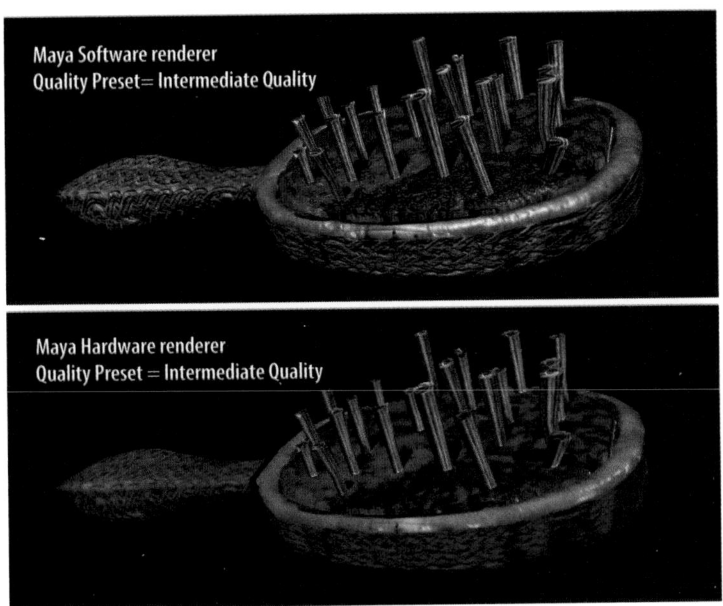

Figure 10.11 (Top) A model rendered with Maya Software. (Bottom) The same model rendered with Maya Hardware via an entry-level graphics card.

The easiest way to set the quality of the Hardware renderer is to use one of the four options of the Presets attribute (Preview Quality, Intermediate Quality, Production Quality, and Production Quality With Transparency). Nevertheless, many of the corresponding attributes are unique and are worth a closer look (see Figure 10.12).

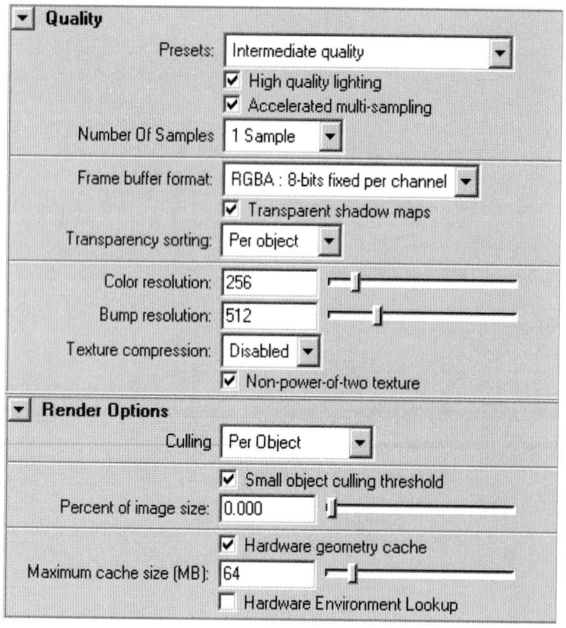

Figure 10.12 A portion of the Maya Hardware tab in the Render Settings window

Number Of Samples Defines the number of subpixel samples taken per pixel during the anti-aliasing process.

Color Resolution and Bump Resolution Control the size of the 2D image that the renderer must bake (pre-render) if it encounters a color or bump shading network that is too complex to evaluate directly.

Culling Controls whether single-sided and double-sided qualities are evaluated per object or are universally overridden. A Small Object Culling Threshold attribute is also provided, allowing opaque objects smaller than the threshold to be ignored by the renderer. (The threshold is a percentage of the render resolution.)

Hardware Geometry Cache When checked, allows the renderer to cache geometry to the unused portion of the on-board memory of the graphics card.

Motion Blur When checked, enables hardware motion blurring. The Motion Blur By Frame attribute sets the time range that the renderer uses to evaluate a moving object's before and after position. The Number Of Exposures attribute determines the number of discrete positions within the time frame that the renderer uses to refine the blur. The higher the exposure number, the smoother and more accurate the result. (For additional information on motion blur, see the section "Applying Motion Blur" later in this chapter.)

Note: In general, the Maya Hardware renderer is superior to Maya's Hardware Render Buffer. The Maya Hardware renderer can render hardware-rendered particles, texture maps, bump maps, displacement maps, and complex lighting. This ability is dependent, however, on the compatibility of the installed graphics card. For a list of graphics cards recommended for Maya, visit `www.autodesk.com`.

Prepping Maya Vector Renders

The Maya Vector renderer can create stylized cartoon and wireframe renders (see Figure 10.13). Although the majority of options are straightforward, a few warrant a more detailed description.

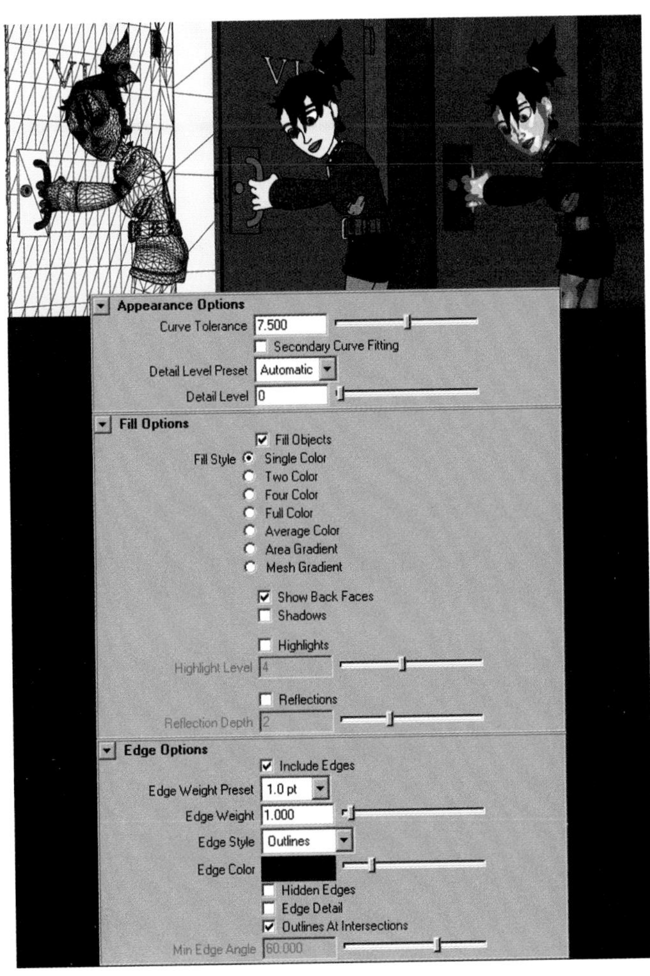

Figure 10.13 (Top, Left to Right) Maya Vector renderer with Single Color and Entire Mesh, Vector with Single Color and Outlines, Vector with Four Color. (Bottom) The Maya Vector tab in the Render Settings window.

Curve Tolerance Determines the smoothness of a NURBS or subdivision surface edge. A value of 0 will leave the edge faceted (as if the surface was converted to a polygon). The maximum value of 15 will smooth the surface to such an extent that it becomes slightly distorted. The Curve Tolerance attribute has no effect on polygon surfaces.

Detail Level and Detail Level Preset Detail Level controls the accuracy of the Vector renderer. A high value improves the quality but slows the render significantly. Detail Level Preset, if set to Automatic, overrides the Detail Level attribute. You can also set the Detail Level Preset to standard quality settings, which include Low, Medium, and

High. If Detail Level Preset is set to Low, small polygons are combined with adjacent polygons, thus negating any fine detail.

Fill Style Controls the solid color that appears on the surface of rendered objects. The Single Color radio button, when clicked, creates a solid color based on the surface material. The Average Color radio button also creates a single color based on the material, but includes shading based on the scene lighting. The Two Color and Four Color radio buttons add additional solid colors based on the material color and scene lighting. The Full Color radio button tints each individual polygon face with a solid color based on the surface material and scene lighting. The Mesh Gradient and Area Gradient radio buttons apply color gradients based on material color and scene lighting. Mesh Gradient and Area Gradient are supported by the SWF format. (See the section "Differentiating Image Formats" later in this chapter.) In addition, you can check on and off Shadows, Highlights, and Reflections in this section.

Include Edges When checked, creates edge lines. The Edge Weight Preset attribute controls the thickness of the line. If the Edge Style attribute is set to Outlines, a line will be created at the outer edge of each surface. If the Edge Style attribute is set to Entire Mesh, a line is drawn along each and every polygon edge. In this case, all polygon faces are rendered as triangles. In addition, NURBS surfaces will have lines drawn at polygon edges derived from the tessellation process.

Rendering with the Command Line

You can launch a batch render with the Maya Software or mental ray renderer from the Microsoft Windows Command Prompt window, the Macintosh OS X's Terminal window, or the shell window of a Linux system. It is not necessary to run the Maya interface. Hence, this method of rendering can be efficient. To achieve this, a Maya `.mb` or `.ma` file need only be saved in advance. At that point, follow these steps:

1. Launch the Command Prompt window (in Windows XP, choose All Programs > Accessories > Command Prompt), the Terminal window (found in the Macintosh's OS X Utilities folder), or appropriate Linux shell window.
2. Switch to the directory in which the appropriate `.mb` or `.ma` file resides. For example, in Windows the command might be

   ```
   cd c:\3d\maya\projects
   ```
3. Launch the software renderer by entering

   ```
   render file_name
   ```

   The Maya Software renderer proceeds using the settings contained within the Render Settings window when the file was saved. You can interrupt the renderer at any time by pressing Ctrl+C in the Command Prompt or Terminal window. You can simultaneously launch multiple renders in separate Command Prompt, Terminal, or shell windows; the renders will evenly divide the available CPU cycles.

   If you prefer to render with mental ray, you must enter this:

   ```
   render -r mr file_name
   ```

The `-r` or `-renderer` flag specifies the renderer used. You can override the file's render settings by using various flags. For instance, you can force the renderer to render frames 5 to 10 with the following line:

```
render file_name -s 5 -e 10
```

To display the lengthy list of render flags, open Help with the following line (see Figure 10.14):

```
render -h
```

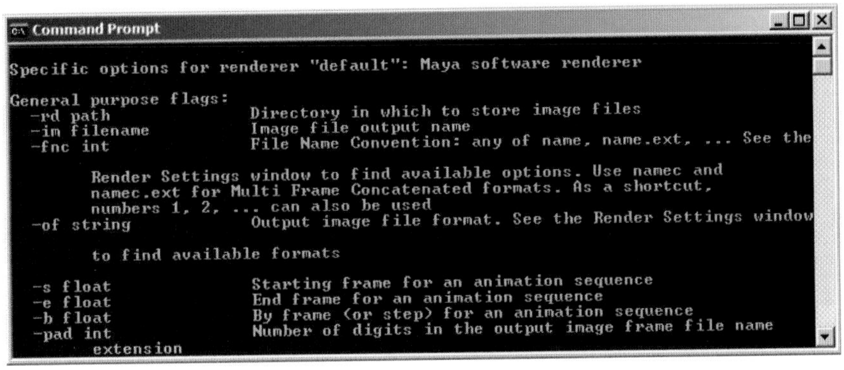

```
Command Prompt

Specific options for renderer "default": Maya software renderer

General purpose flags:
  -rd path              Directory in which to store image files
  -im filename          Image file output name
  -fnc int              File Name Convention: any of name, name.ext, ... See the

        Render Settings window to find available options. Use namec and
        namec.ext for Multi Frame Concatenated formats. As a shortcut,
        numbers 1, 2, ... can also be used
  -of string            Output image file format. See the Render Settings window

        to find available formats

  -s float              Starting frame for an animation sequence
  -e float              End frame for an animation sequence
  -b float              By frame (or step) for an animation sequence
  -pad int              Number of digits in the output image frame file name
        extension
```

Figure 10.14 A portion of render Help, as shown in the Command Prompt window

Organizing the Render

Rendering is the final step of the animation process, yet it requires the same attention to detail as any other aspect of 3D to be successful. Creating clean scene files and establishing appropriate paths to bitmaps are important steps.

Cleaning Up

The speed of any given Maya render depends on the quality of the scene file. If a scene file contains unnecessary construction history, broken nodes, and unneeded geometry, the render will suffer. A quick solution to this problem is to choose File > Optimize Scene Size. By default, Optimize Scene Size deletes unused curves, unassigned materials, orphaned group nodes (those without children), and empty layers. By opening the Optimize Scene Size Options window, you can optimize specific categories by checking or unchecking the category buttons (see Figure 10.15). Use caution when dealing with complex scenes since it is possible to unintentionally delete critical components of character rigs and other advanced setups.

If you are unable to determine why a particular scene is rendering slowly, switch to the Rendering menu set and choose Render > Run Render Diagnostics. The Script Editor opens and displays suggestions for optimizing the scene in question (see Figure 10.16). Although these suggestions can be quite helpful, they are by no means mandatory.

During the modeling process, it is also important to choose Edit > Delete By Type > History when construction history is no longer needed. If construction history remains on a rigged character, for instance, the render time can be significantly increased.

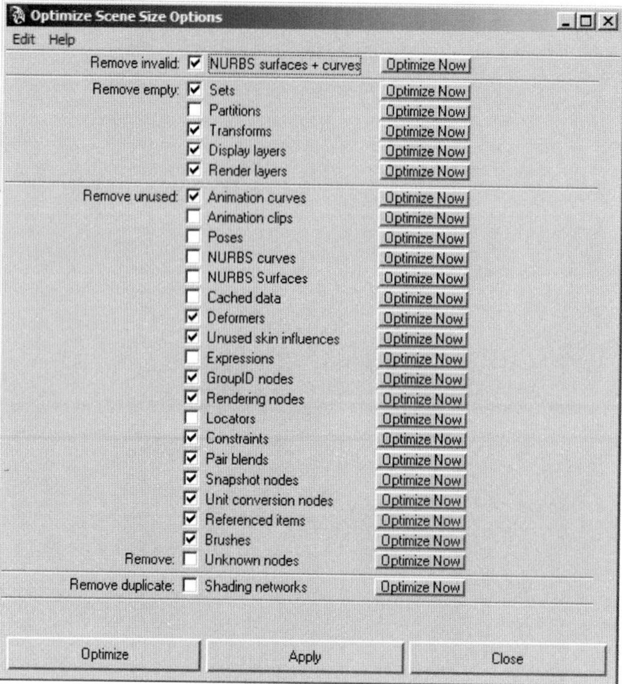

Figure 10.15 The Optimize Scene Size Options window

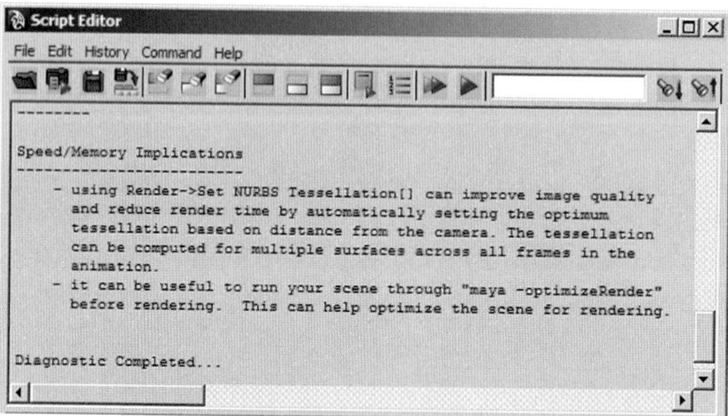

Figure 10.16 A sample render diagnostics message displayed in the Script Editor window

Recovering Lost Bitmaps

Maya .mb and .ma files contain all the elements required for a render—except actual bitmaps. Instead, paths pointing to bitmaps are hard-coded in a Maya file. For example, as shown at the top of Figure 10.17, a .ma file contains the following line:

```
settAttr ".ftn" -type "string" "C:/3D/logo.tif";
```

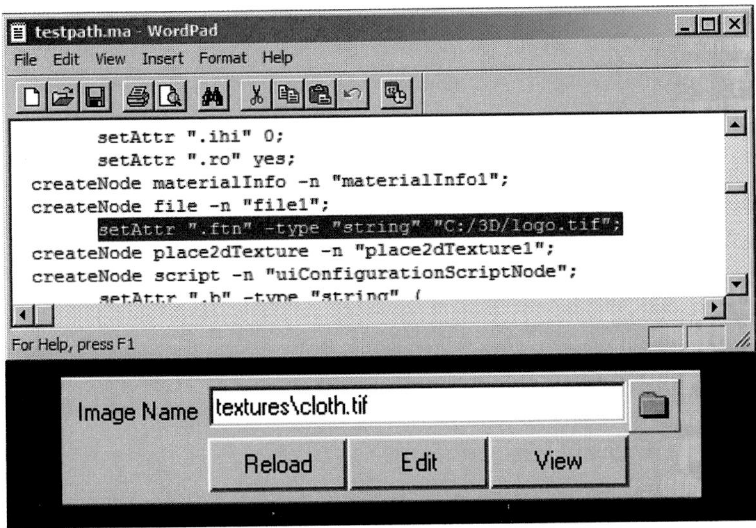

Figure 10.17 (Top) The hard-coded bitmap path of a Maya .ma file, as displayed in a text editor. (Bottom) A truncated path listed by the Image Name attribute of a File texture.

Thus, if the Maya file in question is moved between computers with different drive letters or directory structures, `logo.tif` will be "lost." In this case, the Multilister and Hypershade windows display a black icon for bitmaps that are missing. This holds true even if the project directory has been set through File > Project > Set. In such a situation, Maya displays a truncated path in the File texture's Image Name field (see the bottom of Figure 10.17). Nevertheless, Maya will be unable to find the texture if the drive letter or directory structure has changed.

Fortunately, you can fix this problem by quickly editing an `.ma` version of the file, which is simply text. Using the Find and Replace All function of Microsoft Windows WordPad or an equivalent text editor, replace `c:/` with `d:/` or any other appropriate path. In a similar fashion, you can edit `.mb` files. However, since `.mb` files are binary, a hexadecimal editor is required (see Figure 10.18).

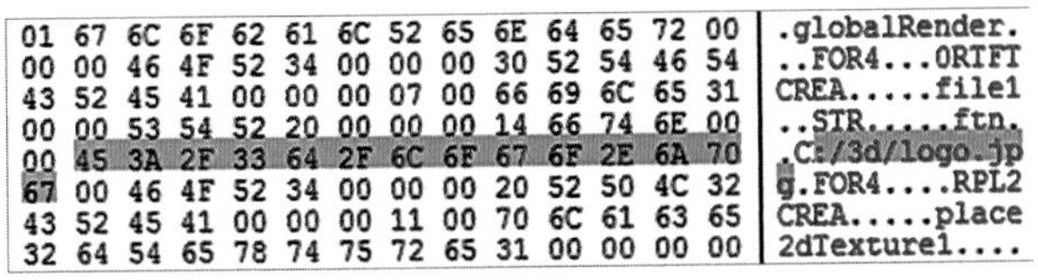

```
01 67 6C 6F 62 61 6C 52 65 6E 64 65 72 00   .globalRender.
00 00 46 4F 52 34 00 00 00 30 52 54 46 54   ..FOR4...0RTFT
43 52 45 41 00 00 00 07 00 66 69 6C 65 31   CREA.....file1
00 00 53 54 52 20 00 00 00 14 66 74 6E 00   ..STR.....ftn.
00 45 3A 2F 33 64 2F 6C 6F 67 6F 2E 6A 70   .C:/3d/logo.jp
67 00 46 4F 52 34 00 00 00 20 52 50 4C 32   g.FOR4....RPL2
43 52 45 41 00 00 00 11 00 70 6C 61 63 65   CREA.....place
32 64 54 65 78 74 75 72 65 31 00 00 00 00   2dTexture1....
```

Figure 10.18 The hard-coded bitmap path of a Maya .mb file, as displayed in a hexadecimal editor

Selecting Image Formats and Render Resolutions

Using the default image format and render resolution is rarely a good choice. To create a professional animation, you should familiarize yourself with compression schemes, image formats, and key differences between video and motion picture technology.

Differentiating Image Formats

Maya Software, Hardware, and Vector renderers can output 30 different image formats. You can select the format by switching the Image Format attribute in the Render Settings window. Although any of the formats can be used successfully in the right circumstance, AVI, QuickTime, JPEG, Targa, and TIFF formats are perhaps the most popular. At the same time, Maya IFF, PSD, Adobe Illustrator, EPS, and SWF formats are designed for specialized tasks.

AVI (`.avi`) and QuickTime (`.mov`) On Microsoft Windows systems, Windows Media Player AVI movies are an available format. By default, Maya renders AVI files with no compression. However, you can choose other compression schemes by clicking the Compression button that appears just below the Image Format attribute. Although AVIs are convenient for short tests, they are not suitable for most renders. If a batch render fails or is intentionally interrupted, the AVI file is permanently lost. In addition, individual AVI frames cannot be checked as the render progresses. Conversely, the QuickTime format is available on systems running Macintosh OS X. QuickTime suffers from the same drawbacks as AVI.

JPEG (`.jpg`) Stands for Joint Photographic Experts Group and is one of the most popular image formats in the world. The main weakness of this format is the lossy quality of its compression, whereby artifacts appear along edges and other high-contrast areas. By default, Maya sets the compression quality of rendered JPEGs to 75 percent. (See the section "Changing Compression Settings" later in this chapter.) Maya does not support CMYK variations of the JPEG format.

Targa (`.tga`) Developed by Truevision in the mid-1980s, this remains a robust and reliable image format. Targas can store an alpha channel and are readable by the majority of digital image and compositing programs. Targa file sizes are relatively large, which is perhaps their main disadvantage. An average 720 × 540 Targa might take up 1.1 megabytes, while the same size JPEG with a 75 percent quality setting will be a mere 60 kilobytes. Not all Targa formats are supported by Maya.

TIFF (`.tif`) Stands for Tagged Image File Format and is another popular format developed in the mid-1980s. TIFFs can store alpha and are similar in size to Targas. The TIFF format has numerous variations and compression schemes, however, and are therefore inconsistently interpreted by various graphics programs. In fact, the mental ray renderer in Maya may return an error when unsupported TIFF variations are encountered as File textures. (Should this happen, convert the image to another format.) By default, Maya TIFFs are compressed with TIFF 6.0 compression. (See "Changing Compression Settings" later in this chapter.)

Maya IFF (`.iff`) A native format developed by Alias. While Maya's FCheck program reads the IFF format, such digital imaging programs as Adobe Photoshop and Gimp are unable to open them. On the other hand, compositing programs such as Adobe After Effects read IFF files. The IFF format can store specialized data (depth, motion, and vector).

PSD and PSD Layered (`.psd`) The standard Photoshop image format. If PSD Layered is chosen, the background color is placed on a Photoshop locked background while the objects are placed on a separate layer with transparency surrounding them. In this case, no alpha channel is provided (even if it is checked in the Render Settings window).

AI (Adobe Illustrator; `.ai`) Converts the scene into a series of editable spline paths. The Maya Vector renderer must be used to output this format. AI files can be read by Macromedia Flash authoring programs.

Note: Maya Software, Maya Hardware, Maya Vector, and mental ray renderers are unable to support all 30 image formats. For a detailed list of which renderer supports what format, see the "Supported Image Formats (Rendering)" page in the Maya Help file.

EPS (`.eps`) Stands for Encapsulated PostScript and can contain both bitmap and vector information. If rendered with Maya Software, a bitmap image is produced. If Maya Vector is used, a vector image is produced. The vector version of the EPS format can be read by Adobe Photoshop, Illustrator, and Acrobat.

Macromedia Flash (`.swf`) A vector image format. All the frames of a Macromedia Flash render are contained within a single file. You must use the Maya Vector renderer to output this format.

RLA (`.rla`) and SGI (`.sgi`) RLA is a legacy Wavefront image format that can store alpha and Z-depth channels. SGI is a legacy Silicon Graphics image format that supports an alpha channel.

A Note on 16-Bit Color Space

The majority of Maya image formats operate in an 8-bit color space (8 bits in red, 8 bits in green, and 8 bits in blue, totaling 24 bits, or 16,777,216 possible colors). In the realm of consumer electronics, this color space is commonly referred to as True Color. At present, the majority of consumer monitors offer a 32-bit variation of True Color. This is a 24-bit color space with an extra 8 bits set aside as an empty placeholder (necessary for 32-bit architecture) or for alpha information. By comparison, Maya16 IFF, TIFF16, and SGI16 are three available Maya image formats that operate in 16-bit color space (16 bits per channel, totaling 281 trillion possible colors).

The human eye is popularly believed to discern 10 million color variations. As such, 16-bit color may seem like extreme overkill. However, many image-processing filters create superior results when operating at a higher bit depth. Hence, programs such as Adobe Photoshop and Adobe After Effects offer the option to work with 16-bit images. Low bit-depth errors are most commonly seen as banding (posterization), where the color transitions fail to be smooth (see Figure 10.19). Although 8-bit color space is satisfactory for many applications, 16-bit color space is superior for any project in which color and color manipulation is critical.

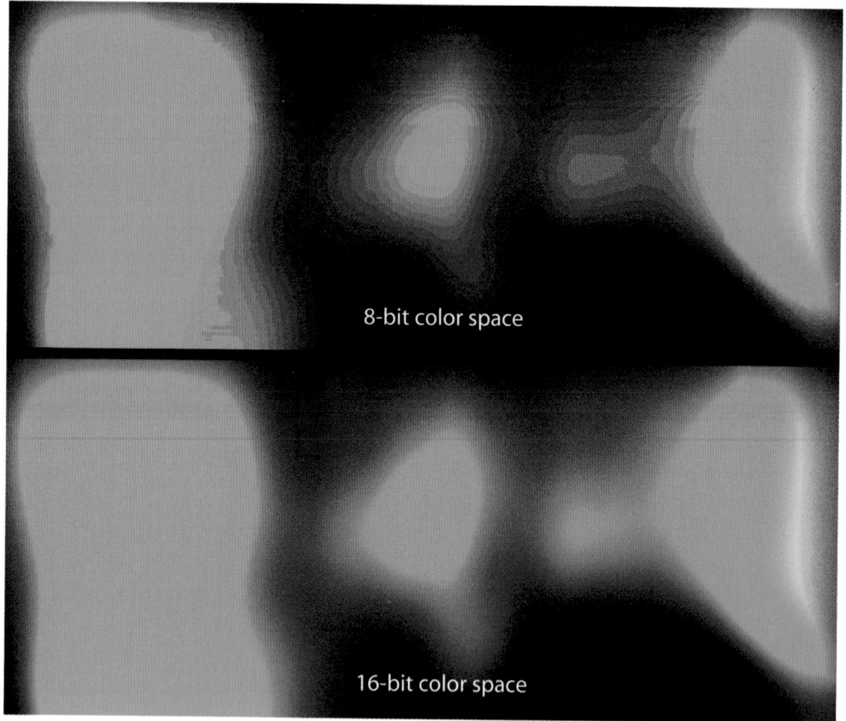

Figure 10.19 (Top) Color banding caused by a Gaussian blur in 8-bit color space. (Bottom) The result of the same blur in 16-bit color space.

Note: Maya supports several floating-point, 32-bit image formats: OpenEXR, DDS, and HDR. In addition, mental ray is able to produce 32-bit images through its Primary Framebuffer. These image formats are designed for High-Dynamic Range Images (HDRI), which are discussed in detail in Chapter 13.

Changing Compression Settings

To change the default compression setting of JPEG and TIFF formats within Maya, you must create an environment variable. Follow these steps:

1. Open a blank text file with Windows Notepad or another text editor.
2. To change the default JPEG compression to maximum quality, add the following line:

   ```
   AW_JPEG_Q_FACTOR = 100
   ```

3. To remove the default TIFF or TIFF16 compression, add this line:

   ```
   IMF_TIFF_COMPRESSION = none
   ```

4. Save the file as `Maya.env` in the default Maya project folder (for example, `C:\Documents and Settings\`*`username`*`\My Documents\maya\2008\`). Be careful to capitalize the word *Maya*.
5. Restart Maya. The TIFF and/or JPEG compression will be based on the environment file.

Oversized Rendering

If time permits, it is always best to render larger than the default size necessitated by a particular project. For example, if an animation is to be created for a video, it is not necessary to stick to 720 × 540. Any multiplier of the 1.33 aspect ratio is equally valid. For instance, 798 × 600 or 1197 × 900 would work equally well. The use of an odd size assumes that the rendered frames will be taken into a compositing program where they can be resized. Since professional animations generally require compositing, oversized rendering can be employed quite often.

Oversized rendering guarantees an animation one very important thing—additional anti-aliasing. This anti-aliasing occurs when the oversized image is shrunk. Compositing programs such as Adobe After Effects must average the pixels of an image during a size reduction. Ultimately, this averaging reduces stair-stepping and other common aliasing problems (see Figure 10.20).

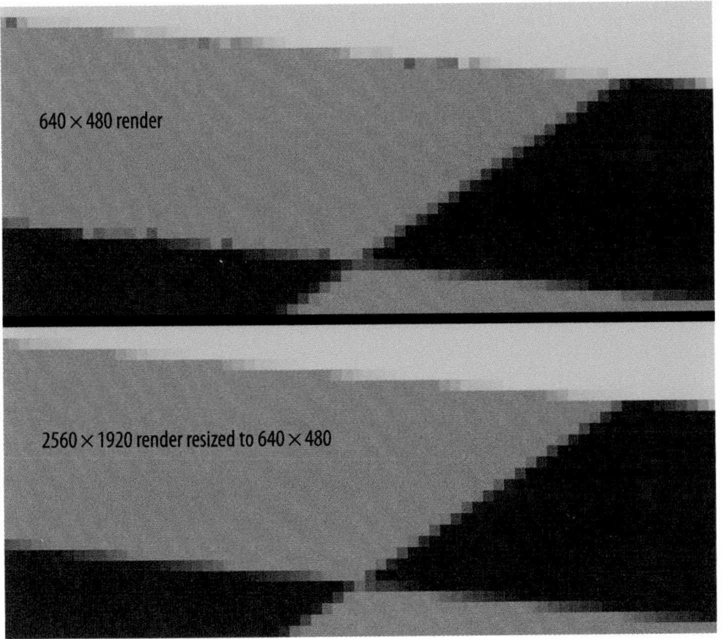

Figure 10.20 (Top) Detail of standard 640 × 480 render. (Bottom) The same image rendered 2560 × 1920 and scaled down.

Creating Depth of Field

Depth of field is the range of distances that encompass objects that appear acceptably sharp. Due to the optical nature of real-world lenses and the physical qualities of the atmosphere, photography and videography rarely produce images that are 100 percent in focus. In contrast, 3D renders are always in perfect focus unless depth of field is used. You can activate Maya's depth of field by checking the Depth Of Field attribute in the Depth Of Field section of the camera's Attribute Editor tab (see Figure 10.21).

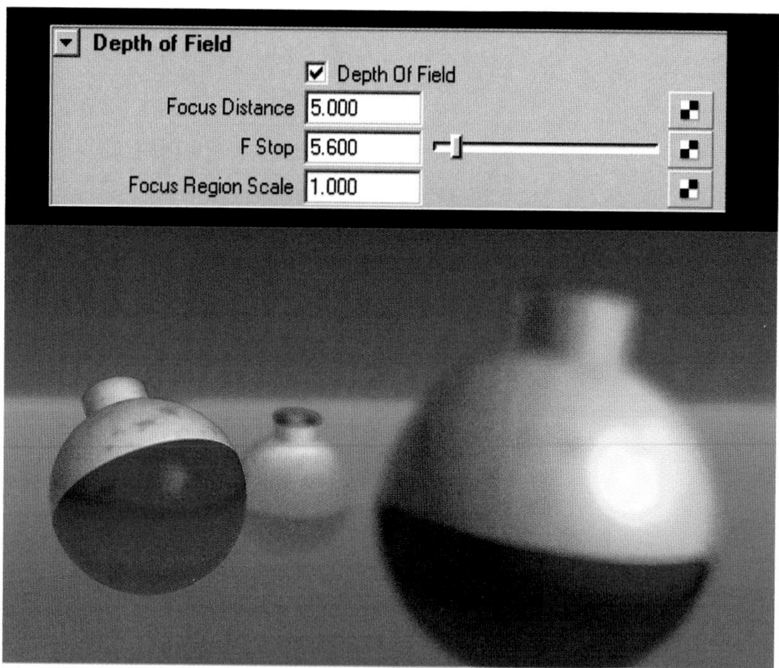

Figure 10.21 (Top) The Depth Of Field section of a camera's Attribute Editor tab. (Bottom) Depth of field in action. This scene is included on the CD as `depth_of_field.ma`.

Maya's depth of field, although generally convincing, can be difficult to set up at times. The following process is therefore recommended:

1. Measure the distance between the camera lens and subject by choosing Create > Measure Tools > Distance Tool (see Figure 10.22). For an accurate reading, place the Distance Tool's first locator at the base of the camera icon lens. Enter the resulting distance into the Focus Distance attribute field.
2. Set the F Stop attribute to the slider maximum of 64. The higher the F Stop value, the greater the depth of field. This will make the depth of field adjustments much easier at the start.
3. Render a test frame. Incrementally reduce the F Stop value and re-render. When the depth of field appears satisfactory, leave the F Stop value as is.
4. For fine-tuning, increase or decrease the Focus Region Scale attribute by small increments. The Focus Region Scale attribute is a multiplier of the depth of field effect.

Note: The F Stop attribute roughly approximates the f-stop of real-world cameras. F-stop is a number that represents the ratio between the diameter of the lens aperture and the focal length of the lens. F-stops are scaled by an approximate factor of 1.4 (for example, f/1.4, f/2, f/2.8, and so on). Each increased f-stop halves the open area of the aperture, halves the amount of light striking the film, and increases the depth of field. The f-stop isn't the only factor to influence depth of field, however. Depth of field is inversely proportional to the focal length of the lens and directly proportional to the distance from the camera to the subject.

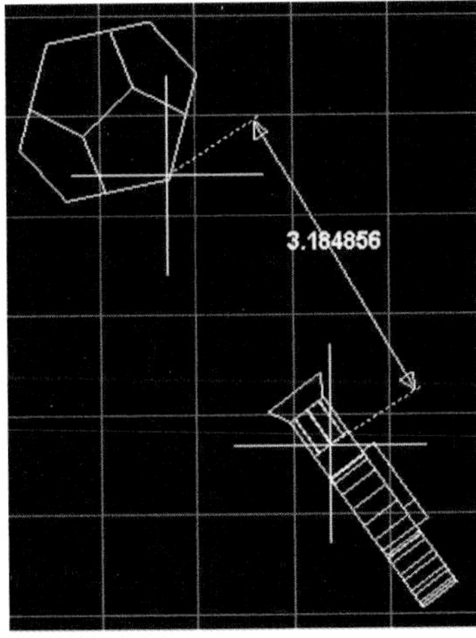

Figure 10.22
The Distance tool used to determine the focus distance

If Maya's depth of field proves unsatisfactory or too slow to render, you can simulate the effect in a compositing program. For example, in Figure 10.23 a still life is rendered with no depth of field. The image is taken in Adobe After Effects and stacked three times within a composite. The bottom layer of the composite is given a strong Gaussian blur. The middle layer has a mask applied to separate out the foreground and middle ground; the middle layer has a medium-strength Gaussian blur applied. The top composite layer has a mask applied to separate the foreground; the top layer has no blur applied. The result is an image with an artificial depth of field. If the elements within the scene are rendered out separately, this effect is even easier to achieve.

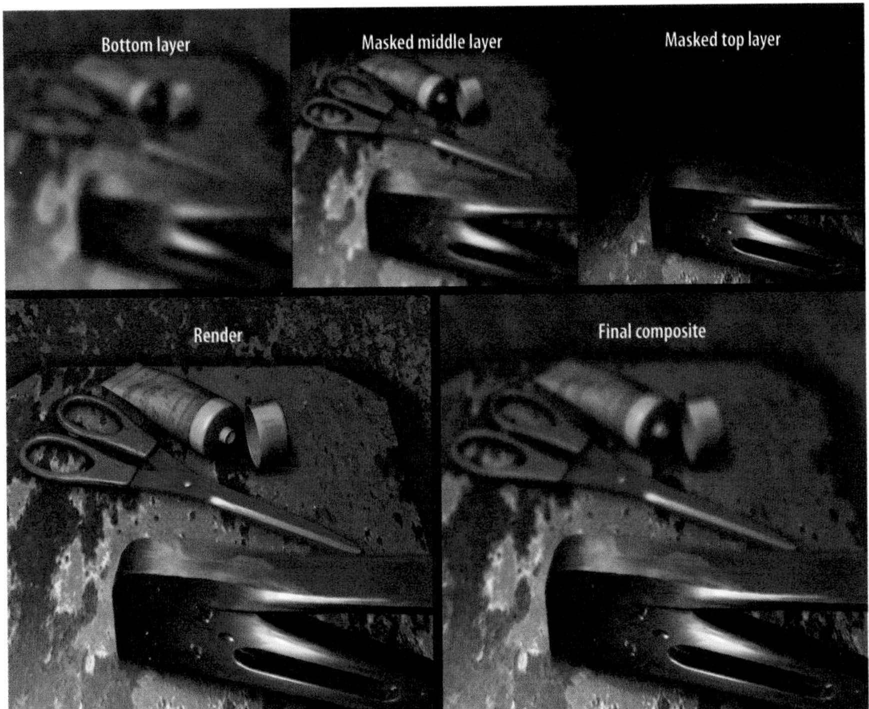

Figure 10.23 An artificial depth of field is constructed by masking multiple copies of a render and applying different strength Gaussian blurs.

In most cases, the artificial depth of field trick is successful because the human brain is unable to differentiate small degrees of "unsharpness" (technically referred to as the "circles of confusion"). That is, the incremental transition from what is in focus to what is out of focus is perceived in relatively coarse steps.

Applying Motion Blur

Motion blur is a streaking of objects in motion as captured by motion picture, film, or video mediums. The effect is an artifact of the time required to chemically expose film stock or electronically process light through a video CCD chip. If an object moves 1 foot during the 1/60 of a second required by a camera to create one frame, the motion blur appears 1 foot in length on that frame. Motion blur is also perceived by the human eye when the motion is rapid. Although the human brain processes information continuously and does not perceive "frames" per se, rapid motion is seen as blurry through various physiological and psychological mechanisms (the exact nature of which continues to be studied and contended).

You can check on the Motion Blur attribute in the Motion Blur section of the Maya Software tab in the Render Settings window. (mental ray motion blur is discussed in Chapter 11.) The Motion Blur Type attribute has two options—2D and 3D. 2D motion blur applies a postprocess blur to the rendered image. The blur is laid between the object's blur start and blur end position in a linear fashion. Hence, the blur is not realistic for objects spinning, weaving, or making rapid changes in direction (see Figure 10.24). Nevertheless, 2D motion blur is efficient and convincing for many animations (and the default settings work quite well).

3D motion blur, on the other hand, samples the moving object at multiple points along its path (see Figure 10.24). 3D motion blur is more accurate than 2D motion blur, but is more time consuming. Unless the anti-aliasing quality is set fairly high, 3D motion blur suffers from graininess.

Note: The 3D Blur Visib and Max 3D Blur Visib attributes (found in the Number Of Samples section of the Maya Software tab) control the number of subpixel samples used to determine if blurred objects are occluding each other.

The Blur By Frame attribute controls the time range within which the blur for one frame is calculated. The following formula is used:

```
Time Offset = ((Shutter Angle / 360) * Blur By Frame) / 2
```

The Shutter Angle attribute, found in the Special Effects section of the camera's Attribute Editor tab, emulates the shutter of a motion picture camera, which is a spinning metal disk that sits between the lens and the film gate. Shutters have a pie-shaped cut that allows light to strike the film. The cut is measured in degrees. The default

144-degree Shutter Angle value is equivalent to a standard motion picture camera that ultimately exposes a frame of film for 1/60th of a second. The larger the Shutter Angle value, the longer the exposure and the lengthier the motion blur streak. Other common shutter angles include 150 and 180.

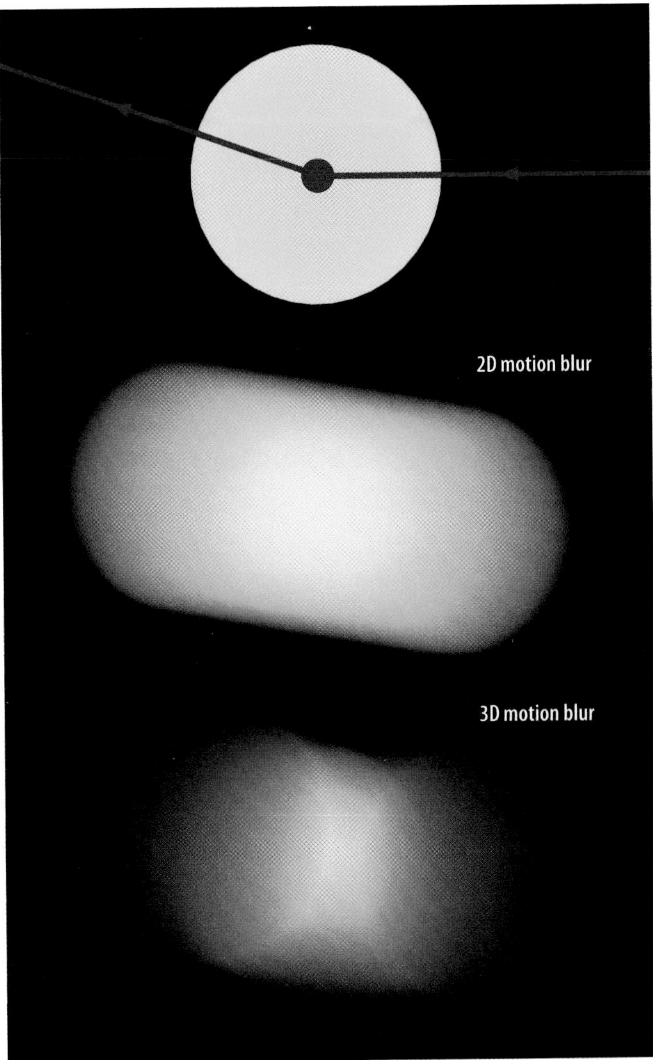

Figure 10.24 A primitive sphere with 2D and 3D motion blur. (Arrows represent the sphere's motion vector.)

Note: You can derive the exposure duration of a frame by employing the following formula:
1 / [(360 / Shutter Angle) × frames-per-second]

If the Blur By Frame attribute is set to 1 and the Shutter Angle value is 144, the following math occurs:

```
((144 / 360) * 1) / 2 = 0.2
```

Thus, Maya looks backward in time 0.2 frames to determine the object's blur start position and forward in time 0.2 frames to determine an object's blur end position. The blur is thereby streaked between the object's blur start and blur end. This effect is clearly visible when an object makes a hard turn and 3D motion blur is used (see Figure 10.24 earlier in this section).

If you increase the Blur By Frame attribute, Maya goes back further in time and forward further in time to calculate the blur. For example, if Blur By Frame is set to 4, the following math occurs:

```
((144 / 360) * 4) / 2 = 0.8
```

If 2D motion blur is activated, the Blur Length attribute serves as a multiplier for the Blur By Frame attribute.

2D motion blur provides several additional attributes:

Blur Sharpness Control the sharpness of the postprocess blur. Low values increase the blur feathering and thus increase the length of the blur streak. High values reduce the blur feathering and thus shorten the length of the blur streak.

Smooth Helps reduce artifacts created in high-contrast situations. For example, if a dark object passes in front of a bright object or background, a dark ring may appear along the edge of the blur streak. Switching Smooth from Alpha to Color eliminates this error but continues to produce a high-quality alpha channel.

Smooth Value Controls the amount of blur applied to the edges of the motion blur streak. Use caution when raising this value above 2, as it may cause static objects to become blurred along their edges.

Keep Motion Vectors If checked, Maya stores the motion vectors but does not apply the blur. This feature is only supported by the Maya IFF image format. You can import the Maya IFF files into a compositing program such as Nuke and use the vector information to create a motion blur during the compositing stage.

Use 2D Blur Memory Limit If checked, places a cap on the amount of memory the blur operation is allowed to use. The number of megabytes is set by the 2D Blur Memory Limit attribute.

Note: Video cameras do not employ physical shutters. Instead, the CCD or CMOS chips are programmed to take a light sample a fixed length of time. This length is referred to as shutter speed and can vary from 1/4 to 1/2000 of a second. Shutter speed also indicates the exposure time of still film cameras.

Step-by-Step: Splitting Up a Render

Professional animators tend to split their renders into layers in order to make their animation projects more efficient. Not only does this habit increase the speed of individual frames, it also ensures that revisions are more easily undertaken. In addition, renders split into layers are more easily manipulated in the compositing process. Maya provides the Display Layer and Render Layer editors to help automate such a process. Detailed instructions for using these editors are included in Chapter 13. In the meantime, a demonstration of the logic involved when splitting a render into layers is included in this section.

The following example is culled from a fully animated, 120-shot music video. Practically every render within the project was split into multiple layers. Although there is no hard-and-fast rule that determines how a render should be divided, the following images offer practical solutions to issues that arise during an animation production. (Note that this does not involve the splitting of the render into shading components, such as diffuse and specular. That approach is covered in Chapter 13.)

Figure 10.25 represents the final composite of one shot. In the shot, a "Little Dead Girl" pulls an "Eyeball Child" up and over a cliff edge. The style is intentionally surreal with fantastic set pieces, characters, and lighting.

Figure 10.25 Final composite

The composite begins with a render of the 3D cliff. Since the camera does not move a significant distance in the shot, only one frame of the cliff is needed. The single frame is then touched up in Adobe Photoshop. Improvements include the addition of scraggly trees in the upper-right corner and the extension of the foreground (see Figure 10.26).

Figure 10.26 Touched-up render of the 3D cliff

The touched-up cliff is imported into an Adobe After Effects composite. The composite is set to 900 × 600, which is a custom variation of the 1.33 aspect ratio. All the renders created for the shot are kept at 900 × 600 to ensure high-quality anti-aliasing. The cliff is quickly split into parts with custom masks (see Figure 10.27). The splitting allows each part to be individually color-adjusted, blurred, and moved into a new position. Specific improvements include an artificial depth of field, trimmed trees in the upper-right corner, and a greater distance between the left and right side of the canyon. A clip-art photo of a sunset sky, color-corrected and blurred, is placed behind the cliff. Since the sky is kept separate, its positional information is keyframed, thereby allowing the clouds to "drift" during the shot.

At this point, the renders of the girl and child are brought into the composite. The girl is rendered by herself, as is the child. This separation allows for greater flexibility in the composite (in addition to speeding up the individual renders).

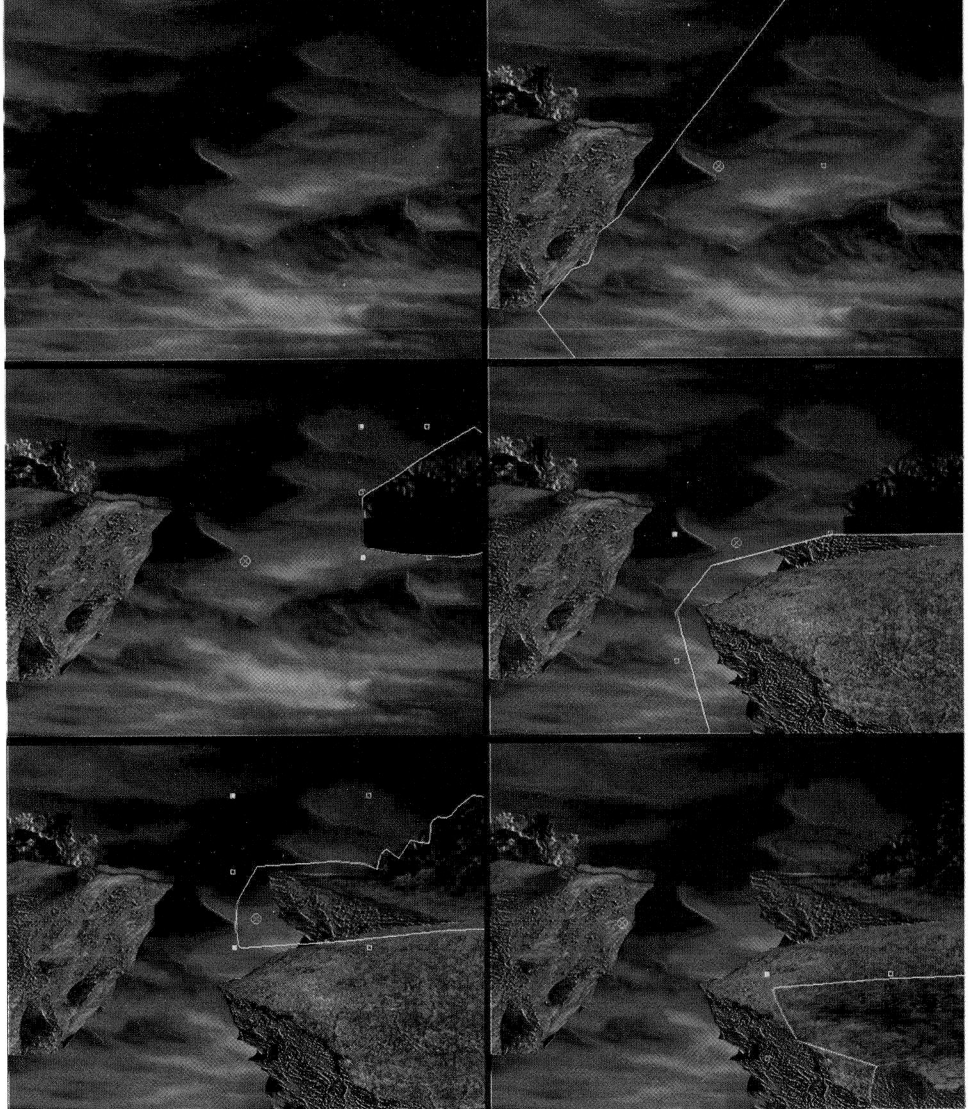

Figure 10.27 The cliff is imported into After Effects, split into parts, adjusted, and reassembled.

Errors in the character setup cause the heroine's left knee to intersect badly with her left boot. To avoid re-rigging, her left boot is rendered separately and placed at a higher composite level (see Figure 10.28). An aesthetic determination also necessitates the rerender of the child with a larger version of the doll he carries. This new render is combined with the old render with the help of a custom mask.

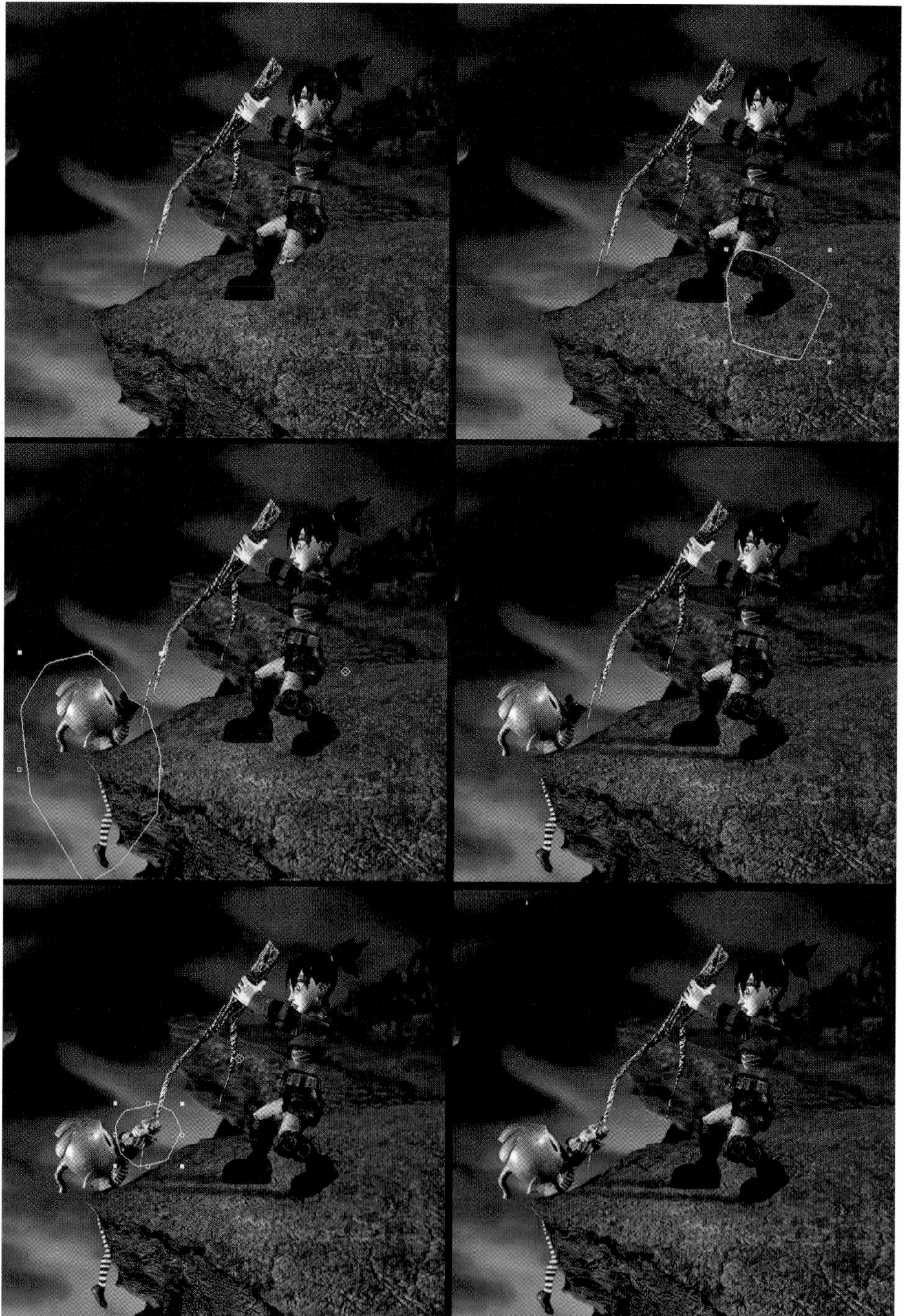

Figure 10.28 Character and shadow renders are imported into After Effects and combined using custom masks.

Shadows are rendered by themselves. To do this, all surfaces in the Maya scene are temporarily assigned to a Use Background material (see Chapter 4 for more information). In this case, the shadows appear in the alpha channel while the RGB channels are pitch black. The shadow renders are dropped directly on top of the cliff layers (see Figure 10.28). Reduced opacity and an additional blur in the composite ensure that the shadows remain fairly subtle. In this case, the shadows are not motivated by a particular light source—they are simply added to give the girl a stronger connection to the ground.

The first composite is placed into a second composite. The second composite is set to 720 × 480 so that the output is ready for digital video editing. Since the first composite was significantly larger, the shot is reframed to improve the composition and avoid parts of the cliff render that remain unfinished (see Figure 10.25 earlier in this section). In addition, the first composite is moved and keyframed within the second composite, thus creating a subtle artificial camera movement.

Conceivably, all the steps of this particular composite can be avoided by rendering the entire shot in one 3D pass. However, such an accomplishment would require additional 3D setup and refinement. Although careful preparation should always be a goal in animation, it is not always feasible due to time and resource limitations. Thus, the composite offers a "quick and dirty" way to fix mistakes and "sweeten" the quality of the renders at hand.

Raytracing with Maya Software and mental ray

Reflections, refractions, and chromatic aberrations are important qualities of materials such as water and glass. The Maya Software and mental ray renderers can provide these qualities through the raytracing process. Although the two renderers share many attributes, mental ray offers many advanced features. In particular, mental ray provides greater flexibility when rendering shadows and motion blur.

11

Chapter Contents

Raytracing with the Maya Software renderer
Creating reflections, refractions, and chromatic aberrations
Motion blur and shadows with mental ray
Raytracing with the mental ray renderer
Reproducing water and glass with Maya Software and mental ray

Maya Software vs. mental ray

By default, Maya renders with the Maya Software renderer. You can switch to the Maya Hardware, Maya Vector, or mental ray renderer by changing the Render Using attribute in the Render Settings window. Although the Maya Hardware and Maya Vector renderers are designed for specialized rendering situations, mental ray can easily handle renders normally tackled by Maya Software. As such, the advantages of Maya Software and mental ray renderers may not be immediately obvious. Therefore, I've included a short list for each:

Maya Software

- Supports the Studio Clear Coat plug-in (Chapter 7)
- Renders rapidly while providing attributes for high-quality anti-aliasing (Chapter 10)
- Offers relatively few attributes and is thus easy to set up (Chapter 10)

mental ray

- Includes Maya Fur and the Maya Hair system in reflections and refractions (Chapter 3)
- Renders bump maps with greater accuracy (Chapter 9)
- Is able to motion blur shadows (this chapter)
- Is able to impart transparency to depth map shadows (this chapter)
- Provides Global Illumination and Final Gather rendering options (Chapter 12)
- Utilizes Maya shaders as well as mental ray shaders (Chapter 12)

Although mental ray's list of advantages is quite long, Maya Software is perfectly suitable for many renders. The trick is to become familiar with both systems so that you can make appropriate decisions at render time.

Raytracing with Maya Software

By default, the Maya Software renderer operates in a scanline mode. To activate raytracing, check the Raytracing attribute in the Raytracing Quality section of the Maya Software tab in the Render Settings window (see Figure 11.1).

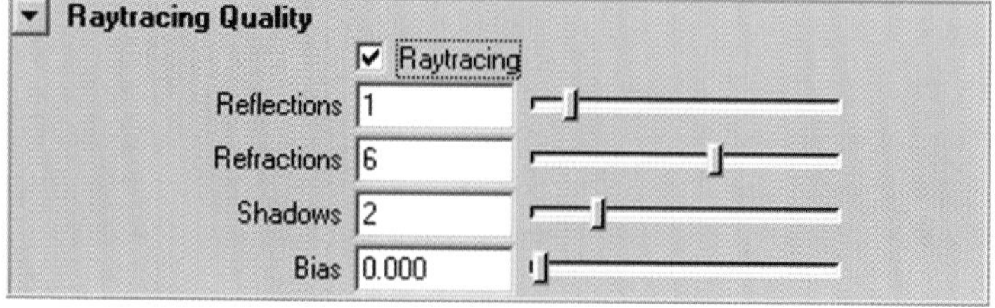

Figure 11.1 The Raytracing Quality section of the Maya Software tab in the Render Settings window

Comparing the Scanline and Raytracing Processes

Before I describe the raytracing process in more detail, the scanline process is worth a closer look. In general, the scanline process is as follows:

- The renderer examines the objects in the scene. The objects within the camera frustum are added to a list and their bounding boxes are calculated.
- The image to be rendered is divided into tiles to optimize memory usage. The complexity of the objects within a tile determines the tile's size.
- Polygon triangles associated with visible objects are processed in scanline order. Each triangle is projected into screen space and is clipped to the boundaries of each pixel it covers. That is, the portions of the triangle outside the pixel boundaries are temporarily discarded. Each pixel is thus given a list of clipped triangle fragments. The fragments are stored in the lists as bit masks, which are binary representations of fragment visibility within a pixel. The algorithm responsible for this process is known as A-buffer.
- The colors of each fragment are derived from the material qualities of the original polygons and the influence of lights in the scene. The final color of the pixel is determined by averaging the fragment colors, with emphasis given to those fragments that are the most visible. As part of this process, fragments are depth-sorted and additional clipping is applied to those fragments that are occluded.

By comparison, the raytracing process fires off a virtual ray from the camera eye through each pixel of a view plane (see Figure 11.2). The number of pixels in the view plane corresponds to the number of pixels required for a particular render resolution.

The first surface the ray intersects determines the pixel's color. That is, the material qualities of the surface are used in the shading calculation of the pixel. If raytrace shadows are turned on, secondary *shadow rays* are fired from the point of intersection to each shadow-producing light. If a shadow ray intersects another object before reaching a particular light, then the original intersection point is shadowed by that object. If the first surface is reflective and/or refractive, additional rays are created at the original intersection point. One ray represents the reflection, and the other represents the refraction. If either ray intersects a secondary reflective and/or refractive surface, the ray-splitting process is repeated. This continues until the rays reach a predefined, maximum number of reflection and refraction intersections. When a reflection ray reaches a secondary surface, the shading model of the secondary surface is calculated and contributed to the original intersection point. Hence, the color of secondary surface appears on the original surface as a reflection. A similar process occurs with a refraction ray, whereby the secondary surface shading model is contributed to the original intersection point. However, the direction that the refraction ray travels in is influenced by the Refractive Index (which is discussed later in this chapter).

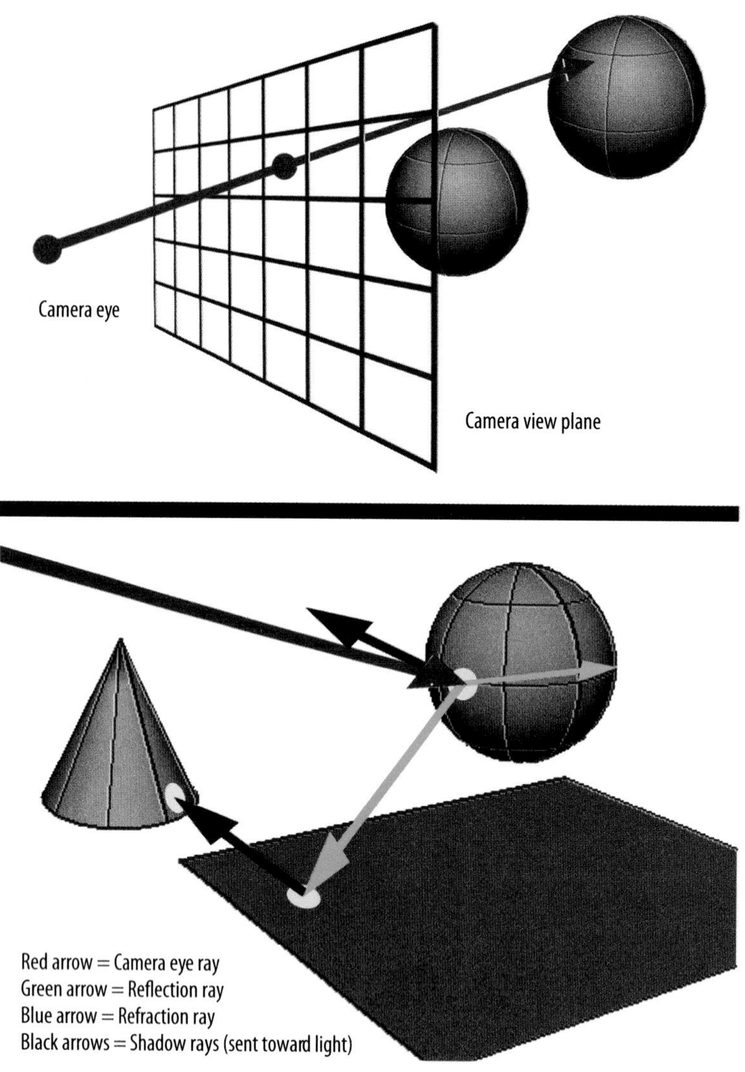

Figure 11.2 Simplified representations of the raytrace render method

Because a single camera eye ray can easily produce numerous shadow, reflection, and refraction rays, raytrace rendering is significantly more complex than the equivalent render with the scanline process. Consequently, the Maya Software renderer combines the scanline and raytrace techniques. If Raytracing is checked on but a surface possesses no reflective or refractive qualities, Maya applies the scanline process and avoids tracing rays.

Another method by which Maya reduces raytrace calculations is through the creation of voxels. Voxels are virtual cubes created from the subdivision of a scene's bounding box (which includes all objects within the scene). Maya tests for ray intersections with voxels before calculating more exact surface intersections. This effectively reduces the number of surfaces that are involved with the intersection calculations. Without voxels, Maya would have to test every surface in a scene.

The Ray Tracing subsection of the Memory And Performance Options section in the Maya Software tab controls voxel creation through Recursion Depth, Leaf Primitives, and Subdivision Power attributes.

Recursion Depth Sets the number of available recursive levels of voxel subdivision. Values of 1 to 3 work for most scenes, with complex setups requiring higher numbers.

Leaf Primitives Defines the maximum number of polygon triangles permitted to exist in a voxel before it is recursively subdivided.

Recursive subdivisions occur locally. Thus, if a voxel is subdivided, the resulting subvoxels are tested for subdivision. If the subvoxels are subdivided into sub-subvoxels, the sub-subvoxels are tested for subdivision. This process continues until all resulting voxels contain a number of triangles that is less than the Leaf Primitives value. At the same time, many of the original voxels and subvoxels may escape subdivision because they always contained a number of triangles less than the Leaf Primitives value.

For example, if Leaf Primitives is set to 200 and a tested voxel contains 1,000 triangles, the voxel is subdivided into 8 subvoxels. Each of the subvoxels is tested. If any single subvoxel possesses more than 200 triangles, it is subdivided into 8 sub-subvoxels.

For efficiency, the number of times a voxel is recursively subdivided is curtailed by the Subdivision Power attribute. In addition, the Recursion Depth attribute sets a cap on the number of available recursive steps.

Subdivision Power The power by which the number of polygon triangles in a voxel is raised to determine how many times the voxel should be recursively subdivided (if recursion is deemed necessary by the Leaf Primitives attribute). For example, if there are 1,000 triangles in a voxel, and the Subdivision Power value is changed from 0.25 to 0.5, the following math occurs:

```
1000 ^ 0.25 = 5.62
1000 ^ 0.5 = 31.62
```

Large Subdivision Power values lead to large results, which in turn create a greater number of recursive subdivisions and a greater number of subdivided voxels. Small subvoxels are inefficient if the majority of their brethren are wasted on empty space. On the other hand, a limited number of large subvoxels are also inefficient if they contain a high number of triangles.

Since Subdivision Power is not intuitive, it's best to change the attribute value by small increments. Maya documentation recommends a setting of 0.25 for most scenes.

Note: A voxel is a form of octree, a data structure in which a node has up to eight children. An octree child is called an *octant*.

Setting Up a Raytrace

The Raytracing Quality section of the Maya Software tab provides Reflections, Refractions, Shadows, and Bias attributes. The Reflections attribute sets the maximum number of times a camera eye ray will generate reflection rays before it is killed off. The Refractions attribute sets the maximum number of times a camera eye ray will generate refraction rays before it is killed off (see Figure 11.3). The limit for both attributes is 10, which is satisfactory for a water glass, bottle, or vase.

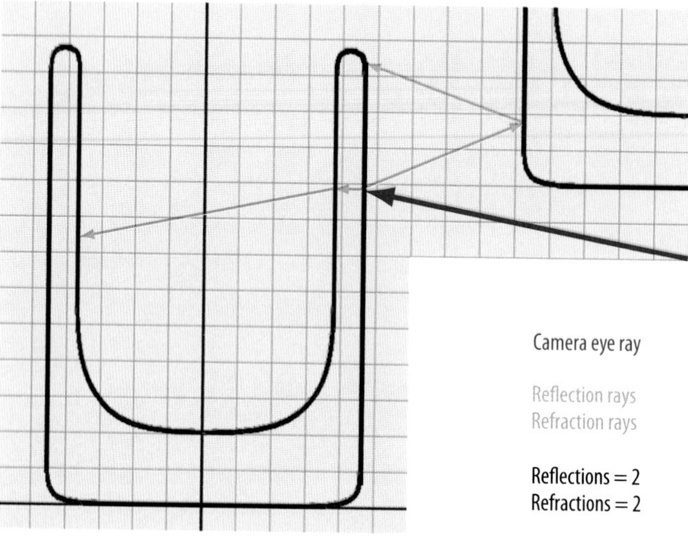

Figure 11.3 Rays generated by a single camera eye ray while the Reflections and Refractions attributes are set to 2

The Shadows attribute, on the other hand, sets the maximum number of times a camera eye ray can reflect and/or refract and continue to generate shadow rays. The higher the value, the more recursive the shadows; that is, shadows will appear within reflections of reflections and refractions of refractions. This attribute only has an effect if raytraced shadows are used. Depth map shadows, whether they are generated by Maya Software or mental ray, will automatically show up in all recursive reflections. If Shadows is set to 0, all raytrace shadows are turned off. A value of 10 will render shadows within nine recursive levels of reflection or refraction (see Figure 11.4). If Shadows is set to 10 and no raytrace shadows appear in reflections or refractions, increase the Ray Depth Limit attribute in the Raytrace Shadow Attributes subsection of the light's Attribute Editor tab. (See Chapter 3 for more detailed information.)

The Bias attribute serves as an adjustment for 3D motion blur in scenes with raytrace shadows. Often, raytrace shadows create dark bands around the center of rapidly moving objects. You can increase the Bias value to remove this artifact (see Figure 11.5).

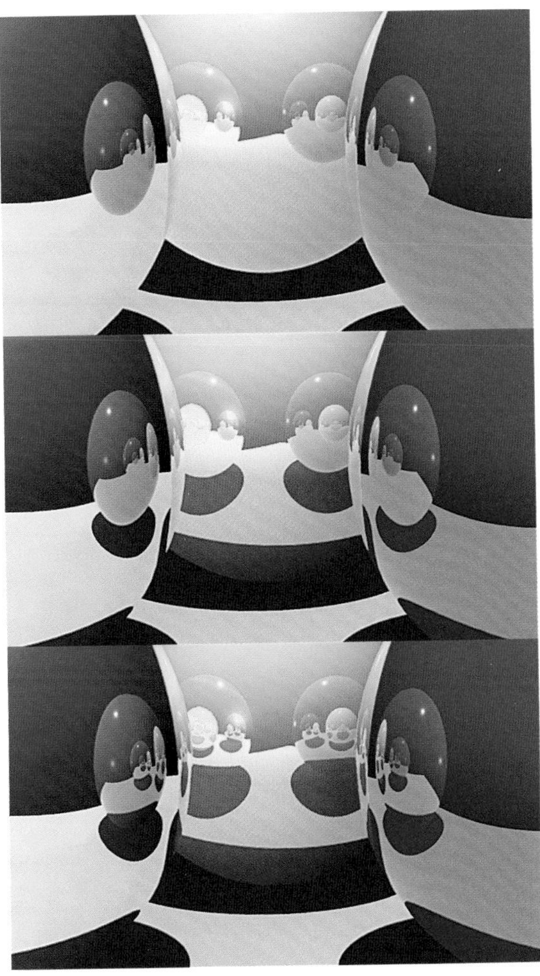

Figure 11.4 (Top to bottom) Spheres rendered with the Shadows attribute set to 1, 2, and 5, respectively. This scene is included on the CD as `shadows.ma`.

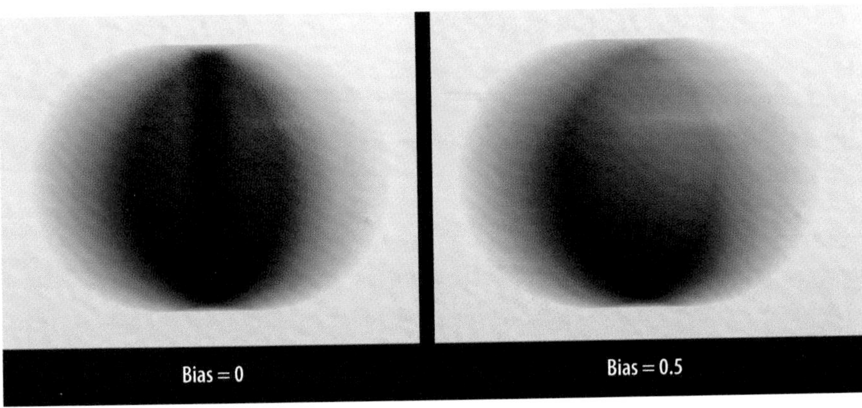

Figure 11.5 (Left) Sphere rendered with raytrace shadows and 3D motion blur. (Right) The same render with the Bias attribute set to 0.5. This scene is included on the CD as `bias.ma`.

Creating Reflections

As soon as the Raytracing attribute is checked, the Maya Software renderer creates reflections for all objects. The amount of reflectivity is controlled on a per-material basis by the material's Reflectivity attribute. This attribute works in conjunction with the Specular Roll Off and Specular Color attributes. If Specular Roll Off and Specular Color are set to 0, there is no reflection. A material's Eccentricity attribute, on the other hand, has no effect on the strength of a reflection and can be set to 0.

Note: Anisotropic materials carry an Anisotropic Reflectivity attribute, which overrides the standard Reflectivity attribute when checked. With Anisotropic Reflectivity, the strength of the reflection is determined by the Roughness attribute. The higher the Roughness value, the dimmer the reflection.

In contrast, the Reflected Color attribute found on Blinn, Phong, Phong E, and Anisotropic materials does not require raytracing. If the Reflected Color value is set to a color other than black or is mapped, a simulated reflection is applied directly to the assigned surface. If the mapped texture is an environment texture, the results are quite convincing (see Chapter 5 for a demonstration). Although a raytraced reflection is more accurate than a texture mapped to the Reflected Color attribute, raytracing is considerably less efficient. In any case, you can map the Reflected Color attribute *and* raytrace at the same time (see Figure 11.6). The color of light reflected in the raytrace process is multiplied by the Reflected Color attribute.

Model created by Torb

Figure 11.6 (Left) Raytraced chrome rim with the camera's Background Color set to blue. (Middle) Same rim with an environment texture mapped to the Reflected Color attribute, but without raytracing. (Right) Same rim with an environment texture and raytracing.

The Reflection Limit attribute (found in a material's Raytrace Options section) is a per-material attribute that sets the number of times a camera eye ray is allowed to reflect off the assigned surface before it is killed. Maya will compare the Reflection Limit to the Reflections attribute in the Raytracing Quality section of the Maya Software tab and use the lower value of the two.

The Reflection Specularity attribute (also found in a material's Raytrace Options section) controls the contribution of specular highlights to reflections. For example, in Figure 11.7 a car rim is assigned to two materials. The spokes are assigned to a red Blinn with its Reflection Specularity set to 0. The outer rim is assigned to a gray Blinn with its Reflection Specularity set to the default 1. Thus, the reflection of the spokes in the rim does not include the specular component. However, if the spoke's Reflection Specularity is returned to 1, the specular highlights of the spokes become visible in the rim reflection. When set to a value below 1, the Reflection Specularity attribute can help reduce anti-aliasing artifacts resulting from recursive reflections that contain a high degree of detail.

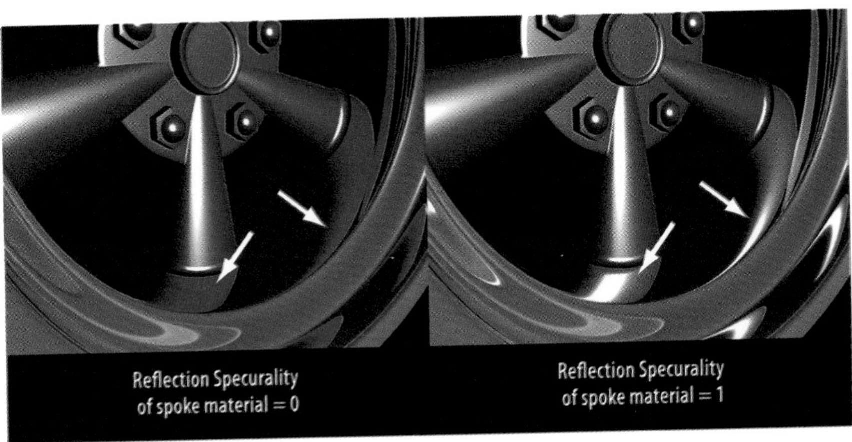

Figure 11.7 The Reflection Specularity attribute of a Blinn material determines whether specular highlights appear in reflections.

Managing Refractions and Aberrations

Refraction is the change in direction of a light wave due to a change of speed. When a light wave crosses the boundary between two materials with different refractive indices, its speed and direction are shifted. The human brain, unaware of this shift, assumes that all perceived light travels in a straight line. Thus, refracted light is perceived to originate from an incorrect location and objects appear bent or distorted. (For more detailed information on refractive indices, see Chapter 7.)

In Maya, refractions are defined on a per-material basis in the Raytrace Options section of the material's Attribute Editor tab. Refraction attributes include Refractive Index, Refraction Limit, Light Absorbance, Surface Thickness, Shadow Attenuation, and Chromatic Aberration (See Figure 11.8).

Refractive Index Sets the refractive index of the assigned surface. The index is a constant that relates the speed of light through a vacuum and the speed of light through a particular material. In the real world, the refractive index of water is approximately 1.33, and glass varies from 1.45 to 1.85. The default value of 1 creates no refraction and is the same as air.

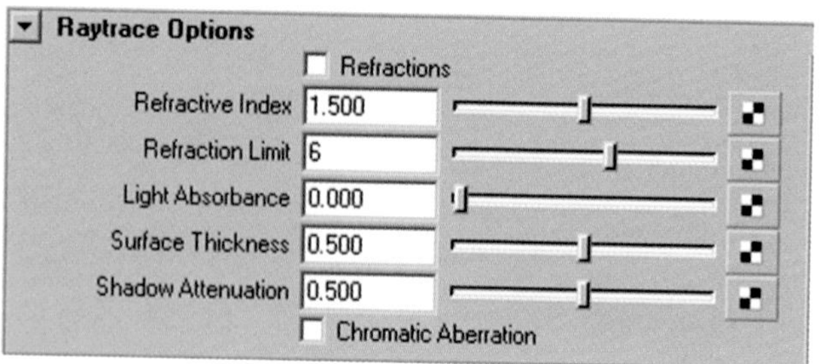

Figure 11.8 The Raytrace Options section of a material's Attribute Editor tab

Refraction Limit Sets the per-material maximum number of times a camera eye ray is refracted through the assigned surface before it is killed off. Maya compares this attribute to the Refractions attribute in the Raytracing Quality section of the Maya Software tab and uses the lower of the two.

Light Absorbance Describes the amount of light that is absorbed by transparent or semitransparent objects. All real-world materials absorb light at different wavelengths (in which case the light energy is converted to heat). When set to 0, the Light Absorbance attribute allows 100 percent of the light to pass through the object. The higher the value, the more light is absorbed by the object's surface and the darker the surface appears (see Figure 11.9).

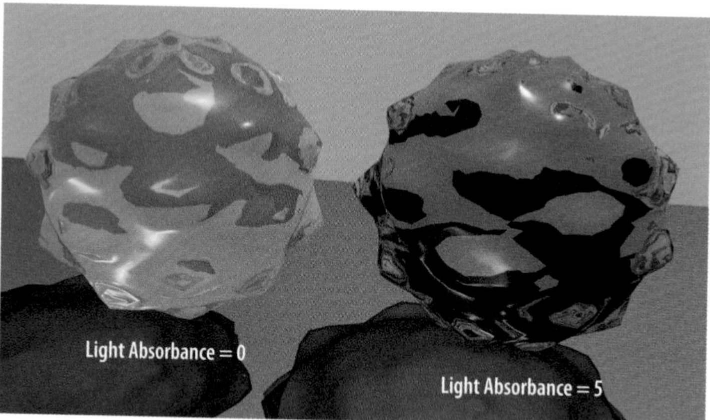

Figure 11.9 (Left) A glass material with its Light Absorbance attribute set to 0. (Right) The same material with its Light Absorbance attribute set to 5. This scene is included on the CD as `absorbance.ma`.

Surface Thickness Determines the simulated thickness of a surface that possesses no model thickness. For example, in Figure 11.10 two primitive NURBS planes are given different Surface Thickness values. Since the left NURBS plane has a Surface Thickness value of 100, the sky color is not visible in its refraction; in addition, the high value creates a magnifying glass effect, which enlarges the table's checker pattern.

Shadow Attenuation Replicates the brightening of a shadow's core and the darkening of the shadow's edge when the shadow is cast by a semitransparent object. A high Shadow Attenuation value creates a high-contrast transition within the shadow (see Figure 11.11). A value of 0 turns the Shadow Attenuation off. The Refractions attribute does not have to be checked for Shadow Attenuation to work.

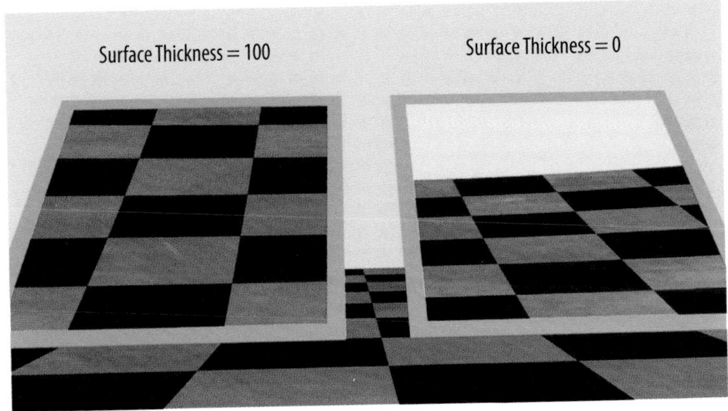

Figure 11.10 The refraction of a NURBS plane is adjusted with the Surface Thickness attribute. This scene is included on the CD as `thickness.ma`.

Figure 11.11 A high Shadow Attenuation attribute value creates greater contrast within the shadow. This scene is included on the CD as `attenuation.ma`.

You can also use the Shadow Attenuation attribute to adjust raytraced shadows that involve materials with Transparency maps. If Shadow Attenuation is left at the default value of 0.5, the part of the Transparency map that is 100 percent white will sometimes cast a soft shadow. At other times, a high Attenuation value may cause the shadow artifact to appear. For example, in Figure 11.12 a directional light casts the shadow of a plane that has a bitmap of a star symbol mapped to its material's Transparency attribute. The black lines in the figure represent the position of the shadowed plane. The red lines represent the edges of the plane as they appear as part of the shadow. The area within the red lines is darkened slightly, even though the Transparency map should provide nothing to shadow around the edges of the star. In this case, Attenuation is set to 1. When Attenuation is reduced to 0, however, the darkened area disappears appropriately.

Figure 11.12 A Transparency map applied to the material of a plane casts a raytraced shadow. The red lines represent the edges of the plane as they appear as part of the shadow. An adjustment of the Attenuation attribute can prevent this area from rendering inappropriately dark. This scene is included on the CD as `attenuation_trans.ma`.

Chromatic Aberration Refers to the inability of a lens to equally focus different color wavelengths. This is an artifact of dispersion, in which different wavelengths of light travel through a medium, such as glass, at different speeds. In effect, this causes a lens to have a different refractive index for each wavelength. Maya's Chromatic Aberration attribute distorts refraction rays, causing colors to shift as shading models are invoked. Points closer to the light source shift toward cyan, while points farther from the light shift toward red and yellow (see Figure 11.13). The aberration is only visible if the Refractions attribute is checked.

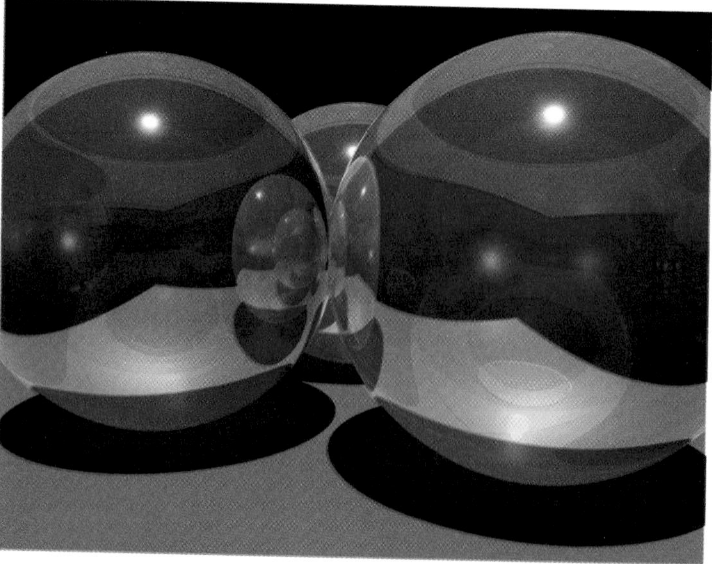

Figure 11.13 The Chromatic Aberration attribute introduces color shifts in raytraced geometry.

Raytracing with mental ray

By default, the mental ray renderer operates in scanline mode. Raytracing is only employed if it is activated as a secondary effect.

Since many mental ray attributes are unique—or at least different in name—it is worth examining some common settings in the Render Settings window. As part of this review, mental ray motion blur and shadows are detailed.

Mastering mental ray Quality Settings

The mental ray Quality Presets attribute, found in the mental ray tab of the Render Settings window, supplies 15 different presets. The presets offer a quick way to set all the attributes within the Rendering Features and Anti-Aliasing Quality sections (see Figure 11.14). For instance, if you set Quality Presets to Draft, the Primary Renderer is set to Scanline and anti-aliasing is kept at a bare minimum to speed the render. If you set Quality Presets to Preview: Global Illumination, Raytracing and Global Illumination is checked for the Secondary Effects attribute; in addition, matching Global Illumination attributes found in the Caustics And Global Illumination section are set to a quality appropriate for a preview. For maximum control, you can set all the Rendering Features and Anti-Aliasing Quality attributes by hand. Descriptions of each attribute follow:

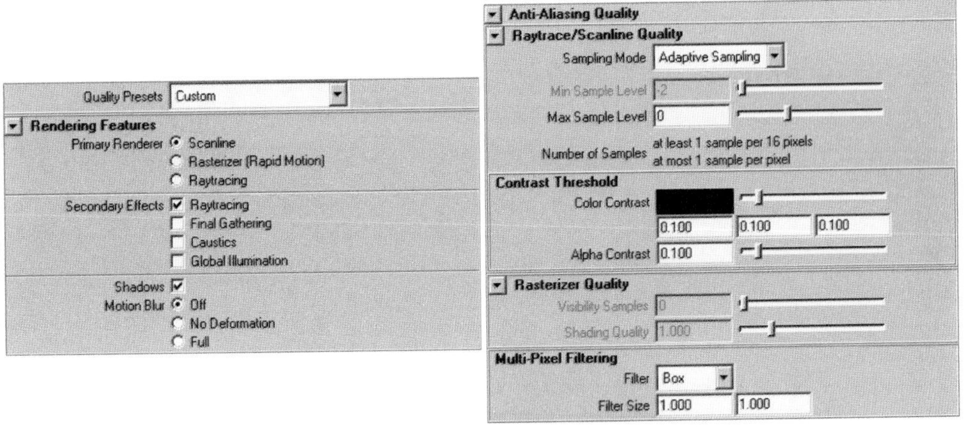

Figure 11.14 The Rendering Features section (Left) and Anti-Aliasing Quality section (Right) of the mental ray tab in the Render Settings window

Primary Renderer Chooses the primary renderer. The Scanline option rapidly renders simple scenes. The Rasterizer (Rapid Motion) option, however, is more efficient when the scene is complex or has numerous motion blurred objects. (The Rasterizer option was previously named Rapid Scanline.) The Raytracing option forces the entire scene to be raytraced. The Raytracing option, by itself, will not produce reflections and refractions—the Raytracing option of the Secondary Effects attribute must be checked.

Note: The Rasterizer (Rapid Motion) primary renderer treats motion blur in a more efficient manner than the Scanline primary renderer. Instead of sampling and shading each visible point of a moving object multiple times along its motion path for a single frame, the Rasterizer samples all objects at a fixed position. The shading information is cached, and then is allowed to "travel" with the object when it is placed at the end of its motion path for a particular frame. Because each visible point has only one shading sample taken per frame, the calculation time is sped up significantly.

Secondary Effect Toggles on and off Raytracing, Final Gathering, Caustics, and Global Illumination. *Secondary* infers that the effects are only employed at a point deemed necessary by the primary renderer.

Shadows and Motion Blur Shadows serves as a master on/off switch for all raytrace and depth map shadows. Motion Blur determines whether motion blur is off or on and chooses the No Deformation or Full method. (See the next section for more information.)

Sampling Mode Sets the style of anti-aliasing sampling. The Fixed Sampling option uses a static number of subpixel samples per pixel. The Adaptive Sampling and Custom Sampling options use a different number of subpixel samples per pixel based on the contrast within the scene. Although Adaptive Sampling allows you to adjust the Max Sample Level attribute directly, Custom Sampling lets you adjust both the Min Sample Level and Max Sample Level attributes. (For more information on anti-aliasing, see Chapter 10.)

Color Contrast A "dummy" attribute that drives Contrast R, Contrast G, and Contrast B attributes. The values of Contrast R, Contrast G, and Contrast B are listed in the three cells below the Color Contrast slider. You can change the values in the cells by hand. Contrast R, Contrast G, and Contrast B set the contrast threshold for subpixel sampling when Sampling Mode is set to Adaptive Sampling or Custom Sampling. If a pixel, when compared to neighboring pixels, does not exceed the contrast threshold set by Contrast R, Contrast G, or Contrast B, the pixel is only sampled one time (assuming that Min Sample Level is set to 0). If the contrast threshold is exceeded, however, the pixel is subdivided and four subpixel samples are employed instead of one. The functionality of this section is similar to the Maya Software Contrast Threshold section, but provides the addition of an alpha channel contrast threshold slider (Alpha Contrast).

Min Sample Level and Max Sample Level Sets the minimum and maximum number of times a pixel is permitted to be recursively subdivided into subpixel samples. A value of 0 equates to one sample per pixel (in other words, no subpixel samples). When Sampling Mode is set to Custom Sampling, you can set the Min Sample Level to a negative number. In essence, this forces the renderer to skip some pixels in the pixel sampling process. For example, a value of –2 will force the renderer to take only one sample per block of 16 pixels. In contrast, a Max Sample Level value of 2 allows the renderer to sample each pixel 16 times. Hence, a Min Sample Level value of –2 and a Max

Sample Level value of 0 is a low-quality render. A Min Sample Level value of 0 and a Max Sample Level value of 2 is a high-quality render. Remember that Min Sample Level and Max Sample Level set a range. The precise values derived from the range, and hence the number of subpixel samples used for a particular pixel, are controlled by the Color Contrast values.

As a simplified example of the sampling process, the following steps occur for a theoretical block of four pixels:

1. Min Sample Level is set to 0. Max Sample Level is set to 2. Because Min Sample Level is 0, the 4 pixels are sampled (and not skipped). With mental ray, each pixel is sampled at its four corners to determine the pixel color (see Figure 11.15).
2. The contrast between pixels sharing corners is tested. For instance, Pixel B has a Red value of 0.9. Pixel D has a Red value of 0.3. The difference between the two values is 0.6. Since Contrast R is set to 0.25 and 0.6 is greater than 0.25, Pixel D is subdivided into 4 subpixels.

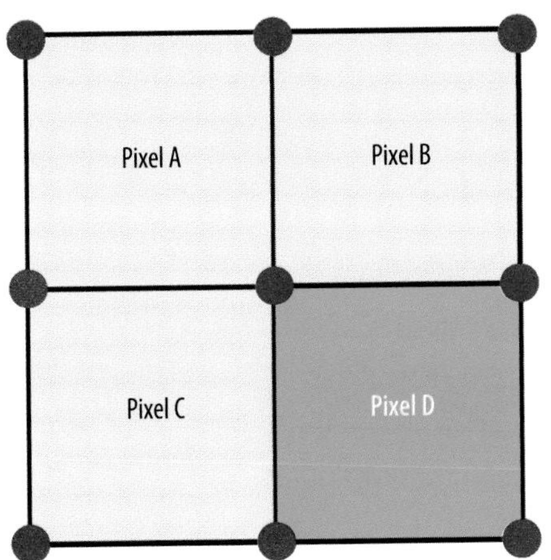

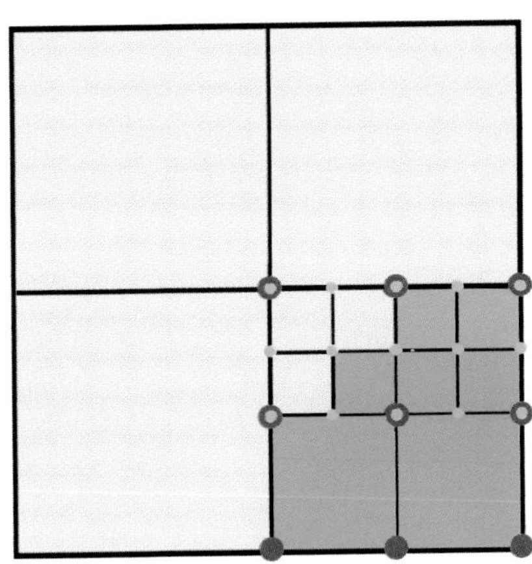

Figure 11.15 (Left) Block of 4 pixels. Red dots are sampled corners. (Right) Pixel D is subdivided into subpixels. Blue dots are sampled corners of subpixels. Two subpixels are subdivided into sub-subpixels.

3. The color of each new subpixel is determined and tested against subpixels sharing its corners. If the contrast threshold is exceeded for any subpixel, the subpixel is subdivided into sub-subpixels. The recursive subdivision stops at the sub-subpixel level, however, because the Max Sample Level is set to 2, which limits the maximum number of subpixels samples per pixel to 16. You can write the math like so:

```
4 subpixels × 4 sub-subpixels = 16
```

4. All the subpixels and sub-subpixels are tested before the renderer moves on to the next pixel. This process also requires the testing of the Green, Blue, and Alpha channels.

Note: The Contrast Threshold section is not available to the Rasterizer (Rapid Motion) primary renderer. Instead, Visibility Samples and Shading Quality are available in the Rasterizer Quality section. Visibility Samples sets the number of subpixel samples used in the anti-aliasing process (a value of 0 defaults to four corner samples per pixel). Shading Quality increases or decreases the number of subpixel samples used in the shading process.

Filter and Filter Size The Filter attribute determines the style of multipixel filter used by the renderer. Multipixel filtering is designed to blend neighboring pixels together into a coherent mass. Such filtering helps to prevent aliasing in the form of buzzing or stair-stepping. You can choose from five styles. Gauss (Gaussian) produces the most thorough averaging but is the slowest to render. Box, on the other hand, is less processor intensive while producing acceptable results. Triangle is similar to Box but produces more accurate results. Mitchell and Lanczos are variations of Gauss that produce a greater degree of contrast. The Filter Size fields, which represent Filter Size X and Filter Size Y attributes, control the intensity of the pixel averaging. As the values are increased, the number of neighboring pixels that are included in the calculation is increased. The greater the number of pixels included in the calculation, the more accurate the averaging. High values may lead to excessive blurriness within the image, however. Unfortunately, the multipixel filter effect in mental ray cannot be turned off. However, Filter Size X and Filter Size Y can be set to 0.01, which makes the filter's impact negligible.

Jitter and Sample Lock Jitter, when checked, introduces systematic variations in subpixel sampling locations within pixels. Sample Lock, when checked, ensures that the sampling pattern is consistent across multiple frames of an animation. Sample Lock overrides Jitter. If neither attribute is checked, samples are taken at pixel corners. Although the default settings (Jitter off and Sample Lock on) for these attributes work in most situations, nondefault settings (such as Jitter on and Sample Lock off) may help solve anti-aliasing problems that other attributes fail to address.

You can access additional sampling attributes on a per-surface basis in the Render Stats section of a surface's Attribute Editor tab. If you check Shading Samples Override, Shading Samples and Max Shading Samples become available. These two attributes override Min Sample Level and Max Sample Level for the selected surface, but function in the same manner.

Using mental ray Motion Blur

Two forms of motion blur are employed by the mental ray renderer: No Deformation and Full (respectively named Linear and Exact in previous versions). No Deformation motion blur is equivalent to Maya Software's 2D motion blur, in that it is unable to accurately portray rapid changes in direction or surface deformation. Full motion blur, on the other hand, plots the motion vectors of each surface vertex and is thus sensitive to deformation. (Unfortunately, Full motion blur handles rapid changes in direction in a fashion similar to No Deformation motion blur.) Attributes for mental ray motion blur are located in the Motion Blur section of the mental ray tab and include Shutter Open, Shutter Close, Motion Back Offset, and Static Object Offset, Motion Blur By, and Motion Steps (see Figure 11.16).

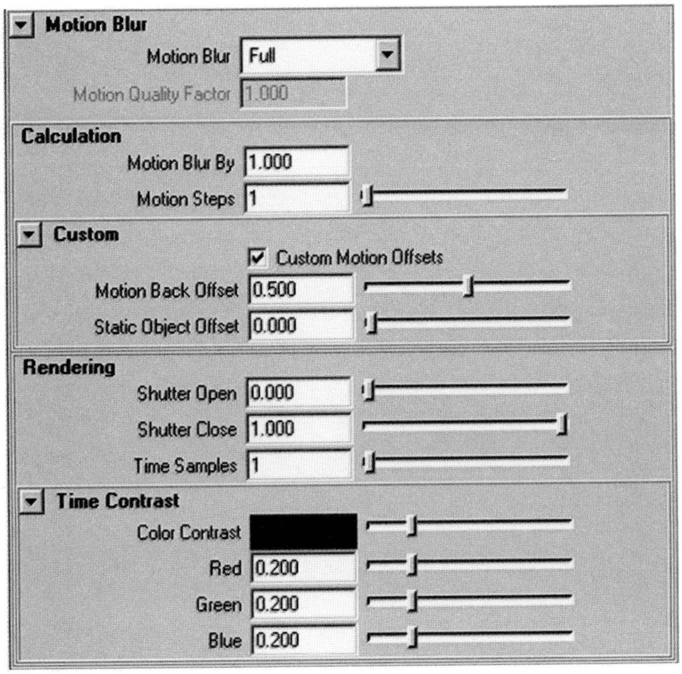

Motion Blur
Motion Blur Full
Motion Quality Factor 1.000
Calculation
Motion Blur By 1.000
Motion Steps 1
Custom
Custom Motion Offsets
Motion Back Offset 0.500
Static Object Offset 0.000
Rendering
Shutter Open 0.000
Shutter Close 1.000
Time Samples 1
Time Contrast
Color Contrast
Red 0.200
Green 0.200
Blue 0.200

Figure 11.16 The Motion Blur section of the mental ray tab in the Render Settings window

Shutter Open and Shutter Close Sets the points at which the virtual shutter opens and closes within the time interval of the frame. If the default values of 0 and 1 are kept, the motion blur calculation utilizes the entire time interval. For example, if the Maya scene file is set to 30 frames-per-second, the object is allowed to travel an appropriate distance for 1/30th of a second, which is indicated by the motion blur trail. If Shutter Open is raised and Shutter Close is reduced, the blur trail becomes shorter as the object is given less time to move for the purpose of motion blur calculation. Prior versions of Maya used Shutter and Shutter Delay for the same purpose.

Motion Back Offset Determines the time interval for the frame examined for motion blur. The default setting of 0.5 causes the renderer to go back in time 0.5 frames to establish the object's start position and forward in time 0.5 frames to determine the object's end position. This jumping back-and-forth in time is visible on the Timeline. When a frame is rendered through the Render View window, the Timeline will automatically hop from the start position frame to the end position frame during the render. However, the size of the hop does not match the Motion Back Offset value exactly. This is due to the following math:

```
Time Offset = ((((Shutter Close - Shutter Open) * Shutter Angle) / 360)
* Motion Blur By) * Motion Back Offset
```

In this case, Time Offset is a variable that represents the size of the Timeline "hop." If all the motion blur attributes are left at their default, the Timeline moves –0.2 frames to the start position and 0.2 frames to the end position. The Shutter Angle attribute, found in the Special Effects section of the rendered camera's Attribute Editor tab, is part of the equation and emulates the setup of a real-world motion picture camera.

Motion Blur By Serves as a multiplier for the motion blur effect. The larger the value, the more exaggerated the motion blur.

Static Object Offset Determines the time used to render static objects. A default value of 0 uses the current frame. Other values allow the renderer to go backward or forward in time to select shading samples for objects that have no animation. Static Object Offset and Motion Back Offset are only available if Custom Motion Offsets is checked.

Motion Steps Sets the number of motion vector segments that are created for moving objects. The higher the value, the more accurate the motion blur.

By default, mental ray motion blur appears extremely grainy. You can remedy this, however, by adjusting the Time Samples attribute (see Figure 11.17).

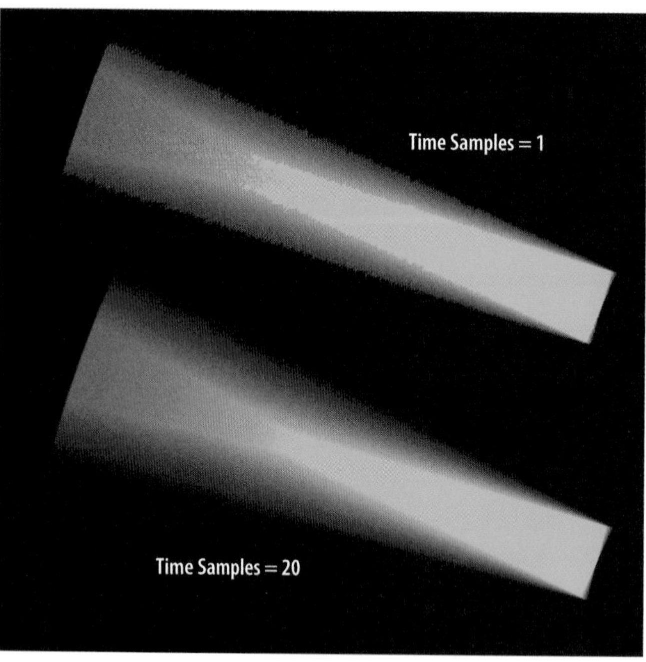

Figure 11.17 Motion blurred stick with two different Time Samples settings. This scene is included on the CD as `mental_motion.ma`.

In actuality, Time Samples is a "dummy" attribute that remotely controls the Time Contrast R, Time Contrast B, and Time Contrast G attributes found in the Time Contrast subsection (these are simply labeled Red, Green, and Blue in Maya 2008). Color Contrast, found in the same subsection, also serves as a dummy remote for

Time Contrast R, Time Contrast B, and Time Contrast G. Ultimately, the Time Contrast attributes determine the number of temporal samples taken per spatial sample. For example, if the Time Contrast attributes are each set to 0.5, then 2 temporal samples are taken per spatial sample per frame. This equates to the formula 1 / Time Contrast.

Controlling mental ray Shadows

Shadows created by mental ray are defined in two areas—the Shadows section of the mental ray tab in the Render Settings window and the shadow-specific sections of each light's Attribute Editor tab.

A light's Use Ray Trace Shadows attribute functions in the same manner for the mental ray renderer as it does for the Maya Software renderer. (Maya Software shadows are discussed in Chapter 3.) However, mental ray supplies separate attributes in the Shadows section of the mental ray tab in the Render Settings window (see Figure 11.18). The Shadow Method attribute controls the method of shadow calculation and has four options: Disabled, Simple, Sorted, Segments. The Simple method creates fast, efficient shadows and is appropriate for most animation. The Sorted method determines shadow order if multiple objects obscure the rendered point from the point-of-view of the shadowing light. With the Simple and Sorted method, shadow rays are generated by the light from the light's origin. Unless a custom mental ray shader is used, Sorted offers no advantage over Simple. The Segments method provides a more sophisticated model whereby shadow rays are traced from the rendered point back to the shadowing light. When the shadow ray strikes an obscuring object, it is terminated and a new shadow ray is born at the intersection. The new shadow ray continues toward the shadowing light (unless it too strikes an object). Each shadow ray, referred to as a shadow "segment," invokes a shadow shader. The Segments method is necessary if software-rendered particles or other volume effects require shadows. The Disabled option turns off shadows.

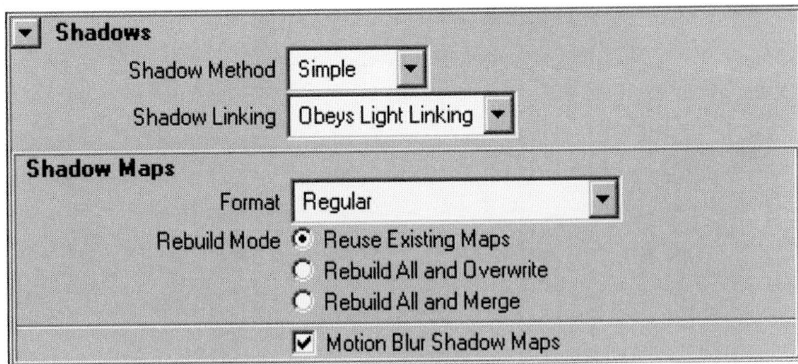

Figure 11.18 The Shadows section of the mental ray tab in the Render Settings window

Raytrace shadows, by their very nature, understand object transparency. However, if depth map shadows are used with the mental ray renderer, object transparency information is ignored. This holds true for standard Maya depth maps, controlled by the Depth Map Shadow Attributes section of a light's Attribute Editor tab, as well as mental ray shadow maps, controlled by the mental ray section of a light's Attribute Editor tab. (For more information on depth map shadows, see Chapter 3.) Nevertheless, you can impart transparency to the depth map shadows by adjusting the Format attribute in the Shadows section of the mental ray tab in the Render Settings window.

If the Format attribute is set to Detail, mental ray takes into account surface properties, such as transparency, when building the shadows (see Figure 11.19). In addition, the Detail option provides superior depth map shadows for motion-blurred objects. If Use Ray Trace Shadows is checked in a light's Attribute Editor tab, the Format option is ignored for that light.

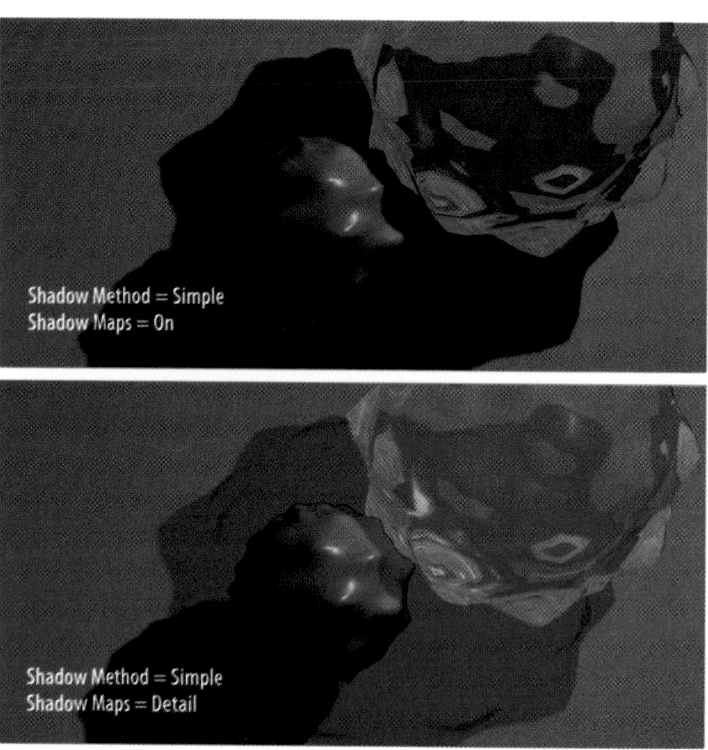

Figure 11.19 A mental ray shadow map with and without the Detail option. This scene is included on the CD as `mental_detail.ma`.

You can also access the Detail option through the mental ray section of a spot, point, or directional light's Attribute Editor tab. If you switch the Shadow Map Format attribute from Regular Shadow Map to Detail Shadow Map, the light overrides the Format attribute in the Shadows section of the mental ray tab of the Render Settings window. When selected, the Detail Shadow Map option opens three additional attributes in the Detail Shadow Maps Attributes subsection of the light's Attribute Editor tab. The Samples attribute controls the number of pixel samples taken at the intersection points of shadow-casting objects. The Accuracy attribute controls the quality of the shadow. Low Accuracy values increase quality but slow the render. An Accuracy value of 0 will allow Maya to choose the best solution for the scene. The Alpha attribute, when checked, forces a scalar (grayscale) shadow.

Returning to the Shadows section of the mental ray tab, the Shadow Maps Disabled option of the Format attribute overrides light shadow settings and turns off every shadow map in the scene. The Regular option turns on standard shadow maps (unless overridden by the Detail Shadow Map option of the light). The Regular (OpenGL Accelerated) option attempts to use OpenGL acceleration to speed up shadow calculations (if available through the system graphics card).

When the Format attribute is switched to Regular, Regular (OpenGL Accelerated), or Detail, the Rebuild Mode attribute becomes available in the same section. The Reuse Existing Maps option retrieves previously rendered shadow maps where feasible. The Rebuild All And Overwrite option creates shadow maps from scratch with each render. The Rebuild All And Merge option retrieves previously rendered shadow maps and updates the maps wherever and visible points have shifted toward the shadowing light.

All mental ray depth map shadow types create motion-blurred shadows when Motion Blur is set to No Deformation or Full and Motion Blur Shadow Maps, in the Shadows section, is checked. Reflected and refracted shadows are equally subject to mental ray motion blur.

Creating Reflections and Refractions with mental ray

By default, mental ray's Ray Tracing attribute is checked. The Ray Tracing attribute is listed twice in the mental ray tab—once in the Rendering Features section and once in the Raytracing section (see Figure 11.20). The two check boxes are linked.

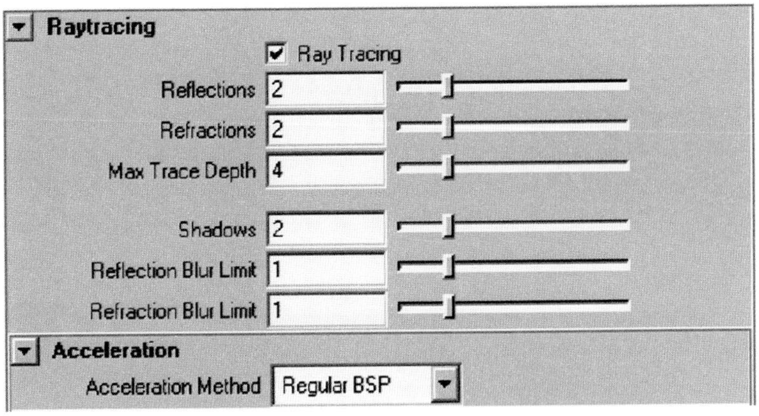

Figure 11.20 The Raytracing section of the mental ray tab in the Render Settings window

The following attributes, found in the Raytracing section, control the rays used for the render:

Reflections Sets the maximum number of times a camera eye ray can be reflected off reflective surfaces. This attribute is overridden on a per-material basis by the Reflection Limit attribute in a material's Attribute Editor tab.

Refractions Sets the maximum number of times a camera eye ray can be refracted through refractive surfaces. This attribute is overridden on a per-material basis by the Refraction Limit attribute in a material's Attribute Editor tab. (Refractions are not created by mental ray unless the Refractions attribute is checked in the Raytracing section of a material's Attribute Editor tab.)

Max Trace Depth Controls the maximum number of times a camera eye ray can reflect off *or* refract through surfaces. This attribute trumps both the Reflections and Refractions attributes. For example, if Max Trace Depth is set to 5, a ray can reflect twice and refract three times before it is killed off.

Shadows Sets the maximum number of times a camera eye ray can reflect and/or refract and continue to generate shadow rays. The higher the value, the more recursive the shadows; that is, shadows will appear within reflections of reflections and refractions of refractions. The default value of 2 allows shadows to appear in a reflection or refraction, but not in the reflection of a reflection or a refraction of a refraction.

Reflection Blur Limit and Refraction Blur Limit Represents the maximum number of times a camera eye ray can reflect or refract and still be considered for a blur. Unlike Maya Software, mental ray can blur reflections and refractions. With the default value of 1, mental ray blurs only the first reflection or refraction but does not progress recursively (see Figure 11.21). The degree of blurriness is controlled on a per-material basis by the Mi Reflection Blur and Mi Refraction Blur attributes, found in the mental ray section of the material's Attribute Editor tab. Reflection Rays and Refraction Rays, in the same section, control the quality of the blur by providing additional shading samples when their values are raised. Because a blurred reflection within a blurred reflection is difficult to distinguish from a reflection with a blurred reflection, a Reflection Blur Limit of 1 works in many situations. Additionally, per-material Reflection Blur Limit and Refraction Blur Limit attributes are provided in the mental ray section of the material's Attribute Editor tab.

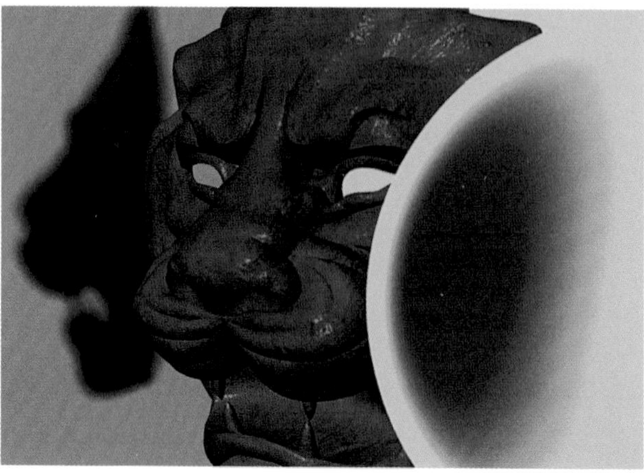

Figure 11.21
A mental ray–blurred reflection and refraction

Reproducing Water

You can describe water by its three main shading components—reflectivity, refractivity, and foaminess—and its three natural phases—liquid, solid, and gas. You can emulate liquid forms of water with custom shading networks and raytracing. You can replicate ice with similar techniques. On the other hand, you can generate water fog with a Light Fog effect or through Environment Fog (see Chapter 2). When replicating these various states of water, the Maya Software and mental ray renderers both have their strengths and weaknesses.

Water as a Liquid

Water, in its liquid form, is either calm or turbulent. When calm, large bodies of water exposed to an intense light source are very reflective. For example, in Figure 11.22 a calm tide pool reflects the sky. Where the water is fairly shallow and is at a perpendicular angle to the viewer, however, the underlying rocks and sand can be seen. This effect is known as a Fresnel reflection and is a result of light moving between two mediums (air and water) with two different refractive indices. (For more information on refractive indices, see Chapter 7.) As such, transparency decreases and reflectivity increases with the viewing angle (the angle between the incoming light ray and the corresponding ray reflected toward the viewer). In addition, the objects underneath the surface are darker than normal since the light received is reduced by sediment within the water.

Figure 11.22 A calm tide pool

In Maya, you can use the Sampler Info utility to determine the angle of a water surface to the camera. A simpler solution, however, involves the application of Ramp textures. For example, in Figure 11.23 a primitive NURBS plane replicates calm water. The outAlpha of a ramp texture (named RampReflectivity) is connected to the reflectivity of a blinn material node (named CalmWater). The outColor of a second ramp texture (named RampTransparency) is connected to the transparency of CalmWater. Since the ramps contain only black and white handles, the reflectivity is the strongest at the top of the plane and the transparency is strongest at the bottom of the plane. The camera's Background Color attribute provides the sky color. The scene works with either the Maya Software or mental ray renderer.

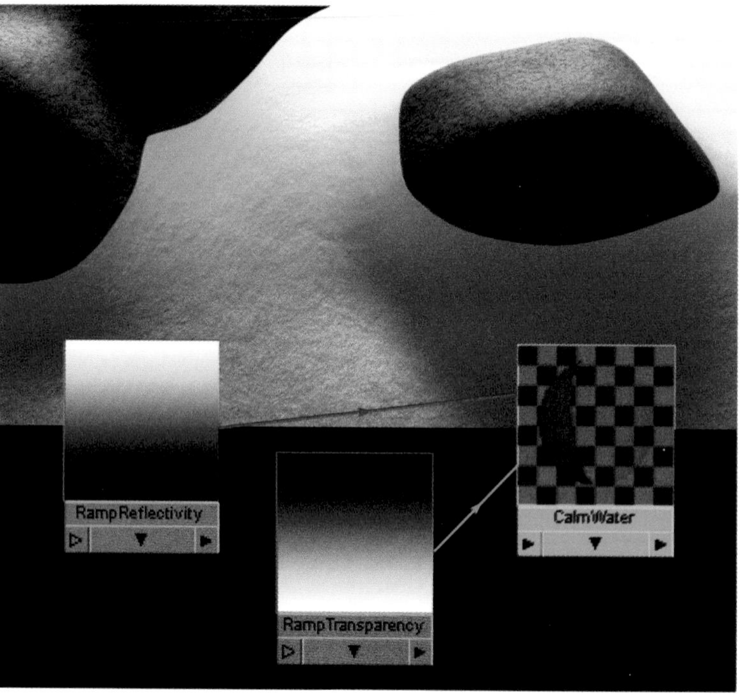

Figure 11.23 Two Ramp textures control the transparency and reflectivity of a NURBS surface. This scene is included on the CD as `calm_water.ma`.

Creating Water Droplets

Individual water droplets, a minute form of calm water, reveal a strong tendency to refract. For example, in Figure 11.24 the weave of the cloth is magnified by each drop. The degree of refraction is defined by a refractive index. Although air has a refractive index slightly above 1.0, water has a refractive index of 1.33. When the water's surface is curved by surface tension, the perceived refraction is stronger than the equivalent refraction provided by a flat surface. The surface curvature acts as a convex lens, causing light rays reflected off the cloth to diverge as they are refracted through the water toward the viewer. In addition, the refraction process creates "hot spots" within the drops. These spots are found in caustic regions. Caustic regions are areas in which light rays are focused by materials such as water or glass. In other words, light rays entering the water drop converge toward a focal point.

Figure 11.24 Water droplets refract the cloth they sit on.

Although the mental ray Caustics attribute is able to produce caustics (see Chapter 12), Maya Software is not. Nevertheless, you can simulate caustics by mapping the material's Incandescence attribute. For example, in Figure 11.25 each water drop is constructed from a NURBS half sphere, which is assigned to a blinn material node (named Water). The outColor of a ramp texture node (named RampIncandescence) is connected to the incandescence of Water. The facingRatio of a samplerInfo utility node is connected to the vCoord of RampIncandescence. The ramp transitions from black to dark blue. Because the center of each drop faces the camera, it receives the dark blue from the top of the ramp, which equates to a slight incandescent glow. The Refractions attribute of Water is also checked and the Refractive Index attribute is set to 3. Although a value of 3 does not correspond directly to real-world water, it produces a satisfactory look. In addition, the facingRatio of the samplerInfo node is connected to the vCoord's two additional ramps (RampColor and RampTransparency). The outColor of RampColor is connected to the color of Water, thus changing the drop color along its edge. The outColor of RampTransparency is connected to the transparency of Water, thus making the drops more transparent in the center.

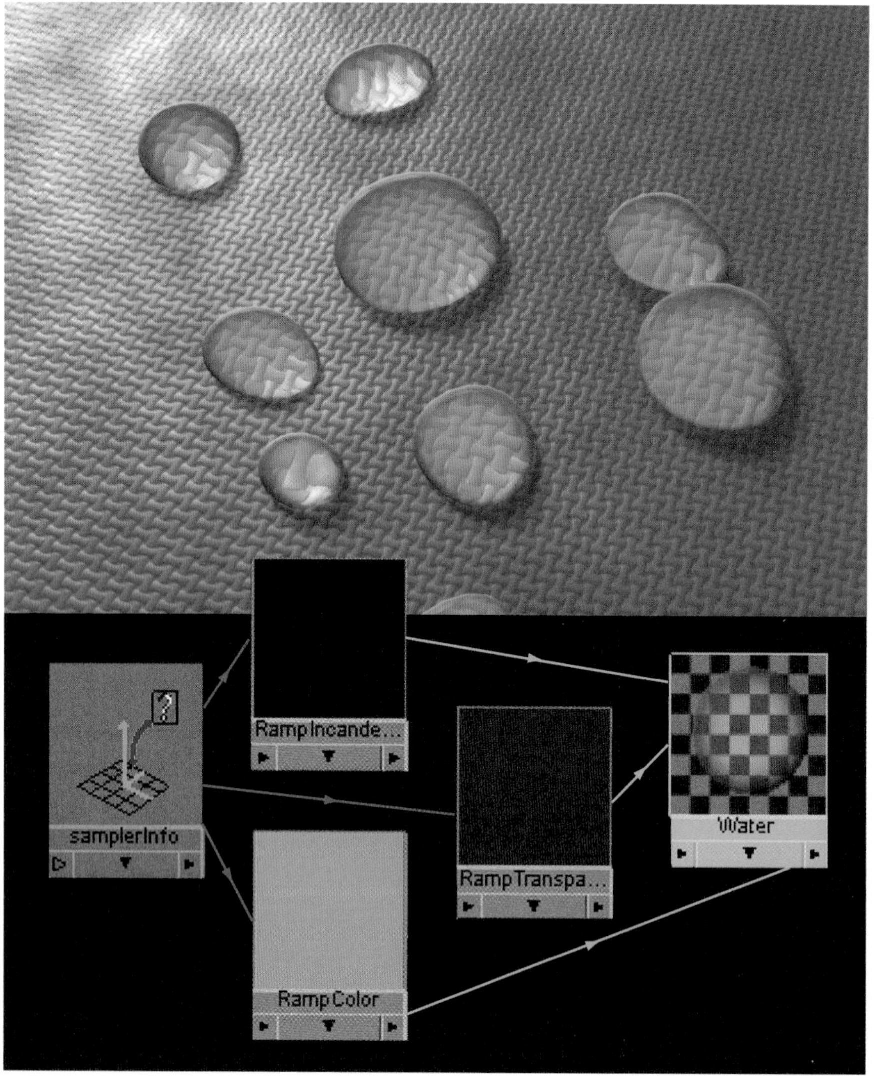

Figure 11.25 (Top) Water drops rendered with Maya Software. (Bottom) The shading network for the drops. This scene is included on the CD as `drops.ma`.

Creating Turbulent Water

Water that tumbles, crashes, or boils creates a great deal of foam. Foam is composed of numerous bubbles. The white quality of foam (assuming the water is relatively clean) is generated by specular highlights appearing on all the bubbles. For example, in Figure 11.26 a wave hitting a rock appears very white. Yet when a small portion of the water is examined, it becomes clear that the white is composed of numerous specular "hot spots" on countless individual bubbles. Although these spots are actually reflections of a bright sky, they are too small and too dispersed to form a reflection that is coherent. By comparison, calm water produces a single large specular highlight in the form of a large, continuous reflection.

Figure 11.26 Water crashes against a rock, producing foam.

The white quality of foam is often exaggerated by rapidly moving water or a lengthy shutter speed of a still camera. If the water is exposed for 1 second, for example, the water has a chance to move a significant distance and thereby create a strong motion blur. For example, in Figure 11.27 the exposure of a waterfall is long enough to allow the foam to blur into monolithic sheets.

Figure 11.27 A long exposure blurs the foam of a waterfall.

Maya's Fluid Effects system is designed to create turbulent lakes and oceans and comes equipped with foam attributes. If the Maya Ocean system is unavailable, bump and displacement mapping on NURBS or polygon surfaces can emulate the look of foam to some degree. On the other hand, Cloud particles, once flowing through a dynamic simulation, can re-create fast-flowing water. For example, in Figure 11.28 a volume particle emitter generates 3,000 particles per second. The Particle Render Type is set to Cloud and the Radius is set to 0.25. Gravity and Turbulence fields pull the particles downward and randomize their direction respectively. The particles are rendered with mental ray. The Motion Blur attribute is set to Full (No Deformation motion blur is unable to blur software-rendered particles). The length of each particle's blue is exaggerated by setting Motion Blur By to 10. Time Samples is set to 10 to help smooth the result.

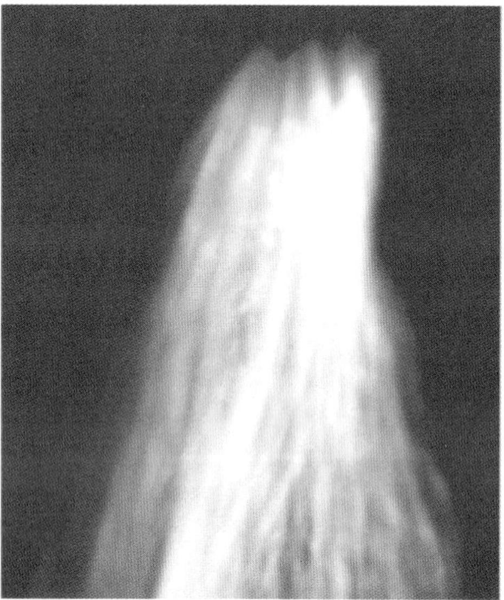

Figure 11.28 Cloud particles replicate fast-moving water. This scene is included on the CD as `waterfall.ma`.

Water as a Solid

When water freezes, it gains new, distinct qualities. For instance, ice cubes, icicles, and other water that is rapidly frozen contain numerous imperfections throughout their mass. Trapped air bubbles, small cracks, boundaries in the crystalline structure, and particulate matter interfere with refractions and reflections. In addition, the convoluted internal structure creates numerous, tiny specular highlights. The end result is a familiar white roughness (see Figure 11.29). The white of the specular highlight is derived from a bright sky or intense camera flash.

You can reproduce the white specular quality of ice in Maya with Water, Noise, and Ramp textures. For example, in Figure 11.30 icicles are re-created with primitive cones hung upside down. Each icicle is composed of an inner and an outer surface. The outer surfaces are assigned to a blinn material node named OuterIce. The outColor of two ramp textures are connected to the specularColor and transparency of OuterIce. The facingRatio of a samplerInfo utility node is connected to the vCoord of the ramp that controls OuterIce's transparency. This causes the icicles to be more transparent along their cores. In addition, a water texture node is connected to OuterIce's Bump Mapping attribute via a bump2d utility node. The Bump Depth value is set to 0.5, thereby reducing the regularity of the specular highlights. OuterIce's Refractive Index attribute is set to 1.1, which is less than the 1.3 assigned to real-world ice.

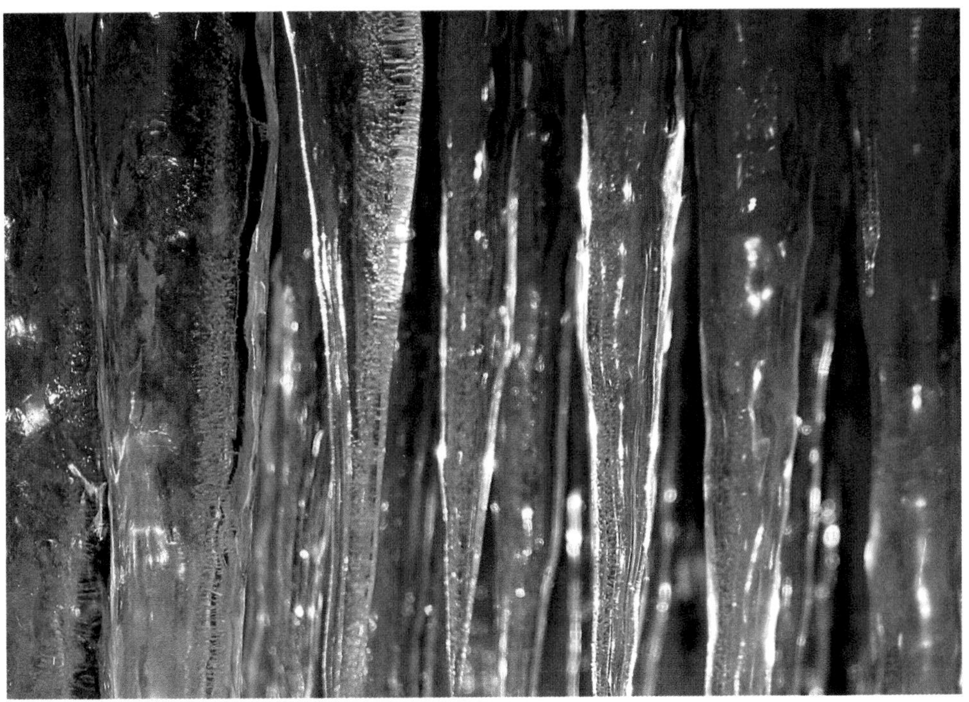

Figure 11.29 Icicles display distorted reflections, refractions, and specular highlights.

The inner surfaces are assigned to a second blinn material node named InnerIce. Two ramp textures are connected to the specularColor and transparency of InnerIce. The facingRatio of a second samplerInfo node is connected to the vCoord of both ramps. This causes the icicles to be transparent and dark along their cores. In addition, a noise texture node is connected to InnerIce's Bump Mapping attribute via a bump2d utility node. The Bump Depth value is set to 36. The Repeat UV of the noise texture's place2dTexture node is set to 10, 4. This creates the crinkled patterns in the center of each icicle. The outColor of the noise texture is also connected to the colorOffset of the ramp controlling InnerIce's transparency. This "dirties" the ramp and makes the transparency inconsistent. The Refractive Index attribute of InnerIce is set to 1.1, causing background icicles to become distorted behind the foreground icicles. The Light Absorbance attribute of InnerIce is set to 20, thus darkening any resulting refraction. Two directional lights strike the surfaces from each side of the screen, highlighting the edges.

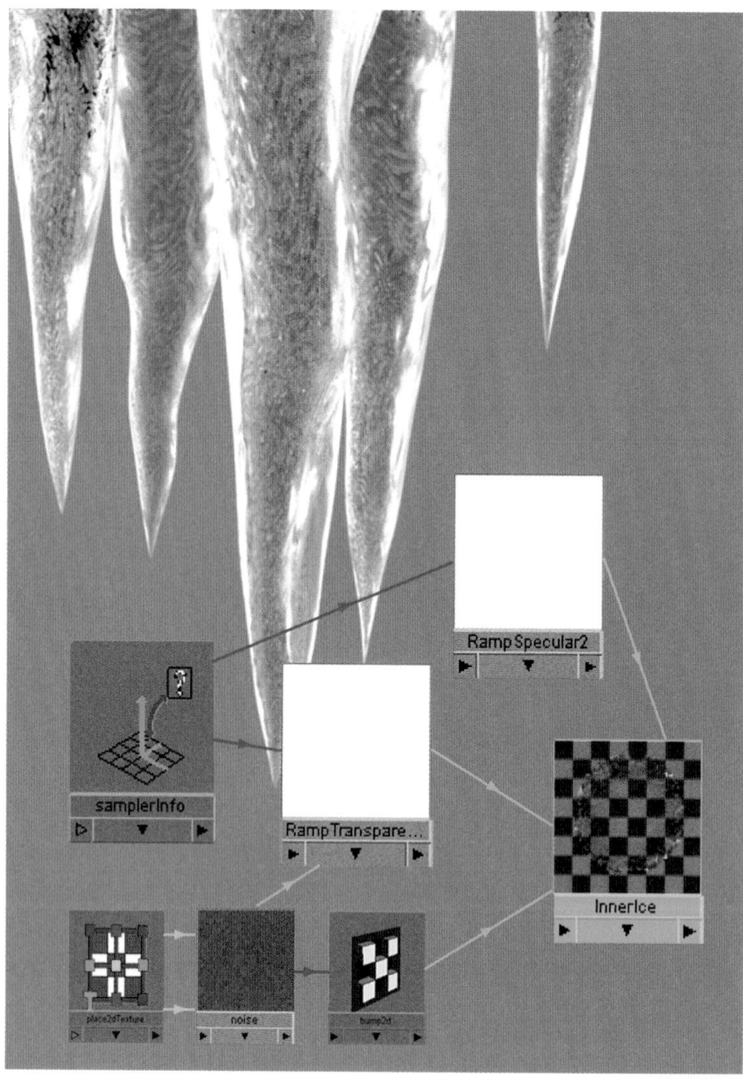

Figure 11.30 (Top) Icicles rendered with Maya Software. (Bottom) The shading network for the inner surface of each icicle. This scene is included on the CD as `icicles.ma`.

Reproducing Glass

Clear glass is difficult to reproduce simply because there is little to it. Due to its high transparency, glass must be indicated through four main characteristics: reflectivity, refractivity, edge reflectivity, and surface grime.

Clear glass is highly reflective, but not to the point that its transparency is completely obscured. For example, in Figure 11.31 whiskey glasses are photographed in a bright exterior. Several sections of each glass carry intense specular highlight streaks. These streaks are the reflections of the nearby wall and sky. Aside from these washed-out highlights, little else of the surrounding environment is visible in the reflections of the glass. This is due, in part, to the relative brightness of the background wall compared to other parts of the environment. The same glass against a dark background with a strong source of light before it would become more mirror-like (this is similar to the glass of a window or a picture frame viewed at night). Whether the background is bright or dark, a percentage of the light rays striking the glass are absorbed and converted to heat or reflected in such a direction that they do not reach the viewer.

Figure 11.31 Reflections and refractions of real-world glass

Glass has a refractive index that ranges from 1.45 to 1.85. The distortion of the background by glass objects is fairly subtle unless the glass is thick or the surface is significantly curved, wavy, or faceted. The lips of glasses and vases often appear darker than other parts of the surface. This due to the high degree of curvature present in a small area. In this situation, a percentage of light rays are reflected away from the viewer. In addition, a strong refraction of a dark table or nearby dark wall is often visible (see Figure 11.32). If the glass is in a well-lit location, a light ring is likely to exist just below the dark ring. This ring is generated by the refraction of intense overhead light source.

Figure 11.32 Dark and light rings around the lips of various glasses

Along the same lines, the vertical edges of a glass are generally less transparent, and thus more reflective, than the section of the glass facing the viewer. This is another example of a Fresnel reflection, where transparency decreases and reflectivity increases with the viewing angle.

The qualities of clear glass apply equally to colored or tinted glass. For instance, in Figure 11.33 a blue water glass shows reflection, refraction, and a dark top ring.

Figure 11.33 A colored, real-world glass

Last, glass is rarely clean. Fingerprints, dust, and other residue reduce the clarity of the reflections and refractions. The clarity is further reduced by any optical impurities in the glass, such as bubbles or inferior materials.

Creating Glass with Maya Software

Aside from the reproduction of various glasslike traits, limitations and quirks of the Maya Software renderer pose additional challenges. As an example, the glass pictured in Figure 11.34 is reproduced in 3D.

When comparing the Maya glass to the real glass, you'll see a number of characteristics are equivalent:

- The refraction of the table through the glass wall
- The vertically stretched specular highlights
- The change in transparency from the base to the rim
- The characteristic dark, refracted rim

The Maya glass is constructed from a single NURBS surface. (The outline was laid out with a NURBS curve and the Revolve tool applied.) The glass is assigned to an Anisotropic material named GlassColor. The Anisotropic material offers the advantage of elongated specular highlights that can be controlled with additional attributes. The Specular Shading section of the material has the following settings:

Angle: 0

Spread X: 34

Figure 11.34 Water glass reproduced with the Maya Software renderer. This scene is included on the CD as `glass.ma`.

Spread Y: 5

Roughness: 0.2

Fresnel Index: 5.4

Reflectivity: 0.1

Reflected Color is mapped with an Env Cube environment texture. The six walls of the Env Cube are mapped with a photo of the real-world from the "point-of-view" of the glass. That is, photos were taken of what was behind, in front of, beside, below, and above the glass. Since the Reflectivity attribute is set to a low 0.1, the cube provides a subtle hint of the surrounding environment. As for the Raytrace Options section, the following attributes are adjusted:

Refractions: On

Refractive Index: 1.33

Refraction Limit: 10

When you're replicating the refraction of a real-world glass, it is important to match the geometry as closely as possible. If the glass walls are a different thickness or the rim has a slightly different shape, the resulting refraction may be significantly different. For example, in Figure 11.35 the vertices of the NURBS rim are adjusted slightly, producing a refraction that does not match the photo. In fact, if the glass featured in Figure 11.34 were constructed with an even higher degree of accuracy, a more appropriate Refractive Index of 1.45 would work. Ultimately, creating the correct look of a refraction in 3D may require the application of a nonrealistic Refractive Index value.

Figure 11.35
When the vertices of the glass surface are adjusted slightly, a significantly different refraction is produced.

Returning to the scene used for Figure 11.34, Light Absorbance is left at the default 0. Although you can raise the Light Absorbance value to darken the glass, the darkening occurs equally over the surface. In this re-creation, the Transparency attribute is instead mapped with a Ramp texture, allowing the base of the glass to appear darker. The Ramp itself has four handles that create a white band in the center of a gray field. This forces the base to be more opaque and the rim more transparent.

Last, the Maya Software renderer has the following settings:

Shading: 2

Max Shading: 10

Reflections: 10

Refractions: 10

Shadows: 2

If Refractions is not set to the maximum value, some parts of the glass turn into "black pits." For example, in Figure 11.36 Refractions is set to 2. The base of the glass becomes solid black because the refraction rays are killed off before they have a chance to intersect all the walls of the glass and reach the table top. The color black is provided by the Background Color of the rendering camera. In Maya, Background Color is the color of empty space.

Figure 11.36 When Refractions is set to 2, the base becomes a large "black pit."

In some cases, black pits are much more subtle. Even when Refractions is set to 10, they can occur with intricate geometry or with surfaces that possess complex angles. In fact, you can see black pits in the upper-left corner of the icicle render in Figure 11.30. In a separate example, a clear glass produces small black pits at its base (see Figure 11.37). The quickest solution is to change the Background Color to something other than black. With Figure 11.37, a brown Background Color helps solve the problem.

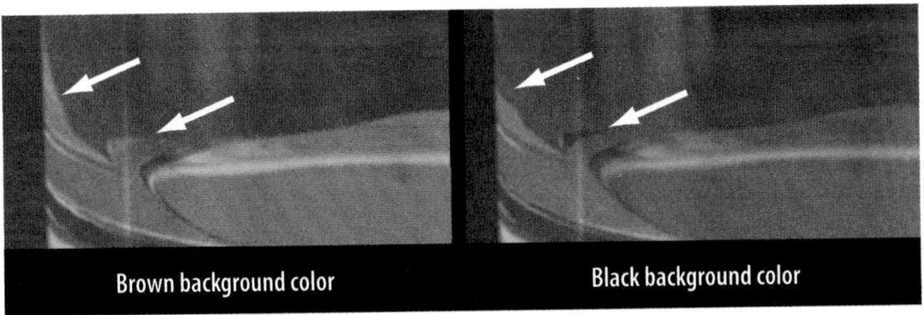

Figure 11.37 Black pits are disguised with Background Color set to brown.

When you compare the Maya glass featured in Figure 11.34 to the real glass in Figure 11.33, you'll see that several characteristics are *not* equivalent:

- The refraction is much smoother on the Maya glass. The refraction of the real glass is slightly wavy due to the variations in the thickness of the glass wall.
- Most important, the Maya glass is missing the hot blue caustics spots at the base. These can be created with the mental ray Dielectric_material shader, which is demonstrated in Chapter 12.

Chapter Tutorial: Texturing and Rendering an Ice Cube

In this tutorial, you will texture and render an ice cube with the mental ray renderer. You will employ reflections, refractions, and custom shading networks to help make the render more realistic (see Figure 11.38).

1. Open `icecube.ma` from the Chapter 11 scene folder on the CD.
2. Create two new Blinn materials in the Hypershade window. Name the first Blinn material **Inner** and the second Blinn material **Outer**. Assign Outer to the OuterIce polygon surface. Assign Inner to the InnerIce polygon surface.
3. MMB-drag Outer into the work area and open its Attribute Editor tab. Set Transparency to 100% white, Eccentricity to 0.1, and Specular Color to 100% white. Check the Refractions attribute. Set Refractive Index to 1.4 and Refraction Limit to 2.

Figure 11.38 An ice cube rendered with mental ray

4. Click the Bump Mapping attribute Map button. Choose a Noise texture from the Create Render Node window. Open the Attribute Editor tab for the new bump2d node. Set the Bump Depth attribute to 0.1.

5. MMB-drag a Ramp texture and a Sampler Info utility from the Create Maya Nodes menu into the work area. Connect the facingRatio of the samplerInfo node to the vCoord of the ramp node. Connect the outColor of the ramp node to incandescence of Outer. Use Figure 11.39 as a reference.

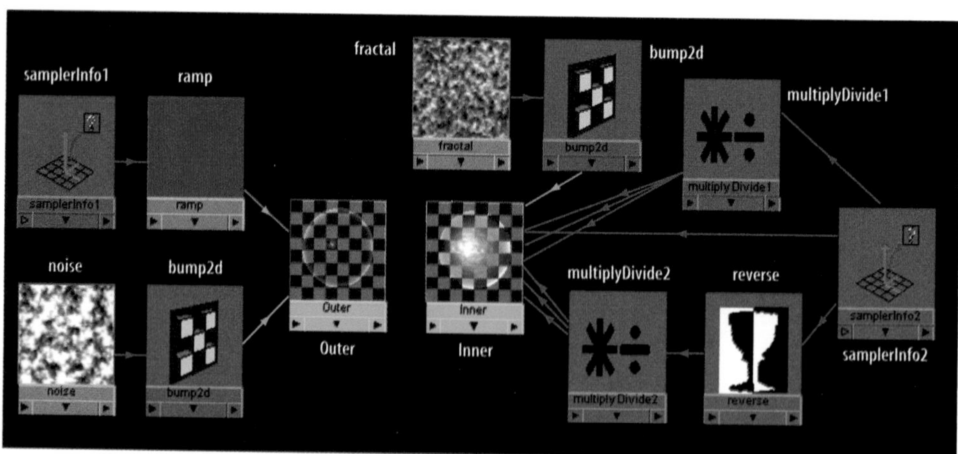

Figure 11.39 The custom shading network for the ice cube

6. Open the ramp node's Attribute Editor tab. Change the Interpolation attribute to Smooth. Delete the middle color handle. Change the top color handle to dark gray. Change the bottom handle to medium gray. Position the top handle two-thirds of the way up the ramp. This ramp will control the bright edge of the ice cube. If the cube edges render too brightly, darken the colors of this ramp. The Outer material is now complete.

7. MMB-drag Inner into the work area and open its Attribute Editor tab. Click the Bump Mapping attribute Map button. Choose a Fractal texture from the Create Render Node window. Open the Attribute Editor tab for the new bump2d node. Set the Bump Depth attribute to 0.2.
8. MMB-drag a Sampler Info, a Reverse, and two Multiply Divide utilities from the Create Maya Nodes menu into the work area. Connect the facingRatio of the samplerInfo node to the inputX of the reverse node. Connect the facingRatio of the samplerInfo node to the specularRollOff of Inner. Connect the facingRatio of the samplerInfo node to the input1X of the multiplyDivide1 node. Connect the outputX of the multiplyDivide1 to the incandescenceR, incandescenceG, and incandescenceB of Inner. Connect the outputX of the reverse node to the input1X of the multiplyDivide2 node. Connect the outputX of the multiplyDivide2 node to the transparencyR, transparencyG, and transparencyB of Inner.
9. Open the Attribute Editor tab for multiplyDivide1. Set the Input2X attribute to 0.3. Increasing this value will create a stronger "glow" around the ice cube's edge.
10. Open the Attribute Editor tab for multiplyDivide2. Set the Input2X attribute to 2.75. Decreasing this value will make the edges of the ice cube cloudier and less transparent. The custom shading networks are now complete!
11. The scene file contains a single directional light named Key. Open the Attribute Editor tab for Key and check Use Ray Trace Shadows. Set Light Angle and Shadow Rays to 5. This creates a soft-edged shadow. Set Ray Depth Limit to 5. This limits shadows to four recursive reflections or refractions.
12. Open the Render Settings window. Switch the Render Using attribute to mental ray. Set the Quality Presets attribute to Draft. Render out a test. If it looks good, switch Quality Presets to Production and rerender. The tutorial is complete! If you get stuck, a finished version is included as `icecube_complete.ma` in the Chapter 11 scene folder on the CD.

12 Working with Global Illumination, Final Gather, and mental ray Shaders

Global Illumination and Final Gather are powerful rendering methods that duplicate many of the physical and optical events common to the real world. For example, the Caustics attribute re-creates reflected specularity. Irradiance attributes, found on standard Maya materials, illuminate a scene in which no lights are present. Global Illumination and Final Gather are available through the mental ray renderer. In addition to a long list of specialized attributes, mental ray provides custom mental ray shaders.

Chapter Contents

Understanding Indirect Illumination

Global Illumination is a lighting process in which virtual photons are absorbed by or reflected off surfaces in a scene. This process is equivalent to naturalistic lighting in which light "bounces" off one surface to the next. (For information on lighting theory, see Chapter 1.)

Although raytracing can trace light paths, the raytrace renderer is unable to mingle colors in a scene. For instance, in the real world, a brightly lit red object will "bleed" red onto the white of a tabletop (see Figure 12.1).

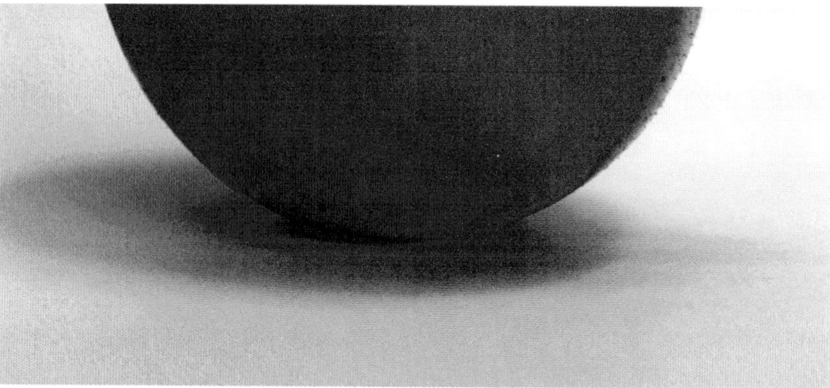

Figure 12.1 Indirect illumination causes the red of an object to "bleed" onto the white of a tabletop.

Raytracing and scanline rendering depend on *direct illumination* techniques. Global Illumination, on the other hand, uses *indirect illumination*. To properly describe indirect illumination, along with color bleeding, a closer look at the mechanics of light is necessary.

Light is a form of electromagnetic radiation that exists as a continuous range of wavelengths. Specific wavelengths are visible to the human eye and are perceived by the human brain as specific colors. At the same time, light is quantified as elementary particles called *photons*, which are discrete units of light energy. When a light wave with a particular wavelength strikes an object, it is absorbed, reflected, or transmitted. Absorption occurs when the energy of a photon is captured by an atom. The capture causes an orbiting electron to temporarily jump to a higher energy level. As the electron returns to a lower energy level, it releases the excess energy as a new photon, which equates to a longer wavelength of radiation. The longer wavelength is felt as radiant heat.

Note: The wave-particle duality of light, to this day, is actively researched and debated. For the sake of simplicity, you can think of light as simultaneously exhibiting properties of a wave and a particle. For 3D animation, critical components of light include light direction, light wavelength (Color and Photon Color), and light energy (Intensity and Photon Intensity).

Transmission, on the other hand, occurs when the photon is absorbed by an atom at a material boundary. The energy is not released by the material immediately, however. Instead, the energy is transferred from one atom to a neighboring atom. This continues until the energy is passed through the bulk of the material to an opposite material boundary. At the opposite boundary, the energy is released as a photon with energy similar to the original photon. Since the energy, and the wavelength, is inherently the same, the light remains visible. Thus, transmission makes glass and similar materials transparent.

Note: All transparent materials incur some degree of refractivity. Refraction occurs when a light wave crosses the boundary between two materials with different refractive indices. As the wave enters the second material, its wavelength, speed, and direction are altered. Hence, refracted objects appear bent or broken. For more information on refraction and refractive indices, see Chapters 7 and 11.

Ultimately, color is not contained within the materials of objects. Instead, color is the result of particular wavelengths of light reaching the viewer through reflection or transmission. Different materials (wood, stone, metal, and so on) have different atomic compositions and thereby absorb, reflect, and transmit light differently. Hence, the red of a red object represents a particular wavelength that the object reflects. In the scenario illustrated in Figure 12.1, the white light of a light source is reflected off the object as a red wavelength. (White light contains the full spectrum of color wavelengths; therefore, the non-red wavelengths are absorbed and converted to radiation interpreted as heat.) The reflected red wavelength strikes the white table, which is made of a different material and has a different atomic structure. Nevertheless, the table reflects pink wavelengths that are closely related to the original red of the object.

Global Illumination can replicate the absorption, reflection, and transmission of light and the resulting mingling of colors. Hence, the system can produce extremely realistic renders.

Note: *Wavelength* is the distance between repeating features of a waveform cycle. *Frequency* is the number of cycles that occur during a particular period of time. When discussing light, frequency is explicitly dependent on the wavelength and speed of the light wave (roughly 300,000 kilometers per second). Hence, the formula is frequency = speed of light / wavelength.

Tracing Photons

To use Global Illumination, you must use the mental ray renderer. In addition, you must employ virtual photons. In Maya, spot, point, area, and directional lights generate photons when the light's Emit Photons attribute is checked (see Figure 12.2). (You can find Emit Photons in the Caustic And Global Illumination subsection of the mental ray section in the light's Attribute Editor tab.)

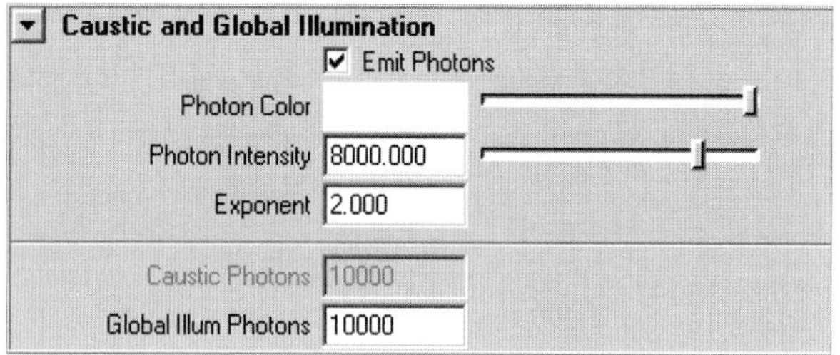

Figure 12.2 The Caustic And Global Illumination subsection of a spot light's Attribute Editor tab

When a scene is rendered, photons are traced from each photon-emitting light to objects in the scene. If a photon "hits" a surface, it is absorbed, reflected, or transmitted (refracted) based on the qualities of the material assigned to the surface. If a photon is reflected or transmitted, it survives with only a portion of its original energy. The amount of energy is determined by the reflection coefficient, which is established by the Reflectivity attribute in Maya.

To simplify the photon-tracing process, many Global Illumination systems, including the one employed by mental ray, randomly cull photons in a process known as *Russian Roulette*. Photons that survive a surface hit through reflection or refraction are given an increased energy that is proportional to the potential energy of all the photons generated by the light source. The photons that are culled and thereby absorbed by the surface have their position, incident direction, and energy stored in a special photon map. The following scenario is a simplified example of the process:

- A light generates 1,000 photons, each with an energy level of 10. The net photon energy is 10,000.
- The photons strike a surface that is assigned to a material with Reflectivity value set to 0.5.
- With the Russian Roulette method, 50 percent of the photons are absorbed and thus contribute their energy to the photon map. The surviving 500 photons reflect off the surface with their original energy level of 10. The surviving net energy is 5,000, or 50 percent of the original net energy of 10,000.
- If the Russian Roulette method is not used, 1,000 photons reflect with a 50 percent energy level, which correlates to the Reflectivity value of 0.5. The net energy level remains at 5,000. However, the calculations are more complex because 1,000 photons must be traced instead of 500.

The absorption, reflection, or transmission of a photon is affected by the shading components of the assigned material. Not only will changes to the Diffuse and Reflectivity attributes affect photon scattering, but Color, Eccentricity, and Specular Color have an equal impact. If a photon survives a hit and is reflected or transmitted, it continues through the scene until it hits another surface. Once again, the photon is absorbed, reflected, or transmitted. This process continues until the surviving photons are stopped by the Max Photon Depth attribute, which defines the number of hits permitted per photon. (Max Photon Depth is located in the Caustics And Global Illumination section of the mental ray tab in the Render Settings window.) Ultimately, the information stored in the photon map is combined with the direct illumination model, which in turn determines the color and intensity of each rendered pixel.

The number of photons generated by a given light is set by the light's Global Illum Photons attribute. You can lower or raise the default value of 10,000 to decrease or increase quality. In addition, you can change the qualities of photons generated by a light with the following attributes (all of which are found in the Caustic And Global Illumination subsection of the mental ray section in the light's Attribute Editor tab):

Photon Color Represents the red, green, and blue components of a photon's energy. Photon Color is a "dummy" attribute. The RGB values of its color swatch are multiplied by the Photon Intensity attribute to produce Energy R, Energy G, and Energy B attributes. You can access these attributes in the Script Editor (for example, `getAttr light.energyR;`).

Photon Intensity A scaling factor used to determine the intensity of photons produced by a light. The default value of 8000 tends to be too high and will often wash out a render. A value of 0 will turn off photon tracing for the light. Photon Intensity should be changed through the Attribute Editor and not through the Script Editor or with a MEL script.

Exponent Simulates light falloff over distance. The default value of 2 replicates natural, quadratic decay. A value of 1 effectively prevents falloff from occurring. Values higher than 2 create a more rapid falloff by artificially decreasing photon energy with distance.

Rendering Global Illumination with mental ray

You can create a simple Global Illumination render with the following steps:

1. Create a still life. Create a spot light and position it over the still life. Open the spot light's Attribute Editor tab. Check the Emit Photons attribute in the Caustic And Global Illumination subsection (found in the mental ray section).
2. Assign the objects to colored Blinn materials. To simplify the process, do not adjust the materials' Transparency attributes.
3. Open the Render Settings window. Change Render Using to mental ray.
4. Switch to the mental ray tab. In the Secondary Effects subsection of the Rendering Features section, check Raytracing (if it's not already checked). Raytracing remotely activates the Ray Tracing attribute in the Raytracing section of the same mental ray tab. The raytracing process is mandatory for Global Illumination.
5. In the Secondary Effects subsection of the Rendering Features section, check Global Illumination. Global Illumination remotely activates the Global Illumination attribute found in the Caustics And Global Illumination section in the same mental ray tab.
6. Render a test through the Render View.

To save time, you can change the Quality Presets attribute to Preview: Global Illumination, which automatically activates Raytracing and Global Illumination in the Secondary Effects subsection and the Caustics And Global Illumination section. (For more information on the Rendering Features section, see Chapter 11.)

Global Illumination will often create a spotty render. Fortunately, you can fix this by adjusting such attributes as Radius and Accuracy, which are discussed in the next section of this chapter.

Keep these additional tips in mind when working with Global Illumination:

- To contribute photon information to the photon map, a surface must be assigned to a material that has a Diffuse attribute. The material's Color value must be higher than 0, 0, 0.
- The first surface that a photon hits is ignored in the creation of a photon map. Nevertheless, the first hit is considered part of the direct illumination calculation.
- Although directional lights can generate photons, they are not recommended. Directional lights possess direction, but no true position. Therefore, when tracing photons, a potentially large numbers of photons may never reach the geometry of the scene and the render is thereby made inefficient.
- Global Illumination works more efficiently with mental ray if there is a complete set. That is, if there is empty space within the scene, some photons may never strike a surface and thus serve no purpose.

Adjusting Global Illumination Attributes

Global Illumination attributes are contained within the Caustics And Global Illumination section of the mental ray tab in the Render Settings window (see Figure 12.3). Of all the attributes, Radius and Accuracy are perhaps the most critical for creating a refined render.

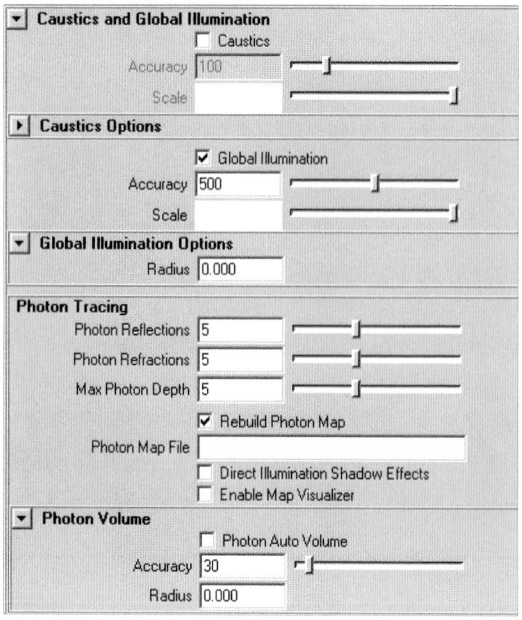

Figure 12.3
The Caustics And Global Illumination section of the mental ray tab in the Render Settings window

Radius Found within the Global Illumination Options subsection, Radius controls the maximum distance from a photon hit that the renderer will seek out neighboring photon hits to determine the color of the hit in question. The default value of 0 allows Maya to automatically pick a radius based on the scene size. Although the default value produces a satisfactory render in many cases, it will often create spottiness (see Figure 12.4). The spottiness is exaggerated in scenes containing complex reflective or refractive surfaces, as the photons are scattered to an even greater degree.

Figure 12.4 Photon hits appear as colored circles. For the left render, each of the two lights generates 10,000 photons. For the right render, each of the two lights generates 200 photons.

In this situation, each circle corresponds to the location of one photon hit. The color of a given circle, however, is derived from the average energies of all the photon hits discovered within the circle. The areas in-between the circles receive no indirect illumination and are thus darker. The circles vary in color because the photon energy levels, stored as RGB, are influenced by the Color value of the materials they encounter while reflecting off and transmitting through surfaces. For example, if a material is green, the energy of the reflected or transmitted photon is biased toward green. Hence, the mingling of colors and color "bleeding" is possible.

Ideally, the individual photon hits should not be visible in the render but should blend seamlessly with each other and the direct illumination. If the default Radius value is producing spottiness, the following steps are recommended:

1. Gradually increase the Global Illum Photons for each photon-producing light.
2. If higher Global Illum Photons values are unable to improve the quality without drastically effecting the render time, manually set the Radius attribute. As a rough rule of thumb, set Radius to a value equal to this formula:

```
[Scene bounding box height] / ([Total number of photons] / 5000)
```

3. Gradually increase the Radius value until the photon hits begin to disappear.
4. Gradually increase the Accuracy value to further blend overlapping photon hits. If Accuracy has no significant impact on the render, continue to raise the Global Illum Photons and Radius values.
5. If a few photon hits remain visible despite high Global Illum Photons, Radius, and Accuracy values, consider using Final Gather (which is described later in this chapter). Final Gather does an excellent job of smoothing out Global Illumination renders.

Balancing the number of photons in a scene with the Radius value is an important aspect of the Global Illumination process. An excess of photons will cause a redundant overlapping of photon hits and an unnecessarily slow render. On the other hand, a limited number of photons with a large Radius will lead to inaccurate indirect lighting calculations.

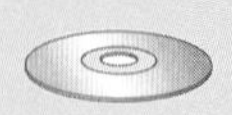

Note: If the proper photon balance is elusive, try the Diagnose Photon tool. The Diagnose Photon tool and Diagnostics section of the mental ray tab are described in section 12.2 of the `Additional_Techniques.pdf` file on the CD.

Accuracy Found within the Caustics And Global Illumination section (directly below the Global Illumination check box), Accuracy sets the maximum number of neighboring photon hits included in the color estimate of a single photon hit. The search for neighboring photon hits is limited to the region established by the Radius attribute. In general, the higher the Accuracy value, the smoother the result. However, Accuracy only affects overlapping photon hits. That is, if the photon count is low or the Radius value is small so that the photon hits do not significantly overlap, the Accuracy attribute will have no effect on the render.

Scale Found within the Caustics And Global Illumination section (below the Global Illumination check box), Scale serves as a multiplier for the Photon Intensity attribute of all lights in the scene. If the slider is set to 50 percent gray, all the photons in the scene will be at half intensity.

Rebuild Photon Map Found within the Photon Tracing subsection, Rebuild Photon Map determines whether photon maps are rebuilt for each render. This attribute should be left checked unless the lighting is finalized and there is no object motion in the scene. If unchecked, this attribute will look for the photon map listed in the Photon Map File attribute field.

Photon Reflections and Photon Refractions Found within the Photon Tracing subsection, Photon Reflections defines the maximum number of times a photon will reflect in a scene. This attribute is overridden by the Max Photon Depth attribute. The first surface encountered is not included in the count. Photon Refractions functions in the same manner but affects the maximum number of photon refractions.

Max Photon Depth Found within the Photon Tracing subsection, Max Photon Depth sets the maximum number of times a photon can reflect *or* refract in a scene.

Direct Illumination Shadow Effects Found within the Photon Tracing subsection, this attribute allows raytraced shadows to maintain transparency. When Direct Illumination Shadow Effects is unchecked, raytrace shadows remain opaque despite material transparency.

Although mental ray provides a Preview: Global Illumination option for the Quality Presets attribute, it does not provide a high-quality preset. Therefore, attributes should be raised individually to improve the render. For example, you can incrementally raise the Accuracy from 64 to 1024 to smooth out photon hits (see Figure 12.5).

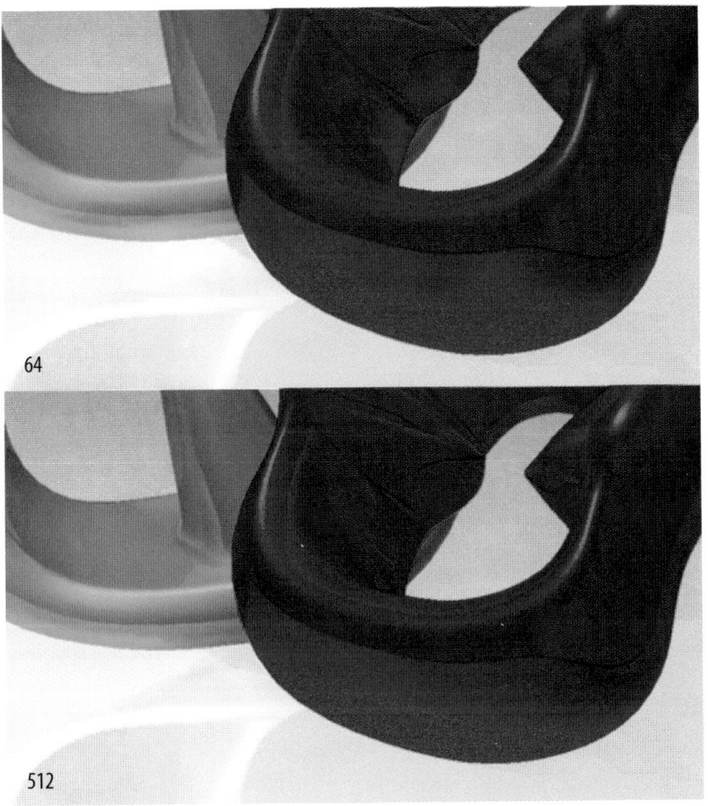

Figure 12.5 (Top to Bottom) Accuracy set to 64 and 512. This scene is included on the CD as `simple_global.ma`.

Enable Map Visualizer and Photon Map File attributes are discussed in the next section. Accuracy and Radius, as found in the Photon Volume subsection, are detailed in "Preparing mental ray Shaders for Global Illumination" later in this chapter.

Reviewing Photon Hits

Unfortunately, photon maps cannot be viewed with FCheck. Photon maps are not image files, but are data files that contain a 3D spatial search structure called a kd-tree. The kd-tree stores the location, incident direction, and energy of each absorbed photon. Nevertheless, mental ray provides a special window to examine data with the maps. Follow these steps:

1. Check the Enable Map Visualizer attribute in the Photon Tracing subsection of the Caustics And Global Illumination section of the mental ray tab. Enter a name in the Photon Map File attribute field.
2. Render a test frame using Global Illumination.
3. Choose Window > Rendering Editors > mental ray > Map Visualizer. The mental ray Map Visualizer window opens. Generally, the new photon map is preloaded into the Map File Name attribute field. If not, click the browse button and retrieve the photon map from the following directory:

   `project_directory/renderData/mentalray/photonMap/`

4. As soon as a valid photon map file is loaded, photon hits are rendered as colored points in the workspace view (see Figure 12.6).

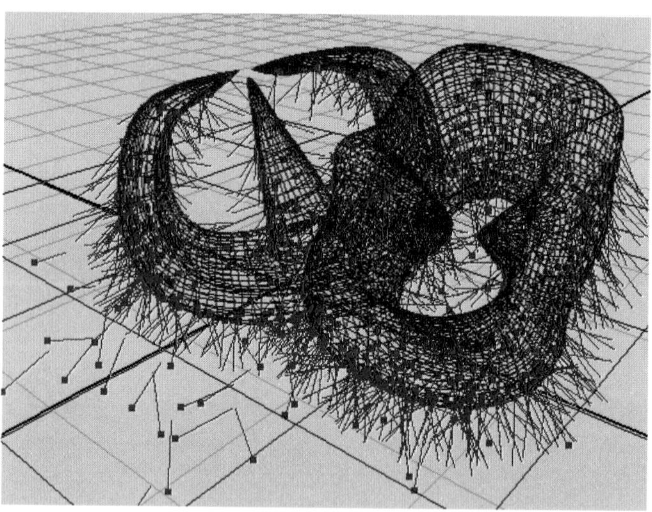

Figure 12.6 Map Visualizer points and direction lines representing photon hits

You can control how photon hits are displayed by changing various settings within the mental ray Map Visualizer window (see Figure 12.7). Sections and attributes of the Map Visualizer window include Photon Visibility, Point Size, Normal Scale, and Direction Scale.

Photon Visibility A section that contains the Globillum Photons, Caustic Photons, and Volume Photons attributes. You can check or uncheck these in any combination to preview Global Illumination, caustic, and volume photon hits. For a description of caustic photons, see the next section in this chapter. For a discussion of volume photons, see "Preparing mental ray Shaders for Global Illumination" later in this chapter. Photon Visibility does not indicate first-surface hits, as they are considered part of the direct illumination calculation.

Point Size Changes the screen size of the points used to represent photon hits.

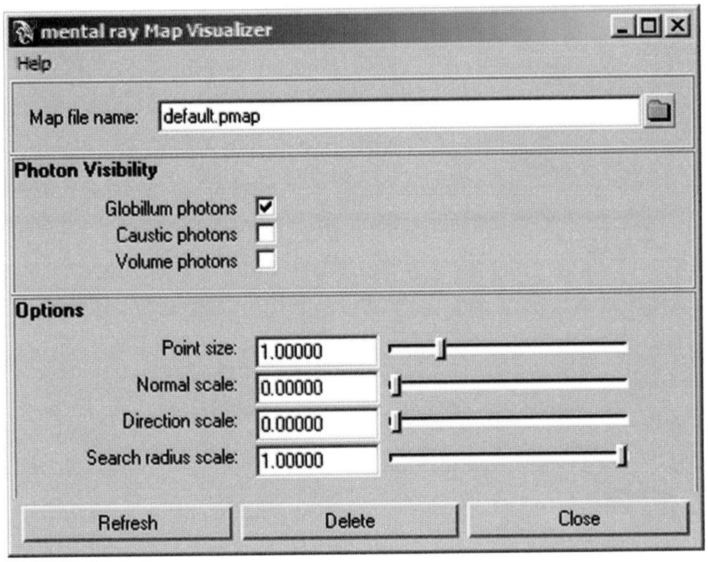

Figure 12.7 The mental ray Map Visualizer window

Normal Scale Displays and scales the surface normals at each photon hit.

Direction Scale Displays and scales lines that represent the motion vectors (incident directions) of photons before their individual hits (see Figure 12.6).

The Search Radius Scale attribute is designed for Final Gather renders utilizing irradiance and is discussed in "Using Irradiance" later in this chapter.

Note: The Enable Map Visualizer attribute creates mapViz and mapVizShape nodes when a scene is rendered with Global Illumination and/or caustics. If you select the mapViz node, you can translate the photon points and lines as a single unit.

Applying Caustics

A major advantage of the mental ray renderer is its ability to provide caustics. Caustics are "hot spots" resulting from light rays focused by the specular properties of materials. For example, caustics are commonly produced by shiny metal, water, and glass (see Figure 12.8). If a 3D material does not possess specular properties, no caustics will be generated by that material.

A special set of caustic photons are used to create caustics in Maya. A caustic photon is emitted by a light in a prerendering process and is traced through the scene until it is reflected or refracted a maximum number of times set by the Max Photon Depth attribute. If a caustic photon encounters a diffuse, nonreflective, nonrefractive surface, it is absorbed and its energy contribution is stored in a photon map.

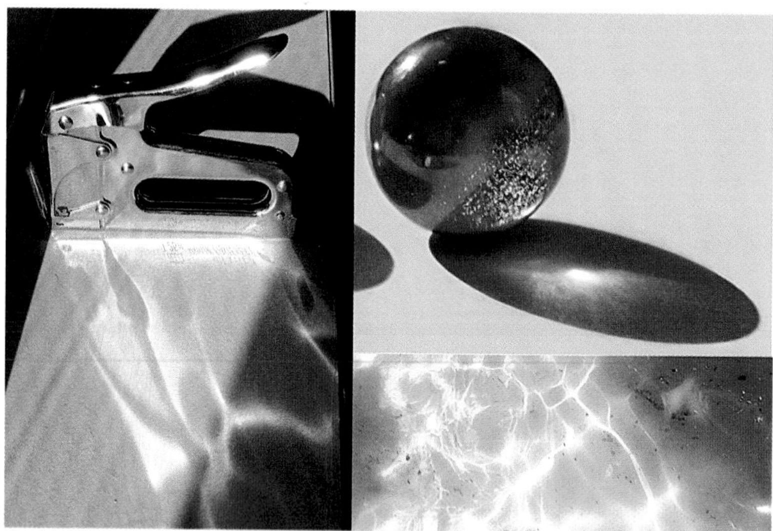

Figure 12.8 Metal, glass, and water produce caustics.

Global Illumination photon maps do not store specular reflection and specular refraction information. Nevertheless, if the Caustics and Global Illumination attributes are checked for a render, the caustic photon and Global Illumination photon information is stored side by side in the same file. You can view the caustic photon hits with the mental ray Map Visualizer window. (See the section "Reviewing Photon Hits" earlier in this chapter.) You can render caustics without Global Illumination if need be. You can activate caustics by checking either the Caustics attribute in the Secondary Effects subsection or the Caustics And Global Illumination section of the mental ray tab in the Render Settings window (both attributes are linked).

The number of caustic photons generated by a given light is set by the Caustic Photons attribute in the Caustic And Global Illumination subsection of the light's Attribute Editor tab. The Caustics And Global Illumination section of the mental ray tab also includes the following caustic attributes:

Accuracy Found in the Caustics And Global Illumination section (directly below the Caustics attribute check box), Accuracy sets the maximum number of neighboring caustic photon hits included in the color estimate of a single caustic photon hit. Higher values produce smoother caustics.

Scale Found in the Caustics And Global Illumination section (below the Caustics attribute check box), Scale serves as a multiplier for the intensity of the caustic. If the attribute is 50 percent gray, the intensity of the caustic is halved. This attribute can also be tinted a color, such as red. If Scale is left white, the resulting caustic color may not match the color of the object creating it.

Radius Found in the Caustics Options subsection, Radius controls the maximum distance from a caustic photon hit that the renderer will seek out neighboring caustic photon hits to determine the color of the hit in question. The default value of 0 allows Maya to automatically pick a radius based on the scene size. An improperly sized Radius will produce spottiness similar to that afflicting Global Illumination. That said, it is not necessary to match the two Radius attributes in the Caustics Options and Global Illumination Options subsections. In general, caustic photon hits occur in small pockets and are not as spread out as their Global Illumination counterparts. Nevertheless, stray caustic hits will occasionally pepper a render. Hence, great care should be taken when balancing the Caustic Photons and Radius attributes (see Figure 12.9).

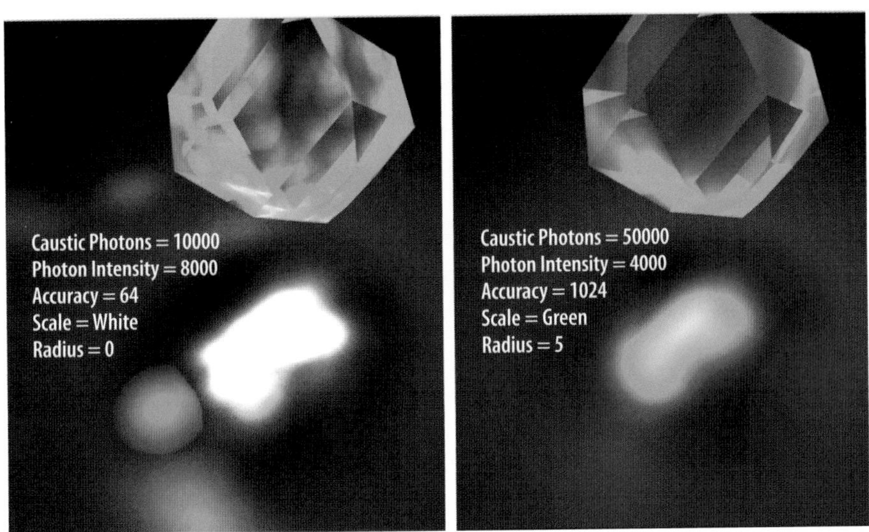

Figure 12.9 Different combinations of Caustic Photons, Photon Intensity, Accuracy, Scale, and Radius attributes create different degrees of caustic detail. This scene is included on the CD as `caustics.ma`.

The Radius attribute is distorted by the refractive quality of a material. That is, the screen size of the caustic photon hit will vary when the material's Refractions attribute is checked and the Refractive Index value is set to a value other than 1. This creates additional difficulties when blending the photon hits.

An additional approach, as suggested by Maya's documentation, requires these two steps:

1. Incrementally increase Radius until there is little change in the render.
2. Incrementally increase Accuracy until the caustic is suitably smooth.

Caustic Filter Type Found in the Caustics Options subsection, this attribute controls the sharpness of the caustic with the application of a filter. The Box and Gauss options produce sharper caustic edges, while the Cone option produces softer results. The effect is subtle unless the total number of photons used in the scene is fairly low (see Figure 12.10).

Caustic Filter Kernel Sets the size of the filter determined by the Caustic Filter Type attribute. The higher the value, the sharper the result; this is most noticeable with the Cone filter option.

Aside from Radius and Refractive Index attributes, Eccentricity, Specular Color, and Reflectivity attributes of involved materials affect the look of the caustic. For example, in Figure 12.11 changes to the Refractive Index, Eccentricity, and Reflectivity of a semitransparent surface lead to fairly substantial variations.

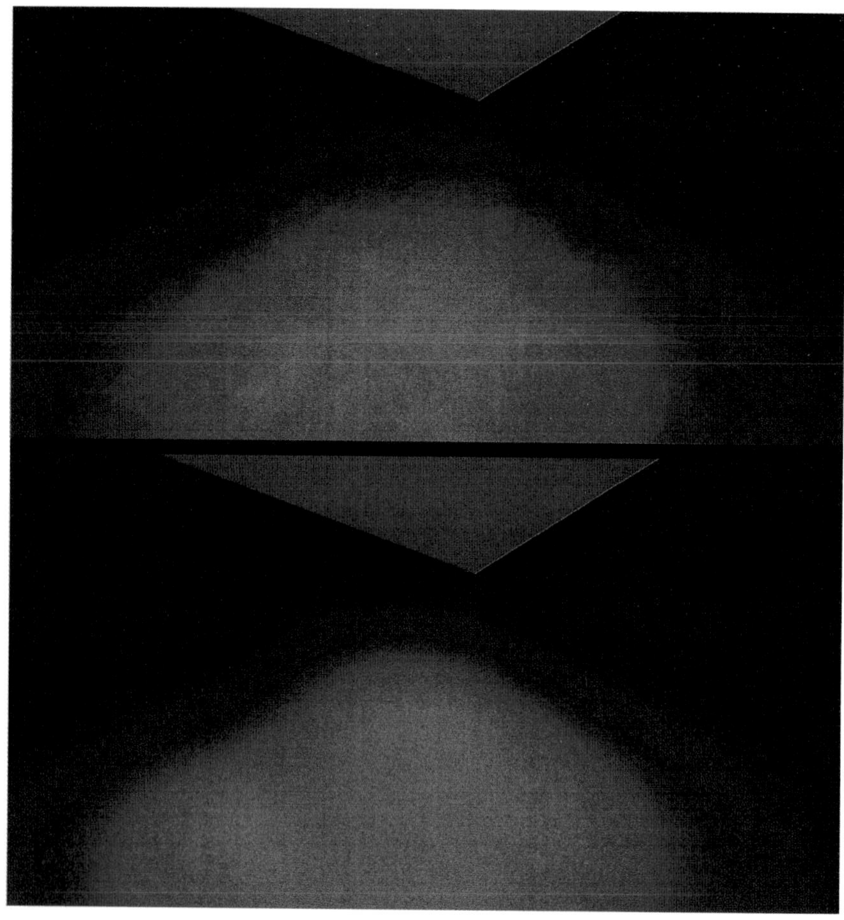

Figure 12.10 (Top) Box filter set to 1. (Bottom) Cone filter set to 1. This scene is included on the CD as `caustic_filter.ma`.

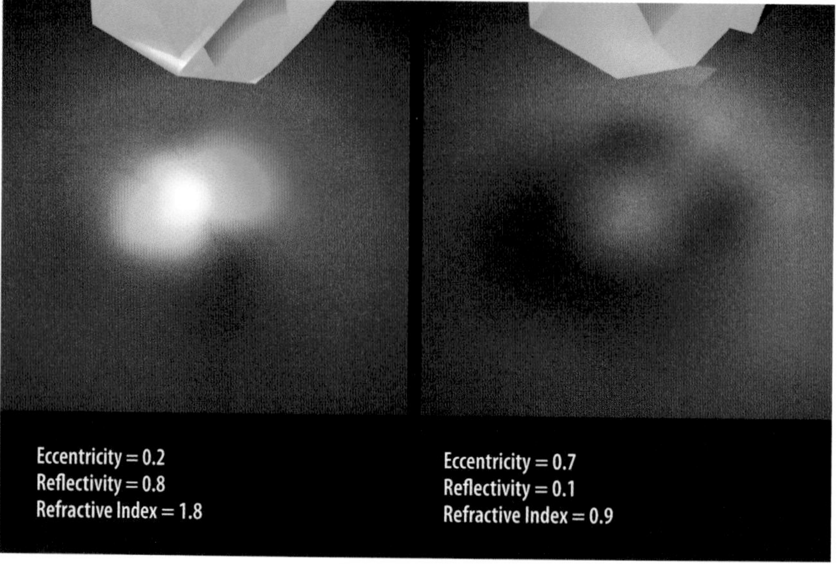

Figure 12.11 Changes to the Refractive Index, Eccentricity, and Reflectivity values of a material lead to shifts in the caustic pattern.

Applying mental ray Shaders

By default, mental ray works with all standard Maya materials. Nevertheless, a large number of mental ray shaders are included with the program. You can find these in the Create mental ray Nodes menu in the Hypershade window or in the mental ray tab of the Create Render Node window. You can assign a mental ray shader to a surface as you would a Maya material. However, you must use the mental ray renderer for the shader to be utilized. In addition, many of the attributes of the mental ray shaders are not intuitive and don't correspond to their Maya counterparts. Thus, descriptions of the most useful shaders and their attributes follow.

Using Dgs_material

The Dgs_material shader provides a physically-accurate shading model by offering Diffuse, Glossy, and Specular attributes. Diffuse represents the diffuse component and determines the base color of the surface. Glossy and Specular control the look of reflections and refractions when raytracing; you can use them individually or in conjunction.

If Glossy is set to black, Specular controls the intensity of the reflection or refraction. The higher the Specular value, the more intense the reflection or refraction. The Specular attribute will not create specular highlights.

If Specular is set to black, Glossy controls the intensity of the reflections, refractions, and specular highlights. The higher the Glossy value, the more intense the reflection and refraction and the larger the specular highlight. In addition, Glossy provides distance-based degradation of reflections and refractions. The degradation is controlled by the Shiny attribute. High Shiny values create a sharp reflections and refractions for objects close to the assigned surface. Low values create the opposite effect. For example, in Figure 12.12, a cylinder is intersected with a plane that is assigned to a Dgs_material. In left render, the reflection and refraction of the cylinder are controlled by the Specular attribute and are thus sharp. In the right render, the reflection and refraction are controlled by the Glossy and Shiny attributes; the reflection and refraction are sharp near the intersection point, but quickly degrade as they travel farther away.

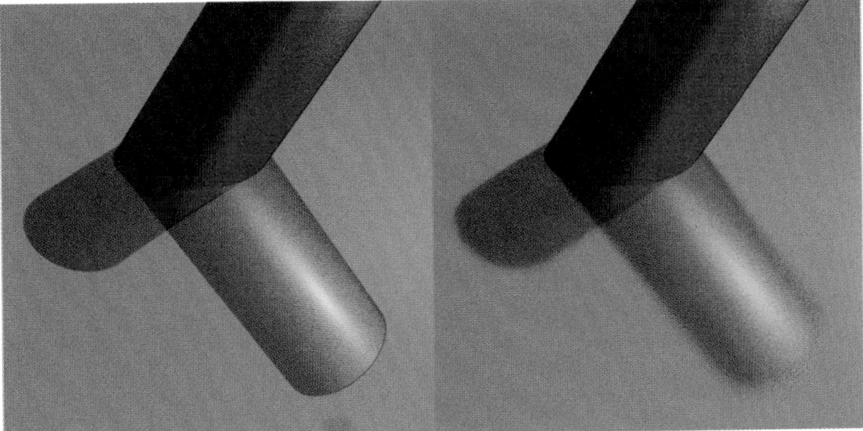

Figure 12.12 (Left) Dgs_material with reflection and refraction controlled by Specular attribute. (Right) Same material with reflection and refraction controlled by Glossy attribute. This scene is included on the CD as `dgs_material.ma`.

If Shiny is set to 0, Shiny U and Shiny V are enabled. Shiny U and Shiny V control the U and V scale of an anisotropic glossy highlight. The Transp attribute determines the transparency. The Index Of Refraction attribute sets the material's index of refraction (this is called Ior in version 8.5).

If Specular and Glossy are used in conjunction, their values are added together and thus produce more intense reflections and refractions. However, the sharpness of the reflection or refraction is controlled by Glossy and Shiny. *Glossy*, as a 3D term, refers to a surface that creates imperfect reflections (one that is less smooth than a specular surface and less rough than a diffuse surface).

Using Dielectric_material

The Dielectric_material shader re-creates a material that is a poor conductor of electricity. Real-world dielectric materials include ceramics, plastics, glass, and some liquids, such as water. In addition, the Dielectric_material shader replicates the interaction between photons and dielectric material boundaries (known as interfaces). Based on angles of incidence and refractive indices of the involved interface materials, a photon will either transmit (refract) through the second material or reflect internally through the first material (see Figure 12.13). The shader refers to the first material as the "inside" material and the second material as the "outside" material. The shader employs Fresnel equations and Snell's Law to determine transmission and reflectance qualities (for more information, see Chapter 4).

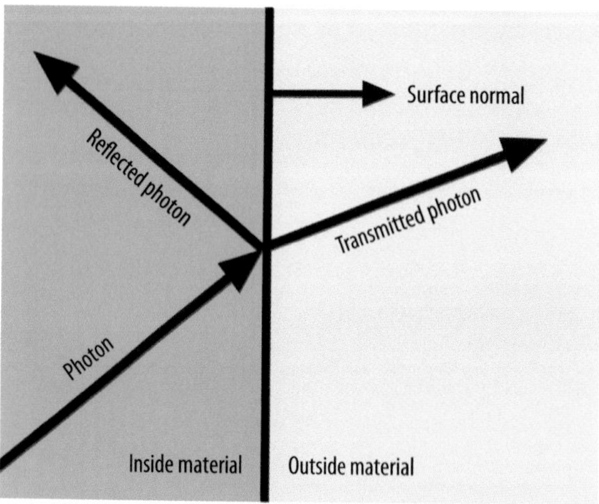

Figure 12.13 The mental ray Dielectric_material shading model

For additional realism, the shader incorporates Beer's Law, which relates the absorption of light by a material to the properties of the material. Thus, the Dielectric_material shader is perhaps the most physically accurate material available in Maya. The attributes for Dielectric_material follow:

Col Represents the percentage of light that will *not* be absorbed when traveling through one world unit of the base or "inside" material. For example, if Col is set to 0.9, 10 percent of the light is absorbed per world unit.

Index Of Refraction The index of refraction for the inside material (called Ior in version 8.5).

Outside Color If Outside Color is set to default white, the interface is assumed to be dielectric-to-air. Thus, the "outside" material, which is air, does not cause a loss of light energy. If Outside Color is set to a color other than white (which equates to a value other than 1), the interface is assumed to be dielectric-to-dielectric. Thus, Outside Color represents the percentage of light that will *not* be absorbed by the outside material that light interacts with after exiting the inside material. The location of the outside material is defined by the normals of the assigned surface (see Figure 12.13). (This attribute is called Col_out in version 8.5.)

Outside Index Of Refraction The refractive index of the outside material (called Ior_Out in version 8.5).

Ignore_normals Bases the entry or exit of light rays through a material on a fixed number and not the alignment of the normals on the surface. This attribute may produce superior results if the model is intricate or otherwise poorly crafted.

Phong Coefficient Controls the intensity of the specular highlight.

Due to its physical accuracy, the Dielectric_material shader has a natural advantage when rendering glass. For example, when the water glass created in Chapter 11 is assigned to a Dielectric_material, it gains more accurate caustic hot spots at the base (see Figure 12.14). Global Illumination is not required.

The main disadvantage of Dielectric_material, and many other mental ray shaders, is the limited number of available attributes. For instance, there's no interactive way to alter the shape or color of the specular highlight of a Dielectric_material shader.

Figure 12.14 (Left) The water glass assigned to a Dielectric_material shader. (Right) The same glass assigned to an Anisotropic material. The left scene is included on the CD as `dielectric_glass.ma`.

Note: If you are replicating a glass filled with liquid, three different Dielectric_ material shaders are necessary. The first shader, assigned to the outside surface of the glass, re-creates the dielectric-to-air interface. The second shader, assigned to the portion of the liquid surface that touches the air, re-creates a separate dielectric-to-air interface. The third shader, assigned to the portion of the glass surface that touches the liquid, re-creates the dielectric-to-dielectric, liquid-to-glass interface.

Using "Mib" Shaders

Shaders that carry the "Mib" prefix represent common shading models. "Mib" shaders are found in the Materials section of the Create mental ray Nodes menu.

Mib_illum_lambert, Mib_illum_blinn, and Mib_illum_phong are stripped-down variations of their namesakes. Each of the shaders carries a Diffuse attribute, which is similar to the attribute carried by Maya materials. Since "Mib" shaders do not possess a Color attribute, you must adjust the Diffuse attribute to change the color. In addition, Mib_illum_lambert, Mib_illum_blinn, and Mib_illum_phong offer Ambience and Ambient attributes. Ambience is a multiplier for Ambient, which is equivalent to the Ambient Color attribute used by Maya materials.

Mib_illum_blinn adds Roughness and Index Of Refraction attributes. Roughness controls the size of the specular highlight. Index Of Refraction does not require transparency or raytracing to function; instead, it emulates the index of refraction that all real-world materials possess, including solids such as metals. (For example, titanium has a 2.16 refractive index.) Index Of Refraction affects the intensity of the specular highlight. To create an intense specular highlight with Mib_illum_blinn, raise Index Of Refraction above the default maximum of 2 and lower the Roughness value.

Mib_illum_phong is similar to Mib_illum_blinn, but replaces Roughness and Index Of Refraction with the Exponent attribute, which controls the size of the specular highlight.

Mib_illum_cooktorr uses the Cook-Torrance shading model and is a physically-based shader. The color of the shader's specular highlight is dependent on the material quality, light color, and the light's incident angle to the assigned surface. Thus, if the surface is animated, the specular highlight is prone to shift in color as it appears at different points along the surface. Mib_illum_cooktorr offers additional control over the specular highlight quality by splitting the Index Of Refraction into Red, Green, and Blue channels. You can assign a different value to each channel and thus make the highlight sensitive to light color. For example, if the light color is pure red and the Index Of Refraction Red attribute is set to 20, the highlight is intense. However, if the light shifts to a green color and the Index Of Refraction Green attribute is set to 1.5, the highlight is dull.

"Mib" shaders share the Mode attribute, which serves as a per-material light-linking system (see Figure 12.15). You can map lights and thereby list them with the Lights[*n*] attribute of the "Mib" material. You can follow two methods to achieve this:

- In the Light Linking section of the shader, switch Mode to Inclusive Linking or Exclusive Linking. The Lights subsection appears. Click the checkered Map button beside the Lights[0] attribute. The Create Light window opens. Select a light type from the list. The light is created at 0, 0, 0 and is listed in the Light[0] field.

- As an alternative, open the Hypershade window. MMB-drag the shader into the work area. Open the Hypergraph Hierarchy window. MMB-drag a light transform node into the Hypershade work area and drop it on top of the shader icon. Choose Other from the Connect Input Of menu. The Connection Editor opens. In the left column, click Message. If Message is not visible, choose Left Display > Show Hidden from the Connection Editor menu. In the right column, click Lights[0] (listed under Lights). Exit the Connection Editor. The light is listed in the Lights[0] field of the shader's Attribute Editor tab. Each time you connect a light, a new Lights[*n*] attribute appears, where *n* is a consecutive number.

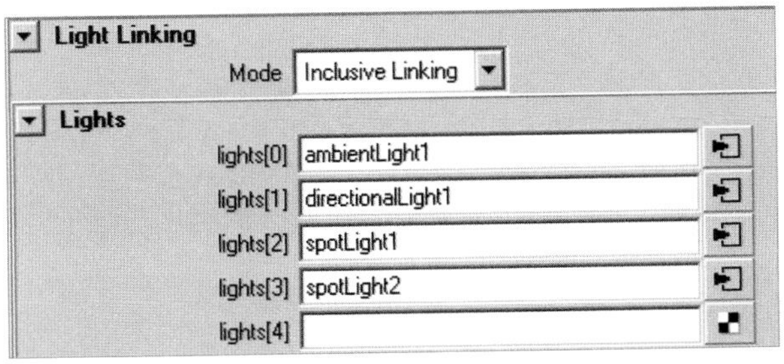

Figure 12.15 The Mode attribute and Lights section of a "Mib" shader. Four lights are listed with the shader.

If Mode is set to Inclusive Linking, only the lights listed with the shader are used to render the assigned surface. If Mode is set to Exclusive Linking, only the lights *not* listed with the shader are used to render the assigned surface. If Mode is set to the default Maya Linking, standard Maya linking, as determined by the Relationship Editor, is utilized.

With Maya 8.5, the Mode attribute is dependent on numeric values. If Mode is set to 0, all the lights in the scene are used to render the shader. If Mode is set to 1, only the lights listed with the shader are used. If Mode is set to 2, only lights *not* listed with the shader are used.

Using "Misss" Shaders

"Misss" shaders undertake subsurface scattering (SSS) by allowing light to penetrate the surface of a translucent object. Translucency is emulated by the Translucence, Translucence Depth, and Translucence Focus attributes of common Maya materials, but is not as physically accurate as "Misss" shaders. Seven "Misss" shaders are offered by mental ray; the most commonly used ones are detailed in this section.

The Misss_fast_simple_maya shader follows its name by providing efficient SSS renders. To apply this shader, follow these steps:

1. Create a primitive surface. Create a light and place it behind the surface so it points through the surface toward the perspective camera.

2. Open the Hypershade window. Switch the Create Maya Nodes menu to Create mental ray Nodes by clicking the down arrow above the left column of material icons. Click the Misss_fast_simple_maya icon. A custom network is automatically created by Maya. Select the Misss_fast_simple_maya shader icon in the Materials tab and assign it to the surface. Create a test render with mental ray. The light penetrates the surface.
3. To reduce the distance through the surface that the light penetrates, open the Misss_fast_simple_maya shader in the Attribute Editor and reduce the Back SSS Depth attribute (in the Subsurface Scattering Layer section). For example, at the left of Figure 12.16 only a portion of a polygon shape receives scattered light; Back SSS Depth is set to a value less than the length of the shape.

Figure 12.16 (Left) Due to a small Back SSS Depth value, only a portion of a polygon shape receives scattered light. This scene is included on the CD as `misss_shape.ma`. (Right) Front SSS Color, set to red, and Back SSS Color, set to green, tints a torus. This scene is included on the CD as `misss_torus.ma`.

4. To adjust the color of the surface that receives no scattered light, change Diffuse Color (in the Unscattered Diffuse Layer section). To adjust the specular highlight, adjust the Specular Color and Shininess attributes (in the Specular Layer section). To alter the color of the penetrating light, change Front SSS Color and Back SSS Color (in the Subsurface Scattering Layer section). Front SSS Color determines the color of the scattered light as it enters the surface. Back SSS Color determines the color of the scattered light as it exits the surface. (Front SSS Color and Back SSS Color are dependent on the camera's point-of-view.) For example, at the right of Figure 12.16 a light is placed in the center of a torus. Front SSS Color is set to red and Back SSS Color is set to green.
5. To remove graininess from the image, expand the Lightmap section and slowly increase the Samples attribute by powers of 2 (32, 64, 128, 256, and so on).

The network created for Misss_fast_simple_maya, illustrated by Figure 12.17, is similar to those created for Misss_fast_skin_maya and Misss_fast_shader. The network includes the following key components:

mentalrayTexture This node writes out a mental ray light map. Light maps are "baked" textures that encode lighting information. When using mental ray SSS, a light map is mandatory.

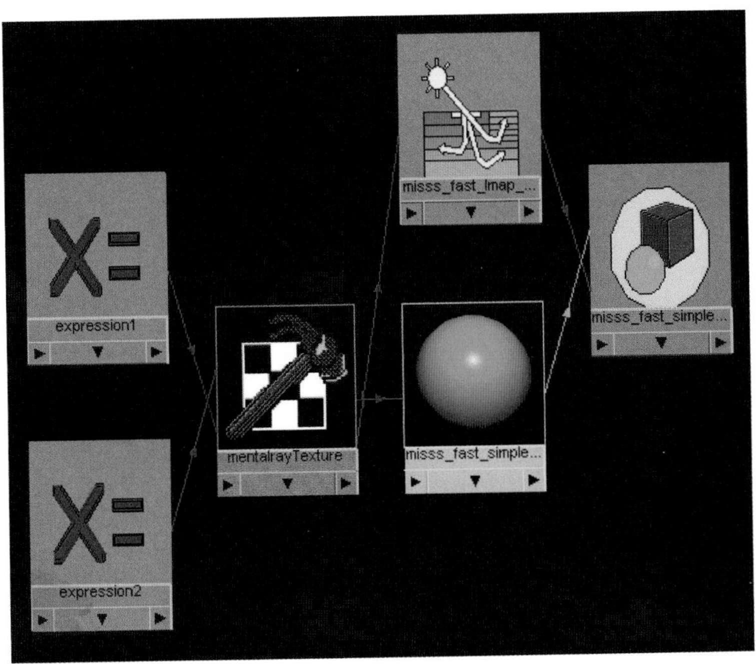

Figure 12.17 The network created for a Misss_fast_simple_maya shader

Misss_fast_lmap_maya This node samples the light map written by the mentalrayTexture node.

Expression nodes Two expression nodes provide values to the File Size Height and File Size Width attributes of the mentalrayTexture node. The mental ray renderer requires that the File Size Width be exactly twice that of the Width attribute found in the Render Settings window.

The Misss_fast_skin_maya shader provides additional attributes to emulate human skin. These include epidermal and subdermal controls. Misss_fast_shader is designed to work with more complex networks that contain the additional SSS shaders, such as Misss_set_normal and Misss_skin_specular.

Using Lens Shaders

The mental ray renderer provides several lens shaders that affect the way in which light travels through the virtual camera lens. For example, Mia_lens_bokeh creates mental ray depth-of-field (see Figure 12.18). *Bokeh* is a photographic term that refers to the out-of-focus quality of an image.

Figure 12.18 Depth-of-field is provided by the Mia_lens_bokeh shader. This scene is included on the CD as `mental_dof.ma`.

To use this shader with Maya 2008, follow these steps:

1. Open the Attribute Editor tab for the camera that is to be rendered. Expand the mental ray section. Click the checkered Map button beside the Lens Shader attribute. Select Mia_lens_bokeh from the mental ray tab of the Create Render Node window. You can find the shader in the Lenses section.
2. Open the Attribute Editor tab for the Mia_lens_bokeh shader. Adjust the Plane attribute, which determines the world distance to objects in focus, and the Radius attribute, which sets the amount of blur (or size of the "circles of confusion"). To improve the quality of the blur, incrementally increase the Samples value.

Physical_lens_dof also creates depth-of-field, but offers only two attributes—Plane and Radius. In order to make the final render suitably smooth with Physical_lens_dof, high Min Sample Level and Max Sample Level values may be required. Physical_lens_dof is compatible with Maya 8.5 and 2008.

Note: The Mia_exposure_simple and Mia_exposure_photographic shaders, listed in the Lenses section of the mental ray tab of the Create Render Node window, are designed for tone mapping and high dynamic range images; they are discussed in Chapter 13.

Using Environment Shaders

Maya cameras carry Lens Shader, Volume Shader, and Environment Shader attributes in the mental ray section of their Attribute Editor tab. As seen in the previous section, the Lens Shader attribute supports mental ray lens shaders. The Volume Shader attribute is designed for volume effects, and is discussed in the next section. You can use the Environment Shader attribute to create effects that automatically involve all objects within the scene. The first approach to using Environment Shader involves the application of an environment lighting system through the use of Mia_physicalsky. The second method involves using a mental ray environment shader.

Mia_physicalsky creates physically accurate outdoor lighting. Although Mia_physicalsky is listed in the lens shader category, you must map it to the Environment Shader attribute. In addition, you must map Mia_physicalsun to the Light Shader attribute of a directional light, which represents the incoming sunlight. The Light Shader attribute is located in the Custom Shaders subsection of the mental ray section in the light's Attribute Editor tab. The Mia_physicalsun shader is located in Mental-Ray Lights section of the Create Render Node window. Most important, Mia_physicalsky requires Final Gather to render (Final Gather is discussed later in this chapter).

Both Mia_physicalsky and Mia_physicalsun carry attributes that re-create atmospheric conditions, such as Haze, Red-Blue Shift, and Horizon Height. When adjusting the attribute values, it's recommended that the same values be applied to any attribute that matches between the two shaders. As an example, the shaders are applied to a scene in Figure 12.19. The decaying shadows, specular caustics at the base of the house, and the green haze over the background are automatically generated.

MODEL BY INKEV1961

Figure 12.19 Mia_physicalsky and Mia_physicalsun shaders provide physically accurate outdoor lighting. A simplified version of this scene is included on the CD as `physical_sky.ma`.

The mental ray renderer provides six environment shaders. You can map each shader to the Environment Shader attribute of the rendering camera. They function in a manner similar to Maya environment textures. For example, Mib_lookup_spherical creates an infinite sphere to which a texture can be mapped. The mapped texture appears in reflections and refractions (assuming the reflective/refractive surface is not surrounded by other surfaces). Although the texture appears in the background of the render, it is not present in the alpha channel. In this way, Mib_lookup_spherical functions like the Env Sphere texture. Mib_lookup_spherical, however, cannot be mapped with a Maya texture. Instead, you must map the shader's Texture attribute with a mentalrayTexture node. In fact, when you click the checkered Map button beside the Texture attribute, a mentalrayTexture node is connected automatically. You can then choose a bitmap file by clicking the mentalrayTexture node's Image Name attribute Browse button.

Mib_lookup_cube6 is equivalent to Env Cube. Mib_lookup_cube1 uses a cube projection, but wraps a single texture around the six walls. Mib_lookup_cylindrical is a cylindrical variation. Mib_lookup_background fits a texture to the camera view on a virtual plane. Mia_envblur, available with Maya 2008, is designed to blur other environment shaders. For example, Mia_envblur is mapped to the Environment Shader attribute of a camera. In turn, Mib_lookup_spherical is mapped to the Environment attribute of Mia_envblur. The result is a blurred environment texture that appears in reflections (see Figure 12.20).

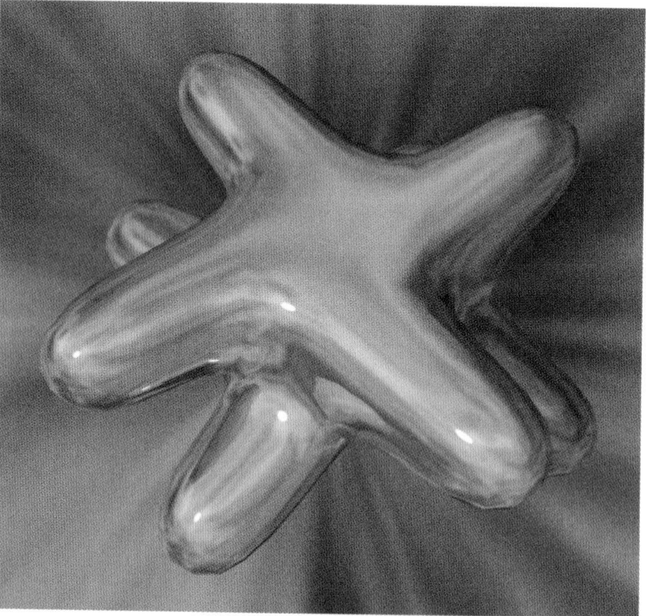

Figure 12.20 Mia_envblur and Mib_lookup_spherical create a blurred environment texture that appears in reflections. This scene is included on the CD as `mia_envblur.ma`.

Using Mib_volume and Parti_volume

Mib_volume and Parti_volume shaders create a volume fog effect within a closed surface. You can find both shaders in the Volumetric Materials section of the Create mental ray Nodes menu. To apply either shader, you must map it to the Volume Shader attribute of the shading group node assigned to a surface. If the shading group node is also connected to a Maya material through the Surface Material attribute, the

Transparency value of the Maya material must be increased for the volume material to be seen.

Mib_volume is an extremely simple fog that carries two attributes: Color and Max. Color represents the color of the fog and Max controls the density. A Max value of 0 will equal 100 percent density. A Max value greater than 8 will create close to 0 percent density.

Parti_volume is a more advanced material that supplies additional attributes to control light scattering and nonuniformity.

Note: Volume materials and effects often refer to the replication of "participating media." Participating media are any media that scatter light. This would include fog, clouds, smoke, ocean water, and so on.

Preparing mental ray Shaders for Global Illumination

If a mental ray shader is used with Global Illumination or caustics, it will be ignored by the photon tracing process unless a connection is made to the Photon Shader attribute of the shading group to which the shader belongs. Maya 8.5 and Maya 2008 treat this necessity in slightly different ways.

With version 2008, some mental ray shaders, such as Dgs_material and Transmat, are automatically connected to both the Material Shader and Photon Shader attributes of a shading group node when they are created. Other shaders, such as those with the "Mib" prefix, are only connected to the Material Shader. With version 8.5, all shaders are connected to the Material Shader attribute, leaving Photon Shader open. In fact, mental ray provides four "sister" photonic shaders that may be used in this situation: Dgs_material_photon, Dielectric_material_photon, Transmat_photon, and Parti_volume_photon. Each corresponds directly to its material or volumetric material namesake. For example, if you want to photon trace with Dielectric_material, you can map Dielectric_material_photon to the Photon Shader attribute of the shading group node (see Figure 12.21). Dgs_material_photon, Dielectric_material_photon, and Transmat_photon are located in the Photonic Materials section of the Create mental ray Nodes menu. Parti_volume_photon is located in the Photon Volumetric Materials section.

Whether a sister photonic shader or a standard shader is mapped to the Photon Shader attribute of the shading group, it is important to match input attributes. That is, the attributes fed to Material Shader and Photon Shader should match. For example, if Dgs_material has a Shiny value of 50 and is mapped to Material Shader, then Dgs_material_photon should have a Shiny value of 50 as it is mapped to Photon Shader.

The mental ray renderer also provides a generic photon shader, Mib_photon_basic, which functions when paired with Dgs_material, Dielectric_material, and various "Mib" materials. Although this pairing cannot provide matched sets of attributes, Mib_photon_basic works well for simple Global Illumination renders.

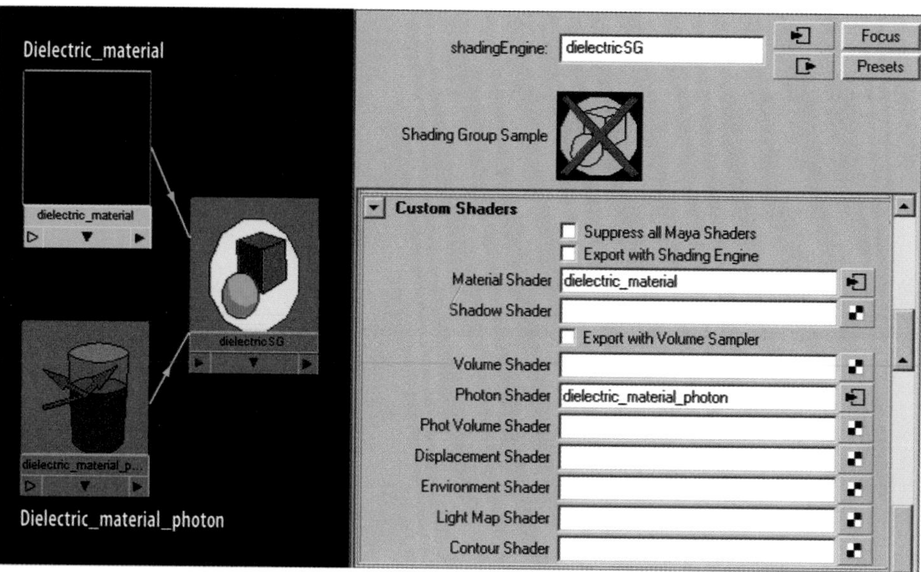

Figure 12.21 Dielectric_material and Dielectric_material_photon materials connected to a shading group node

Two additional attributes are provided by mental ray for rendering volume materials: Accuracy and Radius. These attributes are found in the Photon Volume subsection of the Caustics And Global Illumination section of the mental ray tab in the Render Settings window. You can use these attributes to control photon tracing with Mib_volume and Parti_volume materials. Descriptions of each follow:

Accuracy Sets the maximum number of neighboring photon hits included in the color estimate of a single photon hit. The higher the value, the more refined the render. (This attribute is named Photon Volume Accuracy in version 8.5.)

Radius Controls the maximum distance from a photon hit that the renderer will seek out neighboring photon hits to determine the color of the hit in question. The default value of 0 allows Maya to automatically pick a radius based on the scene size. (This attribute is named Photon Volume Radius in version 8.5.)

Using Final Gather

Although Final Gather is often used in conjunction with Global Illumination, it is not the same system. Final Gather employs a specialized variation of raytracing in which each camera eye ray intersection creates sets of Final Gather rays. The Final Gather rays are sent out in a random direction within a hemisphere (see Figure 12.22). When a Final Gather ray intersects a new surface, the light energy of the newly intersected point and its potential contribution to the surface intersected by the camera eye ray are noted. The net sum of Final Gather ray intersections stemming from a single camera eye ray intersection is referred to as a Final Gather point. The Final Gather points are stored in a Final Gather map and are eventually added to the direct illumination color calculations. The end result is a render that is able to include bounced light and color bleed.

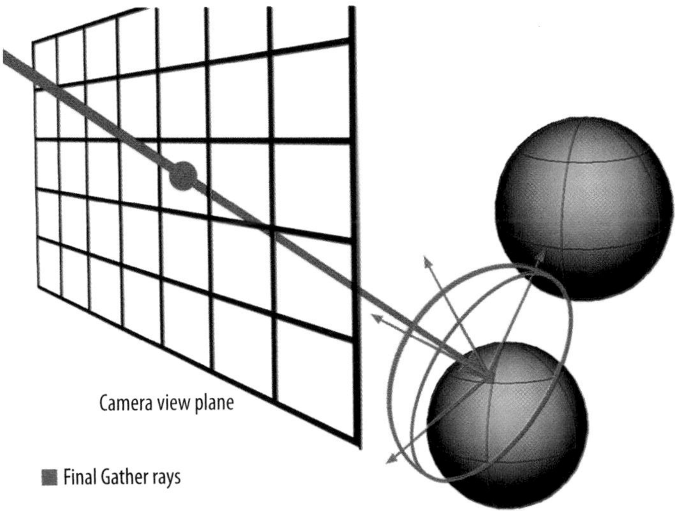

Figure 12.22
A simplified representation of the Final Gather process

During a render, the creation of Final Gather points occurs in two stages. During the first stage, which is precomputational, camera eye rays are projected in a hexagonal pattern from the camera view. Wherever a camera eye ray intersects a surface, a Final Gather point is created. In the second stage, which occurs during the visible render, additional Final Gather points are generated whenever the point density is discovered to be insufficient to calculate a particular pixel.

Ultimately, Final Gather is an efficient alternative to Global Illumination. Final Gather is particularly well suited for scenes in which diffuse lighting is desirable. For example, in Figure 12.23 a character is lit with a single spot light from frame right. The Maya Software render of the scene produces dark shadows. The Final Gather render, however, brightens the dark areas with "bounced" light. In addition, the yellow of the wall and the red of the stage spotlight "bleed" onto the character's hair, cheek, and torso.

Figure 12.23 (Left) Scene rendered with the Maya Software renderer. (Right) Same scene rendered with mental ray Final Gather.

Adjusting Final Gather Attributes

For the Final Gather system to work, the Raytracing and Final Gathering attributes must be checked in the Secondary Effects subsection of the Rendering Features section of the mental ray tab. In addition, Final Gather has a number of unique attributes in the Final Gathering section (see Figure 12.24).

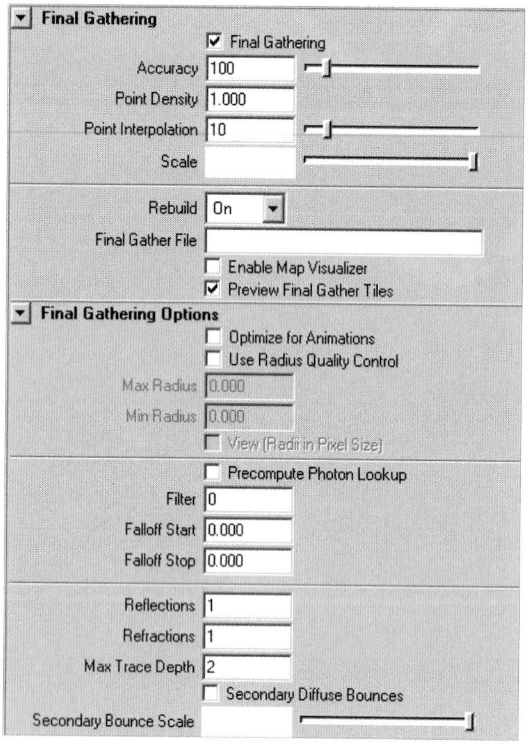

Figure 12.24
The Final Gathering section of the mental ray tab in the Render Settings window

Accuracy Sets the number of Final Gather rays fired off at each camera eye ray intersection. Decreasing this value will shorten the render but will introduce noise and other artifacts. Values less than 200 will work for most test renders, while the maximum of 1024 is designed for final renders. This attribute is named Final Gather Rays in earlier versions.

Point Density Serves as a multiplier for the density of the projected hexagonal grid created during the pre-render stage. Values between 1 and 2 generally suffice. Higher values increase the amount of detail.

Point Interpolation Sets the number of Final Gather points that are required to shade any given pixel. Higher values produce smoother results.

Scale Serves as a multiplier for the Final Gather contribution to the render. You can tint the contribution by choosing a nonwhite color.

Rebuild and Final Gather File If Rebuild is set to On, a new Final Gather map is computed for each rendered frame. If Rebuild is set to Off, the renderer will use the preexisting Final Gather map listed in the Final Gather File attribute field. The map file is stored in the `Project_Directory/renderData/mentalray/finalgMap/` folder. If Rebuild is set to Freeze, the renderer will rely on the Final Gather map calculated for the first frame of an animation and will not update the map as the animation progresses.

Enable Map Visualizer Creates a mapViz and mapVizShape node when a Final Gather frame is rendered. You can view the map listed in the Final Gather File attribute field with the mental ray Map Visualizer (see "Reviewing Photon Hits" earlier in this chapter). Final Gather points are displayed as dots in the workspace view. Point Size and Normal Scale attributes in the Map Visualizer window control the size of the dots and their corresponding surface normals.

The following attributes are found in the Final Gathering Options subsection:

Optimize For Animations If checked, averages Final Gather points across multiple frames. This option reduces the flickering sometimes present with Final Gather renders.

Use Radius Quality Control, Min Radius, and Max Radius If Use Radius Quality Control is checked, Min Radius and Max Radius become available. Min Radius and Max Radius define the region in which Final Gather points are averaged to determine the color of a pixel. If an insufficient number of points are discovered within a region, additional points are created during the render for that region. (The number of required points is determined by the Point Interpolation attribute.) Maya's documentation suggests that the Max Radius should be no larger than 10 percent of the scene's bounding box. Along those lines, the Min Radius should be no more than 10 percent of the Max Radius. If a scene involves intricate or convoluted geometry, however, you can decrease the Min Radius and Max Radius to improve quality. The default value of 0 for both attributes allows Maya to select a Min Radius and Max Radius based on the scene bounding box.

View (Radii In Pixel Size) Forces the Min Radius and Max Radius attributes to operate in screen pixel size. The attribute offers an intuitive alternative to the measurement of the scene in world space.

Precompute Photon Lookup Turns on special photon tracing. In a prerender process, a photon map is created with an estimate of local energies in the scene. The map is used to reduce the number of needed Final Gather points. This attribute will slow the prerender but will speed up the actual render.

Filter Controls a special filter that eliminates or reduces speckles created by skewed Final Gather samples. If a surface in a scene is brightly lit, it can unduly influence energy calculations when intersected by Final Gather rays. A value of 0 turns the filter off. Values between 1 and 4 will soften the render somewhat but will reduce artifacts.

Falloff Start and Falloff Stop Define the world distance from a camera eye ray intersection that Final Gather rays are allowed to travel. Thus, these attributes determine the size of the hemispherical region associated with a Final Gather point (see Figure 12.22 earlier in this chapter). If a Final Gather ray reaches the Falloff Stop distance before intersecting a new surface, the contribution of the ray is derived from the camera's Background Color attribute.

Max Trace Depth Sets the number of subrays created when a Final Gather ray intersects a reflective or refractive surface. A default value of 0 kills the Final Gather ray as soon as it intersects a surface (although the energy contribution from that intersection is noted). A value of 1 allows a Final Gather ray to generate one additional reflection *or* refraction subray. Since Final Gather rays are simply searching for surfaces that might contribute light energy, the Max Trace Depth attribute can be left at 1 or 0 with satisfactory results for most renders.

Reflections and Refractions Respectively set the number of reflection and refraction subrays created when a Final Gather ray intersects a reflective or refractive surface. These attributes are overridden by the Max Trace Depth attribute, which controls the total number of subrays permitted per ray intersection. Reflections and Refractions were previously named Trace Reflections and Trace Refractions.

Secondary Diffuse Bounces When checked, allows indirect diffuse lighting to influence Final Gather points. This attribute is useful for adding light to dark corners or simply increasing the amount of color bleed. Secondary Diffuse Bounces will slow the render significantly. The Secondary Bounce Scale attribute serves as a multiplier for the indirect diffuse lighting intensity.

Using Irradiance

Final Gather does not require lights to render a scene. The system can use irradiance alone. Technically speaking, irradiance is a measure of the rate of flow of electromagnetic energy, such as light, from a per-unit area of a surface. The Ambient Color and Incandescence attributes of standard Maya materials represent irradiance.

For example, in Figure 12.25 a scene is rendered with Final Gather. The Enable Default Light attribute is unchecked in the Render Options section of the Common tab of the Render Settings window. A Fractal texture with an orange Color Gain attribute is mapped to a Blinn's Incandescence attribute, which provides the only light for the scene. Although the ground plane is assigned to a second Blinn material with Ambient Color and Incandescence values set to 0, it reflects the orange energy.

In addition, standard Maya materials carry Irradiance and Irradiance Color attributes in the mental ray section of their Attribute Editor tab. If the Irradiance attribute is mapped, the map becomes an irradiant light source. Irradiance Color serves as a multiplier for the resulting irradiant light.

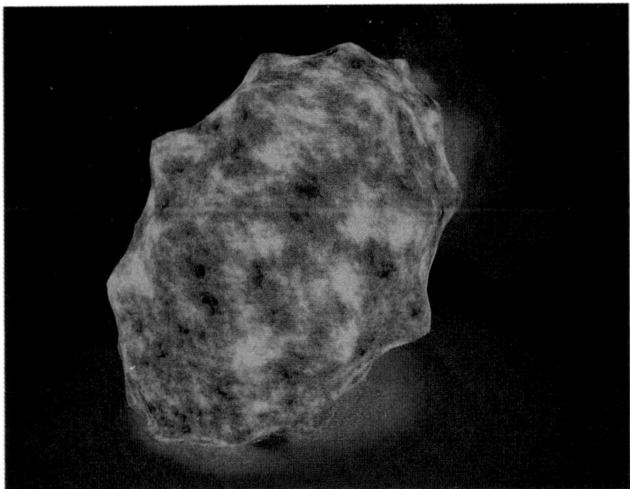

Figure 12.25 A primitive object lights a scene with orange irradiance. This scene is included on the CD as `irradiance.ma`.

You can view irradiant Final Gather points, as well as Final Gather points in general, through the mental ray Map Visualizer window. If a valid Final Gather map is listed in the Map File Name field, the points are automatically displayed in the workspace view as colored dots. The Point Size attribute controls the size. Search Radius Scale controls the density of displayed points; in most cases, it is not necessary to adjust this attribute.

Fine-Tuning mental ray Renders

Although there are no hard and fast rules regarding the simultaneous use of Global Illumination, Final Gather, and caustics, the incremental application of each will make the process less painful. If time limitations prevent the proper application of the Global Illumination process, you can simulate indirect illumination with Maya volume lights and the Maya Software renderer.

Rendering the Cornell Box

To demonstrate Global Illumination, Final Gather, and caustics, we'll use a variation of the famous Cornell Box (created at the Cornell University Program of Computer Graphics in 1984 to test physical-based lighting techniques). This particular box contains two point lights (see Figure 12.26). The Intensity attributes of the lights are left at 1. The floating C shape is assigned to a transparent Blinn with a Refractive Index set to 1.5. The camera's Background Color attribute is set to light red.

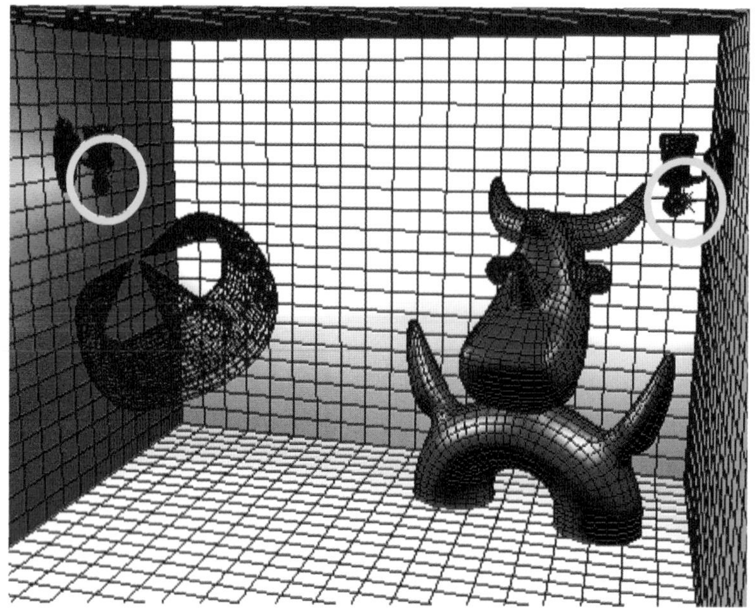

Figure 12.26 A Cornell Box. Yellow circles indicate the positions of two point lights. This scene is included on the CD as `box_start.ma`.

In the first step of the process, the Render Using attribute of the Render Settings window is switched to mental ray. The Quality Presets attribute is changed to Preview: Global Illumination, which checks on the Global Illumination and Ray Tracing attributes. Emit Photons is checked for each light. The lights produce the default 10,000 photons with a default Photon Intensity of 8000. The resulting render has visible photon hits. In addition, the white walls are a dingy gray (see Figure 12.27).

Figure 12.27 The Cornell Box is rendered with preview-quality Global Illumination settings. This scene is included on the CD as `box_step1.ma`.

Since the scene is 10 units high, we'll change the Radius attribute (found in the Global Illumination Options subsection) to 5. (To derive an appropriate value, we'll use the formula listed in the "Adjusting Global Illumination Attributes" section earlier in this chapter.) Since the scene is a bit dim, we'll raise each point light's Intensity to 1.25. The resulting render is significantly smoother (see Figure 12.28).

Figure 12.28 The Radius attribute in the Global Illumination Options section is changed to 5. This scene is included on the CD as `box_step2.ma`.

To increase the realism of the glass C-shape object, we'll adjust the Raytracing section of the mental ray tab. We'll change Reflections to 4, Refractions to 4, and Max Trace Depth to 6; this will allow light to bounce around the scene for a greater length of time. To create a caustic hot spot beside the C-shape, we'll check the Caustics attribute in the Caustics And Global Illumination section of the mental ray tab.

To create a more believable connection between the blue abstract shape and the floor, we'll check the Use Ray Trace Shadows attribute for each light. Although many Cornell Box simulations rely on indirect lighting to create dark areas, raytraced shadows adds an extra level of realism with minimal effort. To make the shadows acceptably soft, we'll set the lights' Light Radius to 2, Shadow Rays to 40, and the Ray Depth Limit to 10. In the resulting render, the blue shape gains a solid contact shadow (see Figure 12.29). A caustic hot spot also appears below the C-shape; unfortunately, individual caustic photons hits are visible.

Figure 12.29 The Cornell box receives caustics and raytraced shadows. This scene is included on the CD as `box_step3.ma`.

To improve the overall quality of the Global Illumination, we'll raise the Global Illum Photons of each light to 25,000. Since there are more photons in the scene, we'll reduce the Radius (in the Global Illumination Options subsection of the Render Settings window) by half (giving us a value of 2.5). We'll also raise the Caustic Photons of each light to 25,000. We'll change the Radius (in the Caustics Options subsection) to 2.5, thus matching the Global Illum Photons. As for other Render Settings window attributes, we'll switch Caustic Filter Type to Cone, Accuracy (directly below the Global Illumination check box) to 1000, and Accuracy (directly below the Caustics check box) to 500. The resulting render shows a significant improvement in the quality of the caustic. However, there are still a few errant caustic photon hits the near the C-shape (see Figure 12.30).

To smooth out the few remaining photon hits, we'll check Final Gathering in the Secondary Effects subsection of the Rendering Features section of the mental ray tab and leave the Final Gathering attributes at the default values. The resulting render is now clean enough to call final (see Figure 12.31).

The Final Gather process thoroughly blends the photon hits. In some situations, Final Gather can make the color bleed extremely subtle. For example, in Figure 12.31 the red and green bleed on the white wall is so faint that it can barely be detected. Nevertheless, the result, particularly around the blue shape, is convincing.

Figure 12.30 The overall accuracy is improved by increasing the number of photons. Nevertheless, a few caustic photon hits are faintly visible, as indicated by the yellow circles. This scene is included on the CD as `box_step4.ma`.

Figure 12.31 The final render with Final Gather. This scene is included on the CD as `box_final.ma`.

Rendering the Cornell Box with Maya Software

You can replicate indirect lighting and the mental ray Global Illumination system with Maya volume and ambient lights. Although the result is not perfect, the render is often close enough to meet the aesthetic demand of a project that is on a tight deadline. For example, in Figure 12.32 the Cornell Box is rendered with the Maya Software renderer with Raytracing checked. The overall lighting is similar to the one rendered with Global Illumination and Final Gather (see Figure 12.31).

To achieve this, five volume lights and one ambient light are placed in the scene (see Figure 12.33). Two large volume lights are placed next to the wall lamps. Their Intensity is set to 2. Two smaller volume lights are placed near the ceiling. Their Intensity is set to 0.2 and their Color attributes are set to red and green. These lights create a false color bleed. One last volume light is placed in the center of the box with an Intensity of 0.2. This volume light creates a soft fill. Volume lights, by their very nature, have a built-in falloff, which is easily adjusted by scaling the light shape up or down. To fill in the underside of the blue shape, an ambient light is placed near the floor with an Intensity of 0.175.

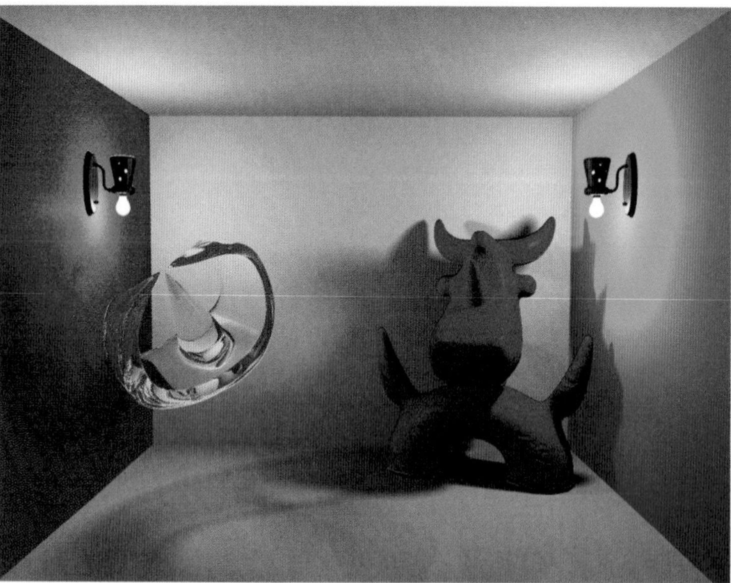

Figure 12.32 The Cornell Box rendered with the Maya Software renderer

The one area in which this technique most noticeably fails is the caustic of the C-shape. The shape's shadow against the left wall is particularly inaccurate. Nevertheless, if caustics are not a critical part of a scene, you can use a similar setup to achieve refined results.

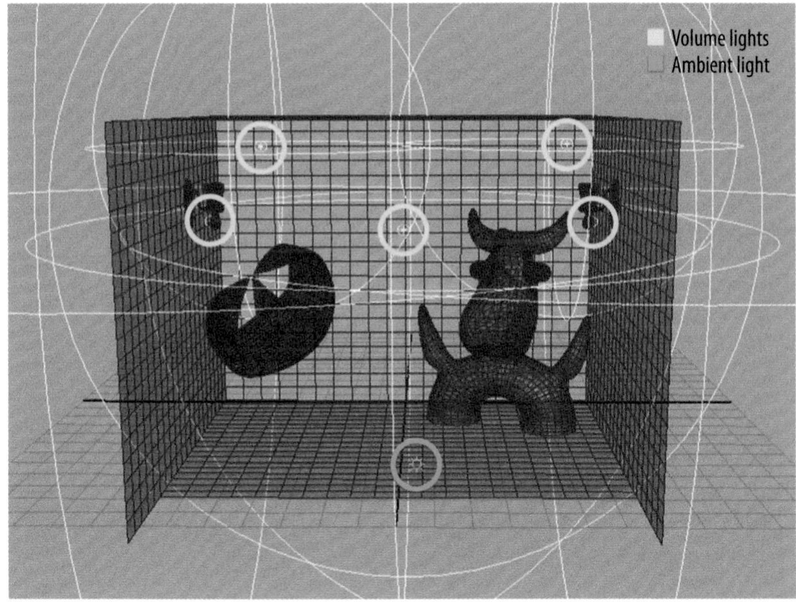

Figure 12.33 Volume and ambient lights are placed in the Cornell Box. This scene is included on the CD as maya_box.ma.

Chapter Tutorial: Creating Caustics with Final Gather

In this section, you will light and render a still life with Final Gather. You will also create a reflective caustic on one of the walls (see Figure 12.34).

1. Open sun_box.ma from the Chapter 12 scene folder on the CD. The scene features a variation of the Cornell Box with three walls and skylight hole.
   In this exercise, all the walls are gray. The floating sun symbol will become reflective metal.
2. Create a spot light and place it directly above the skylight opening. Point the light down so it's perpendicular to the ground. Open the light's Attribute Editor tab. Check Use Depth Map Shadows and change Resolution to 1024. Set the Intensity attribute to 1.5. Check Emit Photons in the Caustic And Global Illumination subsection.
3. Open the Render Settings window. Switch the Render Using attribute to mental ray. Switch Quality Presets to Preview: Final Gather. Change Accuracy (directly below the Final Gathering check box) to 32.
4. Render a test frame. Keep the resolution low at this point. The spot light should strike the sun symbol. Adjust the position of the spot light until it makes an interesting shadow within the box.

Figure 12.34 A skylight creates a reflective caustic.

5. Open the Render Settings window. Check the Caustics attribute in the Caustics And Global Illumination section. Global Illumination is not required to create the caustics. Increase Accuracy (directly below the Final Gathering check box) to 128. It's generally better to increase the various quality settings slowly over multiple test renders.
6. Render a test frame. A yellow caustic should appear on the left wall. Experiment with the placement of the sun symbol to create different caustic patterns.
7. Open the persp camera's Attribute Editor tab. Change the Background Color attribute (in the Environment section) to sky blue. The blue will show up in the sun symbol's reflections. Plus, the color will influence the Final Gather calculations and will ultimately tint the walls. Try different background colors to see what looks the best. Open the spot light's Attribute Editor tab and try different Color values.
8. Open the Render Settings window. Change Accuracy (directly below to the Caustics check box) to 128. Change Accuracy (directly below the Final Gathering check box) to 512. Change Radius, in the Caustics Options subsection, to 0.75. Open the spot light's Attribute Editor tab and incrementally raise Caustic Photons to 50,000. Render a series of tests. Experiment with different (Caustic) Radius and Caustic Photons values. Pick the combination that provides the best-looking caustic.

9. Once you're satisfied with the settings discussed thus far, raise the render resolution to 640 × 480 and the Min Sample Level and Max Sample Level attributes to 0 and 2 respectively. Continue to increase the Accuracy for both Caustics and Final Gather until the walls look smooth. The tutorial is complete! If you'd like to view a final version, open `sun_final.ma` from the Chapter 12 scene folder on the CD.

Texturing and Lighting with Advanced Techniques

You can use high dynamic range (HDR) images to add realism to any render. The RenderMan For Maya plug-in opens up a whole new world of advanced rendering options. The normal mapping process can record details from a high-resolution surface and impart the information to a low-resolution surface. With the Surface Sampler tool, you can create normal maps, displacement maps, and diffuse maps. The Render Layer Editor gives you incredible control over the batch-rendering process.

13

Chapter Contents

Adding Realism with HDRI

HDRI stands for high dynamic range imaging. An HDR image has the advantage of accurately storing the wide dynamic ranges of light intensities found in nature. In addition, Maya supports HDR images as texture bitmaps and can render HDR images with the mental ray renderer. You can even use HDR images to illuminate a scene without the need for lights.

Comparing LDR and HDR Images

A low dynamic range (LDR) image carries a fixed number of bits per channel. For example, the majority of Maya image formats store 8 bits per channel. Maya16 IFF, TIFF16, and SGI16 store 16 bits per channel. Thus, an 8-bit image can store a total of 24 bits and 16,777,216 colors. A 16-bit image can store a total of 48 bits and roughly 281 trillion colors. While it may seem 16,777,216 or 281 trillion colors are satisfactory for any potential image, standard 8-bit and 16-bit LDR images are limited by the necessity to store integer (whole number) values. This translates to an inability to differentiate between finite variations in luminous intensity. For example, a digital camera sensor may recognize that an image pixel should be given a red value of 2.3, while a neighboring pixel should be given a red value of 2.1. LDR image formats must round off and store the red values as 2. In contrast, HDR images do not suffer from such a limitation.

Note: *Luminous intensity* is the light power emitted by a light source or reflected from a material in a particular direction within a defined angle. A bit is the smallest unit of data stored on a computer. Bit depth is simply the description of the number of available bits.

An HDR image stores 32 bits per channel. The bits do not encode integer values, however. Instead, the 32 bits are dedicated to *floating point* values. A floating point takes a fractional number (known as a *mantissa*) and multiplies it by a power of 10 (known as an *exponent*). For example, a floating-point number may be expressed as 7.856e+8, where e+8 is the same as $\times10^8$. In other words, 7.856 is multiplied by 10^8, or 100,000,000, to produce 785,600,000. If the exponent has a negative sign, such as e–8, the decimal travels in the opposite direction and produces 0.00000007856 (e–8 is the same as $\times10^{-8}$). Because HDR images use floating points, they can store values out of reach to LDR images, such as 2.3, 2.1, or even 2.12647634. Thus, HDR images can appropriately store minute variations in luminous intensity.

Note: You can use Maya's Script Editor as a calculator. For example, typing **`pow 10 8;`** in the Script Editor work area and pressing Crtl+Enter produces an answer equivalent to 10^8. (For descriptions of Maya commands, choose Help > Maya Command Reference from the Script Editor menu.) For common math functions, such as add, subtract, multiply, and divide, you can enter a line similar to **`float $test; $test = (1.8 * 10) / (5 - 2.5); print $test;`**.

The architecture of an HDR image makes it perfect for storing a range of exposures within a single file. Hence, the most common use of HDR images is still photography. For example, in Figure 13.1 several exposures of a fluorescent lightbulb are combined into a single HDR image. Any individual exposure, as seen in the top six images in Figure 13.1, cannot capture all the detail of the scene. For instance, in the top-left exposure, the background is properly exposed while the lightbulb is little more than a blown-out flare. However, when the exposures are combined into an HDR image, as is demonstrated at the bottom of Figure 13.1, all portions of the scene are clearly visible.

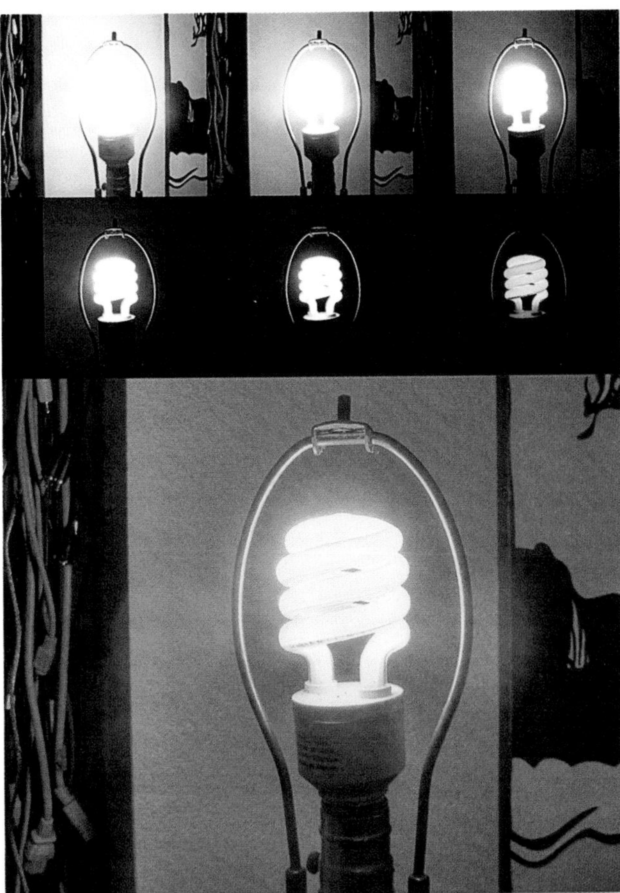

Figure 13.1 (Top) Multiple exposures used to create an HDR image. (Bottom) The resulting HDR image after tone mapping.

The ability to capture multiple exposures within a single file allows for a proper representation of the dynamic range of a subject. When discussing a real-world scene, dynamic range refers to the ratio of minimum to maximum luminous intensity values that are present at a particular location. For example, a brightly lit window in an otherwise dark room may produce a dynamic range of 100,000:1, where the luminous intensity of the light reaching the viewer through the window is 100,000 times greater than the luminous intensity of the light reflected from the dark corner. (On a more technical level, the luminous intensity of any given point in the room or the landscape visible outside the window is measured as *n* cd/m^2, or candela per meter squared; *candela* is the measure of an electromagnetic field.)

Note: On average, the human eye can perceive a dynamic range of 10,000:1 within a single view and perhaps as much as 1,000,000:1 over an extended period of time.

The main disadvantage of HDR images is the inability to simultaneously view all the captured exposure levels on a computer monitor or television. A process known as *tone mapping* is required to view various exposure ranges. Tone mapping is discussed in the section "Displaying HDR Images" later in this chapter. A second disadvantage of HDR images is the difficulty with which an HDR image is created through still photography. Special preparation and software is required. Nevertheless, a demonstration is offered in the section "Using Light Probe Images with the Env Ball Texture" later in this chapter.

Differentiating Bits, Bit Depth, and Dynamic Range

When *bits*, *bit depth*, and *dynamic range* are used to describe a camera or display device, the terms take on different connotations.

When bit depth is used to describe a camera, it refers to the dynamic range capacity of its sensor. For example, a typical digital camera carries a CCD chip that can capture 12 bits per color channel. Therefore, the maximum number of tonal steps that the camera can employ to represent the dynamic range is 4096:1 (based on 2^{12}). In reality, this range is reduced by electronic noise in the system. (Many 12-bit chips only muster a dynamic range of 1000:1.) Thus, the dynamic range for a camera is more accurately described as the ratio of the intensity that saturates the camera to the intensity that lifts the camera response just above its noise level.

When bit depth is used to describe the quality of a display, it refers to the color space capacity of the system graphics processor or card. For instance, most PCs support 32-bit True Color, in which 24 bits are set aside for color and 8 bits are reserved for transparency or other noncolor data. When dynamic range is used to describe the quality of a display, it refers to the ratio of peak white luminance to black-level luminance that a display can produce. For example, an average CRT computer monitor offers a dynamic range of 500:1 to 1000:1. Some LCD and plasma screens fare a little better by producing dynamic ranges closer to 5000:1. Recent developments in LCD technology, as led by BrightSide Technologies and Dolby, promise dynamic ranges of 200,000:1. Regardless of the specific display device, a high bit-depth does not guarantee a high dynamic range and thus the two terms are not intrinsically linked.

An Overview of Supported HDR Formats

Maya supports `.hdr` and OpenEXR image formats. Aside from describing high dynamic range images, the letters *HDR* describe a specific image format that is based on RGBE Radiance files. To differentiate between HDR as a style of image and HDR as a specific image format, I will refer to the image format by its `.hdr` extension. The *E* in RGBE refers to the exponent of the floating point. The Radiance file format was developed by Greg Ward in the late 1980s.

The OpenEXR format was developed by Industrial Light and Magic and was made available to the public in 2002. OpenEXR is extremely flexible and offers both 16-bit and 32-bit floating-point variations. In addition, OpenEXR images can carry an arbitrary number of additional attributes, channels, and render passes (camera color balance information, depth channels, specular passes, motion vectors, and so on). In Maya, OpenEXR is supported by a plug-in. To activate the plug-in, choose Window > Settings/Preferences > Plug-In Manager and activate the Loaded check box for `OpenEXRLoader.mll`. You may then choose OpenEXR (exr), along with HDR (hdr), from the Image Format attribute drop-down list in the Render Setting window so long as mental ray is the renderer of choice. (The Maya Software renderer is unable to render 32-bit, floating-point formats.)

In addition, mental ray is able to read DDS and floating-point TIFF files. DDS stands for DirectDraw Surface and is an image format developed by Microsoft. DDS files are available in 16-bit and 32-bit variations and are commonly used to store textures for games that employ DirectX. Floating-point TIFFs, on the other hand, supply 32 bits per channel. Floating-point TIFFs are widely used in HDR photography, but are often unwieldy for 3D work due to their large file size. (For example, an average `.hdr` image may be 3 megabytes, while the equivalent floating-point TIFF takes up 9 megabytes.) To use DDS images, activate the `ddsFloatReader.mll` plug-in. To use floating-point TIFFs, activate the `tiffFloatReader.mll` plug-in.

Displaying HDR Images

HDR images offer the ability to store huge dynamic ranges. In fact, the RGBE Radiance `.hdr` format can store luminous values between 10^{-38} and 10^{38} cd/m^2. Unfortunately, the entire range cannot be viewed on a computer monitor, which has a significantly lower dynamic range capacity. Thus, in order to view the full dynamic range of an HDR image, it must be tone mapped. Tone mapping reduces the extreme contrast present in an HDR image by averaging radiance values; thus, the process is able to convert the HDR image into an 8-bit LDR image without losing properly exposed areas. For example, in Figure 13.2 a HDR image of a sunset is tone mapped, revealing a proper exposure for the sun as well as the surrounding landscape.

Figure 13.2 (Top) One of many exposures used to create an HDR image. (Bottom) The same HDR image after tone mapping. The sun, sky, canyon, and shadow area are properly exposed.

Several HDR image-processing programs provide tone mapping capabilities, including Photomatix (`www.hdrsoft.com`) and HDRShop (`www.hdrshop.com`). Adobe Photoshop also supports a tone mapping option. To view an HDR image in Adobe Photoshop CS3, follow these steps:

1. Launch Photoshop. Choose File > Open and browse for the HDR image. Photoshop supports the OpenEXR, `.hdr`, and 32-bit floating-point TIFF formats. An example `.hdr` file is included as `tiki.hdr` in the Chapter 13 images folder. (The file has a dynamic range of 7,292:1.)
2. The image is displayed. However, only a limited portion of the dynamic range is visible (I'll refer to this as the *exposure range*). To choose a different exposure range, choose View > 32-Bit Preview Options. Adjust the Exposure and Gamma sliders in the 32-Bit Preview Options window. The Exposure slider determines which portion of the exposure range is displayed. The higher the Exposure value, the higher the selected exposure and the brighter the image. The Gamma slider determines the resulting contrast within the displayed image. Both sliders are measured in stops. A stop is the adjustment of a camera aperture that either halves or doubles the amount of light reaching the film or sensor. For the sliders, each stop is twice as intense, or as half as intense, as the stop beside it.
3. Once the exposure range has been adjusted, you can permanently write out the displayed image as a tone-mapped LDR variation of the original. To do so, choose Image > Mode > 8 Bits/Channel, click OK in the HDR Conversion window, and choose File > Save As.

Note: Technically speaking, HDR images do not store gamma information. In other words, HDR images are not preprocessed with gamma curves in order to make them suitable for a particular display. Instead, HDR images follow the "scene referred standard," which dictates that the format store scene values as close to reality as possible regardless of their ability to be displayed. Eight-bit LDR images, in contrast, follow an "output referred standard," which means that they store colors suitable for an 8-bit display system. (For more information on gamma, see Chapter 6.)

Texturing with HDR Images

Maya supports the ability to use OpenEXR, `.hdr`, DDS, and floating-point TIFF images as bitmap textures (assuming that the `OpenEXRLoader.mll`, `ddsFloatReader.mll`, and `tiffFloatReader.mll` plug-ins have been activated). However, when you load an OpenEXR or floating-point TIFF image into a File texture, the texture swatch may appear solid black or white. This is due to Maya's default selection of an exposure range. To adjust the exposure range, follow these steps:

1. MMB-drag a material into the work area. Map a File texture to its Color attribute. Open the File texture's Attribute Editor tab. Browse for a floating-point TIFF bitmap. A sample floating-point TIFF is included as `tiki.tif` in the Chapter 13 images folder.
2. Expand the High Dynamic Range Image Preview Options section (see Figure 13.3). Switch the Float To Fixed Point attribute to Exponential.

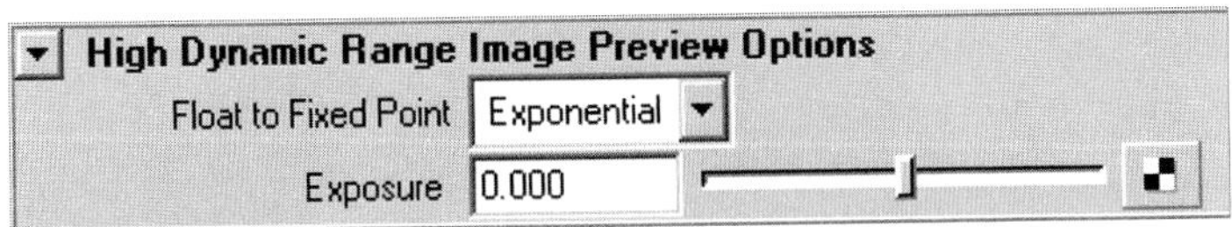

Figure 13.3 The High Dynamic Range Image Preview Options section of a File texture's Attribute Editor tab

3. Adjust the Exposure slider to reveal different exposure ranges. If Float To Fixed Point is set to Clamp, all the values within the HDR bitmap above 1 are clamped to 1 (hence the image may appear solid white). If Float To Fixed Point is set to Linear, all the bitmap values are normalized (that is, the color curves are rescaled to fit the 0 to 1 range).

If you load an `.hdr` or DDS bitmap into a File texture, a median exposure is selected and the Float To Fixed Point attribute has no effect on the texture swatch.

The mental ray renderer is able to render out the full dynamic range of an HDR bitmap used as a texture. This may prove useful when compositing a project that utilizes HDR images. (For example, recent developments in compositing software allow users to interactively "re-light" HDR elements during the composite.) However, additional attributes must be adjusted. Follow these steps:

1. Assign the material created with the previous set of steps to a primitive plane. Light the plane. Open the Render Settings window and switch Render Using to mental ray. Change the image format to HDR (hdr) or OpenEXR (exr).

2. Switch to the mental ray tab. Expand the Framebuffer section. In the Primary Framebuffer subsection, change Data Type to RGBA(Float) 4×32 (see Figure 13.4).

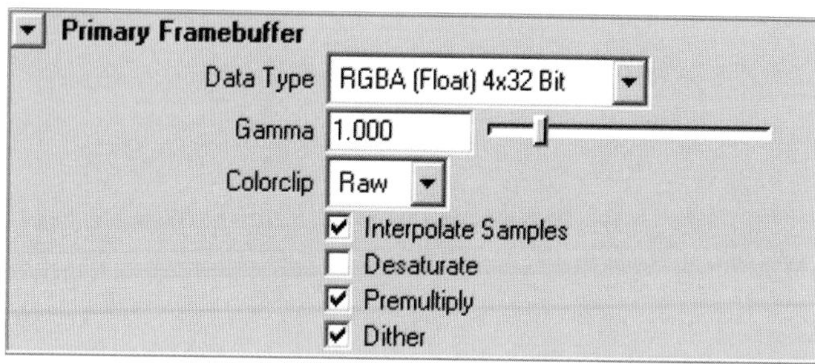

Figure 13.4 The Primary Framebuffer subsection of the mental ray tab in the Render Settings window

3. Launch a batch render by switching to the Render menu set and choosing Render > Batch Render. A fully dynamic HDR image is rendered to the default project directory. To properly view the image, you must bring it into a program that supports HDR images, such as Photoshop, Photomatix, or HDRShop.

Although a mental ray batch render creates an OpenEXR or `.hdr` image with the correct dynamic range, the mental ray preview within the Render View window can only provide an LDR version. Nevertheless, it is possible to view different exposure ranges within the Render View window by following these steps:

1. In the Primary Framebuffer subsection of the mental ray tab of the Render Settings window, change Data Type to RGBA(Byte) 4×8. Render a test frame with the Render View window.
2. Open the File texture that carries the HDR bitmap and adjust the Color Gain. Lower Color Gain values force the renderer to use lower exposure ranges. Render additional test frames. Different HDR images require different Color Gain values. For example, `tiki.tif` requires a Color Gain value in the range of 0.6, 0.6, 0.6.
3. To change the overall contrast of the rendered HDR bitmap, return to the Primary Framebuffer subsection of the Render Settings window and adjust the Gamma attribute. Higher Gamma values darken the mid-tones of the rendered image. Lower values have the opposite effect.
4. When you're ready to batch-render once again, return Data Type to RGBA(Float) 4×32, Gamma to 1, and any adjusted Color Gain to its prior value.

In contrast, when an OpenEXR or floating-point TIFF bitmap is rendered with Maya Software through the Render View window or a batch render, Maya uses the exposure range established by the Float To Fixed Point attribute. In other words, only a small portion of the dynamic range is utilized.

Tone Mapping with mental ray Lens Shaders

The mental ray renderer provides two lens shaders that tone map resulting renders: Mia_exposure_simple and Mia_exposure_photographic. Tone mapping a render is useful when utilizing HDR bitmaps as textures or when surfaces produce super-white values. Applying tone mapping allows you to select a specific exposure range without having to adjust lights or materials. To apply Mia_exposure_simple, follow these steps:

1. Open the Attribute Editor for the camera used to render a scene. Expand the mental ray section. Click the checkered Map button beside the Lens Shader attribute. Select Mia_exposure_simple from the Create Render Node window (in the Lenses section).
2. A Mia_exposure_simple node is connected to the camera and is visible in the Hypershade. Adjust the node's attributes and render a test frame.

In terms of attributes, Pedestal offsets the entire color range of the rendered image, either raising it or lowering it. You can give the Pedestal a negative value. The color range is multiplied by the Gain attribute. To lower the exposure range and thus darken the image, lower the Gain below 1. Compression reduces the color range above the Knee value. For example, if Knee is set to 0.5 and Compression is set to 1, then all color values above 0.5 are scaled toward 0.5, thus reducing the highest values in the rendered image. Gamma applies a gamma curve to make the color range nonlinear. A default value of 2.2 matches most PC computer monitors.

The Mia_exposure_photographic lens shader, on the other hand, is a more advanced tone mapping tool that produces superior renders. It is applied to a camera in the same fashion as Mia_exposure_simple. Many of the attributes, such as Film Iso and Camera Shutter, are designed to match real-world camera setups. Nevertheless, a quick way to lower the exposure level of a rendered image is to enter a low F Number attribute value. For example, in Figure 13.5 a polygon key is assigned to a Blinn with a Diffuse and Specular Roll Off value set to 5. (Any slider can be set to a value higher than its default maximum; see Chapter 6 for more information.) In addition, a second Blinn assigned to a plane has a floating-point TIFF mapped to its Color. As with Mia_exposure_simple, Mia_exposure_photographic tone maps the entire rendered image. (For information on other mental ray lens shaders, see Chapter 12.)

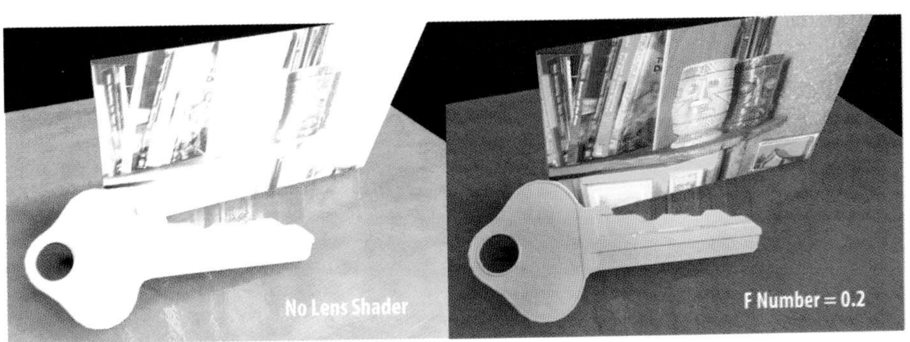

Figure 13.5 A Mia_exposure_photographic lens shader is applied to render. A simplified version of this scene is included on the CD as `mental_exposure.ma`.

Lighting with HDR and LDR Images

Using the mental ray renderer, you can light a scene with an HDR or LDR bitmap image without the need to create actual lights. You can achieve this with Final Gather or Global Illumination with a technique known as image-based lighting (IBL).

HDR images intended for IBL are created in several styles: angular (light probe), latitude/longitude (spherical), horizontal cubic cross, and vertical cubic cross (see Figure 13.6). The mental ray renderer supports angular and latitude/longitude HDR maps. HDR programs, such as HDRShop, are able to convert images into these special formats (see the section "Using Light Probe Images with the Env Ball Texture" later in this chapter).

Figure 13.6 (Top left) Vertical cubic cross HDR image. (Top right) Light probe HDR image. (Bottom) Latitude/longitude HDR image.

Using HDR Images with Final Gather

To illuminate a simple scene with an HDR image, follow these steps:

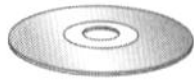

1. Open `man_hdr.ma` from the Chapter 13 scene folder on the CD. Open the Render Settings window. In the Render Options section of the Common tab, uncheck Enable Default Light. If this is left checked, the default lighting will be added to the Final Gather render. Switch the Render Using attribute to mental ray. In the Environment section of the mental ray tab, click the Image Based Lighting Create button.

2. A mental ray Image Based Lighting (IBL) shape node appears in the Lights tab of the Hypershade window. This generates the orange environment sphere that is placed in the workspace view. Open the environment sphere's Attribute Editor tab (see Figure 13.7).

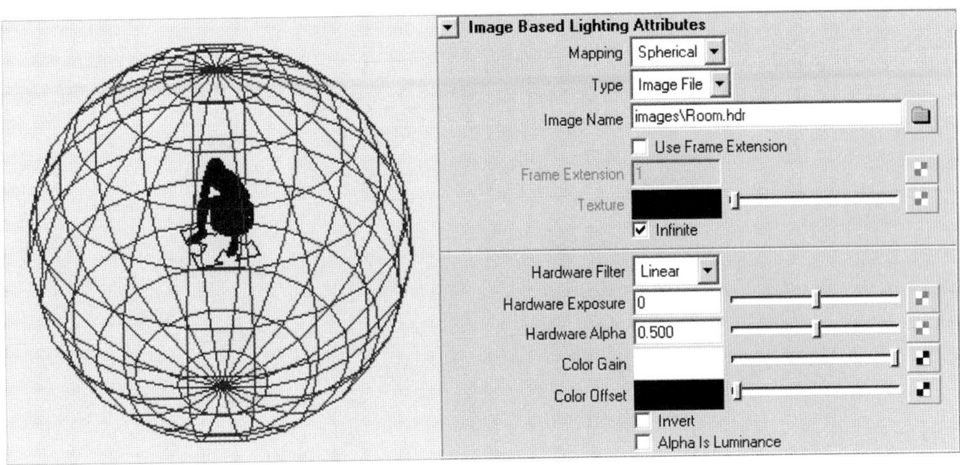

Figure 13.7 An IBL environment sphere and the Image Based Lighting Attributes section of its Attribute Editor tab

3. In the Image Based Lighting Attributes section, click the File button beside the Image Name field and browse for `room.hdr` in the Chapter 13 images folder. Set the Mapping attribute to Angular. Angular and light probe maps, although different in name, represent the same type of HDR image.

4. Return to the Render Settings window. Set the Quality Presets attribute to PreviewFinalGather. Render a test frame. Initially, the scene will be dark. (`room.hdr` features a darkly lit space.)

5. Return to the IBL shape node's Attribute Editor tab. Click the color swatch beside the Color Gain attribute in the Image Based Lighting Attributes section and enter 5 in the Value attribute field of the Color Chooser window (the color space drop-down menu must be set to HSV). This super-white value will raise the intensity of the HDR image.

6. Return to the Render Settings window, switch to the mental ray tab, and expand the Final Gathering section. Change Scale to an HSV value of 0, 0, 5. This increases the intensities of the Final Gather point contributions. Render a test. The mannequin appears brighter, but the light colors are very saturated.

7. One danger of a high IBL shape node Color Gain value is an increased saturation in the color contribution of the HDR image. To counteract this, change Color Offset, also found in the Image Based Lighting Attributes section, to 0.15. Whereas the image color values are multiplied by the Color Gain value, the Color Offset value is added to the image colors. In essence, this adds gray to the image colors, which reduces the saturation. Render out the image. The render is less saturated. A final version of this scene is included on the CD as `man_hdr_final.ma`.

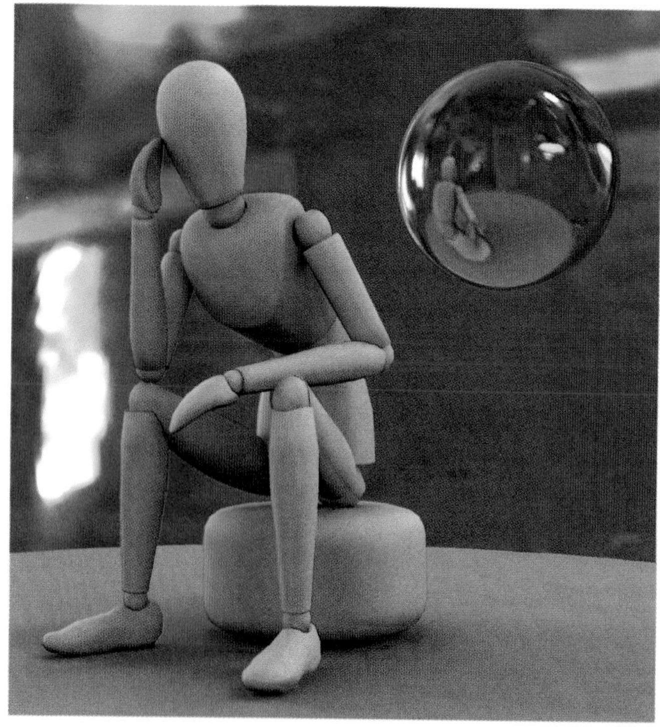

Figure 13.8 A mannequin is lit with an HDR image and rendered with Final Gather. This scene is included on the CD as `man_hdr_final.ma`.

Here are a few traits of the IBL shape node renders to keep in mind:

- When an image is mapped to an IBL shape node, it appears in the background of the render regardless of the camera's background color or clipping plane settings. However, you can uncheck the Primary Visibility attribute in the Render Stats section of the IBL shape node's Attribute Editor tab. If you do choose to leave the IBL shape node visible, it will not appear in the alpha channel.
- In general, renders using HDR images for lighting are not able to produce strong, directional shadows. Nevertheless, you can add standard lights with depth map or raytrace shadows to the scene at any time.
- You can add realism by blurring the resulting reflections slightly. For the image in Figure 13.8, the Mi Reflection Blur attribute of the Blinn assigned to the sphere is set to 3 and the Reflection Rays attribute is set to 6.
- You can adjust the alignment of the reflection by selecting the IBL environment sphere and rotating it in Y. (Scaling and translating the environment sphere will have no effect on the render if the Infinite attribute is checked in the Image Based Lighting Attributes section.)
- If inappropriate dark spots appear in a Final Gather render, adjust the Point Interpolation attribute (found in the Final Gathering section of the mental ray tab of the Render Settings window). Point Interpolation sets the number of

Final Gather points that are required when any given pixel is shaded. For the render in Figure 13.8, Point Interpolation was set to 10.

- To refine the quality of the Final Gather image, raise the Accuracy value in the Final Gathering section of the mental ray tab of the Render Settings window.

Using LDR Images with IBL

Oddly enough, mental ray's IBL system does not need an HDR image to function. You can map any LDR image to the Image Name attribute of the IBL shape node. The main disadvantage is the difficulty of matching the Spherical or Angular mapping techniques, which are designed for HDR images. Nevertheless, a normal LDR image will illuminate the scene with Final Gather. To avoid the mapping issue, however, you can discard the IBL shape node and its corresponding environment sphere. If an LDR image is mapped to the Ambient Color or Incandescence of a material, mental ray's Final Gather system treats the image as indirect illumination. As such, the material to which the image is mapped need only be assigned to a primitive piece of geometry. For example, in Figure 13.9 a polygon sphere is placed around the mannequin. A blurry LDR JPEG of a room is mapped to the Incandescence of a Blinn, which in turn is assigned to the polygon sphere.

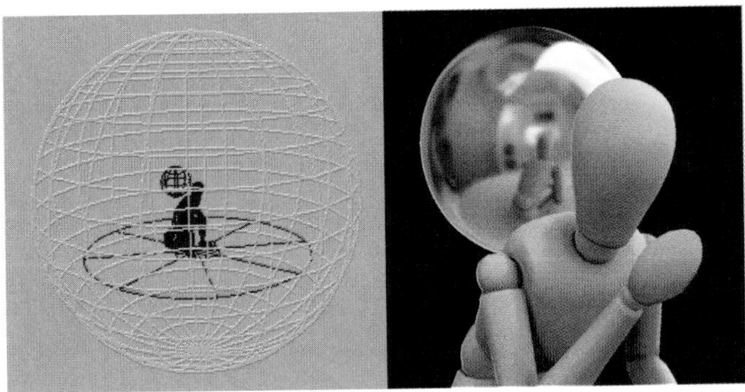

Figure 13.9 (Left) A polygon sphere, assigned to a Blinn with an LDR image, surrounds the mannequin. (Right) The resulting Final Gather render. The Primary Visibility attribute for the sphere is unchecked. This scene is included on the CD as `man_ldr.ma`.

Using HDR Images with Global Illumination

The IBL shape node is actually a collection of three mental ray shaders. The first, an Environment Shader, produces the environment sphere and is used for the basic IBL process. You can use the second, a Photon Emission Shader, to photon trace with caustics and Global Illumination. To do this, you must check the Emit Photons attribute in the Photon Emission section of the IBL shape node's Attribute Editor tab. The Caustics and Global Illumination attributes must also be checked in the Secondary Effects subsection of the Render Settings window. As an example, in Figure 13.10 the mannequin is re-rendered. The mannequin's Blinn material is made semitransparent and given a Refractive Index of 1.4.

Figure 13.10
A mannequin is lit with an HDR image and rendered with Global Illumination and caustics. This scene is included on the CD as `man_hdr_photon.ma`.

Adjustments for the Photon Shader are similar to those of a light and include Global Illumination, Caustic Photons, and Exponent attributes. Global Illumination sets the number of photons produced by the environment sphere. Caustic Photons sets the number of caustic photons produced by the environment sphere. Exponent represents the photon energy falloff. An Exponent set to 2 mimics the real world. A low value causes a more gradual energy falloff. In addition, the Standard Emission attribute, when checked, allows the photons created by the Photon Emission Shader to scatter according to the Global Illumination settings in the Render Settings window. The attribute must be checked when rendering caustics. If Standard Emission is unchecked, only the first hit of each photon created by the Photon Emission Shader is stored in the photon map. Last, the Adjust Photon Emission Color Effects attribute, if checked, makes the Color Gain, Color Offset, and Invert attributes available. Color Gain serves as a multiplier for the photon energy. Color Offset serves as an offset for the photon energy. Invert inverts the photon energy. (An intensity of 1 becomes 0 and conversely 0 becomes 1.)

Using HDR Images with the Light Shader

The third shader carried by the IBL shape node is a Light Shader. By checking the Emit Light attribute in the Light Emission section of the IBL shape node's Attribute Editor tab, you can convert the environment sphere into a light source. The Light Shader creates a series of virtual directional lights across the IBL environment sphere and derives their intensities and color from the IBL image file. The virtual lights are perpendicular to the sphere's surface and point toward the origin of world space.

The Quality U and Quality V attributes set the size of a control texture that generates the virtual lights. For each pixel of the control texture, one light is created. To make the render feasible, the Samples attribute places a cap of the number of lights used. The first Samples field determines the minimum number of lights generated. The second Samples field determines the maximum number of additional lights that are randomly added to make the lighting less regular.

Ultimately, the Light Shader creates diffuse lighting and shadows (see Figure 13.11). Since the Light Shader does not require raytracing, Global Illumination, or Final Gather to function, it renders efficiently and quickly. However, if the Quality U and Quality V attributes are raised to high values, the Light Shader render will slow significantly. At the same time, if the Quality U and Quality V values are set too low, the render will appear grainy.

Figure 13.11 (Left) The mannequin lit with the IBL Light Shader. Raytracing is used with nonreflective surfaces. This scene is included on the CD as `man_light.ma`. (Right) The same scene with reflective surfaces. This scene is included on the CD as `man_light_reflect.ma`.

Using Light Probe Images with the Env Ball Texture

Light probe (angular) HDR images are unique in that they are created by photographing a high-reflective sphere. The sphere offers the advantage of capturing a nearly 360-degree view of an environment. The Env Ball environment texture in Maya, in fact, is designed to support light probe images.

To create a light probe HDR image from scratch, follow these basic steps:

1. Digitally photograph a reflective sphere in a desired location. The example illustrated in Figure 13.12 employs a 12-inch stainless steel "gazing ball" that is sold as a lawn ornament. Take multiple photos with different F-stops and/or shutter speeds to properly expose all areas of the scene.

Figure 13.12
(Top) Five exposures created by photographing a reflective sphere. (Bottom) The resulting tone-mapped light probe HDR image. (The orange and blue colors are derived from the room's lighting and wall color.) The light probe image is included on the CD as `room.hdr`.

2. Bring the photos into an HDR program that supports the light probe format, such as HDRShop. Combine the photos into a single light probe HDR image. (HDRShop includes detailed instructions in its help files.) It's possible to refine the result by taking photos from multiple angles and stitching the photos together. Taking photos from multiple angles allows you to remove the reflected image of the photographer and camera.
3. Export the HDR image as an OpenEXR, `.hdr`, DDS, or floating-point TIFF bitmap.

To use a light probe image with the Env Ball texture to create a reflection, follow these steps:

1. Create a test surface and assign it to a Blinn or Phong material. Open the material's Attribute Editor tab. Click the checkered Map button beside Reflected Color. Choose the Env Ball texture from the Create Render Node window (in the Environment Textures section).
2. Load a light probe HDR image into the Env Ball's Image attribute. If the HDR image is in the OpenEXR or floating-point TIFF format, set the attributes within the High Dynamic Range Image Preview Options section of the file's Attribute Editor tab. If you are using an `.hdr` or DDS image, a median exposure level is automatically selected by the program.
3. Interactively scale the Env Ball projection icon, found at 0, 0, 0, so that it tightly surrounds the surface. Render a test frame. Raytracing is not required.

If the test surface is spherical, a clear reflection of the light probe image will be visible. However, if the surface is faceted or complex, the reflection may be soft and portions of the image may be severely magnified. To prevent this, adjust the Sky Radius attribute of the envBall node's Attribute Editor tab (in the Projection Geometry section). Sky Radius establishes the world distance from the reflective ball to the real-world sky. In the case of Figure 13.12, there is no sky, so Sky Radius represents the distance to the ceiling.

As an additional example, three Env Ball textures are mapped to three Phong materials assigned to three primitives in Figure 13.13. Although the Env Ball assigned to the sphere requires no Sky Radius adjustment, the Env Balls assigned to the helix and soccer ball shape require a Sky Radius value of 1.5. Unfortunately, choosing a Sky Radius value is not intuitive and requires test renders. The Sky Radius units are generic and do not correspond directly to Maya's world units.

Figure 13.13
Three Env Ball textures applied to three primitives. This scene is included on the CD as `envball.ma`.

An Introduction to RenderMan For Maya

RenderMan is a robust renderer developed by Pixar that has been used extensively in feature animation work for over a decade. In recent years, RenderMan has been made available as a plug-in for Maya. (For information on obtaining a copy of the RenderMan For Maya plug-in, visit `http://renderman.pixar.com`.)

RenderMan For Maya can be activated by checking the `RenderMan_for_maya.mll` Loaded check box in the Plug-In Manager window. Once the plug-in is activated, RenderMan appears as an option of the Render Using attribute in the Render Settings window. Like other renderers, RenderMan carries its own set of rendering attributes. However, these are spread among four tabs—Quality, Features, Passes, and Advanced (see Figure 13.14).

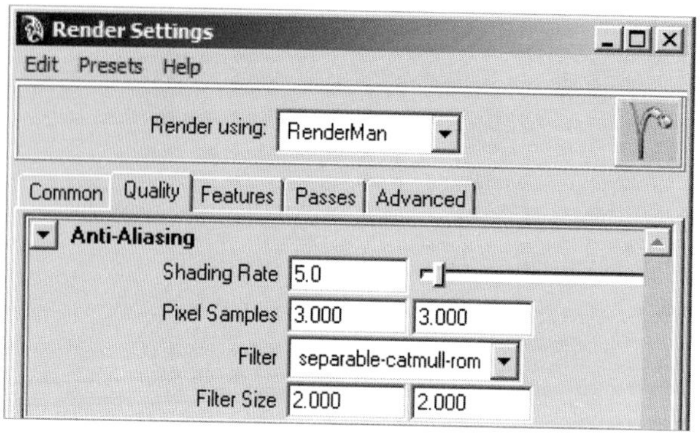

Figure 13.14 RenderMan attribute tabs in the Rendering Settings window

RenderMan is able to render most of the geometry, materials, and effects in Maya, including depth-of-field, motion blur, raytracing, global illumination, caustics, subsurface scattering, HDR rendering, Maya Fur, Maya Hair, Paint Effects, and particles.

In addition, RenderMan offers a large set of specialty render attributes. You can access the attributes by selecting the object you want to affect and choosing Attributes > RenderMan > Manage Attributes from the Attribute Editor menu. The Add/Remove Attributes window opens (see Figure 13.15).

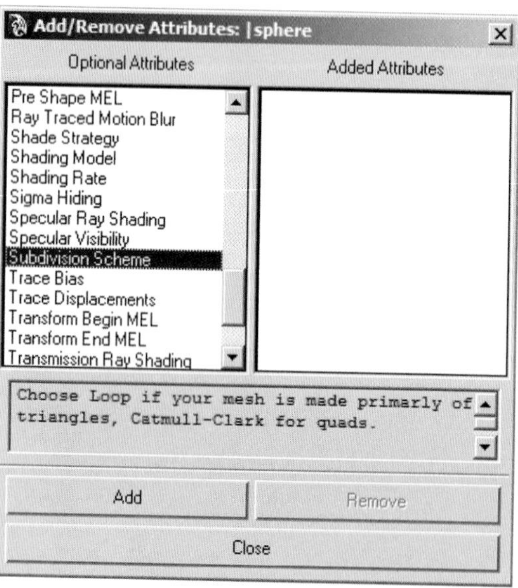

Figure 13.15 The RenderMan Add/Remove Attributes window

Available rendering attributes are listed in the Optional Attributes field. This is matched to the selected object. For instance, a NURBS surface produces a long list of attributes while a Paint Effects stroke produces a short list. To apply an attribute, highlight the attribute name and click the Add button. The attribute is added to the selected object node and is listed in the Extra RenderMan Attributes section of the node's Attribute Editor tab. Available rendering attributes create a wide array of results on a per-object basis, including:

- Raytraced motion blur
- Per-surface control of culling and visibility
- Per-surface control of diffuse illumination interaction
- Subdivision at point of render to negate faceting
- Specialized assignment of NURBS curves and other normally unrenderable nodes to shading groups

RenderMan also provides its own advanced variation of a material editor named Slim. You can launch Slim by choosing Window > Rendering Editors > RenderMan > Slim. Much like the Hypershade, Slim allows you to create and edit materials, textures, and custom connections. However, Slim adds many advanced options not available to the Hypershade. In addition, Slim provides its own set of RenderMan materials, textures, and utilities. Any shading network created in Slim can be exported back to Maya. The new shading network appears in the Hypershade and thereafter is accessible to the RenderMan renderer.

Creating Textures with the Transfer Maps Tool

The Transfer Maps tool can create normal maps and displacement maps by comparing surfaces. In addition, the tool can bake lighting and texturing information.

Normal Mapping

Although normal maps are related to bump maps, there are significant differences:

- Bump maps store scalar values designed to perturb surface normal vectors on a per-pixel basis. In contrast, normal maps store pre-calculated normal vectors as RGB values; normal maps pay no heed to the surface normal vectors provided by the surface, replacing them instead.
- Normal maps are often created by comparing a low-resolution surface to a high-resolution variation of the same surface. Thus, normal maps are able to impart high-resolution detail to a low-resolution surface. Bump maps lack this ability.
- Normal maps are not dependent on specific world units and thereby travel more easily between different 3D programs.

To create a normal map with the Transfer Maps window, follow these steps:

1. Create a new scene. Build a high- and low-resolution version of a single-surface polygon model. (An example file, which includes a simple high- and low-resolution surface, is included as `high_low.ma` on the CD.)

2. Transform the high- and low-resolution surface to 0, 0, 0 in world space. It's okay if they overlap.
3. Select the low-resolution surface, switch to the Rendering menu set, and choose Lighting/Shading > Transfer Maps. The low-resolution surface is listed automatically in the Target Meshes section of the Transfer Maps window.
4. Switch the Display drop-down menu, found in the Target Meshes section, to Envelope. Choose Shading > Smooth Shade All from a workspace view menu. The search envelope assigned to the low-resolution surface appears red. The search envelope is a "cage" in which the Transfer Maps tool searches for source surfaces during the normal mapping process. Initially, the search envelope is the same size as the low-resolution surface. To scale the search envelope, increase the Search Envelope % attribute slider, also found in the Target Meshes section. The search envelope should surround the high-resolution surface.
5. Expand the Source Meshes section of the window. By default, All Other Meshes is listed under the Name attribute. This means that the tool will evaluate all nontarget meshes it encounters within the search envelope. To specify the high-resolution surface as a source surface, select the high-resolution surface and click the Add Selected button. The name of the high-resolution surface appears under the Name attribute.
6. Click the Normal button (represented by the dimpled ball). Choose a destination for the normal map by clicking the file browse button beside the Normal Map attribute. Choose a File Format. Normal maps can be written in any of the standard Maya image formats. Choose Map Height and Map Width values in the Maya Common Output section. Click the Bake And Close button at the bottom of the window.

At this point, the Transfer Maps tool creates a new material, assigns it to the low-resolution surface, and loads the newly written normal map into a connected bump2d node. The Use As attribute of the bump2d node is set to Tangent Space Normals. To see the result, move the low-resolution surface away from the high-resolution surface and render a test. The result should be similar to Figure 13.16.

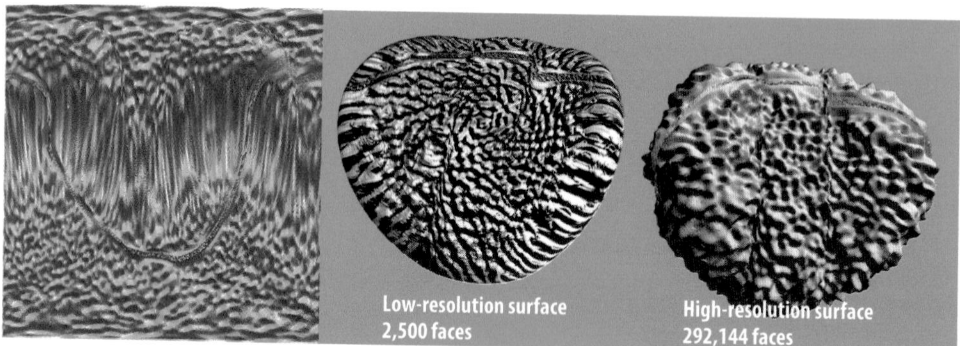

Figure 13.16 (Left to right) Normal map, low-resolution surface with normal map, high-resolution surface. This scene is included on the CD as `normal_final.ma`. The normal map is included as `normal_map.tga` in the textures folder.

To improve the quality of the normal mapping process, you can adjust additional attributes:

Sampling Quality Found in the Maya Common Output section, Sampling Quality sets the number of samples taken for each pixel of the normal map. This serves as a subpixel sampling system. The higher the values, the more accurate the resulting normal map.

Transfer In Found in the Maya Common Output section, Transfer In determines which space the normal map calculations are carried out in. If Transfer In is set to the default World Space, the target and source surfaces can be different sizes. However, they must be positioned at the same world location. If Transfer In is set to Object Space, target and source surfaces can be moved apart; however, the Freeze Transformation tool should be applied while they are positioned at the same world location. If Transfer In is set to UV Space, the surfaces can be dissimilar (different shape or different proportions); however, the surfaces must carry valid UVs for this option to work.

Map Space If the Map Space attribute (which is found in the Output Maps section) is set to Tangent Space, the normal vectors are encoded per vertex in tangent space. Tangent space is the local coordinate space of a vertex that is described by a tangent vector, a binormal vector, and the surface normal. The tangent vector is aligned with the surface's U direction. The binormal vector is aligned with the surface's V direction. If Map Space is set to Object Space, the resulting normal map takes on a rainbow hue. This is due to the surface normals always pointing in the same direction in object space regardless of the translation or rotation of the surface in world space. The Object Space option is only suitable for surfaces that are not animated.

You can also create normal maps through the Render Layer Editor; an example is included in the section "Using Presets" later in this chapter.

Creating Displacement Maps

The best normal map cannot improve the quality of a low-resolution surface's edges. However, the Transfer Maps tool is able to preserve the edge details of the high-resolution surface by creating a displacement map for the low-resolution surface. Steps to create a displacement map are almost identical to the steps to create a normal map:

1. Move the high-resolution surface and the low-resolution surface to the same point in world space. Assign the low-resolution surface to a new material. With the low-resolution surface selected, choose Lighting/Shading > Transfer Maps. The low-resolution surface is listed in the Target Meshes section. Select the high-resolution surface and click the Add Selected button in the Source Meshes section.

2. Click the Displace button. Click the file browse button beside the Displacement Map field and choose a destination for the displacement map to be written out. Choose an appropriate File Format and Map Width and Map Height.
3. Switch the Connect Maps To attribute, found in the Connect Output Maps section, to Assigned Shader. Click the Bake And Close button at the bottom of the window.
4. Move the low-resolution surface away from the high-resolution surface. Render a test frame. In this case, the displacement map is automatically connected to a displacementShader node, which in turn is connected to the Displacement Shader attribute of the material's shading group node.

Unfortunately, displacement maps created with the Transfer Maps tool often produce a "quilting" effect along the original polygon edges. That is, the faces of the low-resolution surface appear to be "puffed out" among the high-resolution surface detail. To reduce this potential problem, follow these guidelines:

- Change the Maximum Value attribute (found in the Output Maps section). Raising the value reduces the amount of contrast in the displacement map. In turn, this reduces the intensity of any quilting artifacts and prevents plateaus from forming when parts of the map become pure white. The ideal value varies with the surfaces involved.
- Increase the Filter Size attribute (found in the Maya Common Output section) to add blur to the map.
- Incrementally raise the Initial Sample Rate and Extra Sample Rate attributes of the target surface. (These attributes are found in the Displacement Map section of the surface's Attribute Editor tab.) This will increase the accuracy of the displacement.
- Adjust the Alpha Gain and Alpha Offset attributes of the File node that carries the displacement map. (See Chapter 9 for more information.)
- Touch up the map in Photoshop. The Displacement Shader interprets a 0 value as no displacement and a 1 value as maximum displacement.

As an example, in Figure 13.17 a displacement map is generated by the Transfer Maps tool using a high-resolution and low-resolution plane. The high-resolution plane, on the left, has 18,342 polygon triangles. The low-resolution plane, on the right, has 72 triangles. In the Transfer Maps window, the Map Resolution is set to 512×512, the Maximum Value to 5, and the Sampling Quality to Medium (4×4). The Alpha Gain of the resulting displacement map's file node is raised to 10. The Initial Sample Rate and Extra Sample Rate of the low-resolution surface are set to 20 and 10, respectively.

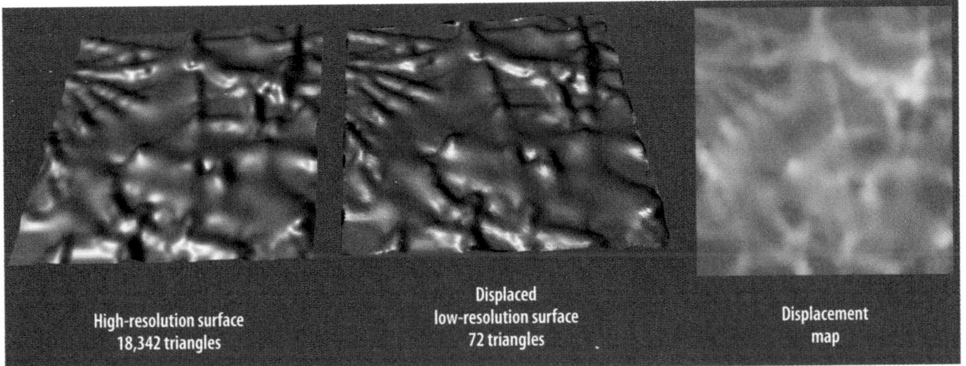

Figure 13.17 High-resolution surface compared to displaced low-resolution surface. This scene and map are included on the CD as `displacement.ma` and `plane_map.tga`.

Baking Lighting and Shading Information

You can "bake" lighting, texture, and shadow information with the Transfer Maps tool. In this situation, a textured source creates a color bitmap for a target surface. The Transfer Maps tool provides two attributes to choose from for this operation: Diffuse Color Map and Lit And Shaded Color Map. Diffuse Color Map simply captures a source surface's color without regard to lighting or shadows. Lit And Shaded Color Map captures all the source surface's information, including specular highlights, bump maps, ambient color textures, and so on (see Figure 13.18). You can map the resulting color bitmap to the low-resolution surface to reduce render times (by avoiding bump mapping, shadow casting, and the like). The use of Diffuse Color Map and Lit And Shaded Color Map attributes is identical to the creation of a displacement map or normal map. The Diffuse Color Map is activated with the Diffuse button, and the Lit And Shaded Color Map is activated with the Shaded button.

Figure 13.18 A low-resolution surface is given detail with a baked texture. This scene and map are included on the CD as `lit.ma` and `lit_map.tga`.

Managing Renders with the Render Layer Editor

Render management is an inescapable part of animation production. Complex projects can easily generate hundreds, if not thousands, of rendered images. The complexity is magnified when objects are rendered in separate passes or when shading components are addressed individually. Fortunately, Maya's Render Layer Editor makes the task more efficient.

Render Layer Overview

The Layer Editor is accessible by clicking the Show The Channel Box And Layer Editor icon on the status bar. The Layer Editor is composed of two sections, which you can toggle between by clicking the Display or Render radio button. The Display section of the Layer Editor is known as the Display Layer Editor. The Render section is known as the Render Layer Editor (see Figure 13.19). You can access the Render Layer Editor directly by choosing Window > Rendering Editors > Render Layer Editor.

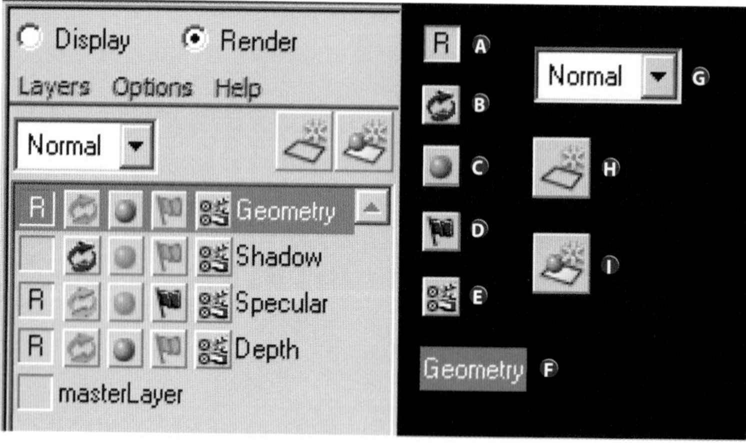

Figure 13.19 The Render Layer Editor

A) Renderable button. If blank, layer does not render.
B) Recycle button. If green, layer does not re-render. If red, layer re-renders. If gray, layer has not rendered since file was opened.
C) Shader icon. If gray, button opens the Hypershade. If blue, a material override is present and button will open the Attribute Editor tab for the override material.
D) Flag icon. If gray, button opens the Attribute Editor tab for the Render Layer Editor and displays the Member Overrides and Render Pass Options sections. If red, an override is present.
E) Controls icon. If gray, button opens default Render Settings window. If red, button opens overridden Render Settings window specific to the layer.
F) Layer name. Blue indicates a selected layer.
G) Blending mode drop-down menu.
H) Create New Empty Layer button.
I) Create New Layer And Assign Selected Objects button.

By default, Maya places all objects on a master layer. The master layer is not visible in the Render Layer Editor until a new layer is created. To create a new layer and assign objects to that layer, you can choose one of these two approaches:

- Choose objects in the scene and click the Create New Layer And Assign Selected Objects button.

- Click the Create New Empty Layer button. While the master layer is highlighted in the layer list, select objects in the scene. Click the new layer in the layer list. The objects will be invisible but will remain selected. Right-click the new layer's name and choose Add Selected Objects from the shortcut menu.

You can add additional objects to a preexisting layer at any time by right-clicking a layer name and choosing Add Selected Objects. Conversely, you can remove objects by choosing Remove Selected Objects. To rename a layer, double-click the layer name and enter a new name in the Name field of the Edit Layer window. To change the order of the layers, MMB-click and drag any layer name up or down the layer stack.

You can edit the layer membership of any object by opening the Relationship Editor and switching to the Render Layers view (see Figure 13.20). You can access this view directly by choosing Window > Relationship Editors > Render Layers. You can add objects to a layer by clicking the layer name in the left column and clicking the object name in the right column. Once an object is included, its name appears in the left column under the layer name. To remove an object from a layer, click the object name in the right column.

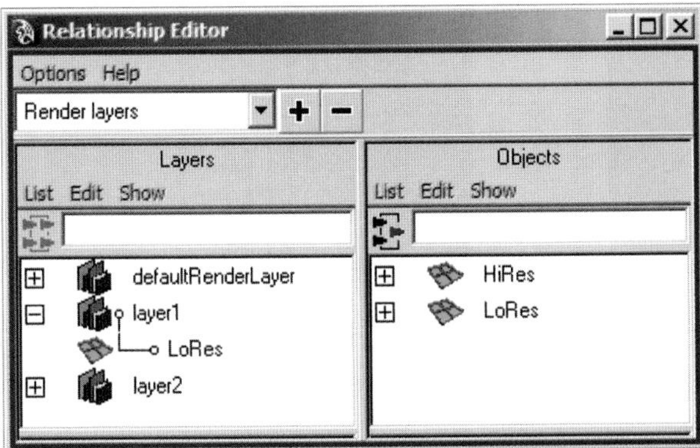

Figure 13.20 The Render Layers view in the Relationship Editor

When a new layer is created, it is rendered by default. To toggle off the render status, click off the R symbol beside the layer's name in the Render Layer Editor.

Maya provides six special effect methods for combining layers. These techniques are accessible through the Blend Mode drop-down menu (see Figure 13.19). The modes correspond to layer blend modes in Photoshop and include Normal, Lighten, Darken, Multiply, Screen, and Overlay. For example, if three layers are activated with the R symbol and each layer has a different blend mode, the final rendered image will contain a blended version of the three layers (see Figure 13.21). This assumes that the Render View window is set to composite. (In the Render View window, choose Render > Render All Layers > ❑ and switch Keep Image Mode to Composite Layers.) Much like Photoshop, the order the layers are blended runs from top to bottom.

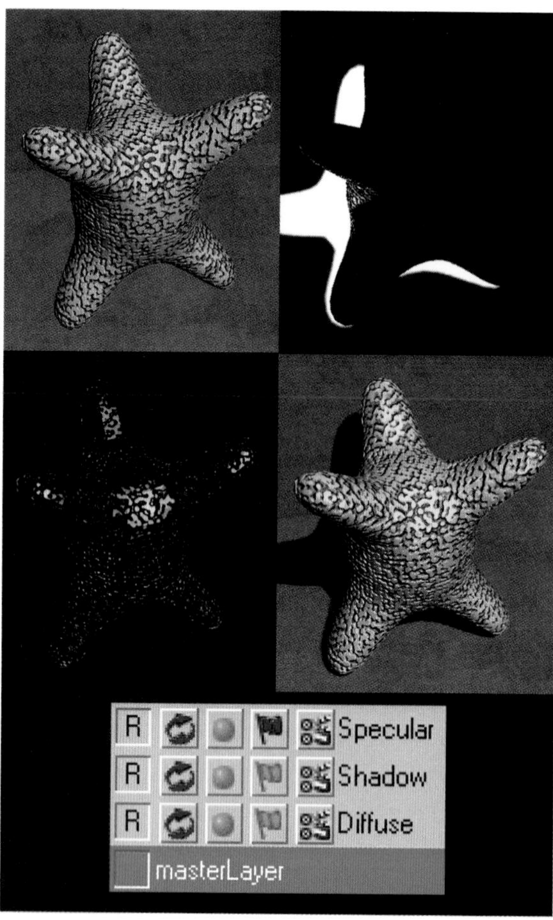

Figure 13.21
(Upper left) Diffuse layer render. (Upper right) Shadow layer render. (Middle left) Specular layer render. (Middle right) Blended layers result. (Bottom) Render Layer Editor. Diffuse layer Blending Mode is set to Normal. Shadow layer Blending mode is set to Multiply. Specular layer Blending Mode is set to Screen. This scene is included on the CD as `layer_blending.ma`.

Note: You can force Maya to save each layer of the Render Layer Editor as a separate layer in a Photoshop file. To do so, switch the Image Format in the Render Settings window to PSD Layered. In the Render View window, choose Render > Render All Layers > ❑ and switch Keep Image Mode to Composite And Keep Layers. When you batch render, a PSD file is written out to the project directory with each render layer on a different Photoshop layer. The Photoshop blending modes are properly set for each layer.

Creating Member Overrides and Render Pass Options

Each render layer that you create receives a long list of Member Overrides. The overrides allow a particular layer to overturn specific attributes of the objects rendered in the layer (these attributes are also known as render flags). The master layer, by comparison, receives no overrides.

To access the Member Overrides section in the Render Layer Editor's attribute tab, click the flag icon beside the layer name (see Figure 13.19 earlier in this chapter).

For example, in the Member Overrides section, you can switch the Casts Shadows attribute from Use Scene to Override On and thus force all objects assigned to the layer to not cast shadows. When an override is activated, the flag icon in the Render

Layer Editor turns red. Additional override attributes control motion blur, visibility, and double-siding.

The Render Layer Editor's attribute tab also contains a Render Pass Options section (see Figure 13.22). Checking or unchecking the Render Pass Options attributes isolates specific shading components. If Beauty is checked, all standard shading components are rendered. However, if only Color is checked, the color component renders by itself. Diffuse produces the diffuse component. Shadow isolates shadows in the alpha channel. Specular isolates the specular highlights. (The Render Pass Options technique will not create an appropriate alpha channel for the Specular attribute.) Splitting an animation into such shading components is a common technique in the animation industry; the resulting renders allow for a maximum amount of flexibility during the compositing process. For an example of this technique, see the section "Step-by-Step: Creating the Cover Illustration" at the end of this chapter.

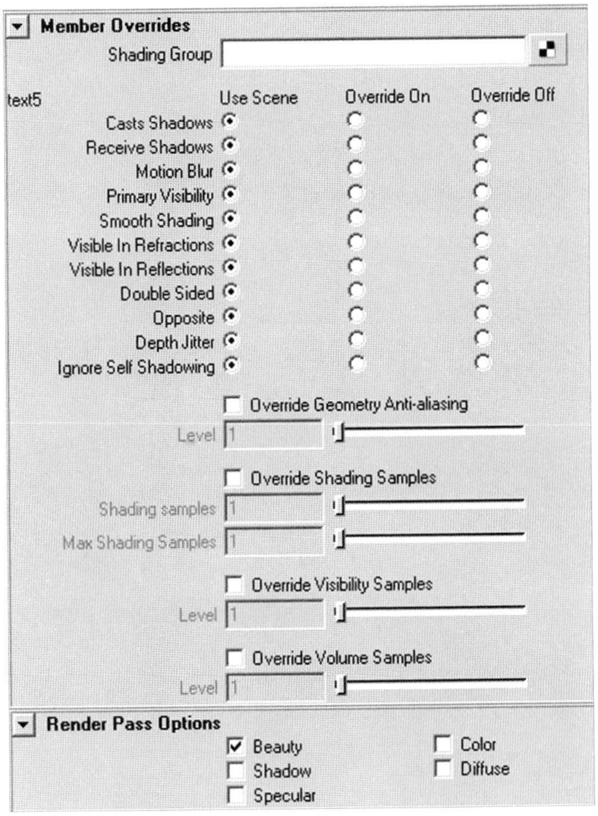

Figure 13.22 The Member Overrides and Render Pass Options section of the Render Layer Editor's Attribute Editor tab

Creating Render Settings Window Overrides

You can override the settings of the Render Settings window per layer by clicking the small "controls" icon directly to the left of the layer name (see Figure 13.19 earlier in this chapter). (The icon features a tiny picture of a motion picture clapboard.)

When the controls icon is clicked, the Render Setting window opens in an override mode. The Render Setting window indicates this by including the layer name in the window title bar (for example, *Render Settings (layer2)*). You can change any of the Render Settings window attributes. However, to make the changes a recognized override for the layer, follow these steps:

1. Right-click over an attribute name and choose Create Layer Override from the shortcut menu. The attribute name turns orange, indicating that it carries an override for the active layer (see Figure 13.23).

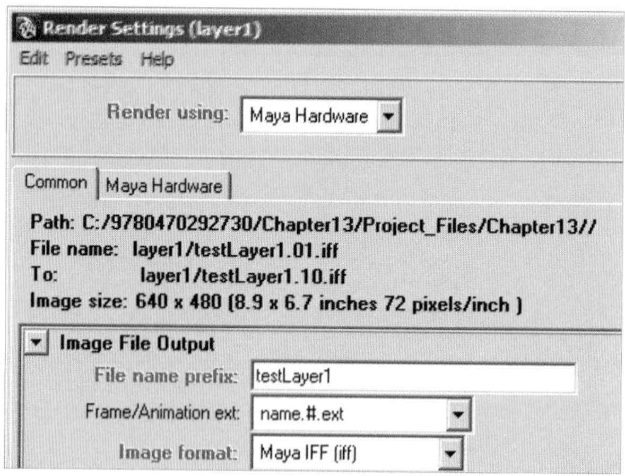

Figure 13.23 The changed title bar and orange font of an overridden Render Settings window

2. Change the value or option for the overridden attribute.

To remove an override, right-click the attribute name and choose Remove Layer Override from the shortcut menu. The attribute automatically takes its value or option from the default Render Setting window.

You can launch the Render Settings window with its layer-centric overrides at any time by clicking the controls icon of a specific layer. You can change all the attributes and options within the Render Settings window per layer, including the renderer used. For example, if a scene features a glass on a table, you can render the glass layer with mental ray and raytracing while rendering the table layer with Maya Software and no raytracing.

The master layer receives its render settings from default Common and render-specific tabs of the Render Settings window. However, once a new layer is created, the default Render Settings window displays tabs for all available renderers. Any attribute that is not overridden for a layer takes its setting from the default Common and render-specific tabs.

Using Presets

The Render Layer Editor provides a series of presets that allow a given layer to be temporarily assigned to a new material and shading group node. All the surfaces assigned to the layer are affected by the assignment. The assignment only occurs on the layer the preset is applied to and does not influence the assignment of materials on other layers.

To apply a preset, right-click a layer name and choose Presets > *preset name* from the shortcut menu. Descriptions of the presets follow:

Luminance Depth Creates a Z-buffer style render in the RGB channel of the image. This is achieved by assigning the surfaces to a Surface Shader material. The material's Out Color is connected to a custom shading network, which derives the distance to camera from a Sampler Info node. You can use Luminance Depth images to create artificial depth-of-field and other "depth priority" effects in a compositing program.

Geometry Matte Generates a solid matte effect in the RGB channels by assigning the surfaces to a Surface Shader material with a 100 percent white Out Color. In the example shown in Figure 3.24, the star shape is assigned to the layer but the backdrop geometry is not. Solid mattes are useful for compositing operations and filters.

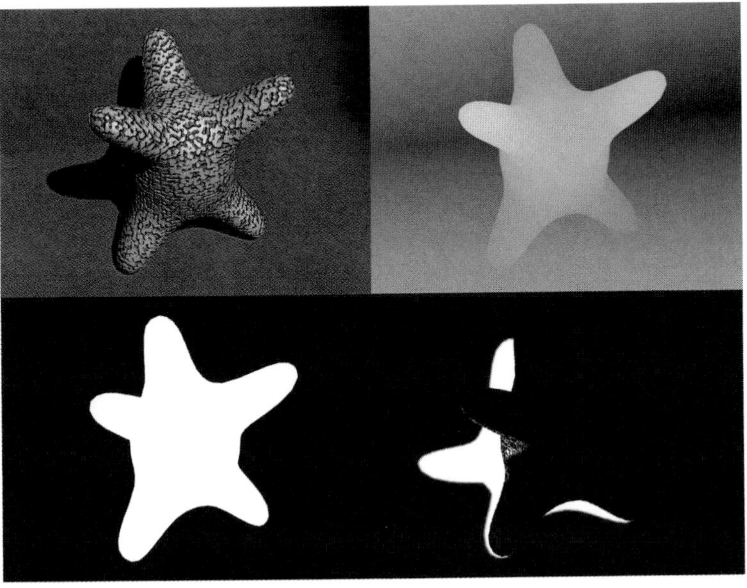

Figure 13.24 (Clockwise, from upper left) Master render layer, Luminance Depth preset, Shadow preset, and Geometry Matte preset

Specular and Diffuse Isolate their namesake shading components by remotely controlling attributes in the Render Pass Options section. (See "Creating Member Overrides and Render Pass Options" earlier in this chapter.)

Occlusion Ambient occlusion refers to the blocking of indirect or diffuse light. Creases, cracks, and crevices on real-world objects are often darker due to indirect and diffuse light being absorbed or reflected by nearby surfaces. In 3D, however, this does not occur automatically. Thus, ambient occlusion renders are useful for darkening renders where they are normally too bright or washed out.

The Occlusion preset achieves ambient occlusion by assigning surfaces to a Surface Shader material with a Mib_amb_occlusion mental ray shader mapped to the Out Color. Unfortunately, it is difficult to blend the Occlusion preset render with the master layer in the Render Layer Editor. Much more control is gained if the Occlusion preset render is combined with a beauty or diffuse render in a compositing program (see Figure 13.25).

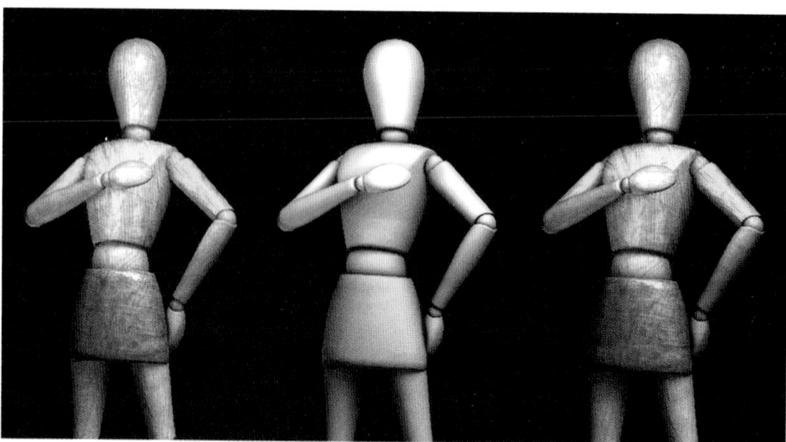

Figure 13.25 (Left) Diffuse preset. (Middle) Occlusion preset. (Right) Occlusion preset render blended over Diffuse preset render in a compositing program. Note the slight darkening of the joints.

Normal Map Renders a tangent-space normal map. You can use the image for compositing operations that require surface normal direction information. You can also map the render to the Bump Value of a Bump 2D utility; the result is similar to a bas-relief (see Figure 13.26). If the Use As attribute of the Bump 2D utility is set to Tangent Space Normals and the mental ray renderer is utilized, the result is fairly clean.

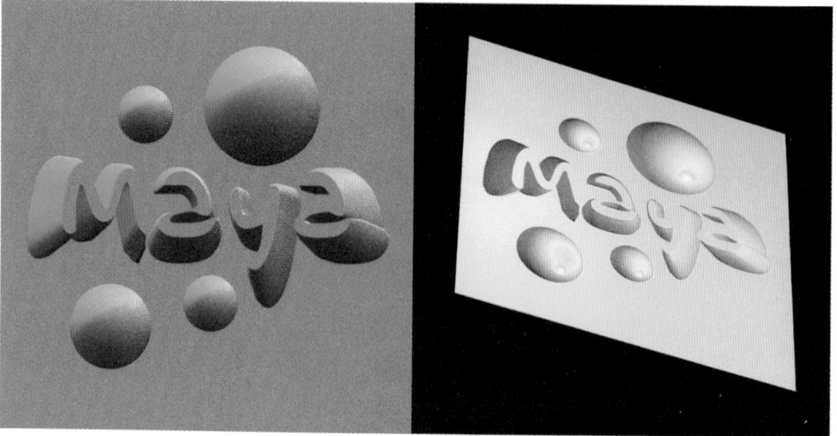

Figure 13.26 (Left) Normal map created with the Normal Map preset. The scene in which the preset is applied is included on the CD as `normal_preset.ma`. (Right) Normal map mapped to a Bump 2D utility. This scene is included on the CD as `normal_relief.ma`.

Creating Material Overrides

You can create your own custom presets by right-clicking the layer name and choosing Create New Material Override > *material*. You have the option to choose any material from the Maya and mental ray library. The new material appears in the Hypershade window, where it can be renamed and edited. The material override will not be active until it is assigned to a layer, however. Once assigned, every surface in the layer is assigned to the override material. To assign the override material, right-click the layer name and choose Assign Existing Material Override > *override material name*. You can access the Attribute Editor tab of a previously assigned material override by clicking the shader icon beside the layer name (see Figure 13.19 earlier in the chapter). You can remove an override by right-clicking the layer name and choosing Remove Material Override.

Step-by-Step: Creating the Cover Illustration

The cover illustration was created specifically for this book. Since the amount of time available to create the render was limited, I combined standard lighting and texturing techniques with various shortcuts.

The model of the woman, known as Masha, was built by Andrey Kravchenko and is commercially available via `www.turbosquid.com`. Masha's polygon count, including clothing, is approximately 45,000 triangles. For purposes of the illustration, however, modeling adjustments were made to the face. In addition, the torso was split into two overlapping surfaces—one for her skin and one for the semitransparent lace shirt. Masha was given a no-frills character rig and posed into place. Other models, such as the spotlights and mannequin, were either culled from the first edition of the book or commercially purchased (see Figure 13.27).

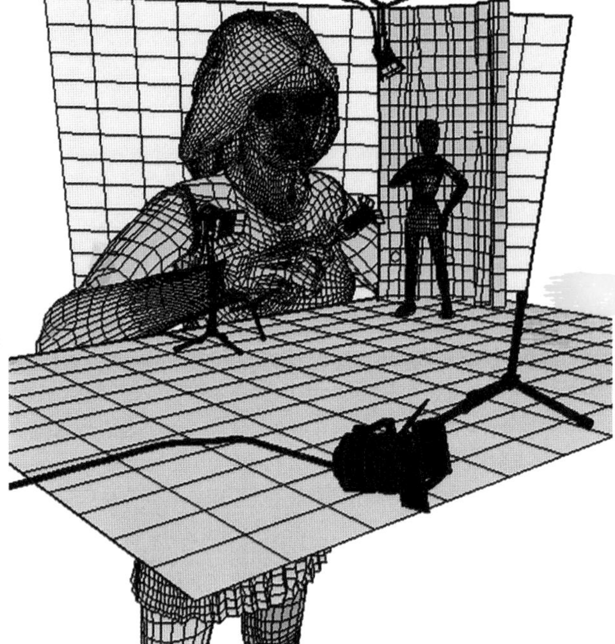

Figure 13.27
The 3D set used for the cover illustration

As for lighting, standard spot, directional, and ambient lights were employed (see Figure 13.28). Two spot lights illuminated the mannequin and represented the throw the prop spotlights. An additional spot light served as a key. A directional light created a rim and represented light arriving from the blue-green background. Two ambient lights shared the duty as fill light.

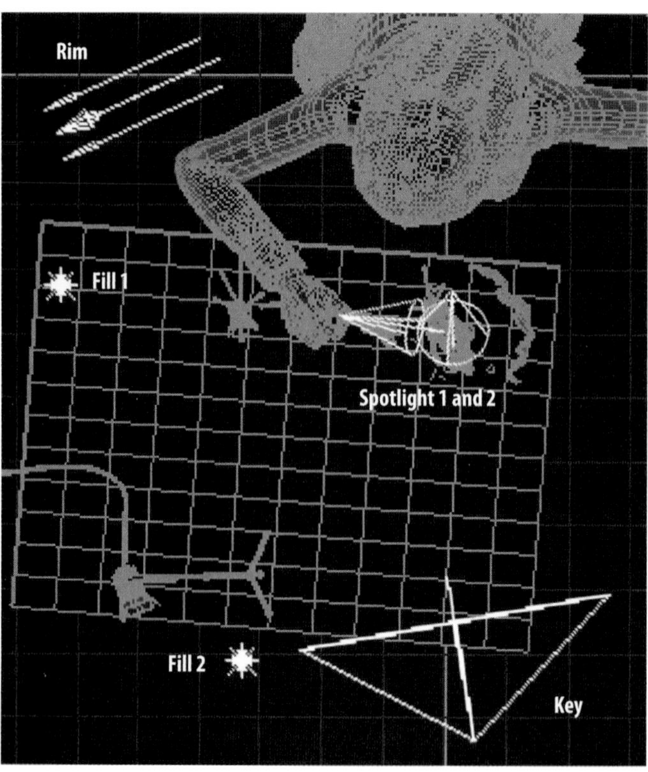

Figure 13.28
Initial lighting setup

The rendering was managed with the Render Layer Editor. This allowed various parts of the scene, such as side curtain, the individual prop spotlights, the mannequin, and various parts of Masha herself, to be rendered out in separate passes. It also allowed for any given layer to have different material overrides and presets applied to further separate shading components. For example, the mannequin was rendered with beauty, diffuse, specular, ambient occlusion, and shadow passes (see Figure 13.29). This diversity of render passes allowed for a great deal of flexibility in the compositing phase, whereby each render was given different sets of filters, color adjustments, opacities, and blending modes.

Each render pass received a different renderer and secondary rendering effect based on its contents and desired result. While some passes used Global Illumination or Final Gather with mental ray, others relied on Maya Software. Global Illumination proved to be the most effective with the mannequin and curtain, while Final Gather proved invaluable for creating warmness for Masha's face. The spotlight props, on the other hand, proved satisfactory with Maya Software.

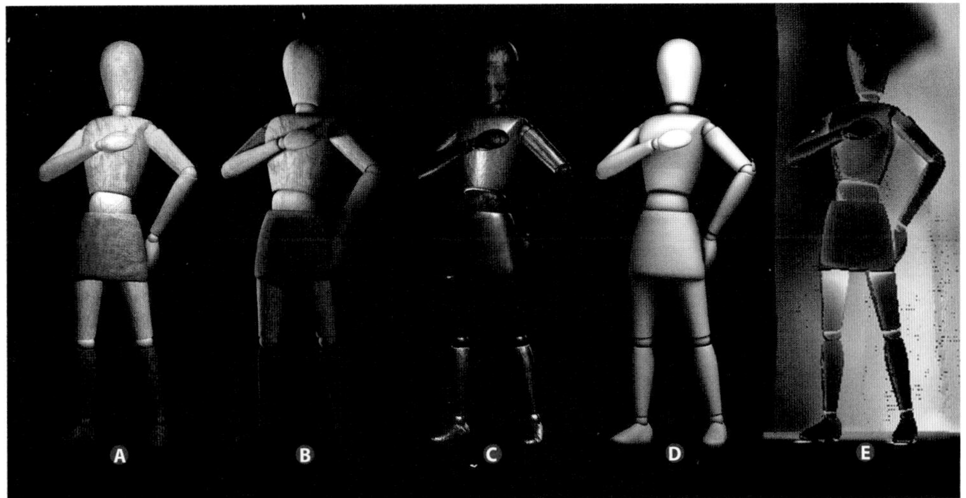

Figure 13.29 Render passes for mannequin shown side by side. A) Diffuse. B) Beauty with alternative lighting. C) Specular. D) Ambient occlusion. E) Shadow (with curtain).

Another advantage of splitting a render into multiple passes is the ability to re-light for each pass. That is, because each render pass was created separately, there was no need to keep the lighting static throughout the rendering process. For instance, lighting that made Masha's face look appealing was not successful for her hand. Therefore, when it came time to create the render pass for the hand, the lights were repositioned. Although the Render Layer Editor cannot keep tabs on the positions of lights, it is fairly easy to save different versions of the scene file. The trick, in this case, is to be explicit with the scene file naming. For instance, any given scene file would follow the naming convention `part_component_version.mb` (for instance, `hand_diffuse_v2.mb`).

The Masha model was accompanied by a set of custom bitmaps. However, these were discarded in favor of new textures. In addition, the UVs of the face were remapped to support more detail. All other surfaces in the scene were assigned to custom materials with custom bitmap textures. In the end, 35 materials were created (see Figure 13.30).

While the majority of material shading networks remained mundane with standard Color, Bump Mapping, and Specular Color connections to File textures, the skin texture utilized a custom shading network (see Figure 13.31). Three different variations of the face bitmap texture were mapped to the Color, Ambient Color, Specular Color, and Bump Mapping. The face bitmaps were further adjusted by blending the File textures with other File, Mountain, or Leather textures through Layered Texture nodes. The Diffuse attribute was controlled by Sampler Info, Remap Value, and Multiply utilities, allowing a custom diffuse falloff to be created; this created the illusion of translucency. Time limitations prevented the use of more accurate subsurface scattering techniques.

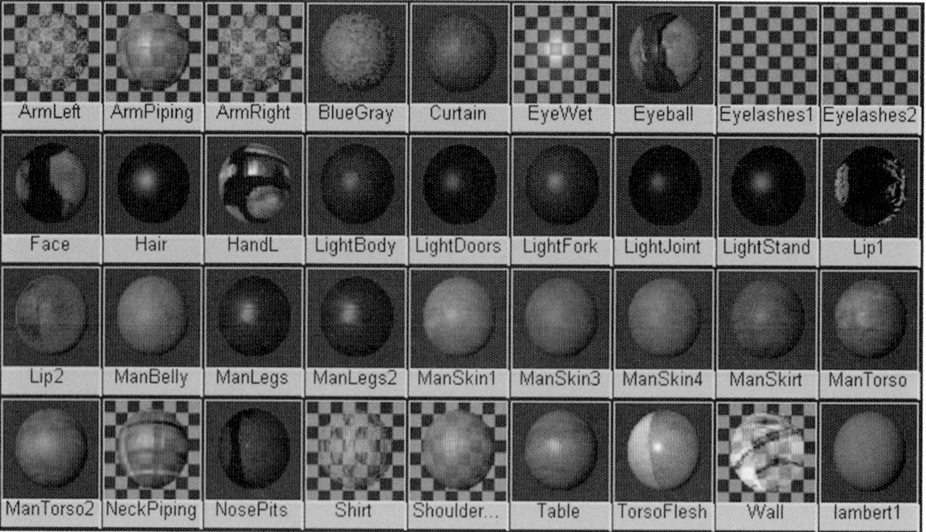

Figure 13.30 Materials created for the scene

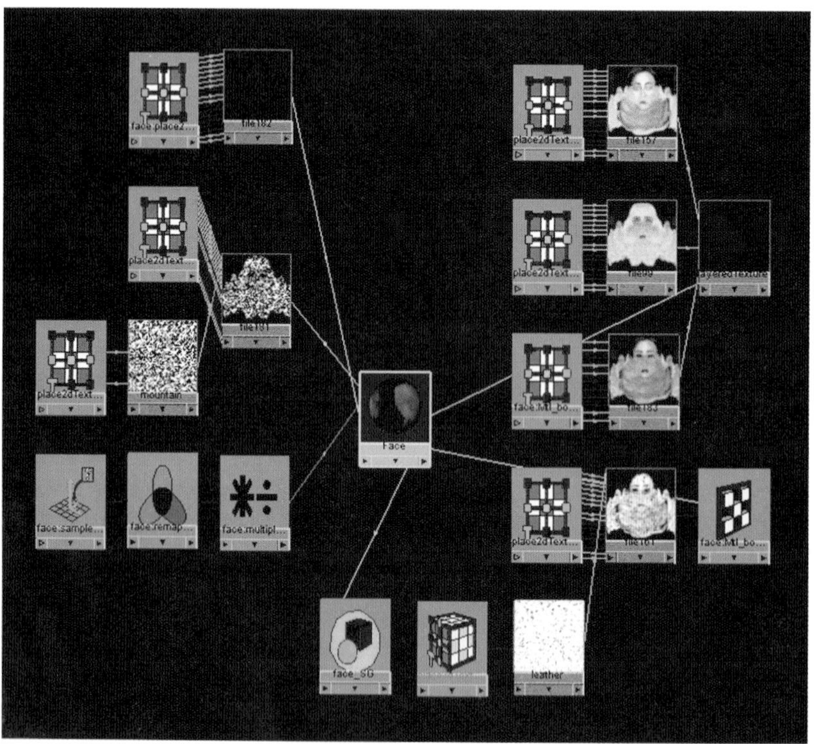

Figure 13.31 Shading network for the face

To create the reflections on the stands of the spotlight props, an Env Sphere texture was mapped to the Reflected Color of an assigned Blinn. A rough draft render of the scene was loaded into the Image attribute of the Env Sphere, providing the basic colors established by the scene.

To create the transparency necessary for the lace shirt, a high-resolution, grayscale bitmap was created and mapped to the shirt material's Transparency (see Figure 13.32). The detail in the map was so fine, however, that rendering high-quality shadows of the lace on Masha's torso proved excessively time-consuming. As a result, the shirt surface had its Casts Shadows attribute checked off and the lace shadows were created in the composite.

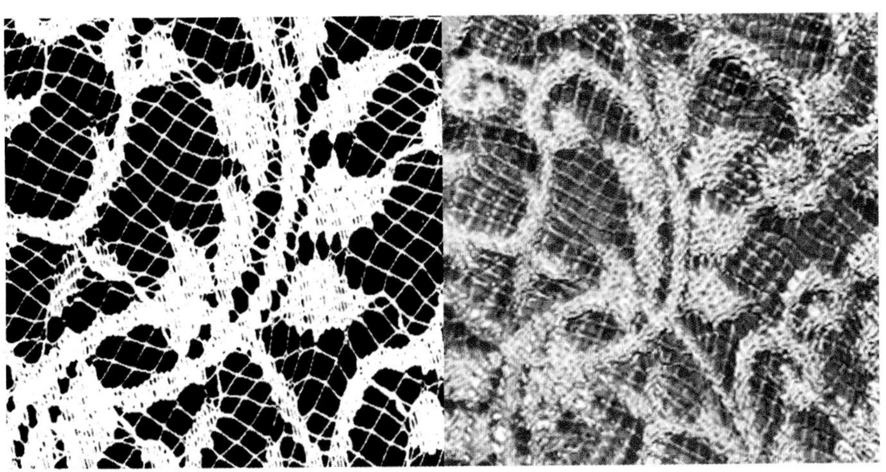

Figure 13.32 (Left) Detail of lace Transparency bitmap. (Right) Detail of lace in final illustration.

Another area that proved difficult was Masha's hair. The original model came with a surface that represented the hair's volume, but had little detail. In order to get a sense of individual hairs, the surface was removed and replaced by Paint Effects system. The Paint Effects were not left in their default state, however, but were converted to polygons. This allowed small sections of the hair mass to be dynamically simulated on a stand-in object, converted with the Modify > Convert > Paint Effects To Polygons tool, and then arranged within the scene. Once several basic hair "clumps" were created, in fact, they could be duplicated and overlapped to create greater complexity. Each clump was created with the hairWetCurl Paint Effects brush with custom attribute settings to give it an appropriate amount of randomness, segments, and curvature (see Figure 13.33). Each clump had approximately 25,000 polygons once converted. The final hair mass contained over

500,000 polygons. The clumps were assigned to a Hair Tube Shader material, which provided a unique variation of anisotropic specularity.

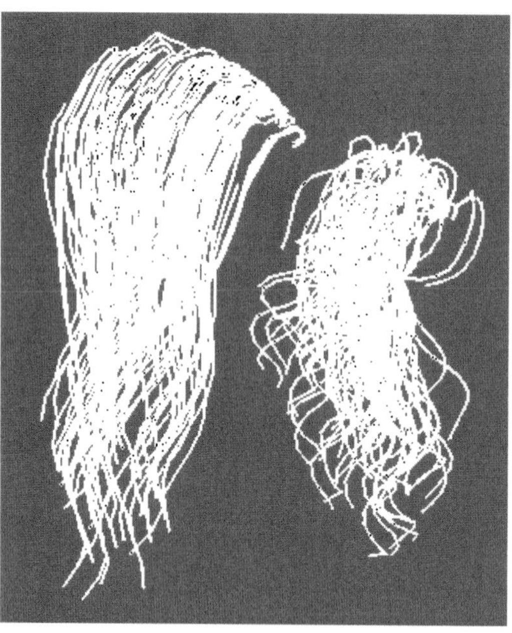

Figure 13.33 Several "clumps" of Paint Effects hair converted to polygons

The final resolution of each render pass was 2130×2130. Render times varied from 10 minutes to 1 hour depending on the complexity of the render layer and the choice of renderers and secondary rendering effects. Images were saved as Targas with an alpha channel. All Targas were brought into Adobe After Effects, where they were adjusted, filtered, combined, and rendered as a final image. The final image was imported into Adobe Photoshop for touch-ups. The total time invested in the illustration was approximately 35 hours. A detail of the illustration is shown in Figure 13.34.

There are many ways to approach any given render in Maya. Although this book has demonstrated various methods, they are by no means the only approaches available. Flexibility and resourcefulness are equally valuable assets when creating 3D. I sincerely hope that *Advanced Maya Texturing and Lighting, Second Edition* inspires you to develop brand-new techniques.

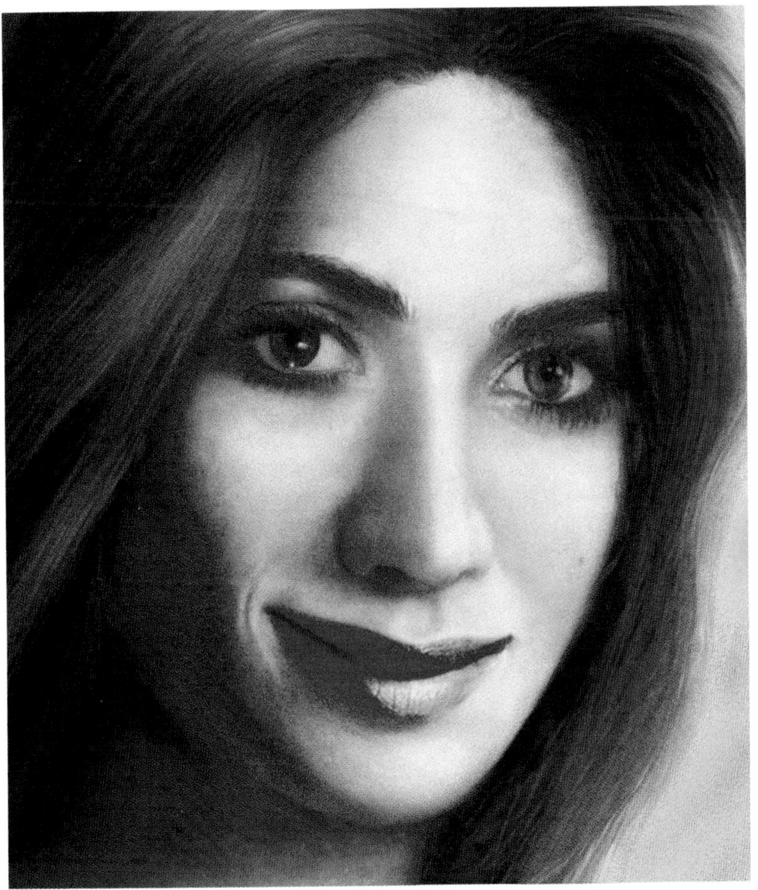

Figure 13.34 Detail of final illustration

Appendix

About the Companion CD

In this appendix:

What you'll find on the CD

System requirements

Using the CD

Troubleshooting

What You'll Find on the CD

The following sections are arranged by category and provide a summary of the items you'll find on the CD. If you need help with installing the items provided on the CD, refer to the installation instructions in the "Using the CD" section of this appendix.

Project Files

All the files provided in this book for completing the tutorials and understanding concepts are located in the Project_Files directory. The following directory structure is used:

Project_Files\Chapter_1\scenes	Scene files and shading networks
Project_Files\Chapter_1\images	Background and HDR images
Project_Files\Chapter_1\textures	Texture bitmaps
Project_Files\Chapter_1\movies	Sample QuickTime movies

The scene files included on the CD have been saved as Maya 8.5 .ma files. The files have been tested with versions 8.5 and 2008. In addition, all the techniques discussed in the book have been tested with versions 8.5 and 2008; any significant differences between the two versions have been noted in the text.

A number of files saved on the CD contain shading networks. When opening a file, you may be surprised to find it void of geometry. Nevertheless, you can access the contained shading network through the Hypershade Materials, Textures, or Utilities tab. If the network is exotic and difficult to access, instructions are included in the text.

Bonus Chapter

An "Additional Techniques" chapter is included and contains advanced techniques that cover a wide range of topics. Although none of the techniques is mandatory for successful animation, reading this chapter can strengthen your knowledge and allow you to be more flexible when solving lighting and texturing problems. Each section is numbered to correspond to the chapter that is most closely linked to the topic. For example, sections 4.1 and 4.2 cover additional applications of the Ramp texture, which was initially discussed in Chapter 4.

The Bonus Chapter requires Adobe Reader to view, so we've also included a link to download the latest version from Adobe's website at http://www.adobe.com/products/reader/.

System Requirements

Make sure that your computer meets the minimum system requirements shown in the following list. If your computer doesn't match up to most of these requirements, you may have problems using the files on the companion CD. For the latest and greatest information, please refer to the ReadMe file located at the root of the CD.

- A PC running a valid license of Autodesk Maya 8.5 or higher. Maya 8.5 requires one of the following operating systems: 32-bit Microsoft Windows XP (SP2 or higher), 64-bit Microsoft Windows XP (SP1 or higher), Microsoft Vista, Red Hat Enterprise Linux 4.0 WS (U5), or Fedora Core 5. Maya 8.5 has additional hardware requirements, which are listed on the Autodesk website (search for "Maya Qualified Hardware" at `www.autodesk.com`).
- A Macintosh running a valid license of Autodesk Maya 8.5 or higher. Maya 8.5 requires the operating system to be Apple OS X (10.4.8 or later).
- An Internet connection
- A CD-ROM drive

Using the CD

To install the items from the CD to your hard drive, follow these steps:

1. Insert the CD into your computer's CD-ROM drive. The license agreement appears.

Note: Windows users: The interface won't launch if you have autorun disabled. In that case, click Start > Run (for Windows Vista, Start > All Programs > Accessories > Run). In the dialog box that appears, type **`D:\Start.exe`**. (Replace *D* with the proper letter if your CD drive uses a different letter. If you don't know the letter, see how your CD drive is listed under My Computer.) Click OK.

Note: Mac users: The CD icon will appear on your desktop; double-click the icon to open the CD and then double-click the Start icon.

2. Read through the license agreement, and then click the Accept button if you want to use the CD.

The CD interface appears. The interface allows you to access the content with just one or two clicks.

Troubleshooting

Wiley has attempted to provide programs that work on most computers with the minimum system requirements. Alas, your computer may differ, and some programs may not work properly for some reason.

The two likeliest problems are that you don't have enough memory (RAM) for the programs you want to use, or you have other programs running that are affecting installation or running of a program. If you get an error message such as "Not enough memory" or "Setup cannot continue," follow one or more of the following suggestions and then try using the software again:

Turn off any antivirus software running on your computer. Installation programs sometimes mimic virus activity and may make your computer incorrectly believe that it's being infected by a virus.

Close all running programs. The more programs you have running, the less memory is available to other programs. Installation programs typically update files and programs, so if you keep other programs running, installation may not work properly.

Have your local computer store add more RAM to your computer. This is, admittedly, a drastic and somewhat expensive step. However, adding more memory can help the speed of your computer and allow more programs to run at the same time.

Customer Care

If you have trouble with the book's companion CD, please call the Wiley Product Technical Support phone number at (800) 762-2974. Outside the United States, call +1 (317) 572-3994. You can also contact Wiley Product Technical Support at `http://sybex.custhelp.com`. John Wiley & Sons will provide technical support only for installation and other general quality control items. For technical support on the applications themselves, consult the program's vendor or author.

To place additional orders or to request information about other Wiley products, please call (877) 762-2974.

Index

Note to the reader: Throughout this index **boldfaced** page numbers indicate primary discussions of a topic. *Italicized* page numbers indicate illustrations.

Numbers

A

B

C

D

E

F

G

H

I

J

K

L

M

N

O

P

Q

R

S

T

U

V

W

X

Z

Wiley Publishing, Inc. End-User License Agreement

READ THIS. You should carefully read these terms and conditions before opening the software packet(s) included with this book "Book". This is a license agreement "Agreement" between you and Wiley Publishing, Inc. "WPI". By opening the accompanying software packet(s), you acknowledge that you have read and accept the following terms and conditions. If you do not agree and do not want to be bound by such terms and conditions, promptly return the Book and the unopened software packet(s) to the place you obtained them for a full refund.

1. **License Grant.** WPI grants to you (either an individual or entity) a nonexclusive license to use one copy of the enclosed software program(s) (collectively, the "Software," solely for your own personal or business purposes on a single computer (whether a standard computer or a workstation component of a multi-user network). The Software is in use on a computer when it is loaded into temporary memory (RAM) or installed into permanent memory (hard disk, CD-ROM, or other storage device). WPI reserves all rights not expressly granted herein.

2. **Ownership.** WPI is the owner of all right, title, and interest, including copyright, in and to the compilation of the Software recorded on the physical packet included with this Book "Software Media". Copyright to the individual programs recorded on the Software Media is owned by the author or other authorized copyright owner of each program. Ownership of the Software and all proprietary rights relating thereto remain with WPI and its licensers.

3. **Restrictions On Use and Transfer.** (a) You may only (i) make one copy of the Software for backup or archival purposes, or (ii) transfer the Software to a single hard disk, provided that you keep the original for backup or archival purposes. You may not (i) rent or lease the Software, (ii) copy or reproduce the Software through a LAN or other network system or through any computer subscriber system or bulletin-board system, or (iii) modify, adapt, or create derivative works based on the Software. (b) You may not reverse engineer, decompile, or disassemble the Software. You may transfer the Software and user documentation on a permanent basis, provided that the transferee agrees to accept the terms and conditions of this Agreement and you retain no copies. If the Software is an update or has been updated, any transfer must include the most recent update and all prior versions.

4. **Restrictions on Use of Individual Programs.** You must follow the individual requirements and restrictions detailed for each individual program in the About the CD-ROM appendix of this Book or on the Software Media. These limitations are also contained in the individual license agreements recorded on the Software Media. These limitations may include a requirement that after using the program for a specified period of time, the user must pay a registration fee or discontinue use. By opening the Software packet(s), you will be agreeing to abide by the licenses and restrictions for these individual programs that are detailed in the About the CD-ROM appendix and/or on the Software Media. None of the material on this Software Media or listed in this Book may ever be redistributed, in original or modified form, for commercial purposes.

5. **Limited Warranty.** (a) WPI warrants that the Software and Software Media are free from defects in materials and workmanship under normal use for a period of sixty (60) days from the date of purchase of this Book. If WPI receives notification within the warranty period of defects in materials or workmanship, WPI will replace the defective Software Media. (b) WPI AND THE AUTHOR(S) OF THE BOOK DISCLAIM ALL OTHER WARRANTIES, EXPRESS OR IMPLIED, INCLUDING WITHOUT LIMITATION IMPLIED WARRANTIES OF MERCHANTABILITY AND FITNESS FOR A PARTICULAR PURPOSE, WITH RESPECT TO THE SOFTWARE, THE PROGRAMS, THE SOURCE CODE CONTAINED THEREIN, AND/OR THE TECHNIQUES DESCRIBED IN THIS BOOK. WPI DOES NOT WARRANT THAT THE FUNCTIONS CONTAINED IN THE SOFTWARE WILL MEET YOUR REQUIREMENTS OR THAT THE OPERATION OF THE SOFTWARE WILL BE ERROR FREE. (c) This limited warranty gives you specific legal rights, and you may have other rights that vary from jurisdiction to jurisdiction.

6. **Remedies.** (a) WPI's entire liability and your exclusive remedy for defects in materials and workmanship shall be limited to replacement of the Software Media, which may be returned to WPI with a copy of your receipt at the following address: Software Media Fulfillment Department, Attn.: *Advanced Maya Texturing and Lighting, Second Edition*, Wiley Publishing, Inc., 10475 Crosspoint Blvd., Indianapolis, IN 46256, or call 1-800-762-2974. Please allow four to six weeks for delivery. This Limited Warranty is void if failure of the Software Media has resulted from accident, abuse, or misapplication. Any replacement Software Media will be warranted for the remainder of the original warranty period or thirty (30) days, whichever is longer. (b) In no event shall WPI or the author be liable for any damages whatsoever (including without limitation damages for loss of business profits, business interruption, loss of business information, or any other pecuniary loss) arising from the use of or inability to use the Book or the Software, even if WPI has been advised of the possibility of such damages. (c) Because some jurisdictions do not allow the exclusion or limitation of liability for consequential or incidental damages, the above limitation or exclusion may not apply to you.

7. **U.S. Government Restricted Rights.** Use, duplication, or disclosure of the Software for or on behalf of the United States of America, its agencies and/or instrumentalities "U.S. Government" is subject to restrictions as stated in paragraph (c)(1)(ii) of the Rights in Technical Data and Computer Software clause of DFARS 252.227-7013, or subparagraphs (c) (1) and (2) of the Commercial Computer Software - Restricted Rights clause at FAR 52.227-19, and in similar clauses in the NASA FAR supplement, as applicable.

8. **General.** This Agreement constitutes the entire understanding of the parties and revokes and supersedes all prior agreements, oral or written, between them and may not be modified or amended except in a writing signed by both parties hereto that specifically refers to this Agreement. This Agreement shall take precedence over any other documents that may be in conflict herewith. If any one or more provisions contained in this Agreement are held by any court or tribunal to be invalid, illegal, or otherwise unenforceable, each and every other provision shall remain in full force and effect.